P9-DTG-251
03780343

BIG EARS

Refiguring American Music

A series edited by Ronald Radano *and* Josh Kun

Charles McGovern, *contributing editor*

BIG EARS

LISTENING FOR GENDER IN JAZZ STUDIES

Edited by NICHOLE T. RUSTIN
and SHERRIE TUCKER

Duke University Press

Durham and London

2008

OKANAGAN COLLEGE
LIBRARY
BRITISH COLUMBIA

BIG
EARS

LISTENING FOR GENDER
IN JAZZ STUDIES

Edited by **NICHOLE T. RUSTIN**

and **SHERRIE TUCKER**

Duke University Press

Durham and London

2008

•

© 2008 Duke University Press

All rights reserved.

Printed in the United States of America

on acid-free paper ∞

Designed by Katy Clove

Typeset in Janson Text by Keystone Typesetting, Inc.

Library of Congress Cataloging-in-Publication Data

appear on the last printed page of this book.

Contents

ACKNOWLEDGMENTS vii

INTRODUCTION
Nichole T. Rustin and Sherrie Tucker 1

PART I
Rooting Gender in Jazz History

SEPARATED AT "BIRTH": SINGING AND THE
HISTORY OF JAZZ *Lara Pellegrinelli* 31

WITH LOVIE AND LIL: REDISCOVERING TWO
CHICAGO PIANISTS OF THE 1920s *Jeffrey Taylor* 48

GENDER, JAZZ, AND THE POPULAR FRONT
Monica Hairston 64

"THE BATTLE OF THE SAXES": GENDER, DANCE BANDS,
AND BRITISH NATIONALISM IN THE SECOND WORLD WAR
Christina Baade 90

IDENTITY FOR SALE: GLENN MILLER, WYNTON MARSALIS,
AND CULTURAL REPLAY IN MUSIC *Tracy McMullen* 129

PART II
Improvising Gender: Embodiment and Performance

FROM THE POINT OF VIEW OF THE PAVEMENT:
A GEOPOLITICS OF BLACK DANCE *Jayna Brown* 157

PERVERSE HYSTERICS: THE NOISY *CRI* OF LES DIABOLIQUES
Julie Dawn Smith 180

"BORN OUT OF JAZZ . . . YET EMBRACING ALL MUSIC":
RACE, GENDER, AND TECHNOLOGY IN GEORGE RUSSELL'S
LYDIAN CHROMATIC CONCEPT *Eric Porter* 210

"BUT THIS MUSIC IS MINE ALREADY!": "WHITE WOMAN" AS JAZZ
COLLECTOR IN THE FILM *NEW ORLEANS* (1947) *Sherrie Tucker* 235

FITTING THE PART *Ingrid Monson* 267

PART III
Reimagining Jazz Representations

"BETTER A JAZZ ALBUM THAN LIPSTICK" (*LIEBER JAZZPLATTE ALS
LIPPENSTIFT*): THE 1956 *JAZZ PODIUM* SERIES REVEALS IMAGES OF
JAZZ AND GENDER IN POSTWAR GERMANY *Ursel Schlicht* 291

EXCLUSION, OPENNESS, AND UTOPIA IN BLACK MALE
PERFORMANCE AT THE WORLD STAGE JAZZ JAM SESSIONS
João H. Costa Vargas 320

"IT TAKES TWO PEOPLE TO CONFIRM THE TRUTH":
THE JAZZ FICTION OF SHERLEY ANN WILLIAMS AND
TONI CADE BAMBARA *Farah Jasmine Griffin* 348

"BLOW, MAN, BLOW!": REPRESENTING GENDER,
WHITE PRIMITIVES, AND JAZZ MELODRAMA THROUGH
A YOUNG MAN WITH A HORN *Nichole T. Rustin* 361

THE GENDERED JAZZ AESTHETICS OF *THAT MAN OF MINE*:
THE INTERNATIONAL SWEETHEARTS OF RHYTHM AND
INDEPENDENT BLACK SOUND FILM *Kristin McGee* 393

BIBLIOGRAPHY 423

CONTRIBUTORS 435

INDEX 441

Acknowledgments

Anthologies notoriously take longer than anyone anticipates. Our first debt of gratitude is to our contributors who not only gave us their writing but worked closely with us over a four-year period on revisions. Their scholarship within and beyond the essays profoundly shaped the collection as a whole. Lara, Jeff, Monica, Christina, Tracy, Jayna, Julie, Eric, Ingrid, Ursel, Joao, Farah, and Kristen: you are awesome.

We would like to thank the photographers and archivists, who produced and provided the images that help to illuminate the theoretical insights of the collection: Cynthia Sesso at CTS Images and the family of Paul Hoeffler, Mark Miller, S. Victor Burgos at Photofest, Nick Morgan at Getty Images, Stephanie Hubbard at Yale, Tad Hershorn at the Institute of Jazz Studies, Peter Bastian, Karlheinz Klueter, Zoran Sinobad at the Library of Congress, Katja von Schuttenbach, and Silke Mehrwald.

The team at Duke is simply fantastic. Their commitment to helping us produce the best possible book was phenomenal. Ken Wissoker and Ron Radano kept us on track with encouragement and thoughtful criticism. Our anonymous readers helped us to shape and refine the book with engaged analysis of each of the essays. Their work was key to our success. Fred Kameny, Courtney Berger, Cherie Westmoreland, Katy Clove, and Lori Harris have been a pleasure to work with every step of the way. Thanks to Ron Radano, Josh Kun, and Charles McGovern for having "big" enough ears to hear a need for gender analysis in jazz studies within the critical paradigm of "Refiguring American Music." We are so proud to be a part of this series and the intellectual project it represents.

We owe a special thanks to Bernard Gendron for the inspirational dialogues during the year of our conference "road show" that led to this collection

Many thanks to Krin Gabbard for assistance in locating film stills, and to Nicole Ishikawa and Kelly Ishikawa for heroic assistance with images and permissions. A big thank you to Mark Cantor for generous consulation on jazz film questions. Thanks to Pete Williams for assistance with the index.

FROM NICHOLE

I learned an incredible amount from the various contributors to *Big Ears*. The quality and variety of work that they contributed indicates their passion for jazz and scholarship. It was a pleasure to work with each of them as they produced the best scholarship possible.

Without the dedication that Tami Albin gave to this project, from its genesis to its detailed conclusion, we wouldn't have been able to produce such a wonderful book. Thank you!

Sherrie Tucker is the best collaborator one could hope for. As the various authors attest, Sherrie has been a mentor and intellectual giant for us all. She is enthusiastic, indefatigable, brilliant, generous, and simply a joy to work with. I strive to be a better scholar and colleague because of her.

Robin D. G. Kelley also deserves many thanks, for he has been a staunch supporter of my work and career ever since becoming my advisor many years ago. He has helped me shape my thoughts about race, gender, and jazz by his example and his mentorship.

I am grateful to my colleagues from the University of Illinois at Urbana-Champaign, where I was able to present some of the material found in my essay for this collection. I would like to single out Dianne Pinderhughes, Pat Gill, William Berry, and Desiree Yomtoob for all their assistance in supporting my writing and research. They made it possible.

I would also like to thank those who helped make laughter and community a part of my academic life — Barrington Edwards, Jessica Millward, Fanon Che Wilkins, Audrey Petty, Cynthia Oliver, Gabriel Solis, Erik McDuffie, Karen Flynn, Kathy Perkins, Alice Deck, Angharad Valdivia, Cameron McCarthy, David Roediger, Richard Pierce, John L. Jackson, Grant Farred, John Gennari, Joao Costa Vargas, and Damion Thomas.

My friends Anastasia Rowland-Seymour, Lucinda Holt, Lydia Holt, Tara Roberts, Sheryl Wright, Ashanta Evans-Blackwell, Melanie Harris-Smith, Aimee Eubanks Davis, Nikole Smith, Jamie Phillips, Sarah Klapmann, Lisa Bowman, Chris Allen, and Laricke Blanchard encouraged and inspired me to keep moving ahead. I celebrate them!

My family—Myra and Alan MacGregor, Karima Rustin, Ahman Rustin, Myisha Gomez, Khadijah DeLoache, Mary Guy, and Helena Paschal—has also been a great help to me during my research and writing, providing housing, food, and fun throughout the process.

My Paschal guys, Marlin, Levinas, and Akil, mean the world to me. Without the demands and distractions that they occasioned—from date nights, to extended visits to the dog park, to diapers and play dates—I wouldn't have known the pleasures of a home life filled with love, laughter, and utter devotion. Because of them I am truly blessed.

FROM SHERRIE

I am grateful to the many students, colleagues, and friends engaged in the dialogues that supported the work and energy of this project. Thanks to the faculty, students, and staff at the American studies program at University of Kansas, especially to my students in "Jazz and American Culture" over the years for the stimulating dialogues that helped me think through much of this work. Among those whose dialogue has been influential for my thinking are Jocelyn Buckner, Amber Clifford, Luba Ginsburg, Monique Laney, Chelsea Schlievert, Megan Williams, and Pete Williams. Terri Rockhold, you rock, you rock.

Many thanks to the Interdisciplinary Jazz Studies Group at the University of Kansas, and to those who participated in our colloquia; particular thanks to Billy Joe Harris, Chuck Berg, Clarence Henry, Kevin Whitehead, Chico Herbison, Philip Barnard, Roberta Schwartz, and Crystal Anderson. I am indebted to the College of Liberal Arts and Sciences and to the Hall Center for the Humanities for research support and for an atmosphere conducive to research.

I owe a special debt of gratitude to the students with whom I worked at Columbia University in "Gender, Race, and Jazz" and in the graduate seminar on gender and jazz studies, especially Monica Hairston, Ben Piekut, Maxine Gordon, Seton Hawkins, Erica Mather, and Jess Pinkham.

I am enormously grateful to Robert O'Meally for the intellectual community he created that shaped so much of our work, the Jazz Study Group at Columbia. Space does not allow for all the names of people whose dialogues shaped my thinking on gender and jazz studies, but let me send out special thanks to Ingrid Monson, Robin D. G. Kelley, George Lewis, Farah Jasmine Griffin, Maxine Gordon, Chris Washburn, Krin Gabbard, Jacqui Malone, Travis Jackson, Billy Joe Harris,

John Gennari, Bill Lowe, Fred Moten, and Guthrie Ramsey. Particular thanks to Yulanda Denoon for her hard work, dedication, and genius at making things happen.

I am grateful to the Feminist Theory and Music scholars for creating and maintaining an intellectual community that has been so important to me: among the scholars I have admired through this circuit are Suzanne Cusick, Ellie Hisama, Susan Cook, Eileen Hayes, Martha Mockus, and Tammy Kernodle.

Special thanks to Ajay Heble for his continuing support of gender as a salient category in improvisation studies, most recently as the director of the Improvisation, Community, and Social Practice research initiative, supported by the Social Sciences and Humanities Research Council of Canada. I am energized by the "Improvisation, Gender, and the Body" team and look forward to our future work.

I am endlessly grateful to Nichole T. Rustin for being the most amazing collaborator imaginable — for her dedication, keen mind, amazing sense of humor, and splendid theoretical contributions to this collection and the field it represents. I approached the idea of collaboration with starry-eyed idealism and she never let me down. I know how fortunate I am to have done this project with you, Nichole!

I want to thank Angela Davis for reaching out to me when I showed up in her course "History of African American Women" as a painfully introverted "returning" student and jazz geek in 1989. I wanted to write about African American women in jazz; she taught me how to listen to interconnected webs of power of gender, race, and class in the music I loved.

To my parents, Marilyn and Roy Tucker, I send my thanks for their genuine interest in all my projects, and for saying "Is it done yet?" and "Don't work too much" all my life.

Finally, the spotlight of my gratitude lands where it belongs: a great big ball of thank-you-for-everything to Tami Albin, best librarian in the world and so much more.

Nichole T. Rustin and Sherrie Tucker

INTRODUCTION

LISTENING FOR GENDER IN JAZZ STUDIES

n jazz circles, if someone says you have "big ears," you have
to feel good about that. "Big ears" is high praise. Players
and listeners (and jazz players are listeners) with "big ears"
are equipped to hear and engage complexity as it happens. Paul
Berliner and Ingrid Monson both emphasized the importance
of listening in their ethnomusicological studies of jazz musicians' perspectives on their practice. As Monson wrote, "The
ongoing process of decision making that takes place in the ensemble perhaps explains why musicians often say that the most
important thing is to listen. They mean it in a very active sense:
they must listen closely because they are continually called upon
to respond to and participate in an ongoing flow of musical
action that can change or surprise them at any moment."[1]

The title of this anthology, *Big Ears: Listening for Gender in
Jazz Studies*, addresses readers and writers as cultural listeners
and takes gender not just as a peripheral, extra, or "special
interest" subtopic in jazz studies but as part of the complex
"action that can change or surprise" which we value and listen
for. By assembling this collection of scholarship in jazz studies
that "listens to," and "takes seriously," a register that is particularly untheorized in jazz studies, we hope to contribute to
the field of jazz studies by advocating ear training that can
listen for gender and by encouraging a critical intervention in
the field of feminist theory and music studies that tends to
focus less on jazz than on classical music, opera, and pop.[2]

Big Ears: Listening for Gender in Jazz Studies is an interdisciplinary examination of gender in the histories, sounds, performances, representations, critiques, and lived experiences of those who, like ourselves, are invested in jazz culture and musical improvisation. Spanning a century of jazz culture and history, this anthology privileges gender analysis as a tool for exploring how the aesthetics of the music have been shaped, directed, and recorded by fans, critics, historians, and musicians and for examining the conditions of possibility that artists have maintained and developed as jazz has grown. We imagine jazz culture in the broadest sense possible and the essays collected here share that vision. That broad scope is grounded by our contributors' responses to the specific question of what we hear when we listen for gender in jazz. The approaches our contributors take to listening for gender reveal a critical commitment to representing the great variety of ways that their subjects dealt with the relationship between gender and jazz in aesthetic and lived experiences. Questioning gender draws attention, as our contributors illustrate, to the body, to race, to social and musical status, to narratives of origin (including that of exception, firsts, tradition), to subjects whose relationships to jazz cross traditional lines of gender, to difference, and to sexuality. Although this is not intended as a women-and-jazz anthology, our focus on gender analysis yields a proliferation of works concerned with women as jazz subjects. It is important to note that we allow this imbalance not in an attempt to "add women" into existing scholarship, but because of the ways these studies demonstrate how gender analysis helps to "listen differently" to areas of jazz culture that are otherwise too easily dismissed as "outside."

When we listened for gender in emerging and established scholarship in jazz studies, we sought work that brought very different assumptions about what a gendered analysis of jazz could and should be. Through a variety of ethnographic, theoretical, musicological, and historical projects, our contributors' interests range from recovering gender as an analytic of marginalization; to connecting a variety of feminist theories to illuminate how we might understand women's participation and reception as musicians in a range of periods, places, and genres; to questioning the relationship between race, gender, and critical authority; to illustrating the tensions between gender, national identity, and communications policy; to defining the dynamics of aesthetics and radical politics or ethics and community; and to underscoring the importance of social assumptions about gender and race in ensemble work. By allowing very different assumptions about gender analysis to coexist, we hope that the anthology serves as a tool for teaching in a number of disciplines as well as paving the way for future volumes dedicated to gender and jazz to develop. We hope as well that our anthology provokes more self-reflection on the part of those writing and researching in jazz studies (a field very conservative about who and what is included), challenging the field to be more representative and articulate about its constituencies. Jazz, as Elsa Barkley Brown (1991) argues, can be a metaphor for writing multilayered and multiphonic histories. *Big Ears* aims at being one of the dissonant polyvocal conversations sounded in the exciting field of "New Jazz Studies."

We decided to do the anthology in 2003, when within a matter of months we appeared together (with Bernard Gendron) on conference panels at Modernist Studies and at the Popular Culture Association. Our experiences at these conferences led us to notice that it seemed no longer true to say that jazz studies lacked scholarship that incorporated gender as a category of analysis or a feminist perspective. We reflected, however, that it still felt that way sometimes to those of us who have been writing about gender and jazz in our disparate disciplines and communities. As we talked, we realized that we had both been thinking individually about putting together an anthology focusing on gender in jazz studies. In the spirit of collaborative jazz practice, we thought the project would be more exciting if we worked jointly and gathered the work of people currently incorporating gender in jazz studies. We began talking up the idea of the anthology, recognizing that we were in a moment when the approach was no longer a critique of a hostile field but of exciting theoretical engagement, and it seemed important to provide a collection that could mark this moment and help us to move to the next, whatever that is. We thought that such a volume would be useful in jazz studies seminars that always seemed to be struggling with gender as "lack" in jazz studies, when gender was included at all. Drawing on networks from our research and conference experiences, we invited scholars from a variety of disciplines and interdisciplinary frameworks who were pursuing interesting avenues of gender analysis and who wrote about the different kinds of music that have been called jazz. We looked to *Uptown Conversation: The New Jazz Studies* (2004), edited by Robert G. O'Meally, Brent Hayes Edwards, and Farah Jasmine Griffin, as a model for how we wanted *Big Ears* to feel intellectually and aesthetically. The pieces we have chosen are of a variety of lengths and styles, and we hope that this introduction will be useful in offering ideas for ways one might read them together, but open enough to imagine other approaches as well as being suggestive of future research directions.

SOLO JOURNEYS

In keeping with our commitment to multivocality, we wish to make visible the different trajectories and stakes that we as coeditors bring to this anthologizing process.

Nichole T. Rustin In conceptualizing my book project, *Jazz Men: Race, Masculine Difference, and the Emotions in 1950s America*, I found myself thinking again about that unvarying metaphor of jazz as democracy and the increasing institutionalization of jazz in academia as a cultural institution. I asked myself over and over, how I could make a persuasive argument about the importance of gender in discussions of jazz in the face of these two "truths?" Thinking through the question led me to reflecting on what attracted me to jazz initially and to issues of access and resources in some of the primary institutions associated with jazz. When I was a girl being introduced to jazz through films — from Diana Ross playing Billie Holiday in *Lady Sings the Blues* to musicals from the 1940s running as repeats on WPIX Channel 11 in New York City — I did not imagine my youthful interest to become a professional one, leading me to co-editing an anthology on gender in jazz studies or writing a book about jazz, race, and masculinity in the 1950s. A committed relationship to the music flourished while I was an undergraduate, when, for nearly four years, I hosted a weekly jazz show on our radio station. Unscientifically, my criteria for choosing the programming ranged from the appeal of a song's title (e.g., "Don't Let Them Drop that Atomic Bomb on Me"), to my preference for a performer's instrument (the bass, my favorite), to another's recommendation of an artist. Graduate school enabled me to explore jazz culture with a scholarly passion, enticed by one of the sustaining metaphors of jazz studies: jazz is like democracy. I thought to pursue that genealogy for my dissertation, but focused instead on questions of race, masculinity, and the life of Charles Mingus Jr. From an examination of Mingus's intellectual project as a black composer, I shifted to a focus on the period of his artistic growth I found most stimulating — the 1950s — when he moved from Los Angeles to New York. The 1950s remains an intriguing period of jazz history, one in which race, gender, and politics informed aesthetic and intellectual arguments about the music and the mark it made on American identity and culture.

New York City remains a locus for understanding jazz aesthetics and cultural politics; the metropolitan area alone hosts three institutions — Jazz at Lincoln Center, Columbia University's Center for Jazz Studies, and Rutgers University's Institute of Jazz Studies — representing cultural, academic, and archival avenues for pursuing research in jazz history. One of the most prominent contemporary musician advocates for jazz and campaigners of jazz as democracy is Wynton Marsalis. On seeing his Lincoln Center Jazz Orchestra in performance, I could at last acknowledge that the jazz democracy he imagined implicitly represents a male collective identity. All male, but interracial, the orchestra reflected boys at play, men enjoying performing and interacting with one another. Not even the classic standby of the girl singer was needed because the radical quality of his orchestra was the fact that it is interracial — white, black, latino speaking the same musical language, grooving to the same beat. Although attention has been paid to Marsalis's institution building and to his ideas about musical tradition, there has been little interest directed toward the issue of jazz democracy as primarily male collective identity. I hope the anthology will, as my own book project seeks to do, challenge those assumptions, making clear the dynamics of gender, class, and race in the communities constituting the cultures of jazz.

The process of writing is, of course, fraught with tensions relating to audience, voice, subject, and community. As I have moved from writing my dissertation to writing my book, I have recognized within myself the need to have something tangible that related to my own intellectual journey. In many ways, the field of jazz studies is deeply rooted and, in many significant ways, it is not. Finding "proof" for the importance or relevance of examining gender and race in jazz has grown easier during the time in which I have been in academia although imagining my place in the field is still sometimes difficult. With *Big Ears*, I hope to create a witness to the feasibility and necessity of exploring gender in jazz studies. Here are a variety of voices examining gender in jazz culture: voices that are, significantly, interested in more than decrying the absence of women or the misogyny of men in jazz or hagiography. I see the anthology in its diversity of subjects and in its promotion of a wide scope of emerging and established voices opening up the often-closed circles of discourse about jazz and its history. I hope the anthology will propose a jazz history in which our understanding of both the frameworks, and the realities, of working and creating as musicians are redefined and sharpened — a collaborative history that would make clear the dynamics of gender, class, and race in the communities constituting the cultures of jazz. I hope that the various approaches will challenge me; introduce me to new artists, audiences, and critics; suggest new avenues of study; and provide a community of like-minded and critically engaged thinkers. Ultimately, I hope the anthology will "prove" that examining gender is a vital and important framework for understanding the music and the culture.

Sherrie Tucker There was a time, not so long ago, when scholars in jazz studies who sounded the words "gender" and "jazz" in the same sentence could get themselves bounced from any number of "clubs." The venues where jazz discourse is played — academic, journalistic, and musical — harbored a chill for those who wished to question the gender-jazz status quo that frequented these clubs. For many of us, we learned that to participate in jazz discourse, one needed to leave one's "gender analysis" at the door.

When Robert O'Meally telephoned to invite me to serve as the 2004–5 Louis Armstrong Visiting Professor at the Center for Jazz Studies at Columbia University, I was elated, naturally. At the same time, I experienced a booming conviction that my "big ears" must be failing me. I could not be hearing him correctly. Nothing in my research process or in my research findings, for that matter, could have prepared me for such spectacular inclusion.

I had to make an excuse to call him back and find a way to get him to say it again. It was not just that it seemed too good to be true, which, of course, it did. But it literally did not seem possible. The field of jazz studies, as I knew it, did not generally invite women into the fold, let alone into prestigious positions. It certainly did not seek scholars with degrees in women's studies, who studied feminist theory and theories about gender and who called for more attention to women and gender in jazz studies at large to anyone who would listen. I had, in fact, just spent a good part of a summer as the brunt of an alarmingly heated listserve debate about whether or not gender and sexuality were appropriate topics for a jazz research discussion. But, apparently, the field was changing, at least at Columbia.

The next thought that kept crossing my mind was the realization that if I had ever imagined I could be accepted in academic jazz studies, I probably never would have written about all-woman bands. I would have wanted to be part of jazz studies so badly, I would have written about something I thought would be valued. My topic and I had been welcomed in women's studies, but I always had found myself being treated as slightly delusional (a romantic seeker of foremothers, someone who had not done her research, or she would have picked a more viable topic) when it came to circles in jazz studies. Studying women in jazz made me nonthreatening too, except sometimes when I suggested that gender would be a "useful category" for jazz scholars generally (following Joan Scott). In those moments, I found few comrades (albeit good ones) and many more skeptics; most of those were dismissive, but some were flat-out hostile. In any case, I felt grateful for whatever turn of events had landed me at the Center for Jazz Studies, and grateful for not anticipating that anything like that could happen.

As someone who studies gender, women, and jazz, I was used to speaking from the margins of jazz studies, not the Center for Jazz Studies. But in 2004–5, I was invited to teach courses in precisely these topics. I taught an undergraduate course entitled "Gender, Race, and Jazz," and a graduate seminar, "Listening for Gender in Jazz Studies," where I worked with remarkable graduate students from Columbia, CUNY, and NYU, whose theses and dissertations involved gender analysis and jazz studies. I had the pleasure of attending classes and events organized by remarkable faculty at the Center for Jazz Studies, all of whom incorporated gender and included women in their analyses and event planning. Robin D. G. Kelley's lectures in "Jazz and the Political Imagination" were revelations in intersectional analyses of race, class, gender, sexuality, nation, and internationalism that always involved listening to music as a critical component. An unforgettable visit from vocalist/cellist/violinist Irene Aebi to George Lewis's proseminar illuminated one fascinating transnational, transgenre, transmedia route through spoken word and creative music. Another highlight occurred at a concert and panel with Lewis, saxophonist/improvisors/composer Matana Roberts, and pianist/songwriter/singer Patricia Barber at Frederick Rose Hall at Lincoln Center. After Roberts fielded the inevitable "gender question" from the audience (standard fare for women who play instruments other than piano), fellow panelist George Lewis stated that he thought it was important to ask such questions of men, not just of women, adding that the prompting of feminist students and colleagues (Ellen Waterman, Julie Dawn Smith, Dana Reason, and Tracy McMullen among them) had led him to think about how gender has affected his career. Farah Jasmine Griffin produced an event honoring Mary Lou Williams, which included lectures by Tammy Kernodle and Father Peter O'Brien, a film presentation by Carol Bash, and a piano tribute performed by Bertha Hope. I produced two public events, one on "all-woman" bands of various time periods, genres, and motivations, and one on women-in-jazz historiography. Nichole Rustin, the filmmaker Kay D. Ray, and the musicians Shanta Nurullah, Carlene Ray, Kit McClure, and Kali Z. Fasteau joined me to make these events memorable and meaningful. I had the honor of serving as Maxine Gordon's faculty adviser as she launched her remarkable "Women Who Listen" oral history project with women jazz fans.

To me, this collection marks an exciting moment when a chilly reaction to jazz and gender scholarship is, well, not exactly unheard of, but at the very least, not the only response one hears. Scholars in jazz studies who incorporate gender analysis may, in fact, experience something of the "Diva Dogs" paradigm coined by the women improvisers in Julie Smith's article in this volume; treated as divas in one moment, dogs the next — but at least we are being heard. For those of us who have been drawn to gender analyses of jazz scenes, sounds, histories, cultures, practices, representations, and discourses, it seems to me that this moment ushers in unprecedented opportunities to hear each other and to be heard, not as salve for projects in which gender analysis is otherwise absent, but as engaged participants in a field that increasingly values dissonance as a mark of its newness. "New Jazz Studies," as the current developments in interdisciplinary approaches to cultural studies of jazz are being called, takes a critical approach to narrative parades of individual geniuses, and pays more attention to the "immeasurably complex worlds through which they moved, and which they helped to shape."[3] This work is not interested in producing grand narratives, but in studies of "moments, meetings, gatherings, gestures, and scenes," frameworks in which analyses of gender can be extremely useful, and that can help us to reframe jazz history in ways that help us to learn more about gender and culture.[4] New Jazz Studies benefits from feminist theory and theories from gender and sexuality studies in its interests in analyzing historical desires mapped onto representations of and narratives about jazz and the connections and disconnections between these and jazz practice.

In other words, it seems to me that many of the turns in "New Jazz Studies" indicate a moment when "gender and jazz" scholars are no longer solely perceived as representing a "special interest" subcategory of jazz studies, but sometimes actually received as sounding precisely the kinds of "wrong notes" that Ajay Heble argues are useful in jazz, jazz studies, and cultural theory beyond, for their ability to "[disturb] naturalized orders of knowledge production," to analyze power, and to explore areas in a variety of jazz cultures (including academic jazz studies) in which difference produces, rather than derails, subjects; and subjects who produce difference attempt to remix power relations.[5]

LOCATING GENDER IN JAZZ STUDIES

Published here are new works by scholars who have been woodshedding on the controversial fusions of jazz and gender, utilizing a variety of styles, theories, and methods, and listening to a vast array of music from diverse histories and cultures and settings. Although many of the scholars included here (and others who could very well be included, but are not, only due to space) have been incorporating an analysis of gender in jazz studies for some time, this anthology is the first collection of essays devoted to our concerted efforts to find ways to analyze gender, as intersected with race and a range of other categories, in jazz studies.

The theme of this collection is "gender and jazz," but in accordance with the mutability and surprise for which each of these categories is famous, the authors approach this thematic fusion from a variety of disciplines, interdisciplines, styles, theories, and methods. One common thread is that none of the articles finds it imperative to prove that gender is an important category of analysis, or that jazz is worthy of academic study, or to prove that women played jazz, or that men have gender. None of the articles assumes gender is a stable category that acts alone, but rather they expect it to bend, change, and reformulate at every turn and understand gender to be coconstituted with other shifting, salient social categories such as race, class, sexuality, ethnicity, nation, etc. All of these pieces are concerned with how to better incorporate gender and race in jazz studies. But how they improvise on "gender" and "jazz" is where the variety is apparent; these are scholars who emerge from diverse fields of dissonance.

In this volume, incorporating a gendered analysis means a number of things. But one thing it most certainly does not mean is to listen exclusively to jazz records by women on week 10 of the class. Neither does it attempt to piece together a coherent account of a "Jazz Tradition" that presents women and men "playing nicely" together from decade to decade, style to style, nor do we consider the pieces included here as composing a separate "Jazz Studies of Our Own" that is only pertinent for specialists who "do gender." Rather, this volume understands "listening for gender in jazz studies" as a practice that is more prevalent than it once was, and that these practitioners hail from a range of disciplinary, interdisciplinary, theoretical, and methodological perspectives. In fact, "listening for gender in jazz studies" is one of the practices that mark this as an exciting moment in cultural studies of jazz.

This collection is not, however, to be mistaken as the "birth" of gender and jazz studies. Just as contemporary women saxophonists and drummers continue to be received as "pioneers," those of us who write about gender and jazz are sometimes tempted to accept praise for appearing out of nowhere. This is flattery that we are obliged to reject as part of our work of "listening for gender" in jazz studies. Indeed, that "origin story," if there is such a thing, begins long before we began our work. One finds traces of it in oral histories with musicians and in the pages of the early newspaper accounts of jazz, as well as in over 30 years of scholarship dedicated to unraveling issues of sex discrimination, marginalization, and the effects of shifting and clashing definitions of masculinity and femininity on whether and how people in particular times and places participated (or did not) in jazz cultures. Because we have been inspired and informed by many of the same articles and books, we would like to take a few pages to summarize some of the pieces that we have found to be extremely important in gender and jazz scholarship.

Much of this earlier scholarship emerged in the 1970s and 1980s as part of the Women's Movement and, as such, must be seen not only as interventions into jazz scholarship but also as part of the development of theories and methods in feminist historiography. These methods opened up techniques for telling "hidden histories" and for revisiting histories we thought we knew, with revised assumptions about who counted as historical subjects. Although the theories and methods associated with "hidden histories," women's history, and histories of gender, sexuality, race, class, "experience," and other social categories have become more complex since much of the early "women-and-jazz" literature was produced, we still consider it important to acknowledge the contributions of this body of research to the gender analyses that are the focus of this collection. Our intent in providing an overview of previous scholarship is neither to celebrate nor to criticize this earlier work, but to provide a kind of map for understanding the routes taken by researchers in the past, many of which were not produced in academic settings. Most of the scholarship that emerged from "women's history" projects received little notice, support, or engagement from intellectual circles and institutions of jazz studies. This scholarship continues to be overlooked, in part, because the rhetorical move of celebration to break the silence resounded more meaningfully in the 1970s and 1980s than it does today, and the usefulness of "uncritical celebration" has been roundly critiqued in feminist scholarship. Yet this work was crucial in paving the way for the work that followed; in addition, we feel that it is important to note how much gender and race analysis is introduced to the field of jazz studies through these works.

A primary preoccupation of jazz historiography has been that of origins and narratives of origins: Where and how did jazz begin? How are new styles developed? A fact commonly accepted has been that jazz is rooted in New Orleans, resulting from the convergence of African and European musical practices. In 1975, an important essay by Susan Cavin appeared in *Journal of Jazz Studies*. In "Missing Women: On the Voodoo Trail to Jazz," Cavin revisited the precursors to jazz in Congo Square in New Orleans, a park that was the meeting place of slaves and their descendents. In returning to the primary documents used by jazz historians to study the practice of drumming, Cavin observes that early jazz historians failed to notice what she calls "the sex variable" in drummers in a site considered to be the "birth" of jazz and suggests that this failure on their part laid the groundwork for subsequent historians to ignore the prominence of women in various jazz scenes.

"Recovery" of women's culture and women's voices as historical actors were important political tactics for feminists of the 1970s and 1980s, but these methods often fell short of attending to differences among women as they were invested in building on commonalities. Although much of the music and musical history "recovered" through "women's music" discourse was acoustic folk music, the 1970s and 1980s also saw a profusion of women's jazz festivals, women's jazz history documentation, reissues of jazz and blues recordings by women, and a feminist-identified revival of the all-woman band tradition of the 1930s and 1940s. The excitement of that time, as well as the critical conversations about who is and is not represented in this celebration of jazzwomen, were vividly captured in the poet hattie gossett's critical article "jazzwomen," written with carolyn johnson, which first appeared in *Jazz Spotlite News* in 1979, then in the feminist journal *Heresies* women and music issue from 1981, and later in an edited volume on women in rock (McDonnell and Powers 1996). In this and other writings about jazz, gossett encouraged us to think about "how it was" when sexism defined women's choices about participating in jazz as musicians, as well as how racism defined women and gender roles, both in the past and in the contemporary times in which they wrote. If "white women are still being promoted over black women," they argued, then how "liberating" was this "current attack on sexism in jazz" accompanying the 1970s women's movement? (gossett 1984, 68). In elaborating on these themes, they argued that both sexism and racism contributed to "black american cultural disenfranchisement," their theory about the cultural appropriation and cooptation of jazz.

Another author who raised such issues has been Val Wilmer. Notably, in her chapter "It Takes Two People to Confirm the Truth" (Wilmer 1977), she explored a variety of tensions in jazz culture, tensions that took place off the stage and out of the recording studio, but nonetheless had a significant impact on jazz artists and their families. Wilmer raised questions such as whether or not it is possible for two artists to thrive in one family; why and how did women become invested in jazz and jazz culture; how do musicians negotiate conflicts between their music and their families; how does the way male musicians negotiate those conflicts influence how their manhood is defined; what do black women want; and how do male musicians understand a correlation between their careers and the race of the women in their lives? The tensions between race, gender, and performance that Wilmer and gossett articulated reflected the contemporary concerns of feminism and black power even as they continued to suggest compelling avenues for analysis.

Such directions are ripe for new research. A recent piece that helped us to think about aspects of the everyday that assist in the marginalization of women's stories in jazz history was Robin D. G. Kelley's essay on jazz wives (Kelley 2002b), which appeared as an obituary for Nellie Monk in the *New York Times*. This article extended some of the issues raised by Wilmer by highlighting the cooperative relationships between male jazz musicians and their wives, specifically those who had profound relationships to the music and the business of producing it. He asked us to consider the "great couples of modern jazz" to rethink the ways that women have influenced and sustained the careers of male jazz musicians. Whether as personal manager, muse, or critic, the wives of jazz musicians played an important role in their husbands' lives and the life of the music, a role that is often discounted and ignored in jazz histories and criticism. Jazz, for Nellie Monk, Bertha Hope, Maxine Gordon, Gladys Hampton, and many other so-called jazz wives, was not only a fact of life for them because of their husbands but also an interest they had come to on their own, often prior to meeting the men who would come to provide their historical definition as "jazz wives."

Women listen to jazz and engage in jazz culture for reasons other than to attract the attention of men. Oral histories that are not necessarily focused on issues of "gender" and "women" deserve re-listening for the treatment of the everyday in which musicians are not always men, and not always isolated from family and communities. New oral history projects that focus on issues of gender and jazz such as Maxine Gordon's "Women Who Listen" project, which aims to collect interviews with women jazz fans, will yield important new information on women for whom listening to jazz has been meaningful, not necessarily as musicians or as "wives," but as audiences. Memoirs of women jazz musicians, women involved in the business of jazz, spouses to jazz musicians, and jazz fans help to increase our perspectives (Cheatham 2006, Wilmer 1989, gossett 1984). Photographs (see figures 1.1 and 1.2) may also help to develop research questions about the underexplored range of everyday jazz life. What does Mark Miller's photograph of pianist Geri Allen and her son Wallace Roney III at a sound check suggest to us about elisions of the everyday in jazz historiography, journalism, and discourse? What do we make of the body language, the silence, the expressions on the faces of the women behind the Count Basie trumpet section in Paul Hoeffler's remarkable reframing of the bandstand?

In the early 1980s, in conjunction with the women's jazz festivals that accompanied the Second Wave Women's Movement, several key book-length studies were published that painstakingly compiled histories of women instrumentalists throughout jazz history. Although not restricted to the category of jazz, *Black Women in American Bands and Orchestras* (Handy 1981) was the first published of this exciting emergence of historical surveys. *American Women in Jazz, 1900 to the Present* (Placksin 1982) and *Stormy Weather: the Music and Lives of a Century of Jazzwomen* (Dahl 1989) soon followed. The three books, taken together, became the classic and still indispensable references for women-in-jazz historians and jazz historians interested in including women in their studies. Although "women's history" may seem hopelessly supplemental today as a political project, it is important to remember that "recovery" of lost histories has been considered an extremely crucial component of many struggles for social justice by groups that have not been considered important enough to count in history. Like Cavin, Handy, Placksin, and Dahl recovered histories of women in jazz from the same archives

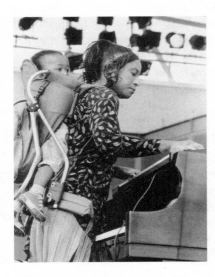

Fig. 1.1. "Wives and Basie Trumpets," © 1960.
Paul Hoeffler, ctsimages.com.

Fig. 1.2. Geri Allen and Wallace Roney III, 1997.
Photograph by Mark Miller.

that had been scoured by authors of histories that assumed women were outside of jazz and, in addition, turned to sites that had been over-looked, such as family bands and school bands (see also Handy 1983). Although documenting lost history is often seen as a "dated" form of feminist inquiry, less "theoretical" than deploying "gender as a useful category of analysis" (Scott 1988), it is also important to note that without an implicit gender analysis, Handy, Placksin, and Dahl would not have been able to open up the jazz history frameworks that had not previously "counted" nor know where to look for the "missing" women.[6] In addition, asking "where are the women" has also been an important route toward finding the gendered spheres of fields thought to be gender-neutral meritocracies; these spheres, incidentally, often include men as well as women (Lara Pellegrinelli makes this point re-garding vocalists in her essay in this volume.)

Not all "recovery" projects of women in jazz have been solely or primarily about rendering women visible in the jazz past and present. Black feminist approaches to studying black women's importance in blues and jazz, for example, have been significant in recovering histories of African American women, not only as "contributors to jazz" but also as precursors to black feminism, as well as in expanding the class param-eters of histories of black feminism focused on the black clubwoman's movement (Carby 1994, Davis 1998, Harrison 1988, Kernodle 2004). Although much of the pivotal work on black women and music has focused on blues women, a recent edited collection reminds us that African American women have been musical producers in many forms of music, not just the blues. In her introduction, the ethnomusicologist Eileen M. Hayes makes the important point that although the scholar-ship on black women and blues is of great significance, anthology prac-tices that render the blues as "the sole representation of black women's musical experience has the unintended effect of muting analytical treat-ments of black women, race, and gender in opera, gospel music, rock, country, jazz, or, for that matter, electro-acoustic music" (6–7). Two ex-cellent pieces on jazz in that volume accomplish far more than to extend the genre focus from "blues" to "blues and jazz." Ethnomusicologist and saxophonist Linda F. Williams demonstrates that in addition to race, gender, and class, intersectional analyses of black women, jazz, and feminism should include generation, age, and genre. Her own research of black women jazz musicians' relationships to feminism pointed out that these factors played an enormous role in the ways in which black women jazz musicians experienced their identities, political alliances, and music-making.[7] Nanette de Jong's interview-based article adds to our understanding of women and gender in the Association for the Advancement of Creative Musicians.[8]

Scholarship on jazz and gender produced after the early 1990s drew from and contributed to feminist musicology a set of practices that emerged as a field to be reckoned with in 1991 with the publication of Susan McClary's iconoclastic (now classic) *Feminine Endings* and the first biannual meeting of Feminist Theory and Music Conference, which was held June 26, 1991, at the University of Minnesota. McClary's methods for analyzing gender and music, including reading music in specific cultural and historical contexts as a gendered discourse, have been tremendously important to scholarship of many musical genres, although more is surely yet to come in jazz studies. Perhaps the most exciting application to date is Robin D. G. Kelley's analysis of how dissonance was differently gendered in 1950s jazz than it was in the operatic and Western classical models analyzed by McClary. Rather than rejecting McClary's methods altogether, however, Kelley draws from her set of analytical tools to explore how gender assumptions punctuated the ascriptions of musical value by critics, musicians, and audiences in 1950s jazz circles, in order to argue that "resistance to order," not "establishment" of consonant order, was considered masculine by those moved by black male jazz musicians in the 1950s, whereas cool jazz was considered "effeminate" (Kelley 1999, 140–41 and n. 2).

Masculinity studies has been another important field of study that has opened up the theoretical possibilities for "listening for gender" in jazz studies. The route, in some ways, has been the reverse of the trajectory of women-in-jazz historiography. Instead of moving from presumed absence to inclusion to gender analysis, writing about masculinity and jazz has traveled from presumed (sometimes conscious and sometimes not) jazz norm to visibility as gender construction. From its birth through the rumors of its death and resurrection, jazz history and criticism has been couched in the language of nation, race, and masculinity. Its early scholars, critics, and promoters danced around notions of racialized masculinity. Their writings evidence what Eric Lott in another context described as a tension between "love and theft," a desire to emulate and advocate for a music that was deeply rooted in black cultural practices and experiences while also seeking to make the music audible or recognizable to white audiences who believed that the highest form of music was the classical genre. Their appropriation of the music led to the designation of jazz as both America's classical music (an appropriate expression for white musicians) and a distinctly black art form. Writers, such as Sidney Finkelstein, Nat Hentoff, Barry Ulanov, John Hammond, Neil Leonard, and LeRoi Jones, began challenging the claims made about jazz and introduced much more complex readings of the relationship between nation, race, and masculinity. Their work reflected the developments happening among the musicians themselves who were challenging assumptions about race, masculinity, and cultural politics in their compositions, their performances, and their own writings in the press and in autobiographies.

Ingrid Monson's "The Problem with White Hipness" (Monson 1995) was one of the most influential and earliest academic articles to analyze white fascination with black masculinity as part of the desire driving representations of jazz. Monson provided us with a conceptual, and gendered, lens for thinking about race and music. We began to ask different sets of questions about what we had been reading in the vast literature of jazz. How could we begin marshalling the disparate works on gender, race, and nation in jazz in such a way that the voices of the black musicians and their representations of the culture and the music held equal authority with those of the white authors who had predominated the written record? Scholars, such as Herman Gray, Robin D. G. Kelley, Eric Porter, Hazel Carby, Nichole T. Rustin, Ron Radano, Kyle Julian, Gerald Early, Krin Gabbard, and others have laid the ground upon which to build our analyses of racialized masculinity in the twentieth century. Again, Kelley's scholarship proved indispensable, as in his often-cited observations of "black male hipsters of the zoot suit generation" as a reminder "that the creation of an alternative culture can simultaneously challenge and reinforce existing power relations" (Kelley 1993, 88). Herman Gray helps us think about the cultural work of public performance of gender, race, and sexuality in the "self representations of Black masculinity in the United states" as "historically structured by and against dominant (and dominating) discourses of masculinity and race, specifically (whiteness)." Urging us to think in terms of difference within difference, of many self-representations of black masculinity operating at once, Gray compares performances of Miles Davis and John Coltrane as "modern innovators in musical aesthetics, cultural vision, and personal style" who "challenged dominant cultural assumptions about masculinity and whiteness" (Gray 1995, 401). Such work not only makes "masculinity visible" but also helps us to think of black musicians as the authors of their own experience, as individuals who negotiated the complex gender ordering of black American experiences and sought and found in artistic expression a critical gaze and a political voice.

Challenging traditional discursive constructions of who is a jazz subject or what counts as jazz reflects many scholars' approaches to situating black artists and audiences in discussions of modernity and modernism. As the music scholar Carol J. Oja writes, new music in the 1920s benefited from being tied to modernism because "the beauty of modernism was that it encompassed no dominating center or clear line of authority. . . . [I]t stood for one basic principle: iconoclastic, irreverent innovation, sometimes irreconcilable with the historic traditions that preceded it." Jazz could then be tied to modern concert music, dance, art, as well as to new ideas about the self and community.[9] Black Americans from the early twentieth century through the postwar period embraced modernity as much as white Americans: access to economic, technological, and social change enabled them to articulate themselves as modern individuals in a modern world. Guthrie P. Ramsey hinges his arguments about black music in the postwar period on the recognition of the experiences of black Americans and their cultural practices as products of modernism. Drawing on Marshall Berman's definition of modernism, which focuses on the efforts of men and women to become *subjects* and *objects*, Ramsey argues that for African Americans, part of "making themselves at home [in the modern world] consisted of the musical expressions that articulated attitudes about their place in the modern world."[10] Ramsey echoes LeRoi Jones when Jones argued in 1964 in *Blues People* that to understand the mindset of black Americans at any historical moment, one need only look to their music, the music which also marked the emergence of a new, modern black subject. Similarly, Angela Y. Davis's study of Bessie Smith, Ma Rainey, and Billie Holiday focuses on how these particular women singers embodied and vocalized their communities' understanding and experience of modern life: articulations of sexuality, violence, urban life, and love characterized the public dialogue found in black music.[11] It is this concept of black music as a public dialogue which has often underscored studies of jazz as participating in modernist discourse. This public dialogue is wide-ranging in scope, taking place within black working-class communities, between "white" and "black" America, and between "America" and the world.[12] Several chapters in this volume, including Jayna Brown's chapter on African American women dancers, locate their analyses in the formation of jazz as a modernist discourse.

Although not explicitly about jazz, Elsa Barkley Brown's "Poly-rhythms and Improvisations" (Brown 1991) provided what is perhaps the most important "ear training" for us in learning how to listen for gender in jazz studies. In developing her argument for jazz as a useful metaphor for writing history, Brown focused on the music's democratic impulse as a model for historians' writing, broadly speaking. She emphasizes the multiplicity of voices present in jazz performance, arguing for the production of conversational narratives in which discordant and harmonious voices are integrated. If Ralph Ellison's "invisible man" speaks for us on the lower frequencies, then Brown seeks a practice of writing that makes all frequencies, and their interconnections, audible. Listening for gender in jazz studies shifts the contours of jazz history: the boundaries and definitions of what counts as jazz sounds and practices, and our awareness of whose bodies are seen and not seen as jazz bodies. From Susan Cavin's call for jazz historians to notice the "sex variable," to the analytical frameworks presented in this volume, what counts as a "gender analysis" has changed considerably. The authors of the following essays are less likely to think of gender as a "sex variable" than they are to think of it as a historically and culturally contingent, perpetual social construction that never acts alone or, in Judith Butler's words, as "a practice of improvisation within a scene of constraint" (Butler 2004, 1).

THE ESSAYS

We've divided the essays, quite loosely, into three broad categories: Rooting Gender in Jazz History, Improvising Gender: Embodiment and Performance, and Reimagining Jazz Representations.

Part I, "Rooting Gender in Jazz History," is as much about tuning our ears to marginalized experiences within jazz history as it is about the restoration of dissenting, outraged, and muted perspectives in jazz criticism. It so often seems that the subjects of jazz history remain fixed on a select group. The essays collected in this part broaden the scope of that history and advance a number of perspectives on how to better integrate marginalized experiences into the story of jazz. Including these essays at the front of the anthology underscores a key aspect of this volume: we wish to emphasize how central women have been to the development of the music as well as to narratives about jazz history and criticism. The authors in this part do not take "gender history" merely to mean writing women into history in separate and supplemental texts, or even neces-

Fig. 1.3. Although gender theorists following Judith Butler maintain that gender is constituted through repeated performance—that all of us, in fact, perform gender all the time—some people also consciously perform gender and sex as part of the job. For three years in the 1920s, Edna Lewis (1907–95) "passed" as a man to play in hotel bands (although local patrons, fellow musicians, bandleader, and hotel owner all knew she was a woman). This is a page from the program from her memorial (January 7, 1996), into which friends lovingly arranged photos from her career. Bottom left: She appears as a "man" because it was deemed more acceptable for her to appear as a man than as a woman horn player in the hotel band. Right: She appears in her silk uniform for another job—playing in an all-woman combo in a Chinese restaurant. Sherrie Tucker Collection.

sarily writing primarily "women's history," but they do consider gender an important analytic of power, especially in the ways difference is produced as normalized hierarchy in sound, social life, historiography, and representation. By challenging traditional discursive constructions of who counts as a jazz subject or even what counts as jazz, these authors draw our attention to a range of issues normally ignored in jazz historiography and criticism, among them the aesthetics of accompaniment; the discordant relationships between women's experiences and reception as jazz subjects — instrumentalists, singers, listeners; and the need to find ways of writing multivocal histories of race, gender, and music.

The two essays that open this part, Lara Pellegrinelli's "Separated at 'Birth': Singing and Jazz History" and Jeff Taylor's "With Lovie and Lil: Rediscovering Two Chicago Pianists of the 1920s," are new scholarship that engage two central concerns of jazz historiography: origins and recordings. They introduce us to new modes of listening and recording jazz history. Pellegrinelli explores the ways in which jazz singing has been ignored within jazz historiography and relegated to a second-class status within jazz culture. Her attention is focused on how certain truths told about jazz history reflect inconsistencies in its history. Pellegrinelli argues that narratives of origins are embedded with gendered narratives, resulting in the marginalization and devaluation of certain aspects within jazz culture. Jazz origins are rooted in singing — blues, work songs, and spirituals — and yet singing has always been viewed in jazz historiography as subordinate to the "higher" art of instrumental music, a predominately male domain. Like Cavin, Pellegrinelli revisits the early jazz history of New Orleans, through anecdote and autobiography, to highlight the centrality of singing to jazz culture. Pellegrinelli asks us to rethink what we have read and what we have heard on recordings to develop a fuller understanding of jazz as a modernist discourse.

Taylor's essay examines the careers of Lovie Austin and Lil Hardin Armstrong, two pianists who were highly successful and influential in the 1920s. Since so much of jazz history relies upon recordings and attention to the soloist, Taylor turns to Armstrong's and Hardin's respective recordings to assess two rarely examined aspects of jazz studies: accompaniment and the impact of gender on the prominence a role such as being an accompanist realizes. Although not all musicologists draw on close analysis of the musical work in this day of the "New Musicology," Taylor finds this aspect of musicological method useful in exploring the dynamics of these women's recorded performances and their influence.

Other essays in this part foreground questions of gender and politics in jazz history. Since the 1950s, jazz historians and critics have highlighted the relationship between jazz and democracy, citizenship, and nation. Few, however, have explored how gender has shaped these relationships either in the United States or internationally. As these authors show, these issues have also influenced ideas about aesthetics, cultural politics, and social issues.

Monica Hairston's essay on Café Society and black female boogie woogie pianists draws us to what many might consider central questions when bringing a gender analysis to jazz studies: What place did female instrumentalists have in jazz culture? How were women constructed and valued as instrumentalists within the community of jazz artists and critics? Although one could potentially respond to these questions with the add-women-and-stir model of jazz historiography, Hairston significantly engages the political and aesthetic choices these particular women made in the context of a vibrant political culture that was linked to the musical culture. She presents these women as social actors. During the 1930s, the Popular Front maintained a cultural dimension and the women Hairston examines, Mary Lou Williams and Hazel Scott, negotiated political, aesthetic, and racial identities within that context. Attending to these women's stories, Hairston lays the groundwork for reading how a diverse community of performers (female boogie pianists) has been critically and historically masked behind narratives of female exceptionality.

Christina Baade links national identity during wartime with radio and the popularity of dance music in her study of Ivy Benson and her Ladies' Dance Orchestra. She integrates a number of issues related to masculinity and femininity in her study, drawing our attention to the complex ways that one defines and is defined by the other in the various cultural "minefields" of the Second World War period. Music as a broad cultural practice and swing as a popular music provide her with the context for exploring how conventional British notions of effeminacy were challenged by a crisis of masculinity and the popularity of female instrumentalists. Authenticity, virility, Britishness, and sentimentality were among the representational "mine fields" Benson and her Orchestra negotiated in their public and popular performances on BBC radio.

Tracy McMullen's essay, "Being Glenn Miller," puts questions of jazz history and cultural politics in stark and almost comical relief. McMullen explores questions of how race is masculinized and reinscribed through an examination of the Yale University Concert Band's reenactment of the Glenn Miller Orchestra. Nostalgia, homogeneity, and musical practice come under scrutiny of what it means for a racially and gender diverse band to reenact mid-century white masculinity in the late twentieth century. McMullen wonders how the contemporary wartime context resonates for those seeking to or compelled to reenact racial roles from another wartime era. Incorporating theories of embodiment and performance in her analysis of historical reenactment, this essay helps to make the transition to our next part and to highlight productive overlaps.

Part II is entitled "Improvising Gender: Embodiment and Performance." "Embodiment" is dangerous territory in jazz discourse, vulnerable to replicating the primitivist history of mainstream reception that celebrated or shunned jazz as unbridled hedonism. Although each of these pieces conveys a critical awareness of the dangers of mapping music associated with black people, women, and/or "the feminine" to embodiment, spectacle, and madness, they also draw from feminist theories of performativity and embodiment as modes of subject formation. As Ingrid Monson wrote in 1997, "the anthropology of the person, the body, and emotion; performance theory; and the anthropology of sexual desire would all seem to provide excellent points of departure for both musicologists and ethnomusicologists in reinvigorated debates about the role of gender in music and culture. What we need are creative applications and syntheses that rethink these ideas through the problem of music."[13]

Jayna Brown kicks off this part by making a compelling case for performance and embodiment as significant categories of analysis for jazz studies that attends to gender, race, and modernism, and for African American dancers not simply as objects to be glimpsed by subjects becoming modern but as subjects accessing particularly modernist perspectives. As Brown argues in her piece on black female dancers as *flaneurs*, performance studies offers theoretical models for reconsidering performers as observers, not simply as the observed, and to acknowledge dancers' "artistic and intellectual interiority," which is denied when, as she puts it, "music is lifted from the flesh." Dance has been especially raced among gendered and devalued categories of jazz studies and has continued to be overlooked in jazz studies despite such excellent scholarship by Jacqui Malone, Katrina Hazzard-Gordon, Brenda Dixon Gottschild, and Susan Cook.

Julie Smith's piece suggests that because music associated with "the feminine" has often been considered "excessive" (McClary 1991), much of the feminist work attempting to reclaim women jazz musicians has focused on instrumentalists proud of dashing stereotypes of "difference" as they played in styles indistinguishable from those of men (Tucker 2000). The flip side to this is the Catch-22 that experimental players face when they are heard as women out of control. Drawing from poststructuralist psychoanalytic feminism, Julie Smith studies the performances of a European feminist trio that improvises on "hysteria" to raise the question of whether sonic spectacle provides opportunities for disenfranchised groups to challenge power relations. Can women who improvise constructions of "feminine hysteria" with their "sonorous bodies" critique the power structures that define them as hysterics?

As with many pieces in this collection, Eric Porter's essay on George Russell's "Lydian Chromatic Concept" could have been placed in any of our parts. It could appear in historiography or in representation (self-presentation), but we have chosen to include it in "Improvising Gender: Embodiment and Performance" for its sensitive analysis of Russell's self-presentation in relation to a critique of reductive discourses of embodiment, madness, and black masculinity at a particular time and place. Russell's "claiming of critical space," according to Porter, is achieved through performing and embodying a self-representation that critiques reductive assumptions about blackness and embodiment and challenges white ownership of "science and technology."

Sherrie Tucker's essay in this volume draws from Ruth Frankenberg's analysis of the "Trope of White Woman" to explore the figure of the white woman singer in the 1947 film, *New Orleans*. By approaching this well-known "jazz film" through a focus on the white woman's desire to embody and perform a black woman's song, Tucker raises questions not only about the film but also about white women's subject formation as "modern," as American, and as sexual, through black music. She begins with representation of a film but closes with the unrepresentability, and therefore unknowability, of alternative forms of white women's subject formation through jazz.

In a sense, Monson's new piece, "Fitting the Part," which was written for this volume and concludes this part, enacts the "creative application and syntheses" she called for in 1997, which would engage theories from "anthropology of the person and the body" and performance theory to learn more about gender and music. By narrating her relationship with jazz and the trumpet, Monson offers a history of experience in the sense that Joan Scott referenced when she wrote, "It is not individuals who have experience, but subjects who are constituted through experience."[14] For Monson, even subjects who do not appear to "fit the part" are shaped through intersecting social categories such as race, gender, class, and sexuality. She also points out that theories of embodiment and performance may help us to understand how social categories are constituted through musical performance.

Our last group of contributors asks us to think about what it means to represent jazz, which is, after all, a practice that all of us who write about jazz are engaged in, even when we write critically. What racialized and gendered tropes are mobilized in various media constructions of jazz performers and jazz communities? How do these constructions, as perceived by audiences, musicians, historians, and critics, impact the ways in which musicians are heard, and, in turn, affect their labor, documentation, places in historical memory? Readers will notice that there is a fine line between the foci of essays in part III, "Reimagining Jazz Representations," and those in the previous part on "Improvising Gender: Embodiment and Performance." Clearly, some pieces in these parts could easily have been included in either one (Porter, Tucker, Monson). However, we found the distinctions between theories of representation and theories of performativity and embodiment significant enough to place these essays into categories that drew into relief their relationships to different strands in current scholarship in gender and jazz studies.

Although "Improvising Gender: Embodiment and Performance" brought together essays that emphasized jazz as a site of embodied subject formation, the pieces in "Reimagining Jazz Representations" shine their spotlights of gender analysis on the desires of viewers/listeners as they are mapped onto performers whose own subject formation may be experienced quite differently. For poststructuralist feminists, this distinction between what Elizabeth Grosz named the "lived body" and the body as a surface "on which social law, morality, and values are inscribed" is itself a construct that must be disrupted and interrogated. For Grosz, it is less useful to think of these two views as opposites — the body as experience versus the body as billboard — than it is to see these as linked in the manner of a Möbius strip. In other words, the blurriness between these concerns in many of the essays in this collection must not be seen as theoretical confusion, but as exemplifying jazz scholarship that joins other feminist projects in finding ways to play both registers at once or, as Grosz puts it, to theorize the "hinge."[15]

For instance, Ingrid Monson's "Fitting the Part," the closing piece in "Improvising Gender: Embodiment and Performance," and the opening essay by Ursel Schlicht in "Reimagining Jazz Representations" both consider women's subject formations through jazz culture as well as the ways in which the bodies of women who participate in jazz cultures are read by others (Monson by her students, Schlicht's magazine correspondents by other fans, readers, and critics). But while Monson asks "How have I [a white woman, trumpet-playing jazz subject] been possible?" Schlicht raises the question of how women jazz fans and musicians in Germany in the 1950s had been rendered illegible except for a brief period when they were represented in the pages of a jazz magazine as articulate spokespersons in a debate that questioned their very existence. As with several other essays in this collection (Taylor, Pellegrinelli, Hairston), Schlicht disrupts a model that assumes jazzwomen are always and only marginalized. Indeed, the pieces in this part take representation as a complex field populated with diverse cultural producers.

João Costa Vargas's essay, "Exclusion, Openness, and Utopia in Black Male Performance at The World Stage Jazz Jam Sessions," draws on ethnography and political theory to examine jazz in one unique jazz club in contemporary urban America. By focusing on who is represented and how in the day-to-day activities of what he describes as a "storefront workshop and performance space," Vargas explores jazz and its relationship to local community discourses and practices. Vargas puts pressure on the question of what it means to look to a male-dominated, public space to address the needs of a larger community. In focusing on black cultural politics and masculinity, Vargas asks how we might challenge the gender bias of potentially liberatory discourses and practices to be found in jazz culture and how we might conceive of an event like a jam session as an issue of representation.

The remainder of the articles turn to representations of jazz in other expressive forms such as literature and film. Farah Jasmine Griffin has contributed a new essay to this collection that presents black women's fiction as an underexplored site of jazz literature that can tell us about what jazz has meant to black women as listeners, readers, and writers in the context of black freedom struggles of the 1960s and 1970s, as well as in the context of black feminism. By urging us to consider fiction that has been largely overlooked by studies in jazz literature, Griffin also opens up the field of studies of jazz representation to a broader range of notions of jazz practice, community, and subjectivity.

Nichole T. Rustin brings a complex gender and race analysis to the more familiar representations of "the experience of the 'jazzman'" in Dorothy Baker's 1938 novel, *Young Man with a Horn*, and Michael Curtiz's 1952 film version. Rustin asks, how has jazz rendered the gendered identifications of "jazzman" and "jazz fraternity," and what have these particular representations of male self-determination and men's homosocial communities meant to different audiences and at different times?

Several of the authors in this collection make the important point that despite marginalization of women in the most prized roles of jazz cultural production and representation, there have existed areas in which women were welcome. The fact that these have been overlooked by both mainstream historians and women-in-jazz historians tells us something about how historians have understood gender and which desires fueled what Hayden White has called "the content of the form" of their respective historical projects. Kristen McGee draws our attention to the large numbers of filmic representations of all-woman bands in the 1930s and 1940s, made for black and white audiences, analyzing a range of "gendered jazz aesthetics."

CONCLUSION

The essays collected here are by no means exhaustive of either the possibilities of gender analysis or work already completed. Scholars who have influenced our thoughts about gender in jazz culture include Hazel Carby, Angela Davis, Krin Gabbard, David Ake, Kathy Ogren, John Gennari, Robert O'Meally, Kevin Gaines, Susan Cook, Penny Von Eschen, Jacqui Malone, Ron Radano, Robin D. G. Kelley, Kyle Julian, Guthrie Ramsey, Herman Gray, and many others. The jazz cultures we have represented range from the traditional to the avant-garde and reveal "feminine" as well as masculine concerns and identities. "Jazz culture" is of this moment and is historically situated; it is improvisational and composed, written and performed. Further, the anthology does not claim to be an exhaustive representation of possible approaches to studying gender in jazz. Rather, we would argue that the intriguing variety of work represented in this volume should draw attention to the traditional invisibility of gender within jazz studies and make us aware of the importance and viability of pursuing gender analysis in future jazz studies. Indeed, not only does the volume contribute to filling a critical hole, it also provides a forum for the voices of women scholars, quite a minority in jazz studies and criticism. Even so, although the majority of contributors are female, we certainly hope readers do not assume that doing "gender" is women's work.

If jazz is an important cultural site of what Olly Wilson (1999) has called "the heterogeneous sound ideal," then the possibility for diverse gender analyses to sound, amid the increasingly complex, nuanced, multi-vocal, textured vocabularies of what is currently being called New Jazz Studies, marks a moment when jazz and gender scholars are not considered irrelevant, or even supplemental to jazz studies, but are crucial contributors of productive dissonance, sounding the textures that help to make jazz studies more jazzlike and more up to the task of studying jazz cultures.

NOTES

1. Monson 1996, 43.

2. Tucker 2001–2, 377.

3. O'Meally, Edwards, and Griffin 2004, 2.

4. Ibid.

5. Heble 2000, 9.

6. Tucker 2006, 2001–2.

7. Linda F. Williams, "Black Women, Jazz, and Feminism," in Hayes and Williams 2007, 119–33.

8. Nanette de Jong, "Women of the Association for the Advancement of Creative Musicians: Four Narratives," in Hayes and Williams 2007, 134–52.

9. Carol J. Oja, *Making Music Modern: New York in the 1920s* (Oxford: Oxford University Press, 2000), 4; Alfred Appel Jr., *Jazz Modernism: From Ellington and Armstrong to Matisse and Joyce* (New York: Borzoi, 2002).

10. Ramsey quotes Berman's definition of modernism as "any attempt by modern men and women to become subjects as well as objects of modernization, to get a grip on the modern world and make themselves at home in it." Ramsey 2003, 97, 104.

11. Angela Y. Davis, *Blues Legacies and Black Feminisms: Gertrude "Ma" Rainey, Bessie Smith, and Billie Holiday* (New York: Vintage, 1999).

12. See Porter 2002; Von Eschen 2004.

13. Monson 1997, 30.

14. Scott 1991, 779.

15. Elizabeth Grosz, *Volatile Bodies: Towards a Corporeal Feminism* (Bloomington: Indiana University Press, 1994), summarized in Chris Weedon, *Feminism, Theory, and the Politics of Difference* (Malden, Mass.: Blackwell, 1999), 120–21.

PART I

Rooting Gender in Jazz History

Lara Pellegrinelli

SEPARATED AT "BIRTH":

SINGING AND THE HISTORY OF JAZZ

In the context of studies that address issues of gender in jazz, singing presents its own unique challenges. Although the vast majority of women in jazz have been and continue to be vocalists, a role that can provide them with tremendous visibility and widespread recognition from audiences, surprisingly little has been done to investigate singing as a gendered domain. The scholarly literature on "women in jazz" has focused almost entirely on instrumentalists: compensatory histories have documented the work of neglected artists, challenged the hegemonic nature of jazz historiography, and raised a host of complex issues faced by women working in a male-dominated field.[1] Indeed, the marginalization of singers by scholars of women in jazz may very well occur because the singers' mainstream popularity complicates or perhaps even eclipses altogether the "stories of devaluation and absence" with which such scholars have primarily been concerned.[2]

Nonetheless, the exclusion of singers from musical canons, scholarship, and the serious press coverage that often provides a critical foundation for these other projects is as deeply entrenched as that of their female instrumental counterparts.[3] For example, some histories, including the most popular textbook for undergraduate jazz courses, completely erase singers.[4] Paul Berliner's landmark ethnography on improvisation, *Thinking in Jazz*, lists only three among his fifty-two interview subjects.[5] Merely a handful of academic articles and biographical studies take singers as their subject, leaving their written documentation in disparate sources: brief encyclopedia articles, album liner notes, magazine and newspaper articles, and publicity materials generated by the music industry. Given the historiographic focus on vocal forms within African-American music broadly speaking — from spirituals and the blues to soul and hip-hop — jazz's almost exclusive emphasis on instrumental music is certainly distinctive, if not peculiar or anomalous.

Aside from the grudging nods afforded a few Swing Era "canaries," ones so prominent that they would be difficult to ignore, singing only factors into the majority of histories as a musical practice common to many forms that comprise jazz's nineteenth-century precursors. An exploration of the ways that historians have represented jazz's so-called birth reveals how gender is embedded in the narratives surrounding this mythical event, ones that contribute to normative concepts, politics, and subject formation in jazz overall. As Edward Said asserts, "beginnings carry weight because they function as sites for the conscious production of meaning, a result of their departure from pre-existing traditions of discourse."[6] In jazz historiography, they effectively fix the marginalized status of women early in a tradition of representation as well as in the musical chronologies themselves. Despite its symbolic and practical importance in jazz's parentage, singing is dropped from historical narratives soon after the music's birth. Having waited for her to deliver her offspring, historians cut the umbilical cord, separating mother from child and enabling the yowling infant to toddle off on his own down the streets of New Orleans.

Most general histories of jazz begin by presenting a variety of precursors, a shadowy morass of genres that goes back to the nineteenth century: spirituals, ring shouts, work songs, field cries, and plantation songs; the European dance forms and operas performed by New Orleans creoles; minstrelsy, the blues, white marching band music, and ragtime. In Rudi Blesh's *Shining Trumpets*, jazz emerges as a fusion of all Negro musics.[7] The jazz entry in Willi Apel's *Harvard Dictionary of Music* traces the music to spirituals, then ragtime and the blues.[8] In Joachim Ernst Berendt's *Das Jazzbuch*, it emerges almost completely from the spiritual.[9] Although Marshall Stearns's classic *The Story of Jazz* includes virtually nothing on jazz singers, vocal forms figure prominently in the book's early sections on the Great Awakening, spirituals, work songs, minstrelsy, and the blues, after which he covers ragtime.[10] Following a chapter on early folk forms, Frank Tirro's popular text *Jazz: A History* divides jazz's precursors into blues and ragtime.[11] In the

Ken Burns PBS series *Jazz*, the blues and ragtime are discussed in a section titled "The Roux" as the two styles that reach New Orleans in the 1890s.[12]

Although the sample presented above is neither systematic nor exhaustive, it readily offers a sense of the literature and the many ways that historians have presented jazz's parentage. While each author paints a slightly different picture, two strands emerge from these gatherings of jazz's ancestors, identifiable as they culminate in their endpoints as its most immediate precursors: the blues and ragtime. The strands are implicitly coded by "instrument" and gender.

The blues, which grows from and contains the African American vocal forms that precede it (with the possible exception of minstrelsy), is linked to emotion; it stands for the expressive side of African American music. Both the statements of early musicians and of historians ascribe a feeling to the blues imparted by race. In Frederic Ramsey Jr.'s and Charles Edward Smith's *Jazzmen*, E. Simms Campbell writes about the blues in similar language to that used by W. E. B. Du Bois in his descriptions of the spirituals. Campbell explains: "To me, they are filled with the deepest emotions of a race. They are songs of sorrow charged with satire, with that potent quality of ironic verse clothed in the raiment of the buffoon. They were more than releases, temporary releases, from servitude. The blues were the gateway to freedom for all American Negroes. In song, the Negro expressed his true feelings, his hopes, his aspirations and ideals, and illiterate though many of them were, there was always a spiritual and ennobling quality to all of the music."[13]

Both men and women sang and played the blues, passed down informally through oral tradition. Many jazz histories, however, only include what are now referred to as the "classic blues," a more polished vocal genre of the teens and 1920s, informed by vaudeville and performed on theater circuits by such women as Ma Rainey, Bessie Smith, and Ethel Waters. The lyrics of the blues were filled with innuendo and double entendre, making them not only an outlet for expressions of emotion but also of sexuality.

The other, shorter strand of jazz's precursors ends in ragtime and represents a largely new, technical side of instrumental practice borrowed heavily from European sources. Although ragtime was popular in instrumental arrangements and as ragtime songs — some trace the genre to minstrelsy and performers who attempted to transfer banjo styles to the piano — jazz histories focus almost exclusively on the virtuosic piano form of the 1890s and the technical prowess of its male performers. These histories give the impression that once African American men gain access to instruments, they abandon the voice in favor of tools that do a more efficient job of achieving musical sophistication, the basis for their musical evolution and potential legitimization in the white world. Unlike the blues, which serves a function akin to the spiritual, the literature on ragtime places an emphasis on secular contexts rather than transcendent musical experience.

The parentage of jazz, therefore, can be read as symbolically gendered: the blues is feminine, a natural product of the untrained voice associated with the body and the sexuality of its performers, whereas ragtime is masculine, associated with instruments as tools and technical skill. Although the specifics of jazz's conception tend to remain as cloaked in mystery as the deliveries of the elusive stork, once jazz is "born," authors drop vocal forms from their histories. Singing either gives birth to the music or perhaps midwifes it, but it does not continue to move forward as part of typical progress-oriented narratives. Although ragtime piano evolves into stride and the instrument is absorbed by early jazz ensembles, the classic blues is almost uniformly constructed as a related yet separate phenomenon, worthy of study as much for the jazz instrumentalists who accompanied these singers as for their own contributions. If we believe our histories, at this early point in the music's development, there were no "jazz singers," only the occasional instrumentalist like Louis Armstrong, whose singing drew directly on his playing and which many dismissed as mere entertainment.[14] Historiography (i.e., instrumental historiography) either confines singers to an inferior social space or simply erases singing from cultural memory from that point forward in its chronology: singing is contained by and at the origins of jazz.

Few scholars have commented specifically on this fracture between the nineteenth century and early jazz. None appears to have acknowledged the division it creates between vocal and instrumental forms — also a division between folk or popular genres and an emerging art tradition — and its significant impact on the erasure of women.

In a review of the *New Grove Dictionary of Jazz* focused on James Lincoln Collier's "Jazz" entry, Eileen Southern criticizes his failure to trace jazz to nineteenth-century instrumental forms, which she puts forth as its real origins.[15] According to Collier, "Of the several streams of black folk music that flowed into twentieth century jazz, the largest comprised vocal forms — spirituals, work songs, field hollers, street cries and other urban forms, and, later, the blues."[16] Southern finds his presentation typical, as I do; it went virtually unaltered in the Grove's second edition published in 2002.

If, as Southern suggests, we need to consider this history as all of one piece, then a variety of primary sources on nineteenth-century instrumental music need to be reexamined and incorporated into our narratives. At the turn of the century, Southern writes, substantive articles about plantation music appeared in the *Musical Gazette* (New York), *Music Review* (Chicago), *Musical Record* (Boston), *Musical Visitor* (Cincinnati), *the Etude, Journal of American Folklore,* and Hampton Institute's *Southern Workman*. Descriptions also appeared in the longer works of a few historians: Louis C. Elson's *The History of American Music* (1904); W. L. Hubbard's *History of American Music* (1908); and Frank Kidson's "Negro Music in the United States" in the *Grove Dictionary of Music* (1907). Southern points out how closely the documentation of some nineteenth-century instrumental music resembles jazz. For example, the journalist George Foster describes a fiddle, trumpet, and drum trio performing in a New York club named for Charles Dickens in honor of his visit to America: "With these instruments you may not imagine that the music at Dickens's place is of no ordinary kind. You cannot, however, begin to imagine what it is. You cannot see the red-hot knitting-needles spurted out by that red-faced trumpeter, who looks precisely as if he were blowing glass. . . . Nor can you perceive the frightful mechanical contortions of the bass-drummer as he sweats and deals his blows on every side, in all violation of the law of rhythm, like a man beating a baulky mule."[17] Furthermore, in addition to primary sources, greater efforts could be made to utilize the painstaking research of scholars such as Dena Epstein, Lawrence Levine, Lynne Emery, and Lawrence Gushee.

Besides the unacknowledged continuum of instrumental music, evidence raises serious questions as to whether the separation of the blues and other vocal forms from early instrumental jazz was endemic to the musical culture at the time or imposed by critics and scholars well after the fact. Arguably, some musical separation between singers and instrumentalists was necessitated by the texture and instrumentation of New Orleans–style music; the voice would have difficulty performing the wildly improvised lines considered its central feature — typically rendered by violin or clarinet, cornet, and trombone — and being heard within such a dense polyphonic texture.

Nevertheless, vocal and instrumental repertory did overlap during the period when jazz emerges, indicating far greater fluidity between

vocal and instrumental domains than is usually conveyed. "Blues singers" sang popular songs from minstrel traditions, vaudeville, and burlesque; folk ballads; and traditional blues. The emerging New Orleans
dance bands played everything: the blues (for dancing the slow drag),
concert pieces, quadrilles, polkas, rags, marches, hymns, popular songs,
and old favorites (such as "Home Sweet Home" and "Listen to the
Mockingbird").[18] Some of the new jazz repertory developed from folk
songs and work songs.[19]

Moreover, performing contexts and their participants overlapped, a
fact that has long been ignored: vocal music was an integral part of the
New Orleans jazz scene. Although anecdotal in character, some jazz
autobiographies, interviews with musicians, and early histories provide
evidence of New Orleans vocal traditions. In his autobiography *Treat It
Gentle*, Sidney Bechet gives the following description of the types of
music one might hear in the famed brothels and saloons, places that
sometimes featured singers: "People have got an idea that the music
started in whorehouses. Well, there was a district there, you know, and
the houses in it, they'd all have someone playing a guitar or a mandolin,
or a piano . . . someone singing maybe; but they didn't have orchestras,
and the musicianers never played regular there. There was Tom Anderson; he had one of those cabaret-like places — saloons. He had practically everything there, card rooms, bar, a hop room — and he had
music. Sometimes you'd hear accordion, guitar, mandolin, sometimes
bass, maybe a violin; other times you'd hear someone singing there."[20]

Ramsey's and Smith's *Jazzmen* mentions that the cornetist Buddy
Bolden — credited by many as the father of jazz and by all accounts a
marvelous showman — would sing with his band. The lyrics were humorous and bawdy, including one for guitarist Brock Mumford titled
"The Old Cow Died and Old Brock Cried."[21] Bolden had his own well-
known theme song: "I thought I heard Buddy Bolden say, 'Funky Butt,
Funky Butt, take it away.'" Describing the main after-hours club in
Storyville, Clarence Williams relates, "Well, at Pete Lala's, everybody would gather every night and there'd be singin' and playin' all
night long."[22] Of the honky-tonks and barrelhouses, Ramsey and Smith
write: "In these dives they dragged out the blues with a slow beat and
fierce intensity. Apparently there were hundreds of Negroes who could
sit down and play and sing the low-down blues. They made up the
words to fit their mood and the occasion."[23]

Numerous women who worked as prostitutes in Storyville's brothels
sang and danced. Jelly Roll Morton describes the "chippies in their

little-girl dresses . . . standing in the crib doors singing the blues."[24] Spencer Williams recalls that Tony Jackson used to work at a house run by Miss Antonia Gonzales, who sang and played cornet.[25] Ann Cook, one of the very first "blues singers," worked for Countess Willie Piazza;[26] a New Orleans Blue Book advertisement states that Piazza "has, without a doubt, the most handsome and intelligent octoroons in the United States. You should see them; they are all entertainers. If there is anything new in the singing and dancing line that you would like to see while in Storyville, Piazza's is the place to visit."[27] The cornetist Bunk Johnson remembered performing with one of these blues women in particular: "I knew Mamie Desdoumes real well. Played many a concert with her singing those same blues. She was pretty good-looking, quite fair, with a *nice* head of hair. She was a hustlin' woman. A blues-singing poor gal. Used to play pretty passable piano around them dance halls on Perdido Street. When Hattie Rogers or Lulu White would put it out that Mamie was going to be singing in their place, the white men would turn out in bunches and them whores would clean up."[28]

Of the fanciest and most expensive houses, Clarence Williams stated, "Those houses hired nothing but the best, but only piano players, and maybe a girl to sing. And there was no loud playin' either. It was sweet, just like a hotel."[29]

Beyond more formal music making, children and presumably other second liners sang along with New Orleans parades; singing fulfilled both a participatory and educational role. Many writings about Louis Armstrong, including his own autobiographies, make reference to the fact that he sang in a vocal quartet in his youth, earning small change on the streets of New Orleans. Bechet reports, "Bunk [Johnson] told me about this quartet Louis was singing in. 'Sidney,' he said, 'I want you to go hear a little quartet, how they sing and harmonize.' He knew I was crazy about singing harmony. He'd take me out to those circuses whenever they came into town and they had any singing in them, and he'd take me to vaudeville and all. Whenever there was some quartet or opera, or some harmony, or some big band somewhere, we'd always go."[30] African American vocal quartets were common in the late nineteenth century and the early twentieth, but as evidenced by an interview with the cornetist Manuel Perez conducted by Robert Goffin, this may have been a distinct phenomenon in vogue in New Orleans. Perez describes a "syncopated evolution. Vocal groups composed of young creoles, or even of whites, such as those of the spasmband, retained the rhythmic aspect of all the badly digested music."[31]

Clearly, these topics would benefit from further research, both a thorough sweep of the secondary literature and renewed efforts to uncover and investigate primary sources. But the question remains, given evidence of the continuity between nineteenth-century instrumental traditions and jazz, why do these early forms so rarely enjoy a place in jazz narratives? If singers and vocal activities were prevalent during the music's formative years in New Orleans and possibly elsewhere, why do they only figure among jazz's precursors? What purposes does their erasure from histories serve?

Of course, the availability of documentary evidence had a substantial impact on the initial establishment of jazz's historiographic tradition. Little information about jazz's nineteenth-century origins or the role of vocals in early music-making activities would have been available to those writing the first, highly influential histories of jazz from abroad: Hugues Panassié, Charles Delaunay, and Robert Goffin. As Europeans who had yet to visit America, neither had they firsthand experience with African American folk traditions nor could they have been familiar with the performance contexts in which singing took place. (For example, Panassié mistakes W. C. Handy's "St. Louis Blues" for a work song.) Their limited focus on the vocals of Bessie Smith, Ma Rainey, and a precious few others reflects the popularity of these women's recordings as well as their wide dissemination.

Both David Stowe and Jed Rasula have rightly critiqued jazz history as a history of recordings, a factor that Sherrie Tucker argues contributes to the conditions for the erasure of women instrumentalists.[32] No recorded evidence exists of these nineteenth-century instrumental traditions, New Orleans singers, or even jazz itself until 1917, the same year the U.S. Navy closed down Storyville's brothels. Although the sources that detail jazz's instrumental precursors await integration into historical narratives, as Gushee points out, specific evidence of jazz's origination is elusive. Little direct testimony survives and a single origin theory proves inadequate for such a complex phenomenon. Many early practitioners and observers failed to recognize jazz as a distinct form from ragtime, or only did so in hindsight.[33]

Aside from the happenstance of available documentation, the absence of instrumental music prior to 1900 and the erasure of vocal music from jazz history thereafter serve the same symbolic purposes. Historians write of the music's "birth" — as if it were an event, a point of arrival — in romantic tones with a sense of wonderment and awe befitting creation myths. It has often been connected with images of water: the "streams of black folk music" described by Collier and, of course, the Mississippi River, a veritable birth canal. As suggested by Said's work, the symbolism of jazz's birth fosters the mythological status of its origination, which can also be placed in the context of African American storytelling traditions and spirituality. To link the subject of this myth with what came before would demystify that which historians have rendered neat, tidy, and to some extent miraculous, like putting cameras in the delivery room. Jazz's birth acts as a clear line of demarcation between it and earlier African American musical forms, conveniently eliminating the historical messiness and arguably necessary for jazz's legitimization as an art tradition.

Importantly, this origination tale would answer those who denied that jazz was both a new, innovative kind of music and an important cultural product invented by African Americans. As inseparable from issues of race, jazz historiographers have had to contend with the same kinds of attacks faced by those who have documented other African American genres. Drawing on Melville Herskovitz's work, Richard Waterman's "Hot Rhythm in Negro Music" finds African rhythm in jazz, as does Winthrop Sargeant's *Jazz: Hot and Hybrid*.[34] Nonetheless, paralleling George Pullen Jackson's white origins theory for the spirituals, Harry O. Brun's *The Story of the Original Dixieland Jazz Band* maintains that jazz was invented by whites, then a long-held theory.[35] According to Scott DeVeaux in "Constructing the Jazz Tradition," historiographers designed strategies to combat such problems: "The depth of tradition, reaching back in an unbroken continuum to the beginning of the century, belies attempts to portray African Americans as people without a past — hence the appeal of an unambiguous and convincing historical narrative: If the achievements that jazz represents are to be impressed on present and future generations, the story must be told, and told well."[36]

An unambiguous and convincing narrative requires a decisive beginning and identifiable, archetypal figures. Attempts to fit into preexisting art music discourses led to a preponderance of "great man" histories, seen in Panassié's *Le Jazz Hot*, Ramsey's and Smith's *Jazzmen*, and Barry Ulanov's *A History of Jazz in America*, among others.[37] In these works, Buddy Bolden emerged with his shining trumpet as jazz's first hero. The anonymity of jazz's nineteenth-century vocal and instrumental forbearers, as well as its early singers, precludes their inclusion in these types of histories, which also privilege the individuality so prized within jazz culture.

Although some historians would simply view jazz as an exotic alternative to western classical music — writers such as Panassié, Blesh, and Sargeant took distinctly antiprogress stances — this symbolic birth also served evolutionary schemas designed to show jazz's forward movement and the progress of the race itself. To be assessed, progress requires a starting point and some kind of measuring stick. As DeVeaux states — it will be useful to follow him on several points — "To be accepted as a kind of classical music, jazz had to be understood as a music that had outgrown its origins in a particular ethnic subculture and could now be thought of as the abstract manipulation of style and technique. Jazz was now to be measured against the 'absolute' standards of greatness of the European tradition."[38] These nineteenth-century vocal forms were the origins that jazz had outgrown; evolutionary schemas do not often attempt to accommodate the voice, typically viewed as a static, unchanging product of the human body.

Whether as raw material for compositions such as black symphonies, a position espoused by Maude Cuney Hare, or as an object of contemplation to be judged on its own merits, jazz moved toward greater sophistication and, explicitly, preexisting constructs of art music. John Work wrote in 1915, "Against the words and ideas of ragtime songs, all moral people . . . have just complaint; but let the spirit of ragtime be changed, and let the writers of it express high ideals . . . and the public, all, would welcome it, and hail it as a new development of the musical art."[39] With the notable exception of Langston Hughes, who believed that African American musical forms should stand on their own feet as legitimate cultural art forms, the writers of the Harlem Renaissance exemplified this view, one being applied to the spirituals at the same time as the beginning of jazz historiography. Despite the emphasis on the form's progress and elevation, in reality, older genres did continue to hold importance and interact with jazz. Although blues underwent stylistic changes and eventually developed into rhythm and blues, the spirituals continued to be performed, sometimes by jazz instrumentalists and singers. A vogue for recording spirituals and other songs with religious themes followed the rise in popularity of figures such as Roland Hayes and Paul Robeson in the 1920s and 1930s, a trend that has gone without comment in the jazz literature.[40]

To better establish jazz's credentials as "serious" art music, historians also divorced the music from its various entertainment contexts. Interest in writing jazz's history was sparked in the late 1930s and early 1940s at a time when a feud raged between those in support of "traditional" (i.e., New Orleans–style) jazz and fans of swing, contemporary music with a devoted mass audience. The debate resulted in music criticism advocating earlier styles that Welburn has suggested is the dawn of jazz historiography.[41] Moreover, it established jazz historiography as an oppositional discourse that valued authenticity over mainstream commercial appeal; the so-called moldy figs asserted that New Orleans jazz was the only "real" jazz. Its performers were depicted as creative if primitive geniuses, where authenticity as a quality of jazz stemmed not only from jazz's rhythmic and improvisatory musical preferences but also from white enthusiasts' fantasies about masculinity and blackness.

As DeVeaux writes, "Only by acquiring the prestige, the 'cultural capital' (in Pierre Bourdieu's phrase) of an artistic tradition, can the music hope to be heard and its practitioners receive the support commensurate with their training and accomplishments."[42] Southern asserts that Collier omits plantation dance music from jazz's precursors because it is considered "trivial," as is much music that accompanies dancing. Similarly, limiting singing to the music's ancestry and constructing the classic blues as a separate phenomenon puts space between jazz (i.e., instrumental jazz) and the taint of consumerism from popular music. This preserves singing and the early forms associated with it as pure and unadulterated, a sacred well for authentic expressions of black culture. It enables them to evoke collective memory and act as a touchstone for instrumental jazz during various stylistic shifts that have since followed. Similar to the images of the Mississippi river that populate stories of the birth of jazz, Marshall Stearns writes in *The Story of Jazz*, "The religious music of the Negro continues to furnish a reservoir of inspiration to the entire jazz tradition."[43] The narrator in Ken Burns's *Jazz*, "Episode One: Gumbo," relates, "The blues became the stream that feeds all streams of American music, including jazz."[44]

This emerging discourse was additionally served by efforts to distinguish jazz from vernacular forms, for, according to Tucker, "to herald vernacular forms that the dominant culture perceived as issuing naturally from black people was deemed less effective politically than to emphasize black musical achievements perceived by the dominant culture as requiring technique and intellect."[45] In many ways, the instrumental emphasis in jazz historiography responds to the prestige value of instrumental music in the western art tradition. Furthermore, the lyrics of vocal music marked them as vernacular, whether the blues or songs borrowed from Tin Pan Alley. Their texts explicitly located them as products of low culture: fun-time music rather than objects for contemplation. Bechet, who tried to defend the spiritual nature of jazz by refuting its origins in brothels throughout *Treat It Gentle*, wrote: "If people want to take a melody and think what it's saying is trash, that ain't the fault of the melody. Sure, there's pieces like Easy Rider or Jockey Blues that have got lyrics you'd call 'dirty.' Lots of them, they're exhibition like, they're for show—a novelty to attract attention. But it's not those lyrics or those blues that really enter into your head. The ones that really do that, they're about sad things—about loving someone and it turns out bad, or wanting and not knowing what you're wanting. Something sincere, like loving a woman, there's nothing dirty in that."[46] Bawdy lyrics—such as Buddy Bolden's theme song—embody the sexualities associated with working-class African Americans. Distancing jazz from lyrical expressions to establish its respectability also distances it from the body.

Finally, these strategies in combination—"great man" histories that render the artist as hero, the divorce between jazz and its entertainment contexts, the removal of its associations with vernacular culture, and, hence lyrics—all contribute to the erasure of women. In general, the ideology of the "artist" gives women and singers little symbolic capital; they may find a place among the muses that inspire male creativity, feeding the wellspring of anonymous folk material from the past, but they rarely count as important historical figures or icons. If demanding art music is made by men for men as connoisseurs, then the elimination of singing as women's primary form of participation helps make jazz into a "serious" (i.e., male) domain.

Moreover, the erasure insures jazz's quest for authenticity and respectability. Although the voice may have been thought "authentic" in terms of its expressions of race, women's blues as performed on the vaudeville and Theater Owners Booking Association (TOBA) circuits as well as recordings were thought to be commercial. Already at this early point in jazz's chronology, women were connected with musical commodification; instead of "blues singers," they were often labeled "comedienne," a reflection of their status as entertainers. The opposition between women's "classic blues" and men's "downhome" blues—less often included in jazz histories but nonetheless a context against which women's classic blues are assessed — renders women's cultural products inauthentic, comparatively speaking, and creates the precedent for women's vocal music as professional "entertainment."

The obvious connections between singing, commodification, and sexuality also proved problematic; based on the evidence in secondary sources about women singers in New Orleans, many appear to have been prostitutes. Jazz's white critics as well as members of the black middle class saw the music as promoting loose sexual mores, racial mixing, and the corruption of youth. Eliminating women from the discourse gives exclusive control over the music and sexuality to men, enabling them to contain the singing body.

Instead of including singers, historians alternatively focus their attention on instrumental practice that resembles singing: talking horns. They emphasize what are usually termed "vocal effects" in the literature: the potential to create microtones, bend pitches, and replicate speech; singing, preaching, shouting, and loud-talk; cussing, whining, squawking, and groaning; growling, whispering, wailing, screaming, and playing the dozens, many of these "primal utterances" said to originate with the voice. Daniel Albright points to this kind of transvestism between forms — "what happens when one art stimulates itself by temporarily pretending to be another species of art altogether" — as being central to modernist artistic investigations, no doubt part of its appeal to Panassié, Delaunay, Goffin, etc.[47] Although histories silence the voice itself in favor of its imitation, singing comes to signify the natural qualities of musicians; Panassié likens New Orleans–style jazz — "primitive jazz" — to "natural, spontaneous song."[48] Rudi Blesh writes: "With no formal training, the Negroes imparted vocal tone to the cornet, trombone, and even the clarinet, though it is an achieved, not a natural, tone with these instruments. Extreme musicality gave the Negroes quick mastery of even these difficult instruments and helped them to surmount difficulties they did not even know existed. Unable to read music, they promptly transformed the marches into Negro jazz just as their forerunners had transformed the hymn into spirituals."[49]

Despite the popularity of a handful of singers with mainstream audiences, singers as a group have been neglected as subjects of scholarly work within jazz studies, including those that focus on issues related to jazz and gender. The primary domain of women's singing has been consigned to an inferior space, contained by and at the origins of jazz in a long tradition of representation. Although instrumental music bearing a resemblance to jazz can be traced to the mid-nineteenth century and singing continued to be integral during jazz's early years in New Orleans, evidence of these traditions has failed to find a place in jazz discourses. Rather, singing disappears from progress-oriented narratives after jazz's birth, its feminized role limited to the music's parentage.

Aside from issues related to documentation, the absence of instrumental music prior to the 1890s and erasure of vocal music from jazz history soon after serve the same symbolic purposes. Although even those who originated jazz failed to recognize the music as distinct from ragtime, the birth crafted by historians responds to a need for a clear point of origination, answering those who would deny that jazz was an African American creation or refuse to acknowledge it as a "legitimate" cultural form. To present jazz as "art music," many authors attempted to divorce it from low culture and the entertainment contexts with which singing was associated, thereby containing sexuality and the female body. Instead, they focused their attention on horns that sound like voices, an elevation of "raw" musical materials.

Although it remains important to understand the strategic importance of these narratives to jazz's acceptance and legitimization, they come with a heavy price: they contribute to the erasure of women and singing, their primary form of participation in jazz. Jazz historiography effectively cements the marginalized status of women early in a tradition of representation as well as musical chronologies. Contemporary historians must continue to challenge dominant discourses for the ways in which they embed gender and impact the representation of women.

NOTES

An earlier version of this text appeared as part of chapter 2, "All the Things You Are: Discourses of the Body, Essentialism, and Historiography in Jazz Singing," in Pellegrinelli, "The Song Is *Who?*"

1. See Handy 1981; Handy 1983; Placksin 1982; Dahl 1989; Tucker 2000.

2. Tucker 2000, 3.

3. The exclusion of singers often extends to men in the field as well.

4. Mark C. Gridley, *Jazz Styles: History and Analysis*, 7th ed. (Englewood Cliffs, N.J.: Prentice-Hall, 1999). Singers are placed in a separate chapter at the end of Lewis Porter and Michael Ulmann, *Jazz: From Its Origins to the Present* (Englewood Cliffs, N.J.: Prentice-Hall, 1993).

5. Berliner 1994. Berliner also indicates which instrumentalists among his participants sing, but I learned through my own conversations with a number of these individuals that they do not identify themselves as singers.

6. Edward Said, *Beginnings* (New York: Columbia University Press, 1985).

7. Rudi Blesh, *Shining Trumpets* (New York: Da Capo, 1946).

8. Willi Apel, *Harvard Dictionary of Music* (Cambridge: Harvard University Press, 1944).

9. Joachim Ernst Berendt, *Das Jazzbuch*, 6th ed. (New York: Lawrence Hill, 1991).

10. Marshall Stearns, *The Story Of Jazz* (New York: Oxford University Press, 1956).

11. Frank Tirro, *Jazz: A History*, 2nd ed. (New York: W. W. Norton, 1993).

12. Ken Burns, *Ken Burns' Jazz*, "Episode 1: Gumbo, Beginnings to 1917" (Warner Home Video, 2000).

13. E. Simms Campbell, "Blues," *Jazzmen*, ed. Frederic Ramsey Jr. and Charles Edward Smith (1939; repr. New York: Harcourt, Brace, Jovanovich, 1977), 105.

14. Billie Holiday is often credited as the first "real" jazz singer who was not also an instrumentalist.

15. Eileen Southern, "A Study in Jazz Historiography: *The New Grove Dictionary of Jazz*," *College Music Symposium* 29 (1989): 123–33.

16. James Lincoln Collier, "Jazz," *The New Grove Dictionary of Jazz*, ed. Barry Kernfeld (London: Macmillan, 1988), 364.

17. George Foster, *New York by Gas Light* (New York, 1850), 73.

18. Collier, "Jazz."

19. According to Ramsey and Smith, " 'Good-by Bag, I Know You've Gone' came from the song sung by the mill workers as they emptied the rice bags. 'Lift 'Em Up Joe' was taken by Joe Oliver from a song of the railroad hands as they raised the rails." Ramsey and Smith, eds., *Jazzmen*, 30.

20. Sidney Bechet, *Treat It Gentle* (New York: Hill and Wang, 1960), 53.

21. Ramsey and Smith, eds., *Jazzmen*, 11.

22. Nat Hentoff and Nat Shapiro, eds., *Hear Me Talkin' to Ya: The Story of Jazz by the Men Who Made It* (New York: Rinehart), 13.

23. Ramsey and Smith, eds., *Jazzmen*, 35.

24. Hentoff and Shapiro, eds., *Hear Me Talkin' to Ya*, 6.

25. Ibid., 7.

26. Ramsey and Smith, eds., *Jazzmen*, 34.

27. Hentoff and Shapiro, eds., *Hear Me Talkin' to Ya*, 10.

28. Ibid., 8.

29. Ibid., 12.

30. Bechet, *Treat It Gentle*, 91.

31. Robert Goffin, *La Nouvelle-Orléans, capitale du jazz* (New York: La Maison Française, 1946), 69–70.

32. Stowe 1994; Jed Rasula, "The Media of Memory: The Seductive Menace of Records in Jazz History," in Gabbard 1995a.

33. Lawrence Gushee, "The Nineteenth-Century Origins of Jazz," *Black Music Research Journal* 14, no. 1 (1994): 1–24.

34. Richard Waterman, "Hot Rhythm in Negro Music," *Journal of the American Musicological Society* 1, no. 1 (1948): 24; Winthrop Sargeant, *Jazz: Hot and Hybrid* (New York: Arrow, 1938).

35. Harry O. Brun, *The Story of the Original Dixieland Jazz Band* (Baton Rouge: Louisiana State University Press, 1960).

36. DeVeaux 1991.

37. Hugues Panassié, *Hot Jazz: The Guide to Swing Music*, trans. Lionel Dowling and Eleanor Dowling (New York: Witmark, 1936); Ramsey and Smith, eds., *Jazzmen*; and Ulanov 1952.

38. DeVeaux 1991, 546.

39. John Wesley Work, *Folk Song of the American Negro* (Nashville: Press of Fiske University, 1915), 38.

40. Louis Armstrong recorded a number of tracks related to religion: the church-styled "The Lonesome Road" (Okeh 41538, 1931); "The Saints" (Decca, 1938); "Shout All over God's Heaven," "Nobody Knows the Trouble I've Seen" (Decca 2035, 1938); and two more "legitimate" sacred recordings with a professional choir, "Bye and Bye" (Decca 3031, 1941), where the band doubles as a choir, and, with a modern gospel feel, "Louis and the Good Book" (Decca 2035, 1958). Many credit Armstrong's recording of "The Saints" with making that song a staple in the popular repertory.

41. Ron Welburn, "Toward Theory and Method with the Jazz Oral History Project," *Black Music Research Journal* 6 (1986): 79.

42. DeVeaux 1991, 526.

43. Stearns, *The Story of Jazz*, 77.

44. Burns, *Gumbo*.

45. Tucker 2002b, 250.

46. Bechet, *Treat It Gentle*, 54.

47. Daniel Albright, "Border Crossings," *Black Orpheus: Music in African American Fiction from the Harlem Renaissance to Toni Morrison*, ed. Saadi A. Simawe (New York: Garland, 2000), xvi.

48. Hugues Panassié, *The Real Jazz*, trans. Anne Sorrelle Williams, adapted for American publication by Charles Edward Smith (New York: Smith and Durrell, 1942).

49. Blesh, *Shining Trumpets*, 160.

Jeffrey Taylor

WITH LOVIE AND LIL:

REDISCOVERING TWO CHICAGO

PIANISTS OF THE 1920s

O n November 16, 1926, Louis Armstrong and His Hot
Five recorded "Big Butter and Egg Man," a tune that
includes, after May Alix's vocal chorus, one of the
most famous cornet solos ever committed to disc. It is an iconic
performance, included in both editions of *The Smithsonian Collection of Classic Jazz*, and appearing in transcription in Gunther Schuller's landmark study, *Early Jazz*.[1] The pianist on the
date was Lillian Hardin, who two years earlier had married the
group's leader to become Lillian Hardin Armstrong.

A year and a half earlier, Ethel Waters, one of the most influential of all American popular singers, had recorded "Craving
Blues," "Black Spatch Blues," and "I Want Somebody All My
Own" for Chicago's Paramount label, accompanied by the record company's house band, Lovie Austin's Blues Serenaders.
Austin was at the piano.

In these recordings, Hardin Armstrong and Austin play a
subordinate and at times nearly inaudible role, although their
energetic chording and occasional solos add greatly to the
overall impact of the recordings. But more to the point, here
are two women who worked with some of the most influential
musicians of the 1920s, who were among the most hardworking and visible black artists of their day. Yet, as *musicians* at
least, they have been largely relegated to the dustbin of history.

In recent years, the issue of gender has moved to the forefront of jazz scholarship, with women finally beginning to find the essential place they deserve in the music's historical narrative. Yet I must confess my initial interest in the work of these two women was sparked simply because they seemed so ubiquitous in the Chicago jazz scene. Everywhere I turned, it seemed their names popped up, especially in newspaper reviews of the time. Yet, outside some discussion in the groundbreaking work of Sally Placksin, Linda Dahl, and D. Antoinette Handy, Hardin Armstrong and Austin have been largely omitted from the story of jazz.[2] More recently, my work has been energized by the excellent scholarship of Sherrie Tucker, whose book on all-girl bands awoke, for many of us, long-silent voices from jazz's past.[3] Tucker, however, wrote of a later period and primarily about women who played instruments other than piano; many, if not most, of the artists she wrote about never made recordings. By contrast, Hardin Armstrong and Austin spent a significant amount of time in the studio during the 1920s and performed with some of the most celebrated entertainers of the decade (see table below). They are heard on some of the most famous recordings in jazz, performances unquestionably part of what has become, for many listeners, the recorded "canon" of the music.[4] Yet, particularly as pianists, their voices have remained curiously silent.

Lovie Austin and Lillian Hardin Armstrong:
Summary of Recording Careers (to 1930)

FEATURED ARTIST/GROUP	LABEL	YEAR(S)
Lovie Austin (born Cora Calhoun; 1887–1972)		
Ida Cox (v)	Paramount	1923–1926
Edmonia Henderson (v)	Paramount/Vocalion	1923–1924; 1926
Ma Rainey (v)	Paramount	1923–1924
Edna Hicks (v)	Paramount	1924
Alberta Hunter (v)	Paramount	1924
Ethel Waters (v)	Paramount	1924
Lovie Austin and Her (Blues) Serenaders	Paramount	1924–1926
Ford and Ford (v)	Paramount	1924
Julia Davis (v)	Paramount	1924
Viola Bartlette (v)	Paramount	1925
Ozie McPherson (v)	Paramount	1925

Butterbeans and Susie (v)	Okeh	1926
Hattie McDaniel(s) (v)	Okeh/Paramount	1926

Austin appears as either piano accompanist or with Her (Blues) Serenaders.

Lillian Hardin Armstrong (1898–1971)

King Oliver's Creole Jazz Band	Gennett	1923 (Richmond, Ind.)
Alberta Hunter/The Red Onion Jazz Babies	Gennett	1924 (New York City)
Louis Armstrong and His Hot Five/Seven; Lil's Hot Shots	Okeh/Vocalion	1925–1927
Butterbeans and Susie (accompanied by Louis Armstrong and His Hot Five)	Okeh	1926
New Orleans Bootblacks/ Wanderers	Columbia	1926
Johnny Dodds (cl)	Brunswick/Victor	1927; 1929
Jimmie Rodgers (v)	Victor	1930 (Hollywood)

Hardin Armstrong was both celebrated and restricted by her fourteen-year marriage to her famous husband. In a familiar version of the "behind every great man" myth, she is most often mentioned in the literature (and quite rightly so) as a potent force in Armstrong's early career, giving him encouragement when his confidence faltered, and played an important role in the jobs her husband landed and the publicity he achieved. She is also often given a nod for her role as a composer, for she wrote or cowrote much of the repertory with which her husband became associated. Yet, as a pianist myself, I felt a natural inclination to explore her life as a performing musician. I found comments about her abilities as a pianist ranging from patronizing to openly derogatory: Schuller, for example, describes her playing as "watery" and her solos as "embarrassing."[5] Even James L. Dickerson, in his recent adulatory but poorly documented biography, admits apologetically that "she was energetic, but, frankly, not a virtuoso performer."[6]

A more shadowy figure, Austin is perhaps best known as co-composer of "Downhearted Blues," one of the most recorded blues numbers of the 1920s; as a performer, she is usually relegated to a footnote. Yet she had at least one enthusiastic admirer in the jazz composer, pianist, and arranger Mary Lou Williams, who gave Austin her own branch on her 1971 "Tree" of Jazz History.[7] Williams also vividly described, with decidedly masculine imagery, the impression Austin left on her when she appeared in her hometown of Pittsburgh on tour: "I remember seeing this great woman sitting in the pit and conducting a group of five or six men, her legs crossed, a cigarette in her mouth, playing the show with her left hand and writing music for the next act with her right. Wow! . . . My entire concept was based on the few times I was around Lovie Austin. She was a fabulous woman and a fabulous musician, too. I don't believe there's any woman around now who could compete with her. She was a greater talent than many men of this period."[8] It is tempting to explain away the relative neglect of these two pianists by simply noting that jazz was, and is, a male-dominated art form. Yet, although it is true that until quite recently jazz's history has been written almost entirely by men, I feel the remarkable careers of Austin and Armstrong deserve a nuanced approach integrating issues of gender and sexuality with both practical and musical concerns. In the following, I suggest some ways of looking at these artists and their working lives that I feel have too often been left out of the historical dialogue. In so doing I raise broader questions about how *non-soloists* — in this case, band members and accompanists — can be appreciated as essential to the story of jazz.

Austin and Hardin Armstrong make an intriguing comparison, despite the distance in their ages (Austin was older by nearly eleven years). They were both born in Tennessee, although on opposite sides of the state (Hardin in Memphis, Austin in Chattanooga), and they both developed an early fascination for black vernacular traditions. Austin and a younger girl who was raised in the same household would sneak off in the early 1900s to hear the great blues singer Ma Rainey (the other girl's name, by the way, was Bessie Smith, who later became "The Empress of the Blues").[9] Hardin seems to have found a strong feel for African-American music in church. In the recorded interview "Satchmo and Me," she described, with typical ebullience, how she would add a heavy beat to the hymns, while the minister looked at her sternly over his glasses.[10]

Both Hardin Armstrong and Austin also pursued classical studies before they became intimately involved in popular music, Armstrong at Fisk University and Austin at Roger Williams and Knoxville Colleges. In so doing, they joined a tradition of classically trained amateur pianists that stretched back to the early nineteenth century. African American women had less frequent and more limited access to formal piano study. Yet the early lives of both Austin and Hardin Armstrong suggest that, like most women of the time, they viewed their musical education not as a springboard for a concert career but as a way of bringing "refined" music making into the home, and they were heartily encouraged to do so by their families. Hardin Armstrong's own meticulously fingered copy of Benjamin Godard's "Au Matin," a light classical work of the 1890s on the order of Christian Sinding's "Rustle of Spring," places her studies directly in the context of nineteenth-century parlor music.[11] Her classical training occasionally surfaced in intriguing ways in her playing, such as in the introduction to "You're Next," recorded by Louis Armstrong and His Hot Five in 1926. Here, a flourish worthy of Liszt or Rachmaninoff is followed by the solid, down-and-dirty "four to the bar" chording that made her a prized member of early New Orleans–style jazz groups. The result, although intentionally humorous, proves what a fine classical pianist Hardin Armstrong must have been.

By the early 1920s, both Hardin Armstrong and Austin had settled in Chicago, where they participated in the vibrant black musical scene of the South Side. Hardin Armstrong worked there with King Oliver's Creole Jazz Band as well as with Louis Armstrong and a variety of other ensembles. Austin led various incarnations of her Blues Serenaders; the group was featured both alone and as accompaniment to some of the decade's greatest blues and vaudeville singers. She secured two long-running and presumably fairly lucrative gigs: the first was as house pianist and music director at the Monogram Theater, one of the South Side's best-known vaudeville houses, where she was first hired in 1913,[12] and then later as a staff accompanist for the Paramount label, for which she made dozens of records.

Such employment in the competitive Chicago jazz scene was highly prized; it speaks to the respect with which Austin's talents must have been regarded. Her job at the Monogram, in particular, was a testament to her versatility although the venue itself was far from palatial.[13] Reviews and advertisements suggest Lovie at the piano may have constituted nearly the entire orchestra. For example, when the owners of the Monogram Theater contributed a brief column about their employees in the *Chicago Defender*, they wrote that "Lovie Austin and Bob Manns [presumably a percussionist] constitute our orchestra."[14] When one considers the variety of acts Austin had to accompany, her resourcefulness is astounding.[15] In addition, at times, Austin herself may have become *part* of the act: intriguingly, in *Black's Blue Book* of 1917 (a directory of the South Side), she is listed in the "Actors and Actresses" category rather than under "Musicians."[16]

Austin's simultaneous employment at both the Monogram Theater and Paramount Records was no accident, for Mayo Williams, Chicago's talent scout for the record label, relied on the theater as a source of talent, finding its unsophisticated setting an ideal breeding ground for the "humble" blues music featured by Paramount's race records, and relied on Austin to keep him informed of new acts.[17] Ida Cox, for example, with whom Austin made her first recordings for Paramount, was discovered by Williams at the Monogram.[18] The very fact that Austin may have influenced who was or was not recorded during the 1920s is a piece of the Chicago jazz puzzle that is usually omitted from the history books.

Austin's precise duties as a "staff pianist" at Paramount are unknown, although she was probably responsible for the relatively simple arrangements featured on Paramount's race records, and one scholar claims she "would sometimes act as an informal musical director, ensuring that musicians were in tune and singers on pitch."[19] Once again, given the detailed study to which many of the Paramounts have been subjected, Austin's impact has ramifications for any scholar's interpretation of early Chicago jazz.

As prominent fixtures on the Chicago scene, both women moved in the same musical and social circles, and knew and worked with many of the same performers. One personality who loomed large in their careers was Jelly Roll Morton, who made several trips to Chicago in the teens before settling there in the 1920s. In "Satchmo and Me," Hardin vividly described meeting Morton for the first time after she had landed a job demonstrating music at a Chicago store, paying as much attention to his ultra-masculine deportment as to his piano-playing: "So, one day Jelly Roll Morton came in. He sat down and he started playing. Ooh, gee, he had such long fingers. And, oh!, in no time at all he had the piano rockin' and he played so heavy and oh, goose pimples are sticking out all over me. I said, "whoo, gee! What piano playing!" So I sat there and I listened . . . I was *so* thrilled. So when he got up from the piano he did something like this as if to say, "Let that be a lesson to you." . . . And it was a lesson, 'cause after that I played just as hard as I could just like Jelly Roll did. Until this day I am still a heavy piano player, and I attribute it to hearing Jelly Roll play."[20]

Austin, who was 3 years older than Morton, seems to have met him somewhat earlier, in the early teens; she once described how he would drop by her house so she could write out his tunes: "Jelly kept all his music in his head, because he couldn't read it. Then, if he had a piece to write down, he'd say, 'Lovie, I want you to help me with this,' and I'd say 'Alright.' And then he'd come over to my house at 3316 Calumet and stay two or three hours, and I would take his music down on paper. That way he got copies he could have published. He wouldn't trust anybody but me. And when I finished, he'd always pay me. . . . When I'd take down his music, he had a way of humming and playing the piano together, and I could get it right away. I was writing a lot in those days, so I could write it just as fast as he could give it to me. Then I'd go over it the best I could to know that it was right."[21] Her comment confirms the recollections of other early jazz musicians that women pianists of the time were in considerable demand for their notation skills and could supplement their incomes by producing scores.[22] Although we now know that written music played a far greater part in the early history of jazz than had been originally assumed,[23] reading music and writing it out are two very different things. The fact that many women excelled at the latter is suggested not only by Austin's comments but also by the lead sheets submitted for copyright after the recording sessions of King Oliver and Louis Armstrong, many of which are in Hardin Armstrong's hand.

Both Austin and Hardin Armstrong seemed influenced by Morton's distinctive piano style, although his impact is more palpable in the latter. As Hardin Armstrong recalls, Morton, although he was capable of tremendous subtlety, also excelled at a rich, dense, almost "orchestral" pianism, which was always undergirded by an irresistible beat. The influence of Morton's solo style is inescapable in a rare 16-bar solo by Hardin Armstrong made during the Hot Five's recording of "My Heart" (see figure 3.1). Just the first four bars of the solo show the debt to Morton. In the first two measures, Hardin Armstrong uses the interval of a sixth in the left hand, a device Morton probably borrowed from blues players of the day, which creates a characteristically thick texture. In addition, in mm. 2–3, Hardin Armstrong moves down stepwise with her thumb while maintaining the B-flat in the bass, another idea found throughout Morton's work. Finally, and perhaps most significantly, one notes the persistent use of octaves to create a melodic line in the right hand; as I have discussed elsewhere,[24] on recording at least, Morton (and later Earl Hines) were among the first jazz pianists to use octaves in this fashion. When these features are added to a powerful touch, with the fingers digging deeply into the keys (a sound that would no doubt

Fig. 3.1. Lil Hardin, beginning of solo on "My Heart." Louis Armstrong and His Hot Five, Chicago, November 12, 1925. All transcriptions by Jeffrey Taylor.

have been characterized in its day as very "masculine"), the connections to Morton are inescapable.

Morton's talent as a vocal accompanist is not often acknowledged, perhaps because he made few recordings with vocalists, but he excelled at this demanding art, as shown by his sensitive backing of blues singer Lizzie Miles in 1929. Although Lovie Austin's solo style (more rarely heard on recording even than Hardin Armstrong's) owes less to Morton (for one thing, she makes far greater use of the staple of 1920s piano playing, the left-hand tenth), I strongly suspect the full sonorities heard in her accompaniments may owe much to his influence, perhaps from hearing him in a similar role.

Morton's presence in both Austin's and Hardin Armstrong's lives is intriguing not just for the apparent influence he had on their piano styles, but because of his somewhat iconic status at the time. The ragtime and early jazz piano soloists had developed a highly competitive, hypermasculine subculture of "ticklers" or "professors" of which Morton was a prominent member. These players were known for their style of dress and their signature musical "routines." They also competed for the attention of women; as James P. Johnson once said, "the tickler's manners would put the question in the ladies' minds: 'can he do it like he can play it?'"[25]

This subculture may have been in part a kind of jazz riff on the cult of the nineteenth-century virtuoso. But long-buried clues from other sources are beginning to suggest it may also have developed in response to the fact that many early ragtime and jazz pianists were gay. One of the most influential of all Chicago pianists, Tony Jackson, was openly so. The drummer Harry Dial, one of the few musicians active in the

1920s to openly discuss homosexuality, noted in his autobiography that male band pianists of the time — even the straight ones — were called "mother" because of the stereotype of their sexuality.[26] He even goes so far as to claim Earl Hines chose his nickname, "Fatha," to make it expressly clear that he was straight.[27] Morton himself expressed some reluctance about learning piano, as it was considered a "sissy" instrument, although he showed touching compassion for Jackson, one of his early idols (when Lomax asked him if Jackson was a "fairy," Morton gracefully deflected the question by answering "well, I don't know if he was a ferry or a steamboat." Not surprisingly, the exchange is deftly papered over in Lomax's book *Mr. Jelly Roll*).[28] The famous "cutting contests" of the teens and twenties, where pianists would aggressively try to outplay each other, sound more like athletic events than musical soirées and had all the markings of a modern-day slam-dunk contest. Developing this masculine fraternity may have been one way pianists could claim for themselves an instrument that had from the previous century been largely associated with femininity.

Hardin Armstrong's and Austin's exclusion from this fraternity may explain why, unlike most important male pianists of the time (Morton, Fats Waller, Earl Hines, James P. Johnson), they made *no* solo recordings or piano rolls during the 1920s. As I have mentioned, even finding solo choruses on band numbers requires some digging. Although some recent scholarship, such as that by Ingrid Monson, has celebrated the interactive nature of jazz, the story of the music has mainly been framed, from Frederick Ramsey Jr. to Ken Burns, as the story of soloists. This is certainly true of the early jazz pianists: although great 1920s artists such as Fats Waller and James P. Johnson are occasionally praised for their ensemble work or their vocal accompaniments, it is the piano solo that remains at the heart of their fame. Perhaps Austin's and Hardin Armstrong's lack of soloing lies at the crux of their relative obscurity. They developed their pianistic talents primarily as ensemble players and accompanists, and their recorded work must be evaluated by somewhat different standards.

In my own work on Austin and Hardin Armstrong, as well as with other pianists I have researched, I have tried to develop some new ways to appreciate the artistry of these musicians as ensemble players and vocal or instrumental accompanists. These modes of performance demand a specialized talent that is not often recognized; as any practicing musician knows, however, being an ensemble player or accompanist, although often a thankless job, requires immense musical sensitivity.

And studying such performances requires a special type of listening, one in which the ear is directed to musical events that, by their very definition, are meant not to draw attention to themselves.

On June 18, 1926, both Austin and Hardin Armstrong were in Chicago's Okeh studios to record with the popular vaudeville team of Butterbeans and Susie. Although neither mentions the other in their reminiscences, the record suggests they knew each other, and one can imagine the two women relaxing in the studio between takes, sharing ideas, and perhaps listening to each other record. One side of the issued recording features the team backed by Louis Armstrong and His Hot Five. Hardin Armstrong is virtually inaudible, obliterated, as she so often was, by Johnny St. Cyr's banjo. But on the other side, a tune (actually more of a vaudeville routine) called "I Can't Do That," Austin is the sole accompanist, playing a role in which she must have been cast often in the duo's frequent appearances at the Monogram. What is immediately apparent in this recording is the sheer density of Austin's style; she is an entire band unto herself. Yet she never dominates the featured soloists with technical artifice, as did many other pianists of the time.[29] Throughout the performance she clearly guides the melody, often spoken by the featured performers, in her right hand, while supplying a rich and unwavering beat with her left.

Austin's work is perhaps best heard, however, in recordings she made in 1923 with blues singer Ida Cox. Although the recording quality is poor, the presence of only one other performer throws her adept accompanying style into relief, and Austin is even given an occasional brief solo (in "Come Right In," her catchy playing sparks a shout of encouragement from Cox: "Spank that thing, Lovie, spank it!"). In "Graveyard Dream Blues," a tune Cox had recorded four months earlier with Austin and Her Blues Serenaders, the pianist imaginatively contrasts rich, bluesy chords under Cox's vocal with a double-time[30] raglike response that includes, in the left hand, chromatic sixths that echo Morton (see figure 3.2). This response provides a humorous comment on the macabre lyrics of the tune and also proves she had pianistic "chops" that rarely surfaced on recordings.[31] Although the passage is not particularly innovative or advanced, it seems exactly *right* for the context — explaining, no doubt, why Austin was in such demand as an accompanist.

In 1927, in the space of just a few weeks, Louis Armstrong recorded the tune "Wild Man Blues" at two sessions, with two different pianists. The first featured Earl Hines, who became Armstrong's most famous

Ida Cox (voice)

(The) Grave dig-ger looked me in__ my eye__ Then I

double-time - - - - - - - - - - - - - - - - -

Lovie Austin (piano)

Fig. 3.2. Ida Cox, accompanied by Lovie Austin, "Graveyard Dream Blues," fourth chorus, mm. 5–8. Chicago, October 1923.

musical partner in the 1920s. The second featured Hardin Armstrong. I first studied these recordings a few years ago while doing work for an article on Hines's and Armstrong's musical and personal relationship. The point there was to show how Hines's more "sophisticated" and "imaginative" accompaniments shone out in comparison to Hardin Armstrong's workaday chording. Many of us, I think, find it difficult not to hear Hardin Armstrong's work on the Hot Five and Seven recordings refracted through Hines's innovative and often deliciously bizarre later work with the same groups. Yet it is intriguing to set this process on its ear and consider instead the *assets* Hardin Armstrong's work lends to these recordings. Hines's moody alternating chords (played with pedal) and far more inventive harmony complement Armstrong's work beautifully. Yet particularly in the second and fourth measures, where Hines seems to evoke Rachmaninoff's C# minor Prelude (a piece that would be found in most piano benches at the time), his work also draws subtle attention to itself. It was this reluctance to remain confined to traditional rhythm section roles that would make the sparks fly in Hines's "Weather Bird" duet with Armstrong a year later and no doubt contributed to his falling out with the trumpeter in the 1950s (see figure 3.3). In Hardin Armstrong's performance, however, her dense on-the-beat chording, very much in the New Orleans ensemble style, provides the kind of unobtrusive, rock-solid foundation Armstrong adored and which accompanies many of his most brilliant solo flights. Note, par-

Fig. 3.3. Louis Armstrong accompanied by Earl Hines, "Wild Man Blues." Johnny Dodd's Black Bottom Stompers, take 2. April 22, 1927. mm. 1–4 of first chorus.

Fig. 3.4. Louis Armstrong accompanied by Lil Hardin Armstrong, "Wild Man Blues." Louis Armstrong and His Hot Seven. May 7, 1927. mm. 1–4 of first chorus (banjo chords omitted).

ticularly, how she completely drops out in the last two measures to let the spotlight fall entirely on her husband. The moment may be read as an act of gendered subservience or simply as that of a gifted rhythm section player who (in the best sense of the phrase) "knows her place" — not in terms of gender roles but in the context of the early jazz tradition in which Hardin Armstrong developed her craft (see figure 3.4).

The relative neglect of Austin and Hardin Armstrong is particularly remarkable in light of the attention given over the years to both early Chicago jazz and the concurrent rise, especially after the "Great Migration" in the mid-to-late teens, of the South Side as something of a city within a city, a true "Black Metropolis," as sociologists St. Claire Drake and Horace Cayton called it in their landmark 1945 study.[32] The role of women in the evolution of the South Side as a unique African American community, which boasted black-owned businesses, black civic organizations, and which held a distinctive relationship to Chicago politics at large, needs to be better understood.

But on a more specific level, even more black women musicians need to be worked into the often-told story of the South Side's influence on the development of jazz: pianists such as Ethel Minor, Ida Mae Maples, Lottie Hightower, Lil Hardaway Henderson, Garvinia Dickerson, and Bertha Gonsoulin,[33] for example, although many never made recordings, were clearly part of Chicago jazz's development.[34] Although documentary evidence is elusive (even basic biographical information can be obscure), one suspects the story of these women, as with Hardin Armstrong and Austin, is not so much one of neglected solo geniuses but of consummate artists and dedicated performers, who worked largely behind the scenes in an interactive setting and played a secondary role to the great male soloists of the period. It is my hope that in the future artists such as these will be folded into the narrative of jazz history and not relegated only to chapters and panels on "women in jazz," however laudable the motivation. Gender studies provide key insights into the work and lives of these women, and ultimately uncovering their stories — not just as women but as *musicians* — may very well challenge long-held assumptions about the early development of jazz, although we may never recover the sounds themselves. Luckily, in the case of Austin and Hardin Armstrong, unlike so many of their gifted but forgotten colleagues, creativity, imagination, and passionate music-making still beckon from the bins at the local record store, internet sites, or wherever jazz reissues may be found.[35] The recordings are historically significant, but, perhaps even more important, they make for sensational listening.

NOTES

This chapter originated as a paper for the Jazz Study Group of the Society for Music Theory, Annual Meeting, Columbus, Ohio, November 1, 2002. It was also presented in revised form at the Institute for Studies in American Music, fall 2002 Speaker Series:

"Music in Polycultural America," November 11, 2002 and at the 2005 Leeds International Jazz Conference, Leeds, UK, March 12, 2005. I am indebted to many for their comments and encouragement during the chapter's evolution, especially Sherrie Tucker, H. Wiley Hitchcock, Henry Martin, Tony Whyton, Ray Allen, and Ellie Hisama.

1. Gunther Schuller, *Early Jazz: Its Roots and Musical Development* (New York: Oxford University Press, 1968), 103–5.

2. Placksin 1982, 43, 58; Dahl 1984, 15, 22; Handy 1981, 40.

3. Tucker 2000.

4. The existence and makeup of a jazz "canon" — one that might be placed on par with the "accepted masterworks" of Western music, art, and literature — is hotly debated today. Recently, at the Leeds International Jazz Conference (2005), keynote addresses by Scott DeVeaux and Sherrie Tucker spoke to this topic. The question is, of course, whether reducing jazz history to a series of "essential" performances (i.e., recordings) honors or reifies a living music.

5. Schuller, *Early Jazz*, 102, 99.

6. Dickerson 2002, xiv.

7. This drawing, reproduced in many places, may be found in D. Antoinette Handy, "Mary Lou Williams: First Lady of the Jazz Keyboard," *Black Perspective in Music* 8 (autumn 1980): 209.

8. Mary Lou Williams, liner notes for *Jazz Women: A Feminist Perspective* (Stash ST 109).

9. Lovie Austin, interview with William Russell, April 25, 1969, Hogan Jazz Archive, Tulane University.

10. Lil Armstrong, *Satchmo and Me* (Riverside RLP 12-120).

11. Montgomery Collection, University of Michigan.

12. Lovie Austin, interview. This section appears transcribed in Russell, comp., *"Oh, Mr. Jelly": A Jelly Roll Morton Scrapbook* (Copenhagen: Jazz Media, 1999), 351. The Monogram actually existed at two different locations, first at 31st and State and then at 35th and State.

13. In her autobiography Ethel Waters describes the Monogram as a "rinky-dink dump," with performances continually interrupted by train noise.

14. *Chicago Defender*, September 29, 1923.

15. The February 3, 1923, issue of the *Chicago Defender* describes the following lineup, at least some of which Austin would presumably have been called on to accompany:

The bill here this week has all the earmarks of a "big time" lineup. One of the best novelty turns that ever graced this house is that of Original Dixie Kid and his trained dogs. "Buster," the dog with the human mind, is about the smartest canine in the show business and some of the stunts which he executes with ease and precision are productive of a great deal of applause. Dixie is assisted by a handsome young lady who is not programmed but who shows that what it takes to send the puppies through their routine she has it. Dustball and Cook, one of the real scream-producing teams on T.O.B.A. [Theater Owners Booking Association] are back and enjoying their usual popularity; they have several new things in their act. Billy Willis, billed as "The One-Man Vaudeville Show," is properly named; Billy does a bit of everything. He has a lot of new talk, some parodies, and other things for which he might be recommended. Billy is a clever gink. Pace, Thomas and Pace, two clever lads and a handsome and talented lady, presenting a singing, talking, and dancing specialty of more than ordinary class and speed, come in for their full share of mitt through their intensive efforts. It is a whang of a show and worth going far to see.

16. Ford S. Black, *Black's Blue Book* (Chicago: Ford S. Black, 1917), 42.

17. Stephen Calt, "The Anatomy of a Race Label, Part II," *78 Quarterly* 1 (June 1989): 22.

18. Ibid.

19. Ibid., 26.

20. Armstrong, *Satchmo and Me.*

21. Austin, interview, 352. It is unlikely that Morton knew nothing about music notation, for manuscripts of his early pieces exist, although in an unstudied hand. It may be that Morton found using Austin to simply be more expedient.

22. Mary Lou Williams noted: "During that period, we didn't have very many readers and this woman [i.e., Lovie Austin] was a master reader." Handy, "Mary Lou Williams," 204.

23. See David Chevan, "Musical Literacy and Jazz Musicians in the 1910s and 1920s," *Current Musicology* 71–73 (spring 2001–spring 2002): 200–31.

24. See my introduction to *Earl "Fatha" Hines: Selected Piano Solos, 1928–1941* (Madison: A-R Editions / American Musicological Society, 2006).

25. Tom Davin, "Conversations with James P. Johnson," *Musica Oggi* 23 (2003–4): 86.

26. Harry Dial, *All This Jazz about Jazz: The Autobiography of Harry Dial* (Chigwell, Essex, England: Storyville, 1984), 47–48. Among pianists in Chicago, Dial names as homosexual Warren Henderson, Alex Hill, Jerome Carrington, Ray Smith, Sammy Stewart, Sterling Todd, Sammy Williams, Jesse Merriweather, and Anthony Spaulding, who according to Brian Rust has also been listed as a woman ("Antonia") in many sources. Brian Rust, *Jazz Records, 1897–1942*, 5th ed. (Chigwell, Essex, England: Storyville, 1982), 1831. I have not seen this "outing" corroborated in other sources, but Dial, who was straight, does make a point of stating that he is more outspoken about these matters than others of his generation.

27. Ibid., 48.

28. The exchange may be heard on *Jelly Roll Morton, Kansas City Stomp: The Library of Congress Recordings*, vol. 1 (Rounder Records CD 1091).

29. An example might be the duets recorded by the clarinetist Johnny Dodds and Tiny Parham in 1927, in which Parham's busy piano technique often seems to interfere with Dodd's improvised lines.

30. That is, with the background beat moving twice as fast.

31. Austin had come up with this double-time idea earlier, for it appears in her June 1923 band arrangement of the tune.

32. St. Claire Drake and Horace R. Cayton, *Black Metropolis* (New York: Harcourt, Brace, 1945).

33. Gonsoulin is a particularly interesting case: a friend of Jelly Roll Morton, she came to Chicago from New Orleans, via the West Coast, and is known primarily as the pianist who replaced Lil Hardin in King Oliver's Band in 1921. See Russell, comp., "*Oh, Mr. Jelly,*" 571.

34. Handy 1981, 160.

35. Lovie Austin's early band recordings appear on *Lovie Austin, 1924–1926* (Classics 756). Her blues accompaniments are most easily found on several reissues by the Austrian Document label, including *Ida Cox, Complete Recorded Works*, vol. 1 (Document 5322). Lillian Hardin Armstrong's recordings with King Oliver, Louis Armstrong, Johnny Dodds, and others are readily available on a variety of reissues.

Monica Hairston

*When the black keys meet the white keys on Piano Avenue, do they music?
They do.* — HAZEL SCOTT, *The Heat's On*, Columbia Pictures, dir. Gregory Ratoff, 1943

Hazel Scott, appearing in her third of five Hollywood film roles,[1] sang the above lyric to a boogie-woogie beat. In this scene of the film — a flimsy vehicle for Mae West of the backstage musical genre — she showcases one of the potential numbers for the musical's producer and financial backer. Even though southern censors (still powerful cultural gatekeepers) demanded that her scenes (along with those of other blacks) be interpolated for easy editing, she was by far the most compelling presence in the film. Miss Scott plays "herself" here, as she does in all of her Hollywood roles. Her performance in this scene, vivacious and stunning, is easy to appreciate simply through the adoring and eager gaze of the two white men for whom she is auditioning. The film encourages this identification, but closer readings suggest musical and political connections, and eventually, historiographical stones left, at time of writing, unturned.

Immediately noticeable is the spectacular nature of the musical number. This film was made when Scott was at the height of her fame as a headliner at Café Society Uptown, Barney Josephson's leftist Manhattan nightclub. In the film, as at Café Society, she is all glamour: red lips and creamy décolletage in a strapless gown. The excitement of the men while watching and listening to her reminds me of an interview that the *New York*

Post nightclub columnist Earl Wilson did with Scott shortly after *The Heat's On* was filmed. The full title of the interview was "Keeping Abreast of Hazel: Hazel Scott Boasts Buxom Bust and Deft Touch on the Piano."[2] Over its course, Wilson remained more interested in Scott's measurements and in the fact that she could get a table at Sardi's than in her music, although the knowledge that she performed boogie-woogie at a nightclub somehow enhanced her appeal.

At what is clearly the climax, if you will, of Scott's filmic performance, she moves — bare back to her audience — back and forth at lightning speed between two pianos, one white and one black. Her neoclassical flourishes and arabesques increase in speed and intensity (and the lids of both pianos rise in response) until — Bam! — a blues progression with a stride left hand brings us back home for the finish. Scott built her fame at Café Society by 'swingin' the classics' and the arguments that work to exclude her from the jazz canon — she didn't play "jazz," she wasn't talented enough, she didn't swing, too commercial, gimmicky — outline terms of contemporary debates about jazz authenticity. Apart from "gimmicky" piano lids, none of these jibe with her performance in the musical. She nailed an incredibly demanding performance — strong left-hand swinging even the rococo — all without breaking a sweat. In this performance and at Café Society, Scott complicated the dualistic and gendered terms we have inherited as a framework for understanding the meaning(s) of jazz and suggested ways that gender and sexuality affected jazz meaning in Popular Front contexts.

The over-the-top conflation of racial and musical imagery in the musical scene points toward something larger as well. *The Heat's On* was made at a time when Hollywood was not only influenced by the ideals of the Popular Front but also shaped them. Leftist directors, producers, and actors labored to create "aesthetics of social significance" that would carry beyond censors and production codes.[3]

Robin Kelley has noted the way in which Birmingham communists inserted a slogan of Popular Front interracialism into "Joshua Fit the Battle of Jericho" that sounds surprisingly similar to her lyric:

Black and White together we'll
Win the vote
Win the vote
Black and White together we'll
Win the vote
Going to build our promised land.[4]

The Popular Front councilman Benjamin Davis of Harlem used the same slogan at his rallies — and Hazel Scott, along with several of her Café Society coworkers, performed at at least one.[5] What was the connection between Scott and the Popular Front contexts to which her film performance pointed? How might the Popular Front have shaped her music or the way it was received and understood? What was the range of potential meanings of Scott's music at Café Society?

A number of historians have explored the connections between the Popular Front and jazz, often with a sustained attention to race, but few have yet undertaken a study of the role that gender may have played on that historical site.[6] This essay aims to sustain and build upon this important body of revisionist work by exploring relationships between Popular Front debates about jazz and the cultural work produced by black female musicians at Café Society, an important nexus of jazz and leftist politics. My focus on Café Society will be framed by close readings of scenes from *The Heat's On*. Consideration of Scott's cultural work in Hollywood and at Café Society — both Popular Front cultural formations — reinforces and clarifies her interventions (and those of other performers) in the musical contexts discussed.

I contend that Café Society's position on the Negro question (as shaped by its participation in the Popular Front) created a space for black women performers, but simultaneously worked to erase or circumscribe their contributions and that this erasure has been inherited by contemporary historians. This chapter concerns itself with (1) the role black women musicians at Café Society played in promoting and rejecting Popular Front cultural aesthetics and politics; (2) how those same cultural politics shaped the reception of these women for different audiences; (3) the kinds of musicking activities, experiences, and representations that connected these women; and (4) the strategies they used to create spaces for self-expression and representations that reflected the experiences of black women.

THE POPULAR FRONT

The Popular Front was a left-wing social movement of the 1930s and 1940s. Although a number of Depression-era and war-related events contributed to its initial success, it became official in name and policy in 1935 when the International Communist Party shifted its focus from revolutionary, working class–based economic transformation to a more evolutionary strategy of broad, antifascist alliance-making. During the last (seventh) Communist International Congress, followers were counseled to join with socialists, industrial and trade unionists, liberals, community activists of various stripes, and "the urban middle class" in solidarity around a pro-labor, antifascist social democratic agenda.[7] This agenda manifested in a number of important and influential ways.

Local leaders representing the Communist Party, American Labor Party, Progressive Party, and the Farmer Labor Party promoted electoral policies that would create gradual legislative social-democratic reform from under or within the New Deal administration. These largely state-specific electoral fronts were complemented by the international nature of the Popular Front's antifascist campaign. The U.S. Popular Front supported the Spanish Republic against Franco during the Spanish Civil War (1936–39) and expressed solidarity (if less material support) with Ethiopia during the course of Mussolini's invasion and with China as Japan made imperialistic inroads.[8] Within the borders of the United States, the antifascist drive took the form of civil rights and antilynching crusades. Perhaps the most significant single example here was the Popular Front's famous participation in the Scottsboro movement.[9] Finally, the Popular Front oversaw the "largest sustained surge of worker organization in American history."[10] One historian called it the age of the Congress of Industrial Organizations (CIO); working-class solidarity was an important aspect of the progressive, multicultural idea of America held by proponents of the Popular Front.

Scholars of Popular Front–era jazz and cultural politics have offered important explorations of the ways in which the Popular Front, spearheaded by Earl Browder's Communist Party, promoted itself as "100% Americanism" and as "20th century Americanism."[11] Positioning themselves as "defenders of the hard-won democratic rights of the masses," Popular Front leaders and activists advanced a vision of America that not only *overlapped* significantly with that of Rooseveltian liberalism but which was, they argued, the logical endpoint of New Deal policy. Jazz played an important role as a cultural arena in which these political ideas played out.

Stowe has suggested that swing was "the preeminent musical expression of the New Deal," a cultural form that — by achieving productive balance between individual and community, by blurring boundaries between high and low culture, and by embodying multicultural ideals about freedom and egalitarianism — was ultimately democratic and, therefore, ultimately American.[12] Michael Denning builds on this assertion by suggesting that one aspect of this "American-ness" was the presence in swing and swing culture of ethnic and traditional musics such as polka, klezmer, blues, boogie-woogie, even classical.[13] This musical example suggests the political overlap; the Popular Front promoted an "assertive ethnic Americanism" that was served well by swing. By constructing a "usable past" — and, here, I would add usable, unifying culture — for ethnic workers, the Popular Front helped them transcend an outsider status that kept them from becoming fully "American." As a cultural manifestation of ethnic Americanism, swing was a powerful symbol and conduit in this process.[14]

Following this musical example, one element that distinguished the laborist pluralism of the Popular Front from the conservative populism of the New Deal was the ideological centrality to the former of black folk as implicitly revolutionary and the extent to which black-white relations shaped policy. Robin Kelley observed that "if there is one thing all the factions of the twentieth-century American Left share, it is the political idea that black people reside in the eye of the hurricane of class struggle."[15] This was certainly the case for an anti-imperialist, antiracist, interracial movement like the Popular Front. This political tenet becomes manifest in the often contradictory ideas about black music, in general, and jazz, in particular, promoted by the Popular Front.

POPULAR FRONT VIEWS OF BLACK MUSIC

Although it had no single party line on the Negro Question, Popular Front politics (guided by the Communist Party of the United States of America, or CPUSA) placed the plight of black folk in the center of their project. During the earlier third period, the black middle class was considered tainted by bourgeois influence. The black working-class masses (largely of the south) were considered, first of all, unproblematically "folk" and, secondly, the progenitors of a pure, authentic, Negro culture.[16] The conflation of the black working class and cultural authenticity continued to appear in various forms during the Popular Front (and, of course, beyond). However, as the CPUSA began to stress interracial unity and Americanism and broaden its alliances to include intellectuals and liberals of the African American middle class, among others, Popular Front cultural priorities regarding black music developed in multifarious and conflicting ways.

For some Communist Party cultural critics, the very existence of jazz could be reduced to the issue of class oppression. In an article entitled

"The Negro In Relation To Jazz," Muriel Reger suggested that "the economic condition of the Negro has much more to do with his propensity for jazz than the shape of his head or any sort of jungle atavism." Opportunities for training, unionization, and a Federal Arts Bureau, in which there will be no race discrimination, Reger adds, will help the Negro take his place among recognized musicians and composers. Setting aside for a moment the disturbing, if tongue-in-cheek, reference to phrenology, we notice here cultural chauvinism veiled as Marxism, in which all musicians, if given sharecroppers' organizations and federal support, would become classical musicians. For Popular Front critics like Reger, only the "simple harmonies" of the blues as folk music or the work of the composer William Grant Still or vocalists Marian Anderson or Paul Robeson were appropriate forms of black music; swing was "debauched."[17]

Like members of the black middle class, some leftist critics became arbiters of cultural uplift of a sort, promoting the imposition of standards of dignity onto black music and the practices surrounding it. In a controversial review, Martin McCall of the *Daily Worker* panned numerous aspects of a 1938 benefit concert:

Members of the Cotton Club show assisted in pretentious musical comedy vocalizing and swaying. . . . Lunceford's orchestra has been known to play effectively, but the gallant spectacle of one trumpeter grinding out high treble notes and two others throwing their instruments in the air and catching them in unison adequately defines the quality of their performance.

"Fats" Waller clowned boisterously as is his wont. When he finally began a very interesting piano solo, it was at once drowned out by scattered jitterbugs. . . . The evening was one of swing as vaudeville, not as musical expression.[18]

This is a rich example of the ways in which vaudeville and certain traditions of black musical comedy were derided, as well as black musical approaches that contained sexual references, clowning, or 'gimmicky' performative effects. In addition, note that serious music should be listened to in a respectful environment of quiet focus — not enjoyed while dancing, vocalizing, or swaying. Spectacle, overt sexuality, and any performatives that draw attention to the body are constructed in opposition to real jazz. Of course, some critics, as Mark Naison points out, simply "still regarded [any] music that dealt with nonpolitical themes as bourgeois and decadent."[19]

In the late 1930s and early 1940s, a school of thought developed that Naison framed as being shaped by generational difference:

During the Popular Front years a group of young American-born Communists, some of them writers for the *Daily Worker*, became convinced that Afro-American music represented the keystone of an American musical culture that was 'democratic' in spirit and form and embodied the best elements of the national character. Unlike previous Communist critics, who saw virtue primarily in protest songs or rural black music undiluted by 'commercialism,' these young turks displayed their greatest interest in black musical idioms which were commercially successful — swing and hot jazz. The Popular Front coincided with an explosion in the popularity of big band dance music, played by black and white bands alike, and some Communists saw a unique opportunity, in identifying with this music, to dramatize the Afro-American contribution to American culture and the cultural benefits of interracial cooperation.[20]

Whether this results from generational differences or political imperative, this view of black music became prominent and influential during the Popular Front and eventually played a founding role in shaping the ideology of mainstream jazz criticism.[21]

For all the inconsistencies of viewpoint, Popular Front cultural critics did identify black cultural production, in general, and music, in particular, as an important issue because the Negro Question was an important one in this context. The Woman Question, however, took a backseat during this era. Popular Front politics ideologically supported equality for women and women's work was central to the cause — especially that of community organizers and garment trade workers — but women themselves were often considered secondary to or outside of the struggle. Although their participation in leftist politics escalated during this era, "gender and sexuality — unlike race and class — were not recognized as sites for the construction of the political subject."[22] In her important work on literary radicalism, Paula Rabinowitz suggests that gender and sexuality, rather than "historically determined and determining structures of oppression," served as metaphors through which class conflict could be imagined by a discursively monolithically male working class.[23] Women in Popular Front jazz contexts seem to serve a similar role.

Popular Front language and ideology were strongly masculinized, thus "[rendering] women invisible or ancillary."[24] The proletariat and proletarian culture were conflated in word and image in leftist representations with the masculine such that workers — industrial unionists — were Men, women's work was "unorganized labor," the bourgeoisie became feminized, and the feminine was understood in terms of the bourgeoisie.[25]

Although women writers did occasionally contribute to Popular Front publications such as the *Daily Worker*, *Direction*, and the *New Masses*, there were no female cultural critics of note.[26] In addition, leftist music critics rarely wrote about female musicians (singers like Bessie Smith were the exception). They also used masculinist and sexualized language to describe music — jazz, in particular. Although not specifically about swing, an essay in the *Daily Worker* concerning the violinist Yehudi Menuhin's union status bears the subtitle: "History's Best Men Have All Been for the Union."[27] "Virility," "masterful," "drive," "force," "ejaculatory," and "lusty vitality" are examples of the descriptive terms applied to swing in Popular Front dailies and weeklies. One review stated that *From Spirituals to Swing*, a concert event I will discuss in more detail shortly, proceeded to prove that jazz has a patrimony which many have tried to deny it: an authentic beginning in the soul of a folk art.[28]

Ideas about jazz in the context of the Popular Front were conflicting, but all privileged African Americans as the most authentic expression of the working class. As such, black music demanded dignity of presentation and respect. Depending on the critic or school of thought, this could mean black folk tunes with classical settings, serious performance demeanors and settings, or — and this view ultimately won currency — swing as the quintessential symbol of interracial cooperation and an Americanism that originated in black working-class culture. As masculinist language was used to give swing "force," "vitality," and "legitimacy," powerful discursive connections were forged among the (black), male working class, jazz, authenticity, and American-ness. Simultaneously, connections among the spectacular, the body, and sexuality were projected onto women performers as a way of marking class difference. Viewed in this light, Hazel Scott's performance in *The Heat's On* achieved important cultural work in its implicit sexualization of class conflict.

FROM SPIRITUALS TO SWING . . . TO CAFÉ SOCIETY

Café Society (downtown location at 2 Sheridan Square in Greenwich Village and, later, Café Society Uptown) owed its existence to the range of social possibilities opened by the Popular Front and was a site where the cultural politics of the movement could be explored and tested. Opened in 1938 by the Bohemian shoe salesman Barney Josephson and billed as "the wrong place for the right people," Café Society was conceived of as a jazz cabaret where music lovers could enjoy good food, political commentary, and top-quality entertainment at a fair price regardless of race. It had several house policies that set it apart from other music venues. These included zero tolerance stances toward segregation and racial prejudice, jazz as the only music featured, and the requirement that 90 percent of the hired talent had to be Negro.

Whether patrons were responding to political sympathies or curiosity, the Café Society left-wing political agenda aided Josephson in attracting his target audience of "celebs, plebs, and debs." An early publicist described the audience thusly: "[On] some nights we would have ex-debutante Brenda Frazier and friends sitting next to a table of longshoremen (a former rank and file longshoreman was Barney's assistant and in charge of the bartenders) or officials from the more progressive trade unions almost cheek by jowl with heads of companies in whose factories their members worked. Our most consistent patrons, however, were people like Budd Schulberg, Lionel Stander, Paul Robeson, Mrs. Eleanor Roosevelt, Lillian Hellman, S. J. Perelman, St. Clair McKelway."[29]

Don Ameche, Billy Strayhorn, Burgess Meredith, Ralph Bunche, Richard Wright, E. Franklin Frazier, and Benny Goodman were also among the guests; some would occasionally perform.[30] Thus, while Café Society eventually attracted as patrons the elite segment of society at which it thumbed its nose, its audience did come to embody the Popular Front interracialism sought and also aided "democratic" networking among left-leaning musicians, politicians, intellectuals, and potential sources of funding.

The conception of nightclub as jazz cabaret, the house policies, and the audience all contributed to the leftist vibe at Café Society. Ultimately, it is the place where Popular Front aesthetics entered the picture; the strongest sense of this was found in the entertainment itself. Barney Josephson, who identified himself as a jazz fan but was no expert on the subject, hired his friend the impresario, talent scout, and jazz writer John Hammond to be in charge of the bookings at Café Society. Between them, they hired and coached a roster of performers that made their Popular Front aesthetic priorities manifest.

The first point of interest is the 90 percent Negro talent house policy. Both Josephson and Hammond held the belief that blacks were inherently better at playing jazz than whites. Josephson simply stated: "We have a definite color policy on music too. Since we feature jazz, and since it is obvious that Negroes play jazz best, practically all of our music is by Negro musicians."[31] This policy clearly reflects the Popular

Front emphasis on African American cultural contributions. Naison notes that "the first laudatory article on 'swing' appeared in the September 12, 1937 issue of the *Daily Worker*; . . . it emphasized that "Negro musicians . . . have been the decisive element behind its history, development, and course."[32]

In line with other cultural arbiters of the time, however, Hammond had very specific ideas concerning the history, development, and course of black music.[33] With the exception of his abhorrence of anything that smacked of the commercial, John Hammond was one of the young, Popular Front 'turks' described by Naison earlier. He had long been associated with leftist causes and organizations, but never claimed allegiance to any party line. His stated investment was in the social justice achieved through the championing of jazz as a universal, quintessentially American art form. However, when the opportunity arose for him to produce a concert featuring black performers, he had more than just good music in mind. Jonathan Bakan uses the term "developmental continuum" to describe the narrative of progress from "simple" to "complex" that Hammond imposed on black music in his famed *From Spirituals to Swing* concert of 1938.

The concert, in line with its title, aimed to present a range of American Negro music to "serious audiences" at Carnegie Hall as art (as opposed to presenting it as entertainment for what the program referred to as "uncritical groups").[34] The program included (in order): a recording of African tribal music, the Mitchell's Christian Singers and Sister Rosetta Tharpe performing spirituals and holy roller hymns, The Kansas City Six performing "soft swing," Sanford Terry on harmonica, several blues performers including Ruby Smith (the recently deceased Bessie Smith's niece), Joe Turner, James Rushing, and Helen Humes, boogie-woogie players Meade "Lux" Lewis, Albert Ammons, and Pete Johnson, Sidney Bechet's band, and Count Basie's band. In choosing the artists he chose, placing them in the order in which he did and framing the concert along a developmental schema, he created a narrative of black musical (explicitly) and social (implicitly) development that would have far-reaching influence.

In addition to the narrative of (racial) progress from "unlettered" to "sophisticated," the near absence of female instrumentalists (Sister Tharpe self-accompanied on guitar being the sole exception) and Hammond's obsession with working-class authenticity as romance should be noted.[35] The historian David Stowe notes that in choosing artists for this series, Hammond tried to avoid those he felt were too commercial or had been influenced too much by white musicians. Stowe quotes him as saying about his *From Spirituals to Swing* roster: "These are artists who, for the most part, have had no formal musical training of any kind, cannot read musical notations, and have never played before white audiences, or in any formal way, before black audiences."[36] Hammond hopes, through jazz, he can publicize the underprivileged social position of most African Americans, but his primitivizing of the artists and his imperialistic need to be "discoverer" and cultural translator of their art form complicates his legacy.[37] In his quest for authenticity, Hammond conflated class and race; for him, racial authenticity was working class and working class, more times than not, was masculinized. The Boogie-Woogie Boys (Ammons, Lewis, and Johnson) became a successful symbol of this conflation. Because it was developed in working-class, often sexualized contexts, performed mostly by black men (at least until the 1940s), and required a dead-on rhythmic sense and a strong left hand, it was associated with a black, male sexuality that signaled a blues-tinged jazz authenticity for many musicians and audiences.

The *From Spirituals to Swing* roster (and conception) famously shaped the first Café Society lineup (from December 1938) and the Boogie-Woogie Boys remained a central attraction for two years straight. Josephson, who had sat in on rehearsals for the concert, cherry-picked Ammons, Lewis, and Johnson along with Sister Tharpe and Joe Turner. Completing the original roster at Café Society were Frankie Newton's Band and Billie Holiday. The club put on three floorshows a night which usually included some combination of the following: an emcee, a celebrity singer like Billie Holiday, individual pianists (sometimes featured with bands, sometimes solo in between other acts), special acts like comics, dancers, or the occasional harpist or harpsichordist, and small bands for dancing.[38] Many styles of music were presented then, and many well-known figures got their start at Café Society: Lena Horne, Pearl Primus, Zero Mostel, Billie Holiday, Mildred Bailey, and Josh White, to name a few. In spite of the variety, "the boogie-woogie piano [was] emphasized and [was] the king of the show."[39]

DESIRE AND THE BOOGIE-WOOGIE QUEENS

Café Society is an excellent site for viewing and analyzing the musical and professional strategies and priorities of Mary Lou Williams, Hazel Scott, and other female instrumentalists. Hazel Scott started at Café Society in 1939 as a replacement for Billie Holiday. When Josephson opened the Uptown branch on October 8, 1940, she headlined there until her marriage to Adam Clayton Powell Jr. Williams worked at the downtown and uptown venues steadily from 1943 to 1947 and off and on after that until the club closed in 1949. This lengthy engagement played an essential role in Williams's creative, social, and political development. She was ambivalent about Café Society's management and the restrictive demands it placed on her musical output, but the steady gig provided her with a consistent income, a professional support system, an expansive fan base, and a stable musical environment that contributed to her creative development.

Williams's Café Society output is often neglected in favor of later achievements it helped enable, such as the composition of her *Zodiac Suite* and her productive partnership with Moe Asch and Asch Records.[40] Her late-night sessions at Minton's (after her Café Society gigs) and her mentorship of up-and-coming (male) bebop musicians, such as Thelonious Monk, Tadd Dameron, Kenny Dorham, and Bud Powell, have also garnered much attention. When the Café Society period is mentioned, however, her musicking experiences are categorized along hierarchies that reflect and reinforce gendered values. Michael Denning's categorization of the music at Café Society may serve as an example of this historiographical tendency. At the same time, it is a starting point for a brief discussion of some of the struggles of representation that the female pianists of Café Society had in common.

Denning's treatment of Café Society's "cabaret blues" as a melding of Popular Front politics and jazz culture is fascinating and well considered.[41] Although it does offer much-needed information on 1930s and 1940s cultural politics in leftist New York, it may also, however, serve as an example of how musical practices, and the socially specific meanings and representations that accrue to them, can fall through discursive cracks.

Denning suggests that "three distinct musics" made up the cabaret blues performed at Café Society: "boogie-woogie piano, the small-group swing bands fronted by women singers, notably Billie Holiday, and the Piedmont blues and gospel of Josh White and the Golden Gate Quartet." The boogie-woogie pianists he mentions are the "Boogie-Woogie Boys" of *From Spirituals to Swing* fame: Albert Ammons, Pete Johnson, and Meade Lux Lewis; he describes the music they played as "hard and driving." The "small groups — Frank Newton's septet and Teddy Wilson's sextet, as well as subsequent bands led by Eddie Heywood, Joe Sullivan, Edmond Hall, and Mary Lou Williams — played a chamber jazz, with the piano's melodic improvisations alternating with the riffs and short solos of the horns." The original Café Society "woman singer" was Billie Holiday, followed by Hazel Scott and Lena Horne.[42] Canonical male figures and gendered categories of activity shape his understanding of music at Café Society. As a result, he reifies the gendered priorities of mainstream jazz discourse as well as the Popular Front ideologies that obscured the specifically gendered contributions of the female keyboardists at Café Society.[43]

For example, Scott did sing but she was first and foremost a pianist of formidable, if poorly marketed, talent. She and Williams alternated as featured pianist for much of her Café Society tenure. Denning implies that Williams was the only serious female instrumentalist and that her musicking was not "hard and driving" but was in stark contrast to that of Scott or Horne. Williams serving as leader in these chamber groups was notable for a woman at the time, but she was sought out and hired by John Hammond, musical director at Café Society, for her Kansas City blues and boogie-woogie skills. Finally, Ammons, Johnson, and Lewis were the first and initially best known boogie-woogie players at Café Society, but numerous female boogie-woogie pianists were featured there through the course of the club's existence, most of whom, including Williams, were treated with similar ambivalence in the contemporaneous popular press. The quantity and quality of these players is noteworthy; they were an important segment of Café Society's entertainment roster because they had popular appeal and their inclusion contributed to the club's political agendas.

As things currently stand, mainstream jazz discourse, traditionally, strategically addresses Williams's excellence as exceptionality.[44] She is often the only female instrumentalist mentioned in popular jazz histories, classroom texts, and high-profile PBS documentaries. She is the *grand dame* of jazz. She is the keeper of a rich, male-focused tradition, its matriarch, its muse. Williams certainly warrants the attention; what is at issue is not her excellence, but the way *exceptionality* in mainstream jazz discourse is couched in gendered terms.[45]

When asked about her experiences as a woman in jazz, Williams often reproduced these attitudes. Her interviews and writings are famously dotted with comments like the following: "As for being a woman, I never thought much about that one way or the other. All I've ever thought about is music. I'm very feminine but I think like a man. I've been working around them all my life. I can deal better with men than women, and I've never heard objectionable remarks from men about being a woman musician."[46] Whether reproduced or rejected, the "exceptionality" model does a disservice to Williams and other women in jazz.[47] It describes her musicking in limited terms and obscures some forms of her excellence as well as the ways in which those came into being. It removes her from her social and historical moorings and overlooks the collective, material, and everyday dimensions of her life. Glorifying her in this way also obscures the quality and quantity of her female contemporaries with whom she may have worked, played, learned, and exchanged support. How might reframing her work at Café Society as a part of a larger category of musical activities of its female keyboardists shed new light on her time there — or theirs?

While Mary Lou Williams and Hazel Scott both had long-term engagements at Café Society, Nellie Lutcher, Rose Murphy, Sylvia Marlowe, Connie Berry, and Dorothy Donegan, who was the "last featured pianist at the Downtown café during the Josephson regime," all performed their boogie-woogie stylings there as well.[48] For the longest time, I imagined Williams as walking the jazz earth alone — one of its sole female instrumentalists. I was happy to find her here surrounded by other women who were, at least at the time, successfully negotiating careers as such.

Reviews of the female boogie-woogie pianists suggest not only that Williams's discursive exceptionalism as we know it was in early stages of development but also that the female boogie-woogie pianists of the 1940s shared similar experiences. Most enjoyed high professional achievement and popularity, and they all navigated conflicting themes and tropes of reception regarding their training, technique, repertoires, and, of course, physical appearance.

By the time Café Society hired Mary Lou Williams, she had already accomplished many of the musical feats that would support her modern-day construction as exceptional. Her precocious beginnings as a child prodigy were well known, for example, and she had become the "lady who swings the band" in Kansas City with Andy Kirk and the Clouds of Joy. While at Café Society, she hosted a weekly radio show on WNEW, and jazz writers like John Martin recognized her as the first boogie-woogie arranger for big bands.[49] However, other pianists could boast of high achievements as well. Shortly after her tenure at Café Society ended, Hazel Scott became the first African American woman to star in her own television show in 1950.[50] Dorothy Donegan was the first to give a concert at Chicago's Orchestra Hall.[51] Press releases and concert notices suggest busy performance schedules for most of these in-demand performers. Even when critics condemned repertoire choices as commercial or "flashy" or performance approaches as not serious enough or too physical, audience members lined up to see their favorite players.

Another major consistency the reviews illuminate is that between the women's repertoires. Virtually all incorporated a large, genre-blurring repertoire of blues, popular tunes, boogie-woogie, swing, and even classical that reflects individual technical command, talent, and flexibility, and "swingin' the classics" is a trope that appeared with great frequency. Although Hazel Scott was perhaps best known for "swingin' the classics," this practice, which consisted of performing well-known classical pieces with a boogie-woogie treatment, was apparently widespread.[52]

There are also similarities of experience and reception in articles and reviews that reveal the attitudes these women had to navigate as female instrumentalists. There were frequent struggles with male managers and producers over artistic agency and career choices. Managers were often in favor of singing as opposed to playing the popular selections; there were also disagreements over lyrics and performative approaches that emphasized sexuality. Although many of the reviews were laudatory, there was an overarching ambivalence about the talented pianists. They were frequently referred to as novelties, their talent qualified by attitudes of amusement and surprise. One *Times* excerpt goes as follows: "Gordon Mercer, of the new General Record Corp. has a surprise up his sleeve for next month's release list — and it's a girl! She's young, good looking, a classical pianist and harpsichordist who knows her Bach, Mozart — and her boogie-woogie."[53]

As that quote exemplifies, there was also an emphasis on looks, a predictable preoccupation that was tied in to contemporaneous racist and colorist values. The white and light-complexioned African American pianists were offered movie roles, but apart from scattered references to their dusky or sepia skin tones, the physical appearances of darker-skinned black women were not commented on. A striking exception is a *Times* description of Rose Murphy: "[She] is a sad-eyed Negress in her middle 30s; a big woman who looks as if she might be handy with the spring cleaning."[54]

Popular Front cultural politics helped enable these women to participate as jazz instrumentalists at Café Society. However, the examples above suggest that they were either conscribed to feminized labor, where they would risk having their work described as being more about sex than music, or explained away — as was the case with Mary Lou

Williams — as an exception to the rule. However, as Rabinowitz suggests, gender produces not only a "difference between" but also a "difference within."[55] Women's boogie-woogie, as practiced at Café Society, serves as a genre within but also distinct from boogie-woogie, as described in mainstream jazz histories. Although the boundaries, icons, codes, and vocabularies overlap, women's boogie-woogie is a "genre marked by its own narrative types and subject positions" and one that "inscribes desire into jazz history."[56] Mary Lou Williams and Hazel Scott serve as examples.

MARY LOU WILLIAMS, HAZEL SCOTT, AND THE POPULAR FRONT CULTURAL POLITICS OF CAFÉ SOCIETY

The historian David Stowe has suggested that authenticity and syncretism (genre-blending and cultural hybridism) were the primary values at Café Society. The experiences of Williams and Scott suggest that in spite of the complexity of their output, the women boogie-woogie players at Café Society were hired because they were perceived as embodying one or the other of these values in gendered ways.

Case Study No. 1: As previously discussed, the views of the Café Society music director John Hammond on black musical authenticity were in line with Popular Front ideologies. For him, authenticity as guiding value was key and the authentic jazz musician was neither white nor commercial, although frequently masculinized. Hammond hoped Mary Lou Williams would perform his brand of authenticity.

He had pursued her for his New York clubs since 1936 and hoped to play a role in shaping her career. With her firm grounding in and recordings of Kansas City blues and swing and boogie-woogie, she was the real article. Better still, her appearance, described in the Times as sinewy, plain, and unassuming, would not distract like Scott's or Horne's. Jobless in New York and without a union card, Williams was finally ready to accept the position at Café Society in 1943, but kept her distance from Hammond; she, like many other jazz musicians at the time, found him patronizing and controlling. She was also wary of his musical preferences and political leanings.

Although Williams did perform at a few Popular Front benefits — including a fundraiser for Benjamin Davis — her attitude about them suggests that she attended them for professional reasons. She had this to say about her time at Café Society: "The only drag in New York was the many benefit shows we were expected to do — late shows which prevented me from running up on 52nd Street to see my favorite modern- ists. Sometimes Johnny Gary (the valet) and I would dig a boogie char- acter coming to take me on a benefit. We'd tear across the street to the 18th Hole and hide real quick under a table till the danger was past."[57]

Although her music was always grounded in blues, she was not inter- ested in performing them night after night, and she felt the same way about boogie-woogie. One *Times* article reads: "If you ask Miss Williams where boogie-woogie came from and what the name means she will tell you frankly that she doesn't know because she isn't much interested in it. She is far more interested in general composing, arranging, and piano playing. Nevertheless, you could not name the top four boogie-woogie players in the field without including her. The others would unques- tionably be Albert Ammons, Pete Johnson and Meade "Lux" Lewis."[58] Here again is the tendency to exceptionalize through masculinization. Although this example is more specific to time and place than Denning's, Williams's musicking has been conflated with working-class, black, male authenticity. Unlike the members of the Boogie-Woogie Boys, however, Williams realized that specializing in the genre would limit career and creativity. "Once, she said, you get known as a boogie player, you've got to play boogie, boogie all the time."[59]

Throughout her time at Café Society, Williams maintained the aura of "authenticity," in part because of her own sense of musical gender, and exhibited syncretic qualities by occasionally swinging classics, but she also managed to stretch or refuse limits placed upon her. She may have been hired to play boogies, but she made conscious and consistent attempts to incorporate those musical elements that interested her — modern, bop-oriented details like augmented intervals and complex, stacked chords, angular melodic lines, and whole tone passages. She also programmed her own compositions whenever possible. A tran- script from a Café Society radio show reveals her strategy. Imogene Coca introduces Williams thusly: "to show you how versatile she is, Mary Lou is going to play her own special mistreatment of Rachmani- noff." We must presume that she proceeded to swing that composer, but later in the program, Mary played a movement from her impressionis- tic, then experimental *Zodiac Suite* about which she had this to say: "From *Zodiac*, I received the name of musician's musician instead of the Boogie Woogie Queen."[60] As her quote reveals, Williams had specific ideas not only about meaningful connections between genre and gender but also about the types of musical practices that could transcend such associations.

Williams's manager after 1964, Peter O'Brien, had this to say about her in reference to John Hammond's limited view: "I don't think she could have conformed to his idea of what the music was supposed to be like. He would have wanted to continue to record her only if she kept playing like the Mary Lou of 1936 and 1938. Here was a really intelligent person, a creative artist who did not produce on demand, but from inside herself. But this was not allowed black women in that period."[61] That Mary Lou Williams was an exceptional jazz musician is not at issue. Understanding the ways in which she navigated what was and was not allowed of her at any given time in relation to the experiences and strategies of her female contemporaries will help illuminate how she became that way.

Case Study No. 2: For Barney Josephson perhaps more than John Hammond, syncretism and the blurring of generic and social boundaries was key. Extremely invested in the Popular Front project of interracialism, he originated and firmly enforced the club's antisegregation policies and sought out acts that he felt mirrored his political views. He featured integrated jazz ensembles, the "cabaret blues" of Billie Holiday ("Strange Fruit" being the best-known example), and smaller acts like the Kraft Sisters, "the Hindus from Englewood," who blended Indian and African American dance styles.[62] Hazel Scott was the epitome of Josephson's aesthetic of syncretism. Her cosmopolitan repertoire and approach reflected the ideals of 1940s New Deal and Popular Front culture.

Young and talented, Scott studied classical piano at the Juilliard Conservatory. In late 1939 she replaced Billie Holiday on Josephson's roster and although she did experiment with and perform in bop style, Scott became best known for singing pop tunes and "swingin' the classics." She gave the "jive" treatment to everyone from Bach to Rachmaninoff and Josephson reported: "When Hazel Scott plays Bach's Prelude in C-sharp minor, that's something!"[63]

Scott's performances of jazz as syncretic and all-American were connected for her black fans at Café Society and elsewhere, with her accomplishments and political commitment. Bop musicians like Dizzy Gillespie are more frequently constructed as revolutionary and anti-assimilationist and are more popularly associated with the Double V campaign, but Hazel Scott actively fought racist practices throughout her career and contributed to Double V concerns. She organized a high-profile campaign against Constitution Hall when the Daughters of the American Revolution would not let her perform there because she was black. She refused to play segregated venues. She lent her talents to a series of V-Discs, and her pinups were second in popularity among black troops only to those of Lena Horne, her coworker at Café Society. Both women were strong symbols of victory abroad and at home.[64]

Horne described her as having the "fiercest sort of racial pride."[65] This trait apparently allowed her to fight back when directors went too far. In *The Heat's On*, the film discussed at the beginning of this essay, Scott and the black cast are featured in a production number called "Caisson Song" in which black women send off their troops (see figure 4.1). The script originally called for all of the women, including Scott, to wear maid's uniforms. Scott refused and, leveraging all her considerable star power, threatened to walk out if changes were not made. Columbia obviously invested little into rehearsal time, set, or props. Regardless, the resulting scene—in which Scott wore a military uniform and the other women wore dresses—was surely read as poignant and meaningful to black audiences who were fighting fascism abroad and racism at home.

Ebony magazine interviewed her in 1945, stating, "Because she refuses to play traditional strumpet and maid roles, Hazel Scott usually plays Hazel Scott in her movie appearances. The confident Scott replied: 'There's one thing about being typed as myself. When people ask me what my favorite role is, I can answer with all modesty—Hazel Scott.' "[66]

Black women of the 1940s had to negotiate numerous conflicting roles. They participated in a black "upwardly mobile achievement ethic" associated with the civil rights push, but they also experienced ambivalence toward those goals. This decade saw the emergence of E. Franklin Frazier's black bourgeoisie, and black women contributed significantly to the trend. Between 1940 and 1950 there was an increase in the number of black women in professional and semiprofessional occupations and a decrease in their numbers as domestic workers. They entered the traditionally feminine fields of social work, nursing, and teaching in high numbers as well as the traditionally masculine arenas of law and politics. More black women were attending college than either white women or black men. Although white women were "freeing working men to fight," joining the workforce was for black women very much about material and social gain directly related to the progress of the race.[67]

Black female members of the new bourgeoisie struggled to negotiate these gains; their ideological positions shifted along with their social

Fig. 4.1. Hazel Scott from "The Heat's On," Columbia Pictures, 1946. Photofest.

positions and they were conflicted over their place in the workforce and the more mainstream, traditional gender roles they were fast adopting. If women's involvement in the workforce was necessary during the war years, immediately following this period, Black magazines like *Ebony* and *Jet* featured articles with rhetorical titles like "Do Career Women Make Good Wives?"

Hazel Scott's musical performances of black femininity successfully navigated these concerns and eased anxieties black women may have had about their shifting gender roles. She integrated the white space of the Hollywood musical with grace and confidence and bridged opposing, gendered performative realms: classical and jazz, intellect and emotion, ladylike propriety and sexy glamor, public and private, technical mastery and natural talent. Unlike the trumpet, which she had played in her mother's band, Scott's instrument of choice (the piano) linked her to narratives of middle-class domesticity and feminine accomplishments. Josephson got his syncretism: her genre-blurring performance style was a democratic mix of high and low or middle-class aspirations and racial uplift. The coy, French-speaking, Rachmaninoff-swinging genius in the designer gown could be seen at Café Society or at a rally for Benjamin Davis. Her performing body took up space, demanded attention, and transcended narratives and ideologies meant to contain her.

While she fulfilled the gendered cultural political work demanded by Popular Front jazz contexts, she also linked these inscriptions of desire to history in ways meaningful to black audiences. In the scene from *The Heat's On* that opened this essay, the gaze of the men in the audience frames Hazel Scott's performance in a way that connects narratives of black female sexuality to class and gender via Popular Front interracial sexual politics. By shifting the frame to include gender as a category of analysis, we see her perform an integrated and autonomous black female subjectivity that asserts female sexuality and desire as coterminous with jazz authenticity. As the men exclaim after her performance: "Isn't she something?"

NOTES

1. Scott's other Hollywood films include *Something to Shout About* (Gregory Ratoff, 1943); *I Dood It* (Vincente Minnelli, 1943); *Broadway Rhythm* (Roy del Ruth, 1944); and *Rhapsody in Blue* (Irving Rapper, 1945). Her French film appearances include *Une balle dans le canon* (Michele Deville and Charles Gérard, 1958) and *Le Désordre et la Nuit* (Gilles Grangier, 1958).

2. Earl Wilson, "Keeping Abreast of Hazel," *New York Post*, November 18, 1943. Reprinted in *Negro Digest*, January 1944, 43–44.

3. The phrase "aesthetics of social significance" is Michael Denning's. See Michael Denning, *The Cultural Front: The Laboring of American Culture in the Twentieth Century* (London: Verso, 1997), 83.

4. Robin Kelley, *Hammer and Hoe: Alabama Communists during the Great Depression* (Chapel Hill: University of North Carolina Press, 1990), 180. My thanks to Robin for pointing out this connection.

5. This was the Davis Victory Rally of 1943. Coleman Hawkins, Billie Holiday, Ella Fitzgerald, and Mary Lou Williams are among the other musicians who participated.

6. Of particular interest here is Robin Kelley's essay "Africa's Sons with Banner Red: on African American Communists and the Politics of Culture, 1919–1934," in Kelley 1994. Kelley offers insightful gender analysis in a revisionist argument that posits African American nationalist and international culture at the center of leftist politics. See also Jonathon E. Bakan, "Café Society: A Locus for the Intersection of Jazz and Politics during the Popular Front Era" (diss., York University, 2004); Denning, *The Cultural Front*; Mark

Naison, *Communists in Harlem during the Depression* (Urbana: University of Illinois Press: 1983); David W. Stowe, "The Politics of Café Society," *Journal of American History* 84, no. 4 (1998): 1384–1406 (Bakan introduces gender as a category of analysis in his chapter on Billie Holiday). For a consideration of concert music during the Popular Front see Elizabeth B. Crist, "Aaron Copland and the Popular Front," *Journal of the American Musicological Society* 56, no. 2 (2003): 409–65.

7. See Denning, *The Cultural Front*; and Naison, *Communists in Harlem during the Depression*. According to Michael Denning, the U.S. Popular Front was not quite a political party in itself and also not merely an unstable coalition between a subordinate, Communist-led "left" and dominant New Deal policy. He suggests that it might best be described as a widespread and influential social movement whose varied participants rallied around a unifying cluster of causes, projects, policies, and issues. One of the central points that Denning makes in *The Cultural Front* is that participation in Popular Front politics was not always directly linked to membership in the Communist Party or even to ideological commitment to Marxism. It was often simply about sharing "the common sense of the day." While it does help explain and emphasize the complexity and contradictions of Popular Front activity (cultural and political), my current understanding is that his revisionist reframing undervalues the centrality and authority of the Communist Party during the Popular Front era. The CPUSA had the most clout, the highest profile, and was the most well-organized institutional formation in the Popular Front.

8. See Kelley 1994.

9. The Scottsboro case involved nine African American boys and men between the ages of thirteen and twenty-one who were falsely accused of raping two white women in Alabama. Popular Front organizations involved in the cause included the International Labor Defense, the legal branch of the CPUSA, and the National Association for the Advancement of Colored People (NAACP), although the latter's involvement was not without controversy. See Naison, *Communists in Harlem during the Depression*; and Kelley, *Hammer and Hoe*, on the Popular Front interpolitics surrounding the Scottsboro case and on the NAACP's initial hesitancy to support the cause.

10. Denning, *The Cultural Front*, 6.

11. See Stowe 1994.

12. Ibid.

13. Ibid., 13; Denning, *The Cultural Front*, 331.

14. See Denning, *The Cultural Front*, 9.

15. See Kelley 2002a, 38.

16. Kelley 1996, 116–17.

17. Muriel Reger, "The Negro in Relation to Jazz," *Direction* 2, no. 1 (1939): 21–22.

18. Martin McCall, "Handy Concert for Milk Fund," *Daily Worker*, November 24, 1938. Incensed by its "arrogant and dyspeptic" reading of the concert, John Hammond demanded a printed apology from the *Daily Worker* after McCall's article was printed. Evidencing Hammond's clout, the *Daily Worker* agreed and also printed his formal statement: "it is highly impolitic for the *Daily* to be a party to insulting treatment of great Negro artists, who, for the first time, are becoming interested in the cause of Democracy and Spain and are contributing their services to help it." *Daily Worker*, December 2, 1938. Naison notes this journalistic dialogue as an example of the conflicting ideas about black music held by leftist critics. See Naison, *Communists in Harlem during the Depression*, 204.

19. Ibid., 212.

20. Ibid., 211.

21. See Stowe 1994; and John Remo Gennari, "The Politics of Culture and Identity in American Jazz Criticism" (diss., University of Pennsylvania, 1993).

22. By the late 1930s female membership in the CPUSA accounted for nearly 40 percent of its total membership. In addition, out of 1,218 attendees at the Second National Negro Congress in 1937, over 500 were women. See Paula Rabinowitz, "Women and U.S. Literary Radicalism," *Writing Red: An Anthology of American Women Writers, 1930–1940*, ed. Charlotte Nekola and Paula Rabinowitz (Chapel Hill: University of North Carolina Press, 1987), 8; and "A Great New Congress," *New Masses*, October 26, 1937. For the quote see Paula Rabinowitz, *Labor and Desire: Women's Revolutionary Fiction in Depression America* (Chapel Hill: University of North Carolina Press, 1991), 60.

23. Rabinowitz, *Labor and Desire*.

24. Denning, *The Cultural Front*, 32. See also Kelley 1996, 121.

25. See Rabinowitz, *Labor and Desire*; and Kelley 1996. Kelley brilliantly argues that especially during the 1930s, these types of gender constructions were a site of commonality for black and white men engaged in leftist struggle. He quotes Elizabeth Faue, who described the labor movement's iconography thusly: "They forged a web of symbols which romanticized violence, rooted solidarity in metaphors of struggle, and constructed work and the worker as male." Kelley 1996, 114.

26. See Stowe 1994; Naison, *Communists in Harlem during the Depression*; and Gennari, "The Politics of Culture and Identity in American Jazz Criticism," on the white, male, and leftist roots of jazz criticism.

27. Mike Gold, "Change the World: History's Best Men Have All Been for the Union," *Daily Worker*, December 2, 1938.

28. See R. D. Darrell, "Music with a Purpose," *New Masses*, February 15, 1938; John Sebastian, "From Spirituals to Swing," *New Masses*, January 3, 1939. While Sebastian

refers to playing styles as "ejaculatory and direct," he at the same time refers to many of the musicians who participated in the concert as "untutored" and "naive."

29. Helen Lawrenson, *Whistling Girl: Candid Confessions of a Chameleon* (Garden City, N.Y.: Doubleday, 1978), 92.

30. Stowe notes that when Benny Goodman did, he often made a point of "conspicuously" borrowing the horn of the African American clarinetist Edmund Hall David. See Stowe, "The Politics of Café Society," 1388.

31. See "Café Society's Biggest Act," *Ebony*, December 1946, 40.

32. See Naison, *Communists in Harlem during the Depression*, 211.

33. His *From Spirituals to Swing* event, backed by *New Masses*, was the second of three major concerts of black music with leftist affiliations and implied historical narratives. Others included the benefit at Carnegie Hall for the Spanish Children's Milk Fund discussed earlier and "Negro Music Past and Present," which took place under the auspices of the American Labor Party. See Naison, *Communists in Harlem during the Depression*, 212.

34. James Dugan and John Hammond, "An Early Black-Music Concert from Spirituals to Swing," *Black Perspective in Music* 2, no. 2 (fall): 191.

35. See Elijah Wald, *Escaping the Delta: Robert Johnson and the Invention of the Blues* (New York: Harper Collins, 2004), 226–27, for his discussion of how William Broonzy was constructed in liner notes, reviews, and Hammond's own autobiography as a shoeless Arkansas farmer. See also Wald 2003 for her excellent discussion of Sister Tharpe and how she negotiated gospel-pop crossover in the 1930s to 1950s. The use of the terms "unlettered" and "sophisticated" is borrowed from her description of the Spirituals to Swing concert.

36. Stowe, "The Politics of Café Society," 1393.

37. In fact, musicians' nicknames for Hammond signified on his patriarchal "authority": the Critic, the Little Father, the Guardian Angel, the Big Bringdown. See Stowe 1994, 58.

38. For more detailed descriptions of the Café Society floor show see George Hoefer, "Café Society Downtown and Uptown: The Wrong Place for the Right People," *Down Beat Music '67*, 12th yearbook, *Down Beat Magazine* (Los Angeles: Maher, 1967), 74.

39. A note about boogie-woogie: During the early 1900s poor, southern, rural laborers — largely lumbermen and sawmill employees — entertained themselves in barrelhouses. Self-taught piano players would perform, often accompanying their own blues singing. While it was not called boogie-woogie at the time, a certain genre of the blues developed in these contexts to meet the need of audiences for faster, more rhythmically complex, instrumental dance forms. Many of these players moved north during the years between the First and Second World Wars as a part of the great migration of blacks in the hopes of

finding better jobs and escaping racial prejudice. In these northern cities the pianists would perform at rent parties, bars, and gambling and prostitution houses. Coming out of this context and adding refinement and technical virtuosity to the genre were three prominent "second generation" players: Albert Ammons and Meade "Lux" Lewis from Chicago and Pete Johnson from Kansas City. The "boogie-woogie King" quote is from Hoefer, "Café Society Downtown and Uptown."

40. Tammy L. Kernodle's treatment in Kernodle 2004 is an exception.

41. Denning, *The Cultural Front*. Denning coined the term "cabaret blues" to make explicit the conceptual influence of the political cabaret on Josephson's jazz club.

42. Ibid., 340.

43. Ibid., 360.

44. I would not normally refer to Michael Denning's work as "mainstream jazz discourse," but the excerpts I use here mirror the tendencies of which I am speaking.

45. Sherrie Tucker suggests that there are two ways in which the presence of women in jazz is typically explained; they fall on either side of the nurture/nature dichotomy. The "always emerging" model explains women's presence in negative terms. There are not remarkable numbers of talented women musicians (particularly instrumentalists) because women have traditionally not been exposed or had access to the environments, instruction and mentorship that create great musicians. The exceptional model, on the other hand, looks to women's nature in explanation: "Women are invisible because they weren't good enough. Playing good enough meant playing like men. Women who play like men are "exceptional women," and exceptional women can enter the discourse without changing it." See Tucker 2001–2, 375–408.

46. Dahl 1999, 349.

47. See Tucker 2001–2.

48. Hoefer, "Café Society Downtown and Uptown," 85. DeLoyd MacKaye, Hadda Brooks, Julia Lee, Cleo Brown, Camille Howard, and Mabel Scott were contemporaries who performed in the same idiom but worked at other clubs (in New York, in Kansas City, and on the West Coast).

49. John Martin, "Inquiry into Boogie-Woogie," *New York Times*, July 16, 1944, SM18.

50. She was closely followed by Hadda Brooks in 1954 on KLAC, Channel 11 in Los Angeles. See John Martin, "Inquiry into Boogie-Woogie."

51. Ben Ratliff, "Dorothy Donegan, 76, Flamboyant Jazz Pianist," *New York Times*, May 22, 1998, A23.

52. For more on swingin' the classics see Stowe 1994 and Bakan, "Café Society."

53. William Russell, "Fem Boogie Artist Act Waxes 6 Hot Ones!" *Jazz Hot*, June–July 1938.

54. John Wilson, "The Café That Gave Us Chee-Chee and Boogie-Woogie, Too." Undated article from clip file on Café Society, Institute of Jazz Studies, Rutgers University, Newark, New Jersey. Especially considering the oppressive historical relationship between African American women and domestic work (in the 1920s and 1930s, some 90 percent of African American women worked as domestics, and until the 1940s we had few other employment options), this conflation of physical attributes with racialized class status is striking but in line with the way engendered class is manifested in Popular Front jazz contexts.

55. Rabinowitz, *Labor and Desire*, 65. She in turn borrows the idea from Barbara Johnson. See Barbara Johnson, *The Critical Difference* (Baltimore: Johns Hopkins University Press, 1980), 55.

56. Ibid., 65–73.

57. Mary Lou Williams, "In Her Own Words . . . Mary Lou Williams Interview," *Melody Maker*, April–June 1954, http://www.ratical.org/MaryLouWilliams/MMiview1954.html.

58. Martin, "Inquiry into Boogie-Woogie."

59. Dahl 1999, 178.

60. Mary Lou Williams, Radio Script for the 7th Anniversary celebration at Café Society, 1945. Mary Lou Williams Archive at the Institute for Jazz Studies, Rutgers University, Newark, New Jersey. For the quote see Dahl 1999, 160.

61. Dahl 1999, 145.

62. Stowe 1994, 1394.

63. Ibid.

64. See Tucker 2000, 227–58. It is interesting to note that in most of the pinups, Scott is posing next to the piano, which makes it impossible to separate her body from her achievements as a musician.

65. Lena Horne and Richard Schickel, *Lena* (New York: Doubleday, 1965), 117.

66. "Bye-Bye Boogie: Hazel Scott Leaves Night Clubs and Moves to Concert Stage," *Ebony*, November 1945, 35.

67. Tucker 2000, 244.

Christina Baade

In December 1942, when Britain had been at war over three years, the British Broadcasting Corporation (BBC) contracted Ivy Benson and her Ladies' Dance Orchestra as its fourth "house" band.[1] The contract was a big break for Benson, and the BBC hoped it would improve program quality while saving money. More importantly, it brought the work of women dance musicians to national prominence, highlighting their contributions to the British war effort. Male civilian bandleaders and *Melody Maker*, Britain's dance band weekly, however, regarded Benson's contract as a threat to an embattled profession, prompting a "storm" of controversy, or what the press began to call the "battle of the sexes and saxes."[2]

The playful appellation downplayed the seriousness of the controversy, as concerning "only" popular music and lady musicians. Like other debates in the period, however, it revealed the divisions and inequalities obscured by the wartime emphasis on a "unitary British national identity," in which everyday people put aside their differences to cooperate with tolerance, good humor, and shared sacrifice in a "People's War."[3] On one level, the battle of the saxes was another iteration of the controversy over work, gender roles, and national service obligations. In December 1941 the government ended reserve occupations for men and began conscripting women for national service. Although it provided individual deferments for skilled men, the implication was that only men in military uniforms embodied fully the wartime ideals of British masculinity.[4] The entry of women into male occupations, especially skilled industrial work, further threatened working men's prestige on the home front, while trade unions worried that the presence of women workers would lower postwar wages. Since it was a primary employer of musicians in Britain, the BBC's decision to hire a women's band on an indefinite contract carried material consequences for male dance musicians. More importantly, the BBC's central role in British society, and radio's wartime status as a key promoter of good morale and national unity, moved the debate over women doing "men's" jobs into new territory — that of morale-boosting entertainment and of popular music, which had a fraught relationship with hegemonic British identity.

There existed in Britain a long history of regarding music as an un-British and effeminate occupation; this, combined with the particular ways in which wartime popular music was constructed as unmanly, made the BBC's recognition of a women's dance band as an equal competitor deeply threatening to male dance musicians.[5] In response to Benson's wartime contract, male bandleaders produced the usual misogynistic imprecations against female musicians, but they also charged that the BBC was failing in its traditional mission of supporting the British musical profession, giving bookings to ladies rather than to deserving civilian men. The wartime emphasis on men serving the nation in uniform, however, weakened their discourse of entitlement: although the BBC and military authorities had deemed dance music, popular song, and dancing crucial for the nation's morale, opinion was more divided about its performers. While the government still maintained the category of reserve occupations, it classified dance music as "inessential," decimating the ranks of civilian musicians. When the call-up intensified in 1942 and 1943, the press alleged that dance musicians — even those belonging to dance bands in the forces like the Royal Air Force (RAF) Squadronairs — shirked their national service duties and implied that they were either unmanly or socially deviant.

With male musicians called up or out of favor, popular music seemed an ideal field for women's advances. The BBC produced numerous programs that featured solo singers as "radio girl friends" for homesick men in the forces, and several women dance band vocalists, most notably Vera Lynn, embarked upon solo careers, claiming greater independence and better remuneration with lucrative recording, film, and variety contracts. Women's bands also had expanded opportunities, but their performances were linked less explicitly with morale-building than those of women singers. Much of the difference resided in the different ways that singers and instrumentalists negotiated the terrain of femininity and wartime citizenship, which existed in uneasy ideological company. As women moved into national service, often with jobs and responsibilities gendered as masculine, the nation became obsessed with maintaining, even heightening, gender difference. In this climate, it was far easier for the BBC to promote female vocalists as morale-building; over the aural medium of radio, women's and men's bands were indistinguishable, whereas vocalists were gendered through the intimate grain of the voice. Indeed, the voices and personas of the most successful wartime singers bridged what Sonya Rose has called maternal and sexualized femininity, evoking both the motherly comforts of home and homeland as well as the romantic companionship of aural pinups.[6] Moreover, singing was a reassuringly feminine occupation (in fact, the challenge usually rested with establishing that it was actually work) in contrast to the technicalities of playing instruments and organizing a band.

Of course, dance bands had to establish themselves through live performance before they entered the realm of radio and recordings. In addition to the visual scrutiny to which women performers were subjected, Benson and her band negotiated a wartime climate in which participation in women's beauty culture was regarded as a duty. According to Pat Kirkham, it symbolized the wartime value of "carrying on," and authorities regarded female attractiveness as supporting the morale of both women and men.[7] Sonya Rose went further to argue that the Ministry of Information stressed the benefits of glamour through the language of class: upper class women modeled the link between good job performance and a well-maintained appearance.[8] In wartime, glamour became a strategy for Benson and her band to assert female citizenship on the stage: it eased the anxieties surrounding women performing nontraditional roles, denoted a specifically feminine mode of competence, demonstrated a willingness to make personal sacrifices for the war effort, and signaled a commitment to boosting morale. Embracing "beauty as duty" ideology involved serious risks, however. Under wartime rationing, it involved significant effort and if taken too far (a judgment left to the unreliable eye of the beholder), it could open practitioners to charges of social deviance — selfish pleasure-seeking, loose sexual morals, incompetence, and un-British, Americanized attitudes.[9]

Although the wartime debates about Benson's contract focused upon gender, questions of class, race, and nationality underlay the controversy — indeed, they influenced any discussion of dance music in Britain. During the interwar period, dance bands and commercial popular music were regarded as American imports that targeted a modernized mass audience, generally characterized as young, working class, and female. Dance music contrasted with music hall and brass bands, considered the more "authentic" expressions of indigenous working class sensibilities, as well as the more discerning tastes of young educated male jazz enthusiasts. With its strong African American associations and the visibility of Jewish songwriters, even dance music performed by British musicians carried foreign associations, as either primitive or lacking in virility, that were alien to respectable, and implicitly white, British manhood. The interwar BBC was hostile to jazz and wary of commercial music, but it supported middlebrow, specifically British dance music in broadcasts from elite West End hotels.[10] In a wartime environment that regarded class privilege with suspicion, the BBC downplayed its references to upper class venues while emphasizing the more populist *palais de danse*. Benson and her band represented a challenge not only because they were female but also because they had honed their technique playing dance halls in Scotland and the north of England, in contrast to the "name" bands in the capital, which dominated broadcasting, recording, and the variety theater circuits in the profession. With their working-class, regional, and populist associations — and even their status as women — Benson's band had the potential to embody People's War ideologies better than the male bands.

The associations of social deviance and un-Britishness remained for wartime dance music, however. Following military setbacks in North Africa and South Asia, authorities blamed popular sentimental songs and the dance bands and singers who performed them for sapping the morale of fighting men as well as civilians, whose contributions also mattered in a state of total war. In July 1942, only five months before contracting Benson, the BBC banned male crooners, overly sentimental female singers, and slushy songs, beginning a largely unsuccessful campaign to increase the "virility" of popular music programming. Further, BBC Listener Research discovered that increasing portions of its audience had grown hostile to broadcast dance music, rendering its morale-building potential more dubious still. While *Melody Maker* and swing fans criticized the commerciality of radio dance music, the broader public protested the overexposure of a limited number of bands, the overplaying of hit songs, the vocal mannerisms of popular singers, and the declining quality of performance. For much of the war, the BBC itself had been concerned that British bands compared poorly with their American counterparts, both in technical ability and in originality; "ventriloquism" of American styles and arrangements was a charge leveled recurrently at British bands. The growing presence of American troops in Britain strengthened the BBC's resolve to define and assert a virile British dance music style, a difficult objective given the genre's strong American associations.[11] Meanwhile, British enthusiasts became obsessed with questions of authenticity in jazz, embodied by the Americans, and swing entered the mainstream of British popular music. Benson thus stepped into a minefield of issues, which centered on the problem of where a ladies' band, however "of the people," fit into the dance music continua of robust virility and effeminate sentimentality, authenticity and commercialism, Britishness and Americanism.[12]

Benson was no pawn in the battle of the saxes: her successes, outlined in *Melody Maker*, and verbal responses exposed the misogyny of her detractors, who reacted with such hostility to her important contract with the BBC. *Melody Maker*'s criticisms of Benson were particularly outrageous because the weekly reversed its own precontract judgments to malign her sound. The debate surrounding the "sound" of Benson's band — its repertory, instrumentation, and style — revealed the inequalities of gender and class that lay beneath notions of a unitary British identity in wartime, along with competing notions of authenticity and function in dance music. As has been the case for many female performers, the discourse about the band's sound existed in tension with that regarding its visual performance. However, the discussion of Benson and her band returned continually to the aural via the invisible medium of radio, the privileged materiality of the gramophone, and Benson's determination to make credible music. As she later reminisced, "I knew I could have gone out with a band that looked pretty and did a few sexy movements but that was second in my mind. They had to play and play well."[13] "Beauty as duty" glamour was not an end, although it was a means. To perform the difficult labor of professional feminine competence, Benson and her players had to negotiate wartime anxieties about women's roles and sexualized femininity; discourses of exceptionalism that classified them as curiosities; and People's War rhetoric of virile Britishness, populism, and morale.

DOING HER BIT: POPULISM, MORALE, AND
THE EMERGENCE OF BENSON'S BAND

Given their hostility toward Benson's 1942 BBC contract, it is striking how warmly *Melody Maker* and the dance music profession received her band in its first two years. As the band became poised for national recognition, several factors contributed to its ability to do so in a manner unthreatening to the status of male civilian bands. First, Benson honed her own and her band's skills on the periphery of national dance music culture, in the industrial North, all-girl combinations, and populist dance palais. Although the band's gender was remarkable in a male-dominated profession, it fell into a reliable tradition of novelty acts as a ladies' band. Second, Benson's musical roots and modest, plainspoken persona were at a premium in the environment of the People's War, which emerged with particular force after the June 1940 evacuation at Dunkirk and emphasized the idea that national unity was based on fairness, cooperation across lines of class, and the contributions of ordinary people. The band's initial lack of aural and visual slickness reinforced its respectability and authentic "of the people" qualities. Even the traits cast as exceptional — Benson's musicality, ambition, and the band's impressive improvement — resonated with wartime discourses of sacrifice, morale-building, and everyday spunk. It was only when Benson entered into direct competition with male bandleaders, at the same time that their masculinity was under attack, that Benson's gender became a problem. With women as a group, she had an uncertain relationship with wartime notions of fairness and British citizenship.[14]

When the wartime press described Benson as a "Leeds girl" from Yorkshire, who had been trained musically by her father, it located her within the working-class culture of the north of England.[15] Like the famous northerners Gracie Fields, the beloved vocalist and comedian, and Wilfred Pickles, the popular newsreader whose voice had diversified the accent of the BBC, Benson was coded as cheerful, genuine, and hard-working, embodying many virtues of wartime British identity. Benson took a suitably feminine route to success as a piano prodigy: her wind-playing father trained her from her third year with dreams of her becoming a concert pianist, and she appeared on the BBC's Children's Hour at the age of nine.[16] She also performed as "Baby Benson" in working men's clubs, which provided affordable alternatives to pubs and offered Sunday concerts — variety shows by semiprofessional entertainers

—for the men and their wives.[17] In her teens, Benson turned from respectable piano repertories and a scholarship to the Leeds College of Art to popular music and the less conventionally feminine clarinet and alto saxophone. Like her male semipro contemporaries, who provided much of the dance music for regional entertainment, she worked a day job, at the Montague Burton tailoring factory, and "play[ed] at social and dance events in her spare time."[18]

For a nation freshly interested in its regional diversity, the industrial north evoked images of indigenous, working-class musicality, embodied especially in working men's brass bands.[19] During the 1930s some girls and women, many of whom came from band families, began to enter the masculine preserve of the bands, whose membership had suffered because of both the depression and the expanding popularity of dance music.[20] Although their progress into leading positions was limited and the language surrounding women players continued to be patronizing well into the postwar period, women players entered into class and musical solidarity with their male counterparts. Although not herself schooled in the tradition, Benson recruited many of her brass players with the help of Harry Mortimer, a leading figure in the brass band movement.[21] Others in her band had wind-playing fathers like Benson: the father of Mae and Norma Birch (both trumpeters), Harry Birch, was principal trumpeter with the band of the Grenadier Guards.[22] Benson later identified a northern music culture that fostered women instrumentalists: "My girls were mostly north country girls, Lancashire, Yorkshire. . . . They loved playing and they loved being in the band and some of them stayed with me for years."[23]

Although brass band culture allowed for the limited integration of women into male ensembles, dance music operated in strict gender segregation. A persistent amnesia seemed to infect most observers, who tended to treat women's bands as remarkable, although, as the *News Review* reminded readers in 1942, women's bands had traveled the British music hall circuit "for donkey's years."[24] Benson was active in the prewar women's band scene: she joined Edna Croudson's Rhythm Girls for 3 years, moved to London in the late 1930s, playing with a three-piece nightclub band, and toured with Teddy Joyce and the Girl-friends.[25] Opportunities expanded for women's bands during the war. *Melody Maker* followed Benson's prominent career closely with news reports, reviews, and mentions in the gossip column, but it also reported on several other all-women's and women-led bands including a band led by Tony Eaton-Parker (a woman and the former drummer for

Ivy Benson), Gloria Gaye and her Glamour Girl Band (who enjoyed a successful season at Covent Garden Royal Opera House), Blanche Coleman (another Covent Garden Royal Opera House bandleader), and the Rhythm Sisters Dance Orchestra led by Archie Pearce (a member of the RAF).[26]

Benson's first role as bandleader followed the gender-segregated pattern of women's bands: her ten-piece combination was part of the touring revue, *Meet the Girls.*[27] Like all dance bands, Benson's band had to balance popular appeal and connoisseur-pleasing performance. *Melody Maker* raised expectations regarding the latter by praising her as the "hottest woman sax-clarinettist in the country . . . one of the few women musicians who really has a sense of swing," an accolade that it did not give readily to British male musicians.[28] Meanwhile, the visual parameters of a women's revue raised other expectations, particularly with its opening in March 1940, near the end of the "Phony War," when bright entertainment was at a premium to relieve a bored population. Everyday women and, especially, entertainers had the duty of looking attractive: a women's show depended upon beautiful performers to fulfill its morale-building function. Since a revue, as opposed to a stand-alone appearance on a variety bill, demanded a degree of integration, Benson's band favored a more commercial approach. It opened the revue in a short scene, accompanied by the pit orchestra; it closed the show with a selection of popular numbers, which included the "amusing" "Hitler, Goebbels and Goering;" and Benson performed as a soloist on saxophone.[29] *Melody Maker* wrote: "It cannot be pretended that the band is a world-beater, but definite improvement was seen during the opening week. . . . Perhaps a mere male should not criticise such a thing, but it does seem that the band might have been dressed more attractively — as it is, the dresses seem rather severe."[30]

The reviewer's assessment was representative of the general attitude toward Benson in *Melody Maker.* On one hand, Benson was a personality and a woman; that she and her band did not project the visual appeal of female singers confounded reviewers, especially in a wartime environment in which women's glamour was a patriotic duty. On the other hand, Benson had serious musical ambitions, and reviewers accorded her fair evaluation, which often included recognition of the band's "improvement."

Melody Maker reinforced its representation of Benson as exceptional by contrasting her musicianship with that of the members of her band. Benson was usually portrayed as a talented — even virtuosic — performer, a savvy manager, and a skilled bandleader. In contrast to her status as a hot player who could swing, only a few of her instrumentalists from the early years, such as the lead trumpet player Mae Birch and the first trombonist Ruth Harrison, were recognized for their outstanding musicianship; none were noted as improvisers. The press portrayed women dance musicians as rare commodities, and Benson was frequently reported to be looking for new talent. Her players were raw materials that, through determination and skill, she would turn into a polished ensemble. Benson's use of inexperienced musicians paralleled the wartime practice of dilution in industry, in which skilled tasks were broken into less demanding components for a new female workforce, neutralizing its threat to the pride of skilled workmen (although unions regarded the deskilling of work and the attendant lower wages as a serious problem). Of course, there were limited opportunities for women to gain dance band experience, even for those with good musical training. Benson was willing to hire inexperienced girls and train them on the job. Sylvia England, a member of the trumpet section, praised Benson: "Ivy was a great teacher. Her determination, persistence, dedication, and knowledge were legendary. . . . By sheer determination and will power she would work with us until we were as good as she wanted us to be."[31] In her role as teacher and chaperone, Benson's relation to her band resonated far more with maternal than with sexualized femininity. She reported, "parents asked me to look after their daughters," but she also emphasized the professionalism of her players: despite their inexperience, they were "more interested in having a job than looking for a husband."[32]

The descriptions of Benson as a musician whose exceptional will could transform the weaker players of her own sex into a band worthy of her talents contrasted with her male contemporaries. The guitarist Ivor Mairants recalled a rehearsal in which the bandleader Geraldo, who enjoyed a long-term contract with the BBC for much of the war, was unable to set the correct tempo for "In the Mood."[33] Even if a "name" bandleader could conduct well, he was unlikely to have maintained his skills as a soloist. In an otherwise lackluster 1941 broadcast featuring several bandleaders, "Detector" declared Benson (see figure 5.1) the virtuosic star of the show: " — a woman — playing a clarinet . . . and SWINGING IT!! In her performance of "Stick of Liquorice," she not only played fast and difficult passages with the technique of a musician, but with a style that marks her as a real swing player."[34] Unlike her male contemporaries, Benson did not have the luxury of leaving matters of

Fig. 5.1. Ivy Benson from "Picture Post," February 3, 1945. Getty Images.

musical skill to her players and arrangers; she functioned as both leader and star performer.

Despite the discourses of exceptionalism that surrounded Benson, she maintained solidarity with the dance music profession, which the call-up had thrown into disarray. *Melody Maker* signaled her commitment in June 1940 with the headline "M.U. Opens Its Doors to Girls' Dance Band (It Will Get Men's Rates)." Sixty women already belonged to the union, but Benson's band was the first to join as a group.[35] Agitation for gender equality in pay was not widespread until 1943; thus the Musicians' Union decision seemed unusually enlightened, although it was hardly disinterested.[36] From early on, the call-up affected dance music disproportionately. Unlike many skilled trades, it was not a reserve occupation; further, it was regarded as a young man's career and young men were the first to be drafted. Band rosters, from name bands in the capital to provincial semiprofessional bands, were in flux, with players leaving at short notice to join the forces. By the beginning of 1941, 80 percent of male dance musicians had registered with the National Service or been called up.[37] Good civilian musicians commanded fees well above the union minimum, whereas professional and amateur dance bands formed in the services that, essentially subsidized by the military, could undercut civilian bands. By agreeing to pay men's rates (i.e., the union minimum), Benson indicated that she would not grossly undercut male civilian bands and demonstrated her dedication to the embattled profession. Portrayed as an example of wartime sacrifice and cooperation, it was a canny decision. With dancing popular and reliable dance bands a rare commodity, paying union rates did not harm Benson's competitiveness with male civilian bandleaders, whose personnel expenses were higher, while it generated goodwill in the profession and made Benson more attractive to potential recruits.

In late 1940 Benson and her band moved from stage shows to dance halls, gaining a contract with the Mecca chain. They enjoyed a residency at Manchester's prestigious Ritz Ballroom, followed by an extended season at the Locarno palais de danse in Glasgow.[38] Top dance halls employed more than one band to provide about 4 hours of continuous music; they also paid well.[39] Dance palais, especially the Mecca chain, were the major employers of professional and semipro dance bands, although dance music enthusiasts stereotyped palais bands as purveyors of uninspired playing and derivative music. Facing wartime personnel shortages and willing to hire lesser known groups, the Mecca chain embraced women's bands: it advertised specifically for small (five-to six-piece) girls' bands for the north of England, while Benson, Coleman, and others enjoyed long-term contracts at important venues.[40] Benson expanded her band to a roster of 14 players, which was unusually large for a civilian band in 1941. West End hotels that had once featured two orchestras of ten to fourteen players each now employed only single bands of five to ten men.[41] Many civilian bandleaders ceased to maintain regular bands; instead, they formed pickup groups or augmented their small ensembles to fulfill broadcasting and recording dates. An attractive spectacle may have helped for revue and palais work, but Benson's firm roster and well-rehearsed ensemble were even more impressive. "It sure will be a novelty for patrons to see a line up which stays the same week after week in these days of call-ups to Army and training centres!" observed *Melody Maker*.[42]

During the war, dance halls, which already carried populist associations, became ready symbols for British good cheer and the uniting of diverse individuals around a common purpose. Dancing exploded in popularity, especially among the young and working class to whom the palais-de-danse offered affordable glamour, escape, and fun. Meanwhile, the styles of palais dancing — and the music it required — underwent significant changes as jitterbugs invaded the ballrooms, American servicemen introduced more rhythmically responsive dance styles, and beginners and crowded floors challenged the preeminence of the complex and space-dependent English style.[43] Swing, which had been a minority taste in Britain before the war, entered the popular repertory as music to be listened and, more importantly, danced to. In October 1943 Josephine Bradley, the doyenne of English ballroom competition dancing, introduced the jive, her modification of the jitterbug, at the Hammersmith Palais, which was a bastion of the English style and the square, strict tempo dance music it required.[44] During 1941, however, strict tempo was still dominant in most dance halls, and palais bands had to play a wide range of repertory. Benson and her band cultivated the versatility essential in the changing climate, with a repertory ranging from waltzes to commercial swing numbers. They also offered dancers variety in instrumentation: while boasting full reed, brass, and rhythm sections, sufficient wind players doubled to bring the string section to seven members when necessary.[45]

In December 1941 Benson and an expanded seventeen-piece band moved from the periphery to London, the entertainment center of Britain. They performed a grueling schedule of afternoon and evening dances at the Royal Opera House in Covent Garden, which served as a Mecca dance palais during the war.[46] *Melody Maker* declared, "Their extensive experience of palais work showed to excellent advantage, and the girls played with a precision and team-work rare in ladies' bands."[47] The band alternated by the hour with Billy Sproud and his band, "one of the most modern little jive bands playing in any dance hall of this type," for a packed audience that included numerous American GIs, who were "all dancing, all happy, full of fun."[48] Throughout 1942 Benson and her band made a series of advances that poised them for national stardom. They made their first radio broadcasts, entered the variety circuit as a stage band under Jack Hylton's prestigious management, appeared in two British-National films (*Hospital Appeal*, which starred the popular Vera Lynn, and *The Dummy Talks*), and became the first female ensemble to perform at London's yearly Jazz Jamboree (a fundraiser that served as a veritable who's who of dance bands in Britain).[49]

Benson's band also began to garner serious criticism from *Melody Maker*. In their radio debut in February 1942 they performed up-to-date Glenn Miller–style arrangements.[50] "Detector" declared: "After Ivy Benson's broadcast last Thursday week, I rang her up and asked her to come clean and tell me the names of the men she'd used to stiffen up the band. Actually, she hadn't used any. . . . Even so, I think it says more than plenty for Ivy's bevy of beauty that I should have been so taken in. I'm not suggesting it sounded like Bob Crosby or Paul Whiteman, but it seemed to me to be at least the equal of most, and better than many, of the male bands we get on air these days. It not only showed a high standard of musicianship, but played with an understanding of dance style that I have no intention of damning with the faint praise that for girls it sounded too good to be true."[51]

Flummoxed by his inability to anchor a women's band in the visual, the radio critic, usually at ease with reviewing bands on the wireless, resorted to suggesting that Benson had perpetrated a ruse and then offered her backhanded compliments. As women entered wartime jobs, sexualized femininity and its visual focus on hair, makeup, dress, figure, and hands helped reassure observers that women doing men's work would not undermine gender difference.[52] When Benson and her band broadcast, however, radio masked their bodies and instrumental performance disguised their voices; the gender of the musicians became problematic for listeners. "Detector," with his expert ears, still sought gender's audible trace, believing a weak performance to be feminine and shocked that women could perform dance music authentically.

Despite his surprise, "Detector" ranked Benson's band among the best broadcasters in the nation, at a point when the quality of bands on the BBC was in crisis. He even deigned to compare her band to American ensembles, although, like most British bands, Benson's still fell short of the (white) Americans. The frame of reference of "Detector" was odd, however. Crosby's band (really a cooperative) had pioneered a much praised big-band approach to Dixieland jazz, although it adopted a more commercial swing style early in the war, and Whiteman was the master of sweet symphonic dance music. Perhaps he was alluding to Benson's versatility and the contrast between the numbers in which Benson's wind players picked up their violins and those in which they concentrated on commercial swing.

Melody Maker's reviewers were more at ease when the band appeared live, and nothing earned Benson warmer reviews than when the performances served patriotic ends. Pat Brand, the gossip columnist and a supporter of Benson, described the band's "shattering success" in the army camps: "The girls have been a real eyeful and earful for the soldiers, as everyone but ultra-modest Ivy would have realized. Particular success has been scored by young Mae Birch, with her trumpet and her personality, and also Ruth [Harrison], the trombonist. Possibly, however, the biggest attraction for the vocal fans has been Kay Yorstan, the Scotch vocalist, who has created a sensation in the camp."[53]

Benson's band offered soldiers the morale-boosting combination of pretty girls and engaging dance music. They fulfilled their national obligations both by looking attractive and by entertaining soldiers during three two-week Entertainments National Service Association (ENSA) tours of military camps. ENSA provided morale-building live entertainment both on the home front and overseas; it was an important employer of entertainers, although its pay scale was notoriously low. Like other leading performers, Benson's motivation in taking on six uncomfortable and poorly paid weeks of labor was not simply patriotism: she needed to do ENSA service to avoid conscription into other areas of national service.[54] Despite their compulsory nature, the tours played a positive role in the band's development, for they brought Benson and her girls into close contact with the forces, a crucial audience for dance music and swing.

Unlike Brand and "Detector," the Northern correspondent Jerry Dawson advocated an egalitarian approach to Benson's band in his review of its stage show at the Liverpool Empire. Because of their exceptional status among "femme" bands, he proposed, "in fairness to her and the girls I must compare the show with only the best of our stage bands."[55] Mention of the band's appearance was a small, but compulsory, matter — Dawson observed only that "the girls were nicely dressed," using visual appeal to signal feminine competence. His detailed critique praised Kay Yorston's personality in a "medley of hill-billies" and the song "I Can't Fish like Annie Can Fish," the band's "beautifully played" Artie Shaw arrangement of "Begin the Beguine," and Benson's "grand tone and technique" in "Valse Vanite." Dawson concluded, "Whilst I can't exactly rave about the show, it was certainly good entertainment and good dance music, and by the time it reaches the 'Jamboree' I have an idea that some of the sceptics will be obliged to eat a little humble pie."[56]

By the fall of 1942, Benson had moved from the periphery to the center of British wartime entertainment. Despite the skepticism surrounding the notion that a women's band could be good, her regularly positive reviews in *Melody Maker*, high fees, and excellent opportunities reflected the uneasy equality with her male competitors that she had attained.[57] Benson was exceptional not only "for a girl" but also for a British dance musician; her swing aspirations drew upon and earned her comparisons with American stars while she gained the approbation of "American swing fans," whom *Melody Maker* treated as arbiters of authenticity in the American form.[58] With her common touch, well-publicized sacrifices, and her band's combination of morale-building music and feminine attractiveness (if not glamour), she embodied British wartime values. On all accounts, Benson was successfully negotiating the risky terrain of musical professionalism, femininity, and good wartime citizenship before the BBC contracted her as its fourth house band.

STORMS OF CONTROVERSY: BENSON AND THE BBC

In the debate that exploded around Benson's contract, *Melody Maker* made the intriguing accusation that the BBC had hired an all-girl band as a publicity stunt (as "a good example, especially to our friends in America"), not because of musical merit.[59] The charge was false, as demonstrated by Benson's earlier positive reception in *Melody Maker* and by internal documents tracing the BBC's decision. Nevertheless, the accusation carried a kernel of truth. In 1942, dance music at the BBC was in crisis. Poor quality performances were part of the problem, but for most of the year, the BBC had been consumed with what it identified as a lack of virility in dance music. The BBC regarded slushy sentiment, characterized by slow tempos, mushy lyrics, and crooning, as demoralizing; thus, in July, it instituted its "crooner ban." Cecil Madden, the overseas entertainment producer, declared, "Male crooners are quite divorced from the reality of the times, and to plug the girls is to show the men [in the forces] that the women are doing men's jobs these days.[60] Although female vocalists successfully combined British women's twin wartime duties of beauty and national service, male entertainers failed to embody wartime expectations of British masculinity, which involved "real" work and a uniform. Dance music was still gendered as skilled, masculine work, but male dance musicians were accused increasingly of shirking their national service obligations. Even dance musicians in forces bands were described in the press as "toy soldiers," who did little real work, and military authorities tried to prohibit moonlighting by musicians in the services.[61] Benson's populist representation as a good wartime citizen was more stable than that of her male counterparts, even with her need to negotiate a masculine profession and proper femininity. Her band's impending national exposure, along with the BBC's stamp of legitimacy, threatened to cast male dance musicians in unflattering relief, and many reacted by questioning whether Benson, as a musician and as a woman, actually deserved the contract. Their stormy response revealed the gender inequalities obscured by wartime discourses of tolerance: critics, in the name of fairness, derided Benson and her band, while the BBC failed to draw upon egalitarian values in her defense.

Given the press coverage of Benson's contract announcement in early December 1942, *Melody Maker*'s allegation of a BBC publicity stunt was not surprising. Overwhelmingly positive, the reports characterized her band as truly feminine, respectable, and committed to the war effort. The Sunday Express commented unfavorably on the male Bands of the Week, which Benson would replace, and announced, "The band now projected should provide better dance music for millions of listeners."[62] Flattering background stories also appeared, reporting Benson to be twenty-six, single, blonde, petite, trained by her father, and interested in languages.[63] The profiles characterized band members through their familial relationships rather than their professional experiences: several players came from respectable musical lineages and the band included two sets of sisters and a mother-daughter trombone section.[64] At a point when women were being conscripted for war work, the press emphasized the band's ENSA service. Most importantly, members had made patriotic sacrifices in their personal lives: six musicians were married to men in the Forces, the lead alto saxophonist's husband was a prisoner of war, and the third trumpet player Briquette Barrois was a Parisian who had escaped the Germans.[65] The band was composed of married women and girls-next-door who did their duty, not a bunch of good-time girls bent on frivolity, an important matter to clarify in a period when the morality of working women was a special concern.[66]

Although charming young women, gamely doing their bit for the war effort, might appeal to the lay public, *Melody Maker* was dubious.[67] Noting that sending Benson to Bristol full time would end the Band of the Week and limit ad hoc broadcasting for other bands, the paper urged the BBC to "consider the claims of others before negotiating for a band which, outstanding as it may be for women, has yet to prove that it can maintain the standard essential for a combination which will doubtless have to take the air many times a week over a considerable period."[68]

Of course the BBC, with its constrained finances and imperative to improve the quality of broadcast dance music, had considered its options thoroughly.[69] Its three resident bands, led by Geraldo, Jack Payne, and Billy Ternent, were serviceable, but the civilian bands booked as Band of the Week often gave underwhelming performances. Few name leaders maintained standing rosters, so the bands that traveled to Bristol to make eight broadcasts over the course of a week tended to be under-rehearsed pickup groups. The BBC believed it could improve its dance music broadcasting by replacing these uneven units with a fourth house band, and Benson was one of the few available civilian leaders with a steady personnel. *Melody Maker* suggested, however, that finance, not quality, motivated the BBC. Benson's players would earn the standard union rate (£12–16 per week), although few male musicians would leave London for Bristol and Band of the Week unless they were paid much more.[70] The paper neglected to mention that male bandleaders — not the BBC — made up the difference, usually by engaging in the dubious practice of song plugging (i.e., taking payments or free arrangements from music publishers in exchange for broadcasting certain songs). It also failed to consider that the players in Benson's band had a narrower range of employment possibilities than their male counterparts. Availability and finance certainly informed the BBC's considerations, but ultimately the BBC chose Benson and her band because they were the best available group.[71]

The reaction to Benson's contract revealed the sense of male entitlement ingrained in the profession. Although *Melody Maker*'s question regarding whether Benson could sustain high standards was valid for any band that the BBC featured over an extended period, it also implied that any men's band had greater claim to a BBC contract. This was not lost upon Benson, who responded by pointing to her band's obvious experience: "I don't see why women should not get a contract. The men say we are not experienced enough for the job, but look how women have gone into other jobs and made good. My band has been together two years and has had much experience all over the country. . . . Admittedly we have only broadcast four times previously, but I leave it to the public to judge what we can do."[72]

Benson supported her argument by drawing parallels with other fields in which women had excelled. Her response resonated with the wartime revival of feminist activity, which gained force during 1943 with calls for equal pay and equal access for women.[73] When women did gain access to better paid and more prestigious work, they often encountered backlash from male workers hoping to preserve their privilege. Benson later recalled, "The men didn't like me getting that plum job. They didn't mind me getting the little ones but they thought that was too big for a girls' band."[74]

Unlike women war workers, who were represented as replacing men in the forces, Benson had beaten male bandleaders in direct competition, and, as fourth house band, she would supplant many of the already meager opportunities for civilian bands to broadcast. The mainstream press hinted at the "heartburning among men's bands that have been passed over," but *Melody Maker* was more blunt: "To say that the profession is perturbed . . . is to put it mildly. Staggered, even enraged, would be a more appropriate word."[75] Not all bandleaders were hostile. Joe Loss, Henry Hall, and Billy Merrin (who had all done well during the war) congratulated Benson publicly.[76] Notwithstanding the limited support, the Dance Band Directors' Section of the Musicians' Union held a special meeting, chaired by Jack Hylton (whose organization managed Benson's band), to draft a protest letter.[77] In a move that nearly overshadowed assessment of Benson's debut, the Directors sent a deputation to meet with the BBC on January 14, 1943, to voice their concerns about the loss of broadcast opportunities for noncontract bands.[78] Benson defended herself and her band against her colleagues' hostility: "We have paid our dues, have insisted on men's rates (not to let the Union down) and have taken jobs — such as a 14 weeks' tour of Service camps for ENSA — that men's bands turned down. I am amazed at the attitude of some of the men."[79] Unfortunately, fair play and service to the war effort did not avert the profession's hostility toward the successful women's band.

With regular broadcasts imminent for Benson's band, the issue of their gender revived and attempts at egalitarian treatment dissipated. The BBC remained silent throughout the controversy, refraining from defending its decision or Benson's qualifications. Finally, before their debut as a house band on January 11, 1943, the BBC's program guide *Radio Times* profiled Benson and her band, although in a distinctly unhelpful manner. C. Gordon Glover, the variety columnist, provided a breezy sketch of Benson's life, mentioned her band's versatility, in passing, and proceeded to dwell on the irrelevant, for radio, effect various instruments had on women's appearances. He concluded, "It either is, or isn't, a pity . . . that the discipline of the microphone will introduce Ivy and her girls to the ear only."[80] In contrast, *Melody Maker* provided a detailed front-page article describing the band's personnel, upcoming broadcast dates, and resume.[81] On the continuation page near the back of the paper, however, the tone changed. With the caveats that Benson could not be blamed for accepting the BBC's offer and that she would do "as well as any leader could with an all-women band," *Melody Maker* went on to criticize the BBC's decision. In a reversal of its judgments throughout 1942, the paper suggested as self-evident that even the best female band "can hardly be expected to compete with the standard provided by even the less outstanding male combinations" in Band of the Week.[82]

Beyond the question of whether women looked pretty while playing the trombone or whether Benson had undercut deserving male band-leaders, the question remained: what did Benson and her band sound like? A day after their debut, the *Daily Express* confirmed the versatility honed in variety and palais work, describing them as "a good band, which can be slow, swingy and stringy[,] or fast and snappy as the conductor herself when she played the clarinet."[83] Others were not convinced of their quality. After four broadcasts, the *Star* found them to be no better than male Bands of the Week. It pointed to what became a recurrent criticism: the new house band played far too much slow music.[84] The problem was endemic in British bands and had helped fuel charges that dance music lacked virility. Benson's preference for slow repertory in broadcasting seemed out of character with her record of versatility. Perhaps she was trying to appeal to populist tastes, influenced by her discovery during her ENSA tour of the preceding summer that camp audiences preferred light music selections to, as *Melody Maker* had put it, "the Shaw arrangements and other super modern stuff that her girls can feature so well."[85] Even Benson's unassailable technique seemed to have faltered. *Melody Maker*'s "Mike" described, "Stick O' Liquorice," which Benson had performed previously to raves, as inadequate: it was "poorly phrased" and "full of fingers and thumbs."[86]

In a scathing review entitled "No Orchids for Miss Benson," "Detector" claimed to offer an objective musical assessment that ignored all hype as well as "personal, sex, and other non-musical considerations."[87] On the air, he argued, the band would be "more listened to than danced to," but it failed to produce "anything really worth listening to." More specifically, the band had poor intonation, it played slow numbers without "finesse," the rhythm section lacked "lift," the brass section's approach to dance music interpretation was "parrot-like," the section playing was "messy," and "the violins — on which women usually excel — make an unbalanced, uninspired section." Benson's band failed in both the manly art of dance music performance and the feminine skill of string-playing, while the wireless medium denied listeners the pleasure of observing the women's band. The BBC had blundered seriously in contracting Benson's band, which was better suited to short stage shows "because it [was] a novelty which inspires sympathy because women dance bands are such rarities."[88] The objectivity of "Detector" about women performers was questionable merely on the grounds of his earlier favorable review, "Girls Who Play like Men," although Benson's band then had been a collection of amazing exceptions, not pathetic deviants.[89]

Even before he began his analysis, however, "Detector" signaled his intentions to cast Benson not only as a poor broadcaster but also as socially deviant. He often awarded "bouquets" to bandleaders who made outstanding broadcasts, but his refusal of orchids for Benson was a reference to James Hadley Chase's *No Orchids for Miss Blandish* (1939), a British gloss on the hard-boiled American detective novel that was "probably the best selling novel of the whole war."[90] According to Orson Welles's summary of the "cesspool" plot, Miss Blandish was a millionaire's daughter held for ransom by a gang, whose female leader decided to hold her until her sadistic son cured his impotence by raping her; after torture and a series of rapes, Miss Blandish was finally rescued but committed suicide just before she was to be returned to her family.[91] By substituting "Benson" for "Blandish," "Detector" transformed his eviscerating review of the band into a very personal attack on the bandleader.[92] With its pinup-style cover and status of defining "the borderline of pornography," the book carried associations of unwholesome sexual excess. In the criminal, exotically American setting, the pampered character of Miss Blandish was too weak to resist her captors and became too damaged to resume a respectable existence as a daughter. Using the book's misogynistic associations, "Detector" recast Benson not as a symbol of People's War commitment but rather as a feminized Other in wartime British society: overly sexual, weak, and alienated from the national family.

The implications of "Detector" were not lost on *Melody Maker*'s readers. A member of the RAF applauded the judgments of "Detector," which "caused much amusement among the boys and myself," whereas an anonymous musician ("A Disappointed Reader") expressed disgust "at the low and libelous criticism" and declared Benson better than the ad hoc "riff-raff" her band had replaced.[93] A Canadian serviceman, who established his credentials by claiming to have heard most of the top American bands, declared Benson better than most British bands, and another respondent questioned his sanity.[94] Meanwhile, the BBC extended Benson's original three-month contract. The announcement was sweetened by *Melody Maker*'s report that the "brilliant bandleader and arranger" Phil Green would play "Sir Galahad" to the band by rescuing its troubled arrangements.[95] Perhaps with the help of a masculine expert, not to mention a respectable romantic narrative, Miss Benson might be saved, after all.

Indeed, the BBC framed Benson's band within the "girl friends to the forces" paradigm that had worked so successfully for female singers and announcers. Unlike audiences at home, who were frequently critical of women's voices on the air, men stationed overseas became enthusiastic followers of female performers, whom the BBC presented as approachable girls-next-door. Stationed in Bristol, the Variety Department's remote outpost, Benson and her band endured difficult conditions to entertain forces around the world: "We broadcast to the troops every hour of the day and night. Sometimes we had to be in the studio at two or three in the morning and you should have seen some of the girls. They were in their night attire with curlers in their hair. If it had been television it would have been hilarious!"[96] Despite the loss of sleep, such broadcasts provided a respite from the demands of glamour. Performing in evening dress was challenging enough in peacetime; it took extra resourcefulness for a ladies' band to look elegant while touring under wartime travel conditions, negotiating clothing rations coupons (performers got no extra allowances), and protecting the reputations of young players. Benson's overseas broadcasts gained limited publicity on the home front, but she received 300 letters a week from servicemen stationed overseas.[97] For men who were not in direct competition with women, the entertainment and companionship offered by Benson's band was deeply reassuring.

Although the band was popular with soldiers overseas, it became the scapegoat at home for ongoing concerns about the virility of dance music. In July 1943, the *News and Times* of Worcester resurrected the problem of manliness and morale-building in the BBC's dance music output: "Of all the bands on the air, there is one for which I have yet to hear a good word. If this lady's band, with its enervating "music" must be inflicted on us, why is it usually put on when there is no alternative . . . ? . . . I am surely not the first to object to this — band."[98] As women, Benson's band might have been incapable of effeminacy, but their performances were marked as sentimental, and they threatened to sap the vigor of listeners.

Benson's vocal section was especially problematic. Her roster of singers was in constant flux, with several departing for other bands, while others were conscripted for factory work. Even worse, soon after Benson began regular broadcasts, the BBC focused its "virility campaign" on screening singers and censored those who crooned, performed in an overly sentimental manner, or adopted American accents.[99] Among the house bands, Benson's was worst hit: her new singer Doris Knight was banned after two weeks, while Kay Yorston, the bass player and a popular, steady force in the vocal section, was chided for her American accent in February and then banned from singing in October.[100] Singers were among the most normative of female performers, but in conjunction with a women's band, wholesome femininity threatened to become excessive sentimentality.

In August, the BBC, in a new fit of concern for the quality of broadcast dance music, commissioned the critic, radio writer, and composer Spike Hughes to assess its contract bands. "From a purely musical point of view," Hughes wrote of Benson's band, "it makes the right noise."[101] The band's faults lay in poor arrangements, repertory decisions, and singers, but in these, it was hardly unique. Hughes suggested that poor sound engineering in Bristol and an infrequently tuned piano had harmed the band's sound. Overall, he asserted, the band had improved significantly. Hughes concluded that the band's critics had reacted to the gender of the players rather than to its actual sound: "There is no way of telling that the players are women. A great deal of prejudice could have been avoided if the sex of the players had never been announced."[102] His solution for avoiding prejudice was unrealistic, and like "Detector," he gendered competently performed dance music as masculine. The BBC's Dance Music Policy Committee more practically attributed some audience prejudices to frequent broadcasts: Benson and her band broadcast to home front audiences five times a week, the same number made by Geraldo and Jack Payne together.[103] For Hughes, Benson's band was "to be overheard, not listened to critically;" it was thus adequate as radio dance music, for it was unimaginable that listeners would use it as anything but background.[104] The Committee disagreed: broadcast dance music was entertainment, and the forces sometimes used it for dancing.[105] However listeners used Benson's broadcasts, providing a "pleasing background to housework, reading or conversation" was very different from her band's work in dance palais, music halls, and army camps.[106]

Hughes's positive, if lukewarm, assessment was matched by a growing consensus in the pages of *Melody Maker* that Benson and her band had improved. In March, "Detector" praised a Benson saxophone solo as "a polished, feeling, and all-around immaculate rendition" that cancelled out his recent criticisms of her clarinet playing.[107] When it announced that Benson and her band would be the resident band for an important new radio variety show, *Melody Maker* noted the band's "very marked all-around improvement" in ensemble, style, and Mae Birch's trumpet solos.[108] The weekly also covered Benson in humanizing personality stories that realigned its portrayal of Benson within codes of People's War selflessness. It reported on the queen's visit to one of the band's rehearsals and how Benson helped an old friend who had lost everything in a fire, concluding "Ivy is undoubtedly the kindest-hearted and most generous kid in our business."[109] *Melody Maker* also printed a glamorous picture of Benson being fitted for a "lovely new dress" for an upcoming benefit concert. Whereas most pictures depicted her in action — conducting her band, playing the saxophone or clarinet, or even exercising one of her greyhounds — this photograph drew on the conventions of the pinup: Benson stood with one hand resting on a hip and the other relaxed at her side, her face turned in profile, and her full body reflected by two mirrors ("you get three views for the price of one").[110] The subtext was clear: fair play and professionalism were not enough for a woman to succeed in the dance music profession. Benson better negotiated her success with a kinder and more glamorous image, reassuring men that femininity and gender differences still survived.

That fall, Benson began to enjoy the benefits that regular broadcasting, with its exposure to national audiences, could bestow. In September, she signed a recording contract with HMV to release two titles per month, alternating popular songs and nonvocal standards.[111] A month later, the band moved from Bristol to London, where the BBC finally rectified its own role in the mixed reception of Benson and her girls by broadcasting them less frequently and in better studios.[112] With their BBC output reduced by half, the band became free to perform in London variety theaters, and Benson soon signed an important contract at London's Palladium as part of an "all-star" program.[113] The contracts were fortuitous, since the BBC allowed Benson's contract to expire in February 1944. Broadcast dance music had declined precipitously in popularity, according to BBC Listener Research, so the Corporation sought to reduce its output. As the most maligned, and expendable, of the house bands, Benson and her girls were the first to go.

In her return to the stage, Benson synthesized her intentions to play serious dance music with the glamorous labor of star female performers. The band earned a solid review from *Melody Maker* for their "bright commercial show," with its "high quality" arrangements that were played with "precision and attack."[114] Although their repertory spanned the stylistic gamut "from sentimental ballads to rhythmic numbers," the reviewer devoted more space to describing the "slick presentation," including the special tropical army uniform adopted by Kay Yorston to sing "Gertie from Bizerte." Any improper implications carried by the "Bizerte" number, for which many blue lyrics, with allusions to promiscuous foreign women, were in circulation, were tempered by the tasteful "red evening gowns and short white coats" worn by the band and Benson's "demure" black.[115] Benson walked the fine line of respectable, sexualized femininity, and *Melody Maker* began to bill the performers as "Ivy and her glamourettes."[116]

National broadcasts not only swelled Benson's popularity but also opened possibilities for women dance musicians as a group. At the end of their extended run at the Palladium, Benson's band went through significant personnel changes before embarking on tour. Veteran players left for other women's bands, while Benson recruited several exciting prospects. The paradigm of female dance music instrumentalists as rare phenomena had shifted, and Benson asserted: "It is a remarkable feature of the times . . . not only the number of girls who are taking up brass instruments, but the number who can play them really well."[117] Benson's band enjoyed a phenomenal reception during its summer 1944 tour of the Midlands.[118] At dance halls in cities including Sheffield and Leicester, the band broke wartime attendance records and played to sold-out audiences, who had paid up to twice the usual fee (the size of the halls ranged from six hundred to a thousand).[119]

In 2000 a nostalgic HBO television drama, *The Last of the Blonde Bombshells*, paid tribute to the glamorous wartime work of women's bands.[120] Judi Dench starred in a plot that traced the bungled reunion of the group, which had disbanded after the war, and hinged upon the antics of the libidinous male ringer who played both drums and the hearts of his bandmates. In contrast to the fictional portrayal, Benson's wartime successes served as a springboard for a vital career in the postwar era, documented impressively on Brian Ravenhill's outstanding website, *Ivy Benson and Her All Girl Band*. Benson and her band toured Europe with ENSA, broadcasted on radio and television, and performed at Allied bases in Germany.[121] As the climate for popular music shifted in the 1950s, driving many dance bands out of existence, "Ivy adapted her style, focusing on the nostalgic sounds of the war years."[122] Over 250 women and girls passed through the band's ranks until 1982, when Benson retired to Clacton-on-Sea, where she performed on organ until her death in 1993. The formula of musical adaptation, competent femininity, and visual appeal remained. As the jazz writer Sheila Tracy, who played trombone with the band in the 1950s, recalled, "My first sight of the Ivy Benson Band was at Lyons Corner House, Marble Arch, and they were wearing orange strapless dresses with green ivy leaves appliquéd down the front. I thought they looked glamorous!"[123]

CONCLUSION: THE PROBLEM OF
SOUND AND COMPETENT FEMININITY

In the critical year of 1943, when the "battle of the saxes" was still fresh in the minds of British dance music fans, Reg Connelly, newly returned from the United States, asserted, "There is no girl in America to touch Ivy as a purely commercial playing proposition."[124] While locating Benson within the devalued realms of the feminine and the commercial, Connelly also positioned her as a virtuosic "playing personality," who was superior in relation to other British leaders and to some things American. It was an unusual claim during a period when British jazz, swing, and dance music enthusiasts embraced American music and rarely asserted the superiority of any British dance musician. Connelly's frame of reference was Phil Spitalny's "Hour of Charm" Orchestra: "Spitalny has a splendid band of glamour girls, of course, and whilst he does his weekly . . . broadcast, this organization is primarily a stage proposition, whereas Ivy's girls are equally good whether they are 'seen or heard.' "[125] For Connelly, the strength of Benson's band was not only its versatility but also its sound, the very quality that had been maligned during their yearlong contract with the BBC. To conclude, I return to the question of what Benson and her girls sounded like during the "battle of the saxes" by way of their twelve wartime recordings, which HMV released on six discs between November 1943 and April 1944.

Although Benson and her girls embodied the wartime ideal of professional competence balanced by sexualized femininity onstage, the economics of recording pushed them into a new ghetto. Because of shellac shortages and the wartime economy, few bands enjoyed recording contracts, and record companies released only a few sure hits each month. Benson's name, made famous over the BBC, could sell records, but HMV distinguished her disks from male bands with a feminized sound. They were "designed to feature Ivy herself as soloist . . . accompanied by a special recording combination consisting of her whole band with the exception of the brass section."[126] Ultimately, the reed section was also excised, leaving the rhythm section and an augmented string section to support the vocalists and Benson's alto saxophone solos. The idea, Tony Middleton suggests, was probably that of Wally Moody, the producer for the sessions.[127] In the process, Benson's band, which was almost uniquely cohesive among wartime British bands, was supplanted by what was essentially a pickup band.

The recording band's string-heavy instrumentation resembled that for Benson's film work, which seemed to have required a feminized sound and image.[128] In preparation for *The Dummy Talks* (1942), for example, she advertised for "three attractive lady violinists," a specification that never appeared in her other calls for players.[129] The feminization of the band's sound extended to its recorded repertory, which obscured its versatility by excluding the swing numbers that it also played. By emphasizing the band's "slow . . . and stringy" aspects, the recordings drew upon the repertory and style that had earned Benson so much criticism for broadcasting insufficiently virile music.[130] In the realm of recording, without a physical presence or even the intimacy of a live broadcast, the projects of presenting women dance instrumentalists as respectably feminine and as energizing were irreconcilable; favoring either approach risked undermining the band's fulfillment of expectations for good female citizenship and morale-building entertainment in wartime Britain. Benson's band succeeded in being respectably feminine, a choice more appropriate for the private, domestic listeners who purchased gramophone recordings than the audience for radio's national, though intimate, address. *Gramophone* described Benson's recordings as "almost too smooth for some tastes, and . . . rather lacking in zip, but withal 'ladylike.'"[131] Rather than distinguish Benson's band as more "down to earth" than her American counterparts, the HMV recordings evoked Spitalny's "Hour of Charm" Orchestra, described by Tucker as "the mental image of billowing dresses and cultured white womanhood conjured by the sweeps and flurries of harps and strings."[132]

Another possible inspiration for the featuring of strings, although not the exclusion of the brass and reed sections, was the American bandleader Artie Shaw. With his artistic imperatives, virtuosity, and beautiful clarinet tone, he was a likely model for Benson, who as a leader-soloist was exceptional in Britain, with its paucity in "the out-and-out virtuoso type of leader."[133] Benson performed arrangements modeled upon Shaw's and featured several numbers associated closely with him, including "Begin the Beguine" and his challenging "Clarinet Concerto."[134] Shaw's critically acclaimed turn to strings between 1939 and 1942 may have inspired Moody's production decisions.[135] However, Shaw's maverick tendencies, impulsive marriages to movie stars, and vocal disgust with swing's commercialism and its fans contrasted with Benson's thoroughly British reputation for hard work and modesty, as well as the negotiations between the commercial and the artistic requirements of a British woman in dance music. Rather than imitating the swinging American, Benson's ladylike recordings appealed to popular British tastes for clear melody, straightforward rhythm, and predictable, unimprovised solos.

HMV's discs were uninspired star vehicles for Benson. The band recorded commercial ballad-foxtrots and waltzes at slow to moderate tempos. With lyrics expressing love, the pangs of separation, and dreams of postwar reunion, the repertory emphasized the same themes addressed by sentimental female crooners. Each of the twelve HMV arrangements was structured around Benson's solo alto saxophone, displaying her beautiful tone and somewhat extensive use of vibrato. She demonstrated her technical control through facile legato playing, but there were no virtuosic fireworks — the tempos were too slow. Improvisation, or even a sense of swing, was also out of the question: Benson usually played the melody straight in the choruses, although she varied the repetitions slightly and offered tasteful obbligatos in answer to the vocal soloists and string section statements of the melody. Only one of the sides, "There's a Ship Rolling Home," a little-recorded tribute to the Merchant Navy, featured the vocalist Rita Williams in the first chorus. *Gramophone* opined, "Probably the weakest feature of this band lies in the vocal section, although smooth, they somehow lack zip."[136] Other bandleaders who lacked star vocalists also tended to bury their singers after the first chorus, but they used more colorful arrangements and featured several instrumental soloists. Benson, with her beautiful melodies played over understated accompaniment, functioned more like a star vocalist than a bandleader in the HMV recordings. Moody's formula rendered the potentially threatening professional woman bandleader into a recognizable figure: the beautiful, melodic, female soloist.

The formula earned Benson good, but unenthusiastic, reviews. "Corny," the commercial (as opposed to jazz and swing) record reviewer for *Melody Maker*, reverted to the old practice of praising Benson for improvement, but he neglected to review her last two wartime discs.[137] The more comprehensive *Gramophone* used phrases like "very pleasant," "without any fireworks," "as usual," and "although sweet . . . too stale."[138] Apparently, the record buying public (or HMV executives) agreed because Benson had only three wartime recording sessions.

One recording stood out, however. "It Can't Be Wrong" was available from five bands and singers when "Corny" (rather backhandedly) singled out Benson's recording: "a nice, not too heavy or over-scored arrangement which features her own never unattractive and even better than usual alto."[139] The ballad-style foxtrot was derived from the love theme in Max Steiner's soundtrack for the film *Now, Voyager*, which starred Bette Davis.[140] The arrangement for Benson's recording cleverly incorporated the theme from the first movement of Tchaikovsky's Symphony no. 6, *Pathétique*, which was featured in the film's diegesis, as a countermelody for the vocal chorus. The popular theme of a well-known symphony would have been comprehensible to listeners, particularly cinema fans who saw the movie several times.[141] Indeed, it hinted at another audience for Benson: young women who also were negotiating the challenges of wartime work and femininity, for whom she was a role model.[142] Referencing the cinema, the song carried the subtext of glamorous American femininity and commercialism. More specifically, *Now, Voyager* was marketed as a women's picture; it portrayed the blooming of a homely spinster, facilitated by a diet, a makeover, and a glamorous new wardrobe.[143] Transformed externally, the Davis character bravely moved beyond societal expectations and eschewed conventional marriage.

This particular song expresses something about the choices made by Ivy Benson as well.[144] Doubly inauthentic, as a British woman, she sought to play dance music — and American swing — with professional credibility. Although bedeviled by critics who tried to trap her in the false binary of male competence and female incompetence, Benson turned her inexperienced ten-woman revue orchestra into one of Britain's top dance bands, aided by the mask of glamour, not the verbal fireworks of an iconoclast like Shaw. On announcing her departure from the BBC (and neglecting to mention its own role in the affair), *Melody Maker* declared: "They took over their duties in the face of a professional storm that would have frightened even the toughest men. But Ivy doesn't come from Yorkshire for nothing. Throughout her year with the BBC, she has taken the hardest criticism as an incentive for improvement, and the whole profession doffs its hat to her for 'taking it on the chin' and coming up smiling with a band that gets better and better."[145] The idioms "taking it on the chin" and "coming up smiling" echoed the 1940 reports of working class East Enders' bravely understated response to the Blitzkrieg, which targeted them with particular severity.[146] Like the East Enders, Benson embodied People's War commitment by not complaining about the underlying inequalities that led to her particular storm. Finally, however, *Melody Maker* acknowledged the sheer hard work of Benson and her band in continuing to perform while under attack from their colleagues, although it was still blind to the challenges of performing glamorous, competent femininity.

An intelligent entertainer, Benson discovered that her audience, especially soldiers, preferred sentiment and worked to provide it. Her band's proud versatility was excised from HMV's ladylike recordings, and even, possibly, from the air. Unlike postwar recordings and broadcasts, the wartime recordings smoothed over her band's other work: their "super-modern" swing numbers, star trumpet soloist, efficient brass section, and the physicality of playing for the troops or dancers at a palais de danse.[147] Nevertheless, balancing her band's visual and aural performances of femininity, Benson for one crucial year helped the BBC to define virile British dance music to serve the war effort. In the process, she laid the groundwork for a long and successful career as the leader of a women's band. Understanding Benson's war work helps us broaden our own understanding of the big band era, along lines not only of gender but also of nationality.

NOTES

My thanks to the BBC Written Archives Centre in Caversham, especially the head archivist Jacquie Kavanagh, for permission to reprint BBC copyright material in this article.

1. Brian Rust's discography lists the band's name as Ivy Benson and Her All Girls Band, but the designation for the ensemble varied in the contemporary press, including "Fem Band," "Benson's Band," the more formal "Ladies Dance Orchestra," and most commonly "Ivy Benson and her Girls' Band." Brian Rust and Sandy Forbes, *British Dance Bands on Record, 1911–1945, and Supplement* (Middlesex: General Gramophone, 1989).

2. Elsbeth Grant, "All-Women Band in 'Storm,'" *Daily Sketch*, December 23, 1942, BBC WAC (BBC Written Archives Centre) Press Cuttings; "Lull in the Battle of the Sexes and Saxes," *Daily Herald*, January 11, 1943, BBC WAC Press Cuttings.

3. Sonya O. Rose, *Which People's War? National Identity and Citizenship in Britain, 1939–1945* (Oxford: Oxford University Press, 2003), 2.

4. Ibid., 179.

5. As Susan McClary has observed, "one of the means of asserting masculine control over [music] is by denying the very possibility of participation by women." McClary 1991, 151–52. For a discussion of how musical pursuits were constructed as problematic to masculine, British identity, see Philip Brett, "Musicology and Sexuality: The Example of

Edward J. Dent," *Queer Episodes in Music and Modern Identity*, ed. Sophie Fuller and Lloyd Whitesell (Urbana: University of Illinois Press, 2002). See also Gary C. Thomas, "Was George Frideric Handel Gay?" *Queering the Pitch: The New Gay and Lesbian Musicology*, ed. Philip Brett, Elizabeth Wood, and Gary C. Thomas (New York: Routledge, 1994), 184–86.

6. Rose, *Which People's War?* 135. See also Baade 2006; Baade 2005.

7. Pat Kirkham, "Beauty and Duty: Keeping Up the (Home) Front," *War Culture: Social Change and Changing Experience in World War Two Britain*, ed. Pat Kirkham and David Thoms (London: Lawrence and Wishart, 1995), 14–15.

8. Rose, *Which People's War?* 133–35.

9. Ibid.

10. Catherine Parsonage, *The Evolution of Jazz in Britain, 1880–1935* (Aldershot: Ashgate, 2005), 67–68.

11. Although their top service bands did not arrive until 1944, the number of American troops in Britain increased from 4,058 in January 1942 to 255,190 in January 1943 and over a million at the beginning of 1944. David Reynolds, *Rich Relations: The American Occupation of Britain, 1942–1945* (New York: Random House, 1995), 99, 103.

12. For a fuller exploration of these issues see Baade 2002.

13. Sheila Tracy, *Talking Swing: The British Big Bands* (Edinburgh: Mainstream, 1997), 30.

14. Rose, *Which People's War?* 5. See also Lucy Noakes, *War and the British: Gender, Memory and National Identity* (London: IB Tauris, 1998), 72; and Denise Riley, "Some Peculiarities of Social Policy concerning Women in Wartime and Postwar Britain," *Behind the Lines: Gender and the Two World Wars*, ed. Margaret Randolph Higonnet, Jane Jenson, Sonya Michel, and Margaret Collins Weitz (New Haven: Yale University Press, 1987), 262.

15. "Women's Band for BBC?" *Star*, December 5, 1942, BBC WAC Press Cuttings; "Women Win," *News Review*, December 24, 1942, BBC WAC Press Cuttings.

16. "Started Young," *Bristol Evening World*, January 7, 1943, BBC WAC Press Cuttings.

17. Ravenhill, *Ivy Benson and Her All Girl Band*, http://www.ivybenson-online.com, accessed January 9, 2005; Richard Hoggart, *The Uses of Literacy* (New York: Oxford University Press, 1957), 125.

18. Ravenhill, *Ivy Benson and Her All Girl Band*.

19. Dave Russell, " 'What's Wrong with Brass Bands?' Cultural Change and the Band Movement, 1918–c. 1964," *The British Brass Band: A Musical and Social History*, ed. Trevor Herbert (Oxford: Oxford University Press, 2000), 115.

20. Ibid., 81–82, 102.

21. Ravenhill, *Ivy Benson and Her All Girl Band*.

22. "The Battle of the Saxes!" *Melody Maker*, January 9, 1943, 1.

23. Tracy, *Talking Swing*, 30.

24. "Women Win," *News Review*. Thanks to the work of Sherrie Tucker's *Swing Shift* and Antoinette Handy's *Black Women*, we know that American women played important roles as instrumentalists during the big band era.

25. Ravenhill, *Ivy Benson and Her All Girl Band*; "The Battle of the Saxes!" 1.

26. "New Girls' Band," *Melody Maker*, March 15, 1941, 10; "Gloria Gaye's Girls Go Touring," *Melody Maker*, July 5, 1941, 2; "Chance for Ladies," *Melody Maker*, July 19, 1941, 2.

27. "Girl Sax-Star to Lead Touring Fem Band," *Melody Maker*, January 20, 1940, 4.

28. Ibid.

29. "Girls' Band Show Starts at Norwich," *Melody Maker*, March 2, 1940, 5.

30. Ibid.

31. Tracy, *Talking Swing*, 35–36.

32. Ibid., 31.

33. Ivor Mairants, interview, Oral History of Jazz in Britain, National Sound Archive 1CDR0003703, July 23, 1996.

34. "Detector," "An Air Band of Bandleaders," *Melody Maker*, July 5, 1941, 4.

35. "M.U. Opens Its Doors to Girls' Dance Band (It Will Get Men's Rates)," *Melody Maker*, June 8, 1940, 1.

36. Rose, *Which People's War?* 116.

37. "Leaders Debate Call-Up of Musicians," *Melody Maker*, February 1, 1941, 1.

38. Pat Brand, "Brand's Essence of News," *Melody Maker*, October 5, 1940, 6; Jerry Dawson, "Northern Gossip," *Melody Maker*, 8 February 1941, 12; "Ladies' Band Scores at Glasgow," *Melody Maker*, March 22, 1941, 9.

39. See James J. Nott, "The Experience of Dancing, Dance Halls, and the 'Dance Culture,' 1918–1939," *Music for the People: Popular Music and Dance in Interwar Britain* (Oxford: Oxford University Press, 2002), 168–90.

40. "Musicians and Bands Wanted," *Melody Maker*, November 29, 1941, 1.

41. "Who's Where in the West End," *Melody Maker*, June 14, 1941, 5.

42. "Ladies' Band Scores at Glasgow," *Melody Maker*, March 22, 1941, 9.

43. See Christina Baade, " 'The Dancing Front': Dance Music, Dancing, and the BBC in World War II," *Popular Music* 25, no. 3 (October 2006): 347–68.

44. "Josephine's Genteel 'Jitterbug' Invades Hammersmith Palais!" *Melody Maker*, October 23, 1943, 1.

45. Brand, "Brand's Essence of News," *Melody Maker*, October 18, 1942, 4.

46. "Detector," "Girls Who Play like Men," *Melody Maker*, February 28, 1942, 6.

47. "Girls' Garden Band Clicks," *Melody Maker*, December 20, 1941, 2.

48. Brand, "Brand's Essence," *Melody Maker*, November 7, 1942, 4; Tracy, *Talking Swing*, 30–31.

49. "Ivy's Girls in Variety," *Melody Maker*, September 12, 1942, 1; Brand, "Brand's Essence," *Melody Maker*, June 20, 1942, 4; "Jazz Jamboree Sold Out!" *Melody Maker*, September 5, 1942, 1.

50. "Ladies Band Airing," *Melody Maker*, January 31, 1942, 1.

51. "Detector," "Girls Who Play like Men."

52. Rose, *Which People's War?* 135.

53. Brand, "Brand's Essence," *Melody Maker*, August 1, 1942, 4.

54. In February 1941 conscription had been extended to women between twenty and thirty-one, which meant that most of Benson's band needed a permit from the Ministry of Labour to continue in the profession. "Women Musicians: Important New Ruling," *Melody Maker*, February 28, 1942, 1. Another option was to hire teenagers: Mae Birch and Ruth Harrison were both eighteen. "Detector," "Girls Who Play like Men."

55. Dawson, "Ivy Benson's Girls in Variety," *Melody Maker*, September 19, 1942, 8.

56. Ibid. The Jamboree itself was judged a somewhat disappointing affair, and Benson's band was mentioned only briefly: they were "astonishingly efficient." "£700 — Money for Jam-Boree!" *Melody Maker*, October 10, 1942, 2.

57. The only negative word was the passing comment by "Detector" that in an October broadcast, "their intonation wasn't so hot." "Detector," "Radio," *Melody Maker*, October 10, 1942, 3.

58. In addition to the cheerful American GIs at Covent Garden, she gained raves when playing for the Halloween Ball at the Washington Club in London. "I was in the ballroom, listening to Ivy and the Girls going to town, and hearing, all around me, such remarks as 'Gee, it's good,' 'Oh, boy, this is solid,' 'Gosh, this reminds me of home,' etc., which coming from American swing fans, is not exactly uncomplimentary to Ivy Benson." Brand, "Brand's Essence," *Melody Maker*, November 7, 1942, 4.

59. "The Battle of the Saxes!" 1.

60. "Anti Flabby Entertainment in Empire Programmes," BBC Internal Circulating Memorandum from Mr. Cecil Madden, Criterion, to DEP, March 11, 1942, BBC WAC S24/14.

61. "Bands in the Forces: The Facts!" *Melody Maker*, February 28, 1942, 1; "RAF Band-Aces Attacked," *Melody Maker*, March 21, 1942, 1; "Sensational Army No-Pay-If-You-Play Order for Musicians," *Melody Maker*, June 13, 1942, 1. Despite the lip service about the importance of dance music for the nation's morale, service dance musicians engaged in an ongoing struggle to prove their usefulness to the war effort, as demonstrated in the Ministry of Information propaganda film *Swinging into the Attack*, which showed the Blue Rockets performing and carrying out difficult training maneuvers. "Official Film with Blue Rockets Gives Lie to 'Toy Soldier' Tales," *Melody Maker*, February 20, 1943, 1.

62. Ernest Betts, "New BBC Band: Stars in 1943," *Sunday Express*, November 29, 1942, BBC WAC Press Cuttings.

63. "Women's Band for BBC?"; "BBC Contract for All-Women Band," *Daily Sketch*, December 12, 1942, BBC WAC Press Cuttings; "BBC Clings to Ivy: All-Ladies' Band Get Resident Job," *Melody Maker*, December 12, 1942, 1; "All-Woman Band," *Empire News*, December 13, 1942, BBC WAC Press Cuttings; "Ivy Benson Is 'Terribly Proud,'" *Evening Chronicle*, December 18, 1942, BBC WAC Press Cuttings; Seton Margrave, "BBC Engage a Girls' Band for Dance Music," *Daily Mail*, December 5, 1942, BBC WAC Press Cuttings. Ravenhill gives Benson's date of birth as 1913, however. Ravenhill, *Ivy Benson and Her All Girl Band*.

64. One set of sisters, Mae and Norma Birch, played trumpet while Billie and Kay Yorston played second piano and bass/vocals, respectively. Ruth Harrison played lead trombone and her mother, Florence, played second trombone.

65. "Ivy Benson Is 'Terribly Proud'"; "Started Young."

66. Rose, *Which People's War?* 118.

67. "New BBC Resident Dance Band," *Melody Maker*, December 5, 1942, 1; "BBC Clings to Ivy."

68. "New BBC Resident Dance Band."

69. Once before, in 1940, it had explored and then dismissed the possibility of employing an all-women's band when the call-up began to affect male dance bands. "The BBC Nearly Had a Girls' Band!" *Melody Maker*, August 3, 1940, 2; and "659" from Streeton, London, to Brown, Variety Booking Bristol, 31 July 1940, BBC WAC R27/21.

70. "The Battle of the Saxes!"

71. The director of variety, John Watt, dismissed replacing the Band of the Week with ad hoc London bookings because of the expense of finding additional studio space in the capital. Because of Bristol's remote location, the cost of forming a permanent Bristol band

led by a veteran bandleader like Billy Cotton or Carroll Gibbons would be prohibitive. Therefore, Benson's band was the best solution for poor quality Bands of the Week in Bristol. "Dance Bands," BBC Internal Circulating Memorandum from Director of Variety to AC(P) London, October 12, 1942, BBC WAC R27/73/1.

72. "Sex Antagonism," *Bristol Evening Post*, January 12, 1942, BBC WAC Press Cuttings.

73. Rose, *Which People's War?* 116.

74. Tracy, *Talking Swing*, 30.

75. "All Women's Band," *Edinburgh Evening News*, December 26, 1942, BBC WAC Press Cuttings; "The Battle of the Saxes!" 1.

76. Grant, "All-Women Band in 'Storm.'"

77. "Leaders Meet on BBC New Dance Band Policy," *Melody Maker*, December 19, 1942, 2.

78. The corporation made one concession to the deputation: it would use mobile units and regional stations to broadcast dance music so that bands touring the provinces would not have to give up work to make a broadcast from London. As *Melody Maker* observed, this was a minor concession, for only a few sessions remained available to ad hoc bands. "Leaders and BBC Clear the Air," *Melody Maker*, January 23, 1943, 1.

79. Grant, "All-Women Band in 'Storm.'"

80. "All things, it was once pointed out by a French savant, were forgivable in a woman save one — she must never look ridiculous. Now, it is my private contention that among the more ridiculous situations in which a pretty young girl can find herself are sitting behind, and pouting into, a bass saxophone; playing the trombone; or squawking through a trumpet with a papier-maché bowler-hat over its end. On the other hand, she looks amiable and elegant in the company of a grand piano or when snuggling up to a violin. So that the odds, so far as a ladies' dance orchestra is concerned, are, as I pointed out to Ivy Benson recently, more or less even. And, being a young woman with a sense of humour as well as of rhythm, she did me the honour to laugh [rather than kick him] and say that she knew what I meant." C. Gordon Glover, "Introducing," *Radio Times*, January 8, 1943, 5.

81. "The Battle of the Saxes!" 1.

82. Ibid., 8.

83. "Woman Conductor Takes BBC Bow," *Daily Express*, January 12, 1943, BBC WAC Press Cuttings.

84. "Band Leaders Lose," *Star*, January 15, 1943, BBC WAC Press Cuttings.

85. Brand, "Brand's Essence," *Melody Maker*, August 8, 1943, 6.

86. "Mike," "Is Their Burbling Really Necessary?" *Melody Maker*, January 30, 1943, 4–5.

87. "Detector," "No Orchids for Miss Benson!" *Melody Maker*, January 23, 1943, 5.

88. Ibid.

89. "Detector," "Girls Who Play like Men."

90. Steve Chibnall, "Pulp versus Penguins: Paperbacks Go to War," *War Culture: Social Change and Changing Experience in World War Two Britain*, ed. Pat Kirkham and David Thoms (London: Lawrence and Wishart, 1995), 140. My sincere thanks to Stephen Heathorn for bringing this connection, and the novel, to my attention.

91. Orson Welles, "Raffles and Miss Blandish," *Horizon*, October 1944; reprinted by *Gaslight*, http://gaslight.mtroyal.ab.ca/Orwell-C.htm, accessed January 11, 2005.

92. The character of Miss Blandish is not developed very thoroughly in the novel: although she shows some spirit at the beginning, shock and the drugs forced upon her soon take their effect. Twice in her delirious mumbling, she repeats, "I wish I were a man." "Detector" viewed Benson's professional aspirations as gender inappropriate; did the novel's punishment of a woman who could voice such sentiments inspire his title at some level? James Hadley Chase, *No Orchids for Miss Blandish* (London: Jarrolds Publishers, n.d.), 85–86, 106–7.

93. LAC S. R. Horner, letter to *Melody Maker*, February 6, 1943, 8; "A Disappointed Reader," letter to *Melody Maker*, February 6, 1943, 8.

94. J. L. Gorman, letter to *Melody Maker*, February 6, 1943, 8; Ronald Landy, letter to *Melody Maker*, February 13, 1943, 4–5.

95. "Ivy Benson Sensation: Famous Male Arranger to the Rescue," *Melody Maker*, February 13, 1943, 1.

96. Tracy, *Talking Swing*, 30.

97. "Still on the Air," *Star*, January 13, 1944, BBC WAC Press Cuttings.

98. "Can You Stand It?" *News and Times* (Worcester), July 12, 1943, BBC WAC Press Cuttings. The week of July 12, the paper was literally correct in two cases; in the remaining three, its figurative accuracy depended upon one's taste in music. Benson broadcast at the following times on the domestic Home Service and Forces Programme: Monday, 11:00–11:45 a.m. (Forces), opposite a schools program, and 11:20–11:55 p.m. (Home) after the Forces Programme was off the air; Tuesday, 10:30–11:15 p.m. (Home), opposite light music; Thursday, 4:20–4:45 p.m. (Forces), opposite Mozart and Haydn string quartets, and 6:30–7:00 p.m. (Home) opposite *Radio Rhythm Club*, a program for jazz enthusiasts; and Saturday, 11:10 p.m.–midnight (Home) after the Forces Programme was off the air. Programme Listings, *Radio Times*, July 9, 1943, 8–18.

99. See Baade 2002, 231–319.

100. Dance Music Policy [Committee] Minutes, September 20, 1943, BBC WAC R27/73/2;

Dance Music Policy [Committee] Minutes, February 23, 1943, BBC WAC R27/74/1; Dance Music Policy Committee Minutes, October 25, 1943, BBC WAC R27/73/2. Doris Knight was reinstated on fast numbers only on January 10, 1944. Dance Music Policy Committee Minutes, January 10, 1944, BBC WAC R27/73/2.

101. Spike Hughes, "Report on the Four BBC Contract Dance Bands and Victor Silvester's Band," August 12, 1943, BBC WAC R27/73/2.

102. Ibid.

103. Geraldo and Payne broadcast in an alternating system in which one bandleader appeared twice while the other appeared three times. R. J. F. Howgill, "Spike Hughes' Report on the Four BBC Contract Dance Bands and Victor Silvester's Band," notes from Dance Music Policy Committee meeting, August 31, 1943, BBC WAC R27/73/2.

104. Hughes, "Report on the Four BBC Contract Dance Bands and Victor Silvester's Band."

105. Howgill, "Spike Hughes' Report on the Four BBC Contract Dance Bands and Victor Silvester's Band."

106. Hughes, "Report on the Four BBC Contract Dance Bands and Victor Silvester's Band."

107. "Detector," "Radio," *Melody Maker*, March 6, 1943, 9.

108. "Ivy Benson's Big Spot in Jack Warner Air Show," *Melody Maker*, July 31, 1943, 1.

109. Brand, "Brand's Essence," *Melody Maker*, April 3, 1943, 6; Brand, "Brand's Essence," *Melody Maker*, May 29, 1943, 6.

110. Brand, "Brand's Essence," *Melody Maker*, June 26, 1943, 6.

111. "Ivy Benson Signs for HMV," *Melody Maker*, September 11, 1943, 1.

112. Howgill, "Spike Hughes' Report on the Four BBC Contract Dance Bands and Victor Silvester's Band."

113. "Stop Press," *Melody Maker*, September 18, 1943, 1; "Ivy Leaves," *Bristol Evening World*, October 1, 1943, BBC WAC Press Cuttings; "Ivy Benson Clicks Season at Palladium," *Melody Maker*, December 11, 1943, 1.

114. "BBC Bands on the Stage: Ivy Benson at Ilford, Billy Ternent at Kingston," *Melody Maker*, October 23, 1943, 4.

115. Edgar A. Palmer, *G.I. Songs: Written, Composed and/or Collected by Men in the Service* (New York: Sheridan House, 1944), 109.

116. "Ivy Benson Leaving BBC," *Melody Maker*, January 15, 1944, 1; Brand, "Brand's Essence," *Melody Maker*, March 18, 1944, 4.

117. "Ivy Benson Makes Changes," *Melody Maker*, April 22, 1944, 1.

118. "Ivy Benson's Plans," *Melody Maker*, May 13, 1944, 2; "Ivy Benson's Provincial Tour," *Melody Maker*, June 17, 1944, 2.

119. "Ivy Benson Smashing Records," *Melody Maker*, July 1, 1944, 2.

120. Gillies MacKinnon, dir., *The Last of the Blonde Bombshells* (HBO Films, 2000).

121. Ravenhill, *Ivy Benson and Her All Girl Band*.

122. Ibid.

123. Tracy, *Talking Swing*, 35.

124. Reg Connelly, "Homecoming Thoughts," *Melody Maker*, September 18, 1943, 3. Connelly was hardly disinterested in matters of Benson's career. Apparently Connelly and Benson met in the seaside resort of Bridlington in the 1930s: "From that moment, he guided Ivy along the path of stardom with his knowledge of the music business and the people who worked in it." They maintained a discreet romance, since Connelly "was married with a handicapped son." According to the memories of several band members, the relationship was an open secret in the profession, but Benson presented herself to the wartime public as single, declaring, "You can't mix marriage with a band." Certainly, Benson had opportunities that no other women's band in Britain enjoyed. Did Connelly promote Benson unofficially, or did he simply mentor her career? Whatever his role, during the period of 1941 to 1943, when Benson got her most important breaks, Connelly was in America on a sojourn that lasted over 2 years. Ravenhill, *Ivy Benson and Her All Girl Band*; and "Women's Band for BBC?"

125. Connelly, "Homecoming Thoughts."

126. "Ivy Benson Signs for HMV," 1.

127. Tony Middleton, liner notes for *Ivy Benson and Her All Girls Band*, Interstate compact disc HQ CD 149 (2000).

128. I have not been able to locate prints of either film that Benson appeared in during the war.

129. "Benson Wants Girls," *Melody Maker*, November 14, 1942, 7.

130. "Woman Conductor Takes BBC Bow."

131. H.S., "Miscellaneous and Dance," *Gramophone*, December 1943, 105.

132. Connelly, "Homecoming Thoughts"; Tucker 2000, 71.

133. Connelly, "Homecoming Thoughts."

134. Brand, "Brand's Essence," *Melody Maker*, August 8, 1943, 6; Dawson, "Ivy Benson's Girls in Variety"; "Ivy Looking for Fem Talent," *Melody Maker*, March 25, 1944, 2.

135. Vladimir Simosko, *Artie Shaw: A Musical Biography and Discography*, Studies in Jazz Series no. 29 (Lanham, Md.: Scarecrow / Institute of Jazz Studies, 2000), 9, 95.

136. H.S., "Miscellaneous and Dance," *Gramophone*, March 1944, 153.

137. "Corny" wondered what had happened at HMV when it "permitted [Benson] to depart from current pops" in order to release "I'm Getting Sentimental over You" and "Star Dust," which even featured a brief "more than adequate guitar solo." As the contract was announced originally, half of Benson's output was to have been nonvocal standards. This was the case in Benson's first recording session on October 14, 1943, which included the two standards along with two pop-oriented numbers, "We Mustn't Say Goodbye" (see note 140) and "The Home Coming Waltz," an infrequently recorded song published by Connelly's company, Campbell Connelly & Co. Ltd., and cowritten by the editor of *Melody Maker*, Ray Sonin. HMV waited four months to release "Star Dust" and "I'm Getting Sentimental over You," however, and Benson recorded no standards in her other wartime sessions on November 4, 1943, and January 21, 1944. Indeed, the standards pushed her into a realm of competition different from the commercial British dance bands (e.g., Ambrose, Carroll Gibbons, and Geraldo) and strict tempo orchestras (Victor Silvester): American swing bands and small British swing combinations. Benson's "pleasant" "I'm Getting Sentimental over You" could not, for the reviewer of *Gramophone*, approach Tommy Dorsey's playing of his signature tune, while her attractive, melodious "Star Dust" lacked the languorous yet swinging finesse of Artie Shaw's 1940 version and the tasteful intimacy of the version that the popular British swing clarinetist Harry Parry and his Radio Rhythm Club Sextet had recorded earlier in the year (which itself was a gloss on Benny Goodman's 1939 recording with his sextet). "Corny," "Glenn Miller's Smashing 'Rhapsody,'" *Melody Maker*, February 19, 1944, 9; "Ivy Benson Signs for HMV," *Melody Maker*; Rust and Forbes, *British Dance Bands on Record*, 65; H.S., "Miscellaneous and Dance," *Gramophone*, February 1944, 137; Harry Parry, *Gone with the Wind*, Empress compact disc RAJCD 840 (1995).

138. H.S., "Miscellaneous and Dance," *Gramophone*, February 1944, 137; H.S., "Miscellaneous and Dance," *Gramophone*, April 1944, 167.

139. "Corny," "James Prejudice," *Melody Maker*, 22 January 1944, 4.

140. Most of the popular songs broadcast and recorded by British bands were American in origin; Hollywood films played an important role in promoting new songs. Benson also recorded "We Mustn't Say Goodbye" from *Stage Door Canteen* (1943), "If I Had My Way," the title song from a 1940 Bing Crosby vehicle, and, on the flip side of "It Can't Be Wrong," "How Sweet You Are," sung by Dinah Shore in *Thank Your Lucky Stars* (1943).

141. See Jackie Stacey, *Star Gazing: Hollywood Cinema and Female Spectatorship* (London: Routledge, 1994), 83–84. It is difficult to obtain statistics, but anecdotally, keen fans would attend a film several times.

142. Paul Aitken has told me anecdotally of his Scottish grandmother, who with her

girlfriends appreciated hearing Benson's all-girl band on the radio. In-person conversation, September 21, 2006.

143. Stacey, *Star Gazing*, 181.

144. In the most literal sense, the film's portrayal of the relationship between Davis's character and a man unable to leave his marriage resonated with the situation rumored to exist between Benson and Connelly.

145. "Ivy Benson Leaving BBC," *Melody Maker*.

146. See Philip Ziegler, *London at War, 1939–1945* (New York: Alfred A. Knopf, 1995).

147. When they performed on the television program *The Music Box*, for example, Benson and her band gave swinging performances of "Lady Be Good" (her signature tune) and "Halleluia," followed by the jump-style "See You Later, Alligator," which featured soloists on tenor saxophone and electric guitar, along with call and response between the vocalist Gloria Russell and the rest of the band, whose members clapped along on the backbeat. The entire band wore satin, off-the shoulder dresses, of course. Kenneth Carter, dir., *The Music Box*, television series, January 18, 1957, Jack Hylton Television Productions, British Film Institute 472721. See also *Ivy Benson and Her All Girls Band*, Interstate compact disc HQ CD 149 (2000).

Tracy McMullen

IDENTITY FOR SALE:

GLENN MILLER, WYNTON MARSALIS,

AND CULTURAL REPLAY IN MUSIC

On April 8, 1994, as part of America's yearlong fiftieth anniversary celebration of D-Day, Thomas Duffy and the Yale Concert Band presented a reenactment of a 1940s Glenn Miller "I Sustain the Wings" radio broadcast in Yale's Woolsey Hall, the site of the original performance. Yale band personnel astoundingly recovered the original 48-star American flag to again cascade down the back of the auditorium; band members donned simulated Second World War era uniforms appropriate to the rank of the musician they embodied, becoming Corporal "Peanuts" Hucko on clarinet or Private First Class Steven Steck on trumpet; and in a dramatic move by the perpetually barbate bandleader, Thomas Duffy returned after the intermission clean shaven (to the particular amazement of his musical charges), with slicked hair and wire-rimmed glasses, all the more to incarnate the famous bandleader. With the spirit of Miller upon him, Duffy led his band through the exact music and heroic war adventure skit performed decades ago for a Second World War radio audience. The event was a huge success, leading to performances at the National Museum in Washington and at the international fiftieth anniversary D-day commemorations in France and England. Described by the band's business manager as their "cash cow," the event continued periodically over the next decade, culminating in a performance for 2004's sixtieth anniversary of D-day.[1]

Such a detailed reenactment partakes of broader trends in our increasingly museal culture.[2] It also coincides with the 1990s swing revival seen in bands like the Cherry Poppin' Daddies, the Brian Setzer Orchestra, and Big Bad Voodoo Daddy, and with another phenomenon that emerged in that decade combining cultural memory and popular music — the "tribute band." Of course, by taking place at a privileged university, as well as the nation's capital and on an international stage, Yale's commemoration was not only popular cultural memory but also a part of the sanctioned national memory of the Second World War. Fiftieth anniversary commemorations of the Second World War closely followed the First Gulf War and its supposed triumph over America's "Vietnam Syndrome." Such remembrances served to supplant dissenting, plural, cacophonous 1960s wartime images with those of a "popular" war, and Yale's reenactment clearly participated in this widespread tendency. But the devil is in the details, and my focus here is on how the intricacies of Yale's production reveal important strategies for enacting and maintaining boundaries that speak to both political and musical gatekeeping. Indeed, the Miller reenactment presents a unique opportunity to undress the cross-dressing and racial-traversing that often attends such nostalgic performances of identity. Contemporary Yale women and men of color would not have been welcome in Miller's original orchestra, and yet in this reenactment, two men of color (trumpet and piano) and four white women (two cornets, trumpet, and tenor saxophone), along with their white male band mates, now take on the identity of a particular white man, wear his uniform, and speak his words, in a spectacle of national consonance.[3] The recreation also enacts a precise gender ritual of big band and jazz performance that I describe as in-passing. I begin by demonstrating in-passing as it is performed by women playing jazz, follow with a dissection of Glenn Miller's constructed white masculinity and its mobilization as a synonym for American nationhood, and conclude by applying my insights on performative nostalgia to the jazz meanings and identities being performed at Jazz at Lincoln Center (JALC) and the consequences such meanings have for the relationship between improvisation and jazz.

WOMEN IN JAZZ AND IN-PASSING

When I discovered Yale's Glenn Miller reenactment, my immediate reaction as a female instrumentalist was to wonder how the women in the band felt. Tenor saxophonist Elizabeth Branch (1997) performing

Private Vince Carbone and trumpeter Else Festersen (1996) festooned in the chevrons of Private First Class Steve Steck struck me as particularly unequivocal examples of the phenomenon I experienced playing saxophone in my faux tux with the "other men" in the band (see figure 6.1). As the only woman instrumentalist in many swing bands, I was expected to blend in with their masculine veneer, whereas the woman vocalist in her beaded gown embodied the "feminine" in our (re)enactment of classic gender roles and heterosexual desire. Thus, I was in some way to "pass" as male, but this did not mean to be overtly butch (unacceptable) or to wear a disguise. Somehow, obeisance to the tradition deeming this position as "male" was necessary without foreclosing my prescribed gender identity as female/feminine.[4] I have termed this move in-passing, as it bears some similarities with the action of "passing" in racial and gender contexts, an activity which has been productively unpacked and theorized by the legal scholar Cheryl I. Harris and the artist Adrian Piper regarding race and Judith Halberstam regarding gender.[5] In-passing relates to passing in that a privileged subject position retains proprietary status, but whereas "passing" entails an undetected and complete (albeit transitory and often uncomfortable)[6] assumption of the privileged subject position, in-passing is a signifying practice that asserts the authority and inevitability of the privileged position while simultaneously allowing the subordinate person to occupy it as a unique placeholder bestowed with honorary status. When placing syllabic emphasis on the in, *in*-passing suggests that the "non-inevitable" person is *in*, she or he participates in the dominant group and has some access to the concomitant privileges. With the emphasis placed on *passing*, however, the term acknowledges the temporary and contingent quality of this participation: the relation with the dominant group is only "in passing," not assured or assumed, and must be continually remanufactured. Thus, in-passing is a form of liminal identity that does not disrupt unified identity, but rather "fashions unity" through its particular signifying practice.

In-passing can best be observed in the uniform(ities) of a ritualized setting: a commemoration or a performance (and part of our postmodern museal culture is that most performances are now "commemorative" in some way).[7] For women in big bands, in-passing requires not calling attention to one's femaleness: in addition to wearing a faux suit, one does not blanch as the conductor calls attention with "Gentlemen!" or point out sexism when he exclaims, "you guys are swingin' like a pair of [tits]!"[8] Here, women perform jazz musically while concurrently

Fig. 6.1. Else Festerson as Pfc. Steve Steck in Yale's Glenn Miller recreation at the International Fiftieth Anniversary of D-Day celebrations, Dinard, France. Reprinted with permission from Yale University Bands.

performing that performance as inevitably "masculine," re-inscribing gender norms rather than embodying progressive action as is usually assumed. The Miller recreation was therefore a ritualized enactment of how women in jazz seem always to have to "play [like] men" in order to play. However, this was not all that was played at Yale.

GLENN MILLER, SWING, AND MASCULINITY

To fathom the import of a Glenn Miller recreation, it is necessary to understand more fully what is being recreated. Performing Glenn Miller is simultaneously a performance of a particular idea of white masculinity, one that Miller himself created and sold to an eager public. Indeed, aligning masculinity with music had been a successful formula in the years preceding Miller's rise.

In his book, *Swingin' the Dream*, Lewis Erenberg argues that 1930s swing big bands effected an assertion of male power that countered the emasculating effects of the depression. Such emasculation manifested itself musically in the "crooner" songs and "sweet" bands of the Depression era and earlier in Paul Whiteman, who had famously made a "lady" out of jazz in his 1924 Aeolian Hall concert in New York. Not dispensing loads of virile "hot stuff," Whiteman instead produced a feminized version of jazz — "cultured," commercial, and conspicuously white.[9]

With the arrival of Benny Goodman and other hard-driving swing bands, Erenberg recognizes the cultural return of men as "patriarchal leaders" directing large units of all-male teams in powerful, virtuosic music. The feminization of popular jazz was not lost on these band-leaders, who often took pains to distance themselves from the form. Goodman himself described sweet music as "a weak sister" that was no match for "the real music of America," i.e., his own band with its roots and inspiration in African American swing bands. Goodman associated his "real music" with a masculinity specifically coded as black: his auto-biographical collaborator, Irving Kolodin, described Goodman's swing as an "inevitable reaction against the white man's jazz of the 1920s."[10] The idea of whiteness as "cultured" (read: feminized), and of blackness and black music as enviably free of this emasculation, was a concern for a white male musician such as Goodman.[11] Although the first popular bandleader to integrate his band on stage racially, Goodman was not interested in hiring *female* instrumentalists of any color. Patti Bown, an African American pianist who auditioned for Goodman in the 1940s, recalls this of her experience: "It was hard for a woman to get a job, a lot of men wouldn't hire a woman. That was a serious, hard thing for me. I knew I could play. They said Benny Goodman was looking for a pianist. I went down there. The people auditioning me clapped like crazy, but he wouldn't hire me. Goodman's musical director said, 'You sure can play, but he won't hire you. He's got some kind of complex about chicks. He thinks they draw too much attention.' Some wicky-wacky preju-dice."[12] Whiteman, white men, and women were aligned in Goodman's mind with the empty spectacle: commercial, sweet, and feminine, all of which signified a lack of talent, integrity, and masculinity. It seems likely that a particularly virulent sexism perpetuated by men toward women in jazz stems from such fears of their own emasculation in the face of a never-attainable black phallus.[13]

Benny Goodman was the first bandleader to racially integrate his band, and his comparatively darker-complexioned swing did not capti-vate an America looking for reassurance during wartime.[14] It was Glenn Miller who took swing and further commodified it for a mass audience, keeping its energy but eliminating any overt references to blackness. Indeed, much like Whiteman, Miller bleached jazz, but this time he retained the normative masculinity. If the masculinity of Paul White-man was white, cultured, and feminized and that of Goodman was of virility born from its relationship to blackness, Miller's masculinity was that of the potent, authoritative white man, cut loose from any threat of blackness or femininity. Miller was a perfect fit for the segregated military, for unlike Goodman, Artie Shaw, Charlie Barnett, or Tommy Dorsey, Glenn Miller never hired a black musician or singer for his band; and his lyrics promoted images of rural, white America, replete with gendered and racial stereotypes that perfectly fed into wartime messages propagated by the Office of War Information selling the idea of the "idealized home front."[15]

Even before Miller became an enlisted man, he was described as a strict disciplinarian, maintaining a demeanor as authoritative and capable as a "General" (Erenberg 1998). Lewis Erenberg cites many such references to Miller's masculine image: "Tall, 'bespectacled and scholarly looking,' he 'was a commanding guy, youthful but mature,' according to his press agent, Howard Richmond, who found that Miller 'looked like security, like all the things I'd never found in a bandleader.' True, 'Mickey Mouse bandleaders looked like security. I'm talking about jazz leaders. To me they always looked like they didn't know where they were going to sleep the next night.' Seventeen-year-old singer Marion Hutton concurred. As her legal guardian, Miller 'was like a father. . . . He represented a source of strength. . . . He fulfilled the image of what a father ought to be'" (Erenberg 1998, 187). And, as Judith Halberstam and others have shown in another context, the acceptance of white masculinity as central takes place through the framing process of others (Halberstam 1998). Other "traveling bands" or "jazz leaders" clearly reference black jazz (either directly or as an inspiration for white jazz leaders) by opposing them to "Mickey Mouse" bands of the popular white variety. By alluding to myths of black masculinity as excessive, profligate, and uncontrolled and thereby unable to provide adequate leadership, Miller's white masculinity is established as reasoned, controlled, and authoritative. Similarly, the "femininity" of Hutton is presented as childlike and in need of strength and guidance. It is Miller's firm patriarchal oversight that contains femininity and its threat of "emotionalism," "incompetence," and "vacuous commercialism" by disciplining it into the safe and only intermittently accessed arena of the beautiful and lyric spectacle. Such analysis is nothing new, but it is important to understand with what desiderata we fulfill our appetite for reenactment.

Miller's patriarchal image was heightened when he enlisted in 1942 and led the 418th Army Air Forces Band stationed at Yale University. For Miller, described in the Yale concert notes as "a man possessed of deep and genuine patriotic sentiment,"[16] enlisting in the army was certainly as much a shrewd business move as any heartfelt allegiance. As Sherrie Tucker has noted, men in big bands, as in other civilian work, would be "scrutinized with the ubiquitous, 'Why aren't you in uniform?'" (Tucker 2000, 42). The Glenn Miller Orchestra had been the most popular band in the nation since 1939 and given Erenberg's convincing analysis of swing bands as playing on patriarchal masculinity, it is impossible to imagine Miller's continued mass popularity without his connection to military service. And although Erenberg describes the move as a sacrifice, he also relates how the AAF Orchestra surpassed even its civilian predecessor in popularity (Erenberg 1998, 182). Indeed, Miller's priorities as an enlisted man privileged business over service. Although assigned to oversee all of the Army Air Forces Technical Training Command (AAFTTC) bands from Knollwood Field, North Carolina, Miller eventually convinced his superiors to allow him to remain full-time at the Yale campus where his officially subsidiary position of leading the 418th AAF Band took place. This post band was to play for daily Review formations, Retreat Parades, luncheon sessions, weekly Cadet Dances and other cadet affairs, enlisted men dances, as well as march to and from ceremonies, and travel to nearby towns to recruit aviation cadets. However, in roughly 8 months, Miller had extricated his band from any post duties (except special occasions) and in early December 1943 transferred twenty-four of his twenty-eight band members into the 2nd Army Air Forces Training Command (AAFTC)[17] Radio Unit, leaving the old 418th to be the post band with a new director and soon renamed the 718th. Miller's priorities for *his* band were gaining national radio shows, playing national war bond rallies (live concerts to huge audiences), attaining overseas radio shows, and eventually, a tour of Europe.[18]

While the stripped and restaffed 418th remained to provide post duties at Yale, Miller's band was now free to function much like a civilian band, but with free passage around the country and the world, free and regular radio play, and free promotion. Instead of playing local recruitment drives in Stamford and Bridgeport, Miller was now touring major American cities like St. Louis and Chicago for national war loan drives and he evaded the 1942–1944 American Federation of Musicians (AFM) recording ban by recording V-discs for the troops (distributed nationally and internationally by the War Department). Miller also recorded six local "test" broadcasts at Yale in the spring and summer of 1943 (the source of Duffy's recreation). Played over WEEI Boston, "I Sustain the Wings" (after the AAFTTC motto, "Sustineo Alas") was soon broadcast nationally over CBS and later NBC under the supervision of the War Department. Miller also worked for months to get permission to travel overseas. On October 13, 1943, "Miller met with Lieutenant General Barton K. Yount to cover several points, the major one being his request that the 418th AAF Band be sent overseas to entertain the troops." In June 1944, the band made the trip and entertained "hundreds of thousands" of Allied soldiers. In describing his work with the bandleader during the war, the saxophonist Hank Freeman recalled, "Glenn was sort of businesslike. It was like he was the head of a big corporation. He had that kind of mind." And indeed, Miller seems to have situated his band in a way that would impress any CEO, guaranteeing huge exposure, a highly sellable image based on patriotism, and an overhead covered by the government. Of course, it cannot be denied that risk was also involved. In taking his band overseas during wartime, Miller did end up paying the ultimate price. He lost his life over the English Channel in what is now believed to be a case of "friendly fire."[20]

Despite evidence of such personal ambition, Miller's marshaling of normative white masculinity assured that such endeavors would be read as "patriotic" or as capable and providing "business acumen" rather than the "crass commercialism" of sweet bandleaders. And it was under such aegis that Miller masterminded the formula for mass popularity perhaps before anyone: create a well-defined and desired image and then replay it, again and again.[21] Miller's drummer Moe Purtill explained that in the early years of the band "we just . . . played [the] same twenty tunes over and over" (Erenberg 1998, 169). But also in the later years, playing for the troops in Europe, Miller continued to repeat. When asked about such repetitiveness Miller responded: "we didn't come here to set any new fashions in music. . . . We play only the old tunes" (Erenberg 1998, 192). Already serving the function of nostalgia, Glenn Miller described his role as providing the fighting boys with a "hunk o' home." Furthermore, Miller insisted that every level of band uniformity be recreated night after night. A fine was levied if uniforms, socks, neckties, or handkerchiefs were not "just right." According to Miller's trumpeter, Billy May, "there was no room for inventiveness. Even the hot choruses were supposed to be the same" (Erenberg 1998, 187). Thus, Miller forged his popular band through the very deployment of repetition and identity. Miller tapped into the desire for the comfort and reassurance of repetition and indeed, of the identical, during troubled times. And what he repeated were images of white masculinity as reasoned and in charge.

Thomas Duffy's obsession with repetition and identity and his fervent attention to detail, therefore, replayed not only the Miller broadcast but also Miller's own repetition compulsion. At the Yale Recreation, identity was in surplus: the identical space, the identical American flag, even Glenn Miller's original secretary was presented to the audience.[22] I term this recreation of a past moment that then becomes bounded — a frozen "hunk o' time" — Replay. Evoking the scopophilic pleasure of the instant replay in sports, Replay in cultural productions offers the same sense of exactness, of the identical, the bounded, the true. It comforts by showing us what we (think we) have seen before and by its ability to play it again; it is a fetishized moment, captured and displayed. Similar formulations include Civil War and other battle recreations, stagings that share the Yale event's preoccupation with place, accuracy, and invocation of an "exact" historical moment. Tribute bands that strive for unerring visual and sonic replication are also examples of Replay (such as the Genesis tribute band the Musical Box, which recreates an exact tour down to the smallest detail, including stage banter and bodily movements from the band's 1973–75 period). Early music ensembles pursuing authenticity or the nostalgico-historical revivals of various jazz periods and styles are less obsessive examples, but the impulse to preserve/find a desired "home" is there. However, the Yale University Replay, with its special claim to political memory through its institutional power, its status as a place of education where plurality is expected, and its sanctioning as a representative body overseas, is a particularly exemplary presentation of Replay. Indeed, the Yale Replay fashions an identity against the pluralities of gender and race, subsuming these differences in a performance that *plays* unity through the medium of in-passing. Most Civil War reenactors are white men who voluntarily take up their pleasure and are averse to racial minorities or women taking on roles that should be "authentically" filled by white men.[23] Unlike battle reenactments or popular swing bands, the Yale band is not so self-selecting, and must accommodate difference within its ranks. It is therefore faced with the dilemma of presenting women and people of color under the banner of unified white masculinity.

Such spectacles of national memory evidence the deep-rooted anxiety with plurality in American culture. In the 1990s, alluding to the Vietnam War became a touchstone for a generalized fear of postmodern pluralities. In the zealous proliferation of "United We Stand" bumper stickers,

Fig. 6.2. Yale Billboard. Reprinted with permission from Yale University Bands.

posters, and commentary, terrified Americans throughout the First Gulf War swore to learn from the lesson of Vietnam: that plurality can defeat a nation, a prospect the frightening specter of terrorism made more dire. As noted above, America's victory in the First Gulf War was hailed as the corrective to America's "Vietnam Syndrome" and this "double victory" segued neatly into fiftieth anniversary celebrations of D-Day and the Second World War. The Yale recreation served, like other Second World War commemorations across the country, not only to return America to its old victorious self but also to "return" it to a world of unity and identity.[24]

This reenactment is functioning as what Fredric Jameson has termed "pop history." In his seminal work on postmodernism (1991), Jameson describes the disappearance of the historical referent in postmodern works, saying of E. L. Doctorow's novel *Ragtime*: "This historical novel can no longer set out to represent the historical past; it can only 'represent' our ideas and stereotypes about that past (which thereby at once becomes 'pop history')."[25] Acting as a cultural ritual, the Yale reenactment binds us together with its representations of nation. And as Mircea Eliade describes in another context (originally pertaining to "traditional" cultures but I now apply the insight to the United States), such rituals cannot be of particulars but enact exemplary archetypes: in the Yale recreation's case, a particular vision of Western culture as white, teleological, unified, masculine, and strong.

Put another way, the Yale Replay is a ritual enactment of the "abstract citizen" of modernity. In her book *Immigrant Acts*, Lisa Lowe describes the contradiction inherent in Western capitalist countries between the need for "abstract labor" and that for "abstract citizens": "Theoretically, in a racially homogeneous nation, the needs of capital and the needs of the state complement each other. Yet in a racially differentiated nation such as the United States, capital and state imperatives may be contradictory: capital, with its supposed needs for 'abstract labor,' is said by Marx to be unconcerned by the 'origins' of its labor force, whereas the nation-state, with its need for 'abstract citizens' formed by a unified culture to participate in the political sphere, is precisely concerned to maintain a national citizenry bound by race, language, and culture."[26] Lowe goes on to describe how the Asian immigrant[27] is a constant threat to the "abstract American citizen" by physiologically bearing the trace of a history (of racist immigration, employment, and social practices) that national memory wishes to forget and of an Other (Asia) that must, by definition, remain outside for the West to establish itself as unified. Forever representing the "foreigner within," Asian immigrants and Asian Americans jeopardize the construction of the unified nation-state. It is spectacles of national memory such as Yale's that attempt to "resolve" the contradiction of particularity (woman, Asian, black) into abstract (white male) by conscientiously enacting the ritual of "particularity" speaking "abstract."[28] Faced with the threat of an "incorrect" reading of the nation-state, national memory attempts to heal the gash through ritual Replay.[29]

Thus, the Miller reenactment fashions a message of unity that depends upon women and people of color "becoming" white men, depicting the practice as completely commensurate. These moments of identity-crossing are thus not "queering," following Butler, or "deviant details," following Lowe; they do not fray the seams of unity and perfect mimesis in their incommensurability, but are more often "obedient transvestism" employed to signify the opposite. Such a reenactment becomes a precise ritual seeking to salve the fear of plurality by presenting women and people of color as obedient "white men," a process that creates the illusion of "plurality within unity" but is in fact only the ceremonial spectacle of the dominant culture speaking itself through the mouths of others ritually vacated of their own position.

However, in the realm of concert hall performance where the audience's gravitational pull always careens toward the past, Duffy's inclination toward Replay is not surprising. A look around the Yale band room lined with past concert posters reveals how seductive the call of Replay is to a contemporary band director who not only must prepare performances each year but also sell them. Duffy frequently mined the patriotic spirit of aging Yale alumni to fill his seats, presenting "Music of the Civil War" or "Stars and Strife: Music of Conflict and Patriotism," but he also arranged music around other themes, as any band director would: school spirit ("Music from the Pens of Yale Composers"), movie themes, church music, or, more problematically, "Memories of the Orient." Faced with a public resistant to new music, it is not much of a stretch for a music director to choose to make the old haunt us that much more palpably by recreating historic details associated with earlier presentations, perhaps in a determined attempt to breathe new life into the endeavor (indeed, Duffy had already filled the post for twelve years in 1994).[30] The director himself is a composer and presents several of his compositions with the concert band annually, obviously sharing in the desire to have new music programmed into concerts. Attempting to balance sales with aesthetic recompense, Duffy, like most of his contemporaries, probably partakes of a delicate game of bait-and-switch, presenting the pop classics, then sneaking in a new or lesser-known work.

Therefore, I hope it is clear that this is not an inquisition into the personal motives of Thomas Duffy. As a highly successful band director and salesman, however, Duffy did divine what people wanted to hear and see, and he balanced that with his own desires as a director and composer. As the band's golden goose and a favorite for fund-raising campaigns (presented as "war bond rallies"), the Glenn Miller recreation obviously enthralled New Haven, Conn. But its national and international exposure also led to reviews in newspapers around the country including the *New York Times* and the *Chicago Tribune*. Expressing the sentiment of the organizers as well as many who partook in national D-Day commemoration events, the Second World War veteran Joseph Dawson told the *Washington Post*: "I thought Vietnam was a stupid war. . . . The whole purpose of this event is to show the world and to show our country that there was a time when our nation moved forward as one unit."[31] The article showed no evidence that the interviewer had solicited a comment on Vietnam; Second World War commemorations bore this connection implicitly. Duffy, like other band directors, indeed, like Miller himself, found success by providing an image that spoke to certain mass sentiments.

SELLING THE IMAGE: JAZZ AS DEMOCRACY

One could argue that the recreation of a Glenn Miller radio broadcast has much more to do with national history and memory than it does with music or music history. But such narratives inevitably intertwine. Even a cursory glance at one music institution, Jazz at Lincoln Center, reveals how historical narratives and iconic American images are mobilized to create meanings of nation and identity. Certainly, the Glenn Miller recreation provides a particularly manifest example of performative history. However, its moves of Replay and in-passing shed light on the less overt, but still highly ideological, performative history taking place at Jazz at Lincoln Center, where as for Duffy and Miller before him, budgetary and other demands entice the institution to reproduce a desired image for large public consumption.

In 1987 the trumpeter Wynton Marsalis, the writer Stanley Crouch, and the scholar Albert Murray were the firebrands behind a Lincoln Center committee that concluded jazz could and should be a permanent and significant member of the large arts institution. Now twenty years later, Jazz at Lincoln Center has grown into a massive organization, the first to expand beyond Lincoln Center's original walls. With 105 full-time staff members, a dozen interns, more than four hundred part-time employees, and roughly three dozen members on its prestigious board, JALC now resides in the new $131 million Frederick P. Rose Hall in the Time Warner Center, where it operates three performance venues and maintains an annual budget of $35 million. Marsalis, the artistic director (and de facto czar), describes the new hall as allowing JALC "to present a face to the world."[32] Marsalis's accomplishments are legion and his emotional, physical, and intellectual commitment to jazz and its importance in America cannot be overstated. However, Marsalis's endeavor to put a "face" on jazz has rallied cries from scholars, musicians, and fans. In a recent article in the *New York Times*, Nate Chinen summarized the basic critique: "Mr. Marsalis was armed with a big idea: that jazz is a model of democratic action, and a prism through which American culture can be understood. This notion, first articulated to him by [Albert] Murray and [Stanley] Crouch, has since been advanced by Jazz at Lincoln Center with the fervor of religious dogma and the adaptability of a political agenda. It served as a central conceit of *Jazz*, the 2001 Ken Burns PBS mini-series that spotlighted Mr. Marsalis not only as a commentator but also as a savior of the tradition. To a certain extent this has become the official story of jazz in the public sphere."[33] Further, the cultural critic Herman S. Gray devotes a chapter in his 2005 book *Cultural Moves* to Marsalis and JALC, arguing that Marsalis's approach to "tradition" is nominal rather than "verbal" (following Nathaniel Mackey),[34] and "canonical" rather than based in a metaphor of "the road and the street." That is, Marsalis considers improvisation more as a category than as a process. He has famously excluded what he considers "commercial" or avant-garde projects from his definition of jazz. Criticisms of Marsalis's exclusionary approach are well known and I do not need to revisit them here.[35] My interest is in how Marsalis performs his desired coherent identity of jazz both on the bandstand and through corporate alliances, and the consequences and conundrums of such an effort. The increased budgetary needs of a large cultural institution, Marsalis's preferred era of "jazz excellence," and his view on the black middle class have all shaped the "face of jazz" that Marsalis is presenting to the world.

However noble and sellable the image of jazz as democratic action may have been to the initial Lincoln Center board and to other supporting arts organizations, JALC's increased income needs are primarily being addressed by corporate sponsors who perhaps find another image of jazz more seductive. Thus, somewhat in contradiction to the image of "jazz as democracy," Marsalis's face of jazz has coalesced around the visage of the sophisticated, upper-class black man.[36] This image can partially be traced to the influence of Stanley Crouch, who has long championed the idea of black middle- (or increasingly, upper-) class values and castigated inner-city black expressions.[37] But it also meets the needs of a white capitalist culture that understands the selling power of black male mystique. Such images of jazz fuel the symbiotic relationship between JALC and its revealing list of corporate sponsors: Cadillac, Brooks Brothers, Altria (formerly Philip Morris),[38] Bank of America, and Coca-Cola. Playing on smoky images of jazz musicians like those captured in the classic photographs by Herman Leonard,[39] JALC and its sponsors sell jazz as a sophisticated masculine accessory. This is not a new marketing ploy in jazz; however, JALC considers itself an educational and historical institution, something its overly sold image does not serve well.

Marsalis confines his definition of jazz's musical style to developments found in 1920s Louis Armstrong, 1930s swing, and the "classic" period of the 1940s and 1950s with artists such as Tadd Dameron, Dizzy Gillespie, and early Miles Davis and John Coltrane. However, this confinement does not partake of the music's tradition of improvisation (as Gray and others have argued); rather, it feeds into the commercialization of jazz that Marsalis ostensibly abhors by presenting jazz as easily digestible consumables. The recent successful marketing campaign built around the "recovered" journals of the fictional pilot/

musician/owner of a 1940s Parisian nightclub, Aerobleu, reveals how black masculine mystique associated with the classic era of jazz trumps historical particularities in the popular imaginary.[40] The All-Music Guide review of the CD states: *"Aerobleu: The Spirit of Cool* is a tribute album to the fictional Parisian club that was a hip spot in the late 1940s. The record contains 15 cuts from artists that would have played the club if it actually existed."[41] Aerobleu was a simulacrum with no original, created to market products imbued with the hip mystique of the jazz club. In much the same way, Marsalis does not need historical particularities to replay his face of jazz; indeed, such elements work against his coherent vision.

For Marsalis, history (or what he would call "tradition") is honored through Replay, i.e., performance tributes to jazz masters that are considered both educational and aesthetic endeavors. In these events, Marsalis is often criticized for his strict adherence to the past—his insistence on "getting it right," rather than taking chances. For example, a reviewer of his recent tribute concert to Louis Armstrong's Hot Five recordings wrote: "The music worked as an homage or a revival. On a deeper level, however, it lacked. The ground covered was too familiar, the treatment clichéd and overly reverential. The wild and wooly spirit of discovery that speaks to us from the original Hot Five recordings was nowhere to be found. Therein resides the central point: That very air of adventure, that ineffable spark of inspiration provides the essence of what makes the best jazz great. It's what separates the original Hot Fives from a skillfully executed, well-meaning tribute. I wish Marsalis had made that point. Unfortunately, I'm not sure he understands it himself."[42] However, in this homage to the Hot Five recordings, which Marsalis considers "the foundation of the organization of jazz improvisation, even as we know it today,"[43] he is content to overlook at least one detail. The pianist in this foundational group and the composer and arranger for many Hot Five and Hot Seven compositions was a woman, Lil Hardin Armstrong. Even in Marsalis's stiff and exact tribute, accuracy to "jazz tradition" overrules accuracies to certain particularized details of the original event. This tribute band, therefore, was filled out with men only. I'm not advocating making the tribute into a "clone band" like the Genesis tribute band described above; indeed, I am not suggesting this is a beneficial way to present jazz at all. I am only demonstrating how Marsalis's reimaginings/recreations perform history through the use of the "exemplary archetype" that men play, write, and are the foundation of jazz. By performing jazz history through Replay,

JALC must then create a special ritual to address the existence of women in jazz.

> *"Jazz is constantly evolving and women have long been instrumental in shaping the landscape of the jazz scene."*[44]

This convoluted and mind-bending statement introducing JALC's second annual "Women in Jazz" Festival has all the doublespeak of a sentence wrested out of a contentious board meeting. Perhaps Lara Pellegrinelli[45] was there to remind the staff that yes, women have been a part of jazz since at least Lil Hardin Armstrong. But the majority would have fought for their carefully constructed image of jazz which could only accommodate women in jazz as, at best, something new. Because of its national status, JALC, like the Yale recreation, is somewhat "forced" to deal with women, to incorporate them into a message that otherwise is oblivious to their existence. Therefore, the only way JALC can work the fact of women instrumentalists into its fiercely manufactured masculine image is by ritualizing women's status as second-class, "lite" versions of jazz that serve to reinforce the boundary of "real jazz." I am speaking, of course, of JALC's annual "Dizzy's Club Coca-Cola Presents: The *Diet Coke* Women in Jazz Festival" (emphasis added). Indeed, it is hard to think of a single other product that bears its marked, attenuated, "feminized," and shadow-self image more precisely than Diet Coke, particularly in its once-a-year presentation on a stage described as Coca-Cola. Could there be a more masterful way to "allow" women onto the jazz stage while simultaneously writing them off of it, or a better way to patently signify women-in-jazz as the continued margin of jazz? JALC certainly masters the antinomy, declaring women "in jazz" while simultaneously writing that women border/lack/want jazz.[46]

Marsalis describes Jazz at Lincoln Center's four main objectives as curatorial, educational, archival, and, what is most important for my analysis, "ceremonial: [to] maintain and revive when necessary the great ceremonies of jazz. . . . We also seek to establish and maintain our own ceremonies."[47] The Diet Coke Women in Jazz Festival is a new national ceremony enacting the ritual remarginalization and re-*lite*-ization of women in jazz, year after year. As the Miller recreation enacted the exemplary archetype of the white male nation, the annual Diet Coke Women in Jazz in Dizzy's Club Coca-Cola provides the exemplary archetype of women perpetually existing outside of jazz. Such a "ceremony" establishes the "truth" of jazz from which all curatorial, educational, and archival endeavors then spring.

"Improvisation has its rules."— *Wynton Marsalis*

In the case of Jazz at Lincoln Center, a coherent image of jazz is perpetually recreated and what does not fit this idea is, by definition, aberrant. But what else is improvisation if not a play between recreation and aberration? A playing that takes what has been said before and "finesses" it? In the introduction to her book, *Undoing Gender*, Judith Butler proposes a way to understand human agency in the wake of psychoanalytic and poststructuralist revelations on subjectivity. Both the metaphor for her chapter title, "Acting in Concert," and her primary answer to where agency can be found, in improvisation, are deeply musical, although Butler herself does not address musical performance as a site of the doing and undoing of identity. Describing gender as "a practice of improvisation within a scene of constraint," she goes on to say that the "possibility of my persistence as an 'I' depends upon my being able to do something with what is done with me" (Butler 2004, 1). Ingrid Monson describes a similar process when she enlists Henry Louis Gates's literary procedure of "repetition with a signal difference" to describe improvisation (Monson 1996, 103). For both Monson (via Gates) and Butler, improvisation turns recreation into aberration; it repeats with a signal difference. Such improvisation recognizes that we cannot deny how we are "constituted, invariably and from the start, by what is before us and outside us" (Butler 2004, 3). Thus, agency is paradoxical, but not impossible. Indeed, such paradox becomes the condition of its possibility.

Certainly, paradox is the condition of possibility at the annual Dizzy's Club Coca-Cola Presents: The Diet Coke Women in Jazz Festival. As mentioned above, women in jazz always face the conundrum of "playing men" when they play jazz, simultaneously writing themselves out as they perform. With the overbearing representational agenda of Jazz at Lincoln Center, one understandable option for women is to avoid the festival and the inscription it makes regarding the status of women and jazz and find other venues and means of expression. Many of the most exciting women improvisers are not within JALC's conservative aesthetic anyway, and, for those who are, women's jazz festivals created by women[48] provide another option as well as the various other (men's) jazz festivals and other gigs that musicians scrap for. Jazz at Lincoln Center is hardly the only gig in town; however, because it is working to establish the national and sanctioned "face" of jazz, foregoing such a venue does assure an even more certain invisibility for women in the jazz master narrative as it is presently being written.

Therefore, it is not surprising that women jazz musicians do aspire to perform at Jazz at Lincoln Center, even if in a separate festival under the sponsorship of Diet Coke. Those women who do secure the opportunity to improvise within JALC's scene of constraint, however, generally lack a desire to highlight their gender doings and undoings, and repeat a common refrain: "I am a musician, not a woman musician."[49] Although the sentiment is understandable given the difficulties and discrimination women instrumentalists face, the lack of recognition of how social worlds *read* them as women musicians (whether they want to call themselves that or not) leads to the inevitable performance of in-passing and the performative (re)marginalization of women in jazz. Without acknowledgement of (the repetition of) gender constraints, there is no foundation to begin to improvise it, to riposte with an "eloquence of aberrance" that is unexpected, new, and refreshing. This is not to belittle the significant musical skills of these musicians. But if improvisation has its rules, they are definitely playing by Marsalis's, and, I assert, are not yet improvising at the highest level.[50] If musical performance is always concurrent with gender, sexuality, and race performance, the most spectacular of our contemporary improvisers may be those whose improvisational range spans the widest. Although there is not enough space to go into detail, I can offer at least a few examples of such artists. Trombonist Abbie Conant consciously performs gender as well as startlingly original trombone and vocal work in her and composer William Osborne's musical theater pieces.[51] The all-female Led Zeppelin tribute band, Lez Zeppelin, provides an exhilarating example of repetition/aberration by recreating "cock rock" in all its titsy glory.[52] Many examples of Butleresque improvisers can be found in theatre, including the work of Anna Deavere Smith and the theater troupe Culture Clash. Dorinne Kondo has described how such artists renarrate U.S. history and complicate identity as they physically embody different races, classes, genders, ethnicities, and even species, performing plurality and complexity, rather than identity and "History."[53]

In the many ways in which "jazz" is typically mobilized, however, the types of improvisation seen in musicians like Conant, rockers like Lez Zeppelin, and theater artists like Smith and Culture Clash will not be

listed under "what we call jazz." Although he claims he is always searching for new ways to "reinvigorate" the institution, the inclusion of such
improvisation into the JALC line up is not the type of revitalization
Marsalis would promote. Routinely criticized for being too musically
mainstream, it is of no great surprise that JALC asserts conservative, fixed
views of race and gender as well.[54] What is interesting is that the conception of improvisation underlies both. Although Marsalis is ceaseless
in his discussions of improvisation, his tendency is to forge, consolidate,
and replay fixed ideas of jazz, masculinity, and blackness.[55]

CONCLUSION

Although I have argued that the image Marsalis assembles around "jazz"
has more to do with the trope of black masculine hipness than "Jazz as
Democracy," the latter remains a dominant theme, and not only at JALC.
The concept of Jazz as Democracy, or the related "jazz as utopian site of
human interaction," can be found in various forms in views that go back
decades and continue to pervade conceptions of the music.[56] However, it
is imperative to understand how what is called improvisation is often
none other than Replay masquerading under its cover. Duffy's Glenn
Miller revival is a form of emulative compulsion that is improvisation's
antithesis. However, in the continual contention over the meaning of
jazz, it is important to recognize that what "Jazz" is clearly becoming,
under the aegis of Marsalis, JALC, Ken Burns, etc., is also Replay, improvisation's antithesis.

   Duffy continued his hortatory military pageant as 9/11 and the Second Gulf War changed the course of American history, making the
revivals ever more frighteningly mimetic. As contemporary events generated a new "wartime atmosphere," the Second World War skit's ex-
hortations to heroism merged eerily with present-day calls to "fight for
freedom." At this point, the questions became more obvious: What did
Duffy and his band feel they were (Re)playing as they conjured images
of a heroic war and reenacted a recruitment skit? How does nostalgia
serve to Replay and entrench values that themselves Replay the same
outcomes? And to whose gain? As JALC creates the national spectacle of
the continual recreation of jazz, who gains from the story being told and
who loses? Although repetition and the "ownership" of jazz seem of
little significance compared to the dire consequences of America's martial repeating, the loss of a meaningful and fertile inspiration for the
practice of improvisation in the public imaginary is troubling. Herman

Gray has called the "canonization of [Marsalis's] specific narrative of jazz in the American cultural imagination [a] crucial [element] in the representation of late twentieth-century American society" (Gray 2005, 50). Ultimately, I come to the same conclusion as Gray: that the "continuing political struggles over how jazz is constructed, represented, and positioned [do] matter." Indeed, all of these staged representations matter. Replay as entertainment performs inevitability, predictability, and identity using stereotypical images as its content. Such images form the ground of our imagination and our action: they reconfirm the presumed "changelessness" of our culture: of Western domination, of stereotypes, of conflict. I believe improvisation can be an antidote to Replay, but only if its edges are continually expanded to include all the types of "aberration" found on our various cultural and musical stages. Through such representations and practices we can perhaps begin to move away from the predictable and deleterious outcomes we have been repeating now for some time.

NOTES

I would like to thank Norman Bryson, Andy Fry, Lisa Lowe, Nichole T. Rustin, and Sherrie Tucker for supplying generous commentary, guidance, and inspiration in the writing of this essay. I also heartily thank Stephanie Hubbard, Yale Band's business manager, for her untiring assistance as I perused the Yale Band archive and pestered her with follow-up questions.

1. Stephanie Hubbard, interview, September 14, 2006. The evening's performance was entitled "Newsreel: Yale Remembers World War II" and included "The Star-Spangled Banner" arranged by Igor Stravinsky, "Salute to the Armed Forces," Gershwin's "An American in Paris," and Sousa's "Hands across the Sea," among others. The Glenn Miller radio reenactment included "American Patrol"; "At Last"; "The Volga Boatman"; "Rhapsody in Blue"; the "Anvil Chorus"; Radio Script: "Uncle Sam's Armorers" from the radio broadcast of June 5, 1943; "In the Mood", "Moonlight Serenade"; and NBC Radio Broadcast, December 1944 (announcing the disappearance of Miller's plane over the English Channel). The recruitment skit featured the work of armorers and began with one of the two main characters singing, "I've got bombs that go jingle jangle jingle." In this chapter I will set the enlistment skit aside and only obliquely address the particularly martial quality of the event.

2. On museal culture see especially Andreas Huyssen, *Present Pasts: Urban Palimpsests and the Politics of Memory* (Stanford: Stanford University Press, 2003).

3. Thomas Duffy used all ten cornet and trumpet players from the Yale Band in the recreation, alternating them into the big band's five slots for each performance. This ac-

counts for the higher number of women in the trumpet section. This personnel break-down is representative of subsequent recreations of the "Glenn Miller AAFTTC Band" over the next ten years, i.e., predominantly white and male with a few racial minorities and women.

4. Sherrie Tucker notes how in the Swing Era "skilled women musicians were described as cross-dressers of sorts: 'the female Louis Armstrong' or 'a Gene Krupa in girls' clothes" (Tucker 2002a, 294). Elsewhere she describes the attempt by Anita O'Day to substitute her sequined gown with a suit, hoping "that the costume change would result in her being 'treated like another musician' instead of as a 'trinket' to 'decorate the bandstand.'" O'Day had to desist when she "was perceived as sexually suspect and worthy of rumors" (Tucker 2000, 57). On O'Day, see also Erenberg 1998, 200.

5. Harris and Piper address the painful and complicated experience of women of color "passing" as white and being exposed to or asked to participate in derogatory and racist remarks perpetrated by white people. Harris theorizes how "whiteness" takes on valuable property status in racist America, while Piper develops methods to intentionally "not pass," gently alerting acquaintances of her subjectivity as a woman of color who has been injured by their racism. Cheryl I. Harris, "Whiteness as Property," *Harvard Law Review* 106, no. 8 (1993): 1707–91; Adrian Piper, "My Calling (Card) #1 (for Dinners and Cocktail Parties)" [meta-performance, 1986–90]; "Passing for White, Passing for Black," *Transition* 58 (1992): 4–32; Halberstam 1998.

6. It is important to acknowledge the differences between racial passing and gender passing. Whereas racial passing almost always entails lesser or greater anguish, "gender-crossers" often experience great pleasure in "passing."

7. Musical examples would include tribute concerts (to John Coltrane or Louis Armstrong, just to name the most recent examples on the JALC schedule), cover tunes, cover bands, and tribute bands.

8. Quoted from a director I worked with in 2000. The word "tits" was not used, rather the director held his hands in front of his chest as if holding two melons and swayed them from side to side. I'm guessing that "tits" is the word he would have chosen, or perhaps "knockers."

9. Erenberg 1998, 11.

10. Benny Goodman and Irving Kolodin, *Kingdom of Swing* (New York: F. Ungar, 1939), 171.

11. This is not to diminish the fact that Goodman grew up poor in the Jewish ghetto of Southside Chicago. Starting in his preteens, Goodman visited black clubs in the Southside to absorb the music there. However, Goodman was obviously considered a white musician, and his desire to align himself with the more swinging black music seems palpable. That his Jewish identity was not a part of his image is clear by the fact that the clarinetist Dave Tarras was billed at the time as the "Jewish Benny Goodman."

12. Dylan Foley, Michael Sofranski, and Edward Field, "The Last Bohemians," images and interviews with Westbeth residents and artists, New York City, 2006 [art installation]. Quote taken from Patti Bown wall panel.

13. A typical quote from a letter to *Downbeat* asks: "Who knows the names of any of the men in Sammy Kaye's band or even if they are men?" (quoted in Erenberg 1998, 77). For more on *Downbeat* and the signification of women as "not jazz," see Tucker 2000 and Tucker 2001–2.

14. The African American pianist Teddy Wilson joined Goodman's onstage trio in 1936, before the integration of major league baseball and the armed services. I do not investigate the extent to which integration hurt Goodman's mass appeal; however, considering that the military itself was still not integrated, the thought of rallying around an integrated band simultaneously symbolizing the unity of America and the fighting troops seems a social impossibility.

15. Songs like "Kalamazoo" and "People like You and Me," among many others, represented America as white, middle class, and rural. For more on swing music of the Second World War era and Office of War Information, see Tucker 2000. Like most white bandleaders, Miller occasionally had black arrangers.

16. Robert Ronzello, "Glenn Miller at Yale." From the Yale University Band Glenn Miller Recreation Archive, 1994.

17. The AAFTTC became the AAFTC when the technical training and the flight training units combined under one authority.

18. This history of Glenn Miller at Yale (presented in this and the following paragraph) is taken from U.S. Army Air Force, "A History of the 418th Army Air Forces Band of the Technical School of the Army Air Forces Technical Training Command Stationed at Yale University, New Haven, Conn." From the Yale University Band Glenn Miller Recreation Archive, 1943.

19. Ibid., 21; Robert Ronzello, "Glenn Miller at Yale," Yale University Band Glenn Miller Recreation Archive, 6; Freeman quoted in Ronzello, "Glenn Miller at Yale," 5.

20. After decades of speculation about bad weather and improper plane maintenance, new evidence introduced in 1985 suggested that Miller's plane was downed by unused ordnance dropped over the channel by returning Allied planes. See Joseph Gustaitis, "Glenn Miller," *American History Magazine*, April 2001, 31–74. Clipping from the Yale University Band Glenn Miller Recreation Archive.

21. The band was awarded the first ever gold record in 1942 for selling more than a million copies of its hit "Chattanooga Choo-Choo" and was America's most popular band from 1939 to 1942 (Erenberg 1998, 188).

22. Immersed in identity, Duffy remarked that he would *not* fly over the English Channel when the band was in Europe, as if his conjuring were begging the mimesis to unfold of itself. Interview with Thomas Duffy, September 18, 2005.

23. Although blacks fought in segregated units, Civil War re-creators deny the actuality that blacks and whites often found themselves fighting side by side in the chaos of the battlefield or that some women also fought. As I will discuss below, authenticity in re-creation is derived from "exemplary archetypes," not particularities.

24. For an interesting discussion on the controversy surrounding Maya Lin's Vietnam War Memorial as it relates to universality, plurality, and the "gash that would not heal," see Lisa Lowe, *Immigrant Acts: On Asian American Cultural Politics* (Durham: Duke University Press, 1996), 4.

25. Fredric Jameson, *Postmodernism: or, the Cultural Logic of Late Capitalism*, (Durham: Duke University Press, 1991), 25.

26. Lowe, *Immigrant Acts*, 13.

27. Lowe stresses that this applies to other immigrants of color as well; however, her particular analysis is of the complexities of Asian immigration.

28. Yale students made jokes during rehearsals for a performance in 2004 about how the "real" Glenn Miller orchestra would not display its Yamaha brand instruments, or, as one student remarked tangentially, have any African or Asian Americans (interview with Clinton Cave, Yale participant in 2004, August 24, 2005).

29. Again, this is a reference to Lowe, *Immigrant Acts*, 4.

30. At the time of this writing Duffy was still the titular band director. He has been on leave from the band since 2005, however, while serving as acting dean of the Yale School of Music.

31. Quoted in Ann Devroy and John F. Harris, "Clinton to Confront Echoes of Reagan on Normandy Trip," *Washington Post*, May 20, 1994, A1.

32. Robin Pogrebin, "New Home for Jazz Gets Mixed Reviews," *New York Times*, January 24, 2006.

33. Nate Chinen, "Jazz in America, to the Beat of a Smooth One-Man Band," *New York Times*, August 27, 2006.

34. Nathaniel Mackey, *Discrepant Engagement: Dissonance, Cross-Culturality, and Experimental Writing* (Tuscaloosa: University of Alabama Press, 2000), 1993.

35. Marsalis came under the intensified scrutiny of jazz scholars after the release of Ken Burns's nineteen-hour documentary *Jazz* in 2001. Marsalis, Crouch, and Murray, along with Geoffrey Ward, were clearly the ideological force behind the documentary, which has been critiqued for its overbearing epic narrative, "Great Man" thesis, conservatism, gender bias, and more. See Scott Deveaux, "Struggling with 'Jazz,'" *Current Musicology* 71–73 (2001–2): 353–74; Krin Gabbard, "Ken Burns's 'Jazz:' Beautiful Music, but Missing a Beat," *Chronicle of Higher Education* 47, no. 16 (December 15, 2000): B, 18–19; Jacques, Tucker, DeVeaux, Gabbard, and Gendron 2001; Laura Macy, "Ken Burns' Jazz: A Discussion with Scott

Deveaux and Krin Gabbard," http://www.grovemusic.com/ grove-owned/music/feature_
jazz/jazz01.htm, accessed May 6, 2006; Steven F. Pond, "Jamming the Reception: Ken Burns,
Jazz, and the Problem of 'America's Music,' " *Notes (Music Library Association)* (2003): 11–5;
Porter 2002; Ronald Radano, "Myth Today: The Color of Ken Burns Jazz," *Black Renais-
sance/Renaissance Noire* 3, no. 3 (2001): 42–56; Tucker 2001–2.

36. In an important article, Ingrid Monson details white fascination with black masculinity in a pursuit of "white hipness" and the influence this fascination has on jazz
historical discourse. See Monson 1995.

37. For example, see Stanley Crouch, *The Artificial White Man* (New York: Basic Civitas,
2004).

38. Marlboros, because the rival manufacturer KOOL is staking a claim for black smokers in
its rap-oriented and hip hop–oriented campaign featuring young men of color DJing or
working the recording studio — although KOOL's annual concert tour *is* called "New Jazz
Philosophy," and one of its ads features a young black man in dreads on the street with his
trumpet and the exhortation "Be authentic."

39. Herman Leonard, *The Eye of Jazz: The Jazz Photographs of Herman Leonard* (London:
Viking, 1985).

40. The journal was available at Barnes and Noble, along with several posters from the
Second World War era and a CD compilation produced by Gene Lees of the musicians
who had ostensibly performed there, including Charlie Parker, Miles Davis, Bud Powell,
Billie Holiday, Sarah Vaughan, and Dizzy Gillespie. Many who saw the Aerobleu para-
phernalia assumed that the nightclub existed and indeed initially the marketers encouraged this confusion. In 2005 many websites did not mention the nightclub's fictional
status, or if they did, it was buried deep in the text. There was even a clarification on
answers.com telling readers that indeed, the nightclub was a figment of the entrepreneur
Brooks Branch's imagination. The restaurateur Steve Schussler was fooled. Seeing an
Aerobleu poster in a record shop, he was inspired to create themed restaurants around the
recreation of the nightclub. In true Baudrillardian fashion, he seemed even more excited
when he found out the club was faked and his simulacra would thus be based on pure
simulacrum. The first Aerobleu was scheduled to open in Las Vegas in 2007; however, the
perhaps overambitious Schussler has had troubles financing the venture. References to
Aerobleu on the web now all acknowledge that the nightclub was fictionalized. See David
Farkas, "Creative Habitat: Steven Schussler's T-Rex Is Just the Beginning of the Concepts Coming out of His Idea Lab," 2006, http://www.chainleader.com/web-exclusives/
schussler.asp., accessed October 1, 2006.

41. Stephen Thomas Erlewine, *All Music Guide Review* (2004), http://www.music.com/
release/aerobleu:_the_spirit_of_cool/1/, accessed September 26, 2006.

42. Chris Kelsey, "Wynton and Louis Armstrong's Hot Fives," 2006, *JazzTimes.com*,
http://jazztimes.com/reviews/concert_reviews/detail.cfm?article=10412, accessed January 10, 2007.

43. John Schaefer, "Wynton Marsalis on Louis Armstrong," *Soundcheck* (WNYC, 2006).

44. It was actually written in 2005 for the inaugural festival by Derek E. Gordon, then president and CEO of Jazz at Lincoln Center. It was dusted off again for the second and appears to be the unstated "theme" of the festival, i.e., confusion, or "How *do* we deal with these women?"

45. Lara Pellegrinelli first highlighted the absence of women musicians at JALC, and it could very well be in response to her writing that the organization created its Women in Jazz Festival. See Pellegrinelli 2000.

46. Sherrie Tucker has a very important article addressing just this conundrum of "women in jazz" (Tucker 2006). Inspired by Norma Coates's work on women in rock (in Whiteley 1997, 50–64), Tucker argues that the margin "women-in-jazz" is a site of potential in its liminal, undecidable, and unlocatable positionality.

47. Jazz at Lincoln Center website, http://www.jalc.org, accessed February 1, 2007.

48. For example, The Many Colors of a Woman Festival in Hartford; the Lady Got Chops Festival at the Jazz Spot in Brooklyn; and the Women's Vocal Series at the Cornelia Street Cafe in downtown Manhattan. These festivals were featured in Bill Milkowski, "Celebrating Their Own: Three Women Jazz Musicians Turned Producers Organize Their Own Grassroots Jazz Festivals," *Jazziz* 21, no. 7 (2004): 60–62.

49. Women's resistance to being considered "women musicians," and indeed to the idea of women's jazz festivals, has been productively documented and analyzed in Tucker 2004a and Ajay Heble and Gillian Siddall, "Nice Work If You Can Get It: Women in Jazz," in Heble 2000, 141–65.

50. Women have to constantly prove that they are "real" musicians, and in describing the moves of in-passing and Replay, I am in part trying to explain the processes of women's perpetual marginalization. For another take on the struggle of women to be accepted as real jazz musicians, see particularly Tucker 2002a, 303–8, and Tucker 2000, 56–57.

51. For more on the work of Conant and Osborne see William Osborne and Abbie Conant, http://www.osborne-conant.org/index.html, accessed October 1, 2006.

52. See *Lez Zeppelin* 2006; http://lezzeppelin.com, accessed October 1, 2006.

53. Dorinne Kondo, "(Re)visions of Race: Contemporary Race Theory and the Cultural Politics of Racial Crossover in Documentary Theatre," *Theatre Journal* 52 (2000): 105.

54. Marsalis's views of race are much more complex than his views on gender. Gray discusses this complexity and how it relates to Marsalis's project in Gray 2005. My point is that in JALC's reduction of jazz to a simplified commodity, its image of jazz becomes aligned with certain stereotypical notions of black masculinity.

55. Marsalis's tendency to forge fixed ideas of jazz is also a central point in Herman Gray's chapter. Whereas Gray describes Wynton's approach as a "canonical project" and advo-

cates "the road and the street" metaphor for conceptualizing the jazz tradition, I describe Wynton as participating in the larger cultural obsession of Replay, something which is the antithesis of the potentialities found in improvisation.

56. For example, in the 1920s jazz was conceived as a "primitivist" antidote to cold Western overintellectualism; in the 1940s it was hailed as a site of racial uplift; and in the 1950s it was sent overseas by the government as a model of democracy. Many current scholars advocate jazz and improvisation as models of democratic interaction. For an excellent anthology on this thought see Fischlin and Heble 2004.

PART II

Improvising Gender:

Embodiment and Performance

Jayna Brown

FROM THE POINT OF VIEW OF THE PAVEMENT:

A GEOPOLITICS OF BLACK DANCE

Artistic expression "from the point of view of the pavement" marks the archetypal experience of modernity.[1]
The figure of the flaneur, dodging rush hour traffic through the streets of the bustling metropole, resonates
throughout the works of cultural critics concerned with the
accelerated rhythm of living and its effects on the senses. The
artist is Baudelaire's poet, the drifting young man, scribbling in
a tattered notebook, sipping coffee in a crowded café. "He"
(the artist is always a *man*) lives a leisurely *vie moderne*, in the
midst of it all, subjecting himself to the bewildering sensorium
of the urban jungle.[2]

According to some definitions of flanerie, modern artistic
expression is defined by an epistemological shift in perspective.
The flaneur gathers his impressions "as latently filmic texts."[3]
This shift in perspective may be visual, but it is also sensorial,
physical. It is not only language but also movement and gesture
that purvey the city's textures. To survive in the city's streets,
the "agglomeration of mass and energy that is heavy, fast and
lethal [and] imposes its tempo on everybody's time," the artist
"must become adept at *soubresauts* and *mouvements brusques*, at
sudden, abrupt, jagged twists and shifts — and not only with his
legs and body, but with his mind and sensibility as well."[4] Although the force of modern technology reshapes the poem,
which becomes supple, fluid, immediate, I suggest that articulations of the modern world are just as readily generated

through other aesthetic vocabularies, through kinetic, haptic, and aural forms of expressivity articulated in and between bodies and locations.

The physical language of dance is a close fit to the urge within critical revisions of flanerie, as it is based on such embodied interaction with the urban environment. Dance scholar Ramsay Burt uses the figure of the flaneur as a useful point of departure, arguing for proper acknowledgement of dance as a modern art form. The celebrated Polish/Russian ballet dancer, Vaslav Nijinsky, he tells us, risked visits to the dives and dance halls of New York City during the 1910s. There he observed black dancers with admiration and brought versions of their dances, such as the Texas Tommy and the Turkey Trot, to the legitimate concert stage. Nijinsky's acts of flanerie were his journeys into the forbidden zones of the city and his poetic interpretation of what he found there. His excursions were like a colonial's journey of discovery in unexplored lands. Black dancers remain nameless, their dancing instinctual, providing the raw material to be molded by Nijinsky's interpretive genius. The music and dance of black people in the cities were soon understood as the pulse of the new age, yet black dancers were continually denied artistic and intellectual interiority.

If "the point of view of the pavement" constitutes the privileged vantage point for modern experience, then working-class black dancers, including those who did not perform for a living, were not merely parts of the hustle and bustle of the modern city but subjects in motion, situated at an advantage for accessing a modernist perspective. They formed their compositions from daily contact with the hustling roadways as they worked the service sectors of the city. Their world is part of a larger set of black diasporic experiences. The constant dislocation, multilocation, and relocation of African peoples around the globe can be described as "to be away from home and yet feel oneself everywhere at home; to see the world, to be at the centre of the world and yet to remain hidden from the world."[5] As the industrializing cities grew, many working-class black people chose the itinerant life of the stage, as it often paid more and offered more independence than life in service. During the same period as Nijinsky's collecting excursions, professional black dancers also expanded their repertoire as they toured the major cities in Europe, Asia, and America. My central point here is that it is not a stretch to recognize black dancers as flaneurs and their bodies' phraseology as flanerie. Considering black people as central agents of artistic interpretation defining modernity opens up the possibility for more finely tuned and sensitive attention to what black dancers compose in their fluid, shifting, constantly moving art. I am looking at dance from 1890 to 1930 here, but such consideration can be useful for examinations of black dance at any historical juncture.

Dancers were acutely watchful. In the 1900s, while living in St. Petersburg and Moscow, Ida Forsyne composed her own interpretation of the Russian peasant dances. "When I got to Russia, I looked especially for heavy women . . . I stole all the steps I could. I liked Russian dancing so much as I wanted to be different than most colored performers . . . I wanted to do a different kind of act," she recalled.[6] 'Stealing' is essential when it comes to expressive arts, yet what is different about Ida's appropriations, I argue, is that they enacted a correlation between the migratory experiences of black people in the United States and the emerging proletariat in Russia as she brought the dances of the former serfs to the center of the new metropolis. Forsyne connected with the rigor of the dances, commenting on how demanding they were and how much discipline they required: "You can't just get up and say, 'I'm going to do Russian dancing.' You can't come up out of a gin mill and do a Russian dance. It's a very strenuous dance."[7]

In New York of the 1920s, the Savoy Ballroom dancer Shorty Snowden was also acutely watchful. He explained the artistic philosophy of his choreography as a state of constant observation, in which he scouted "for anyone dancing in the street or just walking or doing anything that suggests a step."[8]

When we pay attention to the intellectual interiority of black expressive cultures and acknowledge black dancers (vernacular and concert hall professionals) as conscious interpreters, we see that artistic interiority need not be the privilege of the leisure classes. It is not based solely in the individualistic model of the western artist, the lone private thinker. The consideration of black dance that I am describing demands that we understand an interiority that is collective and dialogic. Artistic impressions are perspectives created between peoples, by bodies in motion together. This interiority is the movement between aloneness and communality, between "I" and others in conversation and contact.

THE BLACK FEMALE FLANEUR

Feminist scholars concerned with the formations of modernity offer criticisms of the "explicitly gendered" definition of the modern subject. Women, as Rita Felski writes, were "situated outside processes of history and social change." In their search for models with which to recuperate a female flaneur, feminist critiques look to the actress and the prostitute, women with access to the streets of the nineteenth-century city.[9] But critics such as Felski have argued that despite their presence in the public spaces of the city, working women were not considered artistic interpreters according to the masculinist and middle-class normative model of the modern subject. "True artists" were thought to be governed by the mind and soul, whereas working women were socially defined solely by their physicality. As many feminist interventions point out, women were not seen as modern subjects at all, since "[the] woman embodied a sphere of atemporal authenticity seemingly untouched by the alienation and fragmentation of modern life."[10] Their bodies took on meaning only as products for use and exchange. Although subjecthood was male, women were creatures governed by their emotions, drives, and instincts; they could take impressions but only passively, and they could only mimic. Their bodies were constructed as permeable, understood as yielding to outside meanings in a way the male flaneurs' bodies were not.

Women were particularly available to the world of eyes encountered in the city, as the streets and avenues formed a hall of mirrors in which they were forced to see themselves reflected. "Women see themselves here more than elsewhere," writes Susan Buck-Morss. "Before a man looks at them they have already seen themselves reflected ten times."[11] Taking the analyses of these critics, one would assume that women had no recourse to creative response, no available interpretive strategy. Penned in by oppressive circumstance and the power of such discursive claims, contained by her own reflection in the hall of mirrors and walls of eyes, a woman had limited or no avenues by which to assert her particular viewpoint, her own impressions.

A set of assumptions about the racial and class position of the women who are recuperable as agents of history is housed within the feminist critiques of modernity. They could not be working women, and certainly not black working women. To be a black working woman was to be a nonsubject, purely a body for hire. Anke Gleber contends that proletarian women could not be considered flaneurs, as "the street presented itself to them as a space of transition en route to functional purposes."[12] She argues that the working woman's time was so tightly bounded by duty that she lacked the necessary idle time for poetic reverie. But I question this argument. Considering the time the working woman spent navigating through the city streets, dodging traffic, one might also argue that her perspective on the streets, her sense of the ironies, the cruelty and beauty of the city, and its rhythms — offered views to which the idling white male could never claim access. I contend that for black working women, the spheres of work and artistry informed each other, and the body's labors remained available in both.

At home nowhere and everywhere, black women dancers' modernist renderings were transnational and diasporic. From the mid-1900s up until the time that the First World War broke out in Europe, a community of African American women artists were living and performing in St. Petersburg, touring their acts throughout Russia and Eastern Europe. This community was fostered by a young dancer named Ida Forsyne with her close friends Ollie Bourgoyne and Laura Bowman. Forsyne and Bourgoyne were seasoned variety performers; both had worked since they were children in such important turn-of-the-century troupes as Black Patti's Troubadors. Bowman is best known for appearing in Bert Williams's and George Walker's successful play *In Dahomey*, which ran for six months in London in 1903. This community thrived during a period called the Silver Age of theater in Russia. This was a period of emergence for Russian actresses on the dramatic stage. The urban sphere opened to women, who traversed the streets with new strides.[13] "City living undermined folk customs and weakened traditional family ties, releasing not only women, but children too from the chastening bonds of patriarchal authority," writes Laura Engelstein. "The result was sexual as well as social chaos, the emergence of a new public space inhabited by female creatures with the independence and energy of men."[14]

The flaneur must travel to gather impressions and interpret other worlds. The dancer Ida Forsyne understood the importance of mobility and of expanding one's perspective. She implored other African Americans to "go see something and learn something about the world." Forsyne learned various languages, including Norwegian and Russian. "I went all over. I practiced everyday. I'd have my breakfast and got to the theatre and do a regular act." She toured separately from her husband, the singer Usher Watts. "I was married but I wasn't gonna let him hold me back . . . I went on tour by myself."[15] Ida Forsyne, Laura Bowman, and other performers working out of St. Petersburg would return briefly to the States together following the outbreak of the Russo-Japanese War and the Bloody Sunday uprising of 1905. When the Russo-Japanese War swept near the city, foreigners were warned off the streets and encouraged to leave. "We had special permission to leave, accompanied by the consul and a guard of soldiers who accompanied us all the way to the train and saw to it that we got on," Bowman recounted. She remembered the interchanges held on the train, as they left Russia. "[On the train] one old lady insisted on talking and knowing our history, which Ida and Ollie were telling. They both spoke perfect Russian. When news got out we were on our way to America . . . everybody wanted to ask us a hundred questions. We left that to Ida. She seemed to enjoy it immensely." With Forsyne acting as interpreter, Bowman was able to describe to the Russian passengers the sad sight of soldiers going off to the front and women and children running after them in the streets. Forsyne's skills were essential at the border, where she helped the others negotiate their passports. "We were very lucky to have Ida to interpret," Bowman remembered.[16] They returned to Europe together, in the early part of 1906. Such lost histories give us a quite different model of flanerie, which was created by a group of intellectually and artistically curious young black working women who were itinerant by choice and proclivity. These flaneurs consciously formed a creative community far from "home."

When the First World War broke out in Europe in 1914, Bowman and Forsyne returned to the United States. Ida Forsyne's reentry proved a more difficult transition. Times had changed and she had a hard time finding steady work. "After 1914 I starved to death," she states. "They wanted light-skinned girls . . . when I got back I couldn't get a job nowhere. I wasn't used to the way performers had to do in cabarets here. They used to have to go to the tables and mingle with the audience or do a shake dance at their tables. In Europe there was none of this." For Forsyne, one event underscored particularly the tragedy of her situation at home. Leaving a disastrous appearance in Cleveland, Forsyne sold her signature pair of leather boots, handcrafted for her in Russia, to a vaudevillian performer while on the train to New York. Then Forsyne had to turn to domestic work. "I'd never learned to make beds, cook — couldn't even wash out a handkerchief because I'd never had to but when I got back things were different . . . I got a job dusting furniture at $15 a week and did this for four and a half years." Like many other black women performers, Forsyne had to fuse her domestic work with her stage work. By 1922 Ida Forsyne was working for the Jewish vaudevillian and coon-shouter Sophie Tucker, acting the part of personal maid both on and off stage.[17]

The politics of racial segregation in the United States adds a second layer of awareness to the mouvements brusques of African American people in and around the city streets. In the face of legal and de facto laws that policed their physical movement, black people developed agility, a nimble ability to make it through and around particular zones of the city. Racialized workers had to know the lobbies, dining halls, the luxurious fronts of the city as one did the front area of a stage. They had to have a diligent knowledge of prohibited zones and their hours, know the back stairs, back doors, delivery gates, elevators, restaurant kitchen enclaves, and alleys. These physical experiences of the modern world are also a part of what is articulated through African American dance practices. The particular forms of alienation experienced by African American working people located in the urban terrain, simultaneously marginalized and central (segregated to the *mauvais lieu*, but staffing the service sectors of the city), gave them a necessary perspective, both inside and outside of the rhythms of the city.

Taking into account the physical experience of racial segregation, the places and the moments in which it is negotiated and solidified, helps us to develop a wider definition of performance, inclusive of interactive, dramaturgical, and gestural strategies taking place outside the stage and the cabaret. The laws and rituals of segregation impacted the experience of U.S. city space, leaving a historical palimpsest in concrete and asphalt. Scholars such as Mike Davis, for example, have allowed us to think about the insane and often bloody choreographies of racial zoning ordering city space (in Davis's case, post-Watts Los Angeles).[18] The histories of continual protest and resistance staged in contested urban sites form a kind of counter choreography and impact how we conceive of urban spaces in the earlier part of the twentieth century. As Robin Kelley's work shows, this includes African American people's protest of segregated seating on interstate and municipal buses and their violation of segregation laws in public facilities. Kelley gives an eloquent argument for the history of daily practices of resistance on public transportation and on the job, as well as for African American people's claims to leisure space and time.[19] Both Davis and Kelley insist that we consider the practices of resistance to hazing and zoning laws, such as streetcar boycotts and marches, as central to the formation of urban life.

African American dance offers an impressionistic rendering of rush hour city traffic, in the mouvements brusques of the tap, shuffle, hop, and slide steps that form twentieth-century black dance choreographies. The rush hour traffic did not involve black people in the same way as it did the white-collar workers of the city. Most black people were barred from the workday rhythms that caused it. In the 1910s and 1920s, African Americans were prohibited from most trade unions and from most industrial and white-collar jobs. African American variety performers were not accepted into the White Rats, the union of vaudevillian performers. Black people therefore had the "privilege" of observing traffic from a distance. African American city dwellers were outside of this set of rhythms; yet, often working as maids, cooks, kitchen scullions, bellhops, janitors, and street cleaners, they were supremely situated in the midst of traffic.

New York City was not an "open city." As the skyline was drawn so was the color line; as each towering edifice was built, so were its territories racially zoned and policed. Yet the sections of the city likened to "darkest Africa" were essential to what made this city modern and cosmopolitan. James Weldon Johnson, in his book *Black Manhattan*, develops a history of Harlem (keeping the name given it by the Dutch people who had settled there) positioning it at the center of the archetypal twentieth-century metropolis. "Harlem is not a section that one 'goes out to,' but a section that one goes through," he writes. "In nearly every city in the country the Negro section is a nest or several nests situated somewhere on the borders; it is a section one must 'go out to.' Negro Harlem is situated in the heart of Manhattan and covers one of the most beautiful and *healthful* sites in the whole city. It is not a fringe, it is not a slum, nor is it a 'quarter' consisting of dilapidated tenements."[20] Written in the midst of the Depression, Johnson's words may reflect the anxious aspiration of a black middle class to dissociate themselves, in the eyes of white city dwellers, from negative depictions of their race. But he is also asserting the presence and place of African Americans at the center of the modern world.

Johnson humorously describes white fears of the African American "invasion" of uptown Manhattan in the 1910s. In depicting the irrational fears of the white inhabitants of Harlem, Johnson uses the metaphor of the larger social body to reveal the pathology of racial relations in the United States. He also uses this metaphor to describe the zeal of African Americans buying property in Harlem, for whom such resettlement "became a contagious fever."[21] "Colored people not only continued to move into apartments outside the zone east of Lenox

Avenue, but began to purchase the fine private houses between Lenox and Seventh Avenue. Then in the eyes of the whites who were antagonistic, the whole movement took on the aspect of an 'invasion,'" Johnson writes. "Seeing that they could not stop the movement, they began to flee. They took flight, they became panic-stricken, they ran amuck." Johnson compares the behavior of white people "to that of a community in the Middle Ages fleeing before an epidemic of the black plague, except that their reasons were not so sound. . . . The stampeding whites actually deserted house after house and block after block."[22] Johnson's analogy draws attention to the short history of civilization in Europe. He draws an ironic parallel between African Americans and the historic struggles of colonized peoples elsewhere on the globe, invaded in their own lands by bands of white marauders.

African American creative response to urban space contrasts with the Benjaminian vision of the individual city dweller, experiencing poetic alienation as he strolls aimlessly through the city. In this rendering, the artist is estranged from the crowds of people, his distance the source of his artistic perspective. African American vernacular dance develops from a very different concept of being in a crowd, of the use of city space between strangers. They situated themselves as members of a crowd in particularly creative ways, in their use of public space within their own territories, and their collective incursions in hostile terrain, those areas redlined as off-limits. African American people navigate many types of crowds, face violent forms of alienation, and experience a variety of forms of self-exile, both together and alone. Black flanerie was also about the creative movements necessary in staking collective claim to city space.

Theater audiences were crowds of a specific kind. Each night's audience composition was a cluster of people organized to participate in the formation of that particular cultural moment. In the United States, a theater audience for a black show was a complicated social formation: some theaters would designate a show or series of shows for a black audience, and a section of the seats could be cordoned off for the white members. Sometimes, if it was a show designated for whites only, the balcony, or a section of the back row seats, could be opened to black audience members. Sometimes these seats were available only to the servants of the white members. These choreographies of proximity — how close black bodies were allowed to be to their white fellows and when — made audience formations complex performances in themselves. Audiences were crowds, but there were many other types of crowds; a theater audience was not the same as a crowd on the street. And the theater was not the only place for black gestural vocabularies to form.

For black people, negotiating through or around a midtown crowd called for mouvements brusques that, like any physical impression, could be folded into an act and brought to a theater. But being a member of a Harlem crowd was another kind of crowd experience. It was often a way to link with others and communicate. In such moments, African Americans forged new connections, often with strangers. As Johnson illustrates, certain "condensational events," moments of collective performance in the city space, were recognition of collective presence and belonging in the city.[23] For the working people of Harlem, strolling on Sundays was an important social event. "Strolling in Harlem does not mean merely walking along Lenox or upper Seventh Avenue or One-Hundred and Thirty-Fifth Street; it means that those streets are places for socializing," Johnson writes. "One puts on one's best clothes and fares forth to pass the time with friends and acquaintances and, most important of all, the strangers he is sure of meeting. . . . This is not simply going out for a walk; it is more like going out for an adventure."[24] African American people's experience of "the crowd," at least in the black zones of the city, was not always one of alienation.

Being a member of a crowd, formed in the midst of a larger hostile environment, was often an experience of collective affirmation. In Harlem, funerals were often held at night so people could attend after work. "Frequently after nightfall a slow procession may be seen wending its way along and a band heard playing a dirge that takes on a deeply sepulchral tone," Johnson describes. "But generally these parades are lively and add greatly to the movement, color, and gaiety of Harlem. A brilliant parade with very good bands is participated in not only by the marchers in line, but also by the marchers on the sidewalk . . . keeping step to the music."[25] The funerals of notable African American artists were particularly freighted events, recognizing both individual and collective African American presence in European and American cultural history. The funeral of the musician James Reese Europe, taking place in Harlem in 1919, was the first officially recognized public funeral held for an African American person in New York City history. The funeral held for the performer Florence Mills in 1927 marks another formative moment of collective experience and territorial recognition in the life of New York's black cultural capital.

Parades and protests were overtly politicized events, orchestrated maneuvers that demanded historical recognition. Claiming the modern cities' streets, celebrated as democratic space, asserting a black presence in this space, the territory of the metropole, was to claim a place in the national civic body and to demand the rights extended to all its citizens by the nation's ideological rhetoric. On July 23, 1917, more than ten thousand African American people participated in a silent march organized by the National Association for the Advancement of Colored People (NAACP), in protest of the bloody East St. Louis massacre. On July 2, the streets of black-populated East St. Louis had been burnt and pillaged by white rioters, who had taken the lives of two hundred black people and burnt down the homes of thousands of others.[26] As the ten thousand protestors marched up Fifth Avenue, they laid a blanket of massive silence along one of the nation's central corridors of culture and power. Silence was a powerful dramaturgical strategy; withholding all contributions of expressive culture forced the political recognition of African Americans' actual collective physical presence. At the close of the First World War, James Reese Europe and his 369th Regiment Band led the return of African American soldiers up the corridor of Fifth Avenue. In formal military step, the returning soldiers wound their way uptown, but at 130th Street, they broke with the military step march as the band struck up the syncopated tune "Here Comes My Daddy Now." The crowd rushed out to welcome the men home to Harlem and to assert that Black manhood would have its rightful place in the public sphere.

THE JAZZ AGE

The connection between the body and geographical environment is central to the deeper meanings of dance. The later dances that typified the 1920s as the Jazz Age were African American dialogues on the physical experience of mobility and displacement. The physical vocabularies of African American dance linked the larger movements of migration and work to internal movements of populations within the city. The dances' polyrhythmic constructions conjoined the timed frequencies of rural life, both remembered and current, with the quicker tempos from the urban environment. City life was articulated by the physical phrasing of dances on the streets, in clubs, and on stage. The fast, frenetic pace of the dances refigured the body's relationship to and in city space. Dances such as the Black Bottom, the Charleston, and the Chicago were about the racial formation of places, about folding a continuation of communal memory into the present terrain. In many dances, there was a synec-dochical relation between the sexualized 'zones' of the body and racially zoned territories of the cities and towns in the United States. According to the anthropologist Zora Neale Hurston, the Black Bottom dance originated in "the jook section of Nashville Tennessee, around 4th Avenue. This is a tough neighborhood called the Black Bottom—hence the name."[27]

Earlier, the steps of the Cakewalk dance in the 1890s were physically demanding, but its strenuous high kicks and flourishes played against and within a stylistic of cool grace and elegance. The organizing prin-ciple of the dance and what it parodied was an oscillating tension be-tween restraint and release. The musical pace was usually a waltz, and the challenge to the dancer was to mask the amount of effort the dance demanded. In the 1910s, new bodily phrases developed in tandem with black musical forms evolving out of enclaves in New Orleans, New York, and Chicago, called "ragtime," a term soon capitalized on by the white music-publishing companies. As the new music developed quicker tempos and syncopated rhythms, so did the dances, closely identified with their musical accompaniment. In contrast with the cakewalk, these new dances were explicit exhibitions of athleticism and physical vir-tuosity. Dancers claimed their bodies' physical exertions away from forms of exploitative labor. Sweat and discipline instead produced per-sonal pleasure and exultation.

In the mid-1920s groups of African American dancers formed a dance culture at the Savoy Ballroom, a block-long dance hall in New York City. In league with jazz musicians working there and at other venues in the city, like Small's Paradise, these dancers organized themselves as an artistic movement, consciously building upon the artistry of the past decades of dancers and musicians, who moved and worked within and between cities. Tuesday nights at the Savoy groups of the best dancers developed the lexicons of movement later called swing. Savoy Ballroom dancer Norma Miller began dancing on the streets outside of the ball-room, where she could hear the music, when she was 14 years old and too young to go in. Once inside, she won a number of contests, and manager George Whitey asked her to join his troupe, Whitey's Lindy Hoppers. Miller became their youngest member. Miller recalls the vi-brancy and collective energy that overflowed the Ballroom. "We . . . danced at the Savoy. We created America's only dance and took it around the world, that was what the Savoy represented. People everywhere are dancing that dance today, and it is because of what we created there." Watching the dancers, listening to their steps, the musicians took cues and would often shape their beats and melodies in relation to the dancers. "We knew all the bands, all the musicians, all the music, all the solos, and all the riffs," recalls Miller. "Even at the Harvest Moon Ball, our first dance outside the Savoy, we danced to Fletcher Henderson's swing band." As Miller explains, the dance and the music were cocreative. Dancers helped shape the music of such great bands as Henderson's, and the music was designed with the dancers. "Dancing the Lindy Hop was a very emotional thing," Norma Miller recalls, "and a good swinging drummer could make you sail through a routine, you never got tired because everything was in synch."[28]

The mouvements brusques developed by the black dancers at the Savoy Ballroom were used to denote the democratic exuberance of America. Some of the work written about swing culture in the United States likes to remember the history of swing as heralding a new era of interracial cooperation and cultural exchange. But I am not so sure that we can read swing as proof that the United States was moving inevitably to its promise of full and inclusive democracy. I cannot think of mass cultural amusements as democratic at the same time as they retained exclusionary policies when it came to black people. "The Savoy Ballroom had a policy of welcoming and encouraging white dancers and spectators," David Stowe writes. Of course, the Savoy welcomed white participants; the managers of the Ballroom would be bad businessmen not to encourage the flow of money that white visitors brought in. But this kind of statement obscures the realpolitik of race in the United States.[29] Stowe does not take into account the historical relationship between black dancers and white entitlement. Saturday night was referred to by the black dancers as "Square's Night," and the dancers would laugh about the white "squares" who came on Saturday nights to gawk. The real dancing was reserved for Tuesday nights.[30] "Integration," physical access to any urban space, was a white privilege. Although the lavish Harvest Ballroom annual competitions, organized from 1936, did allow black couples access, the vast majority of the huge dance marathons held in the United States between 1923 and 1933 were segregated, designated solely for white participants. *Black dancers* could be barred, though *their dances* were always welcome. The Black Bottom, the Charleston, and the Lindy Hop were adopted by the chorus lines of Florenz Ziegfeld's *Follies* and in the marathon dances of the United States and England, where white kids danced themselves to injury and death.[31]

The origin tale of the Lindy Hop states that black dancers named the dance after Charles Lindbergh's flight across the Atlantic in 1927. Although this story is not true, the myth became historical "fact" during a marathon open to black couples begun on June 17, 1928, at the Manhattan Casino. This dance followed a marathon, held for white participants only, at Madison Square Garden.[32] The Manhattan Casino marathon ran for eighteen days until the Board of Health shut it down at 4 a.m. on July 4. Only four couples were left in the competition, among them the renowned Savoy Ballroom dancer George "Shorty" Snowden and his partner, Mattie Purnell.[33] Shorty, his partner, and the other survivors went to the Rockland Palace Ballroom, not far from the Savoy, on another night for a series of short contests for which the audience offered a reward to the final winners. The story goes that Fox Movietone News showed up to cover the marathon and decided to film Shorty's quicksilver feet. Someone asked Shorty to explain what he was doing. "The Lindy Hop," Shorty replied.[34] The remembrance of the dance as springing without history from the feet of a sole male dancer belies how Shorty himself describes the moment. "I was really doing the regular steps, just like we did them at the Savoy, several of us, maybe a little faster," Shorty told Marshall Stearns in an interview. "It was the speed that confused them maybe . . . it was new to them." The dancer Ethel Williams describes the "new" dance as evolving out of the Texas Tommy, a dance that she was part of innovating in the 1910s. "[The Texas Tommy] was like the Lindy," she recalls, "but there was a basic step—a kick and a hop three times on each foot."[35] Shorty acknowledges that this dance was the result of individual as well as group expression. "We used to call the basic step the Hop long before Lindbergh did *his* hop across the Atlantic," Shorty continues. "It had been around a long time and some people began to call it the Lindbergh Hop, after 1927, but it didn't last. Then during the marathon at the Manhattan Casino, I got tired of the same old steps and cut loose with a breakaway. Anything you could dream up was okay for the breakaway, you tried all kinds of things. Everybody did the same starting step, but after that, look out, everybody for himself." Shorty's breakaway was his particular eye on/in the crowd, recorded in his body. "I've put together new steps in the breakaway by slipping and almost falling," Shorty reported. In a photo taken just after their award was given, a beribboned Snowden and Purnell with a triumphant bouquet of flowers pose for the camera (see figures 7.1 and 7.2).

Even as a false tale, the story of the dance as a reference to Lindbergh's

Fig. 7.1. Shorty Snowden and Mattie Purnell. Marshall Stearns Collection, Institute of Jazz Studies, Rutgers University, Newark, New Jersey.

Fig. 7.2. Shorty Snowden and Mattie Purnell. Marshall Stearns Collection, Institute of Jazz Studies, Rutgers University, Newark, New Jersey.

flight has important metaphorical resonance. As the first cross-Atlantic flight in an airplane, Lindbergh's well-funded adventure ushered in a new era of technological progress.[36] The crossing of the Atlantic had stood for advancing progress since the traumatic ship journeys made by Africans in the hulls and bowels of ships during their years of enslaved passage. As C. L. R. James argued, the labor of these black bodies was the necessary condition of modernity itself. The brief reference to this sequence of movements by African Americans, as in honor of this new and exciting moment in global transportation (even as a secondary reference), contained the dialectic of violent dislocation and the inevitable gains made possible by mechanical progress.[37] This dialectic is brought home with particular force considering that Charles Lindbergh, the icon of technological progress and innovation, was a profascist Nazi sympathizer, receiving the Iron Cross from the Führer himself around 1938. Not surprisingly, Lindbergh publicly stated his horror that Negroes may have been dancing in his name.

Later versions of the Lindy Hop were developed in the mid-1930s at the Savoy by dancers such as Pepsi Bethel, Esther Washington, Leon James, and Alfred Minns. These dancers formed an avant-garde, setting the pace for professional and amateur dancers internationally. Some joined the troupes organized by Herbert White. White had been a sergeant in the 369th Division and then a bouncer at the Alhambra Ballroom and the Savoy. According to Al Minns, Whitey was "a semi-gangster with ideals . . . [who] knew more angles than a geometrician."[38] Whitey was an agent to seventy-two dancers, organized in troupes such as the Savoy Hoppers, the Jive-a-Dears, and Whitey's Hopper Maniacs (see figure 7.3).[39]

The later Lindy Hop incorporated what dancers called an "air step," in which the feet left the ground and the body took off from the floor. In acrobatic turns, the partners would flip each other over one another's backs and shoulders, defying gravity. The terms around which these movements formed were based in a celebration of athletic repetition and stamina, the body running, spinning, and flying to another level. This was to reshape the effects that hard work could have on one's limbs and their memory. Work, and sweat, could produce forms of communality and joy, rather than alienation and pain.

The Charleston dance also spoke of the physical memory of place, the crucial history of slavery's displacement. It also spoke of the long history of black urban cultural formation, and the long history of black women's urban presence. Charleston, South Carolina, was one of the

Fig. 7.3. Whitey's International Lindy Hoppers. Marshall Stearns Collection, Institute of Jazz Studies, Rutgers University, Newark, New Jersey.

first urban ports of call in the transport of African slaves to the American continent, and the city's geography was organized around the sale of slaves. Black people, slave and free, were fundamentally present in the building of this urban center, creating a culture and economy apart from the owners' households. From the 1700s, slave women controlled the public markets, and their profits allowed many of them to buy themselves and their children out of slavery. Of the city's large free black population of artisans — wagoners, boatmen, blacksmiths — freed black women were a prominent presence, as merchants, seamstresses, boardinghouse mistresses, and prostitutes. The Charleston dance, making its way up the coast, remembered the widely attended illegal and clandestine balls held outside Charleston, which were hosted by this community of urban black women. "City air made free men," and in response to the public prosperity and mobility of black women, the authorities instituted "sumptuary regulations" in an effort to curtail their obvious claims to such freedoms.[40]

Analyses of the dance as a retention of African aesthetic practices may recognize the complexities of the cultural philosophies developed by various African tribes, but miss the very point of it, which is that the dance moves, migrates, and transfigures.[41] Such dance theory has begun to change. Thankfully, as Jacqui Malone points out, "the discourse has moved beyond a search for specific elements to the recognition of shared cultural processes of creativity, based on the notion that 'art moves within people,' and that cultural continuity is never completely broken."[42] But looking solely for continuities causes a kind of freezing of the lens, a loss of historical suppleness and nuance. In looking for timeless universal principles, everything gets lost about the ways black art moves historically across place and time. We risk repeating the very forms of cultural violation we seek to criticize, i.e., the West's versions of black culture as locked forever in an "authentic," mystical, and mythical primitive past. That our words are celebratory corrects nothing, as many of these primitivist renderings are also.[43] Instead, we create an endless list of descriptions, with no force forward. We miss the resonances evident in black daily life; the criss-crossings of various cultures and recognition of the troublesome notion of home, the dodging of many forms of traffic aimed at mowing us down. We can easily miss the ways dances function as multisignifying comments on historical contingency: forced and violent transportation, economic migrations, the formative energies of black people culture-building in the urban centers of the United States.

Rather than thinking simply of a hoped-for recovery of some sense of wholeness, the Charleston recognizes no need for return to "an Africa that is no longer there."[44] The polyrhythms of the dance embody a sense of black being in time, a sense of oneself as existing simultaneously in several different timed and spatial zones. The tensions of movement—rural to urban and transcontinental, both painful and pleasurable—are what the fragmented black body alternately hinges and unhinges itself from.

In a documentary film made in 1958 entitled *The Spirit Moves: Jazz Dance from the Turn of the Century to 1950*, former Savoy Ballroom dancers Pepsi Bethel, Leon James, Esther Washington, and Alfred Minns demonstrate a history of black dance forms — from the Charleston to the rhumba. The documentary is produced, directed, and edited by the Russian dancer and choreographer Mura Dehn, whose disembodied voice narrates the dance study.[45] The white walls and direct lighting provide the atmosphere of a museum, or classroom, as the film aims to legitimate the dances as art forms, worthy of historical preservation. The language of natural history and anthropological study shapes this film's strategy of legitimation, but the experimental camera work — interspersed slow-motion segments, close ups of the dancers' elbows, knees, and faces in soft focus — establishes these dances as forms of modern art.

In the film, Pepsi Bethel and other former members of the Savoy Ballroom crew execute the Charleston. "[The] Charleston in the twenties came as a shock," Dehn narrates, "A complete revolution against the Caucasian grace and body unity. It shattered the body into separate limbs, swinging like a human mobile in a multiplicity of simultaneous but diverse rhythms." The dancers appear in a darkened dance studio space, with arms and legs illuminated. Dehn explains: "To analyze the structure of this dance, we present the abstract design of lights, which are light-bulbs attached to the hands and feet of the dancers. There is a section filmed in double time to emphasize the regularity of syncopation, almost a mechanical precision. The slow motion reveals the classical position of the Charleston dancer's posture, his body almost parallel to the floor. The drummer, Zutty Singleton, is the heartbeat of the Charleston, in his power rhythms of flying drumsticks, arms, head and torso. The dancers are of the generation that created the Charleston, and each has his individual style."

The music for the Charleston was a "new rhythm," the multijoints of the fragmented modern body corresponding with a multisited sense of being in the world. The city was a visual graph of polyrhythmic beats: flashing lights and multitimbre sound that stimulated as well as threatened to overwhelm the human senses. The dancers mapped the city's rhythms, their disembodied hands and legs merging with the points of electric light dotting the avenues. Harnessed by humankind, electricity made possible the mass use of light and sound, and the boundless opportunity for scientific and technological advances. In their illuminated forms, the black dancers infused the synthetic with the sensate. They ushered in the primary force behind modern technology, as it mimicked the effects of magic upon the world, effecting change, both dreaded and hoped for, with lightning-flash quickness and efficiency.

Through dance, black people articulated multiple histories of physiogeographical fragmentation and dislocation. One point from which to chart the physical experience of the modern condition came long before the twentieth century, with the 'shock' of involuntary transportation between Africa, Europe, the American continent, and the islands of the Caribbean. Movement — be it migration, flight, escape, exile, or as an assertion of personal freedom — was a shaping principle, constitutive of African American culture. Their bodies' phraseologies remembered the past, understanding historical movement, as Stuart Hall so adroitly articulates, as a series of ruptures and discontinuities.

The phenomenological experience of modernity came alive through dialogues of shared experience conducted through the body and between bodies. But these were not dialogues dictated by unconscious biological retentions of cultural form. They were not based in an urge to return to a moment *unaffected* by the course of historical change. There is much at stake in keeping our interpretations supple; as Hall writes, "we must not collude with the West which, precisely, 'normalizes' and appropriates Africa by freezing it into some timeless zone of the 'primitive' unchanging past."[46]

Within intraracial dance moments at the heart of the metropole, the black body in motion transfigured itself. The act of transfiguration was about recollecting one's self, under conditions in which to claim community was an enterprise fraught with danger. Recollecting does not mean restoring, for one's self is never recoverable whole and intact. But the collective making of expressive cultural forms was a fundamental tactic for the survival of soul and body.

It is good for us to remember that jazz musicians were in dialogue with dancers. As Norma Miller emphasizes, jazz music and dance were co-constitutive. Black artistic response to the modern world was a collective dialogue: at once aural, visual, and corporeal. When we forget that, we lose sight of the expressionist artistry of many black women and of broader terms with which to consider the modern icon of the flaneur.

NOTES

1. Marshall Berman, *All That Is Solid Melts into Air: The Experience of Modernity* (New York: Penguin, 1988), 197.

2. Ibid.

3. Anke Gleber, "Female Flanerie and the Symphony of the City," *Women in the Metropolis: Gender and Modernity in Weimar Culture*, ed. Katharine Von Ankum (Berkeley: University of California Press, 1997), 67.

4. Berman, *All That Is Solid Melts into Air*, 159.

5. Charles Baudelaire, "The Painter of Modern Life," *The Painter of Modern Life and Other Essays*, ed. and trans. Jonathan Mayne (New York: Garland, 1978), 9.

6. Ida Forsyne, interview by Marshall Stearns, July 21, 1964, Institute for Jazz Studies (IJS).

7. Ibid.

8. George "Shorty" Snowden, interview by Marshall Stearns, New York, 1959. Quoted in Stearns and Stearns 1968, 324.

9. Ibid., 19–20.

10. Felski 1995, 16.

11. Susan Buck-Morss, "The Flaneur, The Sandwichman and the Whore: The Politics of Loitering," *New German Critique* 39 (1986): 128.

12. Gleber, "Female Flanerie and the Symphony of the City," 71.

13. Catherine A. Schuler, *Women in Russian Theatre: The Actress in the Silver Age* (London: Routledge, 1996), 13.

14. *The Keys to Happiness: Sex and the Search for Modernity in Fin-de-siècle Russia* (Ithaca: Cornell University Press, 1992), 275.

15. Ida Forsyne, interview by Cassandra Willis, 1972 (audiotape), James Hatch-Camille Billops Collection, New York.

16. Le Roi Antoine, *Achievement: The Life of Laura Bowman* (New York: Pageant, 1961), 220–22.

17. Ida Forsyne, interview by Marshall Stearns, July 21, 1964, IJS.

18. See Mike Davis, *City of Quartz: Excavating the Future in Los Angeles* (New York: Vintage, 1992).

19. Kelley 1996, 55–75.

20. James Weldon Johnson, *Black Manhattan* (New York: Altheneum, 1968), 146.

21. Ibid., 153.

22. Ibid., 149–50.

23. Joseph Roach, *Cities of the Dead: Circum-Atlantic Performance* (New York: Columbia University Press, 1996), 29.

24. Johnson, *Black Manhattan*, 163–64.

25. Ibid., 168–69.

26. Roi Ottley and William Weatherby, *The Negro in New York: An Informal Social History* (New York: Praeger, 1969), 199–200.

27. Hurston 1998, 44.

28. Miller 1996, 3.

29. Stowe 1994, 42; David Nasaw, *Going Out: the Rise and Fall of Public Amusements* (New York: Harper Collins, 1993).

30. Stearns and Stearns 1968, 321.

31. Carol Martin, *Dance Marathons: Performing American Culture of the 1920s and 1930s* (Jackson: University Press of Mississippi, 1994). In this section I do not mean to ignore the importance of the dance club as a key site where such segregationist policies were potentially contested by both white and black people. Sherrie Tucker's work on the Hollywood Canteen shows us to read these spaces as dynamic. Tucker, "They Got Corns for Their Country: Hollywood Canteen Hostesses as Subjects and Objects of Freedom," conference paper, American Studies Association, Atlanta, November 13, 2004.

32. Stearns and Stearns 1968, 315.

33. Terry Monahan, "'Stompin' at the Savoy': Remembering, Researching and Re-enacting the Lindy Hop's Relationship to the Savoy Ballroom," *Dancing at the Crossroads: African Diasporic Dances in Britain*, 35 [conference proceedings]. Much thanks to Terry Monahan for sharing his findings with me.

34. Stearns and Stearns 1968, 316.

35. Ethel Williams, interview by Marshall Stearns, 1961, file, IJS.

36. The black woman aviator Bessie Coleman deserves historical attention. Coleman, whose mother was African American and father Choctaw Indian, was denied entrance to flight schools in the United States. Coleman went to France and received her training at the École d'Aviation des Frères Caudron between 1920 and 1922. She was the first woman, white or black, to receive an international pilot's license. Coleman died in Florida in 1926 when the dilapidated Jenny she was flying crashed during a stunt exhibition. Sheila Turnage, "Claiming the Sky," *American Legacy* 6, no. 1 (spring 2000): 18–28. See also Doris L. Rich, *Queen Bess: Daredevil Aviator* (Washington: Smithsonian Institution Press, 1995).

37. Scholars have discredited the notion that the dance was named after Lindbergh. But the fact that the dance was quickly associated with Lindbergh's flight is significant and worth analyzing.

38. Al Minns, interview by Marshall Stearns, Stearns and Stearns 1968, 317.

39. Stearns and Stearns 1968, 331. In the late 1930s and early 1940s Whitey's Lindy Hoppers appeared in several films. See Robert P. Crease, "Divine Frivolity: Hollywood Representations of the Lindy Hop, 1937–1942," Gabbard 1995b, 207–28.

40. Ira Berlin, *Many Thousands Gone: The First Two Centuries of Slavery in North America* (Cambridge: Harvard University Press, 1998), 295, 158; Stephanie Camp, *Enslaved*

Women and Everyday Resistance in the Plantation South (Chapel Hill: University of North Carolina Press, 2003).

41. Gottschild 1996, 2003.

42. Jacqui Malone, " 'Keep to the Rhythm and You'll Keep to Life': Meaning and Style in African American Vernacular Dance," *The Routledge Dance Studies Reader*, ed. Alexandra Carter (London: Routledge, 1998), 231.

43. Examples are endless and exhausting, such as the sonorous, self-congratulatory, and ridiculous essays by Rodger Pryor Dodge collected in *Hot Jazz and Jazz Dance: Collected Writings, 1929–1964* (New York: Oxford University Press, 1995).

44. Stuart Hall, "Cultural Identity and Cinematic Representation," *Black British Cultural Studies*, ed. Houston A. Baker Jr., Manthia Diawara, and Ruth H. Lindeborg (Chicago: University of Chicago Press, 1996), 217.

45. "The Spirit Moves," videotape, vol. 1, part I, Mura Dehn Collection, Dance Collection, Lincoln Center for the Performing Arts, New York Public Library. The manuscript for "The Spirit Moves" is in box 37. This collection houses four volumes of filmed black dance footage. Vol. 1, part II, is footage of the aerial Lindy Hop at the Savoy Ballroom. For a short article about Mura Dehn see Karen Backstein, "Keeping the Spirit Alive: The Jazz Dance Testament of Mura Dehn," in Gabbard 1995b, 229–43.

46. Hall, "Cultural Identity and Cinematic Representation," 217.

Julie Dawn Smith

It is in a large part according to the sounds people make that we judge them sane or insane, male or female, good, evil, trustworthy, depressive, marriageable, moribund, likely or unlikely to make war on us, little better than animals, inspired by God. These judgments happen fast and can be brutal.
— ANNE CARSON

Madwomen strain the semiotic codes from which they emerge, thereby throwing into high relief the assumption concerning musical normality and reason from which they must — by definition — deviate. — SUSAN MCCLARY

Maggie Nicols begins by singing a low-pitched, pulsating, yet relaxed drone. Irène Schweizer's piano lines engage with this sound instantaneously, contributing detached phrases that provide stark contrasts to the continuous vocal line. Schweizer's passages move up and down the length of the keyboard, disjunct groupings interspersed with melodic twists and turns that create variable contours of rhythmic fluidity. Joëlle Léandre's sounds oscillate between the high-pitched harmonics and the low tones she coaxes from her bass, as she periodically returns to match the pitch of the vocal drone with a delicate vibrato. At times, she adds elegant pizzicato lines to complement the sonic texture. These introductory sonic gestures allow a luxurious amount of space for the trio known as Les Diaboliques to listen to each other, to attune themselves to their acoustic environment, and to initiate interaction with listeners located throughout the room.[1]

There is a lyrical, songlike quality to the texture as the sounds weave in and out of counterpoint with one another. Individual voices surface — Schweizer's right hand offers the hint of a melody, Léandre conjures harmonic cries as she combines the light touch of finger with bow — and rise above the texture as moments of singular clarity. Nicols's vocalizations unfold into a rhythmical chant fusing with the instrumental timbres creating moments of incantation. She sings fragments of an indistinguishable language that causes Schweizer — attuned to the shift in direction Nicols is making — to increase the intensity of her movement. Schweizer reworks fragments of phrases previously introduced, altering and reshaping their contours to create a pianistic flourish of kaleidoscopic, virtuosic passages. Léandre adds flourishes of her own, demonstrating her brilliant arcato technique.

The intensity quickly transitions into sparse, rhythmic, and repetitive gestures. Nicols returns to the chant, varying it with the delicate and airy high-pitched head tones she skillfully shapes. These shrill yet subtle pitches are matched with Léandre's expressive but equally delicate harmonics and Schweizer's muted plucking of the strings inside the piano. The sparse sonic threads are woven around one another into an economical interface.

Nicols intersperses pseudo-linguistic phrases and punctuates them with her swinging arms and swaying body: visual layers added to the already complex sonic layers created by the trio. The movements are accentuated further by the rhythmic tapping of her feet, amplified by tap shoes. The easy tapping and loose gestures are reminiscent of a puppet whose strings are gradually tightened, as the rhythms become more defined and precise. Schweizer and Léandre provide rhythmic counterpoint to the "foot percussion" — Léandre stretches and slaps the bass strings and occasionally taps the body of her bass with her bow while Schweizer plucks the strings inside the piano to add sporadic chordal accents.

As the rhythms intensify, Léandre abruptly interrupts the rhythmic flow with pronounced vocal outbursts that are punctuated with aggressive strikes on the strings and body of her bass. Nicols reacts as if she is taken aback by Léandre's sudden dramatic turn. She stops vocalizing and stands with an embarrassed smile on her face, as if to apologize for her colleague's demonstrative behavior. Léandre stammers and gags with exaggerated sounds and gestures. Schweizer accents the dramatic moment with clanging hand cymbals which she then slides across the strings inside the piano. The modulating pitch adds an eerie quality that intensifies Léandre's apoplectic vocalizations. Her vocal and corporeal gestures are more and more pronounced, exaggerated rhythmic and gestural stutters that produce a complex polyrhythm of movement, voice, and instrument. The audience is engaged and their bursts of laughter add to the rhythmic counterpoint.

The prolonged and unabashed acting-out is the perfect antithesis to Nicols's silent, apologetic discomfort, which in turn furnishes a contrasting backdrop to Léandre's pathological behavior. The disparity between proper "feminine" demeanor — silent, smiling, repressed, interior, compensating — and abject spectacle — demonstrative, noisy, hysterical, purging — graphically parodies the reality and paradox of the feminine at a visual and sonic level. The interaction provides a split screen for the listener/viewer from which to interpret the duality of female sound and spectacle.

Léandre mimes escape from her affliction by swimming through the thick atmosphere of abjection and despair. Schweizer continues to distort the strings with syncopated, discontinuous sounds. Nicols's embarrassed silence finally gives way to a parody of the song "Zip-a-Dee-Doo-Dah." She begins demurely:

Zip-a-dee-doo-dah
Zip-a-dee-ay
My-o-my what a wonderful day . . .

but moves toward a progressively more sinister subtext, complete with Shirley Temple-esque "spunk" and determination, improvising choreography reminiscent of a Hollywood musical chorus line. As she demonstratively approaches the ending:

Zip-a-dee-doo-dah
Zip-a-dee-ay
Wonderful feeling . . .

she bursts into the frenzied, nonsensical, and angry ranting of a hysteric.

At this point, Léandre's vocals transform into operatic parody while Schweizer expresses her own dramatic flair by generating an extravagant vibrato inside the piano and then striking the lid with mallets for effect. Repetitive rhythms create disjunct vocal lines, as Nicols transitions from hysterical ranting to nonsensical linguistic fragments. These fragments are indistinguishable enough to discourage possible translation: is this a real language or an invented one? She purposefully obscures the phrases to keep the listener slightly off-balance. Adopting a strident tone, Nicols wags her finger at the audience as she lectures, trying to make a point that cannot be fully understood.

The intensity gives way to a sparser texture composed of hesitations and sighs, and, with a fluid gesture toward the audience, Nicols gasps, "Smelling salts please." Her demeanor conjures images of fainting and fragile women: infirm hysterics who succumb to their melancholy. Léandre adds her own anguished vocalizations that accentuate and empathize with Nicols's traumatic turn. As she continues her halting moans, Nicols gives voice to the distress, asking: "Is there a husband in the house?" She mocks the nineteenth-century "marriage" cure for discontented women that continues to resonate in capitalist, heteronormative, middle-class society. Léandre moans with empathy and understanding as Nicols continues her lament: "It's time I settled down. I can't go on like this, wild and abandoned" — a play on the cliché "wild abandon" and women's "wildness." She skillfully shifts the meaning by adding the transitive verb abandoned, moving from agency to victimization. She cries, "Abandoned! Abandoned! Abaaandoned!" with her arms raised high in the air to punctuate her despair.

Léandre accentuates the melodrama with melancholic vocals in tandem with Schweizer's disjointed manipulation of the piano strings. Nicols pauses, looks toward Léandre, considers her misery, and, with a surprising shift that instantaneously alters the focus, turns to Schweizer and asks: "Irène, will you marry me?" This effectively "queers" the moment of her desperation, an "eccentric" request that offers the possibility of an unorthodox resolution. Ever the perfect foil to Nicols's antics, Schweizer ironically responds, "No!" Léandre contradicts with a definitive "Yes!" and she and Nicols embark on a vocal lament of unfulfilled desire that draws from both opera and the blues. Schweizer accompanies them with full-textured orchestral chord voicings that gradually fade into silence, as the wailing gives way to faint sounds, breaths, and silences.

WOMEN IMPROVISERS, SOUND, AND PATHOLOGY

Formed in 1990, the improvising trio Les Diaboliques (see figure 8.1) — "a very strong trio, ohh, la, la" as Joëlle Léandre describes it — is an outgrowth of a series of innovative women's improvising groups that surfaced in Europe during the 1970s and 1980s. Upon the gradual

Fig. 8.1. Les Diaboliques.

Photograph by Peter Bastian.

dissolution in the early 1980s of the first women's improvising collective called the Feminist Improvising Group (FIG), several alumnae of FIG — including the pianist Irène Schweizer, the vocalist Maggie Nicols, the bassoonist Lindsay Cooper, and the trombonist Anne-Marie Roelofs — continued to play together, eventually renaming their improvisational collaboration the European Women's Improvising Group (EWIG). The extraordinary bassist Joëlle Léandre, who had an extensive classical background as well as experience in new music and avant-garde technique, soon joined them. As Anne-Marie Roelofs points out, the acronym EWIG is a German word that means eternal — and the name became a play on the very real and very contrived role of women in western society: "I thought that was great, women go on for eternity."[2]

In 1986, Roelofs and others organized the Canaille festival in Frankfurt to showcase women improvisers, inviting members of FIG and EWIG, as well as several women from a new generation of improvisers emerging on the European scene. The festival was produced in various European cities with local artists and arts groups taking on the responsibility of organizing the event in their respective areas. An improvising collective called Canaille comprised of the pool of women who participated in the various festivals also began touring.[3]

The Intakt Records producer Rosmarie Meier writes in the liner notes to the only available recording of Canaille in Zurich that the active involvement in organizing their own festivals and tours was born of necessity for these women musicians; it was literally the only way they could make themselves heard. She writes: "These musicians have taken their affairs into their own hands, for in these times it is not a matter of course that the[y] get invited to the important festivals of free improvised music." Irène Schweizer translates *canaille* as "something like 'rascal' or 'rabble,' and that . . . sort of captures the mischievous nature of [the] group."[4]

Schweizer traces a line from FIG to EWIG to Canaille, a line that conceivably extends to the trio Les Diaboliques. Maggie Nicols not only sees Les Diaboliques as an outgrowth of previous collectives, she also derives pleasure from playing in this all-woman trio: "I think that the character of this group, obviously the fact that we are women, influences the nature of the music and the particular intimacy and the particular types of relationships between us."[5]

As with the earlier groups of women improvisers, Les Diaboliques continues to struggle with the representation "woman," as well as with class consciousness, soulful creation, and the issues that continue to exist for women in the traditionally male-dominated sphere of free improvisation. Theirs has been a struggle of and for representation and equality underscored by the names chosen to identify each of the groups mentioned above. In this sense, marking each successive group with words that draw attention to their difference as women — feminist, eternal, rabble, diabolical — strategically positions and deploys the sexed female body within the music. As with practitioners of African-American jazz and free jazz who signified on the codes of the dominant culture to bring racial oppression to the fore, the use of the codes associated with gender, sexuality, and the sexed female body by women free improvisers disturbs commonsense notions of freedom, exposes the myth of the level playing field, and highlights practices of free improvisation that are not always "free." For these European women, the complex struggle toward freedom in the music acknowledges the intersections of sexual difference, gender, and sexuality, with race and class, as the basis for improvisational practices.

CONSIDERING THE MADWOMEN

In her description of musical improvisation as "inspired lunacy" and "creative insanity," vocalist Maggie Nicols embraces both the marginal status of improvised music and the marginal status of women who improvise. As many feminist theorists have observed, the sounds that women make (that is, the sounds that are associated with the female body) — including their cries, linguistic excess, improvisations, laughter, and noises — are generally interpreted as pathological and are associated with abjection, abnormality, and insanity.

The poet and theorist Anne Carson suggests, for example, that the interpretation and subsequent dismissal of the sounds women make as "noise" is linked to an entire history of female ritualized banter: the cries of pleasure and pain, the jokes, insults and obscenities, indecent language, blasphemies, shrieking, and laughter sounded during women's ritual practices and festivals in ancient Greece. These rituals are associated with a host of unseemly women, such as witches and lesbians, who were believed to cast evil spells, indulge in vulgar physicality, flaunt their unruly behavior, and, in general incite anarchy. Through these rituals, women orchestrated a vociferous female soundscape that challenged the patriarchal order. To prevent these dangerous public soundings from disrupting the status quo, women's ritual practices were quickly banished to the outskirts of town, away from the normal range of hearing. Exiled to the margins of rational discourse, women were ostracized for breaking the silence with their indulgent and anarchic racket. Ironically, women's cathartic soundings also served a purpose in patriarchy; their noisy catharsis was a purification rite that was believed to purge the abject from the community (Carson 1998, 67–68).

In relation to music, Susan McClary observes that composers historically used "excessive" sounds such as chromaticism, florid ornamentation, and "extravagant virtuosity" — compositional devices that deviate from and provide a stark contrast to the prevailing "diatonic narrative" of the work as a whole — to represent the "madwoman" in opera (McClary 1991, 92, 100). Her analysis of the musical representation of several key women in operas from the seventeenth century to the early twentieth traces the various devices used by composers to frame the sonic excesses associated with the feminine. Such chromatic, ornamental, and virtuosic excesses are, as McClary observes, the sonic corollaries of the abject feminine and are subject to "frames" devised by the male composer. The control of chromaticism within the score was accomplished with a variety of techniques including the elimination of improvisation in the bel canto style and the appropriation of chromaticism as a feature of masculine virtuosity in instrumental styles of music (96, 82).[6] McClary also notes that the figure of the madwoman provided an opportunity for the composer to musically "misbehave" (102).

When considered together, the observations of McClary and Carson demonstrate that the control of feminine excess in/of music is inextricably linked to the control of any "excessive" qualities of sound that escape the carefully constructed frame of logos. Arguably, the ongoing surveillance exerted on music by theorists, critics, and musicologists is part of the larger surveillance exerted on women, their bodies and the sounds they make. This surveillance has made it difficult for women to claim, reclaim, reappropriate, and reinterpret any so-called sonic excess for fear of being associated with madness (read femininity) and femininity (read madness).

RECLAIMING THE MADWOMAN

Yet it is important to challenge the notion that sounds emanating from a female body (or an extension of that body) can only be heard as excessive, noisy, uncontrollable, and hysterical. Beyond the reading of women's sounds as a sign of discursive and/or musical inadequacy, it is arguable that a multiplicity of sonic utterances can be enlisted to express a multitude of subject positions. This is a move toward hearing and interpreting women's soundings as something other than a representation of the inarticulate feminine. Is it possible to utilize excessive sounds as a means of creative communication?

The reclamation and reinterpretation of sounds made by women is not an argument for any kind of direct relationship between the female body and some version of a female or feminine musical language, but for an engagement of/with the sounds and rhythms that are culturally associated with female noise, incoherence, and hysteria, in order to dismantle those very associations and to disrupt linguistic and musical codes. In "Women's Time," Julia Kristeva describes exactly the kinds of sounds and rhythms that exceed musical and linguistic frames as a signifying practice: "to break the code, to shatter language, to find a specific discourse closer to the body and emotions, to the unnamable repressed by the social contract" (Kristeva 1981–82, 25). This is not an outright rejection of language or musical conventions, but an attempt to disarticulate the reductionism that collapses everything (including music) into language and linguistic structures in an effort to open a space where the sexual encoding of sound is broken, hierarchical difference is dismantled, and the multiplicity of sonic difference is realized.

When such noises disrupt our expectations, it serves as a reminder of the libidinal difference that exists at the edge of language and music. This is a space of difference that blurs the boundaries between interior and exterior, existing at the threshold of language where improvising with sound opens the closed ear and stimulates the negotiation and transformation of representation.

Irène Schweizer's distinctive style is a commingling of hard bop and other forms of "legitimate" jazz, South African Kweela and township music, and the experimental forms of free improvisation begun in the 1960s. Indeed, as the only woman to emerge on the European scene for many years and in spite of the fact that she performed regularly with some of Europe's leading male improvisers, she longed for the company of musical women. It was not that Schweizer's playing was any less innovative or virtuosic than her male counterparts; rather, it was her feeling of isolation when she played with a different sensibility and approach to free improvisation, a difference of which she was profoundly aware: "I was always the only woman around. Sometimes there was tension. Men want to show how fast they can play and how much technique they have. So I would have to struggle and also play as fast as possible. I found it too aggressive and competitive at times."[7] Eventually, Schweizer found a form of refuge in the women's improvising collectives of the 1970s and 1980s, communities of women improvisers who encouraged and supported her eclecticism and experimentation, and who provided a space in which her difference could be nurtured: "I really enjoyed playing with women. It was a completely different atmosphere. The interplay, the interaction was quite different than with men. Suddenly there was humour . . . humour was in our midst, we had fun. It wasn't about achievement. We didn't need to show our stuff: I can play this run so fast. . . . It wasn't the technique that was important. It was the expression in the music. What we wanted to say. I liked that."[8]

Schweizer's struggle as a pioneering female pianist can perhaps be also understood in the larger context as a struggle with the constructions of gender, sexuality, and sanity as they relate to the historically constructed relationship between white European woman and the piano. According to Richard Leppert, the piano was an important signifier of domesticity in eighteenth- and nineteenth-century European middle-class life. As one of the central objects owned by the family, it represented the economic and erotic economy of domesticity. The piano was a feminine instrument, a designation that paralleled the conflation of woman with the feminine in the economy of masculine, heterosexual desire. Indeed, the piano was an aesthetic, feminized object, and, as Leppert suggests, "the visual fascination with the piano connects to the scopophilic fascination with women's bodies in art" (Leppert 1993, 155). As was the case with the female body, the body of the instrument represented the contradiction of the feminine in bourgeois society. The materiality of the feminine was fetishized through undue emphasis on the body of the instrument, on its placement within the home, and on its elaborate decoration and stylization, while at the same time the sound of the piano fetishized music as immaterial, its harmonies indicative of the illusive and ethereal feminine. The piano was an ambiguous marker situated somewhere between public and private life, an echo of the ambiguity of the woman it had come to represent (153).

As a passive yet beautiful object that sounds, the piano carried the same kind of danger associated with chaotic feminine sexuality. As Leppert reminds us, the taming of sound through the mechanisms of harmony, unity, and music mimed the confinement of women's sexual agency in the heterosexual family. Indeed, for domesticity to be upheld, the sensuality and the femininity of piano music was confined to a controlled spectacle that effectively covered over sonic feminine danger.

The tension between pianistic propriety — concentration, discipline, respectability, purity, intellect — and impropriety — the spectacle of a sensuousness that was taboo, erotic, illicit, and embodied — produced gestural tensions that reflected the conflict between masculine rationality and feminine irrationality (156). Women players were forever caught in this double bind, required to execute proper performances yet often unable to express their own creativity. The mapping of gender onto music, instruments, women, and their performances was the result of an erotic economy heard in and grafted onto music, "concerned with the arousing and channeling of desire, with mapping patterns through the medium of sound that resemble those of sexuality" (McClary 1991, 8).

For women, this territory was and continues to be difficult to negotiate, especially for those who improvise. Both women and improvisation share an unscripted fluidity, occupying a socially dangerous space that violates the boundaries of masculine and feminine and threatens to disturb representation (Leppert 1993, 143). Indeed, this was the case when Irène Schweizer appeared on the improvised music scene, as Patrick Landolt remarks in Gitta Gsell's film *Irène Schweizer*: "Irène really blasted apart social consensus. That's why she had to bear a lot of hostility in the beginning. Irène, that is Free Jazz and Irène Schweizer and playing with the arms and such . . . that was the enemy personified. And naturally it had to do with the fact that a woman went on stage and did something that didn't suit convention, who in many ways broke with convention. On the one hand, because she went on stage for a solo concert, a solo *piano* concert . . . the holiest of all instruments: the piano. And as a woman performed on stage and made music people thought: 'Wow! This piano will have to be repaired after the concert.' "

A perverse reading of the relationship between Irène Schweizer and her instrument, both marked as feminine, conjures images of a "same sex" duet that disrupts a heterosexual musical economy by highlighting the commingling of vibrating feminine bodies. What does it mean when Schweizer lifts the lid of a piano and plays inside? To open the lid of the piano is to engage in an erotic opening of feminine recesses, an invitation to a direct experience of tactile pleasure and sonic pathology. If the piano is opened wide and sounded by a woman, the very boundaries of sanity are crossed, feminine sexuality is awakened and its sounds become "the root cause of hysteria, the psychological analogue to social anarchy" (Leppert 1993, 171).

Hélène Cixous argues that crossing the threshold of inside and outside in this manner is indicative of an inherent bisexual female imaginary: "it's this being 'neither out nor in,' being 'beyond the outside/inside opposition' that permits the play of bisexuality." This is a libidinal bisexuality that is determined not by sexual partnering, but by the female unconscious.[9] The musicologist Suzanne Cusick goes one step further when she proposes that musicality and sexuality are "psychically right next door" and poses the question: "What if music IS sex?" (Cusick 1994, 71–78).

Freely crossing the boundaries of inside and outside in her improvisations — leaning into the piano's interior to stroke the strings or sitting close by to rhythmically strike the keys outside — Schweizer performs a commingling of musicality and sexuality in which "power circulates freely across porous boundaries; the categories player and played, lover and beloved, dissolve" (Cusick 1994, 79). For Schweizer a sonic blurring of instruments, styles, bodies, resonances disrupts a straight reading of her music: "I consider the piano as an extension of my body and I also consider my piano playing as physical, especially when I play as a soloist. Of course, it's an instrument that I love embracing with my arms and hands, or banging on it hard, according to my actual feelings. The piano has indeed an inside (strings) and an outside (keys) and sometimes I really love to go deep inside it when I play a complete piece on the strings."[10]

Transgressive sounding beyond the normalizing scrutiny of language, symbolic representation, and musical codes may indeed signal female sexuality and the pathological, but it may also be the key to dismantling the frames of reference that define, confine, and eventually silence sonic excess. Investigating the possibility of reclaiming sonic excess requires a historical understanding of the relation between gender, sound, representation, and the most notorious "feminine" sonic pathology of all — hysteria.

Cumulative research on hysteria has uncovered innumerable meanings that have been written, read, rewritten, and reread for over a millennium, producing an "interpretive overload" according to Elizabeth Bronfen in *The Knotted Subject: Hysteria and Its Discontents*.[11] Hysteria has proven to be a mutable affliction and a constantly evolving phenomenon, she argues, because the discursive function of hysteria in medical and aesthetic texts is as important and complex as its nosology.

On an individual level, the hysteric is reported to adapt her symptoms in accordance with changes in her immediate psychosocial situation, a constant mutation that complicates the diagnosis and treatment of her affliction. On a cultural level, hysteria adapts itself to the moral climate of the specific time it appears in history. As Bronfen suggests, hysteria is performative: it performs the representational symptoms of the cultural epoch by pointing to the lack or deficiency in the interpretive system itself. There are no consistent or universal symptoms of hysteria on either an individual or cultural level. Hysteria is a constructed category that reflects the cultural climate in symptoms of the psyche, the body, language, sound, and society. Although hysteria has a medical history, it also has a social history that is embedded within popular culture such that scientific and cultural diagnoses and treatments are inextricably linked to one another. Thus, hysteria is as much an illness of representation as it is an illness of the psyche that reflects the social and cultural context in which it appears (Bronfen 1998, 102–4). It is important to note that the social history of hysteria includes issues related to sound; that is, hysteria is often identified with/as an illness of sonic representation and an inability toward language and meaning.

The story of the identification and naming of hysteria has traditionally been traced back to Hippocrates (Bronfen 1998, 105). Yet, as Helen King claims, recent scholarship reveals that in actuality the "Genuine

Works of Hippocrates" are a collection of texts written by multiple authors, and recent reexaminations of Hippocratic traditions and texts reveal the actual diagnosis of hysteria attributed to Hippocrates is questionable.[12] Medical accounts of the affliction are not merely documents of a fixed disease, but rather a series of texts in dialogue with each other. King suggests that it is only by reclaiming and rethinking all texts associated with hysteria that we can begin to formulate alternative viewpoints, as well as understandings of its variable meanings over the centuries.

The symptoms traditionally attributed to Hippocrates's diagnosis of hysteria have been traced retrospectively to a pathological motility of the female reproductive organs. This "wandering womb" was interpreted as a sign of the dissatisfaction and restlessness of a certain and specific kind of female — the unmarried woman.[13] The dissatisfied womb — considered to be a "small, voracious animal, a foreign body that had dried up, lost weight, and come unhooked" — was believed to roam through the body of a sexually frustrated or dissatisfied woman, such as a widow or "spinster," in search of sustenance (Bronfen 1998, 105). The uncertainty left a woman vulnerable to the demonic possession of animals and animal spirits, producing a symptomatology that ranged from shortness of breath to vomiting, loss of voice, constricted throat, and paralysis of the extremities. From the beginning, the cure for these symptoms — perhaps the most consistent aspect of the discourse on hysteria throughout history — was prescribed with unequivocal fervor: the hysterical woman needed the sobering influence of an authoritative and rational male figure, preferably a husband (Bronfen 1998, 105).

Bronfen reports that in the Middle Ages hysteria became associated entirely with demonic possession. This meant that women's hysterical hallucinations were attributed to the internalization of the diabolical influences of evil spirits. Thus, female pathology was extended beyond the physical manifestations of social deviance; it became an illness with a moral dimension, the hysteric believed to be a deceitful witch who lacked a soul. The prescription for this "daughter of the devil" was severe: she was interrogated, forced to confess, subject to exorcism and other forms of punishment (Bronfen 1998, 106–7).

By the seventeenth century, another shift in the medical discourse on hysteria occurred, as physicians once again turned their "scientific" gaze on female anatomy, attributing a multitude of symptoms to the interaction of vapors emitted by a troubled uterus with other organs. Diagnosis often identified the brain as the organ most directly affected by a miasmic uterus, causing everything from loss of sight to mutism, paralysis, convulsions, fainting spells, and motor impairment, as well as melancholy, anxiety, and discontent (Bronfen 1998, 108). Thus, the mental capacity of the female was questioned, her weak intellect a product of her pathological biology. Although there are some reports that not all physicians sexually encoded hysteria, to the majority, it remained a female affliction, the infirmity of female anatomy and feminine sensibility.

In the eighteenth century hysteria began to reflect bourgeois culture in Europe, becoming the definitive illness of young, sensitive women. These nubile hysterics were subject to uncontrollable sexual impulses, fits of crying and laughter, nervous coughing, and various other symptoms associated with the soft, fluid penetrability of the internal space of the female body as well as with inarticulate, nonlinguistic sound. As Bronfen observes, the leap from the emptiness of the female corporeal space to the emptiness of female moral character — "the spatial density of the body readily converts into moral density" — was well established (Bronfen 1998, 113). The general consensus that hysteria was, for the eighteenth-century female, an illness "owing to an abundance of feeling, an excessive sympathy with her environment, an uncurbed empathy for all that would move her body and soul — but a flow of organic and psychic energy that formed a closed circuit" continued to be traced, by association, to the infirmity of the female body (Bronfen 1998, 114). This is the point at which the ideal of femininity became *the* female malady, making hysteria and femininity coterminous.[14] The hysteric inhabited the feminine just as the feminine inhabited the hysteric.[15]

PLAYING HYSTERIA

Maggie Nicols uses the power of voice to transgress boundaries in a performance situation: to connect audience and performer, to heighten intimacy, to underscore the power of women's sound, and to inhabit hysteria. To inhabit hysteria, a seemingly contradictory notion, is temporarily to dwell on the edge of sanity, a tactic of fluidity. At times, Nicols uses the discourse of the hysteric as a means of expression, playing with broken language, nonlinguistic utterances, and the multilingualism of the hysteric's speech. Inhabiting hysteria in this way questions the constructedness of hysteria and the pathologizing of women's sounds. The hysterical female body that sounds points to the limits of language and music, and the impossibility of representing both sound and the sexed female body. Indeed, Nicols's improvisations constructed from nonscripted narrations, fragmented languages, interrupted monologues, and free associations bypass linguistic and musical conventions. In this sense, Nicols's vocalizations are accomplished with "the *belle indifférence* of a hysteric."[16]

Nicols's improvisations continually demonstrate her facility with sonic free association, swirling narratives that fluidly commingle linguistic and nonlinguistic sounds. She transgresses and reinvents the "talking cure," a psychoanalytic method designed, in the course of Freud's work with hysterics, to purge hysterical utterances by channeling random thoughts into rational speech. She reverses the way we hear the hysteric's multilingualism — challenging the inability to speak an authorized language as pathological — and claims it as a facility with language that reaches beyond language, an improvisation with sound, and a paradoxical communication of the unrepresentable.

Nicols perverts the so-called rational linearity of speech, often interrupting a sentence with a soaring succession of sounds — babble/ gibberish/scat — that imitate language but have no linguistic meaning per se. The listener follows the sounds that weave in and out of language, understanding the contours and the gestures of her articulations. Fluent in several languages, Nicols utters fragments in rapid succession, often shifting from one language to the next in midsentence. Her multilingual narratives are punctuated, at times even hijacked, by invented words and languages, babble, harmonic splitting, rhythmic repetitions, stutters, moans, and shrieks. She gestures, dances, taps out rhythms with her feet, throws body into voice and voice into body.

Nicols's treatment of jazz standards, for example, often embarks on the deconstruction of both lyric and sentiment, perverting the expectations of sound and language to create a subversive transformation. Her perverse rendering of the song *I Love You For Sentimental Reasons* — renamed *Silly Boy* — is a case in point.[17] Nicols improvises and alters the lyrics: "I love you/Ahhhhhh/For sentimental reasons/Treasons-ss/ Ohhhhhh/Ah ah/Through the changing seasons/Ah-ahhhhh Hah/ Ohmushhh/ Ehh/ Ohhhhh/Silly boy."

As in many of the jazz standards Nicols reinvents, she cleverly uses the tradition of quotation in jazz improvisation to its extreme. In this reinterpretation, Nicols parodies the sentimentality of heterosexual romantic love that is often found in the standard jazz lyric, particularly in the songs that cross over into the realm of the "popular." She intones the words "I love you" in an effort to convince the listener of her sincerity. Yet she immediately interjects a "witchy" cry — "ahhhhh" — that rises and falls in an arc before the delivery of the song's *raison d'être*; the motivation of love is "for sentimental reasons." The repetition of the same descending pitch on the words "reason" and "treason" inextricably links them together. Similarly, the insertion of "treasons" suggests that the reason for sentimentality is far from endearing and may prove to be dangerous. "Treasons" is delivered with a snaky "ss" closely following its slow enunciation, conjuring a sinister phallic scene that alludes to the conversation between Eve and the snake in the Garden of Eden — her deal with the devil.

Nicols's voice emits monstrous, eerie sounds that convey a double meaning — she is speaking as both the lover and the beloved, unwilling victim and expectant victor. She underscores the difference by using the onomatopoeia of "mushiness" to betray the subtext of power contained in the lyric. As well, there are frequent collapses into and reliance upon nonlinguistic utterances. At first the sighs and contoured pitches are used to resist the song's sentiments, but they eventually soften into surrender, resigning to the tyranny of romantic love. Nicols avoids complete acquiescence, however, as she utters the words "silly boy" in a whispered, admonishing, and mocking tone. She speaks as a woman who recognizes the immaturity and childishness of the heteronormative social conventions often conveyed through the standard jazz lyric.

As listeners, we are challenged to engage actively with Nicols's perverse sounds and lyrical twists in order to develop new means of translation, interpretation, and understanding, inventing our own ways of listening and sounding that defy linguistic and musical conventions. Nicols's improvisations bridge the distances between sensation and the surrounding environment; as listeners, we too experience immediacy, free play, body awareness, directness, spontaneity, and self-sufficiency: "Babble supplies us with the phenomenon of voice in process of creation."[18]

HYSTERIA AND PSYCHOANALYSIS

The discourses surrounding the diagnosis and cure of hysteria culminated in the nineteenth century, establishing the fortune and fame of heroic medical figures such as Jean-Martin Charcot and Sigmund Freud. Certainly, Charcot built his reputation by staging spectacles of hysteria in his theatrical lectures at the Salpêtrière — a "museum of living pathology" — that regularly featured live hysterics performing their peculiar symptoms (Bronfen 1998, 174).

Sigmund Freud first encountered the performance of hysteria at Sal-pêtrière. Initially, he accepted Charcot's scopophilic method of diag-nosing hysteria, which interpreted visual signs as evidence of pathology. Yet Freud's subsequent work with hysterics led him toward the develop-ment of the psychoanalytic method, a method based on the interpreta-tion of stories told to him by his female patients. Through the narratives of hysterics, Freud eventually linked their symptoms with repressed trauma. Considered to be of a sexual nature, trauma, in Freud's estima-tion, was traceable to sexual abuse or a seduction fantasy and was mani-fested in the fragmentation of language and the breakdown of meaning.

One of the most talked-about hysterics documented by Freud in his case studies is Dora, whose real name was Ida Bauer. In "Fragment of an Analysis of a Case of Hysteria," Freud narrates Dora's complaint that her father was encouraging her seduction by his friend Herr K., in exchange for Herr K.'s complicit silence concerning the ongoing affair between Dora's father and Herr K.'s wife, Frau K.[19] Dora told Freud that she was particularly disturbed by an incident in which Herr K. made advances toward her when she was only fourteen years old. To complicate matters, at least from her father's point of view, Dora devel-oped her own disturbing relationship with his mistress, Frau K., with whom she spent a great deal of time reading erotic literature. Even-tually, her father sent her to Freud for psychoanalysis to make sure she would maintain their complex web of sexual secrets by coming to terms with and finally accepting the advances of Herr K.[20]

Although for Freud psychoanalysis was based on narrative, it was in his estimation the task of the therapist to construct that narrative for the patient. The constructed narrative must, in turn, be accepted by the patient for her to be cured. Dora, however, rejected Freud's narrative: "She flatly denied Freud's narrative embellishments of her story, would not accept his version of her activities and feelings, and either contra-dicted him or fell into stubborn silence. Finally she walked out on Freud by refusing to continue with therapy at all" (Showalter 1985, 319).

Showalter observes that Dora's voice is completely suppressed in Freud's text, an indication that she was merely the object of his observa-tion. Freud's inability to treat Dora as a subject results in his perception of her story as fragmented and incoherent, which, according to Toril Moi, "has less to do with the nature of hysteria or with the nature of woman than with the social powerlessness of women's narratives" (Showalter 1985, 333).

Dora's refusal of Freud's version of her story, as well as her rejection of his treatment, is interpreted by feminists in one of two ways: she was either complicit with patriarchy and pathologically unable to break free from the bourgeois family, or she was refusing her role in patriarchy and her heterosexuality. The question of Dora's collusion with the patriarchal exchange of women or rebellion against it is simply stated: is the hysteric a feminist heroine or a patriarchal conspirator?[21]

This question is addressed, most notably perhaps, in the exchange between Hélène Cixous and Catherine Clément in *The Newly Born Woman*. The section of the book entitled "The Untenable" is a discussion between Cixous and Clément of the political effectiveness of the hysterical figure.[22] Each woman draws different conclusions from Freud's case study of Dora. Cixous finds merit in excess, in the position of the hysteric at the threshold of the symbolic and language, whereas Clément holds little hope for the political power of the hysteric in her attempts to dismantle the system. For both women, the case of the hysteric pivots on the issue of language, on whether the hysteric must embrace symbolic language to break her imaginary identifications or whether she is proof of the notion that imaginary identifications are entrenched in the symbolic.

Clément argues that the hysteric is not only firmly embedded in, but also anticipated and thus is easily silenced by, the symbolic. She insists that the hysteric does nothing more than reinforce the structure of the symbolic, especially in relation to its most powerful institution, the bourgeois family. The hysteric's marginal position is created by the system and anticipated by it, effectively dismantling any possibility of hysterical subversion. The hysteric complains of her powerlessness within kinship structures but her hysterical symptoms do nothing to dismantle that powerlessness. Thus, she is unable to transform her situation through her extralinguistic protest because it lacks the coherence and political capacity of language. For Clément, the hysteric is unable to argue her case successfully.

Cixous, on the other hand, sees hysteria as an effective protest. The hysteric resists her place in the symbolic as a pawn in the patriarchal exchange of women and, in so doing, explodes the symbolic structure, creating viable alternatives for political change apart from language. For Cixous, hysterical identification exists at the threshold of the symbolic, suggesting that "there is something hysterical about every putting-into-words" (Findlay 1994, 330).

The dialogue between Cixous and Clément pivots on the relationship of difference to power and whether this relationship can be (dis)articulated in language. Clément sees the symbolic as being structured by difference in a way that contains it, such that working from within becomes the only possibility for transformation. Symbolic inscription is the only way to bring change to the symbolic.

For Cixous, however, difference exceeds the symbolic, and it is precisely the excess and motility of difference that disturbs and transforms symbolic structures: "There are structures characteristic of hysteria that are not neuroses, that work with very strong capacities of identification with the other, that are scouring, that make mirrors fly, that put disturbing images back into circulation" (Cixous and Clément 1986, 155).

By "making mirrors fly," the hysteric challenges the basic premise of the mirror stage, in which the subject's entry into the symbolic depends upon the abjection of the mother and the repudiation of the imaginary (in Cixous's terminology). The hysteric cannot see herself as abject; it is the system that is based on "blindness, on denial." Thus the hysteric makes sure it is known that she has no place in the symbolic: "Hysteria is necessarily an element that disturbs arrangements; wherever it is, it shakes up all those who want to install themselves, who want to install something that is going to work, to repeat. It is very difficult to block out this type of person who doesn't leave you in peace, who wages permanent war against you" (Cixous and Clément 1986, 156).

The hysteric exposes the fragility and uncertainty of the law and disrupts the myth of symbolic stability. The hysteric's protest brings the "hystericization of the speaking subject in general" to our attention (Findlay 1994, 330). Thus when Cixous states, "Dora seemed to me to be the one who resists the system, the one who cannot tolerate that the family and society are founded on the body of women, on bodies despised, rejected, bodies that are humiliating once they have been used," she recognizes that Dora's hysterical protest has the power to break apart the symbolic (154).[23] The fragmented language she speaks is the fragmented language spoken by all of us — a sounding that is silenced by the law.

ME, MY BASS, AND I

Joëlle Léandre describes free improvisation as "beauty, risk, love, story, life!"[24] To be open to change, to engage interactively with the other, to listen, to experience, to work extremely hard to make your mark in history as a woman are all components that combine to make, in Léandre's words, a *créatrice*. A classically trained musician, she has purposely chosen to dislocate he self from the mainstream classical and avant-garde musical worlds, v hile effectively and creatively maintaining her virtuosity on all fronts. Léandre is a musical multiple personality of sorts — occupying many musical territories simultaneously; shifting their ground; combining fragments of sonic, tactile, gestural, and acoustic elements to shape her individualized improvisational soundscape. At times, Léandre admits that certain people do not understand her work, especially those who confine themselves to singular genres or adhere to accepted styles. Her multiplicity is born of necessity as she searches for creative collaborators: "What I am doing, the people do not always understand. It is jazz, it's not jazz, it is new, you see there is composition, there is improvisation. It is many things."[25]

She describes the improvisational process as a creative amalgamation of sonic fragments and compares this process to the creative process of being human: "I work deeply from fragmentation, this concept. We are more like a kaleidoscope."[26] In Léandre's improvisations, sound and gesture shift, break apart, take on different shapes, and reemerge to create a mixture of textures and polyphonies. Improvisation thus becomes a space of immediacy and displacement, an echo of the "fragmentary, deferring status of knowledge itself."[27] The whole is dependent upon the fragments and vice versa, a spatial and temporal relationship that disrupts the linearity that constructs beginning, middle, and end.

Léandre's fragmentary and complex combinations of sonorous bodies — her bass, her voice, her gestures, her improvisations in various combinations — are layered to produce solo, duet, trio, or quartet textures — multiple voices emanating from one. In the liner notes to Léandre's solo CD, *No Comment*'s composer Sharon Kanach remarks that Léandre is a "one-woman-quartet (Joëlle plus her bass plus her voice plus her composition/improvisation),"[28] an observation Léandre (with a little prodding) confirms: "[The bass] is like a body for me, another body. And some days I talk with the instrument. It's what you need to express. It's an object. First I have to talk in this box in order to talk to the audience. To go in to go out. Sometimes I'm one with the bass. Sometimes I'm two. Interesting. I know in some pieces, in some moments it's like this."[29]

Similarly, Léandre's relationship to sound and music is mediated by the amalgamation of her body and the body of her bass with the resonances of her improvisations: "The duo form is a love story. There is a constant struggle of reaching out to the other — as a matter of fact, my piece of wood, my doublebass and I form a duo. It's a question of intimacy, a sense of touch, a sense of palpable sound."[30]

Léandre constantly (re)invents frameworks for bass playing as well as for improvisation in general, by combining these multiple and shifting sonic selves. Not only are her sounds improvised, but her subjectivity is also improvisational, multiple, her experience fluid, her knowledge fragmentary yet profound. Indeed, Léandre's playing contains an organic quality that works equally with form and content, madness and reason, structure and fluidity in the moment: "Maybe it's unconscious but all the pictures, the movement, the street — you could say the outside — not only the intellectual. No, no, no. Life, life, life, life, life."

Léandre's aesthetic is an aesthetic that finds expression in her multiplicity. Her improvisations offer an opportunity to develop a dialogue with her own otherness: "You can one day decide, I close my door, I want to learn: 'Hey who am I? What do I have to do? What do I want to do?' It's hard to do and difficult to continue to believe. It's not like Ave Maria but Zen maybe," as well as a way to connect with the other outside of herself: "You learn to go to the other one and say: 'Hey, I'm here for you, touch me.' The music is communication, that's all. An expression. [. . .] We learn a lot to meet, to go to the other and say: 'Hey, who are you?' And this happens in improvisation and this is so deep" (personal interview).

HYSTERICAL PROTEST AND THE CRI

The suffrage movement in Europe and the United States is often cited as the reason for the decline of female hysteria in the early twentieth century (Showalter 1985, 326).[31] Yet as Lisa Tickner writes in *The Spectacle of Women: Imagery of the Suffragist Campaign 1907–1914*, a direct correlation can also be drawn between the rise of feminism and the rise of the clinical focus on hysteria.[32] According to Tickner, the reemphasis on "women's essentially *biological* destiny in the face of their increasingly mobile and transgressive roles" acted as social surveillance on women (Tickner 1987, 196). She also observes that, although the etiology of hysteria was no longer linked to a dysfunctional uterus, the connection between hysteria, femininity, and sexuality was not abandoned but reconfigured: "Hysteria was sexual in the sense that the energies of the sexual drive and those originally used to repress it were condensed into the hysterical symptom" (197).

Feminists at this time were characterized by mainstream society as sexually ambivalent, hybrid, socially degenerate, and hysterical (194). The intersection of femininity, sexuality, and hysteria became popularized in the print media and specialized throughout the medical profession and psychiatry, each view reinforcing the other (194). Feminists were caricatured as masculine women or effeminate men cross-dressed in women's clothing: "For half a century or more, feminism and hysteria were readily mapped on to each other as forms of irregularity, disorder and excess, and the claim that the women's movement was made up of hysterical females was one of the principal means by which it was popularly discredited" (194).

The feminine was split into two, as positive images of normal women and negative images of degenerate women were placed side by side as a warning to women who were not content with their proper place. The association of feminists with degeneracy linked gender deviance to the discourse of race in the early twentieth century, playing on the anxieties of the white middle class, specifically on their fear of domination by the racial other (204).

Feminists were often referred to as the "shrieking sisterhood," women who publicly made a noisy spectacle of themselves, disturbed the peace, and threatened violence (194). As Tickner observes, these suffragists strategically adopted this characterization, mapping feminism and hysteria onto each other to effectively deploy the discourse of hysteria as a resistance to traditional roles (197). In other words, feminists often embraced the connection between feminist politics and hysteria in order to give voice to their protests. Similarly, the link between the noise of feminist hysteria and the "pathological" sexuality practiced by feminists (that is, sexuality apart from reproduction) kept the connection between woman's womb and woman's voice intact, challenging the narrative parameters of symbolic expression. Mary Russo suggests that the connection between the shrieking sisterhood and the "bra-burners and harridans of the second wave" links the "grotesque" noise of feminism with the "grotesque" body of women.[33]

Feminists sometimes referred to their noisy protests (the sound of female oppression and dissatisfaction) as "articulate hysteria," the communication of a message that violated the narrative rules of symbolic communication (Showalter 1985, 333). Showalter suggests that for hysterical protest to be effective, language must be transgressed: "Language has played a major role in the history of hysteria; to pry apart the bond between hysteria and women, to free hysteria from its feminine attributes, and to liberate femininity from its bondage to hysteria, means going against the grain of language itself" (290).

Articulate hysteria is contingent on purposeful sounding that freely violates the borders of body and mind, interiority and exteriority. It is a deployment of hysteria that improvises, communicates beyond language, commingles the unconscious and the conscious, infiltrates sense with nonsense, disrupts music with noise. Or, as Heather Findlay suggests "feminism may very well be an *un*consciousness raising, an experience of the role of the unconscious in every symbolic act" (330).

Hysteria, therefore, can be interpreted as a culturally induced performance of a subject's marginality. In contradistinction to Charcot's silencing of the hysteric — "You see how the hysterics cry. One could say this is much noise about nothing" — hysteria can be heard as a noisy performance that speaks volumes. As Joëlle Léandre suggests: "And for me jazz is also a scream . . . *un cri*. When you *cri* — scream yeah? It means a lot of things for me. Politically, philosophically, a part of what, who, a vision of your life, creation, *contestation* — [protest]. [There are] a lot of things included in *cri*: the *resistance*, to resist. And that interests me a lot" (personal interview).

MUSIC THERAPY

Nearing the end of a rapidly paced, technically virtuosic trio improvisation, Les Diaboliques' bassist Joëlle Léandre emerges from the texture and begins to explore the physicality of her instrument. At first, the beauty of the instrument sings through the soaring melody she creates, but soon this sonic luminosity gives way to the darker side of Léandre's experience. Maggie Nicols and Irène Schweizer follow her lead and join Léandre in the creation of a brilliant piece of improvised musical theater.

Slowing down the momentum by bowing at the lowest point on her E string, Léandre conjures sounds that buzz, moan, and stammer. Schweizer leans into the piano and plucks the strings on the inside, echoing Léandre's bass while simultaneously adding a new amalgam of textures. As the piano punctuations become more strident, Léandre's bowing shows more and more evidence of strain. The sounds are disjointed, it is clear that the physical demands of playing her instrument are becoming increasingly difficult for her to negotiate. She expresses her exasperation vocally with slow intermittent moans that match the arduous bowing and the low bass sputters.

Acknowledging Léandre's difficulty, Maggie Nicols turns toward her and empathizes: "Oh, I know, yes I know. I know. Oh, oh, oh, yes, yes, um, um, um." With the addition of percussive tongue clicks, Nicols repeats this refrain over and over again, a soothing, yet chiding mantra that floats atop Léandre's struggle.

The tortured bassist tries to sort out her entangled relationship with the instrument. She questions where her body begins and the body of her instrument ends. She exposes the backside of the bass and compares it to her own backside. She bows across her torso. She climbs onto the bass, wrapping her leg around the c-bout and covering the f-hole with her knee, her foot dangling close to the bridge. She mutters, plucks, whimpers, shakes her head, sighs. Schweizer extracts herself from the piano's interior, sits down on the piano stool and plays a childish, repetitive melody that accentuates Léandre's tantrum. Nicols gestures compassionately toward Léandre and comments: "It breaks your heart."

Empathy aside, Nicols seizes the opportunity to take control of the situation, assumes a more paternalistic attitude, and appoints herself as Léandre's therapist. She encourages Léandre to dig deeper and become more aggressive in her self/bass exploration: "Yes, that's it. Get it out, get it out. Better out than in. Express, discharge, release! Yes, yes. Good, good, good. That's very good, that's it." Schweizer adds dense choral exclamations that buttress the catharsis.

Léandre succumbs to the role of hysterical patient. She scratches bow across bass, blurts out word fragments, gestures to herself, recounts a story that no one can understand. Nicols encourages — "Well done, well done" — and discourages — "I think we'll have to draw to a close now," but Léandre ignores the mixed message and continues to indulge in her melancholy. Her acting out becomes more pronounced and bizarre as she gags, gasps, and groans, and eventually hangs the bow on her nose and squawks. Nicols reiterates more forcefully this time: "I think we're going to have to draw to a close now. That will be £100. Same time next week. You've done some excellent work."

In the end, it is Schweizer, however, who successfully diffuses Léandre's temper with a lush piano solo that seems to calms her. At this point, Léandre assumes a more subdued, introspective attitude as she sings a wordless operatic lament that expresses her distress, accompanied by Schweizer.

Nicols then moves closer to the more passive Léandre. The bassist takes her hand and places it on the bass strings, encouraging Nicols to pull and stretch them as she has in her time of anguish. Instead, Nicols cradles the strings in her hand and begins to stroke the body of the bass, offering it comfort: "She's horrible to you isn't she? Poor thing, she's so horrible." Then turning to Léandre she scolds, "I'm afraid we're going to have to take your bass into care. You are a very bad mother!" As Nicols continues to admonish her, Léandre fixates on the word "bad," stretches it ("baaaaaad"), and repeats it over and over, to create a blues-inflected shout chorus that mimics Nicols's reprimands. Nicols coaxes the bass away from Léandre as she continues to scold: "I'm going to call the police. This bass must be taken to a safe place."

With the threat looming, Léandre abandons the blues for a different strategy. She gestures toward Nicols seductively, raises her eyebrows flirtatiously, puts her arm around Nicols's waist and draws her closer. Nicols, clearly flattered, reevaluates the situation for a brief moment and changes her mind with a sigh: "Well, maybe not." Léandre echoes her, "maybe not," with a knowing mischievous smile. As the pair embarks on a lovers' duet accompanied by Schweizer's luxuriant piano, Nicols strokes Léandre's face and her bass fondly. She has clearly had a change of heart as she exclaims: "What a wonderful pretend family! Yes, yes. You, me, and baby bass, oh darling!" Léandre responds, "I love you," places the bow in Nicols's mouth, and as Nicols clamps down with her teeth Schweizer plays the final cadence.

PERVERSE HYSTERICS

The hysteric's ability to inhabit multiplicity, to expose the inside on the outside, to defy linguistic conventions, to communicate in incomplete sentences, to oscillate between numerous tongues, to speak through the body, and to gesture with silence and with sound have all been strong and consistent markers of pathology in the discourses of hysteria.

Yet Anne Carson reminds us that sonic marginality is the strength of hysteria precisely because it is an articulation that signifies apart from the "control point of logos" and the "dissociation" known as self-control (Carson 1998, 70). She recounts how Freud and Breuer used hypnosis to treat hysterical patients by encouraging them to "speak unspeakable things" in order to transform this symptomatic nonsense "into narrative and rational exegesis of their hysteric symptoms" (Carson 1998, 75). Sound that is "out of control" can conceivably bypass the censorship and conformity imposed by symbolic language and thus is arguably accessible as a useful means of alternate expression for the marginalized subject.

The question is this: if the marginalized subject is clinically or culturally pathologized, can the aestheticization of pathology challenge the very constructedness of that pathology? The mutability of hysteria can be viewed as an opportunity to create a mutable subjectivity — that is, an improvisational subjectivity — able to speak to and speak of the specificity of difference. Sounding the multiplicity and polyphony of individual and collective voices is an aesthetic (re)configuration of hysteria, an outlaw aesthetic that challenges the law from which contemporary "hysterics" — improvisers, feminists, disenfranchised groups, artists, writers, gay and lesbian activists, for example — can challenge power relations through sonic spectacle.

Elaine Showalter cautions that constructing hysteria in aesthetic terms runs the risk of romanticizing the protest of otherness and diluting the political effectiveness of the performance as well as the very real trauma from which it is derived. She stresses the importance of keeping in mind the anger, pain, and desperation that often accompany hysterical "acting out" (Showalter 1985, 335). The danger of staging hysteria under conventional aesthetic conditions — Charcot's theater of pathology, for example — is the danger of overaestheticizing and romanticizing pathology, oppression, and marginalization. Similarly, when aesthetics and hysteria are positioned as coterminous the potential for pathologizing art also exists.

To identify oneself as a hysteric for political, artistic, and acoustic purposes is indeed very different than to be diagnosed as a hysteric from a clinical perspective. Yet the tactic of appropriating hysteria in order to dismantle it has been repeated throughout history. To approach art as an appropriation of hysteria and hysteria as performative are not only powerful tropes for theoretical effect but powerful creative practices as well. The stigmatization of the other as hysteric can be embraced and transformed into an aesthetic that dismantles the very oppressive structures that seek to enforce "normalcy." As Heather Findlay suggests, the "politicized ranting" of feminist, antiracist and queer activists has proved, over the last few decades, to be effective in dissecting and dismantling unequal power relations (Findlay 1994, 345).

The ambiguous territory of subjectivity resonates in hysterical sounds, silences, and noises made in political and artistic practices. These disruptive articulations oscillate unpredictably, creating a sonic difference that finds expression in the hysterical improvising subject. This is the space where the subject is tactically (re)hystericized, where hysteria is perverted, as Kristeva suggests: "We can play our hysterias without necessarily making a psychodrama and exposing ourselves to being the victims of the male order, but with great lucidity, knowing what we do, and with great mastery and measure. That is, perverse hysterics. Very wise."[34] For women improvisers, the perverse playing of and with hysteria is an improvisational practice — the kind of "creative insanity" or "inspired lunacy" Maggie Nicols refers to, Irène Schweizer's impropriety, Joëlle Léandre's multiplicity. No longer is the hysteric an aesthetic object bound to her body, liable to indiscriminate scrutiny and silence, but an active subject paradoxically in control of her hysteria, able to improvise her subjectivity. This improvised, perverse hysteria is the inherent strategy heard in the noisy *cri* of Les Diaboliques.

NOTES

1. The performance described was part of the Time Flies festival of improvised music produced by the Coastal Jazz and Blues Society, November 4–6, 1999. Eleven internationally respected improvisers were invited to play in different configurations during the course of the event.

2. For a discussion of the Feminist Improvising Group see Smith 2004. The members of the Feminist Improvising Group joined in the years indicated: 1977 — Lindsay Cooper, bassoon, oboe, soprano sax; Maggie Nicols, voice, piano; Corine Liensol, trumpet; Georgie Born, bass, cello; Cathy Williams, voice; 1978 — Irène Schweizer, piano; Sally Potter, voice, alto sax. Intermittent: Anne-Marie Roelofs, trombone, violin; Frankie Armstrong, voice; Angele Veltmeijer, flute, tenor, soprano, and alto sax; Françoise Dupety, guitar. The members of the European Women's Improvising Group were: Lindsay Cooper, bassoon, oboe, soprano sax (UK); Maggie Nicols, voice, piano (UK); Irène Schweizer, piano (Switzerland); Anne-Marie Roelofs, trombone, violin (Holland, Germany); Joëlle Léandre, bass (France).

3. The Canaille Festival and Canaille groups are as follows: 1986 — Anne-Marie Roelofs organized the Canaille festival in Frankfurt with Christiane Spieler and Kathi Goth. She invited members of FIG and EWIG (the "first generation"), as well as several women from a new generation of improvisers emerging on the European scene (the "second generation"). The festival was produced in various European cities with local artists and arts groups taking on the responsibility of organizing the event in their respective areas — in Zurich, Irène Schweizer and the group Fabrikjazz (October 1986); in Vienna, Flora St. Loup (November 1987); and in Amsterdam, Maartje ten Hoorn (December 1987).

"First Generation": Irène Schweizer, piano (Switzerland); Anne-Marie Roelofs, trombone (Holland, Germany); Maggie Nicols, vocals (UK); Joëlle Léandre, bass (France); Lindsay Cooper, multi-instrumentalist (UK). "Second Generation": Co Streiff, saxophone (Switzerland); Marilyn Mazur, piano and drums (Denmark); Elvira Plenir, piano (Austria); Flora St. Loup, vocals (France); Maartje ten Hoorn, violin (Holland); Maud Sauer, oboe (Holland); Mariette Rouppe van der Voort, flute and saxophone (Holland); Petra Ilyes, bass guitar (Germany).

4. Marc Chenard, "FMP and Beyond: A Conversation with Irène Schweizer," *Coda* (October–November 1998): 11–13. The recording of the Canaille Festival in Zurich was produced by Intakt Records and is out of print. The women who participated in the Zurich installation of Canaille from the first generation were Irène Schweizer, piano (Switzerland); Anne-Marie Roelofs, trombone (Holland, Germany); Maggie Nicols, vocals (UK); Joëlle Léandre, bass (France); Lindsay Cooper, bassoon (UK); and the second generation: Co Streiff, saxophone (Switzerland); Marilyn Mazur, piano and drums (Denmark); Elvira Plenir, piano (Austria); Flora St. Loup, vocals (France); Maartje ten Hoorn, violin (Holland); Maud Sauer, oboe (Holland); Mariette Rouppe van der Voort, flute and saxophone (Holland); Petra Ilyes, bass guitar (Germany).

5. Les Diaboliques, interview, November 5, 1999.

6. *The Concise Oxford Dictionary of Music* defines bel canto as "a term covering the remarkable qualities of the great eighteenth-century and early nineteenth-century Italian singers, and suggesting rather performance in the lyrical style, in which tone is made to tell, than in the declamatory style. Beauty of tone and legato phrasing, with faultless technique, were the principal ingredients." Interestingly, this definition also eliminates the possibility that at one time improvisation was part of the bel canto style. *The Concise Oxford Dictionary of Music* (Oxford: Oxford University Press, 1980), 62.

7. James Hale, "Irène Schweizer: Many and One Direction," *Coda* 276 (November–December 1997): 15.

8. Gitta Gsell, *Irène Schweizer*, Intakt DVD 121, Switzerland, 2006.

9. Hélène Cixous, "Castration or Decapitation?" *Out There: Marginalization and Contemporary Cultures*, ed. Russell Ferguson, Martha Gever, Trinh T. Minh-Ha, and Cornel West (New York: New Museum of Contemporary Art, 1990), 356.

10. Irène Schweizer, interview, November 5, 1999.

11. Elizabeth Bronfen, *The Knotted Subject: Hysteria and Its Discontents* (Princeton: Princeton University Press, 1998), 101.

12. Helen King, "Once upon a Text: Hysteria from Hippocrates," *Hysteria beyond Freud*, ed. Sander L. Gilman et al. (Berkeley: University of California Press, 1993), 3–7.

13. Helen King, "Once upon a Text: Hysteria from Hippocrates," 3–90, esp. 8.

14. Showalter 1985.

15. Since the origins of hysteria were consistently associated with the female body and with women's lack of moral fiber, impaired intellectual ability, and inferior place in society, the diagnosis of male hysteria was very difficult—if not impossible—to make. Elaine Showalter observes that the cultural resistance to the idea of the male hysteric from one century to the next is so strong that the same symptoms in men consistently generate an entirely different diagnosis than in women.

16. Joseph Breuer and Sigmund Freud, *Studies on Hysteria*, ed. and trans. James Strachey (New York: Basic Books, 1955), 135.

17. Les Diaboliques, Intakt CD 033, 1993.

18. David Applebaum, *Voice* (Albany: State University of New York Press, 1990), 79, 86.

19. Sigmund Freud, "Fragment of an Analysis of a Case of Hysteria," *The Standard Edition of the Complete Psychological Works of Sigmund Freud*, vol. 7, ed. and trans. James Strachey (London: Hogarth, 1953), 7–122.

20. Elaine Showalter, "Hysteria, Feminism and Gender," *Hysteria beyond Freud*, ed. Sander L. Gilman et al. (Berkeley: University of California Press, 1993), 317.

21. Heather Findlay, "Queer Dora: Hysteria, Sexual Politics, and Lacan's 'Intervention on Transference,'" *GLQ: Journal of Lesbian and Gay Studies* 1, no. 3 (1994): 328.

22. Cixous and Clément 1986.

23. Whether or not she used that power is a contentious issue.

24. Léandre made this point during a networking session entitled "Where Are the Women Improvisers?" This session was a component of "V.I.E.W. from the Front," a festival of women improvisers that took place at the Western Front, February 20–23, 1997, Vancouver.

25. Steve Vickery, "Joëlle Léandre: Music Actuelle," *Coda* 243 (May–June 1992): 16–17.

26. Les Diaboliques, interview, November 5, 1999.

27. Toril Moi, "Representation of Patriarchy: Sexuality and Epistemology in Freud's Dora," *Dora's Case: Freud—Hysteria—Feminism*, ed. Charles Bernheimer and Claire Kahane (New York: Columbia University Press, 1985), 187.

28. Sharon Kanach, "Joëlle Léandre: No Comment," *Red Toucan Records* RT 9313-2, 1997.

29. Joëlle Léandre, interview, November 4, 1999.

30. Francesco Martinelli, *Joëlle Léandre Discography* (Pisa: Bandecchi and Vivaldi, 2002), 27.

31. Although, as Juliet Mitchell argues, feminists should not necessarily take credit for "curing" hysteria, since "the historical decline of hysteria has more to do with psychol-

ogy's effort as an institution to break up the diagnostic category of hysteria into other afflictions (anorexia, bulimia, depression, posttraumatic stress disorder) mainly because these disorders can be treated — or so we are led to believe — by less expensive behaviourist therapies." Quoted in Findlay, "Queer Dora," 300.

32. Lisa Tickner, *The Spectacle of Women: Imagery of the Suffrage Campaign, 1907–14* (London: Chatto and Windus, 1987), 195.

33. Mary Russo, *The Female Grotesque: Risk, Excess and Modernity* (New York: Routledge, 1994), 14.

34. Ross Guberman, *Julia Kristeva: Interviews*, ed. Ross Guberman (New York: Columbia University Press, 1996), 46.

Eric Porter

"BORN OUT OF JAZZ . . . YET EMBRACING ALL MUSIC":

RACE, GENDER, AND TECHNOLOGY IN GEORGE RUSSELL'S

LYDIAN CHROMATIC CONCEPT

The last time I taught my cultural history of jazz course, I screened "The Future of Jazz," the final episode of the 1958 television program *The Subject Is Jazz* of the National Broadcasting Corporation (NBC). Hosted by cultural critic Gilbert Seldes, the episode's featured guests were the jazz scholar Robert Pace of Columbia University and the pianist, composer, and theoretician George Russell. I showed the program as part of a class session titled "Jazz Goes to College," in which I attempted to give my students a sense of how jazz's postwar function as a vehicle for cool rebellion and the accumulation of middlebrow cultural capital often came together in interesting ways as the music was embraced by educational and cultural institutions.

"The Future of Jazz" exemplifies the growing academic scrutiny directed to the music. Seldes discusses with Pace a new jazz program at Teacher's College. He introduces Russell as having recently had a composition commissioned by Brandeis University and as teaching classes in "advanced composition" at the School of Jazz at Lenox the following summer. The NBC program also usefully illustrates some of the anxieties that emerged among critics, fans, and musicians at this moment of growing prestige: Has the increased academic attention and institutional support actually improved the legitimacy of jazz? Has something been lost in this process? What does the future hold given the array of experimental practices — drawn from the realm of concert music and postbop idiomatic practice alike — increasingly brought to the art form?

Russell carries much of the burden for charting the "Future of Jazz." The "house band" performs Russell's composition "The Legend of Billy the Kid" — written for and featuring Bill Evans on piano — and afterward Russell explains that he was trying to convey a sense of spontaneity with the piece, a "feeling as though the written music was being improvised." Seldes then asks Russell about his Lydian Chromatic Concept — or "the Concept," as Russell has often referred to it — which he first began working on in the 1940s and which formed the basis for an instructional book titled *The Lydian Chromatic Concept of Tonal Organization*, first published in 1953. Although Russell makes it clear that time would not permit a full explanation of the Concept, he offers the following description that positions it as a device enabling experimental musicians to extend the jazz tradition: "Now the problem in jazz today is to evolve into the subtle harmonic and melodic resources that this chromatic scale affords without losing the earthiness and swing that good jazz is characterized by. The Lydian Concept makes us conscious of tonal gravity. There are essentially two kinds of tonal gravity: vertical, that is tonal gravity inferred by the chord, where the chord infers the tonic, and horizontal tonal gravity, tonal gravity inferred by the scale, for instance the blues scale." Russell goes on to discuss (and analyze musical examples by) Coleman Hawkins and Lester Young as representative of the vertical and horizontal approaches, respectively. Seldes does not quite get it, so he asks Russell to speculate on the future of jazz: "If America has a future," Russell responds, "jazz has a future; the two are inseparable . . . it will certainly be more adventurous tonally. That is, it will be more chromatic. And rhythmically it will be freer, in form it will be freer, more ambitious." Then Seldes, stating that this future can be articulated most clearly through music, introduces the band's performance of Russell's "Stratusphunk," a twelve-bar blues composition that employs the Concept and which Seldes describes as "out there is the tonal stratosphere."

After the screening, when I asked for comments, a student expressed her frustration that, once again, we had a situation where white critics were imposing their own interpretations on this music and that we did not hear black musicians' voices. Others agreed. They were put off by Seldes's Brahmin inflection and his bow tie. They had also listened to me, in previous weeks, talk about critical misrepresentations and black artists' attempts to redefine the terms by which their work was understood. Then someone took Russell to task; she saw him as an interloper, a "white" artist imposing a kind of inauthentic, scientific perspective on what she viewed as an organic expression produced by African-American society. She was unhappy with his centering of composition in jazz performance and his use of the Lydian Chromatic Concept to impose a technical understanding of the work of Hawkins and Young.

It was time to inform these students — and a good number of others in the class, judging from subsequent reactions — that Russell was, in fact, black. That some of these students did not see Russell as black may be explained, in part, by his light complexion, washed out by primitive early television technology and the poor quality of my copy of the program, as well as the chromatic myopia that often comes from not having been around a lot of black folk. (Three out of seventy-five students in this class were black.) But I thought there was more to it. For it occurred to me, and I tried to make this a teaching moment by asking students to consider that they might not have seen Russell as black because his soft-spokenness, precise language, and intellectual demeanor did not fit their conceptions of the archetypal black jazzman. And perhaps his embrace of science and technology ran contrary to their understanding of the kinds of knowledge that informed black cultural practice.

I posed the question as to whether they heard only part of the story. They, like many critics and scholars, understood the racial and class politics of the jazz world, as well as the ways musicians have struggled to gain respect and remuneration, to define the terms of their own existence, and to make their voices heard in ways that have reflected and sometimes informed larger black social and political struggles. But I was not successful in encouraging at least some of the students to step outside of and develop a critical perspective on the raced and gendered mythmaking that has informed the meaning of jazz. We were unable to successfully deconstruct the romantic, heroic, and expressly gendered narratives of black music as cultural resistance and redemptive performance of identity that have been generated in classroom discussions, critical and academic writings, and within the realm of popular discourse. We remained trapped in the gendered and raced authenticating discourse that was so limiting for experimental musicians like Russell (see figure 9.1) who labored in the music business and, quite often, called for new interpretations for the history of jazz and for understanding its place in the world. In other words, Miles Davis made sense as a jazz musician but George Russell did not.

Fig. 9.1. George Russell, Berlin, 1971.
Photograph by Karlheinz Klueter.

This chapter attempts to accomplish what I was not able to do on the fly in the classroom: to develop an understanding of Russell and his Lydian Chromatic Concept (a system that he and others have described as both as a scientific and philosophical system) as a raced and gendered intervention into the discursive and financial economies of the jazz world of the 1950s and early 1960s. I hope to show that once we are able to circumvent the mythmaking surrounding jazz that caused Russell to be unintelligible to my students, we gain a more nuanced sense of the array of critical practices that constituted this cultural framework. My analysis of Russell's deployment of science and technology in his Concept builds from Afrofuturist criticism's insights into the ways that black musicians' articulation of scientific concepts and metaphors, deployment of science fiction tropes, and uses of various technological apparatuses often comment on race, culture, and the category of the human, while also, at times, interrogating, in the words of Kodwo Eshun, "any and all notions of a compulsory black condition."[1] However, I suggest that Russell's theorizing of his own musical project can be read against some of the assumptions of this critical discourse and what we might understand as its occasional complicity with the romanticism fueling black music criticism. In other words, I hope to provide a productive alternative to the raced and gendered modes of cultural critique embedded in the critical field, even as I draw upon its attention to science and technology to better understand the racial and gendered aspects of Russell's intellectual and expressive project.

Russell has been working as a musician, composer, and theorist since the 1940s. He received a fair amount of attention for his composition "Cubana Be/Cubana Bop," which the Dizzy Gillespie Orchestra premiered at Carnegie Hall in 1947. A series of record dates as a leader in the late 1950s and early 1960s also drew notice. He spent the second half of the 1960s in Europe, primarily in Scandinavia, where he began experimenting with electronics, most notably on several recordings of *Electronic Sonata for Souls Loved by Nature*, on which improvising musicians interpret Russell's score and a prerecorded tape of synthesized, ambient, and human sounds. Russell has also spent a significant amount of time teaching music, offering classes at, among other places, the School of Jazz in Lenox in 1958 and 1959 and the New England Conservatory of Music from 1969 to the present. Russell is best known, however, as the creator of the Concept, a theory of improvisation that deeply influenced the development of modal jazz during the late 1950s and early 1960s. He has revised *The Lydian Chromatic Concept of Tonal Organization* several times since its original publication in 1953, the 4th edition seeing publication in 2001.[2]

As in "The Future of Jazz," space does not permit anything approaching a full explanation of the Concept, but a few basics will help this analysis. The Concept is a theory that allows an improviser or composer to identify a series of scales that can be used to express a chord or other harmonic framework (e.g., a series of resolving chords or the key of a piece of music). Russell begins with the idea that the C Lydian mode is a better means of expressing a C major triad than a C major scale, arguing that the Lydian mode is created by a series of perfect fifths beginning with C and that its tetrachords, resolving to G and C, reinforce C as a tonal center. According to Russell, "the major scale *resolves* to its tonic major chord. The Lydian scale *is* the sound of its tonic major scale." From there, Russell locates the "parent scales" that best express other chord values. In other words, if one is trying to express a minor seventh chord, one uses a variation on the Lydian mode to best capture its sonority. But Russell's Concept also allows the improviser or composer to identify five additional scales that can be used, alone or in tandem, to express any chord or harmonic framework, although they do so with increasing dissonance. Taken together, the six scales employ all the notes in the twelve-tone chromatic scale. Thus Russell's system ultimately allows an improvising musician to play any note in the tempered scale, although one is to do so while maintaining an awareness of the "tonal gravity" (i.e., the relative relationship to the parent scale) of the notes one is playing. As his comments about Hawkins and Young in "The Future of Jazz" indicate, Russell explored different types of tonal gravity: vertical, relating to an individual chord; horizontal, referring to a series of chords resolving to a tonic; and supravertical, referring to the tonal center(s) of a piece of music.[3]

As Russell developed his Concept, he was, in a sense, trying to create a theory that did not require a rebellion from its constraints. "The jazz musician," he told an interviewer in 1958, "to some degree, has had to learn traditional music theory only to break many of its rules in practice."[4] As an alternative, Russell developed a system where, as he put it in his book: "You are free to do anything your taste may dictate, for you can resolve the most 'far out' melody since you always know where home is. . . . The Concept does not legislate taste. Hence, there are no 'do's' and 'don'ts' — no laws. It is, rather, an attempt to organize all the tonal materials that the jazz improviser deals with, so that he may choose for himself on the basis of his own aesthetic needs."[5]

Early on, Russell observed that music was a reflection of natural principles and, as such, ideally would provide the practitioner ample freedom to pursue her art free from the restrictions society imposed. Yet he also said that he had been motivated to create the system, in part, out of a belief that existing musical systems and their expressions were embedded with ideological meaning and paralleled social restrictions. In the 1950s, he used familiar language from African American history to describe the limitations of existing music theory. "A theory of any kind demands obedience at first in order to master it. However, a really useful theory doesn't enslave one without making the period of servitude interesting and worthwhile and without eventually freeing its subscribers through its own built-in liberation apparatus. The theory which forces you to rebel against its concepts in order to find freedom is obviously not fulfilling the needs required of it."[6]

In later years, Russell described a kind of coming into consciousness during this period about how the prejudices of Western societies might manifest themselves in music theory. Rules governing musical performance, it began to occur to him, "were just as dogmatic and as narrow-visioned as the laws of other institutions, such as schools and churches."[7]

"Now that I look back," he reported another time, "the traditional music theory always seemed oppressive to me — to my ear and to my essence, to the way that I am. I don't know if I went through all this reasoning at the time, but I do remember my deep emotional feeling about the matter. And in a way it represents — Music is very social, and it can be related to the way Western man thinks about all of life, sort of relegating all of life to small laws, laws of property, and laws of good and bad."[8]

Russell endeavored to derive a system that emerged from his experiences as a jazz musician but could be applied to various forms of music. Looking back at the end of the decade at the development of the Concept in the early 1950s, he said, "I think for the first time I had some inkling of what I was going after: a concept with a soul, born out of jazz and its needs, yet embracing all music created in the equal temperament system."[9] Russell was not so much rejecting Western music theory; he merely sought to ground a new theory in what he deemed less exclusionary aspects of western musical thought. "Equal temperament," he wrote in *The Lydian Chromatic Concept*, "represents an organizational system of great magnitude and one that is relatively free of prejudice."[10]

Russell portrayed the Concept in both specific and symbolic terms as a science. His book is thick with technical terms, some obviously central to traditional music theory, but others (e.g., gravity and relativity) drawn from the physical sciences. Early editions of the book even came with a kind of slide rule for working through the Concept's intricacies. Discussing the Concept's development, he explained, "It occurred to me that musicians were really like physicists or mathematicians in the way they went about solving the problems of improvisation."[11] There was also an ethical component in its empiricism: "It takes a scientist's view toward music. . . . It tries to relate seeing music as a part of nature and coming from nature. Seeing music in a way, emulating universal cosmic laws. It doesn't approach music with the prejudices of bad or good sound, or right or wrong. It just presents the possibilities. It's sort of a physics of music."[12]

RACE, GENDER, POWER, AND JAZZ PERSONAE

Ingrid Monson's essay "Oh Freedom: George Russell, John Coltrane, and Modal Jazz" provides the fullest treatment of the social ramifications of Russell's work from the 1950s and 1960s. She describes his project as a spiritual and intellectual quest: one fundamentally interested in musical and social freedom as it fused modernist musical thought with the "pan-denominational spirituality" developing in African American musicians' communities. As she puts it: "George Russell's music theory and his ideas of spiritual essence mobilized contemporary discourses in the services of needs that were shared by a broader spectrum of the African American jazz intelligentsia: (1) the need to prove the intellectual worth of jazz by demonstrating mastery of the rationalist tools of music theory (thereby undermining the racist idea that the jazz improvisation sprang from the instinctual outpourings of the untutored), while at the same time (2) retaining the romantic trope of music as a means of soulful, emotional, and spiritual transcendence."

The latter part of his project, as with Coltrane's, according to Monson, was oriented toward personal transformation, to the forging of "symbolic links between jazz and the successful anticolonial struggles of India and the African continent," and to the use of music "to break down categories of race, color, and nation."[13]

Building from Monson's analysis, especially her attention to his intellectual quest, I want to suggest that Russell's presentation of self as theorist and romantic artist in his book and other public statements may be understood as a complex kind of gendered, racial, and technoscientific maneuver. Not only did Russell's critical work and compositional strategies seek to expand the parameters of and legitimate jazz performance, they may be viewed as operating at the nexus of both race and gender, an intersection fundamental to the organization of power within the music world. As such, his project simultaneously drew upon and called into question raced and gendered critical orthodoxies while commenting on the social status of musicians laboring in the jazz industry.

As I have argued elsewhere, jazz had by the 1920s expressed the development of two linked musical goals held by many African American musicians: an elaboration and extension of various forms of black folk music through the arts of composition, improvisation, and arranging; and a crafting of an art music that overcame the restrictions of written music by drawing from black vernacular forms. These artistic goals, of course, helped shape and quite often responded to a complex critical discourse in which standards of black musical legitimacy were based, in the most general terms, upon a musician's ability to measure up to standards established in the concert music world, his or her commitment to (and perceived conformity to) the organic wellspring from which black music emerges (tradition, form, community, etc.), or both. The racial dimensions of these authenticating discourses are well known. Not only has each position been informed by a racial logic — the former projecting the desire to transcend blackness in its various social and discursive manifestations, the latter assuming a desire to remain true to it — but they have also formed the basis of modes of perception and debate informing struggles for power and authority among musicians, critics, and business interests.[14]

We must also keep in mind that gender played a significant role in such debates and struggles. For not only have such definitions of good jazz been deeply gendered — owing to pan-cultural, masculinist definitions of artistry and genius, the gendering of musical form in European and black diasporic traditions, the exclusion of women from various kinds of jazz-making and jazz discourse–producing spaces, the special place of jazz as a vehicle for masculine subject formations, etc. — but the jazz world was also a site for masculine as well as racial competition. As African American musicians attempted to gain artistic legitimacy and remuneration, they developed various gendered strategies for presenting themselves as artists in their public performances and, in some cases, in their writing. By the 1920s, some African American musicians presented themselves as romantic artists, masculine subjects who "embraced artistic ideals such as originality, spontaneity, and emotional expression as a way of generating self-respect . . . [and as] a means to power in [an economic] system that exploited black musicians and erased black genius" through both Eurocentric and primitivist (de)valuations of their music.[15]

Over the years, black musicians hoping to gain remuneration and critical legitimacy faced a changing array of challenges due to these raced and gendered definitions of artistry. In the 1950s, for example, the racial logic underpinning assessments of jazz was inflected by and made complicated by the contemporary politics of the art world and broader society alike. Definitions of jazz as high art were embedded with Eurocentric assumptions of postwar modernism as well as with the aura of possibility and the refusal of social boundaries that helped generate the black freedom struggle. Assessments of jazz as an expression of soul reflected not only a decades-old primitivist expectation, as well as its more recent manifestation in beat-era identification with black jazz players, but also the growing senses of cultural pride and political acumen that were central to black politics of the era. Both conceptual frames, deployed in jazz criticism and marketing alike, could be affirming but also quite limiting to African American musicians, whose artistic projects were often more culturally complex than critics and jazz industry types acknowledged.

Charles Mingus, an artist who serially embraced the roles of both "jazz artist" and "serious composer," frequently found himself and his hybrid musical project imperiled both by jazz business perfidy and by what we might call, for the purposes of the present analysis, the art/soul dichotomy of jazz valuation. Thus, in Mingus's writings and public commentary, we find "jazz" varyingly portrayed as an important and unique African American musical achievement and as a symbol of the limitations imposed on black artists by the music industry and critical establishment. The art of musical composition represents in his thought an escape from not only such limitations but also elitism, racism, and alienation. As a means of negotiating the Scylla and Charybdis of art and soul, Mingus frequently embraced the masculinist role of the romantic artist. Whether emphasizing his role as composer or jazz musician, he often described music as "a true expression of the self." This act reclaimed a racial and masculine subject threatened by the material and discursive limitations of the jazz world — even if, in his excessive performance of the role, he sometimes helped reproduce the very stereotypes of jazz musicians as untutored geniuses that he found so limiting.[16]

As with Mingus, Russell's writings and commentary from the period (and later) negotiated the complex discursive field and set of labor conditions presenting themselves to African American jazz players. *The Lydian Chromatic Concept of Tonal Organization*, of course, must be understood primarily as an instruction book for playing music. But embedded in Russell's discussion — in his crafting of the Concept as something with "a soul, born out of jazz . . . yet embracing all music," as well as in his self-presentation as both romantic artist attuned to emotion and theorist committed to the "science" of improvisation — we glimpse a somewhat different strategy. Russell's was, like Mingus's, a project that can be understood as operating within the field of gender, as well as race and economics. Yet Russell was making a somewhat different intervention, voiced through the emotionalism and intellectualism of the romantic artist *and* through the role of the theorist deploying codes from the technoscientific imaginary that played widely during this period.

AFROFUTURISM'S CHALLENGE

New technologies (e.g., saxophones, phonographs, radios, electronic recordings, electric guitars, long-playing records, audio tapes, synthesizers, samplers, computer recording and editing software programs, MP3 files, etc.) have dramatically changed over the years what music is and how it is heard. But if, as Ronald Radano and Philip Bohlman suggest, the very notion of music, as it has been conceptualized in the West and disseminated across the globe, is ontologically and metaphysically understood through the logic of racial difference while informing our sense of what racial differences or similarities are,[17] then it stands to reason that the advent and deployment of these technologies affect how we hear race through music. And, if we keep in mind, to paraphrase Stuart Hall and Paul Gilroy, that gender is one of the modalities through which this production of race and music is articulated, then the audibility of gender in this musical/technological interface should be of concern as well.[18]

In the past decade or so, scholars, critics, and artists have taken up with increasing frequency the question of how race and musical technologies are mutually constitutive, with particular attention to the role of new digital technologies. Herman Gray has recently surveyed this terrain, adding his own important voice as he analyzes "the ways that encounters between new digitally based information technologies and black vernacular musical practices have changed the terms of hearing and, in the process, imagined different notions of blackness through sound." Examining the critical moves of Afrofuturists — whom he describes as a "loose collection of writers, musicians, technologists, critics, and artists" — as well as the musical and intellectual work of the black avant-garde artists Steven Coleman, George Lewis, and Pamela Z, Gray asks that we "consider music more carefully as a potentially productive space of thinking about the relationship of blacks and new technologies. With music as the ground against which to consider this relationship, I think that we might reasonably ask how both new technologies and blackness are transformed in this encounter, and how this creative encounter speaks to the role of cultural politics in the representation and use of new technologies."[19]

As the aforementioned quotation indicates, Gray is in part interested in how such black intellectual/artistic projects "challenge, expose, and unsettle" the ways that race influences the production, uses, and representations of new digital technologies in the twenty-first century. Such projects challenge the unexamined whiteness of digital culture. They similarly call into question the utopian (and often assimilationist) narratives that focus on access to digital technologies as a remedy for black social and cultural exclusions, as well as those narratives that might reproduce such exclusions by assuming these technologies are irrelevant or unfamiliar to black people. Yet, Gray also observes that Afrofuturism, in particular, "use[s] new information and digital technologies to change the terms of a blackness fixed in bodies, place, nation, and even, it sometimes seems, history." He thus raises the question of what insights this project may hold in terms of reconstructing histories of previous encounters between black vernacular practices and emergent technologies, as well as providing a basis for "identifying and breaking codes that hold access to freedom from old narratives and debilitating discourses of black identity."[20]

Before applying the insights of this critical work on black musical technologies to jazz history, we must consider the limitations of the historiographic frame into which we are entering and the possibility that present-day critical projects, even Afrofuturism's, may reproduce those limitations. Scholars have become quite adept at listening to contemporary music for localized and global as well as transhistorical social significations. They have written wisely about how the interface of vernacular practice and technology over the years has reflected transformations in black subjectivities and consciousnesses, spoken of new conditions for black labor and transformations in black political cultures, and given us the tools for theorizing the life of race in ever more complicated ways.[21] Yet the question remains as to whether the tendency to view black musical engagements with science and technology primarily as epiphenomena of social relations, or as guides to self-reflexive scholarly maneuvers, means that we are not hearing an important part of the story — namely, the complex interface of broad histories of alienation and subjugation, localized economic and social forces, and musicians' *own* creative and political aspirations. It is particularly important to keep this in mind when we seek to excavate musical deployments of science and technology that are hidden by mythologies regarding the power and function of black music.

I wonder too about the characteristics of the musicians who figure prominently in this conversation about music and technology. The artists whose engagements with science and technology are most commonly asked to speak to the state of black society and, in some cases, of a liberatory, posthuman future are iconoclastic figures such as Sun Ra, George Clinton, and Lee Perry, whose self-presentation puts them at the edge of madness. I am concerned not only that this situation means that certain kinds of projects (like Russell's) are seldom heard but also that the discourse on black music and technology is contoured in a way that treads dangerously close to reproducing a familiar raced and gendered mythos. For example, I take to be fundamentally true John Corbett's and John Akomfrah's influential assessments of how Sun Ra's, Clinton's, and Perry's use of science fiction tropes (namely, space travel and extraterrestiality) in the subject of their music and the crafting of their public personae are commenting on the alienation of black people in societies structured by racism and creating, in Corbett's phrase, a "platform for playful subversion, imagining a productive zone largely exterior to dominant ideology."[22] But at the same time, I worry that various accounts such as this — even as they are predicated on the idea that investigating engagements with science and technology challenges the primitivist (and racist) assumption that such terrain is irrelevant to the study of black culture — may help reproduce a kind of primitivism (namely, the primitive intellectualism that critics have long ascribed to black male jazz musicians) because of the personalities who represent the conversation. As Monson observes in her assessment of post–Second World War assessments of jazz, "the historically close association between madness, pathology, and racial difference made the image of the jazz avant-garde artist especially prone to appropriation by primitivist racial ideologies."[23]

I am thus interested in drawing from existing scholarly practice concerning black music, science, and technology, but shifting its methodological focus somewhat: from the act of reading musical texts and musicians' personae as relatively unselfconscious reflections of the social to a deeper investigation of how musicians (like Russell) theorized their own practices. This allows us to move from the general analytical attention to the music's symbolic commentary on social conditions and racial and human subjectivity to an enterprise that takes into account why musicians choose to employ certain musical, lyrical, technological devices and what that says about their careers, the genres in which they work, the times in which they lived, the challenges posed by the particular modes of music, and the creative discussions in which they were immersed. I wish to contribute to an alternative genealogy of black musical technologies consistent with Gray's discussion of Lewis, Coleman, and Pamela Z: a move that is organized less around mining musical and personal performances for insights into multiple conditions of blackness than it is around an engagement with a broader range of artists' critical practices for such insights.

The Afrofuturist critic Kodwo Eshun takes us partway toward understanding Russell's engagement with science and technology in his book, *More Brilliant than the Sun*. Eshun professes his interest not in those black musical expressions that speak of redemption or of "a perpetual fight for human status, a yearning for human rights, a struggle for inclusion within the human species," but rather in that of the "Postsoul Era" — in other words, music that "alienates itself from the human" and calls attention to the treachery of the category. Of great concern also are the ways such alien music calls into question and points to the flaws in black music criticism, its humanistic underpinnings, its political certitudes, and its essentialist expectations. "One side of the alien discontinuum is the rejection of any and all notions of a compulsory black condition. Where journalism still insists on a solid state known as 'blackness,' *More Brilliant* dissolves this solidarity with a corpse into a *fluidarity* maintained and exacerbated by sound machines."[24]

Russell's 1968 recording of *Electronic Sonata for Souls Loved by Nature* is the first piece of music Eshun examines in detail, and his analysis relies on the composer's own explanation of his project. By combining prerecorded tape with live jazz performance, Russell, in Eshun's view, "triggered a post-jazz universe," disrupting the romantic and redemptive critical narratives positioning the music as an existential or naturalist response to a machine-tooled modern world. "Instead of invoking jazz as an art, a beautiful soul which defies the military industrial complex, Russell technologizes jazz until it becomes an art-industrial complex." He suggests further that Russell's journey back into a "sonic past," i.e., prerecorded sounds from nonwestern cultures, "is to go forward into a new future."[25]

In Eshun's formulation, Russell's work fits well to support an Afro-futurist data recovery project seeking to challenge the received wisdom about the place and function of black music in the world and the ways that it is so often asked to speak about a "compulsory black condition." But what if we shift our temporal orientation? What if we want to look beyond the posthuman present and future and perhaps direct our attention to a mundane U.S. past, when something called soul and something called art, problematic as the terms were and are, were relevant to Russell and other musicians and worthy of consideration? Again, what is the historical significance — both in terms of contemporary meaning and presentist historiographical and pedagogical concerns — of examining this somewhat earlier fusion of technology and vernacular practice? What if we wish not simply "to go forward into a new future" but also to understand the full historical resonance of "the belief that any valid movement in jazz must be firmly rooted in the past"?[26]

In addition to providing the methodological framework for understanding how one could play better music, Russell's invocation of science can be understood as a raced and gendered intervention in the raced and gendered jazz field of the 1950s and 1960s. We begin to get a sense of the levels at which this deployment of science operated by considering how Russell described his project in ways that are consistent with a post–Second World War "technoscientific imaginary," wherein science and technology were seen not only as threats to humanity for sure but also as the source of the solutions to the problems facing modern society. In an interview in 1960, Russell linked the Concept to other technologies: "You can parallel it to life this way: it reflects man's striving to overcome nature. And nature, I believe, has placed these musical elements, like rhythm and tonality, at our disposal to make beauty out of them. . . . So, it just represents a continuance of man's struggle with nature to accept ever-more complex materials and subdue them, and build art or bridges or atomic bombs."[27]

Timothy Taylor has identified the influence of the postwar technoscientific imaginary on the production, consumption, and critical discussion of music in the United States and France, with an eye toward the racial and gendered ordering of power in the music world. First, he shows how a scientist/*bricoleur* binary, consistent with the formulations of Claude Lévi-Strauss, conditioned the debates between participants in the *elektronishe musik* and *musique concrète* movements. *Musique concrète*'s Pierre Schaeffer was, in fact, very much influenced by the anthropologist, calling his movement "a science of the concrete." In *The Savage Mind* (1962), Lévi-Strauss proclaimed, in Taylor's words, that "bricolage was the process of making culture, making knowledge through a 'science of the concrete.' . . . In other words, the bricoleur begins with materials at hand and makes a structure out of them. The scientist, on the other hand, begins with an overall structure, a concept." Pierre Boulez and other proponents of *elektronishe musik*, on the other hand, deployed the more normative understanding of science to privilege the role of composer in their project while critiquing what they viewed as the less rigorous, less abstract, less in-control aspects of *musique concrète*. This assessment was based in part on the latter's emphasis on collected sounds, quite often from nonwestern, "oral" cultures. "For Boulez and his comrades, then, *musique concrète* wasn't simply an inferior music based on aesthetic grounds of little or no interest to most listeners, or even the lesser of musics in a revitalized postwar economy of musical prestige. Instead, for Boulez and other detractors, *musique concrète* was akin to the music of primitives or, perhaps worse from their perspective, civilized people who had 'gone native.' It was in the position of oral music rather than written; bricolage, not science; premodernity, not modernity."[28]

Taylor also shows some of the ways gender informed the interface of music and technology during the late 1950s and 1960s. As part of his treatment of how "space-age pop music," designed to be played on hi-fi equipment, spoke of a broader anxiety and ambivalence about technology, he discusses how in postwar consumer culture new technologies and scientific innovations were vehicles for masculine identifications. Taylor draws from Michael L. Smith's identification of a rise in "commodity scientism" as "a belief, negative or positive, in the ineffable qualities of science and technology." This ideology was used to market science and technology to the American public, whether they were manifested in consumer goods or nuclear weapons and the space program. Consumers were instructed "to lump together personal and social progress with technology; and technology with new commodities," a process that often relied upon technoscientific jargon and neologisms that could convey a kind of " 'Inside-dopester' status to the consumers." Taylor argues that "commodity scientism in the domestic scene for men is probably best represented by the hi-fi craze of the late 1940s and 1950s." Drawing from the work of Barbara Ehrenreich, he suggests that the hi-fi allowed men to reclaim not only domestic space but also the notion "that *complex* technology was . . . the proper domain of the man." Moreover, in a world where musical consumption, especially art music consumption, could be defined as effeminate, "tinkering with hi-fi sets was one way to avoid such contradictions."[29]

Although Taylor's work does not address the jazz world per se, it does provide important insights into how a racial and gendered logic informed ideas about music and technology during the 1950s and early 1960s. It helps us understand how, at this moment when the use of and familiarity with science and technology increasingly presented a means toward self-advancement and self-worth, battles over music legitimacy could be waged by deploying these racially informed categories and their various Others. Taylor's analysis also encourages us to think about how the deployment of new technologies in music could be a way of asserting one's masculine prerogatives, whether the prerogatives were situated within the realm of heterosocial and homosocial interpersonal relationships or within a broader ideological field of gender formations and identifications.

In addition to being a vehicle for creating higher quality music, Russell's Concept may be viewed as a device geared toward improving the position of jazz players (whether African American or not) laboring in a field coded and often devalued as black. Later in his career, he said that his early involvement with the Concept was in part intended to create opportunities for him to make money writing music. During the 1950s Russell described the need to develop compositional techniques that could once again (as before bebop) significantly influence the art of improvisation. He also said the low pay of the jazz business was forcing musicians into commercial work and preventing bandleaders from conducting adequate rehearsals.[30] The implication then was that the skills available to composers and improvisers through the Concept might provide a means by which quality music could be generated by composers and improvisers alike in an environment that imposed structural impediments to these goals.

Russell's formulation also countered ideas brought to bear on jazz and its practitioners. As Monson notes, framing the Concept as a science disputed primitivist conceptions of jazz, whether negatively or positively valued, by theorizing it as a skilled and rational, as opposed to emotional or instinctual, project. Describing Ornette Coleman's music in 1960 as embodying aspects of both horizontal and vertical gravity, Russell was careful to state that Coleman's artistic choices were a product of reflection. "He knows about these things; he's not just playing that way just because he feels it. He's playing that way because he feels it and knows it too."[31] Such moves challenged the idea that black musicians were products of nature revolting against the machine — a formulation often serving the needs of white hipster observers during this period — as well as the notion that black cultural forms did not have the same legitimacy as European forms because of an assumed "technological absence." As Russell put it later, "For many years jazz has been the victim of bigotry. See, they say it has no technology. But it now has a technology. The Lydian Concept represents a technology and I don't have to look to European theory for that technology."[32]

In the context of the 1950s and 1960s jazz world, in which musicians' struggles to achieve a critical voice often paralleled struggles to obtain fair treatment in the financial realm, Russell's deployment of the Concept as a science and technology should be seen as operating within the field of gender as well as race. Given the way that disputes among jazz musicians, critics, and industry personnel were engaged through modes of masculine competition, as well as racial conflict, the masculine aspects of Russell's performance were central to his challenge to the devaluation of jazz by highbrow critics, primitivist expectations of members of the jazz critical establishment, and the inequities of the jazz business. When Russell claims critical space through an embrace of science and technology, it is a move that should be understood in the context of jazz world debates and within the broader cultural matrix of commodity scientism. At this moment of the technoscientific imaginary's ascendance, when personal and social progress were often linked to science and technology through an array of neologisms and jargonistic phrases, Russell's writing and comments about the Concept draw upon this ideology as they position him as the holder of a kind of insider knowledge. His authority, predicated on the masculinist role of theorist, challenges that of jazz critics. As the inventor and user of this complex musical technology, Russell claims the symbolic empowerment that comes with it for the masculine subject of jazz laboring in the music business. The point here is not to claim that Russell intended to reproduce notions that jazz was a masculine endeavor, but rather to suggest what his strategic deployment of race- and gender-saturated concepts of science and technology meant in the raced and gendered space of the critical discourse of the moment.

But Russell's move here is more complicated. He does not simply abandon the authenticating space of the vernacular when he describes his theory of science and technology. His performance of "Stratusphunk" on "The Future of Jazz" is symbolic of a goal during this period of trying to take jazz into the future by maintaining an attention to its roots. As Russell states on the cover of the album of the same time, "I think my music can best be summed up in terms of my belief that any valid movement in jazz must be firmly rooted in the past. When the roots are plainly identifiable, there is a special excitement that comes with something being new and old music at the same time. This pretty much describes our objective as a band: to build on established jazz; to further it by making broader use of all the materials that are available to us; to create new concepts in the areas of rhythm, tone and form through both composition and improvisation — but always to build and evolve from the best and most valid aspects of what has preceded us."[33] It seems clear that the Concept provided a means of validating yet also negotiating the terrain of the "jazz tradition," defined both through modes of art and soul.

The beauty of the Concept, he argued, was that it allowed maximum entry into the world of chromaticism while still maintaining one's roots. As he put it, "the basic folk nature of the scales is preserved, and yet, because you can use any number of scales or you can be in any number of tonalities at once, and/or sequentially, it also creates a very chromatic kind of feeling, so that it's sort of like being atonal with a Big Bill Broonzy sound. *You Can Retain the Funk.*"[34] The Concept, as his comments suggest, provided a theoretical basis for claiming a place within the tradition while justifying his own attempts to transform it with the tools of modern composition and music theory. Russell's invocation of soul may be read as a sort of defensive posturing, anticipating and perhaps deflecting the essentialist critiques — whether based on a romantic primitivism, avant-garde aesthetics, and/or social relevance — that were often brought to bear on African American jazz players who strayed too far from the modes of blackness and maleness represented by hard bop and soul jazz and in very different ways in subsequent years by free jazz.

This was, to be sure, a difficult maneuver to pull off. During the 1960s, Russell found himself positioned within the raced and gendered critical jazz discourse in ways that simultaneously show the great difficulties of negotiating the art/soul dichotomy and make clear why musicians have been interested in developing a successful strategy for doing so. Although he expressed enthusiasm for Ornette Coleman's and John Coltrane's playing in the 1964 edition of his book and in various interviews from the period, Russell also voiced skepticism toward certain trends in avant-garde or "experimental music." He criticized "free jazz," doubting publicly that some of its practitioners knew what they were trying to express, and he seemed uncomfortable with a musical freedom movement that sought to move beyond the rules he had established for tonal organization and the standards he had set for himself as an artist.[35]

Russell's aversion to free jazz also seems to have stemmed from a fear that adopting that musical stance allowed one to be pigeonholed by critics or musicians engaged in the racial gamesmanship central to politics surrounding the music at the moment. Although critical of racism inside and outside the jazz business, he was at times uncomfortable with the assumption that the "new music" could be understood solely as an expression of black militancy. As he said in 1964, "I don't think the seeds of this new music lie in a racial protest alone . . . it's a cry against the whole social structure. It's a cry for truth. It transcends race — and that can be done, you know. As much as the racial thing is pushed, there are problems that transcend it, which have to do with all of us as human beings . . . We're all being brainwashed, regardless of race, creed, or color."[36] Later, Russell became furious with Dan Morgenstern and other jazz critics after Morgenstern quoted Russell's criticisms of the avant-garde in a 1965 *Down Beat* article. Although not entirely inconsistent with comments he made before and after, Russell believed his words had been taken out of context and that the critique had been exaggerated. He was incensed by the fact that the article featured a picture of Russell with a caption underneath reading, "Avant-garde is the last refuge of the untalented."[37] As a result of this article, Russell found himself among the artists and critics taken to task by Archie Shepp in a letter to *Down Beat* later that year. "I address myself to George Russell," Shepp wrote, "a man whose work I have always respected and admired, who in an inopportune moment with an ill-chosen phrase threw himself squarely into the enemy camp."[38]

Russell was already in Europe when he learned of the controversy. In his response to Shepp and Morgenstern, he tried to counter the uses to which critics deployed his vision. "I don't want to be anybody's darling. I especially don't want to be the darling of a group of men who, after all these years, have suddenly found a use for me . . . to batter a segment of the avant-garde they don't like over the head." Russell also expressed the view that adopting the identity of a free jazz musician might force one to make certain artistic compromises to conform to that image: "The very reason I am in Europe is because I could find no camp or clique to join in the United States where I could express my music without having to embrace the form of popular delusion being sold to the crowd; that is, I could either become a commercial hack or I could play angry, or crazy, or assume one of those other postures that the jazz image-makers love to exploit."[39] In other words, expatriation was a means of escaping artistic compromise, whether a result of conforming to the expectations of the musical marketplace or to the "compulsory black condition" that it encouraged.

CONCLUSION

By proposing a musical science and technology that were "born out of jazz . . . yet embrac[ed] all music," Russell voiced ideas that have much in common with recent critical work. Russell expressed an alternative universalism that was more fundamental and more inclusive than the exclusionary universalism projected by Western musical discourse and, by extension, much scientific and social thought. His was a vision that expanded definitions of human history, creativity, and science and asked black people and others to live according to higher spiritual and political principles rather than by "lesser laws" imposed by modern societies. Russell was, in essence, challenging narrow definitions of the human supported by scientific knowledge and beliefs about black people as irrational beings lacking technologies while simultaneously suggesting that the development of new technologies and modes of knowledge might allow black people to redefine their status as humans and perhaps reconfigure civil society as well.[40]

When evaluating or drawing lessons from Russell's commentary, however, it remains critically important that we analyze it in the historically specific context of his social and creative aspirations. We should understand Russell and his Concept as operating within and responding to the art/soul dichotomy underpinning valuations of jazz. We should also situate him as negotiating the racial politics of masculine authority in the critical discourse around the music and in the economic relationships that helped produce it. Russell's self-presentation as a scientist relied on a dual authority: theoretical knowledge derived from a culturally transcendent science of music and a culturally specific idiomatic grounding. He drew upon the masculine codes that informed jazz artistry, as well as the no-less-masculine field of scientific and technological knowledge as he intervened in the power politics of the music world as well as that of broader society.

R eturning, finally, to my students' reactions to Russell in the "Future of Jazz," I hope that I have suggested an alternative to those assumptions that were implicit in his unintelligibility to them as a black musician. In addition to charting a route to playing better music, the science and technology that he dared bring to jazz represent a strategic response to the raced and gendered authenticating discourses that informed and continue to inform our understandings of jazz and its social significance. It by no means escaped these racial and gendered logics, but his was a move that can also be understood as a hermeneutic for providing insights into how jazz meaning was shaped by them.

Russell's project, then, like other encounters between other technologies and black vernacular musical practices, allows us to hear blackness in different registers. His work from this period does not come easily mediated through the archetypal musician as primitive intellectual but rather demands that we consider him engaged in a self-conscious fusion of technology, science, and the vernacular. As such, it asks us to think about the limitations of "blackness" as a framework explaining the generation of art, and to consider carefully a matrix of meaning revolving around black music and how such meanings relate to the place of black people in the music industry and the world beyond. Russell's project — which simultaneously conforms to and disrupts gendered definitions of jazz artistry — also suggests that investigations of race and racial history in that thing we call jazz require attention to gender as a mode through which race is lived and as a broader field of power that is itself raced.

NOTES

I would like to thank Tori Quiñoñez for research assistance, the University of California Humanities Research Institute for support during the early stages of research and writing, Peter X. Feng for bringing "The Future of Jazz" to my attention, panelists and audience members at the 2002 American Studies Association meeting for comments on a presentation of this material, and Catherine Ramírez for comments on a draft of this essay. Any and all errors, blind spots, misconceptions, etc., are entirely my own doing.

1. Kodwo Eshun, *More Brilliant than the Sun: Adventures in Sonic Fiction* (London: Quartet, 1998), 003.

2. George Russell, *The Lydian Chromatic Concept of Tonal Organization*, vol. 1, *The Art and Science of Tonal Gravity*, 4th ed. (Brookline, Mass.: Concept, 2001). The first volume of this edition focuses on vertical tonal gravity. As of this writing, Russell is working on a second volume dealing with horizontal tonal gravity and supravertical tonal gravity. Earlier editions addressed all concepts in one volume.

3. Ingrid Monson, "Russell, George," *Center for Black Music Research: International Dictionary of Black Composers* (Chicago: Fitzroy Dearborn, 1999), 968–69; Ingrid Monson, "Oh Freedom: George Russell, John Coltrane, and Modal Jazz," *In the Course of Performance: Studies in the World of Musical Improvisation*, ed. Bruno Nettl with Melinda Russell (Chicago: University of Chicago Press, 1998), 149–54; Ingrid Monson, *Freedom Sounds: Civil Rights Call Out to Jazz and Africa* (New York: Oxford University Press, 2007), 287–93.

4. Dom Cerulli, "George Russell," *Down Beat*, May 29, 1958, 15.

5. George Russell, *The Lydian Chromatic Concept of Tonal Organization for Improvisation* (Cambridge: Concept, 1959; repr. with appendix 1964), 27, 49.

6. Cerulli, "George Russell," 15.

7. Pat Wilson, "George Russell's Constant Quest," *Down Beat*, April 27, 1972, 15.

8. Olive Jones, "A New Theory for Jazz," *Black Perspective in Music* 2, no. 1 (spring 1974): 71.

9. Cerulli, "George Russell," 16.

10. Russell, *Lydian Chromatic Concept* (1964), technical appendix A.

11. Francis Davis, *In the Moment* (New York: Oxford University Press, 1986), 172.

12. Ken Linden, "George Russell," *Jazz and Pop*, April 1970, 30.

13. Monson, "Oh Freedom," 156.

14. Porter 2002, 25–32.

15. Ibid., 31.

16. Ibid., 101–48. This presentation of self as masculine, Romantic artist is most evident in Mingus's autobiography, *Beneath the Underdog*.

17. Radano and Bohlman 2000, 1–53.

18. Gilroy 1993, 85.

19. Gray 2005, 149, 153, 162.

20. Ibid., 153–54, 165.

21. Ibid., 218. See Gray's note 9 for a useful account of these issues, key texts, genres, and musicians often considered.

22. John Corbett, *Extended Play: Sounding Off from John Cage to Dr. Funkenstein* (Durham: Duke University Press, 1994), 8; John Akomfrah is the director of the film *The Last Angel of History* (1996), in which prominent Afrofuturist critics, black science fiction writers, and musicians in whose work technology figures prominently are interviewed.

23. Monson 1995, 412. See also Ronald Radano's important discussion of the primitive/intellectual homology in *New Musical Figurations: Anthony Braxton's Cultural Critique* (Chicago: University of Chicago Press, 1996), 261–63.

24. Eshun, 003–6. On this last point Eshun continues, "Today's cyborgs are too busy manufacturing themselves across time-space to disintensify themselves with all the Turing Tests for transatlantic, transeuropean and transafrican consciousness: affirmation, keeping it real, representing, staying true to the game, respect due, staying black. Alien music today deliberately fails all these tests, these putrid corpses of petrified moralism: it treats them with utter indifference; it replaces them with nothing whatsoever."

25. Ibid., 001–6.

26. Such a move, particularly as it concerns the continued relevance of the category of human for black people, is suggested by Andrew Weheliye in his reading of Eshun's work alongside that of Katherine Hayles. His analysis suggests that black references to such

humanist categories as art and soul are not to be dismissed but can be productively investigated in light of their articulations by and through emergent technologies. Weheliye, " 'Feenin' Posthuman Voices in Contemporary Black Popular Music," *Social Text* 20, no. 2 (summer 2002): 25–30. An attention to historical specificity in understanding musicians' dependence on cultural categories is also suggested by Monson's work on Russell. She notes that Russell's embrace of essence and his use of a formalist theoretical paradigm challenge the post-structuralist critique of modernism, essentialism, and universalism. "I would like to suggest that ideas of spiritual essence and universality that circulated within the jazz community in the 1950s and 1960s had little in common with meanings currently attached to these concepts in contemporary critiques of essentialism and that they require recontextualization within appropriate historical and cultural frameworks." See Monson, "Oh Freedom," 156–57.

27. George Russell, "Where Do We Go from Here?" *The Jazz Word*, by Dom Cerulli, Burt Korall, and Mort L. Nasatir (New York: Ballantine, 1960; repr. New York: Da Capo, 1987), 239.

28. Timothy D. Taylor, *Strange Sounds: Music, Technology and Culture* (New York: Routledge, 2001), 55–60.

29. Ibid., 72–81.

30. Jones, "A New Theory for Jazz," 73; Russell, "Where Do We Go from Here?" 234–38.

31. George Russell and Martin Williams, "Ornette Coleman and Tonality," *Jazz Review*, June 1960, 8.

32. Roger Riggins, "George Russell," *Coda* 162 (1978): 11.

33. George Russell, *Stratusphunk*, Riverside 9341.

34. Russell, "Where Do We Go from Here?," 238.

35. Bill Coss, "Afterhours: A Jazz Discussion with Clark Terry, Don Ellis, Bob Brookmeyer, Hall Overton, George Russell," *Down Beat*, November 9, 1961, 19–22, 38; "Tangents," *Down Beat*, June 18, 1964, 14–17, 39.

36. "Tangents," 17. In 1966 he said, "Divisions on the basis of skin color or, for that matter, political color are superficial. For when it gets right down to it, there are but two groups of people in the world: those who will participate in the exploitation of the popular delusions and madness of crowds and those who will not." See "Popular Delusions and the Madness of Crowds: A Letter from George Russell," *Down Beat*, April 7, 1966, 15.

37. "Random Thoughts from George Russell," *Down Beat*, July 29, 1965, 9. Although there is no author listed for this piece, Russell's subsequent comments indicate the author was Dan Morgenstern.

38. Archie Shepp, "An Artist Speaks Bluntly," *Down Beat*, December 16, 1965, 11.

39. Russell, "Popular Delusions and the Madness of Crowds," 14–15. He provided a similar account later: "That movement involved a number of musicians who were caught up in a kind of stream-of-consciousness playing, very angry music and very intense — you know, shouting and screaming — with free use of all kinds of musical resources. And I didn't particularly identify with that movement. On the other hand, I certainly didn't identify with the other direction, the commercial route, which many jazzmen took, some successfully and some not so successfully. So I went to Europe and found employment and found an outlet for my music." See Jones, "A New Theory for Jazz," 67.

40. In 1974 Russell offered the following: "There is a parallelism that can be drawn here: black people in general have a tendency to totally accept laws . . . So, it's O.K. to talk about black liberation and black this-and-that, but nothing is going to change fundamentally in this society which is ruled by laws that are so precious to their makers. One has to question the laws. That's what I did; that's what absorbs me. When Western society tells us that we are not technologically-minded people, couldn't that be absurd? Couldn't we just be involved in a different kind of technology? If we could get some idea of and some appreciation of our own kind of technology — it's very obvious in African art and in the music, and it certainly must be present in other areas of human activity too, if we could develop an appreciation of who we are, it would help rid us of this inferiority complex that's been shoved onto us." Jones, "A New Theory for Jazz," 72.

Sherrie Tucker

"BUT THIS MUSIC IS MINE ALREADY!":

"WHITE WOMAN" AS JAZZ COLLECTOR IN

THE FILM *NEW ORLEANS* (1947)

"The music I've been singing, so traditional, it was new once. And I've been learning to make it mine. But this! This music is mine already!"[1] so gushes Miralee Smith, the white opera-singing, jazz-smitten ingénue played by Dorothy Patrick in the film *New Orleans* (1947), set in 1917. Despite having spent a good deal of the scene talking over the collective improvisation of Louis Armstrong, Kid Ory, Zutty Singleton, etc., Miralee finds her attraction to "authentic New Orleans jazz" rising to a crescendo. Especially moved by the film's theme song, "Do You Know What it Means to Miss New Orleans," as sung by Endie, her black maid (played with palpable unhappiness by Billie Holiday in her only role in a feature motion picture), Miralee rises, eyes glowing, cheeks flushed, and declares, "I'm going to sing that New Orleans song!"

For this act of white-lady impropriety — and not, as we may prefer, for talking over the music — Miralee is (gently) bounced from the Basin Street club. Such a rebuff would crush many a die-hard jazz fan, but not Miralee, whose desire now burns hotter than Buddy Bolden's trumpet calling the children back home. This music is *hers*! She simply *must* feel the song of her black maid moving through her own white-lady body, as indeed, she will, before this musical romance is over. In the film's inevitable, and forgettable, grand finale, Miralee filters the music through her body from the concert hall stage, making jazz respectable and modernizing white womanhood. In the tradition of Paul Whiteman, Miralee makes a (white) "lady out of jazz."

Until recently, the only parts of the film *New Orleans* I had seen were the musical clips containing Billie Holiday—how awful to see her in the maid's uniform, but oh, how her singing transcended Hollywood's limitations—and Louis Armstrong, leading a "Trad" revivalist's dream team of New Orleans musicians including Kid Ory, Mutt Carey, and Zutty Singleton. I doubt that I am alone among jazz fans whose familiarity with those musical sequences had not compelled a further look at the rest of the film. And no wonder: the consensus of jazz and film critics, historians, and aficionados, past and present, is that with the exception of the musical sequences, the film is, as Donald Bogle puts it, "a dreary pedestrian mess." Bogle writes: "Although the story is supposedly about jazz's rise to mainstream acceptance, the real jazz innovators—Louis Armstrong and Billie Holiday—are neatly relegated to the sidelines while the plot follows the lives of the lead white characters, who are uniformly bland."[2]

Although I heartily agree with this critical assessment, I would argue that the juxtaposition of bland white characters with brilliant black musicians is not at all at odds with the film's racial project, nor with those of many "Trad" fans of the 1940s (or with much jazz appreciation since).[3] White blandness and black affect, in fact, are not incidental to this film. The characters with which the white target audience is invited to identify are united by their weariness of European high culture and by their enthusiasm for jazz as played by black musicians. There is something, in other words, about the failure of the film that works in favor of its message: the redemptive promise of authentic black New Orleans jazz for the bodies and souls of white Americans. If the lead white characters in the film were to sit down and watch it with their critics, they might in fact agree with the assessment of their own blandness and the cultural and emotional superiority of Armstrong and Holiday. It is what they do throughout the film.

What is missing if we leave the analysis of the film as musically "bright" and dramatically a "dud" (to cite the headline that didn't do justice to Leonard Feather's explicitly antiracist *Metronome* review[4]) is an assessment of these performances of bland white gaping at creative black musicking as enactments of *power*. Indeed, these acts are facilitated, in large part, through a particular construction of white womanhood as unaware, or "innocent," of her social power. To face the entire

Fig. 10.1. White woman in the foreground. Dorothy Patrick as Miralee, with Arturo de Cordova as Nick, in one of many scenes in which white people eclipse jazz musicians in *New Orleans* (1947). Musicians in the background include Red Callender (bass), Zutty Singleton (drums, back to camera), Charlie Beal (piano), Kid Ory (trombone), Louis Armstrong (trumpet), Billie Holiday, Bud Scott (guitar), and Barney Bigard (clarinet). Institute of Jazz Studies, Rutgers University, Newark, New Jersey.

film, rather than just the musical sequences starring the black jazz musicians, compels us to consider the curious efficacy of the "white lady" in that very enactment of jazz appropriation analyzed in jazz studies as a white masculinist routine. We in jazz studies have gotten rather adept at wagging our fingers at the unconscious primitivism of figures such as Mezz Mezzrow, Norman Mailer, and Jack Kerouac. Women-in-jazz historians like me have been far more interested in recovering women jazz musicians of any race as forgotten historical actors than in retrieving lost histories of white women as jazz appropriators, symbolic or otherwise. Yet, interestingly enough, it is a white woman who is the lead jazz fan, appropriator, and colonizer in the plot of *New Orleans*.

The importance of this topic is, for me, not simply to identify primitivism in the jazz representational past, but to think critically about jazz desire in the present, especially among those who sincerely wish to oppose legacies of cultural imperialism, racial injustice, sexism, poverty, and neglect. For me, this involves interrogating the spheres of jazz scholarship, women-in-jazz scholarship, and jazz fandom that I myself inhabit. The tendency of jazz discourse to occlude ongoing histories of injustice and inequality is a pernicious one. Responding to a 2005 *Time Magazine* article in which Wynton Marsalis emphasized national love of jazz as a moral lever to step up relief efforts after Hurricane Katrina, Salim Washington argued that to consider New Orleans as "the nation's soul only through the lens of culture continues a long tradition of comfort with creating myths that hide much more than they reveal."[5] A century of national love for New Orleans as the birthplace of jazz, for instance, did little to rectify a century of cohabitation of jazz tourism and institutional neglect of poor and black lives in the most flood-vulnerable areas of the city and the wider Gulf region. The lyric "Do you know what it means to miss New Orleans?" will never mean quite the same after Katrina, but the root of its tragic irony — the idealization of moss-draped, gumbo-rich, color-blind egalitarian jam sessions and the concurrent neglect of ongoing structures of race- and class-based unequal life chances — troubles a century of jazz desire.

THE PROBLEM WITH WHITE WOMAN'S HIPNESS

The usual cinematic representations of jazz fans feature white men, as Krin Gabbard makes clear in his recent work on the figure he calls the "Jazz Nerd." Gabbard analyzes the "Jazz Nerd" as a white man who cannot bear any gaps in his collection, and who develops an outside-the-mainstream masculine identity through amassing and organizing and memorizing jazz records, especially those of black men whom the "Jazz Nerd" admires as "hip."[6] For Ingrid Monson, the historical problem with "white hipness" is its tendency to project white desires for affect, authenticity, and sexuality, onto black bodies and black music — so that even when the "hipster" is sincere in loving jazz, he or she may be reproducing elements of the very aspects of dominant constructions of race that shore up white supremacist ideology. Monson draws from Eric Lott's analysis of the continuation of minstrelsy through bohemianism in white men's hipness, but she also notes that "[m]any white women have enjoyed the reputation of black men and women for hypersexuality," adding that "[a]ttention to the particular pathways of identification would no doubt illuminate the cultural issue further."[7]

To critically unpack the "pathways of identification" available to jazz-loving white women historically, it seems to me that we need much more information about white women as performers and audience members of minstrelsy, and as bohemians, hipsters, fans, reformers, and performers of jazz and other forms of black music. Fortunately, a growing body of outstanding work is emerging, notably new studies by Michele Wallace and Jayna Brown, whose works on race in silent film and black American traveling dancers and musicians, respectively, attend to the cultural longevity of the stage and film role of Topsy as a white woman's minstrel staple.[8] Although *Uncle Tom's Cabin* was written by a white woman as an abolitionist text, it became a popular minstrel theme for both black and white minstrel troops and, in white minstrelsy, provided the first stock female blackface role. Brown argues that what white women stood to gain by playing the misbehaving slave girl was "conditional access to realms of expressive freedoms they were otherwise forbidden, carefully contained moments of mischievous disruption to rules and regulations of patriarchal supremacy."[9] Pamela Brown Lavitt's work on Jewish women as coon-shouters, the form that bridged minstrelsy and vaudeville, is another excellent study. Following Michael Rogin, Lavitt argues that immigrant women—Jewish women and Irish women—accessed whiteness through performances of blackness that were not necessarily dependent on blackface, but often on sounding the signs of blackface minstrelsy, while looking white.[10] Their access to white womanhood could be effectively performed through contrast: demonstrating themselves as women who were so white that they could perform counterfeit blackness without forfeiting white womanhood. We can see this on sheet music covers, in which minstrel imagery illustrates the songs, contrasted with cameo inserts of the white woman singer, appearing very Victorian and respectable-looking.[11] This was part of the pleasure derived by audiences, that the woman who sang in the high-pitched "shouting" that was heard as raced and sexually hot was indeed, very, very white.[12]

I expect that white women jazz fans would reject any analysis of their devotion to jazz as appropriation and understandably so. Yet, as one of Maxine Gordon's interviewees in her "Women Who Listen" oral history project of women jazz fans, I have been thinking about how white womanhood has shaped my own pathway of identification as a jazz fan, and it does seem to me that jazz seemed to offer what felt like an "escape" from the social position I continue to inhabit (which, of course, has its privileges in a racist culture).[13] Part of my responsibility then, as a white woman jazz fan, is to lose my "innocence" about the pathways of identification I inherit. I may not *identify* with Miralee's jazz desire, but I need to know its history — especially if I *don't* want to replicate it. In short, although I agree with Donald Bogle that the film is "a dreary pedestrian mess," it is a mess that deserves scholarly attention.

Let us take a closer look at the white woman in *New Orleans*. Again, I want to make it clear that I am not arguing that Miralee Smith reveals what white upper class northern U.S. women jazz fans were really like in 1947 or at any other time. But neither is this representation irrelevant to understanding something about white womanhood and jazz desire. What I want to argue is that this performance tells us something about the cultural legibility of a representation of one kind of relationship of a white woman to jazz — which, in this case, facilitates the "innocent" appropriation of a black woman's song and stumps for "Traditional" jazz during a culture war between fans of "New Orleans" jazz and bebop. I also want to argue that Miralee is not simply an individual film character, but that she occupies what Ruth Frankenberg calls the Trope of White Woman, whose cultural ubiquity makes it difficult to know about, even imagine, and perhaps even to *become*, another kind of white woman jazz fan.

I'm anchoring my reading in Frankenberg's analysis of the recurring, co-constructed, and powerful "family of Tropes," in which White Woman is characterized as vulnerable, innocent, and sexually pure, enabling White Man's cultural value as protector of white womanhood. The trope of Man of Color protects this system of by standing in as white woman's sexual predator — what Angela Davis has called the Myth of the Black Rapist. Alternately, he is rendered sexless and powerless, as animated in Uncle Tom's benign friendship with Little Eva. It is, in fact, the cinematic emphasis of Uncle Tom's devotion to Little Eva that V. J. Jerome identified as the narrative twist that "eliminated" the novel's "endictment of slavery."[14] The recurrence of this relationship in Hollywood cinema has been noted by many scholars including Michele Wallace and F. James Davis, commenting on the "cute" power of little Shirley Temple as a cuddly Confederate in *The Littlest Rebel*, or other roles where the little girl is clearly in charge of her cinematic relationships with Bill Robinson and other black actors.[15] The trope of Woman of Color has the thankless job of enhancing White Woman's purity by representing everything she is not supposed to be: "seductress, fertile, unhygienic," and "always on a slippery slope from exotic beauty to unfemininity and ugliness."[16] Throughout it all, White Woman must remain unsullied by the knowledge that her social position is powerful.

The power of these tropes is not in their accurate reflection of who we are, but in their efficacy in justifying hierarchical social relations and, as Frankenberg puts it, in the fact that they "continue to enlist" actual people into their service with "varying degrees of consciousness and unconsciousness."[17] The family of tropes, for example, makes it very easy for actual white women to become agents of racism without knowing it or wanting to, while identifying as innocent and respectable.[18] Hilary Harris posits that "the imagining and performing" of a genuinely "antiracist white womanhood" could only be achieved through tactics by which white women "fail" at the trope of "White Woman."[19]

I want to argue that the white singer in *New Orleans* animates a jazz-liking white woman whose actions *may appear* to subvert the rules of White Woman and therefore to perform antiracism, but who consistently succeeds at the trope of White Woman and therefore supports the racial hierarchy even as she "champions" black culture. I am going to call this figure the "Jazz Virgin" — to differentiate her from the "Jazz Nerd," while also implying a raced and gendered kinship. The "Jazz Virgin" is a white woman character who is stirred by what she hears in black music — which in this film is construed as sexuality, authenticity, emotion, newness, Americanness, and modernity — while *other characters* serve as her anxious protectors. In this film, it is not only white men who protect white womanhood (as the proxy for racial hierarchy and white innocence), but *all* characters: a black male jazz musician played by Louis Armstrong, a Creole gambling hall owner played by Mexican actor Arturo de Cordova, and the singing black maid so unhappily played by Billie Holiday. So visible is Holiday's displeasure with the role, it is tempting to argue that Holiday resists the trope of White Woman, even if her character does not. But if, for now, we focus on the *character* whose lines Holiday disdainfully recites, then it is possible to argue that all of the characters in the film, at some point or another, try to prevent jazz from entering Miralee's body, or from entering the wrong parts of her body, or to prevent the wrong parts of the music from entering her body. Her protectors know that "too much jazz" signals danger — criminality, sexuality, impurity — and with them, the threat to topple the white woman from her pedestal (and with her, the racial status quo). The *character* who is most ambivalent about the pedestal is another white woman who represents an alternative to the "Jazz Virgin" — predictably, it is the "Jazz Whore" — animated by a fallen white woman aptly named Grace, who has had too much jazz, drink, and sex, loses her social position, and is cinematically punished by getting hit by a car. Interestingly, the fallen Grace, is dark-haired and has a French surname, thus, like the gambling hall owner Nick Duquesnes, is Creole, not quite American, not quite white. Given the history of White Womanhood as the highly charged symbol of white domination in the United States,[20] we must not read this melodrama of will she or won't she "fall" (for jazz) as a story about *individual* taste or character, but as an enactment of racial hierarchy in which protecting White Woman's innocence is central to preserving white power.

ENTER THE "JAZZ VIRGIN"

So let us meet the "Jazz Virgin." We are first introduced to Miralee Smith when she arrives from Baltimore to join her mother in their new home in New Orleans. As the riverboat drifts into the bustling city port, Louis Armstrong plays in a traditional New Orleans–style band on the pier. Miralee is "all ears" from the moment we see her. Soon we will learn that her "big ears" were developed not through "hot" record collecting, but via a route that would be considered appropriate for a woman of her class and race: as a highly trained singer of European art songs. Her social position thus provides: (1) a defining lack of exposure to music outside the western art canon, and (2) an "innocent" ear that enables her to appreciate the "pure" sounds of jazz without knowing their pedigree. As a "Jazz Virgin," her wide-open ears are a *tabula rasa*. *We* recognize Louis Armstrong. The chaperon hears danger, crime, and poor taste. Miralee's ears isolate Armstrong's sound; she is drawn to what she hears and exclaims, "That cornet in that wagon, did you ever hear anything like it?" She is resolutely a different kind of jazz listener than Gabbard's "Jazz Nerd," who *has* heard something like it, knows that it's Armstrong, and can name all the sidemen.

The theme continues as Miralee sets foot in the foyer of the grand antebellum mansion that is her new home — the ubiquitous "big house" of Hollywood southern imagery.[21] Again, she leads with her fine-tuned yet jazz-innocent ears, drawn this time to the sound of Billie Holiday's singing voice, wafting from an unseen room atop the inevitable great marble stairway. She rushes up the stairs, only to be "protected" from jazz once again, when her chaperon and mother — the "jazz biddies," if you will — intervene as the culture police.[22] It is Miralee's mother this time who expresses disdain for jazz. Referring to Endie as "incorrigible" and "full of the devil," she commands the musical maid "never to sing that music in this house." But as soon as the protectors of white womanhood leave the room, it is Miralee who "misbehaves," pressing Endie for more of "that music," despite her mother's ruling. An even greater transgression is Miralee's bid for information about these stimulating sounds. "That music you were singing, what was it?" If "hip" means "in the know," then "hip" she is not. But Miralee yearns to *know*, as well as hear, the music. What is her desire, and how does it drive this narrative about white jazz love?

In some respects, the scene between the curious opera-singing white woman and the knowing jazz-singing black woman could be said to have made progressive inroads into cinematic race relations (simply, the white and black women interact as part of the plot). Just prior to the film's premiere in 1947, the black press, and the popular front and liberal white publications looked forward to promises of positive racial representations. *Ebony* reported: "The producers are out to break some Hollywood records and some stereotypes. There is no footage that Dixie can conveniently chop out; Negro performers appear continuously in scenes with white stars."[23]

As a film made and released in the immediately postwar period, *New Orleans* must be understood as a production that bears traces of wartime *and* postwar representational shifts in terms of race and gender politics in Hollywood. In this scene and others, one could read the splicing together of integration and racial hierarchy as a "rough cut" of an unfinished film about postwar national identity. As such, the integrated scenes also reveal moments of behind-the-scenes struggles portending the Hollywood Blacklist, in which integration was conceived as a sign of communism. Indeed, the first House Un-American Activities Committee (HUAC) hearings lurked around the corner as this film is being shot. And certainly, this integrated scene of White Woman begging modern jazz innovator Billie Holiday to sing a wistful love ballad about the South must be understood as occurring at the cusp of the heated debates among critics and fans in the 1940s, known as the "Jazz Wars."

According to Bernard Gendron, the aesthetic skirmishes over the comparative value of traditional New Orleans jazz ("Trad"), swing, and bebop were not simply expressions of style preference, but "laced with the idioms of commerce, politics, gender, and race," adding that "these idioms must be treated as integral to the newly emerging jazz aesthetic, rather than as mere intrusions or add-ons."[24] To stump for New Orleans jazz in 1946, in other words, was not simply to support "jazz," but to take a side in a battle in which "loving jazz" derived meaning from loving one style and not another.

As tracked by Gendron, the first of these battles, subsiding by 1946, found fans of swing sparring with those of the first New Orleans traditional jazz revival. Considered regressive "Moldy Figs" by swing fans (who saw themselves as modernists), the "traditional jazz" revivalists, or "Trads," saw their music as "authentic" and rejected swing as too commercial. At the same time, a similar war was revving up between journalists and fans over bebop and swing. Only this time, bebop was considered modern by those who liked bebop, and elite and pretentious by those who liked swing or New Orleans jazz. Like Monson and Gabbard, Gendron conceives white men's desires for particular fantasies of black masculinity as critical components within the discursive terrain.[25]

As a period piece set in 1917, and shot in 1946, *New Orleans* functions as a handy time machine that allows its protagonists to become "modern" by advancing music considered "Moldy" by both modernist factions of the 1940s "Jazz Wars." This Hollywood representation of jazz love does not exactly stump for "Trad" in all the same ways, nor for the same reasons, as did the most ardent revivalists, but the context of the 1940s "Jazz Wars" is helpful in understanding the significance of "New Orleans" jazz, and not bebop, as the music that seduces White Woman in this film released in 1947.

If desires for particular fantasies of black masculinities fueled debates of the "Jazz Wars," then what were these dueling desires, and what can they tell us about the construction of the "Jazz Virgin" in *New Orleans* as she begs Billie Holiday for a song? It is significant perhaps to observe that Holiday is not representative of the "Trad" camp and that, in fact, women musicians of Armstrong's and Ory's generations are literally missing from the picture.

Although the Hollywood studios may not have cared about the women of early New Orleans jazz, the "Trad" fans of the 1940s certainly knew some of the female musicians from that era. New Orleans jazz aficionados had located pianist Bertha Gonsoulin, for example, to play at the Bunk Johnson concert at the San Francisco Museum of Modern Art in 1943. If she was still available four years later, Gonsoulin, who had played in King Oliver's band on the West Coast tour in 1921, would certainly have been a more "traditional" choice than the thirty-eight-year-old Californian Charlie Beal who appears in the *New Orleans* film band. An even more obvious choice would have been that more famous Oliver pianist, Lil Hardin Armstrong, who was still living, still performing, and, according to *Down Beat*, whose feelings had been hurt six years previously when Orson Welles had apparently preferred to cast Hazel Scott, rather than ask Lil to play herself, in a film about her former husband.[26] Sweet Emma Barrett was still playing in small groups in the 1940s in New Orleans and would later be picked up by a new generation of revivalists in the 1960s. Singer Lizzie Miles was working as a barmaid but was writing letters to record producers and editors in hopes of making a comeback — indeed, she would become a darling of the second New Orleans revival, along with the pianists Jeanette Kimball and Billie Pierce, also veterans of early New Orleans bands.[27]

If white fascination with black masculinity drives the Jazz Wars, surely, the aging black and Creole of color male musicians from the early days of New Orleans jazz stimulated a different kind of fantasy for white fans, who tended to romanticize them as premodern folk, than did the beboppers of the 1940s. Eric Porter writes that bebop "[m]ark[ed] the emergence of the figure of the modern black jazzman as a defiant, alternative, and often exotic symbol of masculinity" for "black and nonblack observers alike."[28] Beboppers' importance to white hipsters as symbols of "black assertiveness and political demands"[29] highlighted their utility as imagined role models for an "outsider" style that could be *chosen* to substitute for (or supplement) modes of postwar white masculinity. "Trads" and bebop modernists alike tended to fix black jazz masculinity as a sign for something valuable and lacking in white society. But to note the *differences* is to underline the significance of "New Orleans" style as the vehicle for Miralee's transgression as she falls in love with Endie's song and Armstrong's horn.

It is significant that Miralee does not swoon to the music of young Charlie Parker, nor, for that matter, to the music of young Louis Armstrong, but to the music of a middle-aged Armstrong, whose mainstream popularity and familiarity are strong in 1947, who is not perceived as "defiant," and whose character is safely betrothed to her maid. This kinship through servitude renders scenes of mutual respect between Armstrong's character and Miralee as displays of devotion *à la* Uncle Tom and Little Eva. Likewise, it is significant that the song Miralee covets, and eventually takes as her own, belongs to her black maid, whose role is written, if not acted, as a cute but simple-minded, misbehaving Topsy. Just as it is significant that Billie Holiday is cast as the white woman's servant, it is important to note that she sings as Armstrong's talented girlfriend — not as a fellow artist and, certainly, not as a "Modernist" to his "Trad." It is significant that Holiday appears with traditional New Orleans musicians, rather than as an innovator in a modern jazz setting, commanding the respect of "modern black jazz men," nor as a serious artist on a concert hall stage. Certainly, it is significant that the interracial scenes between Miralee and Endie are between mistress and maid.

Even so, it is understandable that *Ebony* would hold out hopes for a progressive film in 1947. The crisis of the Second World War had made possible considerable gains in increasing the scope and dignity of black roles in Hollywood cinema. But, as Anna Everett reminds us, the victories of Walter White, the National Association for the Advancement of Colored People (NAACP), the black press, black actors, and audiences also fulfilled the momentary needs of "the national government and the War Information Office that had ordered filmic images of a happy, multicultural nation unified in battle against the enemy abroad."[30] Just as many of the hopes of African Americans for improved working and living conditions after the war had been dashed, what limited representational gains had been made in Hollywood were repealed.

So, although it is true that the onscreen interaction between Endie and Miralee cannot be eliminated from the film, it is precisely the prominent framing of the maid-mistress relationship that protects White Woman's innocence as she awakens to jazz (and it doesn't hurt that this turns out to be a kind of jazz heard as nonthreatening to mainstream audiences of 1947). Rather than signaling an interracial friendship, the "friendliness" of the maid-mistress relationship performs what F. James Davis calls "racial etiquette," a plantation fantasy of mutual consent.[31] Instead of sternly commanding Endie to cease her singing, as does her mother, Miralee updates White Woman by playfully coaxing Woman of Color to share her culture. Yet, this is hardly a subversion given their power difference and the long history of white fascination with black performance. In line with Brown's analysis of the "conditional access to realms of expressive freedom" that white women gained through minstrelsy, we see Miralee temporarily reveling in her own senses to the sound of Holiday's exquisite *a cappella* phrasing. Eyes aglow, face flushed, Miralee leans toward her singing black maid, lovingly stockpiling each note Endie sings for the moment when she herself may embody this exquisite music.

HOLIDAY'S FAILURE TO ACT

And what is Holiday doing all this time? Mostly, she sings, sounding like the acclaimed song stylist she is in 1946, the jazz singer who had appeared as the first black woman singer at the Metropolitan Opera House two years previously—the Café Society artist who has already recorded the antilynching anthem "Strange Fruit"—the solo concert artist who will debut at Town Hall in a matter of months in a critically acclaimed appearance before a sold-out house.[32] In her nonmusical moments, Holiday vacantly delivers thankless lines like, "Yes, Miss Miralee," "No, Miss Miralee," and "Let me draw you a good hot bath and it will melt away all your tiredness," walking through the part of Endie as though she wants to make sure audiences will not find her believable in this insulting role. Robert O'Meally quotes Carmen McRae's assessment of Holiday's acting: "She wasn't that great. . . . Not that she had any good lines to say. She was *Lady*! The most unlikeliest person to be a maid to *anybody*!"[33] Dorothy Patrick, on the other hand, an actor and not a singer, responds to Holiday as though she sincerely believes in both of their performances as compatible jazz-loving mistress and maid. She begs for a song, and then decides to accompany her maid to a jazz club that evening. Perhaps the most painful moment of Holiday's task in this movie is when Endie protests this uninvited companionship, not out of protection of her own leisure time, but in an attempt to protect white womanhood. Her line could have been right out of *Gone with the Wind* (1939).

"Oh, no Miss Miralee! It ain't fitting for a lady to go to Storyville! 'Ceptin' she's on a slumming party!" Yes, "ladies" are white, in this formulation. In the words of Evelyn Brooks Higginbotham, "no black woman, regardless of income, education, refinement, or character, enjoyed the status of lady,"[34] nor could (known) black performers, however famous, play "ladies" on screen. It must have killed *Lady* Day to deliver these lines, but at least she doesn't mask how much she hates them, a fact well-known to her coworkers on the set. The clarinetist Barney Bigard recalled that she showed up twelve days late for the shooting. "We didn't care and I know Louis didn't worry because, like I said, we got paid to just sit there until she came." For Bigard, her tardiness was a sign of her star power, although he also noted the limits to the privileges it afforded her, in relation to Armstrong. "I mean they had her character all planned out in the script before she even got there, but Louis, well they just let him be Louis."[35] Perhaps when McRae spoke of Holiday as "not so good" in the film, she suggests not that she fails at acting, but that she fails to act. I would argue that her failure to act is a refusal that undermines White Woman—perhaps the only such refusal to survive the finished film. If Endie's lines are designed to uphold White Woman's innocence, then Holiday's resolutely noncommittal speech-acting performs a subversive undertow for that mandatory pedestal.

"Then, hand me my slumming clothes!" chirps a playful Miralee. The moment of Holiday's "cultural move," as Herman Gray might call it, is over, and once again, the "Jazz Virgin" manages to break one set of rules of "White Woman" without failing the larger racial project. In fact, her ability to break the rules without losing the game is itself an enactment of power. Miralee's pathway to jazz, then, trades on a race- and class-naturalized mistress-maid relationship, mixed with "slumming," a mode of white privilege that, like other forms of tourism, affirms hierarchy through exoticizing difference.

WHEN GOOD GIRLS GO TRAD

Krin Gabbard has written about the erotic charge between Louis Armstrong and Billie Holiday in the musical scenes in *New Orleans*, but in my reading, the charge belongs to Miralee, whose female gaze we watch, and then adopt by the end of the "slumming" scene. As she descends into the depths of the Orpheum Cabaret, she can barely contain her physical excitement. As Endie sings with Armstrong and the New Orleans band, Miralee gingerly steps into the club, her eyes bright, lips moist and parted. Like that other adventuresome virgin, Little Red Riding Hood, Miralee is cloaked. Set off by the dark folds of her cape, her face becomes increasingly luminous as she absorbs the music of the black jazz band. The scene is remarkable for its situating of female pleasure in a jazz scene, yet familiar in the sense that white pleasure is made possible through the fetishizing of black men and a black woman.

Two conventions of U.S. entertainment history bear mentioning, as they oil the wheels of the scene at hand. One is the Hollywood tradition of enlisting jazz and blues soundtracks as codes for danger, vice, and crime during scenes in which white women's white womanhood is at stake. Oftentimes, jazz appears to enter the bodies of white women and tamper with their purity, dramatizing anxieties about miscegenation. Audience titillation has long been maximized through the use of jazz and blues soundtracks at moments when white "good girls" fall, overcome by vice, instilling a sense that their demise is intimately associated with the compromise of white racial purity.[36] The most popular examples of this in my "Gender, Race, and Jazz" course hail from the genre of narcotics warning films like *Reefer Madness* and *Marijuana* from the 1930s. Jazz routinely enters the soundtrack as sexual licentiousness and illicit drugs take hold of white women's bodies. Miralee's erotically charged descent into the tellingly named "Orpheum Cabaret" references this cinematic coding, but with a twist, since she does not forfeit white privilege but, in fact, becomes whiter and more powerful as the music fills her body. She is not a reformer like her mother, who wishes to rid the world of jazz, but she does appear to alter the music by inviting it into her body without losing her fundamental "innocence." Her white lady body performs and reforms jazz pleasure at the same time — a powerful raced and gendered achievement that we might call "reformance," which deserves closer scrutiny. It is through a cultural politics of reformance that Miralee differentiates herself from her mother and from Grace, both when she claims the music as her own and embarks on the righteous path to free it from Basin Street.

The other history, which I have already mentioned, is that of women's participation in minstrelsy. Many early jazz musicians and blues performers of the generation so revered during the New Orleans jazz revival of the 1940s got their starts in white blackface or in black minstrelsy. Eddie Garland recalled that the second New Orleans band to go to Chicago (after Freddie Keppard) was a black jazz band fronted by Mabel Elaine, a white woman in blackface who danced in wooden shoes.[37] Although distinct from such performers — Miralee does not seek the vaudeville stage or apply dark makeup — her love affair with jazz does seem to provide the "conditional immunity from the proscriptions of white womanhood" that Jayna Brown argues white women received from minstrel performance. In this way, Miralee's fleeting taste of black music falls in line with legacies of minstrelsy and "coon shouting," in which white women sampled increased sexual and expressive freedom in a controlled environment.

In contrast with the fallen woman, Grace, who had not been content with "slumming," Miralee's brief visits to the Orpheum Cabaret pave the way for her "reformance," achieved by filtering codes of blackness from Endie's song through her own white-coded vocal style. Miralee's rise contrasts with Grace's fall in racialized ways that index the distinction between racial crossings that imply colonial access and those that threaten the loss of white racial purity through miscegenation. So long as Miralee develops in contrast with Grace and upholds the mistress-maid relationship with Endie, she gives up nothing, even as she draws upon Endie's song to aid in her acquisition of a modern, more sexual white identity that is dramatically not her mother's White Womanhood.

When Endie finishes her song, Miralee plies her male lead, the club owner, Nick Duquesne, with breathless questions that flirt with loss of innocence.

Where does such music come from?

Nick begins to narrate the miracle of jazz, but catches himself before imparting the forbidden knowledge of jazz history.

Miss Smith, you're going home?
Not until you tell me.

Miralee's pout proves irresistible to Nick, who begins to lovingly divulge the music's origins in "work songs, the Gold Coast of West Africa, little Christian churches, riverboats. . . ." His own eyes glisten and cheeks flush with the telling.

Although Nick's speech verges on drawing connections between African American culture and class struggle that drew some white leftists to the music in the 1940s, the unpleasant details that would connect those dots are left suitably veiled to Miralee for her to pose her next "innocent" questions.

Why don't we hear more of this kind of music?

Oh, how tempted he is to educate Miralee! But he restrains himself, protecting Miralee from histories of slavery and continuing racism. Instead, he offers the metaphor of "a great big invisible wall that you can't climb over."

The sounds of New Orleans–style collective improvisation swell, as the once innocent and now fallen Grace appears. Nick appears stricken as he takes in the spectacle of Grace, wobbling pathetically in white lace she no longer deserves, a veritable advertisement for the dire effects of jazz clubs on white womanhood. He comes to his senses, regains his resolve to protect Miralee.

But it is too late. Oblivious to Grace's entrance, Miralee has already been transformed by this affective, authentic music and the news of its restraint by an unjust wall. It is at this moment that Miralee's "innocence" and entitlement fuse. Not knowing what makes up "the wall" nor understanding her role in its construction and maintenance, she lovingly declares the music as her own and announces her plan to break through it by singing "that New Orleans song." This is a classic enactment of the power of the Trope of White Woman: to colonize while performing benevolence.[38] Before she can rush the stage, however, she is "rescued" by Nick, who expels her from the club. The rest of the film will be spent reconciling Miralee's epiphany that jazz is hers, with weighty societal concerns about how her jazz love may cause loss of other entitlements for her and other white characters.

Like the "Jazz Nerd," the "Jazz Virgin" collects, and in the film's finale, as I have already given away, Miralee sings Endie's song to an all-white audience in a concert hall, accompanied by two all-white orchestras at once: one classical and one jazz (although, for New Orleans revivalists of the 1940s, Woody Herman's First Herd would be categorized as "Swing" — not a suitable substitute).[39] We hear a little more chest resonance in the finale than we have heard from Miralee's European art song renditions, we hear English instead of Italian, but we do not hear signs of blackness, such as blue notes, speech effects, syncopation, or improvised turns of phrasing or melody or harmonics or timing or timbre, that would popularize other white women singers such as Peggy Lee (who owed a debt to Lil Green) or the Boswell Sisters from New Orleans (who, like the fictional Miralee, learned to sing black music from their maids).[40] But we do not hear an attempt to reproduce black vocal style in Miralee's delivery.[41] And of course, we see no black bodies in this final scene. As jazz musicians in the film, along with jazz and film scholars, have well documented, while the black male musicians were supposed to appear in this final scene, the racial dimensions of red-baiting in 1947 Hollywood would not allow it.[42] Even though Billie Holiday had already been the first African American woman to perform at the Metropolitan Opera House (preceding Marian Anderson), Hollywood of 1947 cannot quite picture a black woman on a concert hall stage.

Nor is there any sign of consciousness in the structure of the film that a professional singer's love for her maid's song could lead to anything like theft. We do not even see the limited gestures toward remuneration that we saw in *Imitation of Life* (1934), in which Claudette Colbert's character, Bea, attempts to insure that her maid, Delilah, played by Louise Beaver, will receive 20 percent of the profits of her own family pancake recipe that is making the white woman rich. (Delilah, of course, refuses, insisting that it is a "gift" and that she does not wish to be financially independent.)[43] But Endie is not even consulted in *New Orleans* when Miralee adds the song to her repertoire. In the final scene, the white opera singer indeed triumphs at New York's Symphony Hall, delivering Endie's song, in her best bel canto belt, dubbed by the white American lyric soprano Theodora Lynch (who, purportedly, had earned money for opera lessons by singing popular songs in the famous all-white Stork Club in New York. By the time of the making of *New Orleans*, Lynch had married J. Paul Getty and was hoping to break into the movies. The off-screen opera singer would, in fact, appear on-screen in future Hollywood feature films. Billie Holiday would not).[44]

Referred to throughout the film as a "blues," "Do You Know What it Means to Miss New Orleans" was written especially for this film in the thirty-two-bar form (AABA) popular song format by a team of Holly-wood songwriters, Eddie D'Lange and Louis Alter. The lyrics resound with the same kinds of "Southern" pastoral nostalgia that Holiday had already dismantled in her powerful delivery of Abel Meeropol's lyrics to "Strange Fruit." In the final scene, backed by an all-white symphony orchestra with two grand pianos *and* Woody Herman's all-white jazz orchestra and an all-white choir, each aggregation carried spectacularly on monumental stage furniture of rotating white columns, Miralee sings Endie's ode to an idyllic South. With lyrics of longing for "moss-covered vines," "tall sugar pines," and the "lazy Mississippi," Miralee woos an all-white concert-going audience to the side of jazz, a music that is theirs whether they know it or not. Thus, a white woman pre-sents the nostalgic song about a happy south stolen from her black maid and jazz is transformed into respectable American culture, as the film swells to its musical big finish without apology or even apparent aware-ness that one might be called for. It is typical Hollywood jazz fare, as analyzed by Krin Gabbard, in which sincere white devotees rescue jazz from black obscurity by trumpeting it from white concert hall stages.[45] Only this time, the colonizing white boy with a (dubbed) horn is a colonizing white girl with a (dubbed) voice.

WHAT DID IT MEAN FOR WHITE WOMEN TO "MISS NEW ORLEANS" IN 1947?

There is, shadowing Miralee's character in this film, a similarly named white jazz-loving woman, Marili Morden (1919–88), whose ex-husband David Stuart is thanked in the credits of *New Orleans* as a consultant. A jazz enthusiast from Portland, Oregon, this Marili migrated to Los Angeles, not following "jazz-innocent ears," as did the fictional Miralee (whose pathway of identification, you may recall, was resolutely free of "hot" records and historical knowledge). On the contrary, Morden's lifelong interest in jazz led her to become an important figure in the West Coast branch of the New Orleans revival, according to the late jazz historian and founder of the Southern California Hot Jazz Society, Floyd Levin.[46] Her third husband, the tuba player Art Levin (no relation to Floyd), asserts that although it was David Stuart who financed the founding of Jazz Man Records in Hollywood in 1939, it was definitely Morden's "knowledge and drive" that were crucial to its success in becoming one of the "BIG trad record stores," along with "Commodore in N.Y, Record Rendezvous in Trenton, N.J. . . . and Ray Averys Record Shack in L.A. [sic]."[47] After her divorce from Stuart, Morden would continue running the store, later operating it and living above it with her second husband, producer Nesuhi Ertegun, with whom she also produced and sold recordings of traditional New Orleans jazz. According to Ertegun's oral history, it was Morden who brought Edward "Kid" Ory out of musical retirement when she urged him to bring his horn to a photo shoot and he unexpectedly ran "through a few choruses . . . the first time he had played the trombone in nine years."[48] A broker, fan, and analyst of the "Jazz Wars," Marili wrote a fascinating analysis of the bitter debates among fans of bebop, "Trad," and swing — offering an economic analysis of scarcity of resources for jazz overall as an explanation of the high stakes of the style wars.[49]

Marili Morden was well enough regarded as a hub of jazz knowledge for Orson Welles to contact her when he sought a traditional New Orleans band for his radio programs in the spring of 1944 (see figure 10.2). She recommended Ory, who assembled the band that Welles employed — many members of which appear in the film New Orleans, a project that Welles is thought to have originated.[50]

What is the relationship between these similarly named jazz-loving white women? Why is it that the one I don't want to emulate so neatly eclipses the one who may have found alternate routes? Morden knew too much about jazz to be classified as a "Jazz Virgin." Was she a "Jazz Nerd?" What were her desires for jazz and how do these fit within the theoretical frameworks explored in this article, for instance, in white desires for particular fantasies of black masculinity? Was Marili hip? Does she offer clues into histories of other jazz-fan negotiations of White Woman? I know little about her, only that she facilitated the connection of Welles and Ory, that she ran an important record store, that she married men who shared her interest in jazz, and that her commitment to jazz, unlike Miralee Smith's, accompanied a commitment to integrated venues for the performance of jazz and blues. As electric guitarist T-Bone Walker's manager, she played a key role in integrating Hollywood nightclubs in the 1940s.

Fig. 10.2. Standard Oil Broadcasts, Los Angeles, 1944. Back row: Ed "Montudi" Garland (bass), Buster Wilson (piano), Marili Morden, co-owner of Jazz Man Records in Los Angeles, Mutt Carey (trumpet), and Kid Ory (trombone). Front row: Jimmie Noone (clarinet), Zutty Singleton (drums), and Bud Scott (guitar). Carey, Ory, Singleton, and Scott appear in *New Orleans*. With permission from Frank Driggs Collection.

To explore these questions, it is necessary to visit one more historical battleground: the climate of diminished civil liberties in the specific forms it took precisely in 1946–1947 in the Hollywood film industry. *New Orleans* was made in the midst of the rise of government-sponsored surveillance that equated racial integration with anti-Americanism.[51] If the finished film ultimately proffers White Woman loving jazz as one kind of sign, an investigation of the film's journey from treatment to final cut is rife with cross-purposes among players we would come to know as the Hollywood left and right. Associate producer of *New Orleans*, Herbert Biberman had been under investigation by the Federal Bureau of Investigation (FBI) since 1941 for Communist activities in Mexico and the United States. Two months after the film's release, Biberman would receive one of the first subpoenas for the HUAC hearings of October 1947. As one of the first "unfriendly witnesses," Biberman was eventually imprisoned as a member of the Hollywood Ten, for refusing to answer questions about his political beliefs and the political beliefs of others. Like Orson Welles, Biberman had supported the

Spanish Civil War and opposed racial discrimination; he was one of those leftists who, as Howard Stamm put it in the case of Welles, raised government suspicions in being " 'premature anti-racists,' much as one speaks of 'premature anti-fascists.' "[52]

Elliott Paul, a writer and jazz fan, penned the original story for the film — a story for which Biberman had great sympathy and hopes. But producer Jules Levey took issue with many aspects of the script and continuously excised the scenes of most importance to Biberman and Paul. In long letters to his wife, the fellow leftist and actress Gale Sondergaard, Biberman described his struggles with Levey. Two months before shooting, Biberman wrote that Levey was "scared to death too many Negroes will come to the theatres to see this picture because there will be so many Negro artists in it...": "He doesn't want their 'black money.' That's really funny — sounds like a capitalist contradiction in terms — he wants *it* — but he's afraid if the theatres draw too many Negroes the whites will stay away. So he hates the performers who are going to be the only draw he will have in the picture. IT'S SIMPLE LUNACY [sic]."[53]

In a letter written the next day, Biberman expressed his rage at learning that Levey had appointed someone other than himself to direct the film. After Busby Berkeley was considered, Arthur Lubin was brought aboard.[54] By this time, the original story that Biberman had developed with Paul had been considerably altered.[55] Soon after taking over the direction of the film, Lubin approached Biberman, wanting to know if he could see the "earlier version of the script" as he had heard rumors that it was "filled with wonderful stuff that was not in this one." Biberman informed him that he should "Ask Levey" and "raise hell, walk out, do whatever you wish," but that the producer had already made it clear that it had "too much Negro stuff."[56]

Film historians have yet to get to the bottom of the relationship of *New Orleans* to Orson Welles's plans for a cinematic jazz epic, but most agree that Welles, in 1941, was working on a jazz project that was to become the fourth episode of *It's All True*.[57] Welles's papers preserve at least some of his jazz research including scripts, notes, and even two drafts of a history of early New Orleans jazz written by guitarist Bud Scott, who appears in the film *New Orleans*.[58] The jazz press ran many stories about the plans for Welles's jazz film, including a report about Lil Hardin Armstrong's disappointment to learn that she would not be cast as herself, but would be played by Hazel Scott, in what was being described as a biography about ex-husband Louis Armstrong.[59] Film and jazz historians have well documented that this Welles film project appears to have been planned in collaboration with Duke Ellington and Louis Armstrong, but was set aside when Radio-Keith-Orpheum (RKO) sent Welles to Brazil.[60] I believe that Brett Wood is at least partially mistaken when he suggests that an undated, unsigned jazz script housed in the Orson Welles Manuscript Collection at the Lilly Library sheds some light on what Welles's version of *New Orleans* would have been like. In fact, the film described in that treatment *was* produced, as *Syncopation*, directed by William Dieterle, shot primarily from October to December 1941 (before Welles's falling out with RKO) and released in 1942.[61]

Another notable representation of a white woman's love of jazz, *Syncopation* depicts a white woman jazz musician/fan named Kit, who at least feels *sorry* that black New Orleans musicians are being displaced by white musicians. Nevertheless, the film retracts antiracist gains by the end, in effect, rendering Kit's sorrow as another version of white woman's "innocence."[62] I cannot take the time here to offer an analysis of this fascinating film, but it is pertinent to note that Kit works in a record store.[63] In the treatment that is archived in the Lilly Library, the film ends with Kit as proprietor of her own record store in New York called "Kit's Music Store — Records of the Old South."[64] In the released film, Kit is shown working in a record store, but it is not clear what kinds of records she sells, nor does she appear to be the proprietor.[65]

Although I am not sure of the connection between the undated script in the Welles papers that became *Syncopation* (1942) and the film project that became *New Orleans* (1947), I will venture a speculation that yet another undated and unsigned script (this one in the Biberman papers) offers a glimpse into what the latter film would have been like if the story as Paul and Biberman created it had been produced. For one thing, the grand finale would not have presented Miralee singing with an all-white orchestra to an all-white audience on a concert hall stage. In stark contrast with that finale scene, this script concludes with Miralee singing "improvised" lyrics with an integrated band that included boogie-woogie pianist Albert Ammons at Barney Josephson's integrated Café Society Downtown. In this script, Endie also sings at Café Society, where Billie Holiday had performed "Strange Fruit," as does the Golden Gate Quartet, so popular with Popular Front audiences in the 1940s. Instead of an ode to a happy pastoral south, the lyrics that flow extemporaneously from Miralee construct jazz just as romantically, but with a different set of hopes. Jazz, in this song, is born of struggle and not yet finished its task of heralding transformations that will result in a more just society:

Born in the land of cotton
Born in Africa, too
Born in the brass of a noisy parade
Born in a gamblin' house, too
That low down song
That I'm singin' now
Tells the world that it's marchin'
Tells the world it's not thru
Tells that world better days are here
For you and you and you.[66]

I cannot guess what this song would have sounded like; it is difficult to imagine how it *could* be sung to boogie-woogie, as suggested by the presence of Albert Ammons, let alone to traditional New Orleans jazz — but if it *was*, the lyrics would not fall outside the hopes invested in either musical style by many 1940s white leftists (see Monica Hairston's chapter in this volume). Traditional New Orleans jazz was not heard as "nostalgic" or "pastoral" to this particular constituency, but valued for its imagined inherent ability to promote social equality. Kid Ory and Barney Bigard were also used on *Crossfire* (1947), another film made by soon-to-be-blacklisted leftists, Adrian Scott (producer) and Edward Dmytryk (director), and the first feature film to address anti-Semitism. That the New Orleans music admired by Welles, Eliot, Biberman, and Marili Morden (Stuart-Ertegun-Levin) — all committed to racial integration — could so easily be seen and heard as something of a plantation fantasy for racial conservatives during the bebop era is an intricacy of the "Jazz Wars" deserving further attention. We can still spot the mostly submerged attempts to present New Orleans jazz as racially progressive (for instance, the Popular Front discourse about jazz as a people's music that we almost hear in Nick Duquesne's speech when he is tempted to educate Miralee), yet it fails to cut the Cold War chill of the final product — epitomized by the White Woman singing her black maid's nostalgic ode to the south in the all-white concert hall without remorse, without losing her "innocence" about the white privilege she represents.

POSTSCRIPT

In a 1951 issue of *Down Beat* appeared a two-and-a-half-page feature on the life and career of the trombonist Kid Ory, written by Marili Ertegun (at the time). She narrated, in great detail, Ory's career from his childhood in La Place, La., up to his Hollywood radio and recording career in 1951. Interestingly, although a photo from the film *New Orleans* has been placed as an illustration to her article, Marili's article makes no mention of the Hollywood film, released in 1947, that brought unprecedented fame to Ory and the other New Orleans musicians, a film in which a white woman with a similar name performed blatant appropriation as love.[67] Likewise, Elliot Paul, credited as originator of the story on which the film is based, made no mention of it in his book, *That Crazy American Music* (1957), although he includes chapters on New Orleans jazz, Louis Armstrong, and Café Society. Two months after the film's gala opening at New York's Winter Garden, Herbert Biberman would receive the subpoena that would eventually result in his imprisonment as one of the Hollywood Ten. Louis Armstrong would tour with New Orleans jazz musicians in conjunction with the release of *New Orleans*, but Billie Holiday was nowhere in sight. She was, in fact, serving time for drug possession at the Federal Reformatory for Women in Alderson, Va. Farah Griffin writes that eleven days after her release on March 16, 1948, "she appeared at Carnegie Hall to a warm, enthusiastic, standing-room-only crowd."[68]

So far, I have argued that the character of Miralee performs the trope of White Woman so successfully that her "love and theft" caper — stealing a black woman's song, filtering blackness from it, and remaking herself as a new kind of modern white American woman — supports, rather than subverts white supremacy. Her innocence (of her social position as powerful) justifies her love. Her ability to believe that her epiphany that "this music is mine already" is universally beneficial, rather than part of a larger imperialist project that divides bodies into beneficiaries and objects, provides the alibi for her theft.

I have also audaciously suggested that this offensive Hollywood representation has something to tell us about jazz desire among actual white women jazz fans. Yet, surely, there were and are "jazz-loving" white women who have loved jazz differently, many of whom have also been knowledgeable about histories of struggle including those who have been committed to antiracism. Yet, I hesitate to turn too quickly to a hopeful recuperation of alternative pathways of identification as traveled by white women jazz fans. Certainly, I want to know more about the alternative declarations of jazz love that white women uttered and acted upon, especially those that have been most effective at "failing" at the trope of White Woman. Yet, even to raise this question, as a white woman, feels dangerously narcissistic, even self-redemptive. My point is not to restore "White Woman" to her pillar of moral superiority.

How did Marili Morden negotiate the trope White Woman? Was she complicit in fetishizing blackness and appropriating jazz, or did she succeed at performing a kind of white womanhood that failed to reproduce white supremacy? Did she sometimes succeed and sometimes fail? Are success and failure overly simple terms for interrogating jazz love?

Sarah Ahmed reminds us that "to be against something is precisely not to be in a position of transcendence," but to work "in an intimate relation with that which one is against."[69] In other words, to imagine oneself as "beyond racism" can counteract one's attempt to oppose it. To this impulse, Ahmed argues: "But race, like sex, is sticky; it sticks to us, or we become 'us' as an effect of how it sticks, even when we think we are beyond it. Beginning to live with that stickiness, to think it, feel it, do it, is about creating a space to deal with the effects of racism. We need to deal with the effects of racism in a way that is better."[70]

In a story recounted by Helen Oakley Dance in her biography of T-Bone Walker, Morden related the sticky story of how she came to manage the electric guitarist's career. She first heard Walker in 1940, in a "tumble down and tilted" nightclub, the Little Harlem, at 114th and Central Avenue, much farther south than the black Central Avenue jazz clubs that attracted the white celebrity crowd. Two African American women, the Brown Sisters, were the proprietors, and Walker was "the apple of their eye," in part because his tremendous popularity had drawn the clientele that built their thriving business. Morden returned many times, usually accompanied by black musician friends, with whom she would occasionally dance. It all came crashing down one evening when, as she recalled, "one of the sisters asked me to stop by her office. 'You're very welcome here,' she said, 'but please — no mixed dancing.'"

"I gaped. Growing up in Oregon I was raised to think we lived in a democracy. . . . I hadn't run into anything like this before. 'My God,' I thought, 'now I know how it feels.'" Out of this experience — described as *her experience of racism* — Morden realized "how stupid it would be for [Walker] to remain in Watts all his life." Her narrative shifts into a success story of how, under her own management, Walker is able to leave the segregated Little Harlem for more lucrative opportunities, thus integrating the top Hollywood nightclubs.[71]

While believing she is performing antiracism — and, in fact, she did play a powerful role in integrating segregated Hollywood clubs—Morden appears to grapple with some of the same issues of the Trope of White Woman that we see so clearly in Miralee Smith. This is the stickier stickiness of white women's jazz desire that we need to know more about. In this account, Morden is apparently baffled by the Brown Sisters' request—but does not explore their motives. She does not appear to consider what other reasons might motivate the Brown Sisters to discourage mixed-race dancing in the club they owned, in a state with antimiscegenation laws still on the books, in a black business district under constant police surveillance, in a city where only white people could imagine daily life as one of integration. The notion that the presence of a White Lady dancing with Men of Color on a dance floor in Watts might justify White Men's police "protection" that harmed the livelihood of Women of Color doesn't seem to occur to her. Yet, she is not completely unaware of her social power and effectively uses it to secure more lucrative bookings for a black artist. In doing so, however, she does not appear to reflect on the impact of her actions on the Brown Sisters and the Little Harlem, as she facilitates new venues for their star, then fights for the right of their clientele—Walker's fan base—to integrate Hollywood clubs. Faced with an imperfect set of choices—to self-segregate in a black club or heroically integrate white clubs—Marili's management of Walker's career provides a sticky scenario different from the blatant appropriation we see in the film *New Orleans*. Yet, the elements are familiar: black music gets relocated to white clubs, black women in jazz culture are eclipsed by a white jazz-loving woman, and a white woman constructs an alternate identity through jazz. I do not mean to dismiss the hard work of integrating Hollywood nor the tremendous amount of support of careers of jazz musicians engaged in by Marili Morden. In further work on white women jazz fans, I hope we can learn more, not only about their "contributions to the music" but also about their struggles with the Trope of White Woman on the messy terrain of jazz desire.

Sometimes as I hear my own white woman's voice teaching "Jazz and American Culture" at the University of Kansas to predominantly white and often sincerely—aspirationally, at least—antiracist students, I wonder how my own body signifies, and I hope I am not simply continuing the work of Miralee Smith making jazz respectable in the lecture hall. I think it is instructive to study Miralee Smith, but I wish I knew more about the trials and errors of Marili Morden.

NOTES

I would like to thank Bob O'Meally and the Center for Jazz Studies at Columbia University for research support; Ellie Hisama, the Institute for the Study of American Music, and Ajay Heble at the Guelph Jazz Festival Colloquium for opportunities to present early versions of this project. An excerpt from this essay appeared as " 'White Woman' as Jazz Collector in the Film *New Orleans* (1947)," *Institute for the Study of American Music Newsletter* 35, no. 1 (fall 2005), 1–2, 13–4. Thanks to Bruce Raeburn for introducing me to traces of historical evidence of the fascinating Marili Morden.

1. *New Orleans* (1947), directed by Arthur Lubin, produced by Jules Levey. associate producer Herbert Biberman, screenplay by Elliot Paul and Dick Irving Hyland. All quotes from *New Orleans* are taken from the Kino Video DVD release (2000), whose liner notes describe the film as a "refreshing rediscovery . . . especially noteworthy for its lack of racial stereotypes, as well as the high caliber of performances delivered by its stellar cast including Louis Armstrong, Woody Herman, Kid Ory, Meade Lux Lewis, etc."

2. Donald Bogle, "Louis Armstrong: The Films," *Louis Armstrong: A Cultural Legacy*, ed. Marc H. Miller (New York: Queens Museum of Art, in association with Seattle: University of Washington Press, 1994), 147.

3. Made in the 1940s, this film takes a clear side in the "Jazz Wars" raging at the time. "Trad" fans, also called "Moldy Figs," invested in early New Orleans jazz as a traditional folk music. See Bernard Gendron's "Moldy Figs and Modernists: Jazz at War, (1942–1946)," in Gabbard 1995a, 31–56; and a later version in Gendron 2002, 121–42.

4. Leonard Feather, "The Reel Armstrong: Musically, 'New Orleans' Is a Bright Film; Dramatically, It's a Dud," *Metronome*, April 1947, 43.

5. Salim Washington, "Has Katrina Failed to Blow the Wool from over Our Eyes?: Why I Disagree with the New Jazz Orthodoxy," *Institute for the Study of American Music Newsletter* 35, no. 1 (fall 2005); in response to Wynton Marsalis, "Saving America's Soul Kitchen: How to Bring This Country Together? Listen to the Message of New Orleans," *Time*, September 19, 2005.

6. Gabbard 2004.

7. Monson 1995, 405.

8. See Wallace 2000 and Brown 2001. See also Michele Wallace, "The Good Lynching and *The Birth of a Nation*: Discourses and Aesthetics of Jim Crow," *Cinema Journal* 43, no. 1 (fall 2003): 85–104. For additional reading focusing on women and minstrelsy see also Kibler 1999 and Lavitt 1999.

9. Brown 2001, 53.

10. Lavitt 1999, 271–75.

11. See for example the sheet music covers of songs popularized by May Irwin, especially "Dar's Something about Yer I Like" and "Dat's Just What 'Expotentisious' Means," viewable on the Library of Congress American Memory website: http://memory.loc.gov/ammem/index.html.

12. Lavitt 1999, 258.

13. Maxine Gordon's ongoing oral history project, "Women Who Listen," will help us to know more about practices of women jazz fans across race, class, and other axes of difference.

14. V. J. Jerome, *The Negro in Hollywood Films* (New York: Masses and Mainstream, 1952), 16. This pamphlet is based on Jerome's lecture of 1950. For more on this Communist Party cultural critic and his work in and about Hollywood see Victor Navasky, *Naming Names* (New York: Viking, 1980), 78–79.

15. Wallace 2000, 150–51; F. James Davis, *Who Is Black? One Nation's Definition* (University Park: Pennsylvania State University Press, 1991), 63–65. I've wondered about this legacy in the relationship between Lisa Simpson and her saxophone mentor, Bleeding Gums Murphy, in Matt Groening's *The Simpsons*.

16. Ruth Frankenberg, "Local Whitenesses, Localizing Whiteness," *Displacing Whiteness: Essays in Social and Cultural Criticism* (Durham: Duke University Press, 1997), 11–12

17. Ibid.

18. Ibid., 15.

19. Harris 2000, 183–209.

20. Davis, *Who Is Black?* 63.

21. For an account of the black film critic Melvin B. Tolson's theory of the "Big House" in American cinema as a technology of American racism, see Anna Everett, *Returning the Gaze: A Genealogy of Black Film Criticism, 1909–1949* (Durham: Duke University Press, 2001), 295–99.

22. Thanks to Tami Albin for "jazz biddies."

23. "*New Orleans,*" *Ebony*, February 1947, 26–31.

24. Gendron 2002, 125.

25. When the essay first appeared in *Jazz among the Discourses*, Gendron included a footnote telling us that he is at work on an essay about "the convolutions of gender in 1940s jazz discourse." This footnote falls out from the essay's next appearance as a chapter in his brilliant *Between Montmartre and the Mudd Club*, but I hold out hope that he does find time to write this intriguing essay at some point.

26. Gabbard 1996, 120–23.

27. For more on women in New Orleans jazz history see Tucker 2004b; Tucker 2006; Dahl 1989; Handy 1981; and Placksin 1982.

28. Porter 2002, 79. See also Kelley 1993.

29. Porter 2002, 84–85.

30. Everett, *Returning the Gaze*, 306–7. See also Thomas Cripps, *Making Movies Black: The Hollywood Message Movie from World War II to the Civil Rights Era* (New York: Oxford University Press, 1993).

31. Davis, *Who Is Black?* 61–65.

32. "Billie Holiday Concert Makes Jazz History," *Down Beat*, March 11, 1946.

33. Carmen McRae, quoted in O'Meally 1991, 145.

34. Higginbotham 1992a, 261.

35. Barney Bigard and Barry Martyn, *With Louis and the Duke: The Autobiography of a Jazz Clarinetist* (New York: Oxford University Press, 1986), 93–94.

36. See for instance Peter Stanfield, "An Excursion into the Lower Depths: W.C. Handy's 'St. Louis Blues,' " in Stanfield 2005, 78–113.

37. Eddie Garland, "Oral History," August 8, 1958, 4, Hogan Jazz Archive, Tulane University. For more on Mabel Elaine's association with the Creole Band see Gene Anderson, "The Genesis of King Oliver's Creole Jazz Band," *American Music* 12, no. 3 (autumn 1994) 283; and especially Lawrence Gushee's masterly *Pioneers of Jazz: The Story of the Creole Band* (Oxford: Oxford University Press, 2005).

38. This trope had enough resonance in the mid-1940s, in fact, that a satirical review of a faux film called "Storyville" included, among its hilarious send-ups of everything that Hollywood typically gets wrong in jazz cinema, the benevolence of a white woman voyeur who pitches in to help rescue jazz when Storyville is destroyed. "One white woman, who has been watching the revival, writes them a check for $10,000,000 to the great jubilation of the cats." This line appears among other hilarities — including the inappropriate casting of Dizzy Gillespie as Buddy Bolden in "Jazz Wars" and the send-up of racist substitutions in the description of Bunk Johnson leading a New Orleans funeral procession followed by the Boston Pops Orchestra in blackface. The review was first published in October 1945 but was reprinted nearly two years later after the release of *New Orleans*, revealing an ongoing refutation by jazz fans of Hollywood representations. Gene Deitch, " 'Storyville': New Movie to Show Real History of Jazz," *Record Changer*, July 1947.

39. Even for jazz fans who are happy to see Herman, this "surprise" is disappointing. As Dave Dixon points out, not only does Herman's orchestra replace Armstrong and others with white swing musicians but the entire big band is wheeled on stage only to be "drowned out by the large symphonic orchestra." Dave Dixon, "Some Reflections on the Film and Its Music . . . ," liner notes, Louis Armstrong and Billie Holiday, *Original Motion*

Picture Soundtrack 'New Orleans,'" Giants of Jazz 1025, Institute of Jazz Studies, Rutgers University, Newark, New Jersey.

40. The Boswells' proximity to blackness was a selling point not lost on *Down Beat* in an article in 1944 that claimed the sisters were "Hep" because of three black women in the household "who sang incessantly: Aunt Rhea jived the spirituals, Aunt Sadie crooned them, and Bertha rocked them to the rhythm of her washboard . . . No wonder the three Boswell girls sang and sang the way they did!" John Lucas, "Cats Hepped by Connee's Chirping," *Down Beat*, October 15, 1944, 3. For a fascinating analysis of the latter see Stras 2007.

41. Interestingly, the stage directions for one early script called for Miralee to deliver her concert jazz song by "blues-shouting, in a throaty voice that penetrates the auditorium," *New Orleans*, April 1946, mimeo script, Herbert Biberman and Gale Sondergaard Papers, 1908–81, U.S. MSS 58AN, box 16, folder 1, Wisconsin Historical Society, Madison.

42. I am continuing to research the politically charged "collaborations" between like- and unlike-minded forces in the creation of this film. For references to these shifts in the making of the film, see for example Laurence Bergreen, *Louis Armstrong: An Extravangant Life* (New York: Broadway, 1997), 429; Gabbard 1996, 120–23; Stuart Nicholson, *Billie Holiday* (Boston: Northeastern University Press, 1995), 153; and Klaus Stratemann, *Louis Armstrong on the Screen* (Copenhagen: Jazz Media, 1996), as well as his *Duke Ellington, Day by Day and Film by Film* (Copenhagen: Jazz Media, 1992), 193–95.

43. I thank Naomi Pabst for reminding me of the pancake recipe and drawing my attention to the interesting comparison.

44. Edwin Schallert, "Career as Singing Star of Screen Dawns Favorably for Theodora Lynch," *New York Times*, April 25, 1948, D, 1.

45. Gabbard 1996, 79–80. Gabbard has pointed out that *New Orleans* is one of many Hollywood films that "wait until the end to elevate white music over black music" (79). Other films with this plot include *The Fabulous Dorseys* (1947) and *The Benny Goodman Story* (1955).

46. Floyd Levin, telephone conversation with Sherrie Tucker, August 13, 2004.

47. Art Levin, e-mail correspondence with Sherrie Tucker, September 6, 2004.

48. Nesuhi Ertegun, quoted from his oral history in Bruce Boyd Raeburn's splendid dissertation, "New Orleans Style: The Awakening of American Jazz Scholarship and Its Cultural Implications" (diss., Tulane, 1991), 161.

49. Marili Ertegun, "Collecting Hot, 1927–1947," *Record Changer*, October 1947, 7–8.

50. Marili Ertegun, "Just Playing Music I Love, Says Kid Ory," *Down Beat*, August 10, 1951. For other accounts of Marili Morden's role in Ory's "comeback" see Bigard and Martyn, *With Louis and the Duke: The Autobiography of a Jazz Clarinetist*; Raeburn, "New

Orleans Style"; Helen Oakley Dance, *Stormy Monday: The T-Bone Walker Story* (Baton Rouge: Louisiana State University Press, 1987); and Ahmet Ertegun, *"What'd I Say": The Atlantic Story: 50 Years of Music* (New York: Welcome Rain, 2001). I am continuing to research these connections. See also untitled script about jazz, n.d., Orson Welles Manuscript Collection, Films, 1939–47, box 22, folder 24, Lilly Library, Indiana University, Bloomington; Bret Wood, *Orson Welles: A Bio-Bibliography* (New York: Greenwood, 1990), 176–77.

51. Larry Ceplair and Steven Englund, *The Inquisition in Hollywood: Politics in the Film Community, 1930–1960* (Garden City, N.Y.: Anchor/Doubleday, 1980), 256.

52. Robert Stam, "Orson Welles, Brazil, and the Power of Blackness," *Perspectives on Orson Welles*, ed. Morris Beja (New York: G. K. Hall, 1995), 236–37.

53. Herbert Biberman, letter to Gale Sondergaard, 1946, Herbert Biberman and Gale Sondergaard Papers, 1908–81, U.S. MSS 58AN, Personal correspondence, box 3, folder 8, 1945–47, Wisconsin Historical Society, Madison.

54. Ibid.

55. Dick Irving Hyland's version dated August 6, 1946, is very close to the finished film, except that Endie's song is structured as a blues, and it is Benny Goodman, not Woody Herman, who eclipses the New Orleans band on the concert hall stage. Dick Irving Hyland, *New Orleans*, typescript, August 6, 1946, Herbert Biberman and Gale Sondergaard Papers, 1908–81 U.S. MSS 58AN, *New Orleans*, box 15, folder 8, Wisconsin Historical Society, Madison.

56. Ibid.

57. Stam, "Orson Welles, Brazil, and the Power of Blackness," 237; Clinton Heylin, *Despite the System: Orson Welles versus the Hollywood Studios* (Chicago: Chicago Review Press, 2005), 126–27.

58. Bud Scott, "The True History of Jazz," and Bud Scott, Thomas Le Blanc, and Dora W. "Bass" Penson, "The True History of Jazz," Orson Welles Manuscript Collection, appendix B, Research Files, Jazz, Lilly Library, Indiana University, Bloomington.

59. "Lil Armstrong Snubbed by Hollywood," *Down Beat*, October 1, 1941.

60. Heylin, *Despite the System*; Stam, "Orson Welles, Brazil, and the Power of Blackness."

61. *Syncopation*, American Film Institute Catalog (2003–6), ProQuest Information and Learning Company (accessed November 25, 2006).

62. This is an excellent example of Ahmed's "Declaration of Whiteness #3: I am/we are ashamed by my/our racism," a "cultural politics of emotion" that shows "we mean well," and "re-posits" the "white subject" as "the social ideal." Sara Ahmed, "Declarations of Whiteness: The Non-performativity of Anti-Racism," *Borderlands* 3, no. 2 (2004).

63. I'd like to thank Krin Gabbard for introducing me to this fascinating film.

64. Untitled script about jazz, Orson Welles Manuscript Collection.

65. Wood, *Orson Welles*, 176–77.

66. *New Orleans*, April 1946, mimeo script, Herbert Biberman and Gale Sondergaard Papers, Wisconsin Historical Society.

67. Marili Ertegun.

68. Farah Jasmine Griffin, *If You Can't Be Free, Be a Mystery: In Search of Billie Holiday* (New York: Free Press, 2001), 75–76.

69. Sara Ahmed, "Declarations of Whiteness."

70. Ibid.

71. Dance, *Stormy Monday*, 50–52.

Ingrid Monson

Over the past few years, I've noticed that some of my students are confused when they notice the apparent mismatch between my white skin, blond hair, and blue eyes and the title of my position — The Quincy Jones Professor of African American Music.[1] For most of my career, I have devoted far more attention to making sure that the knowledge I communicate about jazz history and its inevitable embeddedness in American race relations is first-rate rather than worrying about what I look like. My deeply held belief has been that the history of the music and its musical processes are far more important than my own personal history and that any success I have had in the classroom is probably not because of, but in spite of, who I am. After all, symbolically speaking, I am all wrong: a woman, a trumpet player, a midwesterner, a Norwegian American, a daughter of the white middle class, and perhaps the most damning, a lesbian. Individually, each of these traits is in dissonance with the social history of who has typically written about jazz and with current understandings of who *ought* to be writing about jazz. But collectively, my particular package of social positions presents an apparently impossible portfolio of inauthenticity and unhipness for the would-be scholar of jazz and African American music. Nevertheless, not only has my existence as a jazz scholar been possible, I have actually

thrived to a degree that I could not possibly have foreseen. Consequently, as I look at the confused first impressions of some of my students, the questions I often find myself pondering are "*how have I been
possible?*" and "should the fact that I have been possible be a larger part
of the story that I tell my students?"

TO BE OR NOT TO BE REFLEXIVE

I have never been a big fan of overly reflexive academic writing. Although I have appreciated that part of the reflexive turn (which dates
from the 1980s) that has emphasized taking responsibility for the differences in power between the researcher and the researched and being
honest about the complex human and ethical dynamics involved in the
conduct of ethnographic research, I've been rather suspicious of long
first-person accounts that seem to be more about the researcher than the
subject under investigation. The potential for vanity and self-indulgence
as well as the covering of the slimness of research by making the author
into the principal character have always struck me as highly problematic.
But then I was raised among Scandinavian Americans, a cultural group
notorious for its condemnation of personal display and arrogance. I
seem to have a double standard about this too, since I have never had any
objection to the African American tradition of autobiography and bearing witness that has produced such classics as Frederick Douglass's *Narrative of the Life of Frederick Douglass, an American Slave* (1845), W. E. B.
Du Bois's *The Souls of Black Folk* (1903), Sidney Bechet's *Treat It Gentle*
(1960), Maya Angelou's *I Know Why the Caged Bird Sings* (1969), Charles
Mingus's *Beneath the Underdog: His World as Composed by Charles Mingus*
(1971), and Bernice Johnson Reagon's *If You Don't Go, Don't Hinder Me*
(2001).[2] All of these works have used first-person narration in ways that
powerfully illustrate the very *personal* impact of racism on the daily lives
and culture of African Americans and, by so doing, have challenged
others to move beyond their own complacency.

   Yet the suffering of African Americans at the hands of racism has
always seemed to me of deeper significance in the quest for a just society
than some of the problems I have endured as a woman or a lesbian.
Indeed, my own path through these intersections has taught me that the
quest for freedom as a gendered human being or person of alternative
sexuality will be ultimately shallow without a deeper understanding of
the way race, power, economic privilege, and access to health care shape
and limit the possibilities for personal fulfillment around the world.

I do not think of my path to jazz and the study of African American music as a story that matches the significance and intensity of the struggle for racial justice, but rather as one that illustrates the intersection of three cultural themes whose intersection I am unusually positioned to comment upon. The first is best posed as a question: *just what would an ethical white relationship to African American music look like?*; furthermore, *is there such a thing?* This has perhaps been the central question in my scholarly practice and the one that I have most obsessive-compulsively pursued in all my writings. The second theme is gender — more specifically, why is it so difficult for women to get any respect in jazz? Why despite its celebration of human freedom and communal solidarity does the jazz community more often mention women (especially horn players) as objects of ridicule rather than celebration, even when they equal or surpass their male colleagues in musical erudition? Why is it not only male jazz aficionados who carry this prejudice? The third theme is homophobia and its effect on the experience of the first two themes. To what extent has my social experience as a lesbian shaped my understanding of racism and gender and their complex circulation in the world of jazz? Since I cannot know what my experience in the world would have been if one or more of my subject positions had been different, this is necessarily a speculative endeavor.

BLAME IT ON THE TRUMPET

I doubt that I would be the person I am today if I had not chosen to play the trumpet at the age of ten. I chose it for no good reason, only that it was the sole band instrument I had seen up close and personal. Dick Iebling (at the age of fourteen), the neighborhood paperboy, had shown me his trumpet and I was fascinated by the buzzing of the lips that was required to produce a sound. At least half the fifth-grade trumpet players at Washburn Elementary School in Bloomington, Minn., were girls, so I did not understand that the trumpet was supposed to be a boy's instrument. It turns out that I was quickly recognized as having a "good tone" and a quick grasp of music (aided no doubt by the two years of piano lessons I had had). My early teachers and band directors (all men) were very encouraging of my development on the trumpet and so was my mother; hence, it never occurred to me to drop out of band when I went to junior high school, although almost all the other girls did. My first private teacher was Dick Whitbeck, a Minneapolis trumpeter and composer who served as music director for the Guthrie Theater and was the youngest person ever named to the position (at the age of twenty-four). When I was fourteen years old, Dick took me to a rehearsal of the Doc Severinsen band, which was in town for a concert. I was thrilled to see my first professional rehearsal and meet a famous trumpet player, but this was also my first encounter with the feeling that there was something inappropriate about my being female and a trumpet player. Dick introduced me as one of his best trumpet students and Severinsen replied, "yeah, sure." From the tone of his voice and the way he looked at me, I suddenly realized that he presumed that I was Whitbeck's underage girlfriend, not a trumpet player. As I look back on this now, I realize that Dick's generous attempt to welcome me into the inner world of trumpet players — which was unfortunately answered by Severinsen's sexualized gaze — was simply the first incident in the complex double bind that would follow me throughout my life with the trumpet. Although individual men (especially teachers) were often very supportive, one's ability on the instrument could not guarantee acceptance in or access to the broader fraternity of trumpet players. There was something about being a woman that was disqualifying.

If I had chosen the violin, the piano, or the flute, I probably would have remained in classical music, but it did not take me very long to realize that the trumpet had a far more central role in jazz than it did in the repertory of western classical music. I remember being incredibly disappointed when I played my first Mozart and Beethoven symphonies in an orchestra and discovered that my part was often in unison with the timpani. Worse yet was the fact that in the orchestral repertory, the trumpet often had to count hundreds of bars of rest before entering to play a four-bar passage that consisted of the scale degrees 1 and 5, rather than a memorable melody. Although I was later to play more interesting orchestral parts in the symphonies of Mahler and Strauss, it became evident to me during my years in music school that the trumpet was not a prestige instrument in classical music. Its solo literature was limited; it was not often included as an instrument in the masterworks of chamber music; and the brass quintet literature — although quite in demand for Easter Sunday — would never be considered equal to the string quartet and quintet literature. Twentieth-century chamber works, such as Stravinsky's *L'Histoire du Soldat* or Varèse's *Octandre*, offered some compensation, but as players of loud instruments that produced trails of spit, even male brass players were something of second-class citizens in classical music.

Nevertheless, it was not a trumpet player who brought me more deeply into jazz but a saxophonist — Charlie Parker. I went to the music library at the University of Wisconsin, Madison one day and listened to an album on Verve called *The Essential Charlie Parker*.[3] Side one featured a smoking *Kim*; it was followed by the shimmering strings of *Just Friends*, then *Bloomdido*, *Au Privave*, and *Funky Blues*. To this day, it remains one of my most favorite sequences of Charlie Parker tunes, perhaps because every note of every tune is deeply embedded in my memory. I used to listen to it every morning when I got up. What was it that got me? The astonishing virtuosity, the timbre of the horn, the phrasing with its swallowed, crunched, pointed, and bent notes, and the intensity of the slow blues. *Funky Blues* sent me right over the top with that effortlessly passionate fall that occurs in the first half minute, and those chicken scratch, rooster-call sort of blues phrases that seem to be the very essence of 'making a horn talk.' When I looked for a digital copy of *Funky Blues* recently, I saw that it had been reissued on an album called *Tease: The Beat of Burlesque*.[4] The idea that *Funky Blues* might be heard by some as suitable for accompanying a striptease never occurred to me at 19, or that the deep blues on the saxophone must necessarily be about sex, masculinity, and heterosexuality. To me, it was passionate, amazing, and virtuosic and I wanted to find out how anyone was able to do that.

I had certainly heard about improvisation before. I had been in "stage band" in high school, under the direction of my band director Doc DeHaven, a trumpeter who was one of the most well-known local jazz musicians in Madison, Wisc. I had learned how to swing eighth notes, do falls, and remember Doc explaining to me that the improvising musician had to be able to turn the chord symbols in the charts into solos, but the band itself emphasized reading jazz parts rather than learning to improvise. Doc DeHaven was another in a long line of band directors and teachers who had been very encouraging to me. I will never forget how grateful I was that he released me from any obligation to play in the marching band in my senior year in high school, mostly because he could see how much I hated it.

THE ANTIWAR MOVEMENT

During my high school years, the University of Wisconsin, Madison was a center of anti–Vietnam war activism. Shortly after my family moved back to Madison in the summer of 1970, the bombing of the Army Math Research Center (AMRC) took place and physicist Robert

Fassnacht was killed as a result. Although many antiwar activists and leftists had long been critical of the AMRC's connections to the military, this act of violence caused a split in the movement. Although some rationalized that the Army Math Research Center — through its relationship to the U.S. military — caused the deaths of many in Southeast Asia, others found that the violence that resulted in the death of an innocent person was simply unacceptable.

I had no friends that sophomore year in high school (since I had just moved to town); I found myself taking the bus downtown on Saturday afternoons, listening to music at the Madison Public Library and then wandering down State Street toward the center of Madison's antiwar and hippie cultural district. I remember my excitement as I read my first copy of the famed underground newspaper *Kaleidoscope*, which included not only stories about the antiwar movement and radical politics but also frank discussions of how to have great sex. Over the next few years, I became involved in antiwar and community organizations that led also to my participation in Marxist study groups run by students and activists from five to ten years older than I. My high school French teacher, Mary Rehwald (then Mary Radke), helped make the link to the world of radical politics by putting me in touch with other high school students who were involved in an organization called the Wisconsin Alliance. It was with this group that I formed the friendships that led me to attend all the major antiwar demonstrations that took place during my high school years.

Some of the activists who were about ten years older than I had experienced the civil rights movement in the early 1960s. My friend Toby Emmer, who told me of her experiences doing civil rights organizing in Cleveland, impressed me the most; it was through her that I learned about Fannie Lou Hamer, Odetta, and Bernice Reagon, and I went to their performances or speaking events when they came to town. I still have my LP copy of *Give Your Hands to Struggle* recorded by Bernice Reagon in 1975.[5] Bernice Reagon's *a capella* voice moved me the same way that Charlie Parker had on *Funky Blues*, this time coupled with the moral force of the civil rights movement and the church. Its lyrics went like this: "There's a new world coming, Everything's gonna a be turnin' over, Everything's gonna be turnin' over, Where you gonna be standin' when it comes?" This was all the passion of the blues combined with the conviction, strength, and vision of someone with unflinching moral purpose.

As with many white Americans of my generation, the anti–Vietnam war movement became a path into awareness of the civil rights and black power movements. Since there were not many African Americans in Madison, the black people I encountered during this period of my life were primarily on the stage either as performers or political speakers. Although mixed with rock and roll and folk music, black music also began to be a bigger presence in the social events of the political organizations I was a part of. In the early 1970s, Becca Pulliam, who is now the producer of *Jazz Set* on National Public Radio (NPR), often had dance parties in the house she owned on Madison's East side. It was here that I first heard Aretha Franklin's *Spirit in the Dark* album and danced to the Temptations. The first trumpet solo I learned by ear, in fact, was the one on the Temptations' *Papa Was a Rolling Stone* (1972), and I heard it first at Becca's. Although I remember singing along to the Supremes' *Stop! In the Name of Love* with my girlfriends when I was ten years old, I had been listening to mostly rock and roll (Cream, Led Zeppelin, the Beatles, Janis Joplin, the Rolling Stones, and Jimi Hendrix), horn bands (Chicago; Blood, Sweat and Tears; and Tower of Power), and classical music, before I encountered Charlie Parker.[6]

The merging of the two biggest streams in my life — the politics of the antiwar movement and music — I was thus able to accomplish through my growing interest in jazz. Here I found the passionate musical sound I loved, a repertory that had a big role for the trumpet, and a history that was indelibly linked to the progressive social movements that had preceded and inspired the one I was most directly involved in — the antiwar movement. From Bird, I went on to Miles Davis (and began learning those trumpet solos) and tried to learn a bit about jazz theory, which I got mostly from the bassist Richard Davis, who joined the University of Wisconsin faculty in 1977, the pianist Joan Wildman, who taught a great improvisation course, and my trumpet teacher Bob McCurdy.

The only piece that did not quite fit was that I was a woman on the trumpet. It had never occurred to me that the passion I felt in Charlie Parker, Miles Davis, Bernice Reagon, the Temptations, and John Coltrane had to be gender-coded male when played on the trumpet. The idea that I was rebelling against my gender socialization by loving this music was the furthest thing from my mind. I was simply continuing to play an instrument that I had played since I was ten and combining it with my other interests. Nevertheless, gender socialization was finally doing its work on me. I noticed in college that when I told people I played the trumpet, some reacted as if there was something kind of "queer" about it (women were often just as bad as men in this regard). I did date some men in high school and college and my two most significant boyfriends were both brass players (trumpet and French horn turned guitarist). But it soon became apparent, much to my initial horror, that I was not going to turn out to be a well-adjusted heterosexual. Having finally "got it" that the trumpet was a guy's instrument and that jazz was a quintessentially masculine music, I suddenly felt like a walking stereotype. My deepest attractions to the passions of jazz and the sound of the trumpet were somehow taken as signs of a masculine inner character (lesbian as cross-dressed man), although, to me, these were the sounds of passion and a social conscience that ought to be inspiring to everyone. I have always found the presumptions about women doing apparently 'male things' very curious. Why must the woman who wants to do some of the things that men do (play instruments, have careers, be self-determining) be accused of wanting to "be a man" rather than of aspiring to the same freedom? Why would a person who spent so much of her time studying the musical achievements of men be presumed to be a "man hater," just because she was a lesbian? (In my experience, brokenhearted heterosexual women have the lowest opinion of men.)

As I continued down the path that jazz would lead me on, the apparent "inappropriateness" of who I was began to multiply. To my gender-inappropriate interest in the trumpet would be added the racial inappropriateness of being a white person in jazz. These were the peak years of the black power and black arts movements, after all, and I, like other progressive whites, found myself reading a lot about self-determination — the exploitative history of white people in jazz — and not wanting to repeat the sins of my ancestors. Yes, that was when I naively believed it was possible to be completely different from the white people before us, simply through acts of will and moral righteousness. What surprised me was that I was also considered "inappropriate" in certain respects in the lesbian community of the 1970s. In Madison, Wisc., you were supposed to play softball if you were a self-respecting lesbian and you were supposed to go to "women's music" concerts of performers like Meg Christian, Holly Near, and Cris Williamson (i.e., the Olivia Records roster, before the entry of African American women into the scene). Although I did indeed go to the concerts (not a trumpet to be found anywhere), I found that softball practices conflicted with practicing the trumpet and performing. When one of my friends implied that it was my moral obligation to play softball and asked what was

I doing spending my time playing men's music anyway, I discovered that I was something of an alien in this scene too. Since music was at my emotional core — the thing I needed to do to keep my basic humanity intact — I skipped the softball and practiced like a demon.

BOSTON

Here, I betrayed my deep belief in the deeply held American ideology that our society is a meritocracy that rewards excellence above all else. If I just got good enough, I thought, maybe people would not notice that I played a gender-inappropriate instrument and that I was a white Midwesterner with very blond hair and blue eyes. I think my goal was being tolerated rather than accepted, but this self-consciousness made me kind of timid and scared (as if I were expecting someone to hit me over the head at any time) and, ultimately, kept me kind of isolated. When I moved to Boston to go to the New England Conservatory of Music, I certainly did not advertise that I was of alternative sexuality, but because of it I found myself uncomfortable around both the very straight women (which all the other women in the jazz program seemed to be [there were four of us total]) and the men who wanted to date me. Or was it worse with the ones that did not want to date me? Whichever it was, I also noticed that many of the white men seemed to feel entitled to put me down to my face in ways that none of the African American men did. I also noticed that the other women in the jazz program were unlikely to complain about sexism, so neither did I.

As I reflect on it now, it seems to me that I was much more invested in hoping that the jazz world would be gender-blind rather than color-blind. This was my modernist Achilles heel. I really wanted to believe the rhetoric that in music the only thing that mattered was the music. One of the most disheartening experiences I had at the conservatory was playing in the big band a semester when it was conducted by one of the more legendary sexists on the faculty (a white male). There were only two women in the instrumental lineup that semester: me and a tenor saxophonist. The director liked to tell earthy locker room–style stories that brought out the worst in the men; he was so over-the-top that even the guys told stories about how little respect he had for women. The trumpet section became rather out of control. They would hoot and holler, and one coward had no problem letting the director blame me for the mistakes he was making. Over and over, I felt publicly disrespected and I dreaded going to the rehearsals. By the end of the semester, I thought that maybe I just was not good enough to be entitled to basic courtesy, but then we had a dress rehearsal with a female singer who was scheduled to sing a song with us at the concert. The director fell all over himself being chivalrous to this woman (who, unlike the horn players, was considered to be filling a gender-appropriate role), although everyone could hear that she was not much of a singer. The contrast between the treatment the women instrumentalists had been receiving all semester (the saxophonist was not into bonding over this) and the treatment of the singer was utterly astonishing to me.

When I later heard some of the very same white men who had given me such grief in big band complain that black musicians discriminated against them because they were white, I found that I had little sympathy. It seemed so self-serving. The very same guys who trivialized and mocked female instrumentalists were now charging that African American musicians were discriminating against them. As a woman, I often found myself in an in-between status in this conversation since both sides of this debate seemed to feel comfortable confiding in me. Sometimes, an African American classmate would tell me when he felt that a white guy had a bad racial attitude, did not swing, or lacked passion. Some of the white men, by contrast, would complain about the racial draft they felt from black musicians as if I, as a white person, would be sympathetic. If they were so concerned about discrimination, I wondered, why didn't they ask any women to be part of their bands? I know that if I had said that out loud, they would simply have said that the women were not good enough. I found myself thinking: "funny, that's what I've heard some of the brothers say about you."

On weekends, I began playing in a Latin band that played salsa, merengues, and cumbias. This was to become my first long-term regular gig, and another trumpet player — Frank London — was the one who invited me in as a sub. The lead player was another female trumpet player, Jeanne Snodgrass. When Frank quit this band for a regular gig in another band, Jeanne and I became the regular trumpet players in a band called Ruben Guity y Su Orquesta. People thought we must be sisters or perhaps that we had Latin blood, and it was here that I realized that if I had had another kind of personality (and sexuality), there might have been a way to make being a woman trumpet player work for me. If I had been willing to put on a sexy gown and had gotten off on shaking my booty, I think some of the audience would have really liked it.

This was a family band. Ruben, who was originally from Honduras, was the lead singer and his son Rubencito played the keyboards. The guys in the band protected us from any audience members who had bad intentions and we always felt completely safe in the group. For about a year and a half, I played nearly every weekend at small clubs and social halls mostly in Boston, Lawrence, and Providence: Cindy's in Brighton and the Latin Paradise in Dudley Station were the two most frequent venues. Ruben always wanted to know who was in the audience before he decided which pieces we would play: we needed to play salsa for Puerto Ricans, merengues for Dominicans, and cumbia for the Columbians. Too much of one thing or the other might have offended one of the ethnic groups.

I did not know a thing about clave when I joined the group and here I must step back to underscore that my ability to transgress my gender category was inalterably tied up with class privilege. Because my mother could afford to send me to college, I was able to attend a good music school in a cosmopolitan city. Because my mother was a psychiatrist who had endured a very sexist medical school environment in the early 1950s (and worked throughout her career for the Veterans Administration), she always encouraged me to pay no attention to people's ideas of what women were supposed to do. The primary quality that got Jeanne and me a gig in Ruben's band was that we could read music very well and were technically skilled on our instruments. That we sight-read our parts and seldom took a chart home was something that some of the percussionists in the band found amazing. (This was embarrassing to me since I thought they expressed too much respect for the literate tradition, especially since I had so much to learn about the aural parts of music.) This was a common pattern in the Latin bands in Boston: gringo horn players and Latino percussionists, singers, bassists, and pianists.

It took me quite a while to be able to solo comfortably in clave-based time feels. Jazz phrasing and swing notes just did not work in this more straight eighth style of playing. Long bebop lines did not quite cut it either, but fortunately I began to pick up on the importance of riffs in the style. My favorite trumpeter in Latin jazz was Juancito Torres from Eddie Palmieri's band, who played amazingly singable melodic patterns in the upper register that were so beautifully aligned with clave. I loved going to these gigs in Ruben's band because they brought me into a cultural world I had never seen before — an Afro-Caribbean world that was alive with dancing, food, and amazing music. We always listened to José Massó's *Con Salsa* (on radio station WBUR) on the way to gigs. I learned about performers like Sonora Ponceña, Celia Cruz, Johnny Pacheco, and Gran Combo. I started going to a Latin record store on Tremont Street (near Mission Hill) and, when in New York, to the store that was in the Times Square subway station. I enjoyed knowing something about this music that could not yet be found in mainstream record stores.

In 1980, I was also asked to become a part of the Klezmer Conservatory Band, a group that seemed to arise spontaneously after the spring Jewish music concert at New England Conservatory. Hankus Netsky had asked me to learn the second trumpet part in a piece called *Beym Rebn in Palestine*.[7] I had not heard this music before, but I really loved the piece; this too was passionate music and improvisational. The band was invited to do a gig after the concert and so began the Klezmer Conservatory Band. By the fall of 1980, it became a regular group, and we did our first road gig to play a synagogue in Philadelphia. I loved these gigs too, for the same reason that I had loved being in Ruben Guity's band. It brought me into a world that I otherwise would not have seen. I was overwhelmed, in particular, by the emotional reaction to the music of older people who were often brought to tears by hearing a repertory they had heard little of since their youth. People clapped, danced, cried, and often came up and kissed us after the concerts, although, in the beginning, we did not really play the style very well. I was one of several gentiles in the group and at first I wondered whether it was appropriate for me to be in the band since I was not Jewish. Nobody in the band seemed to feel that way, but I wondered about the audiences. We played for a reformed rabbinical convention in the Catskills about a year after I joined the band. I was thrilled when one of the rabbis seemed to take particular delight in the fact that I was in the band, and, from then on, I decided that if it was all right with a rabbi, why should I worry about it?

The Klezmer Conservatory Band was my most commercially successful gig. Within a year, we had recorded our first album and appeared on NPR's Prairie Home Companion. The band members were like family. We never went out and socialized in Boston, but we were always together on the road and got to know each other very well. Mimi Rabson, Abby Rabinovitz, Jim Guttmann, Hankus Netsky, Judy Bressler, Dave Harris, Charlie Berg, and Don Byron were among the original members of the band, and all were important in shaping the adult I was to become.

Don Byron, who plays the clarinet, was the principal featured soloist in the group. As both gentile and African American, he was often the focus of post-concert commentary. I remember the first time I heard someone come up and ask him whether he read music. Having known Don as a consummately literate musician who was as comfortable with Stravinsky as jazz, this made me very angry. Then there was the time we played at the Boston Esplanade and were killing time after the sound-check and before the performance. I asked to use a telephone and was directed to a pay phone in an area where equipment was stored under-neath the stage. A few minutes later, Don asked me if I knew where the phone was and I told him about the one I had just used. The guards would not let him in (although he explained that he was a performer with the group), and the obviousness of the racial discrimination out-raged me. From incidents such as these, we began a conversation about race, music, and politics that continues to this day.

I too was subject to various categorical assumptions that led to some-times amusing and sometimes irritating questions. One of the funniest conflations of gendered and ethnic assumptions happened when we played a concert in Harvard's Paine Hall. A busload of older people had been driven to the concert and were seated in the back of the hall. Our singer, Judy Bressler, had strawberry blond hair and spoke Yiddish, and I had just had a haircut that had left it on the short side. After the concert, an older woman asked Judy whether the blond boy who plays the trumpet was her son. When Judy told me this, I immediately burst into laughter, because it seemed that the woman had been trying to figure out some way in which I *might* be Jewish. Judy was horrified that someone could think she was that old (it was the woman's poor eyesight, not Judy's looks). Another hopeful questioner had once asked me whether I was related to Rabbi Monson of Montclair, New Jersey.

More infuriating were gendered comments such as the man who came up to me, laughing, and asked whether I knew that I had turned beet red during the performance. Or the man who came up and deliv-ered the backhanded compliment, "I didn't know a girl could ever play so good." By this time, I had begun coming up with snappy answers like, "Well now you know that a girl can play this good," and "You'd turn red too if you played that part." Then there was the time that Judy Bressler and I walked into a bar mitzvah together (I was in a black raincoat with a red lining) and some middle-aged man shouted out, "Oh good the strippers are here." As I look back on this, I think our age had something to do with it. That same man would not have said such a thing to women in his own age group.

When I finally had self-confidence about how I was playing, I was no longer upset by these comments. I had come to realize that no matter how well I played, audiences would always react ambivalently—not because of me, but because of the gendered assumptions in our society about what instruments are appropriate for women to play. Some people would love the transgression, and others would be disturbed by it. These reactions were not personal, but structured by a history and culture that were beyond any individual's control. This was a very liberating realization. Yes, you can try to undermine gendered or racialized presumptions through excellence, charm, a sense of humor, hard work, and generous acts, but you are not going to be able to stop people from making categorical presumptions based on who you are. This insight, I think, was the great turning point in my life and probably the key to all my subsequent success. Insulting presumptions are really not very personal (in the sense of being based on your individual acts and deeds), and the secret to having them hurt less is to know that they are not really about "you" but about categories.

I really should say a little more about this in academic terms. In my courses, I talk about the history of jazz moving from a popular to an art music. The insistence of jazz musicians that they be recognized as artists, and their self-conscious incorporation of musical ideas from both within and beyond the African American "tradition" (from blues, spirituals, and classical to African, Cuban, and Indian), were about breaking out of the stereotyped place that American society had for black music. Musicians were simply not willing to accept the role of black music as nonthreatening entertainment for white people. Black musicians pushed beyond the expectations for their sociological category by virtuosically borrowing from common discourses and musical resources from beyond their ethnic home base and by doing something new with them—things that inalterably expanded the definition of what it is to be an African American artist. The modernist idea of meritocracy, in which talent and excellence are the things that matter most, was one such discourse that jazz musicians mobilized on their behalf. Nevertheless, as numerous political science and sociology studies have shown, race continues to be strongly correlated with residential segregation, a lower life expectancy, and less prosperity.[8] Despite the spectacular achievements of some individuals, in other words, the structural aspects of racial hierarchy tend to shape both the outcome of people's lives and the presumptions that people tend to bring into their encounters with individuals. The same is true for members of other social categories (and their multivariate combinations). This delicate balance between who we are as members of larger collectivities and as individuals is something that the history of jazz makes plain in ways that, in my opinion, have a significance far beyond music history.

MORE THAN THE SUM OF ONE'S CATEGORIES

I was offered a scholarship to New York University's ethnomusicology program and began in the fall of 1985. I could never have imagined when I enrolled that not only would I do well in graduate school but that I also would become a successful academic in a prominent position sixteen years later. The path was not without its bumps, bruises, and collisions, but they did not come from the sources I had anticipated. I had always expected that African Americans would be ambivalent about another white jazz scholar, and so I tried to purge myself of the attitudes that I had heard African American musicians express as sources of exasperation with white people. I never expected the degree of support, generosity, and companionship that I have enjoyed from my African American colleagues. I also expected that being a lesbian would be a tough sell to an African American audience.

My partner and I moved to Fort Greene in Brooklyn in 1986, because we could not afford a place in Park Slope, which was where lesbians who could not afford Manhattan were supposed to live. Fort Greene was a predominantly African American neighborhood, but substantially mixed. We started to meet our neighbors after I locked myself out of the apartment on a cold January day by chasing after the UPS man who had left a package at the wrong address. I was barefoot. DeWayne, a neighbor in the next building, saw my predicament and invited me into his apartment to call my "roommate." He had already figured out that we were gay (or had remarkable gaydar) because as we were waiting for my partner to deliver the keys, he told me about a lesbian couple around the corner and a gay male couple as well. Soon, we were invited to a dinner party, and, a few months later, it seemed that we had become part of a very active Fort Greene social scene. Here, I got to know, for the first time, a lot of African Americans who were not musicians. I noticed that despite the homophobic rhetoric that can often be heard in African American communities, people are actually pretty tolerant as long as you do not constantly pepper your conversation with words like lesbian and gay. We moved into the neighborhood just after the release of Spike Lee's *She's Gotta Have It*[9] and greatly enjoyed recognizing the Fulton Street Mall, Fort Greene Park, and other details of our neighborhood in the film. This was before Lee opened his shop and he was often seen walking up DeKalb Avenue. I loved living in this neighborhood because, once again, it opened my eyes to a world I would not otherwise have seen.

When I began approaching professional musicians for interviews for my dissertation, I was almost apologetic, since I knew that academics were not held in high esteem by jazz musicians. I worried that some would not want to talk to a white person, or that others would not want to talk to a woman, and I was certain that letting people know about my alternative sexuality would not be a wise thing to do (not that they did not pick up on it anyway). In the end, I bonded with the musicians who chose to talk to me in the way I always had: through conversations about music. Once I got people going on a musical topic, they seemed to forget for a few minutes what categories I was a part of. If we got to the topic of race, I seemed to pass some of the basic tests of tolerance and awareness, but I certainly was not perfect. Throughout this long process, I would check in periodically with Don Byron (for a while we had a wedding band together in New York) and then we started having long telephone conversations that usually were about two basic topics: the ups and downs of our respective love lives and race.

The most racially tense moment of my dissertation research was when I tried to organize an interview with a musician through his manager. The manager was an African American man who was quite nationalist in orientation. He called me one night to grill me on my racial attitudes and let me know that being a white researcher was probably an inherently exploitative thing. I tried to explain what I was trying to do with this project in a way that avoided some of the worst of what white people had done before me, but I did not get defensive or accuse him of discriminating against me. After all, why shouldn't he be suspicious of a white researcher that he did not know? I decided to listen and try to figure out what bothered him the most. The idea of a white person "studying" black people for academic credit was one. Wanting to be recognized as being educated in his own right was another. I was quite upset when the conversation was over, because I hated feeling like an oppressor and thought that I would never get to interview the African American musician he managed. When I ran into the musician a couple of months later, I mentioned that I had not called him because his manager did not want me to interview him. He laughed, told me that he had fired his manager, and asked me when I wanted to do the interview. The *pièce de résistance*, however, was six months later when I answered the phone and heard the caller say: "Who is this?" I was a bit startled and said, "Who is this?" It was the manager. He then gave me a convoluted story about how he had seen this number on his notepad, but had not remembered who it was, so decided to give it a call and see who was at the other end. Once we had been through this strange opening, he asked cheerily, "And how is your project going?" I filled him in on what I had been doing and this conversation was just as friendly as the other one had been tense. It felt like a form of apology and I was glad he had called.

Not every racially tense encounter had an outcome like this, but the general scenario has been a far more common experience in my career than racial impasses. Why shouldn't an African American initially roll their eyes when I tell them I'm the Quincy Jones Professor of African American Music? (Non–African Americans do it too.) Perhaps some people have walked away never to return, but, more often than not, people come back, we start to talk and share ideas, and the next thing you know the initial attitude is gone and we're enjoying talking about the music, the continuing saga of race in America, Africa, or how we hope the interminable academic event we are at might soon be over.

TRYING TO BE REAL, NOT EXCEPTIONAL

In general, I have tried to write about jazz and race by trying to avoid a stance that constructs myself as an "exceptional white person." I have always found narratives like Mezz Mezzrow's *Really the Blues* or others that position the white person as a "true friend of the Negro" a form of grandstanding.[10] In many of these narratives, the author invokes a sociological characteristic to mitigate the author's degree of whiteness. Coming from "dark white" or "not fully white" ethnicity (usually Italian or Jewish) is one such background. For other narrators being from a working-class neighborhood, growing up in a black neighborhood, or having so thoroughly internalized African American music and culture that one is no longer culturally white are offered as explanations. Although there is, in fact, a long history of marginalized white people and other racialized groups (Asian Americans, Latinos, Native Americans) identifying with African American music and culture, I question whether these qualities actually collapse the sociological and economic differences among ethnicity, blackness, and class. Although living in the world as a Jew, Asian American, or working-class white person are clearly different subject positions within American society that carry various degrees and combinations of cultural and economic oppression, these positions are not quite the same as those experienced by a person who is black and not light enough to pass for something else.

When I was younger, I also wanted to be "not like those other white people" and found myself sometimes using my familiarity with some aspects of African American life and culture to distance myself from them. Then I started to think about all the conversations I had had with Don Byron and my spouse Okolo Ewunike (who is the love of my life) in which they had been critical of their fellow African Americans who sometimes pretended they were not black by putting on airs. (Don calls this "vacationing.") I did not want to be a white person on vacation. This was not so much about "being proud of being white," but simply recognizing that no matter how familiar I became with African American music and culture, no matter how many individual African Americans invited me into their lives, and no matter how "right on" anything I wrote was, sociologically speaking, I would still be a middle-class person with white privilege, whether I wanted it or not. The only honorable thing to do was be honest about occupying this social position and simply comment as best I could from that vantage point. This is not to say that I have not been culturally transformed in very significant ways by my experiences in African American America, but that I do not walk in quite the same shoes. To me, this is simply a matter of respect. At some point on this journey, I realized that one of the most irritating things to the African Americans I knew was the white person who thought that her understanding of African American music and culture erased all difference.

In my courses, my goal has been to try to have honest and nuanced conversations about race that do not fall into the trap of an either-or paradigm. Drawing attention to the multiple social categories that go into describing any individual (a combination of age, race, gender, sexual orientation, class, national origin, ethnicity, health status, and, undoubtedly, others) and how they combine in the histories of the musicians and other social actors has been crucial to my academic and pedagogical practice. On my down days, I have wondered whether it is ever possible to have a completely ethical relationship to African American music as a white scholar. I have learned a lot from my students who, at Harvard, have included a more ethnically diverse population than at any other institution where I have taught. My favorite moments have been when we get deep into one of the classic problems in interracial communication about African American music (such as charges that

African Americans are excluding non–African Americans by claiming a special relationship to black music) and end up moving from tension to laughter. When illustrating the problem with certain non–African American tropes of argument, I sometimes use an awkward moment in my own past as an example to lighten things up and illustrate how people often learn to communicate across these sociological and cultural categories by making terrible mistakes and learning from them. I have tried to use the fact that I do not quite fit my categories as an example of how people are not fully determined by their social categories; nevertheless, people must still deal with the consequences of such categories every day (i.e., they cannot escape them).

I have sometimes been asked, for example, how people know that I am a lesbian. I have a very ambivalent reaction to this question since it's hard to know whether to take it as a backhanded compliment ("gee, you don't look like a dyke," meaning their stereotype of a butch, I guess), a sign of someone trying to show how tolerant they are ("you do look like a dyke, but I'm so tolerant I wouldn't dream of presuming anything"), or evidence of a presumption that unlike other social oppressions this is a category in which you can more easily "pass" for straight. To me the nature of the social category and the consequences it carries is that you can only 'pass' for so long (no matter what you look like), and then only in the most superficial relationships in your life. In most work situations, friendships, or acquaintanceships in which there is a recurring interaction, people will eventually figure it out whether you tell them or not. What are the signs? It's your everyday chitchat. You don't talk about your personal life or what you do in your free time (you can get a reputation for aloofness if you keep this up too long!); you wear a wedding ring but never mention your husband; you only talk about your personal life with gender-neutral terms (my friend, my partner); you never bring a boyfriend to work-based social events; you don't talk about past boyfriends; you keep talking about "we" without mentioning the name of your partner. All these things start shifting the presumptions of your acquaintances and the people you work with from "straight until proven otherwise," to "queer until proven otherwise." At some point you just start being direct with the people you want to know better. Sometimes they "change" after the news — become more distant, no longer include you in their social activities, or show discomfort in your presence. Sometimes they don't (and they certainly don't change as much as they did thirty years ago).

Like most women, I have been more comfortable going to bat for the injustices experienced by other people than complaining about those I have experienced myself. Yet it is also true that by passionately critiquing racism in all its nuances, I have also been defending myself. I have felt most vulnerable in the world as a lesbian, and although the jazz world has a very long way to go in its acceptance of women and alternative sexualities, I have also been touched by the tolerance I have experienced when I have least expected it. Being hired as the Quincy Jones Professor was the ultimate experience in this regard. It is not as if my colleagues in African American studies and music did not know what they were getting after all. I am living proof of the fact that the jazz world and African American America are far more tolerant of people like me than they ever get credit for. I must single out Henry Louis Gates Jr., in particular, because he does not have a homophobic bone in his body. The most frustrating aspect of all the news coverage of Cornel West's and Anthony Appiah's departures from the university was that African and African American Studies continued to be presented in the press as an "affirmative action" discipline that was essentially a cover for African Americans hiring other African Americans. Why has media coverage never given my African American colleagues the credit for the complexity with which they practice affirmative action and cultural diversity? I wrote some friends shortly after I had moved back to Massachusetts and said that I suddenly felt that all of the things that had simply made me "weird" as a young adult now made me endearing. This is not because my experiences as a white woman trumpet player who loves jazz and hates racism are so exceptional, but that the moral dilemmas, categorical complications, and ethical soul-searching that attended this all-American journey are all too common.

I could have lived a more ethnically appropriate life after all, as I once joked with my students. I could have been a ski instructor and really fit the part. (This is no joke: I really was an excellent skier growing up.)[11] Blonde hair, blue eyes, a Scandinavian name — I could have really worked that angle. (By this time, the class is on the floor.) But I would not trade this other journey for anything in the world.

NOTES

1. The money for the chair was donated to Harvard University by the Time Warner Endowment and hence the full, official title of my position is even more complicated: the "Quincy Jones Professor of African American Music, supported by the Time Warner Endowment." I am neither the personal appointee of Quincy Jones, nor an employee of

Time Warner, but simply a professor hired jointly by the Department of African and African American Studies and the Department of Music at Harvard University.

2. Frederick Douglass, *Narrative of the Life of Frederick Douglass, an American Slave* (New York: Laurel, 1997 [1845]); W. E. B. Du Bois, *The Souls of Black Folk* (New York: New American Library, 1969 [1903]); Sidney Bechet, *Treat It Gentle* (New York: Hill and Wang, 1960); Maya Angelou, *I Know Why the Caged Bird Sings* (New York: Random House, 1969); Charles Mingus, *Beneath the Underdog: His World as Composed by Charles Mingus* (New York: Alfred A. Knopf, 1971); Bernice Johnson Reagon, *If You Don't Go, Don't Hinder Me: The African American Sacred Song Tradition* (Lincoln: University of Nebraska Press, 2001).

3. Charlie Parker, *The Essential Charlie Parker*, Verve V6-8409 (1961).

4. *Tease: The Beat of Burlesque*, Verve 439302 (2005).

5. Bernice Johnson Reagon, *Give Your Hands to Struggle*, Smithsonian Folkways SF 40049 (1997 [1975]).

6. Aretha Franklin, "Spirit in the Dark," *Aretha Franklin, Queen of Soul: The Atlantic Recordings*, New York Atlantic Studios, March 10, 1970, Atlantic R2 71063 (1992); The Temptations, "Papa Was a Rolling Stone," *The Temptations: Emperors of Soul*, May–June 1972, Motown 31453-0338 (1994); The Supremes, "Stop! In the Name of Love," March 1965, Motown 012 159 415-2 (2000).

7. Klezmer Conservatory Band, *Yiddishe Renaissance*, Vanguard Records VCD 79450 (1981).

8. See, for example, Jennifer L. Hochschild, *Facing Up to the American Dream: Race, Class, and the Soul of the Nation* (Princeton: Princeton University Press, 1995); David O. Sears, Jim Sidanius, and Lawrence Bobo, *Racialized Politics: The Debate about Racism in America* (Chicago: University of Chicago Press, 2000); Michael C. Dawson, *Behind the Mule: Race and Class in African-American Politics* (Princeton: Princeton University Press, 1994).

9. *She's Gotta Have It*, dir. Spike Lee, Island Pictures 440 083 635-3 (1991 [1986]).

10. Milton "Mezz" Mezzrow and Bernard Wolfe, *Really the Blues* (New York: Random House, 1946).

11. I was a member of the Blizzard Ski Club in Minneapolis, which had several levels of ski instruction labeled by color. As you passed each test, you were awarded a new color. These were, in ascending order, green, yellow, blue, red, brown, white, low black, and top black. I still have my top black pin.

PART III

Improvising Gender: Representation

Ursel Schlicht

"BETTER A JAZZ ALBUM THAN LIPSTICK"

(*LIEBER JAZZPLATTE ALS LIPPENSTIFT*):

THE 1956 *JAZZ PODIUM* SERIES REVEALS IMAGES

OF JAZZ AND GENDER IN POSTWAR GERMANY

We believe that jazz in itself contains some factors that impede a woman's understanding, while the man finds access to this music much easier: And this is because jazz itself is unfeminine. . . . Basically, each very precise and motored exact rhythm contradicts the essence of the woman, who rather follows a different rhythm — the living, irregular rhythm of nature. Let's imagine a column of men marching in the same rhythm — this is nothing extraordinary. A column of exact marching women, on the other hand, has an unnatural effect, and borders on the ridiculous. Applied to jazz: a man who sits all night at the drum set looks natural. A woman at the drum set looks disconcerting.[1]

The 1950s saw an unprecedented transformation of Germany. On May 23, 1949, the three zones occupied by the Allied Forces became the Federal Republic of Germany (FRG). Just a few months later, the German Democratic Republic (GDR) was founded on October 7, 1949. While the West rapidly developed into one of the most productive industrial nations within a decade of formation, the East was marked by an effort to eliminate all social and economic bases of German fascism, and the transition to a socialist regime in the early 1950s.

From 1945 to 1949, women played an especially crucial role

in reconstructing the country. The *Trümmerfrauen*, the women in the midst of the rubble, began to clear the destroyed towns and cities with their bare hands. Independent, strong, hardworking and literally laying the foundation for rebuilding the nation, the Trümmerfrauen (see figure 12.1 on page 298) were in every sense picking up the pieces of what *Hitlerdeutschland*, Hitler's Germany, had left.

No matter how hard German women worked to face this monumental task, it did in no way amount to a new level of women's liberation. In the West, ideas of "ideal womanhood" changed radically backward to home and hearth (*Heim und Herd*). Although every working hand was needed during the 1950s — immigrant "guest workers" were hired from Turkey and 30 percent of the workforce consisted of women — laws were such that married women had to get official permission from their husbands before they could accept a job. The idea of women in the professional world was not welcome, and those who persevered and maintained a high profile would be excluded from ideals of German womanhood.

During the first years of the Hitler regime, the Nazi ideologues fostered the ideal of a devoted, patriotic mother, serving her family, community, and, when needed, standing ready to support the regime every step of the way. Since the latter involved activities in sharp contrast to idealized motherhood, there is no clear-cut image of "the woman of Nazi Germany." The propagandists tried to uphold the "mother cult" image of the early years, but when women were desperately needed to prepare for the war, gradual changes were installed. Women first served as volunteers in agriculture; however, in 1935, this became mandatory, no longer a volunteer activity, and the work increasingly comprised labor in armories. In 1939, some women already served as *Wehrmachtshelferinnen*, i.e., a woman took over the work of a soldier, often in communications, so that a man could fight at the front. Women participated in the horrors of concentration camps. Quite a few female Nazis even volunteered. As of 1942, all women had to work in armories, if needed. From 1943, the Nazis completely ignored protection of mothers, and any woman available up to the age of fifty had to join the army.[2] There were many women of course who developed strategies to resist serving the Nazi regime.[3]

As Germany surrendered unconditionally to the allied forces and millions of German men were dead or prisoners of war, German women were extremely vulnerable to the foreign men taking over the country. A taboo and still not fully addressed to this day are the brutal mass rapes women had to endure.[4] The early postwar years were all about survival, and women had to be inventive.

Jazz may seem a remote concern in this context. However, ever since the first sounds of jazz had traveled to Europe across the Atlantic, there had been small but dedicated European audiences fascinated by jazz music and its culture. The music inspired numerous European composers in the 1920s, found enthusiastic audiences, and many jazz fans stayed loyal during the war years, when jazz was among the many art forms officially labeled "degenerate" and forbidden by Nazi ideologues. The well-known passion for jazz of highest-ranking Nazis notwithstanding, it could become risky for the regular citizen to listen to jazz.

Jutta Hipp, widely considered the single most important jazz pianist in Germany in the early 1950s, recalled how dangerous and, at the same time, vital an activity it was to listen to jazz. Born in Leipzig (in the zone that became East Germany), she was a teenager during the war and listened to jazz at night on the BBC: "I'd sit there in the dark and copy off the tunes they played, but it wasn't allowed. My parents were always scared. We always had to keep the lights out because of the bombs."[5] Looking back at this time, she wrote in a letter to Marshall Stearns in 1956: "You won't be able to understand this . . . but to us, jazz was some kind of religion. We really had to fight for it and I remember nights when we didn't go down to the saved cellar [safe cellar/bunker], because we listened to records, we just had the feeling that you were not our enemies, and even though the bombs crashed around us (with the time, you get used to it, but never again!) we felt saved [safe], or at least, if it [had] killed us, we would have died with nice music."[6]

Listening to jazz symbolized a courageous distance from Nazi ideology and any "German" values that were used and distorted by National Socialism. In postwar Germany, jazz took on an important meaning as it symbolized liberation from the Nazi regime. German jazz fans could not wait to connect with the American forces. Many of them had listened to the British and American radio stations during the war. Hipp recalled being utterly disappointed once she and her friends found out that not every American soldier was a jazz fan! She was convinced that once the American troops arrived, they'd love to be greeted with jazz music—but to her surprise that did not happen: "The funny thing is that when the first Americans came to my hometown, my brother and me, we only had a phonograph and we said 'When the Americans come, we're going to play all our American records and they'll be so gassed, they'll be so happy.' We opened all of the balcony doors wide, and they came by and we played our records, and we invited some to the house but they didn't care for it at all — they were all hillbillies."[7]

In 1946 Jutta Hipp fled from Leipzig to the Tegernsee area in the Alps in Bavaria, part of the American zone. She lived in the small town of Fürstenfeldbruck for several years and settled in Munich sometime between 1949 and 1951. She had studied visual arts in Leipzig and first tried to establish herself painting signs for GI shows. During intermissions, she played piano, and it was her piano playing that became her means of survival. She played for American troops all over Bavaria and played in a circus for a while. Hipp actually hardly knew how to play jazz at that point. In Munich, trumpeter Charly Tabor became a mentor and helped her improve her jazz skills. She met the Viennese tenor player Hans Koller, who became her most important musical collaborator. The Hans Koller quartet with Hipp on piano quickly became one of the best combos in the country. Hipp relocated from Munich to Frankfurt sometime during 1952.[8]

Frankfurt emerged as the most vibrant and innovative center of German jazz and attracted a number of musicians who shaped the postwar scene. During the war years, dedicated jazz musicians around drummer Horst Lippmann had managed to keep playing and networking; they even founded the Hot Club Frankfurt in 1941 despite the Nazi repression. When the American forces arrived in destroyed Frankfurt on March 28, 1945, it took the musicians only nine days to make contact. Trumpeter Carlo Bohländer went to the American authorities and presented a letter written in English that listed the repertoire of American titles of the Hot Club Combo of Frankfurt to ask permission to perform. The authorities, impressed with the knowledge of this young German who obviously already sympathized with American culture during the war, gave him special permission to perform with his band. The Hot Club Combo of Frankfurt was the first German band licensed to perform.[9] The musicians began to play for American audiences and were increasingly in demand.

Hot Clubs, initially a forum for jazz fans to participate in regular listening evenings, presentations, and lectures, originated in France (1932) and spread through other European countries. They were often attended by both musicians and fans, where listening and discussions about the exciting but still rather obscure music from America took place, sometimes also concerts and jam sessions. By 1950 twenty Hot Clubs existed in the three occupied zones that made up West Germany, as well as several clubs in the Eastern zone that became the German

Democratic Republic. The membership consisted of small and dedicated circles devoted to studying each and every detail of the music and the artists. Most of the clubs documented their activities meticulously, so that the programs and evolution of each club can be traced clearly. This allows valuable insight into not only the activities but also the values of jazz musicians and fans, which is important here in regard to examining gender difference and women's access to jazz. Bernd Hoffmann, who has researched the activities of the German Hot Clubs in great detail, gives an example of a Hot Club's membership with the club in Würzburg: lists show that their members were between sixteen and twenty-eight years old, and that they were mainly students, employees, and tradesmen, but no artisans. The club had thirty members; 15 percent were women, so four or five members must have been women.[10] An important concept in studying the music was to learn how to tell "real," "authentic" jazz from popular dance music. Louis Armstrong's tone, phrasing, scatting, or Duke Ellington's individualized orchestral colors were examples of "authentic" jazz. (The Hot Club de France, founded in 1932 by France's most prominent jazz critic, Hugues Panassié, is still active today and on its website still subtitled *Association des Amateurs de Jazz Authentique*.)

German audiences were particularly fascinated by the rhythmic energy of jazz, the player's expressiveness on stage, and the art of improvisation, which were elements that provided an exciting contrast to Western classical music and German vernacular styles. In both prewar and postwar media, jazz was frequently described in derogatory terms such as jungle or Hottentot music and carried clichés about blackness and exoticism. The idea that black artists created jazz generated and complemented a wealth of primitive fantasies about black sexuality and wildness. Reviews conveying distorted images of jazz and jazz musicians were often accompanied by cartoons of black men in raffia skirts and the like. Hot Clubs, on the contrary, would issue newsletters with detailed information about musicians, records, styles, and concerts. Ideas about the art of collecting records (the scrupulous study of the minutiae of recordings and performances) occupied Hot Clubs from the start. These activities, the club members believed, lent the study of jazz an intellectual, scientific aura. Hot Club members hereby wanted to emphasize their love and respect for the music and to counter denigrating clichés surrounding jazz prevalent since prewar years. In the first years after the war, the Hot Clubs in Germany were under control of the Allied Forces, and the clubs sought good relations with them. A letter to the authorities by Dietrich Schulz-Koehn, the president of the Hot Club Düssel-dorf, stated that "these meetings are strictly scientific and serious; there is no dancing or 'behaviour as on a party' [sic]."[11] An example of the strict rules of conduct is stated in the bylaws of the Hamburg Anglo-German Swing Club (AGSC), one of the biggest clubs with strong ties to the British Forces and numerous British members: "Dancing at meetings is forbidden at all times . . . Intoxicating liqueur will not be brought to meetings at any time."[12] By the mid-1950s, a number of Hot Clubs witnessed a transition from pure study groups to forums where live music, jam sessions, and dancing were included in the activities. Club members debated, however, how to remain morally respectable, how to study and present "real," serious jazz, and how not to give in to com-mercial types of jazz that attracted dance audiences. Many clubs went to great lengths to distance themselves from so-called Swing-Heinis, a derogatory term for young men who embodied the more expressive aspects of jazz, "who don't look at jazz as music, but as fashion and excuse for excessive behavior." Curiously, "serious" jazz often was lim-ited to swing. The more conservative members rejected bebop, the music as well as the pronounced fashion statements of the boppers. Despite their admiration of earlier innovators such as Armstrong and Ellington, this did not necessarily translate to similar appreciation of Charlie Parker or Dizzy Gillespie.

Postwar jazz audiences were roughly divided into a generation who had secretly listened to jazz under the Nazi regime and who saw jazz as a sophisticated, intellectual experience, and a youth culture who em-braced jazz as a progressive lifestyle brought by the American liberators that included dance, fashion statements, and new visions of redefining German culture. Jitterbug and boogie became increasingly popular, much to the dismay of conservative German commentators who wor-ried about German respectability. In *Jazz, Rock, and Rebels*, Uta Poiger, in her analysis of postwar American culture in Germany, described how the new dance styles were perceived as excessive and threatening to a woman's good reputation. "To some West German commentators, the respectability of female jazz fans was even more questionable than that of males," Poiger wrote. "Contemporaries criticized girls who hung out on streets and who danced boogie as potential sexual delinquents." In terms of gender and jazz, she commented: "While East and West Ger-man discourses on (American) westerns centered on fears of male over-aggression, debates around jazz and American dances evolved around worries about weak men and overly sexual women."[13]

The exotic connotations and clichés surrounding jazz music and culture, as well as the expressive qualities of the music and the musical practice itself, were, of course, in contrast to images of traditional bourgeois German femaleness (protected, innocent, orderly, sexually passive) and early Nazi propaganda. Incongruously, many of these traditional ideas of gender inspired by nineteenth-century bourgeois culture mixed with Nazi "mother cult" images prevailed, despite the fact that women's roles and realities had changed dramatically during the war and after.

In 1952, the German Jazz Federation was founded. The drummer Horst Lippmann, one of the most active and progressive-thinking musicians of the time, had been a driving force toward founding a nationwide network of jazz. In October 1951, during a meeting of Hot Clubs from West Germany and West Berlin, the first president was elected. In May 1952, the bylaws were accepted by the membership, and twenty-one Hot Clubs and Jazz Clubs became a part of the German Jazz Federation. Just one year later, in May 1953, the Frankfurt Hot Club under the leadership of Horst Lippmann organized the first Frankfurt Jazz Festival, which became the primary German Jazz Fest for many years.[14]

Jutta Hipp (see figure 12.2) was already earning high recognition and won the "Podium Jazz-Referendum 1952–1953" poll for best German jazz pianist in March 1953.[15] On March 6, she opened in Frankfurt for Dizzy Gillespie with the Hans Koller Quartet, but she was not officially featured at the Jazz Festival in May. She was present, however, and participated in the jam sessions. The following year, she played at the Jazz Festival in Frankfurt with her own band, the Jutta Hipp Combo, and also appeared in Sweden, Denmark, and Yugoslavia.

In January 1954 Leonard Feather listened to the Jutta Hipp quintet for the first time in a club in Duisburg. He knew about Hipp and had tried to find her: "After our concert that night [in the nearby city of Düsseldorf], Billie Holiday, Buddy de Franco and some others slipped away in the company of Horst Lippmann. As we entered a crowded cellar in Duisburg, music floated up to our ears that we could hardly believe was the work of five Germans. . . . Jutta's American visitors were all amazed almost beyond belief. Hearing good music played in Sweden a week earlier had been no surprise — but to encounter the finest European jazz we had discovered thus far, played in a country that had been deprived of the sight and sound of real jazz during so many years of Nazism and war — this was incredible!"[16]

Fig. 12.1 Trümmerfrauen photo from *Die Frau von Heute* 15 (1947): 5. Reprinted with permission from Stiftung Archiv der deutschen Frauenbewegung, Kassel, Germany.

Fig. 12.2. Jutta Hipp, 1953–54. Collection of Katja von Schuttenbach.

Feather and Lippmann arranged for this quintet to record three months later in Frankfurt, and the record was distributed by Blue Note Records. This was the first time a white, female recording artist appeared on Blue Note Records. The record was entitled *New Faces — New Sounds from Germany: Jutta Hipp and Her Quintet* (Blue Note BLP 5056). Feather also arranged for a visa for Jutta Hipp for the United States, and she arrived in New York on November 18, 1955.

In *Jazz Podium*, West Germany's premier jazz magazine, Jutta Hipp was frequently mentioned and writers expressed much pride for her achievements in Germany and later in New York. *Jazz Podium* was founded in 1952 and was aimed at providing thorough information on all aspects of jazz.

In the April issue of 1956, an article appeared called "Zur Diskussion gestellt: Die Frau und der Jazz."[17] For the first time since the magazine's inception, and, as it turned out, the only time for many years to come, a discussion on women and jazz took place. Its instigator, Peter Kunst, was a jazz fan and director of a German Hot Club. He expressed frustration that very few women attended his programs and rarely came back a second time. Kunst wanted to open a discussion. His article reproduced a multitude of stereotypes about jazz and gender, such as decrying the "inappropriate" behavior of young women who dared to enter the exotic field of jazz music. Peter Kunst invited a fellow staff writer, Marianne Knueppel, to respond. She and other women readers jumped on the occasion to offer their views: jazz fans, writers, and musicians responded with letters to the editor, among them Jutta Hipp, the Austrian vibraphonist Vera Auer, the French ragtime pianist, jazz writer, and lecturer Martine Morel, the jazz writer Madeleine Gautier, the German journalist Eva Windmöller, the *Jazz Podium* contributor Ingigerd Fuelle, and Rosemarie Wiebe, who wrote as a passionate jazz fan. This unique series offers detailed insight into gendered perceptions of jazz in 1950s (West) Germany.

"PRESENTED FOR DISCUSSION: THE WOMAN AND THE JAZZ"

> *Each rule has its exceptions, however, the old assessment keeps suggesting itself, that jazz is a purely male concern. Sure, in reality, jazz produced good and esteemed women jazz musicians and singers, but in the far greater number of only-jazz-consumers, the woman demonstrably plays a rather modest role. Why are there so few true female jazz enthusiasts?*[18]

"Presented for Discussion: The Woman and the Jazz" is worth a closer look from a linguistic standpoint. The words *woman* and *jazz* both appear in singular, suggesting absolute, finite meaning. In the German language, the articles *die* and *der* are gendered, *die* signifies a feminine noun, *der* signifies a masculine noun. (A third article, *das*, is neuter, closer to the English *the*). So *die* Frau is "feminine," and *der* Jazz is "masculine." The title thus implies: how would *the (feminine) woman* fit into *the (masculine) jazz*? Where was the "appropriate" place for women in the world of jazz?

A title such as "Women and Jazz" (*Frauen und Jazz*) would have left the meaning of each word more open. The way definite articles were used in this title, however, suggested that there might be one clear answer as to how "the woman" fits into "the jazz." Furthermore, the title implied an open discussion on women in jazz. Kunst acknowledged that "sure, in reality, jazz produced good and esteemed women jazz musicians and singers," but this was not his concern. He did not name a single woman artist, vocalist, or instrumentalist in his article, but asked, "Why are there so few true female jazz enthusiasts?"

Kunst discussed this question in great length, focusing on three topics: (a) gendered education and access to jazz, (b) important properties of a jazz fan, and (c) the "nature" of men and women. First, he pointed out profound differences in education of girls versus boys and explained how considerable restrictions in a girl's upbringing made it virtually impossible for an adolescent girl to have access to the jazz world. "No doubt the question of upbringing is a factor," Kunst wrote. "The young generation makes their acquaintance with jazz in the beginning *Sturm und Drang* period, when they try to burst through the traditional bourgeois sleeve. To try to suppress this explosion of the up-until-then childlike mind would be to fight (the yet more powerful) nature." He then states the contrasting attitudes toward teenage girls and boys: "Without a doubt one allows a boy in his transition from child to manhood a much greater understanding, whereas a girl in her adolescence is literally kept on a chain, so that under the critical observation she does not find an opportunity to go over a wall."[19]

As the director of a Hot Club, Kunst was confronted with the fact that almost no young women frequented his club because parents would find it unsuitable. He regretted this reality: "Time and again young ladies are brought by their friends to my, God knows, moral club events, without attending a second time. The repetitious answer to my questions as to why was, "The parents did not allow it. Jazz fans were not the right company for her daughter."[20]

Peter Kunst's analysis, although expressing compassion for the adolescent girls not allowed to attend his Hot Club, took a surprising turn by turning to "nature" to explain fundamental differences between men and women as jazz fans. "Natural" gender difference is a recurrent topic in all letters sent in to *Jazz Podium*, reflecting a mindset that long dominated in Western thought. In eighteenth-century anthropology, the progressive ideals of Rousseau regarding nature and subjectivity that embraced male adolescent rebellion served at the same time to narrowly define "nature" and polarize gender difference. Nature, psyche, and character became almost synonymous. The feminine was defined as being motherly, nurturing, emotional, chaste, and oriented toward the domestic sphere, an efficient strategy to confine women to the private and keep them out of the public, professional, political realms of society. This created and legitimized a type of ideal womanhood, the housewife and mother, which had not previously existed in such clearly defined boundaries. Thus, "nature" and "natural" gender differences frequently served in both the humanities and the sciences to explain and justify imbalances of gender and power.[21]

Peter Kunst had just arrived at a point in his argument where the next logical step would have required a call for profound societal change. Unable to reconcile ingrained concepts of gender difference and the real-life repercussions of young women not attending his programs, Peter Kunst shifted to a peculiar argument about gender and jazz fandom, i.e., the "nature" of the jazz fan. The quintessential passion and skill of any true, "authentic," male jazz fan is to compile a record collection.

A man possesses in a much more pronounced manner the drive to collect something. Philatelists are common among men, however, rare among women. A true jazz lover will sooner or later become a record collector. Once the young man got through his sweat cure at the jazz concert hall, he would often go and choose a hot boogie from his record dealer, to also be able to delight in this music at home. Soon he'll know Lionel Hampton and Earl Bostic inside-out, and, lo and behold, soon enough there will also be a HOT FIVE in the record cabinet, or a DAVE BRUBECK. And if he does not drift to a new "thing," a new friend of jazz will have matured, whose intellectual development can be assessed according to his continuously adjusting and refining record collection.

Once he collects and relishes in this wonderful world of complete contemplation, he will have really matured. It does not matter how high the number of records, nor how famous . . . solely love and understanding make him a true jazz fan.[22]

Kunst conveyed how in the sophisticated field of jazz, a true fan had to display a profound and quite obsessive dedication to collecting records and would study each and every detail of the music. The quality of a fan's record collection indicated the degree of his intellect. The hierarchy of this intellectual development is clearly defined: from dance music, a "hot boogie," one moves to the more accessible jazz pieces by Earl Bostic, and then one reaches the higher spheres such as Louis Armstrong's Hot Five. Kunst explained further that the "nature" of women would not allow for such an activity: "A woman will never be such a collector. If at all, she will have some sort of a nesting drive, which gives her the impulse to assemble a dowry. Surely she will also buy a record from time to time, but she does not buy the record to really own it. Maybe she will pay the 4 bucks [German marks] to follow just this particular whim, but this record will in its own way stay alone and will not trigger this almost fanatic and systematic drive to completion, which would in such case be manifested in a male buyer (that is to say, if he is a jazz fan)."[23]

This argument is quite stunning for the shift it marks in Kunst's reasoning. Earlier on, Kunst complained that "one thus does not credit the girl, who normally proves far more mature than a boy of the same age, with the ability to make her own free decision, a privilege that is granted to the junior much faster and without much consideration." However, he did not draw the obvious conclusion that if girls and women were granted equal opportunity to listen and study this music, they would attend his Hot Club and this subject of discussion would be unnecessary. In the second half of his article, each difference in behavior is explained ultimately by a "natural" cause. In not qualifying these differences in sociopolitical terms, Kunst avoided any overt criticism of prevailing societal norms; if he were to analyze his own facts, he would have had to call into question the foundations of gender in German society. Despite his use of strong language ("a girl in her adolescence is literally kept on a chain"), he was not calling for change. Kunst's effort to sound serious, scientific, and reasonable also reflects the pseudo-scientific mindset of the die-hard "authentic" Hot Club scene.

The letter ended with the big question of why, despite all of the above, there were in fact "true female jazz enthusiasts" and what to make of them. Peter Kunst was on friendly terms with quite a few.

"What to think of the women who somehow did get acquainted with jazz, and why do we perceive the female jazz fan to be, to put it mildly, 'completely different' than our male colleagues?" he asked and answered as follows: "I again have to draw from my personal experiences. The "jazzfan-esses" in my circle of friends are without exception closely befriended, married, or in other close contact with a jazz enthusiast. Normally, however, it is characteristic to the female sex to subordinate herself to the male influence, and so I come to the assumption that the alleged enthusiasm is not altogether sincere but rather a compromise or an adjustment over time."[24]

There remained no way for a woman to be a jazz fan and to be taken seriously. The *enthusiasm* was "alleged," and the opinion about any given piece of music was a "compromise" of male intellectual influence and female sentiment. Once more, Peter Kunst felt obligated to elaborate further, to base his conclusion on some "facts." His listening examples are exactly analogous to the above-mentioned process of intellectual development — listening through light and easy examples first to access the higher realms of expertise.

The contributions of women to discussions about jazz I detected to be as either an opinion of a third party or as expression of the female sentiment. This sentiment is no doubt more honest, but decides — if it is really female — in by far the most cases in favor of a less jazzy example. Tommy Dorsey's silky trombone will thus enjoy greater popularity than the vital outburst of John Higginbotham's horn, and, deep inside, the female sentiment will lean much further towards Frank Sinatra than towards Louis Armstrong. I do not have any doubt that a woman is also capable of reading this scale of musical expression in jazz, because she rather willingly accepts the guidance of a clever expert; however, the essence of such attacks on the female intellect is surely the confession: "You know, Big Bill Broonzy is really tremendous, and Leadbelly is one of the greatest singers, but, I just think Bing Crosby is delightful![25]

Listening with a "female sentiment" meant preferring a "smooth" piece over a "hot" one and by extension meant not understanding the "real" thing. It might be no coincidence that the above examples of the "hot" artists are black men, whereas the "smooth" ones preferred by the "female sentiment" are white men. None of the authors of these letters to *Jazz Podium* addresses race directly. However, in light of the widespread stereotyped views of blackness as exotic and wild, and of jazz as an exotic black music, it seems plausible that "smooth" is coded for "white" and "hot" for "black." Furthermore, the way Peter Kunst set up this argument implied that women would not advance beyond the early stages of intellectual development (!).

"Maybe our colleague Marianne Knueppel would like to comment here on this subject?" reads the final sentence. Kunst seemed genuinely interested in other points of view on the subject. His reasoning fell in three different categories: (a) the analytical, such as the clear observation that adolescent girls are highly restricted in their upbringing; (b) the belief in "natural differences," such as binary divides of male, intellectual record-collecting, and female "nesting instinct;" and (c) the derogatory, as in his conclusion that the woman jazz enthusiast is an oddity, her opinions a compromise, dependent on male guidance.

"WOMEN AND JAZZ: IT'S OK TO TALK ABOUT IT:"
RESPONSES BY READERS, CRITICS, WRITERS AND MUSICIANS

The Staff Writer Ingigerd Fuelle Responds All seven responses to Peter Kunst's article printed in *Jazz Podium* in the following issues were written by women. Given that women had hardly a voice in the jazz media, the number of letters to the editor was impressive.[26] The first response came not from Marianne Knueppel, to whom Kunst's invitation was addressed, but from Ingigerd Fuelle. *Jazz Podium* introduced her as a staff writer based in Bonn, the new (and initially just temporary) capital of West Germany. Fuelle titled her letter "Women and Jazz: It's OK to Talk About It." The connotations of the German *Man kann ruhig darüber sprechen* imply that this is a far-out, possibly even a taboo, topic.

She discussed the various obstacles met by jazz fans, in general, and women jazz fans, in particular, without ever overtly identifying herself as a jazz fan. Could it be that Kunst's article was intimidating? Would one really want to appear as an exception, an oddity, a woman jazz fan? At the same time, Fuelle was a staff writer for *Jazz Podium*, which signified competence in the world of jazz, and her letter clearly implied that she spoke from experience. Her very lengthy and wordy introduction showed the unavoidable failure of a woman to be equally accepted, no matter which route she chooses to try. Fuelle did not address the subject of jazz directly. Instead, she created an analogy, a story of three schoolgirls in a boys' class. None of them succeeded in being excellent and in being accepted as equal within the class. The overprotected girl who studied only at home alone would have no interaction with her classmates and soon became an outsider. The average girl student who participated in group homework with the boys and contributed a correct answer now and then might have a chance: "At least possible that she succeeded." Fuelle implied that being average might not be enough for a girl to receive appropriate credit and notice. Lastly, the talkative girl craving recognition would be the center of interest, but would not be thorough and smart enough to achieve good results on the homework. So the boys did not respect her.

The class functions as a metaphor for a male-dominated society, for the public realm, and for the jazz scene. Women in 1950s Germany had been pushed back into the home front, despite their roles during and immediately after the war: As the Nazis needed women on every level of their warfare, ideas of what was "appropriate" quickly adjusted. Millions of men were absent, so women's responsibilities shifted considerably. The immediate postwar years were characterized, in part, by the hard labor of the Trümmerfrauen under grueling conditions. However, once the men came back from prison camps and the country began to function to a point where the economy took off to what became the German *Wirtschaftswunder*, the "economic miracle," women were quickly discouraged from the public sphere. The idea of "ideal womanhood" changed radically toward a subordinate status: married women in Germany were not allowed to work without their husbands' permission. Public versus private quickly became, once again, the primary societal divide between men and women in 1950s Germany. Academic — or artistic — excellence by a woman was a solitary achievement, and outstanding achievements by women rarely had any significant impact in the public sphere.

Ingigerd Fuelle, informed by her understanding of being a jazz fan, demonstrated how these situations continued in the real life of a woman jazz fan. She argued that developing a true understanding of jazz was an almost insurmountable science. To acquire a comprehensive collection of jazz records meant years of devotion and intense study. The collector was constantly at risk of making wrong choices such as buying items that were too commercial, not acquiring the latest important releases, or owning an obscure record that did not list the lineup, where one might not know all the tunes and personnel featured. As a consequence, each "jazz beginner — especially a young one whose opinions do not sparkle with maturity or who tends to show off circulating opinions that are considered competent as one's own — is in need of constant help and guidance from an expert."[27]

In that respect, Fuelle found that women who became jazz fans "through marriage" — the category Peter Kunst established in his last section — had a definite advantage. Fuelle stated that upon marrying a jazz fan, a woman could expect: "A more or less large record collection is placed in front of them (no, the number of records is really not doing it, but the content), not to forget the jazzologically advanced instructor (today one can expect this), and then the development unfolds relatively smoothly — given that the interest has already been there in the first place." The size and quality of the record collection was mentioned first; the husband instructor seemed secondary. However, if, over time, this married woman jazz fan proved really well informed, she faced another and rather serious challenge: "the poor spouse might then run the risk of being called 'unfeminine.' "[28]

In her lengthy article, Ingigerd Fuelle never offered direct personal experience. Indirectly, however, she situated herself in the category of female jazz fans who "have enough love for this music to take an intense interest in it by themselves." Apparently, she was one of the very few from the "old school," when "jazzology" was completely new territory. From her vantage in 1956, the new generation of young jazz fans had it comparatively easy to find guidance, expertise, and records. Five years earlier, in 1951, a "*female who stepped into a jazz club*" would be met with a similar amazement. At that time, "only the most unwavering found access to the Grail." To be so well informed indicates that she must have been among those few. Another hint that she was advanced in this science: "Even later, given the variety of the field, one never ceases to learn." She portrayed the average woman as a follower, i.e., not initiating, passive: "A woman — admittedly — does not like to take on a pioneer role. If she does something along those lines, she will promptly cause astonishment, more or less gently." While maintaining a careful distance regarding her own role in jazz throughout, Fuelle implicitly constructed herself as "exceptional" and conveyed that she belonged to the inner circle. Fuelle concluded:

The real women jazz record collectors, who have grown beyond the beginner status? One finds them despite all of this, and I will assume that they are not abnormal human beings. Looking closely, they just had a bit more courage to start earlier. If some of them participate less in discussions, they might be even better listeners. Maybe they prefer to do their homework without the detail of occasional hair-splitting?

No offense, I know well that exchanges on this subject are necessary from time to time. . . . This is why colleague Marianne Knueppel was not the only one who felt compelled to comment. Heartfelt, Your Ingigerd Fuelle[29]

Whereas Peter Kunst also alluded to the joy of contemplation while listening to the beloved music, Ingigerd Fuelle emphasized the hard work. She found a way to justify a place for women in this "Grail." Her writing is largely convoluted and defensive, but she offered a subtle critique of the motives and practice of male jazz fans. In her conclusion, she talked about women jazz fans as a group, almost a community. Perhaps she intended to communicate a coded encouragement for other women to follow their interest? Given how often her arguments remained implicit and nonconfrontational, they might indicate her experience and expertise in being guarded and protective of her space in jazz.

Rosemarie Wiebe: A Letter from a Jazz Fan A short and concise letter from Rosemarie Wiebe appeared in the following issue. Unlike Ingigerd Fuelle, Wiebe clearly identified as a jazz fan. She addressed her letter to "Dear Peter Kunst!" and went right into commenting on his article: "You pinned me in the last paragraph of your article as 'being an exception.' Now, I cannot refute you directly, however, I do think that there are certainly females who concern themselves with jazz without being in a "liaison" with a jazz fan just for jazz's sake."[30]

She discussed Peter Kunst's main threads — gendered education, "natural" characteristics of gender, and the science of collecting jazz records. She took the debate to another level, particularly on gendered differences in listening to music. In comparison with the previous letter by Fuelle, Rosemarie Wiebe's perspective was straightforward, clear, and refreshing: "Marianne Knueppel asked me whether I believe that men listen differently to jazz than we do. On no account do they have a "special ear" for jazz! Still, they will certainly listen to it in a different way. A man will listen in on things with a much more awake 'mind.' Since a woman can rely on her feelings to listen, she will be superior to the man in that she hears what is 'true,' and what effect. However technically perfect something may be — the male intellect still analyzes feverishly whether it might be something brand new and incredible — and a faness may say matter-of-factly: it does not speak to me!"

This is the first of several instances where Wiebe states an advantage of being a woman jazz fan: it offers the possibility to listen more independently, more free of defined yardsticks. This topic of listening also raises a different question: Was there a chance that these women jazz fans listened to women musicians? In the United States, the "Rosie the Riveter" phenomenon enabled women to thrive as jazz musicians. All-female swing bands—from the International Sweethearts of Rhythm to the bands of Ada Leonard, Rita Rio, Sharon Rogers, from Phil Spitalny's Hour of Charm to the Darlings of Rhythm and countless small combos on the USO camp circuit—were widely popular. But hardly any of them ever recorded. A fan like Rosemarie Wiebe might have been excited to listen to the Sweethearts of Rhythm, but the canon of the available recordings consisted primarily of male artists. Records by female vocalists were available, and, with some luck, recordings by Mary Lou Williams. In fact, play lists of Hot Clubs did at times include tracks by Mary Lou Williams. Unfortunately, the letters to *Jazz Podium* do not reveal whether and to what extent the fans listened to women musicians. Wiebe continues, "And the female fans have another advantage over the male: they enjoy a certain fool's freedom. I have it as well and am glad for it—given our yearning for freedom."[31]

Wiebe wrote with a strong sense of solidarity and community toward women, and with a humorous tone, while putting forth how strongly women were considered inferior ("Given our yearning for freedom."). There is no indication that Wiebe herself felt inferior: on the contrary, she found a way to acknowledge gendered difference with self-esteem and certainty. Repeatedly, she reclaimed common derogatory stereotypes against women jazz fans such as the alleged inability to understand and assess a piece of music independent of male guidance, and attributed new meaning, as in her conclusion: "You say, dear Peter, that I collect with male fanatism. May I correct you: I collect with female fanaticism, meaning first and foremost what I 'like' (Men would, after all, collect what got many stars!). I am surprised then once in a while, when I hear from "experts," that this disc or the other that I bought is, in fact, 'good.' And then I think to myself, begrudgingly and with a superior smile: jazz really is a male affair!"[32]

BETTER A JAZZ ALBUM THAN LIPSTICK

Better a Jazz Album than Lipstick is the extensive, two-page response coauthored by the twenty-year-old *Jazz Podium* staff writer Marianne Knueppel and Eva Windmöller, editor of the then well-known German film magazine *Star Revue*. Eva Windmöller also wrote music reviews and various articles for the *Stern*, one of Germany's most widely read weekly magazines. In their leading paragraph, the authors made it clear that only the serious, devoted jazz fan willing to sacrifice much time and money to conquer this sophisticated field is worth their attention: "It is true: there are hardly any women with a serious interest in jazz — who are not just interested, but willing to penetrate this subject matter as a field of knowledge, to make an effort towards jazz, to spend money on records and to sacrifice time, much time indeed, to listen to this music and to belong to it. Because only this really serious type of jazz fan — let us better say "jazz friend" — should be our subject of interest. We think that there are explanations for this. Of course only a general view is possible — there are exceptions to every rule."

For the first time in this series, jazz was discussed as an art form. Knueppel and Windmöller portrayed jazz musicians as "ambassadors of American culture," who brought jazz to the world through performances in concert halls, radio programs, and records. The authors found that therefore information about jazz was available, and ignorance about jazz could not be excused by lack of access to all these options. "No exterior circumstance prohibits or impedes any girl from an interest in jazz." However, this did not mean that women had the same shot at becoming jazz fans: "There are other factors at work."

One such factor is the cultural foreignness of jazz. In the first subsection, entitled *Jazz: Accepted but Offside*, the two writers pointed out that because jazz was rooted neither in European music nor culture, a serious interest required "a renunciation of the ordinary, an excursion into the unusual." Rather than emphasizing how the widespread German admiration of the exotic element in jazz could be attractive to a woman listener, they argued that the unfamiliar cultural context made it more remote for women to become serious fans. They bluntly stated that this is where "the women fail, because it does not occur to them to conquer new territory under difficult circumstances."[33]

Making a general statement that women are not curious or adventurous shows their attitude toward "all the other women." Unlike Rosemarie Wiebe, the authors talked about "the women" without a notion of community and repeatedly with a denigrating tone. Between the lines was their frustrated need to distance themselves from identifying with such unadventurous women.

The second topic was gendered listening. Here, Knueppel and Windmöller changed tone and seemed to emulate Rosemarie Wiebe's straightforwardness and clarity. "We believe that colleague Peter Kunst has looked at the connection between jazz fans and collecting in the wrong light," they wrote: "We want to leave it open as to whether collecting is a typical masculine or feminine property. But we want to ask: Who would be a jazz fan just for the sake of collecting? First of all,

LIEBER JAZZPLATTE ALS LIPPENSTIFT

DIE FRAU UND DER JAZZ, so betitelte Peter Kunst einen Aufsatz, der im Jazz-Podium Nr. 4/V, 1956 zur Diskussion gestellt wurde. In den folgenden Heften veröffentlichen wir bereits einige Beiträge, in denen aus der Sicht der Frau zu diesem Thema Stellung genommen wurde. Heute lassen wir einen Kommentar folgen, den unsere Mitarbeiterin Marianne Knueppel gemeinsam mit Eva Windmöller, Redakteurin der bekannten deutschen Film-Zeitschrift „Star-Revue", verfaßt hat.

Es ist wahr: Es gibt kaum Frauen, die sich ernsthaft für Jazz interessieren — und nicht nur interessieren, sondern auch gewillt sind, in die Materie als Wissensgebiet einzudringen, sich um den Jazz zu bemühen, Geld für Platten auszugeben und Zeit, viel Zeit sogar, zu opfern, um dieser Musik zuzuhören und ihr zu gehören. Denn von diesem wirklich ernsthaften Typ Jazzfan — sagen wir besser „Jazzfreund" — soll hier ja nur die Rede sein. Wir glauben, es gibt Erklärungen hierfür. Natürlich kann nur Generelles gesagt werden — Ausnahmen gibt es zu jeder Regel.

Ehe wir auf den Jazz speziell zu sprechen kommen, überlegen wir uns einmal, wie es mit anderen Interessengebieten als Liebhaberei bei den Frauen aussieht. Obwohl eine Frau im allgemeinen nicht zu ernsthaften Hobbies neigt, wollen wir ihr diese jedoch nicht ganz absprechen. Aber hat sie ein Steckenpferd, so wird es sich stets um etwas handeln, was mit dem alltäglichen Leben in irgendeiner Verbindung steht, was einen praktischen Wert oder Nutzen hat, oder was ihre eigene Person angeht. Selbst wenn ihr „center of interest" ein geistig anspruchsvolles Metier ist — wie klassische Musik, Theater, Literatur, Malerei — so sind dieses ihre vertraute Gebiete, an die sie im Laufe ihrer Erziehung herangeführt worden ist und die traditionelles Kulturgut darstellen, zu welchem sich eine Frau genauso wie ein Mann ohne weiteres hingezogen fühlen kann — sei es aus einer eigenen gleichgelagerten Begabung oder einem anderen Motiv heraus.

Leben, wo er nicht seine Wurzeln hat. Um sich für diese Musik zu entscheiden und ihr zu folgen, bedarf es — wie von Kollege Peter Kunst schon gesagt — einer Abkehr vom Alltäglichen, einer Exkursion ins Ungewöhnliche. Das ist nicht nur für den Jazz zutreffend, das gilt für jede Extravaganz. Und da scheitern die Frauen, denn es kommt ihnen nicht die Idee, unter Schwierigkeiten Neuland zu entdecken.

Es wurde der „Sammeltrieb" erwähnt, den der Mann angeblich von Natur aus in besonderem Maße mitbekommen haben soll, und welche Eigenschaft ihn im Gegensatz zur Frau quasi zum Jazzfan prädestiniert. Wir glauben, Kollege Peter Kunst hat die Verbindung Jazzfreund und Sammeln in einem falschen Licht betrachtet. Ob das Sammeln eine typisch männliche oder weibliche Eigenschaft ist, wollen wir noch dahingestellt sein lassen. Aber wir möchten fragen: Wer ist denn Jazzfreund um des Sammelns willen? In erster Linie liebt man doch die Musik, und die Tätigkeit des Sammelns ist nur eine sekundäre und gar nicht einmal erforderliche Begleiterscheinung. Der Besitz von Platten gibt uns die Möglichkeit, unabhängig die geliebte Musik zu

Fig. 12.3. *Jazz Podium* (September 1956): 9. Institute for Jazz Studies, Rutgers University, Newark, New Jersey.

one loves the music, and the activity of collecting is a secondary and not even required concomitant. Owning records allows us to listen independently to the beloved music. But it is the music the discussion is focused on, not the record. Those who collect for the sake of collecting will become philatelists or other such collectors of rarities — but not jazz fans."[34]

Here, they used the inclusive "us," showing that they are indeed competent listeners and lovers of jazz. Read through the lens of feminist criticism, their article contains quite a few conflicting views, discrepancies between parts where the authors expressed confidence and certainty as women jazz fans and stereotypes about female weakness and incompetence. Their next subtitle reads *"Jazz is Unfeminine."* They wrote: "We believe that jazz in itself contains some factors that impede a woman's understanding, while the man finds access to this music much easier: this is because jazz itself is unfeminine."[35]

What follows is a discussion of the "nature" of jazz, and, in turn, gendered differences regarding the music itself: "Let's imagine a column of men marching in the same rhythm — this is nothing extraordinary. A column of exact marching women, on the other hand, has an unnatural effect and borders on the ridiculous. Applied to jazz: a man who sits all night at the drum set looks natural. A woman at the drum set looks disconcerting."[36]

Rhythm was certainly the most exotic element in jazz to European ears at the time. Compared to other musical genres and styles, jazz is perhaps the music where rhythm is the most individualized, where each player develops a personal time feel and where that sense of time most strongly characterizes someone's individual playing. A listener recognizes particular players by identifying the degree to which someone lays back or plays on top of the beat, the extent to which a rhythm section creates tension, or how a musician retains her feeling of time in relation to the others. Rhythm is a primordial element of each instrumentalist's and vocalist's personal sound. Billie Holiday, for example, is considered one of the primary jazz innovators because of her strong personal laid-back and ever-flexible timing. Rather than her voice, it was perhaps primarily her timing and phrasing, along with her depth of expression, that became such an important influence on jazz. So to connect jazz drumming to military marching indicates that the authors might not have had a chance to listen to a great variety of jazz drummers. Although Knueppel and Windmöller did not cite examples of music, they must have been familiar with the important American swing drummers and possibly also with the musicians who played at the Frankfurt Jazz Fest. In 1956 they might also have known bebop drummers. (Hot Clubs, however, apparently favored swing over bebop, judging from the available playlists.) Jazz, in particular rhythm, signified masculinity and seemed particularly exotic to Knueppel and Windmöller. However, this strange but fascinating music appealed to them. The more they situated jazz as inaccessible but highly desirable, the more they conveyed the image of tasting a "forbidden fruit."

The notion of "nature" is a dominant subject in their article, and, similar to the previous letters, "nature" enters the discussion when all other explanations fail. Basically, each very precise and motored exact rhythm contradicts the essence of the woman, who rather follows a different rhythm — "the living, irregular rhythm of nature."[37] Beliefs about this "irregular rhythm of nature" circulated in many cultures in a multitude of expressions, assuming a female interconnectedness based on menstrual cycles, lunar orientation, etc. Whereas an earlier wave of feminists had worked to establish a political consciousness of women's issues, populist literature on "new femininity" and esoteric self-exploration flooded bookshelves in Europe and the United States in the

1970s and 1980s. (Ironically, during that wave of new femininity, percussion circles became a popular mode of musical self-expression for women.) Binary constructions of gender ("rational" versus "natural") remained unquestioned, as in this *Jazz Podium* discussion. Since such constructs served as arguments to maintain women's inferiority, they carry a dangerous potential for backlash.

Knueppel and Windmöller continued to emphasize how "unfeminine" the field of jazz is: "Real and sustained interest in jazz requires objectivity, matter-of-factness and the ability to abstract. Again, three entirely non-feminine qualities," they began. "Women listen with their feeling, without analyzing why they like something or not. Their thinking is more subjective, self-oriented than men's."[38]

Although these sentiments might also allow for a reading in which gendered differences could coexist and deserve equal merit, the authors maintained a denigrating tone toward women, in general: "In any case, a woman will not easily think about whether a chorus is good or bad. If she even bothers to find out what that is — a 'chorus.'" Although jazz required that one had to immerse oneself deeply into the "field" to learn how to hear jazz and although the authors clearly saw themselves as competent, they reiterated how "the women" would rarely invest themselves seriously in any field. They took their argument one step further: if women would go and develop a profound interest in any field, they would prefer an area that would be aesthetically beautiful and "non-problematic." Jazz was already seen as highly sophisticated, not easily accessible, culturally unfamiliar, complex, and problematic, and now the authors characterized jazz as not beautiful (!). "She will seek to avoid the problematic," said Knueppel and Windmöller. "Jazz cannot fulfill this condition, since he ['the jazz'] is not 'beautiful' in our traditional sense. What certainly [naturally] should not be a value judgment."[39]

Knueppel and Windmöller arrive at the same question Peter Kunst had asked. The last caption read: *Willingness to Sacrifice — What for?* Why on earth would any woman devote herself to jazz? The sacrifices, the work, the effort, the problems, the inherent difficulties! What was the point? "And then he ['the jazz'] makes great demands toward his 'victims' — intellectually and also financially (if one thinks what you forego in order to buy another record or a good concert ticket!) — and one dedicates every free moment to this! Why all that? What does jazz give back as equivalent? One gets what one knows to extract out of it, its value is non-material. ['It' stands for jazz in each case. 'It' could also be translated as "him," since jazz is referred to with a masculine article in the German language.] Those who are bewitched by it will gladly do whatever it takes. But there is no purpose, an intention is not behind it. It is a breadless art, 'for its own sake,' and given these trials and tribulations, this absolute devotion and effort, a woman is not up to the task."[40]

In the final section, *The Female Jazz-Type and the Male Colleague*, the authors revealed themselves as women "who really love jazz with complete devotion, know the matter quite well and would rather spend their last 5 marks on a record than on a lipstick." They described themselves, as well as all other women jazz fans they had encountered, as "individualists searching for something and finding the incredibly rich world of jazz." For the first time in their letter, there is a notion of joy and fulfillment outweighing the effort and hard work. It is refreshing to learn about the authors' feelings and to read about their longing for acceptance as jazz fans.

Even the most dedicated woman had to be "twice as decided, twice as enthusiastic, intelligent, and enduring" to stand her ground against the men. For the first time in the debate *Die Frau und der Jazz*, there was an explicit call for change: "And for all that, all we want is to simply be treated by our male colleagues as jazz fans!"[41]

FOUR STATEMENTS FROM PROFESSIONALS

The series ended with excerpts from four letters by Jutta Hipp, Vera Auer, Martine Morel, and Madeleine Gautier. Unfortunately, each is limited to one paragraph. The editors of *Jazz Podium* might not have expected so many responses and announced that these four excerpts would conclude the subject of *The Woman and the Jazz*. Hipp, the most professional musician of these four and at the peak of her career at the time, felt that her colleagues treated her as equal — because they did *not* treat her "like a woman," i.e., they would not hold the door for her or help her into her coat. Hipp also considered Lorraine Geller, Terry Pollard, and Elli Frankel as equal to men. For the first time in the entire series, (and, significantly, this was the first time a musician entered the discussion), references to other women jazz musicians were given. In 1956, Jutta Hipp already lived in New York and recorded for Blue Note Records. Her perspective was different from those of all the other writers in this series of letters. Vibraphonist Vera Auer had not experienced such unequivocal acceptance, nor had she made as much of an impact on the scene as Jutta Hipp. They say "good for a woman," Auer sighed. Both musicians disagreed with the shortcomings attributed to women in all previous pieces. For example, Auer argued that on the dance floor "the female youth displays much better rhythm than the male," therefore, disagreed with Knueppel and Windmöller's arguments about rhythm ("a woman at the drum set looks disconcerting").[42]

Martine Morel was introduced as a ragtime pianist and as someone who had a large record collection at her disposal, who gave lectures and wrote articles about jazz. This description portrayed her as a competent jazz expert first, rather than a musician at Jutta Hipp's level. Madeleine Gautier had written about jazz "for many years" which made her a jazz expert. During the 1950s, she wrote for *Jazz Hot*, the most important French jazz magazine. However, instead of learning about her record collection, we learn that she was married to Hugues Panassié, at the time the most prominent jazz critic in France, who owned a huge and famous record collection. Did that make Madeleine Gautier perhaps merely a "jazz fan by marriage?" Unfortunately, we do not get any information as to how Morel or Gautier developed their interests and acquired their skills. Even more than Knueppel and Windmöller, Morel and Gautier wrote as if in denial of their female gender. "One very rarely meets a woman with a real passion for something, who has a vocation, like a man," wrote Morel. Gautier was even more condescending: "many women are egocentric and in love with themselves — to the extent that they cannot concern themselves with anything that goes beyond their own little persona. . . . Some have nothing in their brain or in their heart — and they don't listen, and they will never learn it."[43]

Since these are just short excerpts, it is hard to tell how each person viewed herself as a woman, as a writer, or as a jazz fan. The statement by the most professional musician, Jutta Hipp, exudes the most unconflicted and positive feeling. Hipp was then the most immersed in the music itself, living jazz was her daily reality. For Gautier and Morel, jazz might have been more of an intellectual area with most of the listening taking place at home in front of a record player. Perhaps they were less part of a community than Hipp and had less of a chance to come in contact with independent women who could inspire them? If so, Gautier's and Morel's derogatory views could possibly be read as an example of how perceptions were most stereotyped when there was the most isolation from like-minded peers.

In conclusion, the number of women's voices in a medium like *Jazz Podium* is as fascinating as the variety of their views. Each woman situated herself in the context of jazz in a unique way, and each contributed different facets as to how to think of "the woman" and her possible place in "the jazz." The most prominent topics were gendered education and how to find access to and quality information about jazz. Records were the primary medium, of course, because of the necessity to own or to have access to a record collection, but possibly also because listening to records could be done independently and in private or semipublic settings. Regarding print media, liner notes were important sources of information as well. *Jazz Podium* as the primary magazine was indispensable; all seemed avid readers. Marianne Knueppel and Ingigerd Fuelle were even regular contributors.

Each woman constructed herself as an exception to norms of femininity and womanhood. However, each one found her own way to negotiate a space that allowed for a serious interest in the music without being ostracized from male peers as unacceptably "unfeminine." Some presented themselves as adventurous explorers, whereas others inserted disclaimers about their seriousness and moral standards to maintain a balance of justifying their femininity while defending their interest in and love for the music. For the latter, it seemed to be difficult to reconcile their interest in jazz and their femininity and seemed to require distancing themselves from women in general.

Several letters went to great lengths, pointing out gendered differences in listening to jazz and collecting records. Rosemarie Wiebe offered a refreshing view compared to the serious mindset prevalent in the Hot Club scene. Jazz as a metaphor for liberation and progressiveness clashed with the Hot Clubs' meticulous rules and practices, where very little mention was made about the emotional content of the music; the emphasis was on studying hard to become an "expert." The culture of collecting records and minutiae about lineups, titles, facts about the artists, etc., conveys a mindset that reflects the dominating "masculine" values (i.e., objective, rational, and serious), but lacks the spontaneity, vibrancy, and emotional liveliness of the music itself. In that respect, learning that Rosemarie Wiebe enjoyed a fool's freedom to listen to what she liked (rather than to what was considered important), that Marianne Knueppel and Eva Windmöller owned records because it enabled them to listen independently (rather than to buy because a certain record should be in a jazz fan's collection), or that Vera Auer observed that women on the dance floor look more comfortable than men provides an interesting counterpoint to the focus on systematic hard work.

However, with the exception of the very short statements from Jutta Hipp and Vera Auer, all women contributors overwhelmingly retained the notion of jazz as a sophisticated, exotic, foreign, and hard-to-discover terrain. The exotic character is only partially attributed to jazz as black music. Unlike more populist mediums, these writers show admiration for jazz artists without emphasis on race, and the examples mentioned include black and white American as well as white European musicians. This is consistent with the writings in *Jazz Podium* at that time.

As in the male discourse on jazz, the women writers used constructs of the "rational" versus the "natural" to explain and, to a large extent, justify societal gender norms. This shows how deeply ingrained were some fundamental ideas of both gender and jazz: the majority of the letters perpetuate (more or less subtly) a denigrating view of women, i.e., of women who did not aspire to the advanced spheres of the sophisticated jazz expert. The conflict between being taken seriously and being accepted is not resolved, and the authors do not clearly identify societal strategies at work to maintain women's inferiority and strengthen male dominance. Each author, including Peter Kunst, grappled with the core imbalance of gender and power in German society without coming to terms with it. They identified issues of injustice, but the cultural climate was not ready for a public debate demanding equality for women and fundamental change.

Listening for the subtleties of how each woman managed to succeed in creating her niche, whether expressed in a yearning for freedom or spending everything to buy the latest record and sacrificing the lipstick, gives an idea of the covert rebellion that began to emerge. Transporting their personal feelings into a public debate might have strengthened a sense of secret community with other like-minded women jazz fans. All women, musicians, critics, and fans found a way to live a side of their personalities through jazz, a cultural sphere that, according to the predominant ideology, was morally questionable, loaded with connotations of sexuality and exoticism, and thus most definitely inappropriate for "young ladies," as defined by the prevalent German ideals of womanhood. This microcosm of women's perceptions of jazz also shows how exotic even a personal interest in jazz culture was, let alone the idea of actively participating as a musician. "The woman" did not really belong in "the jazz." Women had to create their own space, and judging from these letters, to a large extent, it was a solitary activity at home in front of a record player, where women could listen "independently" and discover the music, each in her own way.

NOTES

1. Marianne Knueppel and Eva Windmöller, "Lieber Jazzplatte als Lippenstift," *Jazz Podium* 5, no. 9 (September 1956), 9. The tone of these writings is dated, clumsy, and full of idiomatic expressions no longer in use in today's German. I translated these articles and letters into English, and while the language is fascinating, the English translation can only approximate the feel of German in the 1950s.

2. http://www.martinschlu.de/nationalsozialismus/frauen/11Frauenforschung.htm (accessed June 27, 2007).

3. This is a complex and fascinating topic addressed in many works of research on resistance against the Nazi regime.

4. This topic has only begun to be addressed in gender studies in recent years. However, a book of an anonymous woman in Berlin talking about the horrors of mass rape by the Russian Army appeared as early as 1954 (in English) and 1959 (in German). Forgotten for years, the book was finally reprinted in German (Eichborn, 2003) and English (Picador, reprint edition, July 2006): Anonymous, "A Woman in Berlin: Eight Weeks in the Conquered City: A Diary."

5. Sally Placksin, interview with Jutta Hipp, liner notes to *First Ladies of Jazz*, Savoy LP 1202.

6. Jutta Hipp, letter to Marshall Stearns, January 12, 1956. [Katja von Schuttenbach, formerly Katja Kaiser, made me aware that 12.1.1956 is the German rendering of January 12, 1956. Hipp thus wrote this letter two months after she arrived in the United States.] With permission from the Institute of Jazz Studies, Rutgers University. See also Ursel Schlicht, "Jutta Hipp (1925–2003), Homage to an Early Trailblazer," *IWJ Quarter Notes: The Newsletter of International Women in Jazz* 6 (Sept 2003); and " 'Women Cook—But Not in Kitchen': Frauen im Jazz: Eine kommentierte Bibliographie," *Jazz Newsletter* (Jazz-Institut Darmstadt), no. 6 (1994): 5–64.

7. Sally Placksin, interview with Jutta Hipp, liner notes to *First Ladies of Jazz*, Savoy LP 1202.

8. Much of the details about Jutta Hipp's postwar activities are provided thanks to the excellent research of Katja von Schuttenbach in her graduate thesis "Jutta Hipp—Painter, Pianist, and Poet" (Rutgers, May 2006).

9. Jürgen Schwab, *Der Frankfurt Sound: Eine Stadt und ihre Jazzgeschichte* (Frankfurt am Main: Societäts Verlag, 2004), 53.

10. Bernd Hoffmann, "Zur westdeutschen Hot-Club-Bewegung der Nachkriegszeit," *Jazz in Nordrhein-Westfalen seit 1946*, ed. Robert von Zahn (Köln: Emons, 1999), 68. See also Hoffmann: " 'Als wertvoll' anerkannt: Jazz in NRW," *Studie zu den spielstätten aktueller*

Musik in NRW, ed. Reiner Michalke (Köln: Büro für innovative Kulturprojekte und Kommunikation, 2003), 17–53.

11. Hoffmann, "Zur westdeutschen Hot-Club-Bewegung der Nachkriegszeit," 67.

12. AGSC 1949, 81, quoted in Bernd Hoffmann, "Broadcasting House / Musikhalle: Hamburg 36, der Anglo-German Swing Club: eine programmatische Skizze," *Musikwissenschaft und populäre Musik*, Versuch einer Bestandsaufnahme, ed. Helmut Rösing, Albrecht Schneider, and Martin Pfleiderer (Frankfurt am Main: Peter Lang, 2002), 223.

13. Poiger 2003, 57, 56.

14. Arndt Weidler, "A New Beginning — am Anfang war die Idee: Über den Streit, wer die Idee hatte die DJF zu gründen," http://www.djf.de/verband/history/gruendung.php (accessed September 18, 2006).

15. Katja von Schuttenbach states that according to *Jazz Podium* (Germany), March 1953, 14–16, Jutta Hipp obtained sixty-seven votes, followed by Paul Kuhn with forty-eight votes.

16. Leonard Feather, liner notes to *New Faces, New Sounds from Germany: The Jutta Hipp Quintet*, Blue Note 5056.

17. Peter Kunst, "Zur Diskussion gestellt: Die Frau und der Jazz," *Jazz Podium* 5, no. 4 (April 1956): 13, 16.

18. Ibid.

19. Sturm und Drang, a movement in German literature that embraced and built upon Rousseau's ideals of subjectivity and nature, is an idiom to describe the adolescent rebellion against established norms; it is best exemplified by Goethe's *Die Leiden des jungen Werther*. It is sometimes translated "storm and stress," but the English translation does not fully capture the German connotations.

20. Kunst, "Zur Diskussion gestellt," 13.

21. Regina Becker-Schmidt and Axeli-Knapp, *Gudrun: Feministische Theorien zur Einführung* (Hamburg: Junius, 2000), 26.

22. Kunst, "Zur Diskussion gestellt," 13.

23. Ibid.

24. Ibid., 16.

25. Ibid., 13.

26. While I do not have statistics on how many women wrote for jazz magazines, I did compile an annotated bibliography on women in jazz in 1994 and examined all major jazz magazines in English, German, and French for their writings about women in jazz. Until the late 1970s practically all pieces were by men, with very few exceptions.

27. Ingigerd Fuelle, "Frauen und Jazz: Man kann ruhig darüber sprechen," *Jazz Podium* 5, no. 6 (June 1956): 18.

28. Ibid., 17.

29. Ibid., 18.

30. Rosemarie Wiebe, "Die Frau und der Jazz" (Leserbrief), *Jazz Podium* 5, no. 7 (July 1956), 10.

31. Ibid.

32. Ibid.

33. Knueppel and Windmöller, "Lieber Jazzplatte als Lippenstift," 9.

34. Ibid.

35. Ibid.

36. Ibid.

37. Ibid.

38. Ibid.

39. Ibid., 10.

40. Ibid.

41. Ibid.

42. Jutta Hipp, Vera Auer, Martine Morel, and Madeleine Gautier, "Nicht für voll genommen? Vier auf dem Gebiet des Jazz tätige Frauen äußern sich," *Jazz Podium* 5, no. 9 (September 1956), 5.

43. Ibid., 6.

João H. Costa Vargas

EXCLUSION, OPENNESS, AND UTOPIA

IN BLACK MALE PERFORMANCE AT THE

WORLD STAGE JAZZ JAM SESSIONS

LIEMERT PARK, LOS ANGELES, FALL 1997

It was Billy Higgins's first appearance at Thursday night's jam session in a long time. Still recuperating from major surgeries, he was extremely thin and talked and walked with difficulty. His smile was the same, as was his affection toward all of us gathered to celebrate him. He played the drums most of the night, from about 11 p.m. to 2 a.m. He also sang a few songs as he played the guitar. He made it a point to let all musicians — about twenty of us — come on stage and perform at least a couple of songs with him. His playing at the drum set was as crisp and fast and melodic as ever. He set up the tempo for "A Night in Tunisia" and cued the rest of us to come in. Just relax, he said. So we did, in spite of the furious pace. He nodded in appreciation and reassurance. We were doing fine, and began to settle in the changing grooves, alternating between an Afro-Cuban feel and a fast-paced hard bop, pushing forward. Higgins at times interspersed his drumming with scats as he accompanied one of the improvisers on the horns and piano. The atmosphere at the Stage was one of communion, celebration, intensity, and solemnity. Drenched in sweat, as soon as we finished the song, he called Coltrane's "Impressions," and off we were again, this time even faster.

Friday, as usual, I made my way to Crenshaw Blvd.'s mosque, for the Juma Prayer. To my surprise, Higgins was there. I knew he was a Muslim, but hadn't seen him there in the previous months since I started attending. He was in his wheelchair, and after trying to kneel a few times, decided to stay seated. Once the Juma was over, Higgins and I started to talk, commenting on the previous night's jam session, his trip to Brazil, and how he was coping with his health problems. At this point, the mosque's imam, Dr. Khalilullah, with whom I had talked only briefly before, joined the conversation, wrapping his arms around both of us. A few minutes into the dialogue, Dr. Rizza Khalilullah interjected:

"Young brother, let me see if I get this right. You're saying last night you played a few songs with the greatest jazz drummer ever; then you two meet again here today. Very interesting, isn't it? What does all of that tell you?"
"I don't know," I responded.
"Well, Allah is talking to you. When are you going to convert?"

The ethnographic vignette above condenses many of the themes I explore in this essay. The social practices and musical performances centered on the World Stage weekly jam sessions reveal norms according to which public spaces and the greater society operate. Billy Higgins and Rizza Khalilullah, immersed in transnational webs of music, religion, and male blackness, embody modes of sociability that characterize everyday interactions in Leimert Park. As well as revealing cherished conceptions about art, solidarity, and spirituality — especially as they express positive blackness — the vignette also, if only surreptitiously, suggests internal dilemmas black communities experience as they confront the effects of imposed marginalization. Among such dilemmas is the prominence that black males have in the area's musical spaces. Because this prominence is seldom discussed by the men who physically and symbolically dominate Leimert Park, it excludes women and other men who are not considered worthy of inclusion in their circles of sociability. Leimert's musical performances and the social contexts within which they take place are necessarily embedded in — and in critical dialogue with — the historical structures of discrimination, and the class, generational and gender tensions among blacks living in the inner city.

To describe and analyze Leimert's sociability practices, I will take the following steps: first, I focus on the jam sessions by paying attention to the general performance dynamics, the musicians, the sounds, and some of the evaluation parameters shared by the audience and performers. In the second part, I analyze Leimert sociability as it is enacted in the jam sessions as well as in the neighborhood's public spaces. As ideal types, the ethics of openness and the exclusivist posture allow us to understand how blackness can both preclude and incite progressive politics. Openness and exclusion produce boundaries of blackness, whether through confrontational utterances that exclude whites, women, the poor, and those deemed amoral, or whether via artistic performance that engages audiences and invites participation. (Ethnographic evidence of such exclusions and openness permeates the essay, examples of which are the common disdain with which black male improvisers and audiences see white musicians and black women performers, and the willingness on the part of artists, such as Juno Se Mama Lewis, to address and dialogue with young black persons often considered dangerous and disrespectful.) Indexes of blackness deemed respectable, such as social class, urban space, gender, sexuality, and age, become concrete in the dominant perspectives shared among those socializing in Leimert Park. Yet, as this essay will offer, because such indexes are constantly in process, elaborated, and self-critical, they point to liberating possibilities, to a utopian social world that is both aware and committed to overcoming prejudice, patriarchy, and male-centrism. Improvised black music can be seen as a privileged conduit for emancipatory practices and thoughts — even when unmistakably permeated by principles and attitudes that frontally contradict radical liberation and decolonization. Contradictions notwithstanding, Leimert's social utopia rests on revisions of the past that rely on emancipatory visions of the future as much as they build on already existing black radical traditions.

Throughout this chapter I will be employing the ethnographic present tense. This is not to diminish the time-specific quality of the research I conducted between January 1996 and August 1998, when I participated regularly in the World Stage's jam sessions while working in South Central at the Coalition Against Police Abuse. Rather, my intention is to preserve that very specificity and give the reader a sense of the social processes that were taking place in Leimert Park during that period. Many significant changes have materialized since then.[1]

The World Stage storefront workshop and performance space occupies a prominent place in Leimert Park, a gentrified area of north South Central Los Angeles adjacent to the Crenshaw and Baldwin Hills districts. With its tree-lined streets, well-maintained houses, Afrocentric restaurants, galleries, shops, cafés, and clubs, the Village — as Leimert Park is also referred to — is the epicenter of a black cultural renaissance that has been taking place since the 1980s.[2] Founded by the jazz drummer Billy Higgins and the poet Kamau Daaood, the World Stage provides a place for all-night rehearsals, jam sessions, clinics conducted by veteran jazz players, and performance showcases for new bands.

Men dominate the jam sessions at the World Stage. A few women participate, usually as singers. The antipathy that instrumentalists often express toward singers, however, has less to do with the fact that the singers are women than with the fact that singers usually request odd keys which they want to perform. Players of different ages participate in the World Stage jam sessions. A regular bass player in his seventies performs in the same venue that hosts young men in their late teens. On average, twenty people attend the sessions. Although black males make up a majority of those playing, a typical night sees from one to four whites, and perhaps a few Latino or Asian American musicians as well. Players from China, Indonesia, Japan, Sweden, Denmark, England, Canada, Australia, Russia, Brazil, Poland, Israel, South Africa, Mexico, Cuba, Argentina, Italy, Spain, France, Germany, Colombia, Haiti, and from various U.S. states appeared at the venue during the time of this research.

On a given Thursday night, at about 11 p.m., the weekly jam session starts to heat up. The musicians play well and together, negotiating occasional difficulties with serious enthusiasm. The tempo builds from tune to tune, as improvisations become more daring and inspired. The audience follows with foot tapping, syncopated finger snaps, and words of appreciation. Warm applause follows each solo.

Attracted by the excitement, a small crowd of about twenty people gathers in front of the performance room's large front windows. The two small plastic tables and chairs set on the sidewalk are quickly taken. People standing outside the club exchange words about the tunes and the players' names, commenting on each improviser's approach. A considerable part of this growing audience consists of musicians who begin negotiating their way to the stage as they talk about the ongoing music. Tentatively, they assemble the group of instrumentalists who will perform next. The rhythm section of piano, bass, and drums is more difficult to put together because trumpet, alto, and tenor saxophone players abound in greater numbers. On a good night, at least six different combinations of players take the stage. Ensembles usually consist of the rhythm section and three different horn players. The management allows each group three songs, but enforces the rule only for less experienced players.

PAYING DUES

The musicians who participate in jam sessions at the World Stage are in a process of musical growth and change. Hardly beginners, they have mastered the mechanics of their instruments, know chord changes and melodies of at least half a dozen jazz standards, and command the basic theories of and approaches to improvisation. Those who lack command of their instrument stand out as exceptions. Unless they improve their playing substantially and demonstrate progress as time goes by, they will be ostracized and are not likely to come back. Some who take part in the Stage's sessions have no intention of performing professionally, not even part-time, but they are exceptions. If a player has aspirations to earn money by performing with other musicians, however, the jam sessions constitute a substantial site for learning, developing, and establishing social connections, all of which are essential for success.

Musicians describe this process as "paying dues," a phrase also utilized in situations outside of music. Just as most of the amateur musicians feel frustrated about not being able to play more often, frustrations with jobs, relationships, families, communities, and the wider society require struggle and learning.[3] "Paying dues," in this sense, suggests awareness of the inevitability of individual and collective predicaments marked by adversity. Many of the jam sessions regulars have had, or are still struggling with, alcohol and drug dependency. Unemployment and financial difficulties pose problems constantly. Failed relationships, illnesses, and brushes with law enforcement can have calamitous consequences. These shared conditions permeate conversations at the Stage, but they also emerge in the music. Sensitive renditions of standard jazz tunes can evoke these shared experiences of hardship. Soul, in these instances, expresses what the musician has endured. It conveys to the audience the sense that the player shares with them a large range of emotions grounded in black collective social life. In the context of the jam sessions, soul and paying dues, although not the same, can refer to a set of common experiences and sentiments and are thus sometimes used interchangeably.

Paying dues and soul, however, evoke more than just hardship and joy expressed through particular styles and aesthetics. Soulful renditions of tunes and paying dues also communicate a sense of resiliency and transformation. They demonstrate that the musician, in spite of the technical difficulties related to the music and in spite of his or her condition as part of a racialized group that has been historically discriminated against, is still able to make a statement and thus persevere. Indeed, it is the trying, the very searching for music-expressing group and individual conditions that constitutes one of the most appreciated elements of the jam session for the musicians themselves and for their active listeners. When moved by the sounds they hear, people in the audience talk back to musical phrases, call for dynamics, incite riskier approaches, and applaud the musicians' efforts. Soul, in this case, constitutes sensitive and recognizable effort. It has more to do with how much energy one puts into a performance than with how aesthetically pleasing the result of this effort may actually be, although, of course, aesthetics and style are important. "I feel you, brother," or "I feel you, sister," in the context of improvising thus relates to a shared set of sentiments and styles that links listeners to the musician's efforts.

At the World Stage, most musicians strive to find their sound, master scales, memorize chord progressions, comprehend improvisation theories, improve their timing, understand jazz conventions, and become better performers. Yet, the idea that what counts the most is the emotional and technical *effort* one puts into music still serves as a powerful incentive to carry on, to find and express pleasure, to develop one's abilities, and to overcome musical, personal, and social difficulties.

Paying dues, therefore, involves more than the necessary and arduous learning process that musicianship requires — the so-called woodshedding. For those participating in the Stage's jam sessions, paying dues also implies being aware of, discussing, and attempting to convey musical constraints and possibilities that are lived by African Americans. The musical and social life of Leimert can be comprehended as commentaries on each other and, in this way, illuminate further aspects of the world views of Village regulars.

Given the numerical and symbolic dominance of self-described respectable black males in the jam sessions, it should not be surprising that the aesthetic principles guiding these performances and their appreciation derive considerably from this group's raced, classed, gendered, and sexualized shared perspectives. It is only a testament of my experiential limitations during my work in L.A. that, although I attempted to be critical of the dominant black male world views, I accomplished little as far as bringing women's voices to the Village's interactions. The analysis and critique that I present, therefore, are at best internal challenges insofar as I am obviously speaking as a relative insider. I stress "relative" because of my non–African American background (I am a light-skinned black Brazilian) and "insider" because of my gender.

All of which is to say that the emotions mostly valued at the jam sessions, even when accentuating traits not necessarily connected to hegemonic male heteropatriarchal expectations (vulnerability and subtlety, for example, about which I will talk more below) have a clear point of origin in Leimert's black male universe. I can therefore only speculate on how such emotions and the shared views on paying dues are challenged by the presence of women, the non-black, and the African Americans not considered respectable by those who dominate Leimert's public arenas. As I suggest toward the end of this essay, certain modalities of black maleness in Leimert seem to be open to that which in principle threatens it. This openness can be seen as an indication of challenges that critical black women and those who are excluded from the universe of respectability successfully wage against the self-containment of dominant modes of black maleness.

EVOKING JOHN COLTRANE: SOUNDS AND SOLEMNITY

More than weekly meetings of amateur musicians, more than occasions when individuals have an opportunity to express their musicianship and sentiments, the jam sessions at the Stage quite frequently realize a metaphysical quality that transcends these given, more immediate facts. Many of the Stage's black male musicians attempt to evoke the mood produced by John Coltrane's latter performances, those where he was accompanied by McCoy Tyner on piano, Jimmy Garrison on bass, and Elvin Jones on drums. This lineup, formed in 1961 and active until 1965 — when Jones and Tyner left as the saxophonist insisted on ever more experimental approaches — became the quintessential John Coltrane Quartet.[4]

At the Stage, it is not so much Coltrane's modal approach and his use of Arabic and Indian scales and moods that are emphasized, although these traits are at times employed with considerable skill by some of the more advanced players. Fundamentally, most musicians try to perform Coltrane's spiritual intensity and musical seriousness through their personal renditions of tunes.[5] These renditions may not immediately connect with Coltrane's playing in terms of tone, melody, tempo, and harmony, but they conjure Coltrane's passion and dedication. Several amateurs confided to me that this kind of intensity served as their main goal and constituted the reason for the importance given to Coltrane's work. A tenor saxophonist in his mid-fifties expressed his desires, "Man, if I can have *that* energy, blow my soul out of the horn, I'd be God damn happy. . . . I don't have to sound like Trane or anything like that, but just blow with that type of vibe, you know what I'm saying?" This particular person was sometimes rather efficient in invoking a Coltrane-like energy (which was made even more evident when he employed eastern-inspired scales in his improvisations), and those who listened to his moving renditions would confirm his success by linking his effort with the celebrated musician: "The brother was sounding like Trane tonight, just burning and playing the shit out of his horn."

It is an indication of the racial, gender, class, and sexuality character of such statements and performances that black males, presumably heterosexual and self-defined as respectable middle- or working-class, seem to have almost a monopoly over the possibility of satisfactorily expressing the spirit of Coltrane. It is quite telling that the few women who then participated at the World Stage seemed to perform only non-Coltrane standards. This was the case of a black woman pianist, who was a school teacher and a private piano instructor, in her mid-fifties, who regularly played in the jam sessions and was respected as a musician. The same was true for two black women singers, one a college graduate in her early thirties and another one in her seventies, a retired city administration worker; both were celebrated as performers, and yet, as far as I can tell, did not venture into the vocal songs Coltrane helped popularize during his requested partnership with baritone Johnny Hartman — I'm thinking of "Lush Life" and "My One and Only Love," among others.

Although the music produced at the Stage mostly by black males may not immediately suggest a technical connection with the more spiritually oriented phase of Coltrane's life and work, the underlying motif of Coltrane's spiritual guidance dominates the sessions. It is rather emblematic of the Stage's dominant stance, however, that although songs such as "Wise One," "Acknowledgment," and "Resolution" remain favorites commonly held up as exemplars of Coltrane's spiritual force, they are seldom played during jam sessions. Most of those who take part in the sessions do not know those songs well, making it difficult to perform them regularly. Moreover, it is the spiritual and musical intensity emanating from his famous quartet that matters most for the amateur musicians regarding Coltrane's sounds — especially those he recorded in the last two or three years of his life in albums such as *Crescent* (recorded in April and June 1964) or *A Love Supreme* (recorded in December 1964). It frequently happens that compositions from an earlier period of his life, from a period that is not immediately associated with the spiritual force of Coltrane's latter phase, are performed with the intention of compensating, as it were, for the conspicuous absences. This means playing earlier songs at a fast tempo, allowing for "outside" solos — not being too rigid with chord changes and time — and most of all, evoking pulses, rhythms, and lyricism that are associated with the author of *A Love Supreme*. It is under these conditions that tunes such as "Impressions," a fast-tempo thirty-two-bar modal song that utilizes two minor scales, and "Blue Train," "Mr. P.C.," and "Equinox," each a minor twelve-bar blues, can be heard in almost every session, performed mostly by black males, sometimes by nonblack males, and rarely, if at all, by black women.

These evocations, however, may hardly be perceptible to someone who does not know the players' intentions or their personal likings. Even when readily recognizable "Trane licks" are employed — note and articulation clichés and tone idiosyncrasies — they do not automatically transform a song's interpretation into a worthy acknowledgment of Coltrane. One of the most experienced amateur saxophonists at the Stage listened to a particular white male piano player and at first agreed with most of those at the session that he sounded good. The piano player's phrasing with fourths chords (instead of the more common triads) and use of his left hand creating low pedal points were clearly based on McCoy Tyner's playing as it appears in several recordings with Coltrane. But, on second thought, the amateur saxophonist noted that the young white piano player was lacking something. "You know, the cat's got the theory and shit, but it's not happening. . . . You know why? It's too cute. . . . Yeah, too cute." By this, the saxophonist meant that the piano player, in spite of his expertise, was not approaching the songs and transmitting emotions in manners that were compatible with (what he considered to be the legacy and essence of) Coltrane. "He's playing without feeling. Trane wouldn't be happy with this, you know. It sounds too clean, too easy, you know what I'm saying?" The others agreed. The white piano player, after all, knew the techniques — the notes, chords, and some of the articulation tricks that made his playing resemble Tyner's — but he did not produce emotions that gave meaning to such techniques in expected ways. Furthermore, the fact that the piano player seemed to be aloof when performing did not help his case. As a middle-aged drummer added: "He ain't giving it a shit either, check it out. What is he all smiley for, huh? Fuck that shit!"

PATRIARCHY, BLACKNESS, AND AESTHETIC JUDGMENT

Belittling comments such as "playing cute" rarely are directed against black men or women. As well as implying lack of commitment to the music, "playing cute," when directed to black men, has the effect of questioning not only one's social and racial belonging but also one's heterosexuality. "Playing cute" can be particularly insulting since it is a quality often associated with children and women — associations that threaten to undermine the prized virility of black male musicians. Furthermore, "playing white" and "playing cute" are often interchangeable, which makes accusing somebody of "playing cute" an automatic challenge to a person's blackness.

Although the charge of "playing cute" questions a black man's heterosexual masculinity, it does not do so for a white man, or at least it is not stated with this primary purpose. From black men's perspectives at the Stage, white men are already considered less virile than black men. Thus, the sexual content of "playing cute," when applied to a white musician by a black person, can be redundant, only reaffirming what is already known. In the obviously black patriarchal context of the jam session, therefore, what is important is the "non-black" quality of "playing cute." I did not witness any such comment directed specifically at the black women musicians. Yet, I can speculate, based on conversations I had with various male musicians, that if a black man were to say that a black woman was "playing cute" he would not consider it as offensive as it would have been if directed to another man — from his perspective, it does not question the woman's heterosexual orientation. It implies a wrong approach to the music. The sexist and homophobic character of these judgments is evident. Among African Americans, jazz has historically been a black male–dominated arena, where standards of performance and behavior that do not conform to accepted forms of black masculinity are marginal at best. In such a heteronormative male-centric context, where black men are the overwhelming majority of performers, when not producing satisfactory results, blacks and nonblacks, men and women may be charged with "playing white," "not swinging," "not saying nothing," "just going through the [chord] changes," or not "putting feeling into it." These principles are fairly consistent and held by most of the regulars of the Stage. No musician, however, is ever going to specify what constitutes the essence of "swing," "feel," or "happening." It is assumed that jazz musicians who venture to the Stage should be familiar with the basics of swing and consistently express it through their instruments. Still, the expectations go well beyond expression. Fellow musicians and audience members know when, for example, an evocation of Coltrane's spirituality is worthy of praise.

This process, through which a player's accomplishments are judged, is thoroughly dependent on both technical proficiency and the local context — not only the generalized appreciation of Coltrane but also the gender-specific shared sentiments that emanate from the consciousness of being part of an oppressed racialized community. Recognizable musical patterns aside, identifiable pleasures, as well as suffering and struggle, must be conveyed in one's playing. Ideally, these sentiments are transmitted effortlessly, and this is the mark of a master, a great musician. Among amateurs, however, it is habitually better to convey struggle than ease, for ease risks being quickly confused with alienation from shared sentiments, even when these sentiments are happiness and joy.

Shared sentiments provide the ultimate standard by which improvised music is judged. This does not mean that nonblacks are unable to produce valued, meaningful sounds, but it accentuates the necessary burden they face — to understand, show willingness to learn, listen, and, of course, empathize with sentiments that constitute the core of the music. Although specific rhythms, scales, modes, and other technical devices may serve as clues regarding a musician's inclination, these technical facts only become meaningful when used as conduits for the expression of recognizable and cherished emotions.[6]

An unmistakable belief in the irreducible and ultimate superiority of the black experience is ubiquitous in the Village. "Playing cute" offends precisely because it excludes the accused from the valued universe of blackness — a universe that is decisively grounded in patriarchal gender and sexuality definitions. Yet, manifestations of exclusivist postures do not happen unchecked. The notion that the same parameters of evaluation should be applied to all, regardless of social, gender, and racial belonging, functions to counter some of the excluding effects the emphasis on male blackness as artistic performance entails. Blacks and nonblacks, men and women, have their musical efforts evaluated according to the same principles. To be praised, one has to produce aural statements that evoke certain techniques and shared sentiments. Such sentiments, from the perspective of black male artists, are thought to be specific to the black experience, and it may be argued that this fact alone reinforces the exclusivist stances mentioned earlier. In practice, however, this is not what usually takes place. Nonblacks, women, and persons who do not feel compelled to subscribe to heterosexual forms of self-presentation can and, in fact, do produce sounds that are much appreciated by the mainly black male audience of the Stage. Examples of this are the acceptance that an older, retired white piano player enjoyed among the most proficient horn players; the sincere admiration that an openly gay black man singer, a hairdresser in his thirties who had a salon nearby, commanded when he performed; and the respect the few regular black female performers enjoyed during the sessions. Still, skepticism toward nonblacks is conspicuous. After all, compared to blacks, and considering the effects of historically imposed segregation, it is less likely that nonblack musicians will have interest or the ability to express the types of socially shared sentiments in forms that are valued in this imagined black community. Nevertheless, there are nonblacks who effectively cross the line, so to speak. Understanding and performing music thus present the possibility of relativizing race barriers. Although it is a relativization based on black-specific gendered and sexualized experiences, it points to the possibility of acquiring socially specific knowledge and sentiments irrespective of one's personal background. In this sense, the meaningful performance of improvised music bears unmistakable kinship with what I call an ethic of openness as it is espoused by most of the local well-known artists, as I will show later in the essay.

Paradoxically, the heteronormative male-centric parameters Leimert regulars utilize to evaluate improvisation question some of the principles we might expect from a patriarchal community. By emphasizing sensitivity and vulnerability — traits that are antithetical to dominant patriarchal expectations of control and confrontation — the appreciation of jazz performance in the Village draws on a set of values that allows for a view of manhood that is not exclusively dependent on hegemonic expectations.[7] Although "playing cute" refers to aloofness, "soul" is often associated with a musician's demonstrative involvement in the performance. In addition, unexpected renditions of standard themes sometimes build on emotional exposure, which is also greatly valued. Gentleness and understanding are as important to one's profile as a jazz musician as the most easily discernible and often sexist brashness, resilience, and bravado. Thus, as much as black maleness is based on easily discernible patriarchal values, it also depends on elements which, in theory at least, question its very male-centric foundations. That is to say, the ethic of openness is energized by forces that have the potential to radically reconfigure how not only art but also belonging and community can be conceptualized and experienced.

PUBLIC NORMS OF RESPECTABILITY: EXPANDED DIMENSIONS IN TIME AND SPACE

The social heterogeneity of the World Stage's participants extends beyond age, race, and ethnicity, featuring people of heterogeneous occupations, levels of education, and places of residence. At the time of the research, such heterogeneity did not translate into gender variation. These spaces are obviously black male–dominated. The few women, mostly black, that participate in the networks are the exceptions that confirm the male norm. Some of the African American regulars live in the adjoining gentrified Leimert Park, Baldwin Hills, and Crenshaw neighborhoods or in nearby Inglewood. Yet, working-class and poor blacks also participate in the jam sessions and in chess games set on the sidewalk outside. They come to see friends, tell stories, and exchange conversation about cars, dating, and job opportunities. Some of these less affluent blacks live in nearby neighborhoods. One does not have to walk more than a mile east or south to be in the more deteriorated parts of South Central. Others make the trip from Long Beach, Pasadena, or other pockets of black residences in the greater metropolitan area. They usually carpool or, more commonly, take several buses and/ or the train. For the less well off, the $3 cover charge at the Stage can be prohibitive, and they either have to borrow money from someone or talk to Don Muhammad — the Stage's director and the person responsible for collecting the money — to see if he will let them pay the following week. Blue-collar workers, clerks, janitors, and the unemployed, young and old, interact with doctors, lawyers, dentists, teachers, and professors. Leimert Park constitutes a unique black public space in South Central, one that, although male-dominated, is marked by social, racial, ethnic, and generational multiplicity.

During twenty-six months of observant participation in Leimert Park, I explored the form and content of the area's public norms. In the process, I encountered a form of blackness that stood in sharp contrast to those that prevailed in the tenement populated mostly by low-income women where I lived and in the highly politicized, male-dominated atmosphere at the Coalition Against Police Abuse, where I worked.[8]

This version of blackness revolved around the normativity of nuclear male-headed families, clearly delimited gender roles, a valorization of employment, obeying the law, gaining formal education, owning property, and achieving economic well-being. Black middle-class patriarchal norms of respectability, evident in a wide array of conversations and behaviors in the Village's public interactions, became even more obvious because they often emerged in direct opposition to images of women, despised black gangsters, hustlers, the poor and unemployed, and sex workers. An ethnographic vignette illustrates some of these norms.

We were outside the World Stage, about six of us, all black men, jam session regulars, listening to an ensemble that was not particularly appealing. Some of us sat on the plastic chairs arranged around a matching table. Suddenly, a few shots echoed in the air, and a car sped by us. Without a word, almost automatically, we were all on the floor, heads turned toward the street, looking for signs of more shooting or speeding cars. The musicians were obviously not attuned to the events in the street—the music did not stop. We got up slowly. One of the men present, a nurse and multi-saxophonist in his forties who often showed up for the jam sessions in his work clothes, was very upset. He expressed his disdain for what he thought were young gang members. "Lock them up, all of them, that's what we need," he said in a voice that was still not his regular loud tenor. Another black man, in his early sixties, who was a lawyer and always dressed sharply for the occasions, agreed with the statement with a nod and an expression of palpable disgust. As we resumed our interrupted dialogues, I noticed that the main theme had become what made Leimert Park so special to these men, whose ages ranged from the mid-twenties to mid-seventies. They seemed to agree that the Village, unlike other areas of South Central, was a place of respectability, pride, and lawfulness.

As those men were discussing what they considered the bases of upstanding blackness, they were clearly excluding from their respectable social networks those young men seen as criminals, "punks," as they would put it. The geographical connection that was made between the young men and their alleged place of residence—what Stage regulars often referred to as the "deep ghetto"—reinforced the shared sentiment that the Village stood in sharp contrast to areas of South Central considered dangerous and deteriorated.

The symbolic and spatial imbrications that were contained in these particular experiences and images of Leimert Park were also laden with class, generational, and gender perspectives. The gendered perspectives were less obvious in the drive-by shooting incident, but clearly connected to them. The comments about the young shooters were made by men who valued the Village because it provided a social and cultural space in sharp contrast to the areas of South Central they considered deteriorated, inhabited by the poor, the unemployed, sex workers, and gangsters. I was reminded of such views when I told these men where I lived—an area that they often called "the deep ghetto," which in their experience and imagination was replete with drugs, violence, and female sex workers. Leimert Park's perceived value, from the perspective of those men, was also clearly associated with it being a predominantly male space: few women could be seen in the performance spaces, cafés, and in the streets, especially during the jam sessions. To the physical near absence of women corresponded a predominant, obviously male-centered, patriarchal gaze that presented itself as unproblematic. Men's opinions on what constituted ideal families, relationships, and public spaces such as the Village invariably posited women as those to be possessed, controlled. The few women who circulated in Leimert were either respectable beyond doubt (as in the case of the jam session regulars, or acquaintances whose known personal life details classified them as such), or suspicious-looking (unaccompanied, considered unkempt, or not well known). More than sociological accuracy, what this simple typology reveals is the normative basis from which it stems: men's own views on women, irrespective of the women's own opinions of themselves or of those men.

Two forces especially influenced these norms. First, pride in particular forms of expressive culture — especially jazz music, visual art, and poetry — worked to build an understanding of black identity grounded in achievement, artistic innovation, and intellectual complexity. Second, the presence and popularity of Muslim religion, ideas, and values, deriving from Al-Islam and the Nation of Islam, among other sects, promoted a culture of dignity, respectability, and mutuality. Within music, these commitments could reinforce class distinctions, privileging jazz over hip-hop and blues. Yet — and in these moments the black male patriarchal norms of respectability were challenged and relativized — recognized local artists also encouraged and championed artistic expressions emanating from young women and men who lived in the poorer parts of the black ghetto.[9]

The dominant public norms at Leimert Park envision a black community expanded both in space and in time. The Village's public life incorporates stories, art, and peoples from a wide range of regions of the United States as well as from various countries of the world. It also cultivates a black historical legacy through its sociabilities and artistic venues. Leimert's cultivation of an international black culture stretches back to the political era when Malcolm X and other proponents of Black Power made their call for an international community of solidarity formed by the oppressed of the world.[10] Most of the area's respected artists, restaurateurs, and entrepreneurs — blacks, mostly men in their late forties and early fifties — developed their trades and outlooks during the 1960s, and the framework of Pan-Africanism proposed then, coupled with the civil rights movement's claims for social justice and solidarity, certainly made an impact. Those who work, perform, and socialize in the Village share knowledge about a collective experience of oppression that links them to others around the world. In Leimert, more than anywhere else in South Central, a sense of belonging to a community that is larger than the city, the state, and indeed the nation predominates.

The Al-Islamic emphasis on the international character of the Muslim community shapes the appeal of art, clothes, instruments, and books from various parts of the world, especially the African continent. In the mosques, Muslim restaurants, and in the streets, men and women (more so during the day than at night, when the Village becomes markedly male-dominated) can be seen wearing African- and Eastern-style clothing. Muslims run many of the shops that import these clothes from various nations on the African and Asian continents, notably Nigeria, Pakistan, Indonesia, and India. Yet, not all men and women who dress in African and Asian costumes are Muslims. Nor are the shops scattered throughout the Village that sell such clothes run exclusively by Muslims.

JUNO AND THE ETHIC OF OPENNESS

Conjoined with Islamic influences, a generalized gaze that looks outward to transcend the local characterizes the dominant culture of Leimert. A few storefronts away from the World Stage, a small shop specializes in international objects including African tapestry, hats, tunics, vests, shirts, bracelets, and rings. Two men run the shop — a black Muslim who regularly attends the mosque on Crenshaw Blvd. and a black man in his early seventies originally from Louisiana who is a devout Catholic, a drum master, a trumpet player, and an artisan, named Juno Se Mama Lewis. One of the most charismatic and well-known public figures in Leimert, Juno, as he was known, is respected partly for his age but mostly for his storytelling and eventful life history. The shop is an almost obligatory meeting point for the area's regulars. Musicians, visual artists, poets, and passersby all gather around Lewis at different times of the day. Some of the participants in jam sessions, me included, make a habit of stopping by before going to the World Stage.

Juno participates sporadically in the sessions. When the music suits his demanding standards, he will show up with one of his multitude of trumpets — instruments to which he has been dedicating his craftsman-ship and musicality for the last ten years or so — and captivate the au-dience with his mix of improvisational wit and theatrical performance. Juno's presence is greatly treasured at the Stage's larger events, which usually take place on Friday and Saturday nights, when he appears as a guest artist during presentations by professional jazz groups. Juno lends his enthusiastic support to local unknown musicians by being present when they perform at the World Stage or Fifth Street Dick's. Always dressed exquisitely in his own mixture of West African, Creole, and Eastern costumes, warm and friendly even with strangers to the locale, Juno provides a focal point of admiration, recognition, and respect for the locals.

Juno has patented several models of drums he has invented over the years, but he is best known for his musicianship. He played and re-corded, among others, with John Coltrane. His percussion-playing and vocals appear on Coltrane's 1965 record *Kulu Se Mama*, titled after the homologous poem written and performed by Juno in the open-ing track.[11] In *Kulu Se Mama*, Juno sings his verses in Entobes, an Afro-Creole dialect, and plays several types of African percussions: the Juolulu, water drums, the Doom Dahka, bells, and a conch shell.

Juno's persona invokes a variety of places within the United States and abroad. The list of instruments he played during the *Kulu Se Mama* sessions speaks of a strong connection to the African continent — a con-nection that is maintained to this day through his playing, manufactur-ing, and teaching of drums. He acquired his mastery of Entobes, the Afro-Creole dialect he speaks, during his childhood in Louisiana. As well as reinforcing the links with his African ancestry, the dialect accen-tuates Juno's more recent roots in this country. Juno often speaks about growing up in New Orleans, the large number of people who migrated from there to Los Angeles in the 1940s, and his unusually large family. He often visits New Orleans and comes back with more stories about the music, the food, and feasts. He muses on the many Creole Parades he has attended — the dancing, the rhythms, and the music — and de-lineates for us in rich detail the wonderfully different pulses of New Orleans, where brass bands take to the streets at every funeral, and funerals become popular feasts of dance, music, and umbrellas. "It's the Second Line kind of thing, you know what I'm saying?" Standing up, he moves his long arms and hands as if he were gently digging an imagi-nary hole in front of him: "That's the rhythm. And man, once it starts, you're in it." He starts to move his feet slowly, closes his eyes, and, looking up to the sky, draws a smile of nostalgia. "Forget everything else because now you're part of the rhythm. You're part of the crowd."

The multiple references that pervade Juno's performances and storytelling permeate the Village's public spaces and interactions. Juno both feeds from and decisively contributes to the vitality and range of this collective material. His small shop expresses and solidifies Leimert's practices of expanded community. It contains objects from Morocco, Senegal, Ghana, Benin, and Nigeria. Patrons listen patiently to Juno talking about the artifacts while he works on his drums or his latest musical passion, trumpets. The people who gather in the small shop to listen to him revere his experiences with John Coltrane, Miles Davis, and other famous jazz musicians of the 1950s and 1960s. Juno satisfies part of their curiosity with his firsthand knowledge of celebrated musicians' idiosyncrasies. He directs his storytelling, however, to what he considers more important issues. As he describes Coltrane's mannerisms, dedicated practice sessions (said to have regularly consumed sixteen hours a day), and altruistic spirituality, Juno manages to make statements about the need to preserve and encourage not only jazz but also black art, in general. "Music, visual art, and poetry have healing powers," he claims: "they bring out the best in every individual and unite different people through shared appreciation." Juno emphasizes Coltrane's interests in Eastern religions and music: "Trane had that thing with Eastern scales — you can hear it all the time, especially with the soprano saxophone. I think Miles Davis was the one who gave Trane his first soprano, just before they split. . . . And then in the end Trane was seriously into Hinduism, you know what I'm saying? So all that shows in his music. How many people around the world *heard* what he was saying? A lot, black, white, yellow, blue. . . . So that was Trane. He was like that."

The message Juno delivers establishes that the production, appreciation, and enjoyment of meaningful art ideally requires a higher level of spiritual existence. It requires tolerance, open-mindedness, historical awareness, and goodwill. World Stage founder and drum virtuoso Billy Higgins exemplifies this fusion of technical, personal, and spiritual achievement for Juno. "He wasn't born like that, you know. Billy's worked a lot on all his stuff. You can feel him when he speaks, you feel him when he listens to you. Coltrane was kind of an angel — everybody who met him felt the same — and Billy's got that type of vibe. He's nice to everybody, works a lot with the kids; he even gave one of his drum sets — the one that was at the Stage, remember? — to a young kid, and man, his playing is so fresh, so meaningful." He sees Higgins as a spiritual reservoir, a great musician, of course, but most of all, a source of inspiration for life.

As Juno weaves into his stories references from the African continent, India, New Orleans, Los Angeles, from the past and the present, he emphasizes the foundations of the expanded community. He considers black art, especially what George Lewis refers to as "Afrological" music, as having the capacity to connect different peoples and parts of the world through shared appreciation of rhythms, colors, words, harmonies, and emotions.[12] His own personal contacts with artistic icons, coupled with a cultivated knowledge about black experiences in various parts of the United States, render his anecdotes a repository of values. These values carry a utopian model of public interactions which demands a special type of sensibility, nurtured in and through art. I should emphasize that, in spite of the universal claims made through this utopian model, the principles that stem from Juno's narratives are unmistakably rooted in — indeed, well express — a black male–centered gaze that is shared and celebrated by many at the Village. We will see below how his gaze is a variant with respect to a less plastic, more excluding perspective that is also held by black males who socialize in Leimert.

Although the political aspects of this utopia may not seem evident, they can be grasped most fully in the very fact that the imagined community to which Juno alludes challenges accepted ideals, beliefs, and practices about national borders, racial identity, and cultural purity. Black art is not for blacks only, Juno often says, adding that there is no room for prejudice in any artistic expression. The utopian public sphere created by Juno, Daaood, and Higgins, to name only a few of Leimert's central public and artistic figures, challenges not only hegemonic forms of classification and knowledge but also deeply ingrained beliefs held by some African Americans about the irreducible character of the black experience. Juno values, preserves, and transmits the accomplishments of blacks from various coordinates of time and space, but he also posits hope for a better future to be built from the capacity — indeed, the responsibility — blacks have to utilize their knowledge, art, and sensibilities to accomplish social and personal betterment. By de-essentializing and, at the same time, cherishing blackness and African diasporic cultures and histories, the utopia that Juno so eloquently (albeit seldom explicitly) narrates and embodies helps define Leimert's public sphere.

This utopia depends upon telling and listening. Juno and other musicians, poets, and artists draw respect, admiration, and emulation from others, indicating the special communicative dimension of this community. Through artistic expression, storytelling, and active listening, Leimert's public sphere enacts a metacommunicative system to build a community of shared sentiment. This includes explicit commentaries about social injustices, but proceeds more often through allusions to yearning, mourning, pleasure, joy, and hope, which constitute the community.

Fleeting though it may be, the character of this community of sentiment becomes activated in performances by competent artists and storytellers. It also emerges during the jam sessions at the World Stage and in the midst of conversations between people in the streets, cafes, mosques, and restaurants. Emotions conveyed through various kinds of social performances cement a shared vision of an alternative future, communion, and comprehension exercised through a learned disposition for openness.

THE EXCLUSIVIST STANCE

The ephemeral nature of storytelling, music, art, emotions, and openness makes this part of the Village's codes fragile and easily obscured by other more assertive stances. The disposition for openness coexists uneasily and often in direct contradiction with intolerance toward difference: that associated with what is considered gang culture, but also differences attributed to nonblacks. Employing concepts and predispositions that readily resonate with stereotypes about social outcasts held by blacks and the wider society, the community becomes susceptible to class and sexual prejudice, gender blindness, and racial essentialism. Although this stance shares some of its limitations with the ethics of openness—the unselfconscious male-centric gaze being a case in point—its logic makes an internal critique more challenging.

Racial essentialism here means the tendency among some of Leimert's regulars to associate relevant and aesthetically pleasing cultural production with (and only with) a specific blackness. Because the notion of an exclusive community mingled with black essentialism is mostly defended by patriarchal (mostly male) persons who see themselves removed from the disadvantaged social segments of South Central, it generates aversion to women as well as to poorer (especially younger) blacks and, of course, nonblack racial groups. The cultivation of connections with Africa through interest in history, travels, and art and the cosmopolitanism that is associated with Islam—these very same elements that are central to the ethic of openness so vivid in the lives and works of Leimert's public individuals — ironically become instruments through which (what is considered) the true, irreducible essence of blackness is to be found, cherished, and elevated above all else.

These essentialist tendencies often manifest themselves openly in public and confrontational ways. Members of the Nation of Islam organize Saturday rallies in the triangular green area at 42nd Place, Crenshaw Boulevard, and Leimert Boulevard, a location at the very geographical center of the Village. One speaker at a rally attended by about one hundred men wearing business suits and women in partial veils exhorted the audience to take personal responsibility, to support, and, if possible, to start a black business, and to make donations to poor African countries. The speaker charged that whites in the United States conspire to oppress blacks and make them break their ties with their original motherland. The speaker concluded that whites — especially Jews — were responsible for blacks' wretchedness and self-hatred, and that only by dissociating themselves from the wider society and surpassing the "white man" would blacks overcome their state of imposed inferiority.[13] Applause and cheers followed. I recognized several people in that audience from the Shabazz restaurant and from jazz presentations in the area.

Direct and confrontational, the exclusivist attitude demands that its supporters appreciate black art, history, and sociability while, at the same time, rejecting all that falls outside of the ensuing Afrocentric universe. It is an attitude that searches and reaches out at first, but then raises walls around the newly found treasures to safeguard their purity. As the followers of the Nation of Islam made clear at the rally, they believed that the economic and cultural survival of black Americans requires them to define unmistakable boundaries and to purge from those boundaries all that is considered not worthy. Although this attitude provides a clear sense of purpose and pride for blacks, many of whom are not necessarily members of the Nation, it nevertheless operates on — indeed, it amplifies — historical chasms both within the inner city and between the inner city and the wider society. Black exclusionary stances reaffirm separatism based on race, gender, sexuality, class, age, place of residence, and education, for example. The solidarity that flows from these exclusivist stances precludes engagement in the appreciation — or even consideration — of difference. It is a solidarity marked by strict rules of belonging. In spite of the cosmopolitan components within other currents of Islam, this leads to a monologic rather than dialogic existence, to a closed and exclusionary ideology.[14]

The form and content of the ethic of openness, on the other hand, suggest new possibilities. In contrast to the exclusivist posture, which seeks difference (i.e., Eastern and African cultural traits) to affirm sameness and cohesiveness, the dialogical stance is characterized by a permanent state of restlessness.[15] Through evocation, storytelling, empathy, and emotions, through media that are almost ethereal compared to the in-your-face exclusivist approach, those espousing the (meta)communicative ethic express their discontent against rigid, stereotyped forms of classification. They affirm that the black young and poor are not threatening; that nonblacks need not be despised, feared, or pitied; that cultural difference is to be seen as potentially productive; and that past and present sufferings can be inspirational. Indeed, the past for them serves as a repository of accumulated knowledge from which insights regarding mutual understanding can be drawn. The ethic informed by these postures, based on claims of the universality of human understanding, is essentially plastic. Thus, nothing could be more appropriate than plastic, malleable forms of expression—forms that are constantly searching, experimenting, questioning—to express, precisely, such a plastic ethic.

LEIMERT'S UTOPIA

The tension between exclusivity and openness in Leimert manifests itself in contradictions and ambiguities, rather than in discrete, atomized opposing camps. In everyday life, most of Leimert's regulars stand somewhere between the postures expressed by Juno, Billy Higgins, and Daaood, on the one hand, and by those emphasized by more radical followers of the Nation of Islam, on the other.

Both stances, however, emphasize black male agency. Both visions assert a crucial need for black people to determine the form and content of the lives we desire. Historical forms of oppression have systematically rendered blacks as *objects* of control, surveillance, and critique. In sharp contrast, the projects that can be observed in Leimert Park radically affirm blacks as *agents* of our own destiny.

Leimert Park's residents and regulars often mobilize around issues that impinge on their community.[16] One of the first local meetings held to discuss allegations that the federal government participated in the trafficking of crack cocaine in South Central took place in Leimert's Vision Theater. The influence of Islam in Leimert reflects this collective spirit. Most Muslims and sympathizers of Islam in Los Angeles had to *become* believers or sympathizers, after being raised in other religious atmospheres. They had to make a choice. It is rare for black Angelenos (as I suspect for blacks in the United States in general) to be born in non-Christian families. Appreciation of black artistic forms, the cultivation of racial pride, and interest in black history are all acquired perspectives that demand *action* from individuals. As tense as Leimert's public places, norms, and utopias can be, they nevertheless seem to be invariably rooted in the assertion of black agency and the active work of individual and collective change.

Intolerance toward race, gender, class, and age differences as well as marked suspicion toward those who lived in areas considered degraded were some of the most readily observable traits of Leimert's social life. Nonblacks and poor blacks, as well as women and non-heteronormative persons, were viewed as having personal essences that, in principle, placed them in different and distant worlds across which communication and understanding were, if not impossible, at least very difficult. A social environment conspicuously devoid of significant numbers of women, the Village is also indisputably male-centric and by default patriarchal in how men relate to each other and to women.

Although this intolerance is more directly connected to the exclusivist stance, in which a version of Afrocentricity analyzed above plays a central role, it is also manifested in the plastic and apparently more accepting perspective based on the ethic of openness. I propose that both the exclusivist stance and the ethic of openness draw on the politics of respectability that strives to define virtuous blackness. Boundaries of blackness, to use a term developed by Cathy Cohen, thus become the object of such politics of respectability.[17] Seemingly more fluid and permeable according to the ethic of openness and correspondingly rigid and confrontational in the modes put forward by the exclusivist stance, the resulting boundaries of blackness, however, end up doing the same cultural work: delimiting, enclosing, and guarding more or less stable notions of what blackness is and should be. Whether through confrontational utterances that exclude whites, women, the poor, and those deemed amoral, or whether via artistic performance that engages audiences and invites participation, excluding boundaries of blackness are consolidated inasmuch as they rely on the valuing of specific social class, urban space, gender, sexuality, and age as respectable and necessary indexes of blackness. The dominant perspectives among those living or socializing in Leimert Park pointed to clear lines of social division.[18] On one side of the line stood the middle- or working-class males considered respectable, and their community; on the other side of the line stood those who needed to be policed and whose version of blackness had to be silenced.

Thus, in most cases, those individuals deemed to be on the outside of 'acceptable blackness' — because of their addiction, sexual identification, gender, poor financial status, or relationship to the state — are often left with two choices: either find ways to conform to 'community standards' of membership or be left on the margins where individual families and friends are expected to take care of their needs. In this case, the shared primary identification of group members, while still active, is mitigated by other identities such as underclass, homosexual, drug addict, or single mother. Further, these intersecting identities are used as signals, imparting judgments about the indigenous worth or authenticity of certain group members. Targeted members of oppressed communities are thus confronted with a *secondary process of marginalization*, this time imposed by members of their own group (Cohen 1999, 75).

Such intolerance, however, did not occur unchecked. In Leimert Park, solidarity emerges from a generalized openness, storytelling, music, visual arts, and a variety of discourses based on a clear sense of belonging to streams of history that both include and extrapolate the confines of the here and now and of one's immediate social networks. This solidarity is actualized in the daily heterogeneity of ethnic, racial, and social backgrounds of those who participate in the jam sessions and those who can be seen in the streets, mosques, bookstores, small shops, and restaurants. As it emphasizes histories, agencies, and the various corresponding communities, this solidarity and the ethic of openness that accompanies it provide antitheses to various forms of exclusion and essentialism.

Although this ethic of openness is primarily based on theories and practices of black men belonging to specific economic and cultural cliques such as artists, entrepreneurs, and other professionals, it nevertheless constantly subjects itself to self-scrutiny, reformulation, and transformation. As a process, the ethic of openness, as it materializes via storytelling, poetry, and music, is well suited for expressing vulnerability. It is this vulnerability that, in my view, projects the ethic of openness as an enabling conduit through which its problematic reliance on notions of patriarchal middle-class blackness — which excludes from its radius women, the poor, the nonblack, gays, and lesbians — can be challenged and overcome. By opposing the certainties and resulting exclusions deriving from patriarchal values, the ethic of openness embraces change, self-reflection, and dialogue.

I stress Leimert's more progressive outlooks because they embody political potentials that are also present in other black social settings in which I participated in South Central. What takes place in Leimert thus offers useful insights into both the present predicament of the inner city and some of its possible futures. Rather than constituting merely relief to the hardships of everyday life in the inner city, the jazz and the sociabilities around the jam sessions present us with understandings of our past, present, and, most importantly, of an undetermined yet desired future. Such indeterminacy, open-endedness, and will to engage in dialogue — all grounded in passion for social change and justice — provide a blueprint for social transformation that refuses to accept the already given, the easy solutions. As part of a black creative tradition that is still in the process of becoming — or, as Graham Lock would put it, "a dance between the moment and the stars"[19] — Leimert's progressive stance points to an utopia whose contours are in permanent negotiation.

NOTES

I respectfully dedicate this essay to the living beautiful spirits of Billy Higgins and Juno Se Mama Lewis.

1. Billy Higgins and Juno Se Mama Lewis, among others, have died. Fifth Street Dick's, a café and jazz club right around the corner from the World Stage, owned and run by Richard Fulton, closed shortly after Fulton's death. For an analysis on ethnography and how it represents reality and time, see for example Johannes Fabian, *Time and the Other: How Anthropology Makes Its Object* (New York: Columbia University Press, 2002 [1983]).

2. This characterization is not exclusive to blacks who live in the area. The *Los Angeles Times* has described Leimert Park as "a center for African American culture in Los Angeles" that "has blossomed in recent years." Peter Y. Hong, "Merchants Rally against Parking Meters," *Los Angeles Times*, May 4, 1997, B, 3. See also Frank Williams, who presents the area in similar terms. Williams, "The Poet of Leimert Park," *Los Angeles Times*, September 23, 1997, B, 2.

3. I utilize "amateur" to differentiate from "professional." The amateurs at the World Stage are not able to make a living off music. But this distinction does not necessarily

describe amateurs' musical abilities or their performance experience. While Most of the amateurs who play at the World Stage are conscious of their technical deficiencies, especially when compared to established musicians, they have an extensive experience playing not only at the Stage but also in various restaurants, cafés, clubs, and hotels in Los Angeles, in other cities of the United States, and occasionally abroad.

4. "The Coltrane Quartet . . . was the most influential band of the post-war period. It was the one group that amalgamated all the threads that had gone into creation of Black music up to that point and did so in a musical way, based on the traditions of the great jazz heritage . . . The unique tone and the hypnotic mood that John Coltrane established the minute he started to play have become the norm." Wilmer 1977, 31, 32. It is significant that the June 1998 issue of *Down Beat*, one of the most widely read jazz and blues magazines, featured a cover article on Coltrane's enduring legacy. Howard Mandel noted: "The sound and spirit of John Coltrane fills the air. Although the man himself died of liver cancer 32 years ago this July 17, two months short of age 41, his music and his personal example still exercise their profound effect, having an impact on the music we call jazz greater than any single figure since Charlie Parker . . . It is not just the release of *The Complete 1961 Village Vanguard Sessions* that brings Trane's deep, fleet, probing sensibility to the fore. There are also a flood of homages that refresh our memories and perspectives on his work, streaming from artists as diverse as [the white virtuoso tenor saxophonist] Michael Brecker (playing "Impressions") and [the singer] Kevin Mahogany in a February concert of Coltrane's music with the Carnegie Hall Jazz Orchestra, [Miles Davis's former alto saxophonist] Kenny Garrett (on *Pursuance*, featuring Pat Metheny), [the British guitarist] John McLaughlin (*After the Rain*, with Elvin Jones and Joey DeFrancesco), the ROVA saxophone Quartet and guests (*John Coltrane's Ascension*), Prima Materia with Rashied Ali, Dave Liebman, Benny Colson, and other Arkadia Records artists (anthologized on *Thank You, John!*, released early this year)." Howard Mandel, "Louder Than Words: The Enduring Legacy of John Coltrane," *Down Beat*, June 1998, 20.

5. For a thorough analysis of the relation between Coltrane's spirituality and the structure of his compositions and use of musical techniques, see Lewis Porter, *John Coltrane: His Life and Music* (Ann Arbor: University of Michigan Press, 1998). Among other convincing and creative examples of the spiritual-technical connections in Coltrane's work, Porter juxtaposes the words in Coltrane's poem "A Love Supreme," which appears in the liner notes to the disc of the same name, with Coltrane's solo in "Psalm," the last song of the disc. "A comparison of the poem with Coltrane's improvisation reveals that his saxophone solo is a wordless 'recitation,' if you will, of the words of the poem, beginning with the title 'A Love Supreme'" (244).

6. Such argument can be extrapolated from Frank London Brown, "McDougal," *Phoenix Magazine*, fall 1961, reprinted in *Black Voices: An Anthology of Afro-American Literature*, ed. Abraham Chapman (New York: New American Library, 1968). For a historical analysis of black masculinity focusing on Charles Mingus, see Rustin 1999.

7. Similarly, bell hooks (2004) sees the blues as one of the few outlets for nonpatriarchal

forms of black male expression of emotions, in which vulnerability and sensitivity are seen as valued aspects of artistic performance.

8. See for example João Costa Vargas, "The Inner City and the Favela: Transnational Black Politics," *Race and Class* 44, no. 4 (2003): 19–40.

9. Reaching out to hip-hop culture constituted an important part of the work of the local poet (and former professor at California State University, Northridge) Kamau Daaood. At the time of my research, Daaood, who was in his late forties, had shaped his art in the Underground Musicians and Artists Association (UGMAA), made up of not only poets but also musicians and visual artists, and part of a fertile black arts movement that followed the Watts rebellions of 1965. The poets Wanda Coleman, Odie Hawkins, Eric Priestly, K. Curtis Lyle, Quincy Troupe, Emory Evans, and Ojenke, to name a few, participated in this group and most took part in the work of the Watts Writer's Workshop in the late 1960s as well. The jazz pianist Horace Tapscott and his "Pan-Afrikan Peoples Arkestra" (influenced by Sun Ra's Solar Arkestra) both inspired and participated in this cultural movement. See Horace Tapscott, *Songs of the Unsung: The Musical and Social Journey of Horace Tapscott*, ed. Steven Isoardi (Durham: Duke University Press, 2001).

10. See for example Malcolm X 1973.

11. Recorded in Los Angeles in 1965, *Kulu Se Mama* had an unusual personnel roster: aside from his regular rhythm section, the pianist McCoy Tyner, the bassist Jimmy Garrison, and the drummer Elvin Jones, Coltrane added the drummer Frank Butler, Pharoah Sanders on tenor saxophone, Donald Garrett on bass clarinet and bass, and the percussion and vocals of Juno Lewis — all playing simultaneously. A drawing of Juno and a transcription of "Kulu Se Mama (Juno Se Mama)," his poem that gave the record its title, illustrate the inside cover of the original LP. The date, location, and substance of the recording are no accident. The radical, experimental character of *Kulu Se Mama*, with its iconoclast stances toward bebop's usual time, harmony, and improvisations, can be readily associated with the post-uprising cultural climate that included, among others, the no less radical experiments undertaken in Watts by local poets and musicians. Coltrane's innovative approach to rhythm and his obvious search for greater freedom in tonality can be contextualized, and indeed acquire further meaning, within the effervescent political and artistic expressions of the mid-1960s. I thank George Lipsitz for pointing out that Frank Kofsky made a similar argument in his *Black Nationalism and the Revolution in Music* (New York: Pathfinder, 1970).

12. For Afrological music and improvisation see Lewis 1996.

13. This of course is only *part* of the Nation of Islam's complex messages. For articles on the organization's outlooks see Benjamin Playthell, "The Attitude is the Message: Louis Farrakhan Pursues the Middle Class," *Village Voice*, August 15, 1989, 23–31. See also Henry Louis Gates Jr., "The Charmer," *New Yorker*, April 29–May 6, 1996, 116–31. Both articles seem to agree that the Nation of Islam's main support — if not its moral principles — comes from middle-class blacks. "Farrakhan's level of support among black Americans

is vigorously debated. If you gauge his followers by the number who regularly attend mosques affiliated with the Nation of Islam and eschew lima beans and corn bread, they are not very numerous. Estimates range from twenty thousand to ten times that. On the other hand, if you go by the number of people who consider him a legitimate voice of black protest, then ranks are much higher. (In a recent poll, more than half the blacks surveyed reported a favorable impression of him.) The [Million Man] march was inspired by the Muslims, but not populated by them. Farrakhan knows that the men who came to the march were not his religious followers. They tended to be middle class, college-educated, and Christian. Farrakhan is convinced that those men came to a 'march called by a man who is considered radical, extremist, anti-Semitic, anti-white' because of a yearning 'to connect with the masses.'" Gates, "The Charmer," 128.

14. According to the Holy Qur'an and many Islamic scholars, the religion of Al-Islam, as it is practiced today by an estimated one billion people, including members of a dozen mosques in South Central, was revealed to and systematized by the Prophet Muhammad in Arabia about 1,400 years ago. Al-Islam is based on the Sunnah (Way) of the Prophet Ibn Abdullah, believed to be the last Messenger of Allah. The Nation of Islam, on the other hand, is a American phenomenon. It was founded in 1930 in Detroit by Wali Fard Muhammad, also known as W. D. Fard. Fard taught Elijah Poole, who later changed his name to Elijah Muhammad, and made him his spokesman and representative.

15. A similar point, albeit made in a more general manner, can be extracted from Paul Gilroy, *The Black Atlantic: Modernity and Double Consciousness* (Cambridge: Harvard University Press, 1993).

16. For example, in April 1997 a group of approximately twenty-five small business owners and neighborhood residents rallied against the city's intention to install additional parking meters in the area. "They liken the parking meters scheduled to crop up in two city-owned lots, to weeds that could destroy their cultural garden spot." Hong, "Merchants Rally against Parking Meters." The photograph that accompanied the article showed a mix of shop owners, artists, and residents carrying large signs expressing their demands. There were persons wearing African and Eastern clothes, there were African drums being played, and there were those wearing standard clothing.

17. Cathy Cohen, *Boundaries of Blackness: AIDS and the Breakdown of Black Politics* (Chicago: University of Chicago Press, 1999), esp. chapter 2.

18. For a historical analysis of how the northern urban black middle class in the 1920s engaged in policing practices as it focused on the migrating working class and especially on young black working-class women coming from the south, see Carby 1992.

19. Graham Lock, *Blutopia: Visions of the Future and Revisions of the Past in the Work of Sun Ra, Duke Ellington, and Anthony Braxton* (Durham: Duke University Press, 1999), 184.

Farah Jasmine Griffin

"IT TAKES TWO PEOPLE TO CONFIRM THE TRUTH":

THE JAZZ FICTION OF SHERLEY ANN WILLIAMS

AND TONI CADE BAMBARA

Published in 1977, Valerie Wilmer's *As Serious as Your Life: John Coltrane and Beyond* (alternately called *As Serious as Your Life: The Story of the New Jazz*) continues to be one of the most important books about the lives, aesthetics, and politics of the Coltrane-influenced generation of "free jazz" musicians. Wilmer's book is one of the first and still rare instances to also call attention to the family lives of musicians as well. She devotes two chapters to women in the New Music.[1] While one focuses on the difficulties faced by women musicians, the other, titled "It Takes Two People to Confirm the Truth," is primarily concerned with the women who are the musicians' partners, wives, and companions. In this way, *As Serious as Your Life* is an important precursor to contemporary scholarship on the music, which seeks to understand the musicians and the music they produce in the context of the communities that support and sustain them. In addition, in her attention to gender and the roles of women as musicians and domestic partners, Wilmer also anticipates developments in the field as well.

Contemporaneous to Wilmer, a number of Black women writers, including Sherley Ann Williams and Toni Cade Bambara, also began to develop works of fiction that turn our attention away from the bandstand to the women who attend performances, the women in the booth or at the tables in the club, and the women who share domestic space with the musicians. And yet, with the exception of Gayle Jones's *Corregidora* and Toni Morrison's *Jazz*, few of these writers appear on syllabi, as symposia topics, or in a myriad of recent anthologies devoted to jazz literature.[2]

My understanding of jazz literature is informed by Sascha Feinstein's definition of jazz poems: "A jazz poem is any poem that has been informed by jazz music. The influence can be in the subject of the poem or in the rhythms, but one should not necessarily exclude the other."[3] So, for our purposes, jazz literature includes poems, novels, short stories, and literary essays that reference the music and musicians as central to the work's form or content.

Significantly, women have received attention as writers of jazz poems and a number of them appear in jazz poetry anthologies, including Jayne Cortez, Sonia Sanchez, Ntozake Shange,[4] and Harryette Mullen. It is therefore surprising that Williams and Bambara have not yet made it into this emerging canon. Rarely, if ever, are they included in listings or bibliographies of jazz and literature.[5] Bambara's short story "Medley" appears in only one of the anthologies devoted to jazz literature, Marcela Breton's *Hot and Cool: Jazz Short Stories* (1990).[6]

Nathaniel Mackey's epistolary series of novels features women as musicians and Candace Allen's novel *Valaida*, inspired by Valaida Snow, is about a female instrumentalist. The protagonist plays violin as well as trumpet. Mackey's creative and critical writings are central to any discussion of jazz fiction and in all probability Allen's novel will begin to receive the attention of scholars as well.[7] Consequently, fictional female jazz musicians should begin to gain the attention of critics who study jazz fiction. However, to my knowledge, Sherrie Tucker's pioneering essay, " 'Where the Blues and the Truth Lay Hiding:' Rememory of Jazz in Black Women's Fiction" (1992), which focuses on works by Bambara, Maya Angelou, and Xam Cartier, is the only critical work to focus on jazz fiction by women specifically.

Quite possibly, stories by Bambara and Williams are not included in emerging canons of jazz fiction because they center the voices of women who are not instrumentalists but who share their lives with the musicians. Inspired by Wilmer's example, this essay will posit two such stories, "Tell Martha Not to Moan" by Sherley Ann Williams and "Medley" by Toni Cade Bambara, as jazz literature. Both authors use fiction as a vehicle that allows them to respond to discourses surrounding the music, be they other forms of fiction or stories and stereotypes that abound within the jazz community. Furthermore, each author sheds light on aspects of jazz communities often unseen in writings about the music.

Including these stories in the emerging canon of jazz literature or in interdisciplinary studies of the music will challenge or alter many of the major paradigms used to discuss that literature. In one of the best critical works on jazz fiction, *The Color of Jazz: Race and Representation in Post-War American Culture* (1997), Jon Panish compares representations of jazz and jazz musicians by Black and white writers during the 1950s and early 1960s. Panish argues that "black and white Americans differ fundamentally in their use and understanding of jazz as an African American cultural resource . . . [and that] these differences are linked to racial developments in the social, economic, and political spheres during this era."[8] Focusing on representations of Greenwich Village, Charlie Parker, jazz performance, and improvisation in the works of writers as diverse as Jack Kerouac, Amiri Baraka, Ross Russell, and John A. Williams, Panish argues that "in most general terms, white texts tend to romanticize the jazz musician's experience, stereotype jazz heroes, dehistoricize and decontextualize the development of the music, and emphasize competitive individualism over any sense of community. Black texts, on the other hand, tend to present the jazz musician as an admirable but complicated figure; set the development of the music in a clear tradition that is continually repeated and revised; make connections between the music, the musician, and social experience; and inextricably link the accomplishments of the individual with the success of the community" (Panish 1997, xix).

In *Blowin' Hot and Cool: Jazz and Its Critics* (2006), John Gennari also posits important differences between Black and white critics and jazz writers although he is more concerned with critics than with writers of fiction. Gennari's argument is more nuanced than that of Panish in that his distinctions are less Manichean. According to Gennari, "Across lines of color . . . a romanticism imbues every [white] jazz critic's engagement with the music." Nonetheless, "it has been crucial for . . . these critics to use their white privilege on behalf of the musicians" (8–9).

In " 'Where the Blues and the Truth Lay Hiding:' Rememory of Jazz in Black Women's Fiction" (1992), Sherrie Tucker focuses on jazz fiction by Black women writers, whom she credits with creating an alternative historiography to that posited by jazz critics and historians of the music. Tucker's essay anticipates many of the arguments she makes in her important study of women jazz musicians, *Swing Shift: All Girl*

Bands of the 1940s (2000). According to Tucker, writers such as Maya Angelou, Toni Cade Bambara, and Xam Cartier create "a site in which we find a record of meaning, as well as existence for Black women in the field of jazz." This project, Tucker argues, runs counter to conventional jazz criticism and histories in that the women "depict jazz as being part of Black women's lives and Black women as part of jazz."[9]

In *The Color of Jazz*, Panish is writing about texts of the 1940s and 1950s and although he does cite a few women writers, he is primarily interested in men. The stories of Williams and Bambara are just as influenced by their times, the late 1960s and early 1970s. Neither woman romanticizes the musicians; however, in the case of Williams, the potential success of the individual musician is in direct opposition to the success of the community as it is represented by the woman and child he leaves behind. Neither woman focuses on the singular virtuosity of the musician. Tucker calls our attention to women as musicians and historians of the music, and, in so doing, she posits an alternative figure and history to those found in conventional works. This essay will focus on women as members of jazz communities and as partners who refuse to romanticize the musician and insist upon highlighting his relationship to others. "The Sister until very, very recently was unconcerned, unappreciative and deaf to jazz. She knew that a Black jazz musician would never make a dollar or get ahead or give her any concern or consideration, as she always demanded of a Black husband. She is a matriarch, but her values are the establishment values in this country: the fine home, the big car, and the front" (quoted in Valerie Wilmer, *As Serious as Your Life*, 191). Valerie Wilmer attributes the above quotation to a woman, "white herself, but married for years to one of the great Black bass players." According to Wilmer, the woman's view (not unlike that of the Moynihan Report) represents the traditional attitude toward Black women. (I am not sure where Naima or Alice Coltrane or Fontella Bass would fall in the above categorization.) Wilmer writes that this is an attitude that began to change because of the Black Power Movement: "But this was in the 1970s, after Malcolm X, after Stokely Carmichael had informed women that their position in the movement should be 'prone,' and after the Black woman's consciousness had been stirred to realize the importance for the man's self-esteem of rejecting the privileged role she is alleged to have enjoyed in white society by virtue of her sex. Although the evidence that she is equally exploited and frequently more so than the Black man has been clearly expounded, the pressures on Black women to support the man, whether or not he is able to provide, are very strong" (191). In the remainder of the chapter, Wilmer focuses on a number of Black and white women who are married to or live with musicians. Williams and Bambara write against both the image of Black women as materialistic and bourgeois and the pressure to accept Black male patriarchy. Bambara also challenges the notion of Black women as unappreciative or unconcerned about the music. Both writers give us characters that frequent jazz clubs. In spite of Abbey Lincoln's well-known angry assertion that "We are the women whose bars and recreation halls are invaded by flagrantly disrespectful, bigoted, simpering, amoral, emotionally unstable, outcast, maladjusted, nymphomaniacal, condescending white women,"[10] neither Bambara nor Williams seems concerned with the presence of white women. In fact, white men and women are all but absent in their social milieu. These writers were both self-proclaimed Black feminists/womanists and along with Alice Walker, Toni Morrison, and Ntozake Shange, they were among the primary architects of the renaissance of Black women's writings in the 1970s and 1980s. Like these other writers, they were primarily concerned with what Hortense Spillers calls the "intramural" relations between Black people, mothers and daughters, men and women, and women friends.

The Black Woman: An Anthology (1970), edited by Bambara, is a founding text of this literary movement, informed both by the Black freedom struggle and the feminist movement. *The Black Woman* is a showcase of a new generation of Black women poets, novelists, critics, and scholars. It included works by Walker, Audre Lorde, Nikki Giovanni, Abbey Lincoln, et al.; it also included Sherley Ann Williams's first published story, "Tell Martha Not to Moan." Originally published in the *Massachusetts Review* in 1968, "Tell Martha Not to Moan" exhibits many of the qualities that characterize Williams's later work. The central character, Martha, is a single welfare mother; her lover, Time, is a jazz musician. Ordinarily invisible to novelists, politicians, and the mainstream public, or else viewed only as a sexual being who is dependent on the tax dollars of the middle class, Martha is here the protagonist of the story. Although she is not the first working-class or working-poor woman to appear in Black fiction, she is unique. Unlike Ann Petry's working-class heroine, Lutie Johnson, Martha is not an ambitious, noble, and chaste member of the "deserving poor." She is not even working-class. Unlike Annie Allen of Gwendolyn Brooks's collection of poetry of the same title or Maud Martha in Brooks's novel *Maud Martha*, Williams's Martha does not speak in the poetic language of the western literary tradition. Martha is a sensual young woman who has a child out of wedlock and who chooses to live with her lover outside of marriage as well. She is sensual and funny but lacking in self-confidence. Her language is the eloquent Black English that Williams grew up hearing. "My mamma is a big woman, tall and stout, and men like her cause she soft and fluffy-looking . . . since I had Larry things ain't been too good between us. But—that's my mamma and I know she gon be there when I need her. . . . Her eyes looking all ove me and I know it coming" (47).[11] Without lapsing into stereotypical dialect, Williams presents Black speech in much the way that Zora Neale Hurston did with the Black southern language of Janie in *Their Eyes Were Watching God*.

"Tell Martha Not to Moan" gives us a woman who ultimately wants the stability and security of a stable family and relationship. However, unlike the dismissive remark in the Wilmer text, it lends complexity to the character by charting her personal history and fear of abandonment. At the story's opening, Martha's mother confronts her with a series of questions about her second pregnancy: "When it due, Martha?" "Who the daddy?" After Martha responds, "Time," her mother asks, "That man what play piano at the Legion? What he gon do about it? Where he at now?" This series of questions by a woman who some may consider a matriarch portray a mother's concern for the well-being of her daughter and unborn grandchild. They immediately set up an authoritative voice that questions Martha's actions and Time's integrity. This interrogation ends with "Martha, you just a fool. I told you that man wasn't no good first time I seed him. A musician the worst kind of man you can get mixed up with" (48).

Mamma's voice is the voice of authority not only because of her age and experience but also because she sets the frame of the narrative. Consequently, her characterization of Time makes the reader suspicious of him even before he enters the narrative. Her voice haunts but does not dominate the remainder of the story. Martha's interior voice is the dominant one of the narrative.

Williams provides her readers with insight into Martha's inner self, her limitations as well as her aspirations. At eighteen years of age, she is the very young mother of a toddler, not yet fully mature and lacking a sense of direction. Her lover, the piano player Time, is the complex intellectual—a frustrated black artist in a racist society. In her critical work, *Give Birth to Brightness*, Williams devotes an entire chapter to the figure of the Black musician in Black American literature, "The Black Musician: The Light Bearer." Published in 1972, *Give Birth to Bright-*

ness explores works by Amiri Baraka, James Baldwin, and Ernest Gaines. Interestingly, the book focuses on male writers and very masculinist folk forms, figures, and themes. Her central argument is that Black male writers have created a brilliant literature that provides "a vision of Black life." In the brief time that Time is in Martha's life, he does bring light and enlightenment as well as a vision of Black life. He possesses a politicized racial consciousness that Martha lacks.

Not only is Time a bearer of the tradition of Black music, his appearance and his appreciation of Martha have identified him as a "conscious" brother. Martha recalls the first time she sees him. She and her friend Orine are in a club called "The Legion" and Time is the new pianist. She remembers: "First time I ever seed a man wear his hair so long and nappy. — he tell me once it an African Bush — but he look good anyway and he know it." At the end of the set, he approaches her saying, "You, you my black queen." Martha takes "Black" as an insult. . . . "I ain't black. . . . I just a dark woman." The Black consciousness movement seems not to have reached her small southern town. Time tells her, "What's the matter, you shamed of being Black? Ain't nobody told you Black is pretty?" (30). In this exchange, Williams reveals a number of things about her characters. The musicians play for a Black audience and Time steps off the bandstand like a preacher from the pulpit. He is more politically and racially aware than Martha for whom Black is not yet Beautiful. He both names and claims her: "Yeah, you gon be my black queen." "On the first night of their meeting he informs her of his plans to go to New York: "Up in the city they doing one maybe two things. In L.A. they doing another one, two things. But, man, in New York, they doing everything. Person could never get stuck in one groove there. So many things going on, you got to be hip, real hip to keep up. You always growing there" (53). He is an ambitious and cosmopolitan man in possession of a clear vision of his desires and his future. Later that evening (or in the wee hours of the following morning) in a moment of postcoital bliss, he shares his dreams with Martha: "I uptight on the inside but I can't get it to show on the outside. I don't know how to make it come out. You ever hear Coltrane blow. . . . He showing on the outside what he got on the inside. When I can do that, then I be somewhere. But I can't go by myself. I need a woman. A Black woman. Them other women steal your soul and don't leave nothin.' But a Black woman" (55).

Time plans to fit Martha into the larger vision he has of his life; his political sensibility if not his emotions tell him that she is the woman to fill his slot because she is Black. He is the voice of a masculinist Black nationalism. Although his vision for his life and his music includes Martha, there is no place for her child, Larry, for whom he seems to hold resentment.

As their relationship develops, Time introduces Martha to the music, to aspects of Black history, and to a community of musicians who treat him as a kind of high priest. Time is consistently able to articulate his vision for his future. Martha is not; throughout the story, she is often rendered mute or inarticulate. He consistently paints a portrait of his vision, a vision inspired and informed by his nationalist politics. In contrast, she thinks, "It seem like all I got is lots little pitchers in my mind and can't tell nobody what they look like." She too has something inside, but as with Morrison's Sula, she lacks the means to express it.

If Time is resentful of Martha's devotion to her child, she is sometimes jealous of his music. It is a jealousy that comes to a head in the closing pages of the story. Listening to Time's conversation with other musicians, she realizes he is used to having a woman who provides for him while he pursues his music. Later he asks her what she wants out of her life and then, "What are you doing on welfare?" Having found her voice at his encouragement, she replies: "What else I gon do? Go out and scrub somebody else's toilets like my mamma did so Larry can run wild like I did? If [my no good daddy] had gone out and worked, we woulda been better off" (62).

Martha has been abandoned by a father who did not provide and a mother was forced to do so by being the primary breadwinner. Time attempts to explain the role of "the man" in constructing the limited opportunities of both her and her father. Martha explodes: "You always talking bout music and New York City, New York City and the white man. Why don't you forget all that shit and get a job like other men? I hate that damn piano" (62). Like the "Sister" of the above quotation, Martha challenges, indeed assaults Time's dream and his music. But unlike the "Sister," she is not one-dimensional and materialistic. She is a woman already abandoned by her own father and the father of her child. She is a woman who relies on welfare, a woman not only deserving of affirmation and love but also deserving of a partner who is committed to building a life with her and sharing financial responsibilities, a partner who is able to accept her child and take care of his. Time is the devout musician, the politically conscious intellectual, but he is also a man who abandons his responsibility to his lover and their unborn child to fulfill his responsibility to the music. In the story's closing pages, Martha, pregnant with yet another child, sits awaiting his return. In "Tell Martha Not to Moan," music and mobility belong to the male musician, but language and storytelling ultimately belong to Martha. The first-person narrative puts control of the story in Martha's hands. Finally, the story, as it is rendered by Williams if not by Martha (for it is unclear how conscious Martha is of the implications of her telling), seems to anticipate Toni Morrison's quotation at the end of *Song of Solomon*. As the protagonist, Milkman, celebrates the ability of his ancestor to fly back to Africa, his lover Sweet asks, "Who'd he leave behind?"[12] Both Morrison and Williams remind us that Black male flight, be it literal or figurative, often results in abandoned wives, children, families, and communities.

Interestingly, in later works, Sherley Ann Williams's female characters possess both music and mobility. Dessa, of the novella "Meditations on History" and the novel *Dessa Rose*, is a fugitive slave who sings spirituals that communicate her plans for escape. In *Peacock Poems* (1975) and *Some One's Sweet Angel Child*, Williams creates a series of blues poems in the voice of Black women. In *Peacock Poems*, she begins her experiment with blues forms and presents poems of a woman's wandering the United States with her newly born son, John. *Some One's Sweet Angel Child* includes poems inspired by the life of Williams's muse and model, Bessie Smith.

It is not insignificant that although jazz does not provide Martha a means of mobility nor form, the spirituals (in a blues form) and the blues provide both for Williams's later characters and for her own creative voice as well. In this way, she is not unlike Alice Walker, Gayle Jones, or others, for whom the classic blues singers serve as models for independent, creative, and mobile women.[13]

Toni Cade Bambara refuses to surrender jazz form. In her work, the music offers possibilities for women as well. In "Medley," she does not give us a female instrumentalist, but she does give us a female musician. She also challenges certain conventions of jazz fiction, especially that of the heroic, mobile male musician, and she rewrites the scenes of virtuosic musical performance as well.

Much jazz fiction turns on the virtuosic performance of an individual musician. James Baldwin's "Sonny's Blues," Ann Petry's "Solo on the Drums," and Paule Marshall's *The Fisher King* are but a few examples of fiction that makes use of this trope. "Medley" was first published in Bambara's second collection of short stories *The Sea Birds Are Still Alive* (1974).[14] Also written in first person, "Medley" is the story of Sweet Pea (a nickname she shares with Billy Strayhorn), who has decided to leave her lover, Larry, a bass player. Sweet Pea has been on the road and returns to domestic chaos that helps to confirm her decision to leave. She enters, takes a look around the apartment, and decides to leave again: "I could tell the minute I got in the door and dropped my bag, I wasn't staying. . . . I definitely wasn't staying. Couldn't ever figure out why I'd come but picked my way to the hallway till the laundry-stuffed pillow cases stopped me. Larry's bass blocking the view of the bedroom" (103).[15]

When he calls from the bedroom, "That you, Sweet Pea?" she responds, "No, man, ain't me at all. . . . See ya around" and closes the door. We later find out that she informed him of her intentions before leaving. The bedroom that the two share is blocked by his bass. It would seem to suggest that the music stands in the way of their intimacy . . . but this proves not to be the case, for much of their physical and emotional intimacy takes place in the shower where they make music together.

When she leaves the apartment she meets friends at the jazz club they often frequent. Once there, she shares the following with the reader but not her friends:

Larry Landers looked more like a bass player than old Mingus himself. Got these long arms that drape down over the bass like they were grown special for that purpose. Fine, strong hands with long fingers and muscular knuckles, the dimples deep black at the joints. His calluses so other colored and hard, looked like Larry had swiped his grandmother's tarnished thimbles to play with. He'd move in on that bass like he was going to hump it or somethin, slide up behind it as he lifted it from the rug, all slinky. He'd become one with the wood. Head dipped down sideways bobbing out the rhythm, feet tapping, legs jiggling, he'd look good. Thing about it, though, old Larry couldn't play for shit. Couldn't ever find the right placement for the notes. Never plucking with enough strength, despite the perfectly capable hands. Either you didn't hear him at all or what you heard was off. The man couldn't play for nuthin is what I'm saying. (105)

As a musician, Larry Landers is all style and no substance. He never gets called for gigs. He is, however, a good man and devoted partner; he is not the kind of musician who won't share household expenses or chores. Unlike Larry, Sweet Pea, a manicurist, is in constant demand. In fact, one of her regulars, a gambler, hires her to keep his hands well groomed on a week-long trip to Mobile, Birmingham, Sarasota Springs, Jacksonville, and Puerto Rico. As with Martha, Sweet Pea is also a single mother, of a daughter who is away at boarding school. Her goal is to find a home for herself and her daughter. By week's end, she has earned the $2,000 she needs to do so.

Even before she leaves for her trip with the gambler, Sweet Pea informs Larry of her intention to leave him. On the eve of her departure, they engage in a musical conversation that serves as the story's only virtuosic performance. Throughout their relationship, Larry and Sweet Pea sing and pantomime tunes in the shower. Unlike other scenes of virtuosic performance that focus on gifted individuals whose voices soar above the ensemble even as they are supported by it, Bambara gives us virtuosity as dialogue, conversation between a man and woman. The music, the quotations, and the improvisations contain all of the couple's anxieties, fears, and desires.[16]

Throughout the duet, they negotiate the terms and the end of their romance. There is no speech, no quotation marks, and no verbal exchange. Instead, he provides the rhythm and the chord changes, and she sings the sometimes wordless melody. She starts with "Maiden Voyage" and he joins her doing a "Jon Lucien combination on vocal and bass, alternating sections, eight bars of singing words, eight bars of singing bass." Larry insists on "I Love You More Today Than Yesterday" followed by a series of love songs. Inspired by Larry's laying "down the most intricate weaving, walking, bopping, strutting bottom," Sweet Pea takes the melody up and out, away from the love songs. "Took that melody right out of the room and out of doors and somewhere out this world." The music travels for her, clearing the way and Larry continues to provide her the foundation and support she needs even as he pleads his case. She returns to sing "Deep Creek Blues" as a means of acknowledging his pain. Even so, she notes: "Found myself pulling lines out of songs I don't even like, but ransacked songs just for the meaningful lines or two cause I realize we were doing more than just making music together, and it had to be said just how it stood." Larry returns to "I Love You More Today than Yesterday," but Sweet Pea refuses to join him. She is "elsewhere and likes it out there." Instead of joining him, she ends with " 'Brown Baby' to sing to my little girl." "Brown Baby," written for Oscar Brown Jr.'s infant son, Oscar Brown III, was first recorded by Mahalia Jackson in 1960. Nina Simone and Lena Horne recorded it as well. By inserting this song into her improvisatory narrative, Sweet Pea is linking herself with a number of Black women singers and articulating her dreams for her daughter. The story ends with her lullaby to her child, so as with Martha, Sweet Pea chooses her child over her lover, but unlike Martha she possesses both music and mobility.[17]

Both Sherley Ann Williams and Toni Cade Bambara are writers strongly influenced by Black music. For Williams, the blues eventually came to dominate her aesthetic sensibilities. Bambara finds her inspiration in jazz, the music that often plays a significant role in her fiction. Furthermore, she is also inspired by the music's rhythm as well, often referring to some of her stories as "pieces written in 6/8 time."[18] Both women, writing as Black feminists/womanists, challenge received notions of Black women and their relationship to jazz music. Although Martha seems to fit the role of the woman who cannot support her man's aspirations, Williams does not demonize her. Instead, she painstakingly allows us to see the conditions that make her desires for financial and emotional stability perfectly reasonable. Bambara gives us a woman who understands the music well enough to use it as a means of communicating difficult and complex emotions. Both stories expand our notion of gender and jazz by insisting on the significance of the women who make their lives with the musicians and the music.

NOTES

1. The New Music, also called free jazz, avant-garde jazz, or the New Thing, refers to the music first produced by Coltrane, Ornette Coleman, Cecil Taylor, and Albert Ayler in the 1960s.

2. Gayl Jones, *Corregidora* (New York: Random House, 1975); Toni Morrison, *Jazz* (New York: Alfred A. Knopf, 1992).

3. Sasha Feinstein, *Jazz Poetry: From the 1920s to the Present* (Westport: Praeger, 1997), 2.

4. While Shange's poetry is included in studies or anthologies of jazz poetry, her novel *Sassafrass, Cypress, and Indigo* (New York: Picador, 1996) also prominently features the music and musicians. The same is true of her play *For Colored Girls Who Have Considered Suicide When the Rainbow Is Enuf* (New York: Scribner, 1997).

5. While I have been able to find no reference to Sherley Ann Williams's "Tell Martha Not to Moan," Toni Cade Bambara's "Medley" appears in at least two bibliographies: Marcela Breton, "An Annotated Bibliography of Selected Jazz Short Stories," *African American Review* 26, no. 2, (summer 1992), 299–306; and Richard N. Albert, *An Annotated Bibliography of Jazz Fiction and Jazz Fiction Criticism* (Westport: Greenwood, 1996).

6. Marcela Breton, *Hot And Cool: Jazz Short Stories* (New York: Plume, 1990). The story does not appear in Richard Albert's *From Blues to Bop: A Collection of Jazz Fiction* (New York: Anchor, 1992) or David Meltzer's *Reading Jazz* (San Francisco: Mercury House, 1993).

7. Nathaniel Mackey, "The Bedouin Hornbook," *Callaloo Journal*, March 1987; Allen

2005. Maya Angelou's "The Reunion" has received little critical attention. The story focuses on Philomena Jenkins, a pianist. Published in Baraka and Baraka 1983.

8. Panish 1997, ix.

9. Tucker 1992, 26, 27.

10. Abbey Lincoln, "To Whom Will She Cry Rape," in Bambara 2005, 95 [orig. pub. as "Who Will Revere the Black Woman" in the 1st ed. of the anthology (1970)].

11. All citations for "Tell Martha Not to Moan" are from Bambara 2005.

12. Toni Morrison, *Song of Solomon* (New York: Alfred A. Knopf), 328.

13. In this list we might also include the critics Deborah McDowell (see her introduction to Nella Larsen's *Quicksand/Passing* [New Brunswick: Rutgers University Press, 1986]); Hazel Carby (1994); and Angela Davis (1998).

14. Toni Cade Bambara, *The Sea Birds Are Still Alive* (New York: Random House, 1977).

15. All quotes from "Medley" are from Toni Cade Bambara, *The Sea Birds Are Still Alive*, Vintage ed., 1982.

16. Significantly, Tucker's reading of the shower duet focuses on Sweet Pea's musical choices as a jazz canon that "included Black women along with men in [the] history of jazz," 38.

17. "Brown Baby" also became part of Brown's repertoire and he would sing it throughout his career:

"As years go by I want you to go with your head up high
I want you to live by the justice code
And I want you to walk down freedom's road
You little brown baby"

According to Brown, the DJ who first played "Brown Baby" on the radio was told to remove it from his rotation list; it was removed from the shelves of a number of record stores as well.

18. 4/4 dominates in jazz, but triple meter is in no way rare. Songs such as "All Blues," "Footprints," and "Afro-Blue," all standard fare for musicians participating in jam sessions, are all in triple meter. In fact, with the exception of hip-hop, most genres of Black music make use of triple meter. I am grateful to conversations with the musicians/composers/scholars Guthrie Ramsey, George Lewis, and Salim Washington for helping me to clarify this point.

Nichole T. Rustin

"BLOW, MAN, BLOW!": REPRESENTING GENDER,

WHITE PRIMITIVES, AND JAZZ MELODRAMA

THROUGH *A YOUNG MAN WITH A HORN*

ow does race make a man and how does a man become an artist? The basic characteristics of an ideal jazz man, often a young man with a horn, include musical superiority and individual personality. The ability to express individual personality develops from a continually maturing engagement with the intricacies of musical style and the articulation of a rare consciousness of oneself. Ralph Ellison explains it as a musician "achieving that subtle identification between his instrument and his deepest drives which will allow him to express his own unique ideas and his own unique voice. He must achieve, in short, his self-determined identity."[1] Quite a promising thought that freedom in discipline creates the possibility for discovering and exercising a "self-determined identity." The trope of the "young man with a horn" provides an enduring narrative within jazz hagiography and the critical literature on the history of white musicians within jazz culture. What I attempt to suggest throughout this essay is that this image of coming of age allows the racial purification of jazz origins as a cultural practice and enables white musicians to have a "personality" within the music. Although I have in mind the larger problem of examining how black men and white men talk differently about or differently experience[2] jazz, here I focus on exploring constructions of white masculinity and the defining impact of black cultural practices on them.

In the frontispiece of her 1938 novel *Young Man with a Horn*, Dorothy Baker explains that the "music" rather than the "life" of Bix Beiderbecke inspired her story.[3] The premise for her novel differs from those consciously evoking jazz figures such as Michael Ondaatje's *Coming through Slaughter* and John Clellon Holmes's *The Horn*. Baker wanted to give her *experience of the music* some textual shape. Her understanding of the music and her efforts to capture its meaning reveal less of a commitment to recording the details of Bix's life than to conceptualizing how a young musician comes to devote himself to jazz and what the effects of that devotion are. Consequently, jazz cultists find her portrayal off the mark. Universally condemned for being a poorly veiled story about Beiderbecke's life, *Young Man with a Horn* seems to insist on being read as a roman à clef. The marginalia littering my library copy identify the "real" people characters must have been based on — "Venuti," "Bud Freen," "B.G. [Benny Goodman]," and "[Paul] Whiteman." Taking her title from Otis Ferguson's 1936 essay on Beiderbecke and making her protagonist an alcoholic seems to belie her claim that she did not base her novel on Beiderbecke's life. One can almost hear in the criticism leveled against *Young Man with a Horn* hints of dismay that once again a woman has gotten it wrong. She failed to capture the experiences of a jazz musician, presenting instead "a turgid little drugstore novel with a hero like no jazzman living or dead. Recommended for laughs, to any reader who knows music and musicians."[4] Even those who acknowledge Baker's claim of inspiration continue to view the story as a feeble life history of legend Beiderbecke. Tragically dead at twenty-eight from alcoholism and pneumonia in 1931, he lies at the center of "white" jazz hagiography.[5] The prominence of Beiderbeckian hagiography haunts interpretations and constructions of white jazz musicians and musicianship in their "real" and fictional appearances.

Most of the criticism about Baker's story centers on the film released by Warner Bros. in 1950, starring Kirk Douglas in the title role and directed by Michael Curtiz. Big band critic George T. Simon reviewed the film not long after it was released. For him, "what could have been a good, authentic, and convincing film and which gives early indications of being one gradually deteriorates into a second-rate, cliché-ridden melodrama."[6] Hoping for a more accurate representation of Beiderbecke's music, Simon condemned the film for its inability to capture *what he heard* when he listened to Beiderbecke. Simon expects a lot considering that Otis Ferguson could himself only revert to the imprecise language of religious conversion and patriotism to describe the catalytic effect of Beiderbecke's sound. According to Ferguson, the music's energy can only be "marveled" at precisely because "there is no way of describing it. . . . Why waste time with words and poor copies? One hears it, and is moved and made strangely proud; or one does not, and misses one of the fine natural resources of this American country."[7] Here, we see the conflict between representing the experience of music and using the measure of experience to evaluate interpretations of the music. The power of jazz to be affective, i.e., to evoke emotional cues, determines how "authentic" and/or "successful" its critics will view it as.

Perhaps that is why I remain fascinated by the story about race and masculinity Baker tries telling in her novel. I am especially intrigued by the translation of that story into a narrative suitable for exposition in film. Both versions of *Young Man with a Horn* negotiate contemporary discourses about race, artistry, and masculinity within jazz culture, and each version presents the contradictions inherent in representations of such discourses. Although transformed from a novel about white voyeurs to a film about domestic melodrama, *Young Man with a Horn* ultimately remains the story about the perennial problem of rendering the experience of the "jazzman" visible. How is he made recognizable as a man and artist; what are the terms we are willing to accept as "authentic" representations of the culture; how is the question of individuality, so central to ideas about originality and authenticity within jazz, resolved? Can a non-musician be articulate about the meaning of the music? In addressing these conceptual questions about meaning created around jazz, gender, and race, my essay pursues two ends. The first engages the articulation of masculinity and whiteness through jazz at two distinct historical moments and the second suggests the relevance of "jazz" for reflecting contemporary contests over the meanings of race and masculinity. In particular, I am interested in how interpretations of white jazz and a young man's coming of age by novelist Dorothy Baker and director Michael Curtiz reveal complicated discourses about gender, primitivity, and identity that jazz hagiography often hides. Within this larger critical project, I aim to look specifically at the construction of definitions of masculine fraternity. Since the practice of jazz depends on relationships between musicians,[8] the notions of fraternity and intimacy are central to the effective performance of the music. Understanding how "outsiders" imagine these relationships helps us to consider the important question of how jazz enables gendered identifications.[9]

With her title, *Young Man with a Horn*, Dorothy Baker suggests that her protagonist's story could be the fate of any young male musician. It is cautionary in that the protagonist, Rick Martin, winds up nameless and faceless, merely a whisper on some old recordings passed among record collectors attempting to relive the past, to gain access to that inner circle who recognized a "musician's musician." Despite efforts to grow artistically, Rick's music always retained "an element of self-destruction." The narrator, himself featureless, tells us that Rick's story "has the ring of truth and an overtone or two. It is the story of a number of things — of the gap between the man's musical ability and his ability to fit it to his own life; of the difference between the demands of expression and the demands of life here below; and, finally, of the difference between good and bad in a native American art form — jazz music. . . . The story ends with death" (3, 4). Sadly, only the narrator and two Negroes[10] — Smoke Johnson, a drummer, and Jeff Williams, a bandleader — mourn Rick's death. Here, in the narrator's lamentation, Baker articulates both the promise and failure of the great idea about jazz. In jazz music, we find the realization of U.S. ideals about democracy embodied in sound. In jazz history, integration triumphs and represents a social ideal toward which the nation continually strides.[11]

If, however, jazz culture is all about the success of integration, then *Young Man with a Horn* attempts to mark the experience of that integration. And, if *Young Man with a Horn* tells the story about the death of a forgotten jazzman, then the failure of democratic ideals occurs because of the continuing ambiguity which race presents in contemporary life. To be clear, throughout jazz history, musicians across racial lines have transgressed social mores and articulated innovative musical ideas which have shaped the practice and performance of jazz music. However, in writing the complexities of that history, jazz critics, biographers, and historians have shied away from fully engaging what the experiences of this complex racial and gendered world meant to those within that cultural sphere. Reverting to an ideal of jazz as having already achieved "democracy" obviates the examination of the conceptual differences in what that "democracy" looks like. Thus, the ways in which Baker and Curtiz imagine jazz, race, and masculinity and the resistance to those representations by jazz critics present us with one vital site for understanding how the cultural place of jazz is negotiated and transformed. Their work is especially useful for understanding the tensions around defining masculinity in a world in which social change disrupts normative gender roles and ideals.

Although written toward the close of the New Deal era, *Young Man with a Horn* reflects the "Jazz Age" and life in the United States during

Prohibition. The period was marked by both conservative and radical approaches to the experience of modernity. With the United States transforming from a predominantly rural country to an urban nation, new ideas and opportunities for leisure activities blossomed. Movie theaters, dance halls, and speakeasies, among other activities, gave Americans across racial, class, and gender lines access to new types of entertainment. The danger, of course, was the potential for over-indulgence. The long campaign to enact Prohibition was realized in 1920 and was aimed at tempering the excesses of alcoholism. However, it seemed only to abet a more hedonistic lifestyle among those willing to seek their pleasures illegally. The young writers, dubbed the Lost Generation, who seemed to best capture the tenor of the era did so by evoking the energy of the wildly popular and controversial music of the period — jazz.

Discussions of jazz culture were fraught with contests over its potentially criminal influence, the evidence of its art, and the dangers of intimate interracial contact. Both white and black people debated, censured, and promoted the influence of jazz on contemporary life.[12] For white avant-garde writers and artists, jazz represented a productive avenue for experimentation, given that their audience "*believed* jazz performance could transmit the values of a simpler past into the furious present." On the impulse by artists to view jazz this way, Kathy Ogren explains, "Experiencing jazz could release and rejuvenate buried emotions or instincts, thus liberating an inner, and perhaps more creative person."[13] At the same time that black culture could be seen as an escape, black people were mobilizing a political culture to challenge on all fronts the verity of the black primitive. From national efforts to enact a federal antilynching law and protest the unmitigated power of racists to international efforts provoked by the increasing power of fascists, black men and women — including entertainers, athletes, intellectuals, and soldiers — presented a new critical cultural politics.[14]

Kathy Ogren aptly describes the 1920s as enmeshed in a jazz controversy: "For many Americans, to argue about jazz was to argue about the nature of change itself."[15] As Americans attempted to articulate a modern image of the United States divorced from a European heritage, cultural forms, particularly music, were sites of continuing and vehement debate. Widespread economic and social changes in the wake of the First World War provoked this yearning for an idealized "American" character or self. Jazz found itself at the center of the debates. White American criticism about jazz revolved around the supposed inferiority of black people and the consequent disbelief that they could actually create a music that was superior to that of the European classical tradition. Even more problematic was that this black-oriented music would come to represent "American" music. Ideally, the democratic impulse of the American character would appropriately define American music. Jazz detractors believed it appealed to the instincts rather than the higher levels of creative possibility men were capable of. Despite evidence to the contrary, these writers also believed that jazz would prove a passing fad, that it was compositionally limited and already in a state of decline; as Daniel Gregory Mason argued, "In melody and harmony jazz is commonplace at best, at worst desolatingly cheap and banal. The only individual thing about it is the rhythmic trick by which it attacks certain notes too soon, by anticipation." Comments such as these were not uncommon. An invasion of the cultural body politic, jazz's influence could be tempered only by a more redemptive music — the overtly "emotional" character of jazz needed civilizing if it were to be a suitable representative of American life and a rejection of the decadence of modern European culture.[16]

Concurrent with the writing and publication of *Young Man with a Horn*, jazz criticism rapidly developed as a professional practice, and the genres recognized as constituting jazz expanded as well. These developments and explorations within the genre were anxiously and vigorously debated by fans and critics, each determined to codify jazz practices. Jazz fans passed the litmus test of authenticity when they recognized the music as an art and listened with rapt attention to live and recorded performances. Meanwhile, American jazz advocates increasingly found venues for their work. British and French writers, who had, since the end of the First World War, published reviews, profiles, and analyses of jazz in their own countries, exerted a deep influence over these writers.[17] White jazz history (and ultimately criticism) was premised on the idea that it developed out of respect to (read by many as imitation of) black New Orleans jazz; and it often sees its greatest achievement in swing, which provided the soundtrack for the 1930s and 1940s, supplanting Dixieland as the dominant mainstream "jazz" form. Swing appeared to capture the most democratic impulses of American culture, and its popularity also revealed how central business concerns were to the practice of jazz.[18] As white jazz history demonstrates, the attempt to produce a "real" jazz history met the unavoidable contradictions of racial identity and cultural forms. Baker's novel explores the tensions between the practice of jazz as an art and a commercial product, the impact of race on the development of a musician, and struggles around the codification of expertise and knowledge about jazz.

Young Man with a Horn narrates Rick's growth from a neglected boy to a dead drunk who was once briefly famous. Throughout, Baker both questions and reasserts dominant ideas about jazz culture and its participants. A coming-of-age tale, Rick's journey to adulthood focuses on the promise and failure of relationships and the foundational problem of a dysfunctional family. Born in Georgia, Rick is soon orphaned. His mother dies in childbirth and his father abandons him ten days later. His father's brother and sister raise Rick and the three of them move to Los Angeles when he is eight years old. There, they leave Rick to his own devices. While his aunt and uncle work, he spends his time between school and home where he reads voraciously. Just as he is about to enter high school, the intellectual passion he had channeled into reading finds direction in music. Rick discovers musical community on the Central Avenue jazz scene and family with a young black man named Smoke Jordan. They meet at the bowling alley where Rick replaces pins and Smoke works as an on-again, off-again janitor. Being a small fourteen-year-old, this was the only job Rick could get to finance his purchase of a trumpet from a local pawnshop. Rick chose to become expert on the trumpet, rather than the piano on which he first learned to play, because the horn was "something you could keep around with you, so you could pick your own time to play it" (28). The trumpet thus represents his continuing sense of isolation and its omnipresence proves a barrier to intimacy, a point that the film explicitly stresses.

Not only does Smoke's and Rick's relationship represent racial transgressions, it also marks the crossing of geographical boundaries within the city itself, a primary dynamic within jazz history. The centrality of Central Avenue to the development of the themes of the novel cannot be overlooked or underestimated. Known as "Little Harlem," it was the entertainment and financial locus for black life in Los Angeles and Watts for most of the first half of the twentieth century. During the 1920s, Los Angeles boomed with the growth of the film industry. While the city seemed a frontier of possibilities, the realities of segregation and racism often proved otherwise for the blacks, Mexicans, and Asians living there. Although many musicians, such as Charles Mingus, Buddy Collette, Dexter Gordon, and Britt Woodman, idealized their youths in Los Angeles and Watts as integrated, their experiences as working musicians revealed the deeply segregated nature of daily life in Los Angeles. Through leadership at the local level across the nation, the American

Federation of Musicians (AFM) regulated job opportunities for many musicians. As was the case in most cities, the Los Angeles locals were segregated. The white local controlled all of the opportunities for musicians outside of the small radius of Central Avenue, which headquartered the black local. These two locals did not amalgamate until 1953, indicative of the long contests over what democracy and American musical culture could mean.[19] And while the depth and quality of black male and female jazz artists working and living in Los Angeles before the Second World War were extensive, West Coast jazz is normally linked to the postwar period when white musicians such as Dave Brubeck, Gerry Mulligan, and others were seen as counteracting the effects of bebop and the "aggressiveness" of black musicians on the personality of jazz.[20] Baker draws us into Los Angeles's pre–Cool jazz scene and competing ideas about what constitutes a "real" jazz sound and an ideal jazzman.

The overarching problem for Baker is interpreting white men's attraction to jazz music and exploring its effect on the development of a young man trying to be a musician. What then are the types of gendered identifications jazz enables? Baker implicitly defines whiteness alternately as lack, absence, or sterility, while simultaneously suggesting that blackness enables emotional freedom. Navigating between these images of racialized masculinity proves the most significant problem for Rick's emergence as an artist. The dialectical character of Rick's actions, his desire for a relationship with Smoke, and the narrator's attempts to unearth what that desire signifies must frame our reading of gender in the novel's depiction of jazz culture. The relationship between Smoke and Rick begins with a shared attraction to jazz, and it is in this exploration of their interest in the music that they realize a space for sharing speech and the intimate details of life that friends communicate. Baker suggests that it is Smoke, or black men, who have to initiate and eliminate the boundaries for fraternity, while white men establish its definitions. In other words, Baker's interest in the transgression of racial lines allows for recognition of the sameness of the experiences of "masculinity" for black and white men. Likewise, jazz critics argue that the cultural setting for jazz performance enables an understanding that beneath the appearance of difference, men are motivated by the same desires and needs.

However, for Baker, as I will argue through a discussion of the stages of Rick's coming of age, this promise of masculine fraternity has not yet reached its full maturity. I see three stages Rick must advance through to successfully achieve that "self-determined identity" which Ellison described. First, Rick must come to recognize the commonality of gender which "race" obscures through his developing a friendship with Smoke. Music provides an entrée to that fraternity which allows them both to communicate and to share experiences. Second, having come to appreciate the inherent qualities of the music he has learned to play with Smoke, Rick has to reconcile that appreciation with his experiences in a commercial dance band and the racialization of musical practice he finds there. Third, having to some extent achieved a consciousness of self, Rick finds himself having to deal with a new type of intimacy, that between lovers, with his music. This final stage determines whether or not Rick becomes a man with a horn.

Baker draws us to emerging discourses that race is more a descriptive term than a physiological category. Race becomes nothing more than an "adjective" for those who, by participating in jazz culture, articulate their desire across racial boundaries. Race is still a process, however. Rick alternates between coveting what he sees as Smoke's good life — Smoke has a number of sisters and brothers, his parents are still married and at home — and feeling chagrined that he could desire the family life of a "nigger." A "coon, no getting around that, with a face that shone like a nigger's heel," Smoke was "African by nature, too, slow and easy" (21). Their relationship, however, establishes a closeness that enables Rick to "forg[e]t in no time at all that there was such a word as coon" (31). The two were "without descriptive adjectives, [they were] just two people" (44). They cement the friendship by sharing the experience of their first cigars. By offering Smoke cigars and cigarettes, Rick, the younger of the two by four years, tries to prove his maturity with the person he views as an idol or big brother, and bridge the invisible line between black and white men. When Smoke thanks Rick for the cigar by saying it was "mighty white" of Rick, "Rick let the adjective slide across his consciousness without going deep enough to nick him. . . . The whole thing [their friendship] was easy now" (34). Despite his growing acceptance of racial difference, "the mutuality of sameness" that Robyn Wiegman examines, Rick still fantasizes that he could be the Other. "Though he would have preferred black to white for his own color, still he heard generations of his lily-white kind turning over in their graves to tell him he was crazy" (46).

The more time they spend with one another, the less rigid the color line becomes and the less likely Rick will be able to fit into either the black or white world. Only in the "integrated" world of jazz can Rick feel truly comfortable. Gayle Wald's reading of Mezz Mezzrow's *Really the*

Blues, an autobiography of jazz and racial conversion, argues that "white Negro masculinity" is as much about making the "antihegemonic choice" to identify with the Other as it is about preserving the "racial authority of white masculinity." Further, she questions what it means to be able to choose racial identifications. Preserving the authority of white masculinity reveals the endurance of concepts of racial essentialism, so that even in the depiction of the adoption of black cultural practices, tropes of the black primitive shape its representation.[21] Mezz Mezzrow is not unlike Baker's Rick in that both insist it is possible to stop thinking in terms of race. However, Baker's Rick does not see himself as becoming black physically in the way that Mezzrow does; he imagines himself as figuring out how to play as well as black musicians despite being white. Rick wants a black sound, not a black body.

The problem of defining race resurfaces when it means defining musical styles and not individuals. To be an effective jazz musician, the narrator tells us, one must be a man who has something important to say. Echoing a persistent narrative within jazz criticism and history, Baker offers that "real jazz" is never composed but a spontaneous expression of emotion. This measure of authenticity within jazz draws on tropes about race and primitivity and offers an explanation to the attraction of black musicians to Rick. The narrator admires Rick because of his desire to be "true" to his music, and it is precisely because of this desire that the place of white men within jazz troubles the narrator. The narrator muses, "In the first place maybe he shouldn't have got himself mixed up with negroes. It gave him a funny slant on things and he never got over it. It gave him a feeling for undisciplined expression, a hot, direct approach, a full-throated ease that never did him any final good in his later dealings with those of his race, those whom civilization has whipped into shape, those who can contain themselves and play what's written" (9). Being true to his music places Rick in a bind. How can he use his trumpet to express what he feels without losing the social and cultural discipline of whiteness?

Rick rejects the demands of the commercial white dance orchestra to devote himself to the more emotional and thus potentially more individual sound of "hot" jazz as musical expression. Listening to Jeff Williams's band encourages Rick on this path and the band teaches Rick things he never before understood about race and manhood. To explain the pull of Williams's music, the narrator undertakes a long dissertation about the ephemerally ethnic differences (like those between "chowmeins") characterizing the Memphis and New Orleans jazz styles. The

New Orleans type that Williams's band excels at is, according to the narrator, "like black magic," and because the musicians play "everybody in at the same time," the band develops "psychic responses to each other" (42–44). Although an egalitarian structure, the genre nonetheless proves problematic for the narrator because in embracing this black magic, Rick becomes confused about racial propriety. The narrator rationalizes the contradiction between black "music" and black "men" by suggesting that Rick's unwavering devotion to Smoke, Jeff, and the others causes his inevitable psychological disease. Rick's defenses were weakened not by drugs, seductions, or capitalism (5), but by his interactions with these implicitly primitive folk.

Through Rick, Baker also reveals the objectification of black men within jazz culture and the racial anxiety provoked by that representational process. The desire Rick feels in looking at black men takes him completely by surprise and is an entirely unfamiliar experience. This looking initially emasculates Rick because it suggests that black men elicit sexual desire. For example, after hearing Smoke talk about his friend Jeff Williams, Rick wants to know what he looks like. Rick attributes Smoke's reluctance to describe Jeff to an inability to make Jeff distinguishable from other Negroes to white eyes. In other words, it seems that Smoke cannot articulate racial difference. But Rick realizes his misreading when he finally meets Jeff. That first night Rick can barely restrain himself from gazing at length at Jeff. Jeff's beauty shocks him, and Rick realizes that the reason Smoke hesitated to describe him was that it would mean sexualizing Jeff. Rick then "marked him for later inspection. No need to stare at him like a housewife at a movie actor; not right now at least, full face and in the presence of all" (56–57). This proved the right course of action because he avoided revealing his desire, or questionable manhood, to the band.

Baker also suggests that there is a moment when Rick begins to understand how the limitations of his emotional experience affect his ability to see other people. According to the narrator, Rick "was as intuitive as a woman and spontaneously tactful as few women are" (60). Although she condemns Rick's looking because of the evidence of feminine sensitivity, she implies that the (white) masculine gaze is potentially both feeling and objective because of it. If Rick can translate the emotional acuity he feels at this incoherent stage of thwarted pleasure into his music, he might be the ideal man. However, we have known from the beginning that he has not grown enough to master this work. Rick learns how to interact with other men based on the popular culture of the period. Unfortunately, the clichés of contemporary music teach Rick to conceive of others in sexual terms. The inadequacy of popular song lyrics to express emotion stunts Rick's ability to communicate; they express only the broadest of feelings and are not evidence of what some philosophers call higher-level emotions or his own lived experiences. Rick would not desire a friendship with Smoke if not for his own desire to be a musician. In Smoke, Rick recognizes both his "Negro" and his white selves. His relationship with Smoke requires that he grapple with his emotions and longings, that he recognize that the music he desires to play is generated by his lived experiences, however troubling a prospect that may seem.

The demands of family and real life continually distract Smoke from pursuing his art and prove the vital distinction between him and Rick. Often out of work and responsible for contributing to the family's livelihood when working, Smoke cannot save enough money to purchase another drum set. More tragically, he is not self-motivated. Smoke has the talent but not the desire necessary to make himself a success, and some attribute his stalled career to his lack of maturity. Jeff Williams, a hero to both Smoke and Rick, admitted to Rick, "I sure do wish something would get him jarred loose. Everytime I hear him play it gets me sort of sore he won't do anything about it. Seem like he won't grow up and get onto himself" (65). Smoke's big chance comes with the death of Ward, the drummer in Jeff Williams's band. Jeff wants him to join the band, but Smoke is reluctant and conflicted about taking Ward's place. Smoke's lack of initiative frustrates Rick to no end because all Rick can think about is performing. After exploding at Smoke, telling him that he is blowing his chance, Rick realizes that Smoke is grieving and needs comfort rather than anger. When he attempts to confront Smoke about his lack of initiative, Rick finds himself completely confused. "All I meant was you're a good man on drums and now Jeff needs one, and you're really good. Why I said it is I like you better than anybody. Damn it, honey, don't cry anymore or I'll have to too. I'm sorry I said it and I didn't mean it." Comforting Smoke was his first time engaging "tenderness directly." The narrator tells us that it worked well enough so that one was "reassured and the other exculpated and neither one embarrassed, although the one had certainly wept like a nervous woman and the other had fallen into the wrong terminology" (81–82). Emotional vulnerability and range are not part of Rick's experience and this lack will ultimately affect his ability to express his individuality as a man and performer, a hallmark of what emerging discourses view as jazz musicianship and personality.

Although Rick finds an ideal job with a chair in a white dance orchestra, his ideas about music and discipline were learned from his former bandmates and thus make him an unsuitable member of the orchestra. "The fascination of making music was on him like a leech," (72) enabling him to "strike into the deep levels of a[n instrument's] subconscious" (117). Rick is often anxious around the men in the orchestra because his ideas about music conflict with theirs. Rick's assertiveness when discussing musicians he enjoys impresses the other band members because of the connoisseurship his pronouncements reveal. The quality of his performance leads to some discussion of "blackness" and jazz. He blushes when, after listening to him play, the collegiate bandleader Jack Stuart offers faint praise of his playing before Rick and the rest of the band. Jack says, "You certainly play whorehouse piano, fella, and nigger whorehouse at that" (117). When a trombonist offers that white and black bands are to be considered in separate categories, Rick finds the argument intriguing. "That's a funny thing. You'd think any white man could learn to play as well as a negro. Well, I think a white man could do it, all right, if he'd only try hard enough to. But these negroes don't even seem to have to try; they're just born that way" (119).

The orchestra sees music as a means to make money, meet women, and entertain, not as a vocation or obsession. Rick's experiences with the band (recounted in book 3 of the novel) bring into relief the questions about racialization, commercialization, and jazz that I alluded to earlier as an important point in the coming-of-age tale. There were no regular rehearsals for the band the first week before their stint at the beachside resort. Instead of promoting a professional attitude toward their gig, Jack, "straw boss over ten musicians" (124), "was first of all a collegian, and with him the going was always easy. And that first week was more like a fraternity house-party, stag and unfettered, than anything else" (122), leaving them all with sunburns. As opening night approaches, Jack establishes the rules: they are a dance band, playing tunes in such a way that the fraternity and sorority crowd could learn the Charleston first and foremost. The band was "playing to our own kind of a crowd, and we won't be playing one steps for a bunch of snaky Jews and department-store girls" (125). When the question arose of whether they were to play the arrangements as written, Jack stood firm.

His was not "a coon band" and he did not want it to sound like one: improvisation would not be tolerated. Until Rick told him that Art Hazard was a black musician, Jack believed his favorite trumpeter was white. Shattered to learn this, the narrator explains, "Jack seemed mixed up. He was beginning to feel the gin. 'You mean to tell me a white man would play in a coon band?. . . . You mean Art Hazard isn't a white man?' Jack said, his jaw way down" (131).

The white musicians see Rick as black because his musical style identifies him as such, and the power of the "black" makes it extremely difficult for him to be treated white. As the summer progresses, most of the boys in the band begin dating different girls at the resort. Consequently, a new arrangement takes place where a smaller group of like-minded (hot jazz–oriented) musicians, led by Rick, take over, while the other musicians dance with their dates. In the process, Rick's sound proves to be a popular draw. Jack's jealousy begins to grow. When given the chance to get rid of Rick and save face, Jack seizes it. A national orchestra leader, Lee Valentine, comes to hear Stuart's band — not, as Jack believes, because he's heard great things about it, but because he needs a new trumpeter and Rick's friend Jeff Williams recommended him highly. Although Jack could not see it, Rick immediately recognized that "in the eyes of Lee Valentine (Jeff Williams was) a musician, not a negro. Valentine could be free of the fraternity boy standards of Jack Stuart" (151). That first evening, Jack and Lee have a talk, and the next day Rick finds himself a member of Valentine's band. The narrator explains, "It had been a cash deal the night before; Jack had released his part of Rick for four-hundred and seventy-five dollars in currency. The roll was in his pocket. Rick was sold whether he knew it or not. He had become, overnight, the property of Lee Valentine" (155). Would Jack have "sold" his share in Rick had Rick not produced such a hot and popular sound? Perhaps, but Baker implies that it would not have been the case since he is bought by the one man familiar with the Negro sound and able to appreciate its potential financial rewards.

The very instability of the narrator's presence (the writing alternates between the narrator's point of view and the third person) suggests Baker's own difficulties in articulating the differences between the races and the impact of race on the music. Toni Morrison's discussion of the white literary imagination sheds light on Baker's difficulties. Morrison argues that white writers' fabrication of "an Africanist persona" provokes an "extraordinary" and "powerful exploration of th[eir] fears and desires" as well as a "revelation of longing, of terror, of perplexity, of shame, of magnanimity." Particularly telling is how much the American national character is defined "through and within a sometimes allegorical, sometimes metaphorical, but always choked representation of an Africanist presence."[22] Because the narrator connects Rick's demise to the influence of the Negroes with whom he associated, we are led to conclude that the very idea of interracial contact is psychologically compromising and terrifying. The narrator's perspective suggests that the taboo of intimate interracial contact presents the most vexing issue for participants within jazz culture. The narrator's ambivalence about the contact originates in her ambivalence about the social context which Rick turns away from and which, as we will see, Amy (his future wife) runs toward. "Civilization" in this novel concerns the disciplining of one's personality. The narrator's inability to support completely Rick's or Amy's choices results in the conflicted representation of those choices in images of dread, fear, and contagion.

The introduction of love seems to imply a mature self, a pursuit of a self-determined identity. This new intimacy between lovers seems capable of superseding the intimacy of his male friends. Rick once wondered when he would meet a girl capable of provoking complicated things like the stars above the Pacific on a black night, showing a "cool brilliance." With Rick's love interest, Amy North, Baker attempts to alleviate the intellectual and biological danger jazz presents. Amy's presence suggests an avenue Rick can travel out of the jazz subculture back to the proper white social world in which differences between the races are rigidly maintained. Intimate interracial contact is taboo, and jazz and psychoanalysis are its substitutes.[23] Sharing with Rick the formative history of a troubled home life, Amy grapples with her own ambivalence and anger toward her father's ineptitude as a physician and her mother's subsequent suicide. Desiring some way to channel the isolation and intellectual curiosity that consume her, she turns at last to medicine and psychoanalysis, a profession that reveals to her both scientific and imaginative truths. She tells Rick "that thought is what matters, or thinking, the mind in any event, is what matters. The world is in men's minds" (183). After recounting her disappointing experience of having fifty-nine poems rejected by a small journal, she came to realize that it was a "good thing, too, a very most fortunate thing to have happened because you don't find out anything about what's true by lolling around in a girls' school writing what you think might be. You find it by going to disordered minds, looking deep into them" (184–85). The disordered mind is positively beautiful and astonishing, according to Amy, and it is not be found in the sphere that so intrigues Rick, the black primitive. Amy rejects the black primitive, here characterized in the figure of Smoke's blues-singing sister, Josephine, for what she finds to be the infinitely more compelling paradox of a white primitive (187, 189). She takes Rick on as an analytical project, decides to marry him, and later moves on when, apparently, she "reforms." Like those who went slumming in Harlem nightclubs, Amy desires and rejects the self-esteem Rick has apparently discovered in his trumpet. The narrator explains, "The truth probably was that she married Rick because she would have given her eyes to have what he had, to have one firm ability and along with it the intimate, secure knowledge that it was worth something. She may have thought (she had her mystical side) that by marrying him she could share this depth with him, like sharing his name" (191–92).

Although Amy functions in the novel to resolve some of the unconscious dread around interracial contact, she ultimately fails in this role. She has the accoutrements of civilization — education, reproductions of French moderns, a piano — but she does not have an autonomous identity. Her problem, one that she is well aware of, is that she has no individual voice. She looks constantly for substitutes — poetry, art, medicine, alcohol, Rick — and continually fails to find meaning in herself. Rick's infatuation with her blinds him to her emptiness until one evening when she plays the one piece that she knows, Debussy's *Clair de Lune*, on the piano seven times impeccably, "her shoulders naked and white, . . . her face tense above the music." Rick is immediately struck by a new awareness of her — she reveals herself to be the "sublime grotesque" (193). The evening she eagerly asks him, after an extended estrangement, to invite Smoke, Josephine, and Jeff over after his gig to play for her new friends underscores his new understanding (195, 201). When Rick sees these new friends, who view jazz as little more than an amusement, he has a moment of clarity, he feels unburdened, and "free of Amy after all the poison she fed him" (202). He rejects her dilettantism, elitism, and voyeurism. Finally, he understands that she saw him as little more than a curiosity. Amy subsequently disappears from the text. Her departure suggests the impotence of whiteness and heterosexuality for rescuing Rick from the influence of black men.

To give meaning to her experience of the music, Baker probes the question of racial transgressions. Although seeming to desire to represent integration, her elegiac ultimately maintains racial boundaries. Rick longs for that emotional vulnerability (or freedom) that makes his black friends real musicians. Once Rick, a sometime Negro, leaves the black world of Central Avenue, all his troubles begin. As he does not have a life outside of music, he finds himself unable to cope with the exigencies of the "real world." Technically able, Rick is emotionally stunted; he cannot turn his experience into music. As soon as he joins the white world of dance music, he begins his descent into hell. Amy drives him to drink, his black friends achieve fame and fortune while he ends up penniless, and his music is emotionless. There is no happy ending for a man who wishes to abandon his racial heritage — he cannot succeed in a white world or be fully comfortable in a black one. So, how does the white primitive of the Jazz Age find new life in the 1950s?

Jazz history, or more precisely jazz hagiography,[24] owes its life to the artist's profile, the primary mode by which the pantheon of the jazz canon is constructed and the qualities of the art and the musician explicated. Although most who have undertaken the writing of jazz history did not see themselves as substituting the sanctification of musicians for the writing of their biographies, the effect has been the same. While the merits of artists included in the canon are debated unceasingly (the nature of the fan's and often the historian's project), slight critical attention is paid to the way in which the profile contributes to the gendering and racialization of discourses about jazz culture. The language of 1950s hagiography, in particular, posits "jazz" as the resolution of contemporary crises in white masculinity and evidence of interracial cooperation. The metalanguage of race functions through hagiography to mark jazz culture as a man's world and to abrogate differences between men. Evelyn Brooks Higginbotham argues that race has a totalizing effect which "precludes recognition and acknowledgement of intra-group social relations as relations of power."[25] The inescapable tensions around any foregrounding of "race" within jazz culture suggest this totalizing effect. Because the desire for hagiography is so compulsive for jazz experts, "uninformed" representations are always conflicting with "real" experience. As a result, writers find themselves fighting over what are the most accurate or truthful presentations of jazz musicians. In the process, they fail to acknowledge how gender informs those models. Exclusion of women is certainly a critical point to examine in their debates, but just as profound is the negotiation of the feminine within constructions of masculinity and manhood in jazz. In a period when "race" dominates the social and political discourse, the problem of the "feminine" becomes even more interesting.

The highly disciplined art of jazz, practiced by black men revered for their ability to be simultaneously emotional and masculine, beckoned to those who hoped to flee the psychological pressures of life in postwar America.[26] This understanding of jazz marked a subtle shift from 1920s constructions of black people and jazz as a primitive source of revitalizing truth and emotional freedom. With the increasing prominence of jazz as an art, jazz was less an escape to the primitive than a return to "civilization," where the dichotomies of emotion and reason, nature and culture coexisted. All the contradictions about masculinity seemed resolvable in Cold War jazz culture — one could be patriarchal and egalitarian, one could feel and be stoic, one could be disciplined and abandoned.

Down Beat's contributor Ralph J. Gleason found editing his collection *Jam Session* (1958) edifying on two levels. It allowed him a chance to track the development of jazz criticism and reportage in the United States, and it enabled him to collect the most insightful pieces of that literature into an accessible format. His introduction makes clear that jazz had a history and that it required a canon. His title alludes to a *lieu de mémoire* — the jam session — to evoke "the golden age, time past," in which the myths and practices of jazz become history.[27] Gleason had decided he would not duplicate any material from two recently published anthologies in his own. The exceptions were essays by Otis Ferguson and George Frazier, each about white musicians.[28] The Ferguson essays are classic models of impressionistic writing about jazz, while the Frazier piece illustrates attempts at realistic portrayals of the "jazz personality." Ferguson's "Young Man with a Horn" painted a portrait of a young white coronetist named Bix Beiderbecke. According to Gleason, this essay, originally published in 1936, "brought jazz out from behind the iron curtain of prejudice and ignorance. This was an important piece, one that attracted the attention of many and was of great aid in spreading the gospel of jazz through the world of arts and letters where Ferguson was so widely read." Gleason's celebratory tone openly addresses the centrality of ideals of integration and exceptionalism to discourses about jazz in the Cold War United States. Dying in the Second World War secured Ferguson's prominence as the martyred proselytizer for jazz and its progressive racial politics. Jazz, a metaphoric gauge of the nation's health and racial politics at any given moment, serves also as a bulwark against the nation's disease and disintegration.[29]

In the process of rereading his scrapbooks and hunting through secondhand magazine stores and libraries, Gleason reassessed the quality of the writing as well as the power of memory. Gleason's interest in jazz developed after being struck by measles and, consequently, confined to his bed where the only amusement available during his convalescence was a radio from which the strains of black big bands captured his attention. Turning from his own memories as laying the groundwork for a career as a critic, his new insight into "race" enabled him to see how the work he once revered as brilliant appeared "as a whole, . . . corny now, maybe even Jim Crow, at the least somewhat out of focus."[30] Despite the trace of racism, he still felt there to be some merit to pieces once revered. Gleason implies that as his ideas about race, characterized in this instance as knowledge of "Jim Crow," became more sophisticated or complex, his understanding of jazz culture changed accordingly. The combination of experiences — memory of sickness, development of a career, and awakening of racial consciousness — suggests that the sites of analysis and debate about what jazz signifies find their conceptual roots in the desire to retrieve one's own past in the context of creating a historical memory. Additionally, we see that the problem plaguing the long history of legitimizing and professionalizing jazz as an art is the inevitable question of race both as an interpretive framework and as a fact of experience.[31]

Michael Curtiz, prolific director of femme fatales, charming beauties, and tough guys for Warner Bros., released his version of Dorothy Baker's novel in 1950. Although the range of Curtiz's work, including the award-winning films *Casablanca* (1942) and *Mildred Pierce* (1945), suggested his facility with different types of subject matter, jazz critics found he resorted to the clichés of melodrama rather than the unfolding of authentic experience in his exposition of a musician's coming of age. A single viewing of the film testifies to its concern with adhering to the genre characteristics of melodrama,[32] in this case, with redeeming an alcoholic rather than satisfying the concerns of hagiographers. While the film explores the same coming-of-age story that Baker published in 1938, it situates the protagonist within contemporary discourses of race and masculinity. Whereas Baker grappled with the influence of blackness on the psyche of a white man, the film examines the cohesiveness of the family structure. The narrative centers on the problem of fitting the "individual" into the collective, represented by the role of the soloist in the dance orchestra. The distinction between the two concepts of beset white masculinity illustrates different ways of thinking about jazz. As in the 1920s when "jazz" seemed a catchall for debates about the changing dynamics of postwar American life, so bebop has come to represent an ideological site for debating the meaning of jazz's promise of integration and democracy in the post–Second World War United States. The central critical narrative of "bebop" is that it ruptured the democratic culture of swing by reverting to race to measure authenticity and avant-garde potential. These cultural and historical shifts in jazz performance and social conditions were again seen as emblematic and also prophetic of the nation's political climate. Thus, Ralph Gleason could argue, "when that integrated jazz world fell apart, it foreshadowed the end of the civil rights movement as it has been structured, and both races fell away into a deeper exploration of their own inherent urges and drives."[33] For many critics, cool jazz served as a representational foil for the increasingly dominant images of separatist and racial divisions among jazzmen. Despite its seeming achievement of merging feeling with discipline, cool jazz did not create a new representational future for jazz. The bebop/cool jazz debates did reveal the racial dynamics within jazz culture and allow for a coherent ideological site on which to define and challenge prevailing assumptions about jazz and the social world in which it operated.

In fact, for the film to give new meaning to the role of white musicians within jazz culture, it is imperative that Rick Martin find a space in an orchestra. For Rick, as a protagonist in a 1950s melodrama, the solution to problems resides in the reestablishment of a cohesive and functioning unit which he, as the male hero, can dominate. Rick finds his peace once he realizes that his music cannot solely sustain him. Because of an ill-fated romance and marriage, Rick loses his innocence, becoming an alcoholic and thus nearly destroying what might have been his best hope at a real life. The band is his only family, a point established early in the film when we learn that orphaned and neglected by his sister, his guardian, Rick finds nurturing relationships with a group of black musicians who play Dixie in a back-alley nightclub in Los Angeles. The visual images which the film employs to mark Rick's search for a family life parallel one another. Rick grows up lonely and without anything to occupy his time. His sister is uninterested in him and the last time that we see her is the evening she leaves with her date, telling Rick that he has to either go back to school or get a job. Despondent, Rick leaves her apartment by the fire escape and walks through the neighborhood, kicking a can, until he comes to the mission where indigent men gather for meals, warmth, and ministering. Peering into the window, Rick is entranced by the sound of the piano played during the sermon. He walks in and sits in a pew, tapping out the melody on his legs. Here, we begin to see Rick's face brighten at last, the first time in the movie when the lighting does not cast a shadow on him. Each night, he returns and after everyone leaves he teaches himself to play the piano. He stays until a bum rises up from a pew to tell him to quit banging on that piano.

For a couple more scenes, we see Rick out and about in the city, visiting a pawnshop to pick out a trumpet, working in a bowling alley resetting pins to pay for the horn. We do not see him return to his sister's apartment, but the image of returning home is recalled on the evening he ascends the ladder outside Club Dixie to peer into the window and watch Art Hazard and his Dixie Pickers play. Through the smoke and haze of the club, we see Hazard spy the young boy, curious about what he is doing there. When the dancers leave and the band continues to jam, Rick loses his footing and drops to the ground at the same time that the nightclub door swings open. Hazard greets Rick and welcomes him into the club to join them. The film repeats the image of Rick and the fire escape in this latter scene to underscore Rick's desire for a place to belong and be welcome. As Hazard welcomes him, introducing the band, offering him food, asking him what he would like to hear them play, Rick is treated as an equal, as someone whose company is desired. He is also treated as a member of a family, treatment he never received at home.

When asked if his parents would miss him at this late hour, Rick responds, "I don't have any real folks . . . ," and from then on, Hazard takes on the role of confidant and teacher. From him, Rick learns how to play the trumpet he is able eventually to buy with Hazard's help. They return together to the pawnshop where Hazard gives his approval of the instrument Rick has chosen and splits the cost with him. Outside the shop, Rick offers him a cigar, thereby sealing their friendship and celebrating a new beginning. The next several scenes show Hazard teaching Rick to play and we see his pride as Rick's natural talent blossoms. As Rick grows older, however, we sense, from the worried look on Hazard's face, that he is devoting too much time to the horn. One evening Hazard visits Rick in his room, bare of most everything except a bed, phonograph, records, and his trumpet. Here, we sense Rick's continuing loneliness, something which he is himself able to ignore by devoting himself to learning his music. Despite his surrogate father's admonitions that he would be better off with "wife, kids, money in the bank" instead of a jazz career, Rick decides he must keep trying. Rick has little choice, it seems, as the voice-over notes a bit earlier: "He was cut out to be a jazzman the way the righteous are cut out for the church."

Although the film is narratively uninterested in considering jazz as an integrated culture, it is concerned with how to regulate the black sound of jazz. Swing seemed to proffer a solution but it proved illusory under the "aggressiveness" of bebop and the aesthetic shifts that it precipitated within jazz. Tortured by its own ambiguity over what "jazz" is, the film must, as Krin Gabbard argues, kill the black father.[34] From Archie Mayo's 1944 film *Sweet and Lowdown*, to Warren Leight's 1996 stage play *Side Man*, the enduring trope of family to anchor 1950s jazz masculinity both in terms of respectability and artistry remains constant despite the fact that melodrama prohibits the representation of men capable of the intimacy which family demands. Rather, in turning what was a novel about interracial relationships into a film about sexual relationships among white people, the film redirects Baker's interest in male identity and homosociality into a story about maintaining the family structure, a site of order and control during the postwar period. If white Americans were discontented with civilized life in the 1920s, by the 1950s, the potential absence of civilization (threat of the bomb) makes it a much more desirable condition. The film has less of an "anti-jazz" project than an "anti-bebop" project. Released during the waning of debates about bebop and its impact on jazz, the film poses the question of how musical passion might be directed or channeled in such a way as not to consume or emasculate the musician. The film covertly and perhaps unwittingly suggests that black musicians are emasculated by the entrenched racism of contemporary society, that black musicians will never achieve the greatness that others such as Rick Martin will. Unlike earlier attempts by white men to "refine" jazz, as with Paul Whiteman's efforts to make jazz a lady,[35] Rick discovers how to bring the sweet and hot sounds of jazz in concert. He masculinizes jazz.

Race is integral to understanding stories about jazz. While still a story about the gap between "man's musical ability" and the "demands of expression" in this life, the film demonstrates the way in which ideas about race and jazz are reconstructed for a 1950s audience. The most significant shift was making a novel about the nature of race relations within jazz culture into a movie about individuality. Hoagy Carmichael is the only "real" musician playing a musician in this fiction film, a role which some would say enables the film to suggest a pseudodocumentary feel. He is, as jazz film scholar Krin Gabbard describes it, "curiously diegetic and extradiegetic." Hoagy Carmichael's character Smoke functions to raise the question of homoeroticism and intimacy in the band. There are two love triangles in the film, the first implicit among Jo, the singer, Smoke, and Rick and the second, much more explicit among Jo, Rick, and Jo's friend Amy. This latter triangle defuses the ever-present threat that Smoke represents to notions about masculinity and respectability. Beside Jo, Smoke is the only person who really understands what Rick is talking about, what Rick ultimately desires. Jo tells Rick to find a hobby, a domestic interest. She understands his desires as a musician since she makes her living as a singer, but only so much. She is, after all, the proper love choice concerned with family. Smoke encourages Rick in his jazz quest. The film establishes Smoke's position as sexual threat and "uncivilizing" influence in a number of scenes.

Rick's first major job is with Jack Chandler's dance orchestra. Although Chandler warned the musicians that they were not to play any "blues or lowdown jive," just strictly dance music, Rick winds up doing just that out of boredom with the stock arrangements. Whereas Baker's novel explains clearly that Chandler thinks of the "blues or lowdown jive" as "whorehouse, nigger music," the film interprets jazz as a site for sexual and masculine rivalry. After a set, Chandler leaves Smoke in charge of the band as he rushes off to confront Jo for being distant since the arrival of Rick. Back on stage, Rick encourages Smoke to form a smaller sympathetic group to play "our type of music." The sympathy is defined not just in the type of music they like to play, but in the camaraderie they feel with one another. The musicians in this smaller band, like the musicians playing with Hazard, look at each other, smile, and encourage one another by nodding their heads. They are grouped around the piano, their bodies relaxed and moving to the rhythm. This behavior is in sharp contrast to the dance orchestra as a whole where everyone sits rigid in their respective rows, eyes fixed upon Chandler's baton.

Predictably, Chandler fires Rick immediately. Rick threatens him both sexually and musically, despite Rick's reluctance either to take his place with Jo or to lead the band. Later that evening, Rick leaves town with Smoke by his side. The triangle of Jo, Smoke, and Rick is established in the scene where Jo tries to persuade Rick to ask for his job back. She had spoken to Chandler about it and thought he would take him back. Rick declines and she leaves. The competition between Jo and Smoke is made evident when, outside of Rick's room, we see Smoke watching Rick's door, hiding from Jo. He sees her crying as she runs down the stairs. Sensing his chance, Smoke moves out of the shadows to wait with his suitcase in hand. Smoke's plan is transparent, as we see from the smile playing about Rick's face. The next few scenes depict

Rick and Smoke together, playing for a dance show, driving across country in a convertible singing a duet about an eroticized male, "loving Sam, the Sheik of Alabam."[36] A fight in a bar on Christmas Eve with some gangsters leads the two to part ways, depicted in a tearful goodbye at the train station. Smoke wants Rick to come home with him, but Rick declines, eager to pursue his artistic vision without further dallying. The cliché of ill-fated love and the primacy of family is played out. The train pulls out with Smoke between the cars staring back after Rick, who returns his gaze. Smoke will eventually return, but only because he has the chance to be in a band with Rick again, to renew their covert family life. Toward the end of the movie, just at the beginning of Rick's mental and physical breakdown, we see him turn away from the intimacy he has shared with Smoke in these travels. Earlier that day, Rick learned that Art Hazard died after being run down by a car. Rick went to his job performing with the Phil Morrison dance orchestra, and flubbed during the set. After the set and back in the locker room, we are treated to a little beefcake, surely a way to take the edge off the gaze which Smoke directs toward Martin. Smoke, who was also playing with Morrison thanks to Rick's intervention, suggests it might not be too late for Rick to make up with Phil after their blowup. Rick says no, he has had it; music is not a business for him. Smoke asks if he can come along and Rick again says no; he advises Smoke to keep his good job and die rich.

Young Man with a Horn was early in the careers of Kirk Douglas, Doris Day, and Lauren Bacall (see figure 15.1). Most shots of Doris Day put her in a soft glow, framing her blonde hair and all-American beauty. Like her singing, Jo is sweet and her voice revealingly clear. She contrasts dramatically with the darkness and mystery of Lauren Bacall's Amy North, who is studying to be a psychiatrist. Jo is desexualized when she transitions from black to white in the film. In Baker's novel, Jo and Smoke are siblings. Jo is characterized as a blues singer, connoting sexual looseness and aberrance. In the film's "purification" of Jo, "jazz" is cleansed of its connection to the sexual underworld and repositioned in a wholesome social world. It is Jo's maternal instinct and nurturing inclinations that aid Rick in his return from the brink of death. With Jo, Rick finally realizes his goal of making sense while he plays. Her talents and desires are nonthreatening. The band is family. Although there are hints of sexual tension between Jo and Rick when they first meet, that tension is never resolved on screen. We know that Jo recognizes her first rival in his trumpet. In fact, she warns Rick that their marriage is a

Fig. 15.1. Doris Day, Kirk Douglas, and Lauren Bacall in *Young Man with a Horn*. Warner Brothers, 1950. Photofest.

dangerous one when they talk about music and other mature interests and hobbies. The second rival, Amy North, just seems to sneak up on her. She acknowledges Amy's position. Smoke has come to town to work and to rejoin his friend. They commiserate with one another about losing Rick.

Amy North's character is central to the film achieving its ends for two reasons. The film is a melodrama about a young jazz musician's rise and fall; it is also a male-oriented account of a social problem—alcoholism. Amy North's role as the femme fatale brings darkness and mystery into Martin's innocent world. Her sexuality and independence are seductive and dangerous. As Jo warns Rick, albeit too late, Amy will hurt him. The pain affects his music, which he thought separate from his daily life. Amy's presence also articulates the debate about the role of jazz in defining American cultural practices. When first meeting Rick, Amy admitted that she did not care for jazz. She had not come to Galba's to listen to the musicians but to study the faces of the people caught by that unnamed "something about jazz that releases inhibitions, a sort of cheap mass-produced narcotic." Furthermore, she was not impressed by cultural arguments made for it. "Oh I know it's supposed to be our native art, cotton field, the levees, old New Orleans and blues in the night." In this scene, the three are physically positioned in a triangle around the table, both Jo's and Rick's attention focused on Amy, who does most of the speaking. She continues to speak, but is cut off as the owner Galba comes over to ask Jo to sing a song. As Jo sings, her old friend Amy observes with contempt, a shadow cast over her mouth, that Jo is "so simple and uncomplicated, so terribly normal." Rick falls in love with the complicated Amy, and their problematic relationship plays itself out.

Whereas in the novel Rick winds up disgusted and horrified by Amy, in the film, he pities her, and this moment marks his coming of age. As in the novel, Amy has a party for her society friends at which she hopes to parade Rick, as their entertainment, a thing to be observed. He walks in one evening to find her playing *Clair de Lune*. Her back to him, she does not see how he shakes his head. When they talk, she tells him about the party, tells him it is to celebrate her "glorious failure" at medical school. Because of his friend Art Hazard's funeral, he arrives after the party is over. He moves from pity to anger when he sees how little she really cared for him. They fight and he leaves, the marriage over, his confidence shattered, feeling once again alone. The collapse of family brought about by Hazard's death and Amy's betrayal causes Rick to turn to alcohol.

The film taps into the strategy of jazz biopics to propel the second half of the narrative. Jazz biopics often depend upon the same domestic arrangements endorsed by 1950s melodramas. They also depend upon the realization of an individual's voice within a group. For melodramas from *The Glenn Miller Story* to *Gene Krupa*, the musician ideally finds his fulfillment not in the music but in the power of a wife who encourages and challenges him because she believes in him. Glenn Miller tells Helen that she has to hurry to New York to marry him because he cannot wait any longer. Once she arrives, his career begins in earnest — she pushes him to return to his Schillinger studies in composition; she saves the money that bankrolls his first foray as a bandleader; and lastly, she serves as his muse. From that point on, Miller's success is assured even after his disappearance during the Second World War. Throughout *Young Man with a Horn*, we are aware of a similar process of domestication. Rick's preference for "that mumbo jumbo jazz" clouds his judgment and portends his downfall, but Rick is redeemed because he seems able eventually to choose the "right" woman. Leaning on Jo during his recovery from pneumonia and alcoholism insures his future as a musician. The failure of the domestic experiment with Amy suggests that the only place in which a man can thrive musically and sexually is in the band with people who know and feel what he is trying to say. Both life and work entail domestic compromise. *Young Man with a Horn* concludes ambiguously, suggesting a happy ending but leaving us nevertheless uncertain about Rick's future. Does he wind up with the girl? Can he make the dance band profitable while playing his music? In the final scene, as Rick joins Jo at her recording session, the other musicians look on encouragingly. For the moment, jazz is domesticated, the white musician is linked with the maternal mate, and Smoke, the representative of aberrant sexuality, is infantilized, the adopted child of a patriarchal white universe.

CODA

In 1991 Spike Lee released his film *Mo' Better Blues* about black jazz musicians, claiming that he would tell the story of jazz differently. In some very important ways, he does. It is no accident that the nightclub around which most of the story takes place is named "Beneath the Underdog." Lee thus calls to mind Charles Mingus's autobiography and his criticism of the competing financial and artistic interests of musicians and those controlling performance venues and recording opportunities.[37] By centering his story within a black jazz world, Lee also allows a space in which the different perspectives of black (male) musicians can be articulated. Although the debate about whether jazz is "black" animates the movie, different ideas about what constitutes that blackness are circulated both narratively and visually. *Mo' Better Blues* has the potential for exploring how jazz musicians relate to one another in the homosocial context of jazz.

Heterosexuality is so overdetermined in the film, however, that there are only the merest glimpses of what masculine fraternity might mean. As a result, like the film version of *Young Man with a Horn*, *Mo' Better Blues* ends up a male melodrama. Lee's story resolves itself within a domestic scene. The domestic arrangements reestablish patriarchy, the sublimation of women's desires and voices, and the othering of competing masculinities. *Young Man with a Horn* envisions the band as a domestic site that allows for the presence of a viable white masculinity that embraces, albeit subtly and covertly, both the feminine and the homo-erotic. *Mo' Better Blues* also constructs the band as a domestic world, but because its presence is limited to the site of the nightclub and not the family, it is nonproductive. In the end, Bleek's sexual and musical rival/friend, Shadow Henderson, establishes his own band in which *he allows* his girlfriend, Clarke Bentancourt, a place to sing. Throughout the movie, Henderson has advocated playing what the people want to hear and not what he necessarily wants to play. While Henderson achieves fame and fortune, Bleek achieves inner peace and a new resolve about the place of music in his life. He marries and fathers a child. In this way, Lee suggests that jazz culture is emasculating because the real jazz musician finds his "important thing to say" in the home and the fathering of a son. He also implies that black men can only define themselves as sexual rivals. In moments when a creative approach to the nature of fraternity can be offered, the narrative retreats to either sexual gamesmanship or physical brutality. Lee offers us the potential for exploring masculine fraternity, however, in that he tells a story about musicians trying to figure out the meaning of who and what is a black jazzman. What is needed is to contemplate new ways of telling stories about race, masculinity, and jazz that exist on a continuum of homosocial relations.

NOTES

1. Ralph Ellison, "Golden Age, Time Past," *Living with Music* (New York: Modern Library, 2000), 60–61.

2. See Scott 1988, 773–97.

3. Dorothy Baker, *Young Man with a Horn* (New York: Houghton Mifflin, 1938).

4. Ralph Berton, *Remembering Bix: A Memoir of the Jazz Age* (New York: Harper and Row, 1974), 405; Nina Baym, "Melodramas of Beset Manhood: How Theories of American Fiction Exclude Women Authors," *American Quarterly* 33, no. 2 (summer 1981): 123–39.

5. Barry Ulanov writes, "By 1938, when Dorothy Baker's highly fictionalized and best-selling life of Bix, *Young Man with a Horn*, was published, he had taken on some of the qualities of a minor god, and to many musicians he was and still is jazz incarnate . . . To see (musicians and fans) sit around a phonograph and listen to beat-up copies of old Paul Whiteman records on which Bix plays, or to some of Bix's own records in even worse condition, is to watch men transfixed." Ulanov 1952, 128. For example, Richard Sudhalter's *Lost Chords* (New York: Oxford University Press, 1999) attempts to reintegrate

white musicians into the jazz canon, which he argues has been done a disservice by critics who insist upon centering jazz within African American cultural history and, consequently, become theoretically dependent on a faulty blues-based premise to explain the music.

6. George T. Simon in *Metronome*, February 1950, 15.

7. Otis Ferguson, "Young Man with a Horn," in Ralph J. Gleason, *Jam Session: An Anthology of Jazz* (New York: Putnam, 1958), 48.

8. For an ethnomusicological approach to this see Monson 1996.

9. See also Wald 1997.

10. I use the term "Negroes" as it comes up in Baker's novel and is appropriate historical usage. Otherwise, when making my own commentary, I use either "blacks" or "African Americans."

11. See Stowe 1994; Stanley Crouch, "Blues to Be Constitutional: A Long Look at the Wild Wherefores of Our Democratic Lives as Symbolized in the Making of Rhythm and Tune," in O'Meally 1998.

12. For example, David Levering Lewis, *When Harlem Was in Vogue* (New York: Knopf), and Ann Douglas, *Terrible Honesty: Mongrel Manhattan in the 1920s* (New York: Farrar, Straus and Giroux, 1995). Douglas argues that "white consciousness of the Negro's rights and gifts (however severe the limitations of that consciousness) and black confidence that Negroes could use white models and channels of power to achieve their own ends (however mistaken time would prove that confidence to be) reached a peak of intensity in the 1920s never seen in American history before or since" (5). If, as she suggests, Freud's writing in the 1910s, 1920s, and 1930s was to advocate atheism, then jazz completely fails with its obsessive cultish desires.

13. Ogren 1989; Lawrence W. Levine, "Jazz and American Culture," in O'Meally 1998. See also Neil Leonard, *Jazz and the White Americans: The Acceptance of a New Art Form* (Chicago: University of Chicago Press, 1962). "At the heart of the jazz musician's behavior (in the twenties) was an absorption in esthetic experience which made the new music their main source of happiness and morality" (60).

14. Penny Von Eschen, *Race against Empire* (New York: Cornell University Press, 1997); Brenda Gayle Plummer, *Rising Wind: Black Americans and U.S. Foreign Affairs, 1935–1960* (Chapel Hill: University of North Carolina Press, 1996); Barbara Savage, *Broadcasting Freedom: Radio, War, and the Politics of Race, 1938–1948* (Chapel Hill: University of North Carolina Press, 1999); Ted Vincent, *Keep Cool: The Black Activists Who Built the Jazz Age* (London: Pluto, 1995).

15. Ogren 1989, 7. See also Paul Allen Anderson, *Deep River: Music and Memory in Harlem Renaissance Thought* (Durham: Duke University Press, 2001), for extended discussion of black thought about music, the dynamics of black life, and national identity in the interwar years.

16. Daniel Gregory Mason, "The Jazz Invasion," *Behold America!* ed. Samuel D. Schmalhausen (New York: Farrar and Rinehart, 1931), 499. See also Macdonald Smith Moore, *Yankee Blues: Musical Culture and American Identity* (Bloomington: Indiana University Press, 1985).

17. See Ron Welburn, "American Jazz Criticism, 1914–1940" (Ph.D. diss., New York University, 1993); John Gennari, "Jazz Criticism: Its Development and Ideologies," *Black American Literature Forum* 25 (fall 1991): 449–523; DeVeaux 1991. See also Hugues Panassié, *The Real Jazz* (New York: Smith and Durrell, 1942); André Hodeir, *Jazz: Its Evolution and Essence* (New York: Grove, 1955); Alain Locke, *The Negro and His Music: Negro Art Past and Present* (New York: Arno, 1969 [1936]).

18. Brian Priestley, *Jazz on Record: A History* (New York: Billboard, 1991); Erenberg 1998. See Stowe 1994; and Bernard Gendron, " 'Moldy Figs' and Modernists: Jazz at War (1942–1946)," in Gabbard 1995a, 31–56.

19. See Bryant et al. 1998; Michael B. Bakan, "Way Out West on Central: Jazz in the African-American Community of Los Angeles before 1930"; and Ralph Eastman, " 'Pitchin' up a Boogie': African-American Musicians, Nightlife, and Music Venues in Los Angeles, 1930–1945," both in DjeDje and Meadows 1998; Bette Yarbrough Cox, *Central Avenue: Its Rise and Fall (1890–c. 1955): Including the Musical Renaissance of Black Los Angeles* (Los Angeles: BEEM, 1996); Lawrence Gushee, "New Orleans–Area Musicians on the West Coast, 1908–1925)," *Black Music Research Journal* 9, no. 1 (spring 1989): 1–18; Tucker 1996–97; and Buddy Collette, *Jazz Generations: A Life in American Music and Society* (London: Continuum, 2000), for attempts to redress this historiographical absence.

20. David W. Stowe, "Jazz in the West: Cultural Frontier and Region during the Swing Era," *Western Historical Quarterly* 23, no. 1 (1992): 53–73; Robert Gordon, *Jazz West Coast: The Los Angeles Jazz Scene of the 1950s* (London: Quartet, 1986); Ted Gioia, *West Coast Jazz: Modern Jazz in California, 1945–1960* (Berkeley: University of California Press, 1992).

21. Wald 1997, 119.

22. Toni Morrison, *Playing in the Dark: Whiteness and the Literary Imagination* (Cambridge: Harvard University Press, 1990), 17.

23. Freud explains that taboo is characterized by the "dread of contact with it" as well as an ambivalent attitude: "He is constantly wishing to perform this act (the touching) [and looks on it as his supreme enjoyment, but he must not perform it] and detests it as well" (38). The instinct is to find substitutes. "The basis of taboo is prohibited action, for performing which a strong inclination exists in the unconscious" (41); it has "contagious power" which encourages temptations, imitation. Sigmund Freud, *Totem and Taboo* (New York: W. W. Norton, 1989).

24. Neil Leonard, *Jazz: Myth and Religion* (New York: Oxford University Press, 1987).

25. I am drawing on Higginbotham 1992a.

26. See for example Editors of *Look* Magazine, *The Decline of the American Male* (New York: Random House, 1958).

27. Pierre Nora, "Between History and Memory: Les Lieux de Mémoire," *History and Memory in African American Culture*, ed. Geneviève Fabre and Robert J. O'Meally (New York: Oxford University Press, 1994), 284–300; Ralph Ellison, "The Golden Age, Time Past," *Living with Music: Ralph Ellison's Jazz Writings*, ed. Robert J. O'Meally (New York: Modern Library), 50–64. Of course, Gleason's is not the only attempt at canonizing — *The Art of Jazz, Jazzmen, The Jazz Word, A Treasury of Jazz*, the *Smithsonian Collection of Classic Jazz* — one could go on and on with examples of edited collections which imagined themselves to bring together the most central conceptual, artistic, and musical discourses about jazz in a definitive or at least suggestive fashion. See also Krin Gabbard, "Jazz Canon and Its Consequences," in Gabbard 1995a, 1–28.

28. This despite his own speculation that it might be possible to eliminate white jazz musicians "from the history of the music without altering its development in any significant way." Ralph J. Gleason, *Celebrating the Duke, and Louis, Bessie, Billie, Bird, Carmen, Miles, Dizzy, and Other Heroes* (Boston: Little, Brown, 1975), 5.

29. Gleason, *Jam Session*, 44. See also Poiger 2003, 162–67; and Von Eschen 2004.

30. Gleason, *Jam Session*, 12.

31. I am here drawing on Fanon 1967, in particular the chapter "Fact of Blackness."

32. Jackie Byars explains that melodramas of the 1950s "exhibited and examined the dialectics between class politics and sexual politics, between capitalism and patriarchy. Their material was everyday life, where values and ethics — and conflicts over them — are forcefully expressed." They also exhibit a desire to identify "a cohesive social code." For these melodramas most male- or female-oriented issues could be resolved within a domestic structure, and the ideology of that structure can be manifested in ways other than a traditional family. Male melodrama resolves the problem of finding freedom within the system. She writes: "In each, as the deviant male character is finally reintegrated into the domestic and communal order, the order is redefined. In depicting deviance, therefore, these films forcefully portray the range of the permissible, the norm, the ideal." Significantly, the narrative pattern of male melodramas presents men's problems "in the sphere of the 'social,'" and so we see that the real problem, "the healing of the shattered family structure," has an external solution. Jackie Byars, *All That Hollywood Allows: Re-reading Gender in 1950s Melodrama* (Chapel Hill: University of North Carolina Press, 1991), 8, 11, 116, 129.

33. Gleason, *Celebrating the Duke*, xxii–xxiii.

34. Gabbard 1996, 73.

35. See for instance Early 1994, 163–206; Paul A. Anderson, "From Spirituals to Swing:

Harlem Renaissance Intellectuals, the Folk Inheritance, and the Prospects of Jazz" (Ph.D. diss., Cornell University, 1997), chapter 5; Scott DeVeaux, "The Emergence of the Jazz Concert, 1935–1945," *American Music* 7, no. 1 (1989): 6–29.

36. See McCracken 1999.

37. See Charles Mingus, *Beneath the Underdog: His World as Composed by Charles Mingus* (New York: Vintage, 1991 [1971]); Brian Priestley, *Mingus: A Critical Biography* (New York: Da Capo, 1983); Rustin 1999; Porter, "Out of the Blue: The Challenge of Black Creative Musicians, 1945–1990" (Ph.D. diss., University of Michigan, 1997).

Kristin McGee

THE GENDERED JAZZ AESTHETICS OF *THAT MAN OF MINE*:

THE INTERNATIONAL SWEETHEARTS OF RHYTHM

AND INDEPENDENT BLACK SOUND FILM

The International Sweethearts of Rhythm, world famous all-Colored girl's orchestra . . . are an absolutely unequaled combination of charm and of talent. — *New York Age*, December 11, 1948, 10

Frequently praised by critics and fans alike, the International Sweethearts of Rhythm gained a reputation not solely for their unparalleled musical capabilities but also for the visual image that they presented: one of charming, talented, respectable jazz musicians who proudly showcased their diverse cultural backgrounds and races. Indeed, the group was frequently depicted in press releases as a group of talented jazz women representing the beautiful "black and brown" races of the world. Since the release of Sherrie Tucker's (2000) book on the all-girl jazz bands active during the 1940s as well as D. Antoinette Handy's (1983) earlier historical account of the International Sweethearts of Rhythm, jazz scholars, feminists, and fans of the unprecedented predominantly black, all-girl band from Piney Woods, Mississippi, I have come to know a great deal about this hard-swinging, professional female band which was extremely popular during the 1940s.

In this essay, I examine the musical and visual performances of the International Sweethearts of Rhythm in an all-black-cast film entitled *That Man of Mine* (1946) in the context of independent black musical films and black theatrical forms.[1] By connecting the musical, gendered, and racial representations of these jazz women with other gendered performative texts during the 1930s and 1940s, I suggest that both William Alexander, the independent African American director of the film, and the female musicians of the International Sweethearts of Rhythm exploited the combined musical, visual, and narrative capabilities of sound film to propose a more flexible identity for female jazz musicians, one which began to challenge proscribed racial interactions by featuring the unprecedented culturally and racially integrated International Sweethearts of Rhythm in 1946.

The International Sweethearts of Rhythm's many musical appearances in *That Man of Mine* draw from a unique tradition of all-black-cast musical films dating from the 1920s but also acknowledge more dominant white musical film conventions and styles which were popular during the 1930s and 1940s, including the "making of a musical" film formula. Alexander's presentation of the International Sweethearts of Rhythm reveals both his intimate knowledge of black musical film genres from the 1930s and 1940s, including the all-black-cast film musicals such as *Cabin in the Sky* (1943), the short subject and sometimes avant-garde jazz films like Duke Ellington's *Symphony in Black* (1935), as well as familiarity with the commercially dominant and predominantly white-cast Hollywood musicals of the 1930s and 1940s epitomized by the lavish Busby Berkeley musicals.

I further argue that the particular choices for representing the International Sweethearts of Rhythm in *That Man of Mine* were more likely influenced by prior and persistent visual, cultural, and racial representations of African American female performers than by the world-famous African American male jazz bands, like those led by Duke Ellington and Louis Armstrong, who similarly traveled abroad during the 1930s and 1940s. Most pervasive of these various African American representations were the highly caricatured and hypersexualized 'Jezebels,' the controversial but popular black chorus girl acts (the Cotton Club dancers, for example), and the multitalented, headlining stars like Josephine Baker and Valaida Snow, who often began their careers with black theatrical companies as chorus girls and eventually headlined these productions, often traveling and working abroad in mixed theatrical settings for predominantly European audiences (Brown 2001, Haney 1981, Francis 2004).

Feminist scholars have begun to unravel the controversial yet prominent status of performing women and especially blues singers and chorus girls during the 1920s and 1930s. Hunter (2000), Harrison (1988), and

Carby (1994) investigate the racial and social politics and ideologies mediated by theatrical blues women in a variety of contexts including black music theater circuits, dance halls, race recordings, and Hollywood films. Other scholars take seriously the influence of African American theatrical stars and especially chorus women upon American culture during the 1920s and 1930s, including Brown (2001), Bogle (1980), Woll (1989), and Francis (2004). By examining chorus girls' relationship to mass-mediated performance contexts and by further illuminating the sheer volume of discourse surrounding the "chorus girl problem," writers like Brown (2001), Glenn (2000), and Latham (2000) uncover the radical gender transformations initiated by these highly popular and profitable gendered performances.

Jayna Brown's dissertation, for example, reveals how African American chorus girls, in particular, symbolized many of the paradoxes of the Jazz Age as these women simultaneously espoused financial and social independence, but were frequently criticized in the conservative black press as profiting from dominant white fantasies. By investigating reviews of these productions, Brown reveals the heavily debilitating proscriptions by white audiences for black female performers who were made to enact a certain imagined idea of "colored folk" or African indigenousness during the 1920s and 1930s (Brown 2001, 240). According to Brown: "Black women variety artists performed versions of racialized femininity prefigured in earlier periods of colonial expansion that circulated throughout the world. Discourses of scientific racialism and romantic nationalism constructed fantasies of a black folk, sprung from the soil of the United States. Linked to European and British fantasies of African and colonial female subjecthood, both eugenicist fears and miscegenationist desires were mapped onto the light-skinned bodies of the colored chorus girls" (Brown 2001, 220).

Brown's research focuses upon the widely popular African American female entertainers of the 1920s and 1930s, a particularly prominent time period for African American theatrical performers. It is likely that the International Sweethearts of Rhythm would have been conscious of the kinds of female representations that circulated during the two preceding decades of rapid growth and experimentation because of the international prestige of black musical and theatrical forms. Moreover, the International Sweethearts of Rhythm frequently performed in variety revues and stage shows (in film houses) and thus had firsthand exposure to female stars like Valaida Snow and the famous dancing "chorines."

The Sweethearts would have also been privy to the time-tested practice within the dominant entertainment industry of looking to black sources for regeneration and inspiration whereby white theatrical productions often borrowed, imitated, and reformulated urban black artistic forms like jazz dance and black musical forms like blues, ragtime, and jazz. Susan Glenn and Angela Latham point out the racial and sexual complexities of white chorus girls' performances, many of which imitated dance styles from celebrated black jazz and theatrical artists, incorporated blackface routines, and often favored hot jazz accompaniments, a musical genre which inspired a variety of racialized associations by vaudeville fans, journalists, and theatrical promoters (Radano 2000, Rogin 1996, Agawu 1995). While white chorus girl acts performing on variety revue circuits earned more than black chorus girl acts, they also contended with certain dominant notions of performed sexuality, blackness, and its assumed association with jazz and popular dance. Their performative choices were more flexible than for black chorus girls who also performed in white variety revues, in black and tans, or in short subject musical films.

Since the 1940s some of the musical sequences from *That Man of Mine* have been rereleased at various times: first as soundies during the mid-1940s and then during the 1980s and 1990s, both soundies and musical scenes from the film were incorporated into various compilation films, documentaries, and videos on the subject of women in jazz. During the 1940s the independent film producer William Alexander cut and recast musical numbers from *That Man of Mine* as short subject musical films and then sold them to be distributed as soundies by the Soundies Distributing Corporation of America. For example, Alexander's short subject film *Harlem Jam Session* (1946) consisted of three numbers from *That Man of Mine*: "Harlem Jam Session," "Don't Get it Twisted" and "Just the Thing."[2]

In the mid-1980s, at the onset of the third-wave feminist movement,[3] filmmakers Greta Schiller and Andrea Weiss produced and directed a documentary about the International Sweethearts of Rhythm (1986) in collaboration with female jazz collector and record distributor Rosetta Reitz. The film incorporated several of the soundies recut from *That Man of Mine* in combination with other film footage, interviews, photos, and a historical narrative of the International Sweethearts of Rhythm's profound and radical breakdown of racial and gendered barriers during the 1940s.[4] In 1990, Rosetta Reitz included the International Sweethearts of Rhythm's filmed recording of "Jump Children" (not featured in *That Man of Mine* but recorded the same year) in her *Women in Jazz* compilation video, which also included the vocalists Billie Holiday, Rosetta Tharpe, Ida Cox, Nina Mae McKinney, and Rita Rio and her Mistresses of Rhythm. Finally, in 1993 another collection of all-girl bands was released on a video entitled simply *All-Girl Jazz Bands* (Storyville 1993), a film which included selections by the International Sweethearts of Rhythm and several others by Ina Ray Hutton and her Melodears, Lorraine Page and her Orchestra, and Rita Rio and her Mistresses of Rhythm. Accordingly, interested feminist jazz scholars, fans of the International Sweethearts of Rhythm, and sound film scholars may have unwittingly encountered scenes from Alexander's original 1946 film *That Man of Mine* from any of these soundies, compilation films, documentaries, and videos.

Within this chapter, I highlight the early relationship of music to sound films and historically contextualize female jazz musicians' durable and flexible relationship to film which dates from the late 1920s. In the second section, I present a detailed historical and cultural analysis of *That Man of Mine* while highlighting the International Sweethearts of Rhythm's contributions to the film. I then compare the practice of sidelining by all-girl bands to the professional filmed appearances of the International Sweethearts of Rhythm. Finally, I examine the lack of scholarship written about the International Sweethearts of Rhythm's musical films and, more generally, about all-girl bands in film, especially considering the large number of musical films produced during the 1930s and 1940s.

INTRODUCTION — SOUND FILM AND ITS RELATIONSHIP TO JAZZ

At the close of the Jazz Age, many Hollywood productions recruited the most popular jazz bands to record soundtracks for their "talking," "singing," and "dancing" films in an attempt to profit from the growing public taste for big band music (Stowe 1994, 94–140). As the plushest theaters and cinema palaces were rewired with "talkie" sound equipment, they continued to accommodate live performances of popular music. Thus, these new "talking" films not only afforded more complex narrative and dialogue structures but also featured soundtracks of popular bands and cameo appearances by celebrated jazz personalities. One way to promote popular jazz bands entailed recording arrangements for a film's soundtrack and then contracting these same bands to provide opening and intermittent music sets to these films. Similarly, all-girl bands performed in big city theaters in New York and Los Angeles even if a film's soundtrack was recorded by a male band. The number of all-girl bands performing in movie theaters both before talkies and after therefore suggests that their relationship to the film industry was firmly established prior to their appearances in short subject films in the 1930s and 1940s (McGee 2003).

SOUNDIES AND ALL-GIRL BANDS AND ORCHESTRAS

During the 1940s many of the most successful all-girl bands were recruited for film as featured acts on the newly invented soundies.[5] These three-minute musical films were projected inside Panorams, the most popular of the various film projection machines, which were simply mass-produced jukeboxes designed for local viewing of internal film projectors. From 1941, these early film boxes were strategically positioned in hotel lobbies, cabarets, theaters, bus stations, ballrooms, and nightclubs and remained fixtures of popular culture for the next six years. Soundies became an attractive medium for the promotion of lesser-known and new musical acts as they could be cheaply, quickly produced, and widely distributed to businesses throughout the United States and abroad to military bases.

The novelty of these sound film boxes, in combination with the interest of Roosevelt and Mills in reaching the widest possible popular audience, encouraged a degree of experimentation and diversity in musical genre and subject matter. Vaudeville acts, hillbilly songs, patriotic hymns, all-girl bands, "hot" jazz bands, gospel songs, operatic arias, flamenco dancing, "gypsy" campfire songs, and burlesque stripteases made the grade in this mishmash of musical material. In addition to the various lesser-known and more "exotic" numbers were performances by celebrated popular theater and radio entertainers like Cab Calloway, Lena Horne, Doris Day, Duke Ellington, Bob Hope, Lawrence Welk, Dorothy Dandridge, Count Basie, the Mills Brothers, and Bill Robinson.

The producers of soundies encapsulated the many diverse cultural and ethnic musical genres of the day, as well as what they perceived to be the most exotic, comic, and bizarre. However, soundies were not immune to the frequent exploitation and misinterpretation of these many "ethnic" music cultures, exhibited previously by the Hollywood film and music-recording industries. Such was the appeal of the films of Borrah Minevitch and his Harmonica Rascals (*Boxcar Rhapsody*, 1942), which depicted Bohemian hoboes stealing liquor and living in boxcars; or of skits with Creole female cross-dressers, comedians in blackface, and musical cartoons such as *Hot Frogs* (1942), which layered voice-overs and musical recordings of famous jazz musicians, including Louis Armstrong and Fats Waller, over the highly racialized caricatures of frogs and monkeys.

Even admitting these overtly racist musical presentations, the sheer diversity of soundies' subject matter suggested a rather bold and inclusive racial hiring practice in the context of a largely segregated 1940s American culture. President Roosevelt's integrationist and progressive political aspirations undoubtedly influenced James Roosevelt Jr. (co-founder of Soundies Distributing Corporation of America) and par-tially inspired his company's interest in presenting a democratic and pluralist American musical culture. Indeed, President Roosevelt had declared that music could inspire "a fervor for the spiritual values in our way of life and thus . . . strengthen democracy against those forces which subjugate and enthrall mankind" (Erenberg 1998, 184). Despite their sometimes exoticized, sexist, and racist presentations, soundies were revolutionary, not in their often crude and hasty film techniques, but rather in their willingness to present a multiethnic, cosmopolitan, and pluralist coalition of music, dance, comedy, and drama during Second World War America.[6]

The first release of Globe Production Soundies actually chose one of Hollywood's leading all-girl white bands, the Lorraine Page Orchestra, to sideline to a recording of Victor Young's radio orchestra for its 1940 debut. Lorraine Page's all-girl band was one of five original acts filmed for the Soundies Distributing Corporation of America. The Music Maids, a female vocal group, were the fifth of these original acts to be released by Globe Soundies Production.[7] The Music Maids lip-synced or rather, in film industry lingo, "sidelined" over the prerecorded per-formance of Victor Young's orchestra, who also recorded all of the original music for this first Globe Production series.[8] During the 1940s, the interest and potential appeal of all-girl groups (whether real or staged) is evidenced by Soundies selection of no fewer than two female films of the first five released.[9]

The nearly simultaneous emergence of sound film with race films, race records, and "ethnic" record series in the 1920s introduced a mar-ket strategy that became the model for the subsequent 1940s music films, thereby perpetuating racial, ethnic, and language demarcations of earlier recordings and full-length films. Soundies, which were presented in a series of eight three-minute acts, were designed to cater to particular communities, neighborhoods, cultures, and races. Black artists were grouped together and catalogued in a separate "Negro" section.[10] African American soundies, rather than being shipped weekly to Panoram operators, were included in the special-order items constituting the "M" series of extra Negro subjects and were available by special order only.[11] Jazz film historian Mark Cantor asserts that owners of Panoram machines were given the choice of selecting from two possible formats on a weekly basis: a preassembled or a custom reel of eight films. He suggests that most patrons would have likely ordered the preassembled reel which may have included soundies by a variety of artists including black artists, country artists, and other types of variety performers.[12]

Because of the influence of vaudeville, white all-girl bands were frequently packaged with a variety of "novelty" acts featuring dancers, comedians, and singers of jazz and ballads. These may have been promoted anywhere in the United States and especially to army camps at home and abroad after 1942. Some of the other all-girl bands (all white except the International Sweethearts of Rhythm) fortunate enough to be recorded for soundies or short subject films were Phil Spitalny's Hour of Charm Orchestra, Ada Leonard and her All-Girl Orchestra, Dave Schooler's 21 Swinghearts,[13] Rita Rio's Mistresses of Rhythm, the International Sweethearts of Rhythm, and Thelma White and her All-Girl Orchestra.

THE INTERNATIONAL SWEETHEARTS OF RHYTHM AND INDEPENDENT BLACK FILM

> *Pretty Margie Pettiford, one of the 16 charming and talented girls who make up the International Sweethearts of Rhythm, America's versatile all-girl orchestra.* — *New York Age*, April 1, 1943, 10

The International Sweethearts of Rhythm was one of only a few predominantly black all-girl bands to perform in soundies and short subject films during the 1940s.[14] William Alexander, an entrepreneurial black filmmaker from New York, first filmed this band under the auspices of his Alexander Productions Company. Alexander was one of a few black filmmakers to be employed during the Second World War by the Office of War Information for the purpose of creating patriotic black films to bolster morale for the soldiers at home and abroad. Together with

Hollywood veteran Emmanuel Glucksman and Claude Barnett, founder of the Associated Negro Press, Alexander's news reporting firm
"All-America" was the only predominantly black-owned film company
to actually survive the war (Cripps 1993, 132). The black film historian
Thomas Cripps locates the impetus for Alexander's patriotic films during the war: "Why not, said an agency report on black morale, make a
few 'morale building all-Negro films' and play them off in ghettos and
'camp movie houses that served exclusively black soldiers.' In this way,
said an owi man, they might exploit 'all-Negro' theaters and their midnight shows by engaging 'a private company' . . . to do films glorifying
Negro military heroes, something in the manner of 'Sergeant York' or
even 'Abbott and Costello' comedies 'with an Army background.' "15

Like other black filmmakers of the 1930s and 1940s, Alexander worked
in collaboration with established liberal white producers, most notably
Emmanuel Glucksman. During the war, Alexander was recruited by the
Office of War Information (owi) to make black films for the United
States Army Signal Corps for use in Panorams at army camps and in
black communities in an effort to bolster morale and to entertain and
support black troops abroad. Together with Glucksman, Alexander successfully produced the *American Newsreel Magazine* film series under
their entrepreneurial All-American Films firm. Cripps identified these
white corporate "angles" as necessary partnerships for black entrepreneurs and filmmakers who were otherwise prohibited from or had little
access to state-of-the-art motion picture facilities, much less the necessary relationships with the major theater chains to garner much-needed
contracts in the North and South for showing privileges.16

Alexander's film reveals a connection to the earlier "uplift" and "race
pride" aesthetics articulated by Harlem Renaissance writers, political
leaders, and filmmakers who promoted and encouraged African Americans' educational and cultural contributions for the improvement and
advancement of the race. By incorporating themes of race pride and
uplift through self-betterment, creativity and moral conviction, black
sound filmmakers reinterpreted a strategy first articulated during the
mid-1910s. Since the silent film era, black filmmakers had incorporated
themes of racial pride and uplift as well as represented the assimilationist
aspirations of black elites and the black middle class as they attempted to
create more positive and serious race representations in film.

Jacqueline Najuma Stewart (2005) illuminates the movement by
black-owned film companies to support and program black films with
uplift themes during the silent film era. As early as 1916, the Lincoln

Motion Picture Company and the Micheaux Booking and Film Company "appealed to Black audiences by focusing their efforts on producing 'high' dramas rather than 'low' comedies."[17] Film theater management's advertisements similarly urged their patrons to carefully consider the bookings advertised by theaters in black neighborhoods and to further resist the "so-called all-colored comedies," which according to these advertisements would allow would-be patrons to "save that dime as well as your self-respect." One ad even purported that "Some day we will have race dramas which will uplift, instead of rotten stuff which degrades" (202). According to Stewart, both Lincoln and Micheaux promoted and advertised race pride films like *The Realization of a Negro's Ambition* (1916) and *The Trooper of Troop K* (1916), films which were thought to have "contributed positively to the advancement of the Race" (203). Alexander's interest in creating serious films which depicted African Americans as upstanding, diligent, and creative individuals remained consistent with the aesthetic and cultural aspirations of earlier filmmakers and film promoters like Micheaux and Lincoln.

After the war, William D. Alexander was the only black filmmaker to successfully distribute black-cast short subject musical films internationally. From Mark Cantor's *Jazz on Film* website,[18] we learn that Alexander was one of the only producers to make short subject films[19] independently from MGM, RKO, Universal, Monogram, Twentieth Century Fox, Republic or Paramount. In May of 1946, Alexander organized the Associated Producers of Negro Motion Pictures to broaden the scope, financial mobility, and exposure of race films. Alexander initiated the Associated Producers of Negro Motion Pictures after the war perhaps to centralize and advertise more effectively his films and those of other entrepreneurial black filmmakers and perhaps, to some extent, to publicize black films made in combination with influential white producers like Dudley Murphy, Ben Hersh, William Forest Crouch, and Sam Coslow.

Alexander's probable exposure to the International Sweethearts of Rhythm during their international Second World War United Service Organizations (USO) tour must have inspired his first feature all-black-cast film immediately after the war. Moreover, it was Alexander's own wartime American Newsreels Inc. film company that released two other music-centered feature films which included sidelining female bands, *Tall, Tan and Terrific* (1946) and *The Big Timers* (1945). Hollywood films during and after the war also capitalized upon the mass appeal of swing and, consequently, scripted the most popular big bands into their musical plots. Many more of these same bands became famous during the war while performing at army and navy bases in Europe and at home. Bands like those led by Harry James, Glenn Miller, and Duke Ellington were scripted into Hollywood musical numbers with musically talented stars like Sammy Kaye, Bing Crosby, and Maureen O'Hara. Benny Goodman and the Count Basie Orchestra were featured in a number of "swing"-inspired patriotic films including *Sweet and Low-down* (1944) and *Stage Door Canteen* (1943) respectively. Following the model of these Hollywood music genre films, Alexander chose the International Sweethearts of Rhythm, one of the most celebrated and requested American all-girl bands, for his postwar film debut.

Like many film directors, Alexander efficiently recut musical numbers from his feature films and sold them to the Soundies Distributing Corporation of America who then distributed them as soundies during and after the war. Soundies of the jazz artist Billy Eckstine were recut from Alexander's *Rhythm in a Riff* (1946), and Dizzy Gillespie shorts were refashioned from the feature *Jivin' in Bebop* (1946). He probably envisioned cutting the musical numbers performed by the International Sweethearts of Rhythm out of *That Man of Mine* (1946) for release as soundies or as musical shorts. Indeed, four musical shorts of the International Sweethearts of Rhythm were produced and released as soundies in the mid-1940s under the auspices of the Associated Producers of Negro Motion Pictures or as "Alexander Production" releases. The filmmaker's competitive desire to market and distribute all-black films was most successful in his widespread distribution of black musical shorts and soundies.

THAT MAN OF MINE (1946)

That Man of Mine, an all-black-cast four-reel film, released shortly after the formation of Alexander's Associated Producers of Negro Motion Pictures in 1946, espoused the same moralistic tones of wartime patriotism, but displaced themes of loyalty to country with loyalty to race. On one level, the tensions in the film parallel the real-life challenges faced by black filmmakers attempting to compete with Hollywood genres. Some black filmmakers opted to recast tried-and-true formats like the glamorous 1930s musicals, simply injecting them with more appropriate cultural and racial themes. Others, like Spencer Williams, began cultivating new genres that more specifically addressed the contradictions of black patriotism in light of America's continued segregationist policies.[20] Although Alexander's film remained consistent with the goals set out by the postwar audiovisual movement, which included members of the American Council on Education, the Educational Film Library Association, and the American Film Center, promoting social change through film and broader and greater presence of black characters in Hollywood,[21] it failed to garner much critical response either positive or negative upon the film's release.

In contrast to dominant Hollywood films, Alexander's presentation of the Sweethearts is unique in his portrayal of these women as serious musicians. The opening scene reveals a discussion between two very sophisticated and educated African American businesswomen about the possibility of auditioning the Sweethearts for the proposed production. We are then transported to the main theater upon the set of a day-time rehearsal where the Sweethearts are presented in professional day clothes, each wearing something different and casually working out some details before warming up on a thirty-two-bar form. When asked to play, the band breaks into a jam session with the first chorus blown by the first trumpet player (probably Edna Williams). The trumpeter plays a couple of rotations, then passes it to the pianist Johnny Mae Rice before the tenor soloist Vi Burnside blows a final chorus supported by the band's climatic shout chorus. The Sweethearts opening number was unusual in its showcasing of many jazz soloists, as opposed to the flashy, fast-paced, and complicated arrangements presented by some of the predominantly white all-girl bands of the era. This contrasted markedly, for example, with Ina Ray Hutton's prior film appearances in *The Big Broadcast* series (1936), where the band often plays fast-paced arrangements of jazz, ragtime, and Tin Pan Alley. Also, Phil Spitalny's Hour of Charm Orchestra was celebrated for its technical proficiency and ability to play both classical and jazz arrangements.[22]

The band's second number features the bandleader and vocalist, Anna Mae Winburn, singing a medium tempo blues. This arrangement exemplifies the succinctness of Basie-esque arrangements. Finely tuned saxophone unison phrases weave the vocal stanzas together. Then the two lead trumpet players face off in a short improvised conversation in two- and four-bar breaks. Finally, the effervescent Tiny Davis sings a rougher-style blues with the band chanting "All right" in response to Davis's "How 'bout that jive?" The song ends with a flashy trumpet solo full of bravado and physically demanding, repetitive high-note riffs as the woodwinds showcase difficult runs and falls.

Perhaps in response to Tiny's witty and raucous blues rendition, the

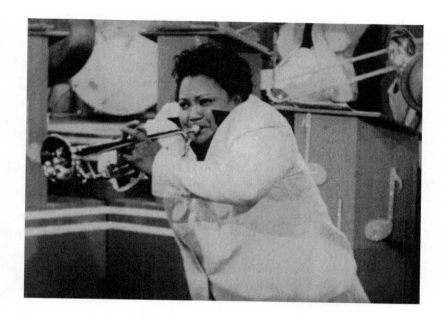

Fig. 16.1. Tiny Davis, trumpet, International Sweethearts of Rhythm, *That Man of Mine*, 1946.
Broadcasting and Recorded Sound Division, Library of Congress.

two women directors then ask for another number requesting "nothing too derogatory," a comment which further signaled the "uplift" politics as well as a self-consciousness of prior black female sexual representations in film. Vi Burnside begins this final audition number with four choruses of sixteen-bar blues. As the blues fade out, we are returned to the office of the male producer and male director. Here, the men debate the merits of serious acting and high drama versus music and dancing. At one point, the doubtful producer interjects "You've got to have the best of everything. . . . So what else do you have but a bunch of dancers and a girl band?" Here, the script betrays some of the residual stereotypes regarding female creativity and musicianship from Jazz-Age African American theatrical performances. The third scene opens with the band auditioning for the male producer and director, again with a musical piece featuring many of the band's accomplished soloists. This time, the arrangement delivers a more arranged and chromatic jazz piece in contrast to the earlier riff-based swing performance and is propelled by the heavy downbeats of the guitar and bass.

The next scene cuts again to the director's office where they debate the aesthetics of the potential film. Should they create high drama or sex appeal and glamour? The debate comes to a fore with the firing of the lead actress (performed by Ruby Dee in her first film appearance), who has proven herself in various serious dramatic roles, for another woman, more glamorous and sexually appealing, but who is also less experienced and much lower on the social stratum. The final act begins with another hot number by the Henri Woode jazz band performing an extremely up-tempo jazz arrangement with complicated, chromatic melodies more akin to bebop than swing or blues as two excellent jitterbug dancers enter the stage, following the patterns, melodies, and rhythms of the musical phrases with a finesse, athleticism, and accuracy uncommon for social dancers. The Woode band is a smaller seven-piece band and sounds more contemporary, even avant-garde compared to the Sweethearts.

Soon after, the Sweethearts reenter in full evening attire for their final audition, this time performing a highly complicated jazz arrangement at lightning speed as if to compete with Woode's difficult arrangement. This complicated piece affirms the women's technical expertise while also revealing their versatility in a number of musical idioms from jazz to blues and from swing to "symphonic" arrangements. The movie ends with the producer opting for the original serious actress who is also fiancée to the director, as opposed to the less talented, socially suspect, and sexually promiscuous street entertainer. As if to legitimate the film's timid progressive gender angle, the Sweethearts are simultaneously congratulated for their professionalism and musical expertise and are consequently chosen as the featured musical act.

In his representation of women in *That Man of Mine*, Alexander both invokes and critiques the western literary trope of "fallen" woman and virtuous wife, or in Hollywood vernacular, "slut" versus "sweetheart." Alexander further complicates this dichotomy by both sanctifying more prevailing feminine representations, favored by prominent black filmmakers, of "respectable" black womanhood in black films as well as destabilizing dominant Hollywood and theatrical associations of black female entertainers as either hypersexualized theatrical performers, chorus girls, and jazz singers or desexualized "Mammies." He does so by paradoxically presenting a range of female characters including promiscuous theatrical entertainers and dancers as well as morally upright and highly educated businesswomen. In this respect, both Alexander's and the International Sweethearts of Rhythm's musical choices directly responded to representations of African American female bodies inscribed within vaudeville and variety revue performances of the Jazz Age and the many spectacular musical films produced during the 1930s and 1940s.

The black feminist scholar Hazel Carby probes the female representations of African American women's bodies during the first half of the twentieth century as they were depicted in editorials, literature, and in the works of celebrated Harlem Renaissance writers. Carby claims that women's bodies became contested subjects because they symbolized so many of the traumatic ruptures experienced by African Americans during and after the great urban migration. Accordingly, women's bodies embodied many of the contradictions of urban American culture as they became sites for white male desire, fantasies of miscegenation, and performative symbols of lost colonial subjects. During the 1920s and 1930s, mass-mediated African American performances incorporated images of primitive, exotic, and libidinous beings, whereas their innovative jazz dances and vocal performances were simultaneously appropriated by the dominant culture for their spontaneity and creativity (Carby 1992).

Since the emergence of sound film, racialized characters had frequently been cast in Hollywood films in binary oppositions: sometimes black female actors were hired to evoke promiscuity and, in their most extreme sexualized roles, to evoke the forbidden white male desire of miscegenation. Conversely, their characters often required the exaggerated and outmoded plantation character of the desexualized "Mammy."[23] In Alexander's film, women represent a range of these extremes and are therefore depicted in more complicated ways, as women are cast in a variety of roles from cultivated and upstanding businesswomen to uneducated, promiscuous, and highly sexualized theatrical dancers and jazz singers.

Significantly, the Sweethearts' position in the film is secured only after they have proven themselves as serious musicians and not as sex objects, visual images, or merely as a "bunch of girls" with all of its allusions to novelty acts. Alexander's presentation of female musicians self-consciously negates the female stereotype favored in other predominantly white Hollywood films, which consistently presented white women musicians as feminine objects on display, musical threats to male musicians' cohesion and innovation, college students, or fill-ins for those male musicians abroad.[24] Although the moral dilemma of the film implies a broader dialectic with other all-black-cast films as well as white film genres and themes, it does so by implicating the purported socially redemptive power of music and a slightly more realistic representation of musical women. However, as female musicians, the Sweethearts are required to audition for the majority of the film before they are accepted as serious jazz instrumentalists. The Sweethearts' constant "auditioning" status contrasted with other swing-centered narratives featuring male bands, where the professionalism and skill of male musicians like Duke Ellington or Glenn Miller were accepted a priori. In *That Man of Mine*, women are eventually treated as individuals both in their musical endeavors (but only after they have proven themselves as capable improvisers) and in their abilities as dramatic leading actresses. This was indeed striking in contrast to presentations of female musicians in Hollywood films of the 1940s.

Although the International Sweethearts of Rhythm are the only known example of a predominantly black, professional, all-girl band on film from this era, their presence confirms alternative artistic and political movements countering the more visible depictions of white all-girl bands in Hollywood films. The black independent film producer William Alexander most likely chose the band because of its commercial appeal and its profound popularity with black audiences. However, either consciously or not, Alexander introduced another image of jazz, one which involved a group of serious female musicians and presented them as such. Here, the women of the International Sweethearts of Rhythm are afforded a more complex relationship to the world of male jazz musicians. The women are presented as professionals and as improvisers, yet they remain dissociated from the greater jazz community of juke joints, bars, and nightclubs. In *That Man of Mine*, the Sweethearts are both feminine, as they perform in conservative full-length gowns, and serious improvisers. However, their relationship to the greater jazz community is never fully referenced.

Favoring the "hot" side of the jazz spectrum, most of the soundies and film appearances by the International Sweethearts of Rhythm dedicate ample time for improvisation and featured spots by the band's many fine soloists, including the tenor saxophonist Vi Burnside, the trumpeter Tiny Davis, and the drummer Pauline Braddy. Indeed the band's first musical selection in Alexander's short four-reel film *That Man of Mine* (1946) merely presents "rhythm changes" (thirty-two-bar song form), which highlight each and every capable jazz soloist in the band. Moreover, the band's conductor, Anna Mae Winburn, is consistently presented as a bandleader and singer and never as a mere sex object. Although many musical selections feature improvised solos, the band also performs a good number of "flash" jazz pieces which exhibit their technical skills and solo- and unison-playing abilities. Both the Melodears and the Hour of Charm orchestra also performed a few "flash" jazz pieces to impress their audiences and perhaps, more importantly, to dispel widespread beliefs that women could not play with as much agility and technical proficiency as their male jazz counterparts.

The film's portrayal of these women creatively addresses their interracial makeup. Rather than directly addressing the mixed and more worrisome white, black, Asian, and Latina band constituency of the group, the film presents them as an "all colored girls" unit. Shots of the band effectively obscure the "whiteness" of a few of the members with dim camera shots, and hairstyles and makeup further blur racial signifiers.

Sherrie Tucker discusses the conscious representation of the International Sweethearts of Rhythm as simultaneously "international" and "all-colored" — a strategy which contained powerful meanings for African Americans during the war, many of whom experienced more racism and sexism at home than abroad. According to Tucker, the Sweethearts' internationalism was not of a "generic variety" but rather suggested "non-European international alliances between people conceived of as black and brown" (Tucker 2000, 185). This alignment with internationalism further proffered their connections to other prominent African American entertainers, jazz musicians, writers, and travelers who gained prestige, status, economic stability, and political prominence performing abroad via the transatlantic routes (Gilroy 1993). Further, the all-colored descriptor was one way of asserting race pride and racial uplift, which enabled the racially mixed constituency of the group to become a self-determined act. In this particular sense, internationalism prioritized the "blackness" and "colored-ness" of the group over the whiteness of some of its members. Indeed, while touring in the Jim Crow South, white women were frequently forced to wear hairstyles, makeup, and sometimes even black greasepaint to disguise their whiteness (Tucker 2000).

SIDELINING ALL-GIRL BANDS

A number of purely commercial all-white films attempted to profit from the highly successful all-girl spectacles by provocatively arranging groups of models pretending to play instruments (a practice known as "sidelining") to the syncopated popular songs and to the hottest jazz recordings. In *Swing It, Mr. Schubert* (RCM Productions 1942), Carole Adams and the Glamourettes, touted as "America's most gorgeous girl band," was one such nonplaying, sidelining, all-white "band" who dramatized a race-inflected commentary on the high-art, low-art dichotomy so often satirized in Hollywood musicals during the 1940s.[25] In this musical film, the Glamourettes pretend to perform a medley of swung Schubert themes recorded by the prolific and well-respected John Kirby Sextet.[26] The juxtaposition of this musical arrangement sidelined by provocative and sexy female models effectively satirizes the upper-middle-class amateur musical expectations for white women while also extending a popular 1920s and 1930s trend of rendering jazz arrangements of classical themes (à la Paul Whiteman) established in vaudeville and musical revues, two musical forms which drew heavily from nineteenth- and twentieth-century minstrelsy.[27] Although it is clear that most of these women have no musical experience, the film does feature two female pianists who actually do play and both perfectly replicate the short but technically challenging improvised solos recorded by pianist Billy Kyle which are clearly memorized to synchronize the film's audio score.

The women's costumes further satirize the Victorian sartorial expectations of the film's title as women perform in shimmery, satin, cleavage-revealing two-pieces and V-shaped split skirts with oversized (in relation to the skimpy bodysuits), ballooning shoulder coverings — the only Victorian sartorial gesture. Indeed, these unbalanced garments would have been an uncommon band uniform for both male jazz musicians and socially "respectable" white female amateur musicians. Rather, their physical appearance relied upon the sensual and revealing costumes worn by chorus girls and all-girl spectacles of variety revue and burlesque, which appropriated jazz and blues musical accompaniments to provide the necessary soundtrack of "sex and sleaze" as these provocative, highly sexualized groups of anonymous women uniformly danced and fulfilled Americans' desire for the perceived libidinal release and pleasures of jazz and swing.

During the 1940s nonperforming African American all-girl bands also sidelined for all-black-cast films but seemingly for much different cultural and gendered purposes. *The Big Timers*, an all-black-cast film released in 1945 (also released on William Alexander's American Newsreel Films Inc.) is a short, forty-minute musical feature, which provides a thinly veiled plot to facilitate the filming of an informal variety revue, hosted by Gertrude Saunders and her USO performing colleagues.[28] The appearance of the small seven-piece all-girl band, the "All-American Girl Band," occurs rather abruptly in the film as they magically materialize at the moment that Gertrude Saunders introduces her newly found Sugar Hill acquaintances to her USO performing friends. The performers gladly interrupt the dinner party to showcase a few numbers from the revue in the intimate confines of Saunders's hotel apartment.

The film's foreword proclaims the director's alliance, so to speak, with the "poor folks who work for the rich folks on Sugar Hill." Inexpensively produced on the set of a hotel in Fort Lee, N.J., the film introduces a young and beautiful Francine Everett as "little" Betty Washburn, a promising, young musical theater singer whose musical education has been supplemented by the hard-earned savings of her mother (performed by Mabel Page), who is also one of the hotel's maids. In the film, Betty's mother conceals her daughter's low economic status from the fiancé's extremely wealthy and socially superior family by pretending to own the hotel apartment of Gertrude Saunders (the leading USO performer). To establish her credibility, Washburn's mother hosts a formal dinner for the wealthy fiancé's parents. Of course, the plot is foiled when Gertrude Saunders returns home early to find the two families dining in her apartment. However, a working woman herself and sympathetic to the young women's musical aspirations, Saunders agrees to "play along" as Betty's aunt. Eventually, the hotel management is privy to the shenanigans and interrupts the after-dinner variety revue much to the dismay of Betty's mother.

During the variety revue scene, Stepin Fetchit performs a dual role as drunken porter/waiter and featured specialty artist. He eventually joins the USO revue, delivering a comical rhyming rap at the piano as he accompanies himself with a simple stride left hand. He then enters "stage left" in front of the magically appearing all-girl band to deliver one of his characteristic routines as he pretends to slide and stutter, only half-delivering his shuffle with oversized shoes and high-waisted baggy pants.

Although it's obvious that the small, seven-piece band is not actually playing and further that they are not real musicians, the film does attempt to create an impression that perhaps there *could* be an all-girl band that would indeed perform jazz and even take improvised sixteen-bar solos. At one point, during the band's featured number, "Start Swinging," the lead reed player stands up to take two choruses on the clarinet. Close-ups of her face make it abundantly clear that she does not perform. Her brief solo is followed by an even shorter four-bar solo performed by the trombonist (clumsily edited in the film), also with several close-up shots. Most of the "instrumentalists" are light-complexioned African American women, with the exception of the trombonist. The film's cramped set, which could not have accommodated more than these few women, contradicts the film's sound track, which clearly features a full sixteen-piece big band.

Here, the all-girl band functions simply as a sidelining group of beautiful women. This fact is made evident, first, by these women's inactivity and awkward mouth positions and, second, by the incompatible arrangement of instruments which contrasts with the sound track's full-sounding, big-band instrumentation. Most of the women fit the dominant aesthetic for chorus line women as they are slim, light-complexioned, and highly feminine in their presentation as they are adorned with elaborate updos and a variety of white silk and satin sequined and lace gowns. The producers, however, timidly suggest a real female band by presenting two close-ups of instrumental solos, first on the clarinet and then on the trombone. The politics of the color line must have contributed to the visual arrangement of these nonplaying sideliners as the slimmest and most light-complexioned women are presented in the front row or two. As the camera highlights the beautiful visages of these two women while they each thinly mimic the motions of two brilliantly delivered "hot" blues choruses, it is clear that Pollard attempted to create a 'moment of disbelief' by presenting female musicians who can improvise and perform hot jazz, even if these lovely sideliners are rather unconvincing in their "air instrumentals."

Tarzana, the following female USO performer, starkly contrasts with the refined and stoic romantic ballads performed by Betty Washburn. The "Whoopie Dancer" delivers her characteristic solo "jungle" number performed in black ostrich-feather shimmy skirt and black-and-tan diamond-studded bodice. She is petite and dances barefoot with a cooper bracelet banded tightly around her ankle. Tarzana performs a combination of jazz moves and "jungle steps," and eventually as the music slows to half-tempo blues, she performs her typical "slow drag" routine. Although Tarzana's hybrid cosmopolitan choreography combining the well-tested routines of the stage, modern dance innovations of the dance hall and established moves of burlesque may have fit well into the gendered aesthetics of USO camp shows, her performance in this intimate, domestic space for New Jersey's elite African American society seems a bit bizarre. At the risk of speculating, I argue that Alexander resolved the potential dilemma of reinscribing racist stereotypes by presenting a variety of African American performing women in both *The Big Timers* and *That Man of Mine*, teasing the boundaries of mass-mediated feminine tropes while also incorporating well-worn theatrical acts such as the ever-so-nuanced "Tarzana" to connect this film with earlier black revues and black-cast musicals.

The jazz women's costumes are also significant in that rather than wearing Women's Army Corps (WAC) military uniforms, as both the International Sweethearts of Rhythm sometimes did while touring with the USO and the WAC band always did while on tour (Tucker 2000, 250–58), these women wore expensive jewel-studded full-length gowns. Their highly feminized appearances contrasted with the white side-lining women in the Glamourettes soundies and also avoided the primitivist and jungle-inspired, skimpy chorus line attire.

The film never introduces the all-girl band. They are simply anonymous USO entertainers; therefore, their presence is normalized and legitimated by the public's familiarity with other all-girl bands, white, black, and mixed, who performed on the USO camp circuits, including the International Sweethearts of Rhythm (at that time engaged in their 1945 USO camp show tour of Germany and France). Moreover, I argue that, by 1946, the novelty appeal of all-girl bands was beginning to wane as the public was by then familiar with the hundreds of real and professional 'girl' bands that had been performing in America's USO camp shows, dance halls, vaudeville theaters, ballrooms, and movie palaces for the last two decades.

It appears that African American all-girl bands did not frequently appear in early black-cast musical films. The film *Tall, Tan and Terrific*, however, released in 1946 and also directed by Bud Pollard and released on Alexander's All-American Newsreel, Inc., provides a second example of a sidelining African American all-girl band.[29] The film's title directly references the physical and visual requirements for African American chorus girls, who were permitted auditions only if they were "tall, tan and terrific," implying that they must be taller than five feet six inches, light-skinned, and under twenty-one years old (not to mention terrific dancers). In *Tall, Tan and Terrific*, the all-girl band is introduced as the "All-Girl Golden Slipper Band" simply named after the film's Harlem nightclub. Throughout the film, the band is cast as the supportive house band for the many established theatrical and variety revue performers employed to entertain the club's well-heeled clientele. Some of these performers included Mantan Moreland, Francine Everett, Barbara Bradford, and Dots Johnson. The sidelining all-girl band is placed far out of view to prevent a close reading of these women's instrumental capabilities; nevertheless, it is clear from the women's hand movements, sitting positions, and faces that they are not real musicians. There are no close-ups and the band is presented merely as the nightclub's house band which provides intermittent jazz sets, primarily of the sweet sort, as well as musical accompaniment for the many singers, chorus girl acts (the Gorgeous Astor Debutantes), and comedy routines.[30]

The few examples of all-girl "bands," which upon viewing revealed groups of gorgeous women poised with band instruments, were perhaps the most surprising and startling of the types of female jazz performance documented on film. Often in the Hollywood examples, the women sported the most revealing and sexy costumes. Other soundies presented white women marching in similar leggy costumes with instruments pulsating in time to patriotic marches or big band jazz arrangements of the most popular tunes. In each of the previous examples, white all-girl bands are not depicted as jazz musicians but merely as models or "Sweethearts on Parade" presumably for the boys abroad.[31] These performances to the 'hottest' jazz arrangements intimated a certain racialized transgression as white women in minimal costumes sat seductively and passively. Here, unconscious associations of hot music with miscegenation and with the overtly sexualized images of black jazz dances portrayed in theatrical and Hollywood film contexts must have contributed to these films' appeal.

The women's appearances in the black musical films, however, are more functional. They simply provide musical accompaniments which support the many specialty numbers, vocalists, and comedic routines. Moreover, their attractive physical appearances (according to the color line dictates of the 1940s) provided pleasing visual backdrops for the various featured variety and theatrical entertainers including theater and film stars Stepin Fetchit, Francine Everett, Barbara Butterbeans, and Rudy Toombs. Rather than acting as sexual props for hot jazz, their appearances relied more upon normalized ideas of 'substituting' female bands. This contrasted with dominant fixations of black rhythm, miscegenation, or images of anonymous and sexy choreographed feminine configurations often featured in Hollywood scenes or specialty vaudeville acts.

The International Sweethearts of Rhythm's several musical performances in Alexander's 1946 four-reel film *That Man of Mine* clearly mediate the various hegemonic, racial, gendered, and musical constraints for women of color during the 1940s. As jazz instrumentalists, the International Sweethearts of Rhythm are treated as capable improvisers as well as versatile musicians as they perform a wide variety of genres from blues to jazz, ballads, and highly arranged up-tempo flashy, theatrical numbers. However, in contrast to these women's musical maturity, their film's early indictment of the International Sweethearts of Rhythm as "just a bunch of girls" effectively sabotages their professionalism, especially as they are forced to repeatedly audition for the film's directors. Moreover, their anonymous status, in contrast to other, film-featured male jazz bands like those of Duke Ellington and Glenn Miller, fails to position them within the greater jazz community of composers, bandleaders, arrangers, and musicians working within interconnected and international networks of nightclubs, theaters, ballrooms, and cabarets.

Clearly, Alexander adopts dominant Hollywood film conventions with his "musical within a film" plot. However, he also incorporates well-tested black theatrical characterizations as well as countervailing filmic and cultural representations inspired by black film genres as he includes a wide and complex range of feminine personas in his film. Chorus girls, stage singers, educated businesswomen, respectable wives, morally suspect dancers, and "all-girl" bands all appear with equal prominence, even as they perpetuate the stereotypes that they have previously represented in black musicals like *In Dahomey* and films like *Cabin in the Sky* and *Symphony in Black*. Significantly, Hollywood genres during the 1940s did not permit such a wide range of feminine personas for women of color.

The International Sweethearts of Rhythm's refusal to abide by the strict dictates of segregated performing groups by employing women of the "international" races of 'Black and Brown' reinforced their sense of cultural uplift and pride, which they then transmitted to their fans in the predominantly black theatrical circuits. Although they are described at various times in the film as an all-colored band, this descriptor can be read radically as a positive assertion of "race pride" and as an assimilation strategy enabling the International Sweethearts of Rhythm to employ Jewish women, Chinese women, and Latina women, who then willingly and sometimes out of necessity adopted a "colored" identity while touring the Jim Crow South.

Anna Mae Winburn's cool and collected conducting style (as she typically faced the audience and not the band), her sexy, form-fitting, full-length gowns and her subtle, but highly swinging vocal renditions also reinvigorated and challenged the physical and visual expectations placed upon other African American headlining stars like Josephine Baker, Lena Horne, and Billie Holiday. These leading women presented a complex mix of coded performances, which could be as liberating, uplifting, creative, and ingenuous as they were "exotic," "primitive," and sexualized (Brown 2001, Carby 1992, Francis 2004, Harrison 1988). The professional jazz women of the International Sweethearts of Rhythm would have been privy to these various representations, techniques, and strategies as they performed their variety of ballads, jazz arrangements, and blues, including the film's title song, "That Man of Mine."

Although jazz scholars have begun to investigate the medium of film and its treatment of jazz bands (Gabbard 1995b, Gabbard 1996), few have explicitly identified the unique relationship of women's jazz bands to early sound film. Moreover, contemporary histories and documentations of jazz films rarely mention the all-girl bands. Indeed, one of the few reference works on jazz in film, David Meeker's *Jazz in the Movies*, cites a few films of Ina Ray Hutton and Her Melodears but none of the other all-girl bands (Meeker 1977). Male musical giants like Louis Armstrong and Cab Calloway, who became famous as entertainers and musicians, owed much of their initial success, in part, to the powerful medium of film.

The question as to why women musicians and bandleaders never fully achieved the same longevity in their careers after their brief episodes in film remains largely unasked. However, for the women instrumentalists of the International Sweethearts of Rhythm, their involvement in the smaller jazz community, in the larger African American entertainment industry, and in the broader culture industry certainly requires an integrative analysis, which takes into account the wide range of gendered performances visible during the most revolutionary and expansive period of the media industry. Performative expectations for female jazz musicians working inside and outside of Hollywood and the nationally organized theatrical circuits during the 1930s and 1940s required women to negotiate musical considerations in conjunction with the more complex feminine and racialized expectations. In this respect, women were certainly filmed not merely to be heard, but to be seen. In contrast to the internationally successful 1920s and 1930s black theatrical and musical women, who often negotiated historically established expectations for racialized female caricatures in the all-black-cast musical films, and finally to representations of jazz women in Hollywood films, one could argue that the Sweethearts' many musical and visual appearances in *That Man of Mine* began to disrupt such confining characterizations. However, the hundreds of pre-1940s advertisements for black, mixed, and white all-girl bands, many of whom were never recorded for film or for record companies, suggest that the jazz scene and the larger culture industry offered other less-mediated performance opportunities, and especially for African American jazz women during the first half of the twentieth century.

NOTES

I would like to thank Sherrie Tucker, Mark Cantor, Celia Cain, and Phil Bohlman for their many readings of preliminary drafts and for their expert suggestions for improving this chapter. The still from *That Man of Mine* was graciously provided by Zoran Sinobad of the Library of Congress. An extended version of this article will appear in my book *Some Liked It Hot: Jazz Women, Race and Representation in Film and Television* (Middletown: Wesleyan University Press, forthcoming).

1. *That Man of Mine*, 1946. Associated Producers of Negro Motion Pictures Inc., an Alexander Production, produced by William D. Alexander, directed by Leonard Anderson. In *Swing Shift*, Sherrie Tucker discusses a few films from this period by the most affluent all-girl band, Phil Spitalny's Hour of Charm Orchestra. The Hour of Charm created short subject films for two of the largest film companies, Universal and Warner Brothers (as Vitaphone) during the 1930s and 1940s. I have compiled a filmography of all-girl bands from the 1920s, 1930s, and 1940s, which documents over seventy short subject and feature-length films with appearances by these bands. Most of these films were discovered after reviewing an extensive catalogue of non-indexed "soundies" at the Library of Congress and by viewing private collections of jazz films. I am especially grateful to Fred MacDonald of MacDonald and Associates for allowing me to view films of Dave Schooler and his 21 Swinghearts, Rita Rio and her Mistresses of Rhythm, and Lorraine Page's all-girl orchestra, among others.

2. *Harlem Jam Session*, 1946, featuring the International Sweethearts of Rhythm, Associated Artists Productions.

3. There is much discussion and disagreement concerning the particular period within which third-wave feminism first gained critical reception. I suggest that the film com-

pilations produced during the 1980s of "women in jazz" are drawn from second-wave impulses, but that these works emerged while new forms of scholarship were under way, which attempted to more thoroughly examine the racialized contexts within which women performed and worked during these early decades (1930–50). Moreover, radical women of color called for new forms of subjectivity in their critique of second-wave feminism for privileging Eurocentric subjects and for ignoring issues of ethnicity and race. The feminist works of scholarship *Ain't I a Woman?* by bell hooks, *This Bridge* by Cherríe Moraga and Gloria Anzaldua, and *Home Girls* by Barbara Smith are often recognized for illuminating these shortcomings and altering the forms of feminist writing and critique during the 1980s and 1990s. Catherine M. Oor, "Charting the Currents of the Third Wave," *Hypatia* 12, no. 3 (1997): 30.

4. Albeit not always conceived of in feminist terms during the 1940s, as Tucker (2000) elegantly points out in her discussion of the film.

5. As pointed out by the jazz film historian and archivist Mark Cantor, the term "soundies" is often confused with other types of short subject films made during the 1940s. According to Cantor, soundies refer only to those three-minute films projected in Panorams; these machines were engineered and distributed by Mills Novelty Company in Chicago, which utilized a 16-mm motion picture projector that "allowed films to be rear-projected via a system of mirrors" (Cantor's comments to this chapter, August 21, 2006). Other film projector systems produced during these decades were Vis-O-Graphs, Featurettes, and Nickel Talkies; all of these projected various formats of short subject films.

6. Feature films, inspired by the variety and multicultural diversity of these musical shorts, began incorporating a greater diversity of music and dance by leading black, Latino, Jewish, and white artists into their predominantly white Hollywood productions. Louis Armstrong, America's favorite trumpeter, vocalist, and jazz personality, cameoed in such films as *Pennies from Heaven* (1936) and *Atlantic City* (1944). Benny Goodman and Count Basie appeared along with Kay Kyser in *Stage Door Canteen* (1943) to entertain an interracial group of American GI jitterbuggers. Hollywood's most enduring war classic, *Casablanca*, scripted a black actor and professional drummer, Dooley Wilson, as Sam, the pianist, singer, and bandleader of an all-white orchestra at Rick's Café American, a haven for refugees from the Nazis (Erenberg 1998, 184). According to the American Film Institute, Dooley's sometime musical partner and pianist Elliot Carpenter dubbed his piano parts, playing behind the scenes. Apparently Wallis, the producer, suggested tailoring the part of the piano player for either Hazel Scott or Lena Horne, to no avail. AFI, search *Casablanca*, 1943, and then under "Note": http://film.chadwyck.com.proxy.uchicago.edu/cgi/htxview?template=basic.htx&content=frameset.htx (accessed August 31, 2006). "Shine" was composed by Ford Dabney and Cecil Mack.

7. Many of the soundies of all-girl bands were discovered in Maurice Terenzio, Scott MacGillivray, and Ted Okuda, *The Soundies Distributing Corporation of America: A History and Filmography* (London: McFarland, 1991). Several others were discovered at the Library of Congress from an unpublished and unindexed catalogue of soundies donated on

deposit from Green Tree Productions. Finally, other films were graciously offered for viewing at the McDonald & Associates Film Archive in Chicago.

8. Thanks to Mark Cantor for informing me that the music for this soundie was recorded by Victor Young's radio orchestra and not Dick Winslow's band.

9. Sidelining was the practice of having actors or real musicians appear in a film with instruments but not actually playing. However, many lesser-known as well as well-known studio-supported male jazz bands also participated in sidelining during the 1940s. Dick Winslow's was one such band that provided soundtracks for some of the sidelining, or rather "staged" all-girl acts released on soundies. For a brief definition of sidelining, see "Frequently Asked Questions about Music for Film, TV and Multimedia," *Film Music Magazine*, August 11, 2005, http://www.filmmusicworld.com/faq/13.11.html.

10. This was gleaned from Terenzio's "Introduction" (*Soundies*), which detailed the grouping of music and entertainment in the soundies catalogue by race, genre, or ethnicity.

11. Mark Cantor quoted in Tucker 2000, 352 n. 6.

12. Mark Cantor's written comments to this chapter, August 21, 2006.

13. Doris Swerk, saxophonist with Dave Schooler's 21 Swinghearts, confirmed that the band was sponsored by Elliot Roosevelt for their many soundies. Because of their affiliations with Roosevelt, the band performed on the same circuits as bands such as Tommy Dorsey, Benny Goodman, and Jack Teagarden. Interview with Doris Swerk, December 29, 2002.

14. In addition to the International Sweethearts of Rhythm, Mark Cantor points out that jazz films were also made of the Vs, an African American quartet from this period.

15. "Report on Negro Morale," n.d., marked "confidential," entry 3, box 65, "Negro" folder, Bureau of Intelligence, OFF, RG 208, NA-MD, cited in Cripps 1993, 132 n. 12.

16. Thomas Cripps, *Black Film as Genre* (Bloomington: Indiana University Press, 1978), 38. See also Cripps, *Slow Fade to Black* (New York: Oxford University Press, 1977).

17. Jacqueline Najuma Stewart, *Migrating to the Movies: Cinema and Black Urban Modernity* (Berkeley: University of California Press, 2005), 202.

18. This was gleaned by searching "William Alexander" from the homepage in Mark Cantor's Jazz on the film's website in 2003: http://www.jazz-on-film.com. However, the search engine is no longer part of this site.

19. Even those short subjects not distributed by Soundies Dist. Co. were referred to as soundies.

20. Williams directed *The Blood of Jesus* in 1940, which addressed the perils of sinful living and paid tribute to African American traditional life and black Southern piety.

21. Thomas Cripps, *Hollywood's High Noon: Moviemaking and Society before Television* (Baltimore: Johns Hopkins University Press, 1997), 137.

22. See also the Hour of Charm's "Jazz Etude" performance in *When Johnny Comes Marching Home* (1943, Universal) and their short subject film *Musical Charmers* (1936, Paramount) as well as Dave Schooler and his 21 Swinghearts in the soundie "The Night Ride" (1941).

23. See for example representations of the blues women and jazz singers Bessie Smith in *St. Louis Blues* (1932) and Nina Mae McKinney in *The Devil's Daughter* (1939). Thanks also to Sherrie Tucker for her comments on this section with regard to Hollywood representations of stereotyped black female characters like the Mammy and the Jezebel.

24. See Tucker 2000 and McGee 2003 for analyses of Hollywood films which present all-white female bands like Phil Spitalny's Hour of Charm, Lorraine Page's Orchestra, and Ina Ray Hutton and Her Melodears, and rely more upon these types of "substituting" and "collegiate" representations.

25. *Swing it, Mr. Schubert*, 1942, RCM Productions, featuring Carol Adams and the Glamourettes, produced by Sam Coslow, directed by Josef Berne, and distributed by Soundies Distributing Company of America Inc. See for example the films *Rhapsody in Blue* (1945), which featured mixed genre (classical and jazz) musical numbers by the pianist Hazel Scott and mediated some of the high-art, low-art debates of the era. In the film, the work of Gershwin was presented as both popular music, borrowing black and jazz influences, and high art (symphonic music) and was featured in American concert halls as Whiteman performed Gershwin's music for the famous concert at Aeolian Hall in 1924. See also appearances by jazz musicians in Hollywood musicals like *Doctor Rhythm* (1938), a film which also satirized "long hair" music and juxtaposed jazz alongside more "respectable" symphonic concert hall performances. Other swing-inflected films which satirized high-art and low-art distinctions were *Two Girls and A Sailor* (1944, Gracie Allen performs a comic classical concerto), *The Fabulous Dorseys* (1947), *King of Jazz* (1930, Paul Whiteman), *A Song Is Born* (1948, featuring Danny Kaye as a musicologist and the musicians Benny Goodman, Louie Bellson, and others as "field subjects" in the five musicologists' investigations into the origins of jazz).

26. According to the jazz film scholar Mark Cantor, the John Kirby Sextet was highly active during the period 1938–46, recording both "hot" jazz and jazz and swing interpretations of classical themes for recordings and broadcasts. Cantor argues that these were not at all satirical, but rather "serious re-investigations of melody and theme." Thanks to Cantor for alerting me to this example.

27. However, Cantor also argues that this would have not been perceived as satirical, considering that many highly respected male jazz bands like the John Kirby Sextet frequently incorporated serious jazz orchestrations of classical themes into their repertoire.

28. *The Big Timers*, 1945, directed by Bud Pollard, All-American Newsreel Inc.

29. Both films of African American sidelining all-girl bands were brought to my attention by the feminist jazz and all-girl band scholar Sherrie Tucker.

30. *Tall, Tan and Terrific*, 1946, directed by Bud Pollard, All-American Newsreel Inc.

31. *Sweethearts on Parade* (credits are missing) is a patriotic musical short created most likely for soldiers abroad. It features uniformly dressed women in patriotic bodysuits marching in time to military marches. The women are not dancers or singers but merely models who resemble each other as they make various textbook formations with military props such as guns and batons.

Bibliography

Agawu, Kofi. 1995. "The Invention of African Rhythm." *Journal of the American Musicological Society* 48, no. 3: 380–95.

Ake, David. 1998. "Re-masculating Jazz: Ornette Coleman, 'Lonely Woman,' and the New York Jazz Scene in the Late 1950s." *American Music* 16, no. 1 (spring): 147–66.

———. 2002. *Jazz Cultures*. Berkeley: University of California Press.

Allen, Candace. 2005. *Valaida: A Novel*. London: Virago.

Baade, Christina L. 2002. " 'Victory through Harmony': Popular Music and the British Broadcasting Corporation in World War II." Ph.D. diss., University of Wisconsin, Madison.

———. 2005. " 'Something Extra for the Boys': 'Radio Girl Friends,' the BBC, and Forces Broadcasting, 1940–1944." In *Floodgates: Technologies, Cultural (Ex)change, and the Persistence of Place*, ed. Susan Ingram, Markus Reisenleitner, and Cornelia Szabó-Knotik, 3–23. Frankfurt am Main: P. Lang.

———. 2006. " 'Sincerely Yours — Vera Lynn': Performing Class, Sentiment, and Femininity in the 'People's War.' " *Atlantis: A Women's Studies Journal / Revue d'Études sur les femmes* 30, no. 2: 36–49.

Baldwin, James. 1961. "The Black Boy Looks at the White Boy." In *Nobody Knows My Name*. New York: Dial.

Bambara, Toni Cade, ed. [1970] 2005. *The Black Woman: An Anthology*. New York: Washington Square.

Baraka, Amiri, and Amina Baraka, eds. 1983. *Confirmation: An Anthology of African-American Women*. New York: Quill.

Barkin, Elaine, and Lydia Hamessley, eds. 1999. *Audible Traces: Gender, Identity, and Music*. Zurich: Carciofoli.

Berkman, Franya. 2004. "Divine Songs: The Music of Alice Coltrane." Ph.D. diss., Wesleyan University.

Berliner, Paul. 1994. *Thinking in Jazz: The Infinite Art of Improvisation*. Chicago: University of Chicago Press.

Bogle, Donald. 1980. *Brown Sugar: Eighty Years of America's Black Female Superstars*. New York: Da Capo.

Bronfen, Elizabeth. 1998. *The Knotted Subject: Hysteria and Its Discontents*. Princeton: Princeton University Press.

Brooks, Daphne A. 2006. *Bodies in Dissent: Spectacular Performances of Race and Freedom, 1850–1910*. Durham, N.C.: Duke University Press.

Brown, Elsa Barkley. 1991. "Polyrhythms and Improvisation: Lessons for Women's History." *History Workshop Journal*, 85–90.

Brown, Jayna. 2001. "Babylon Girls: African American Women Performers and the Making of the Modern." Ph.D. diss., Yale University.

———. 2006. " 'Dat Var Negressen' Walaida Snow." In "Recall and Response: Black Women Performers and the Mapping of Memory," ed. Brown and Tavia Nyong'o. Special issue, *Women and Performance: A Journal of Feminist Theory* 16, no. 1 (March): 51–70.

Bryant, Clora, et al. 1998. *Central Avenue Sounds: Jazz in Los Angeles*. Berkeley: University of California Press.

Butler, Judith. 1990. *Gender Trouble: Feminism and the Subversion of Identity*. New York: Routledge.

———. 2004. *Undoing Gender*. New York: Routledge, 2004.

Carby, Hazel. 1987. *Reconstructing Womanhood: The Emergence of the Afro-American Woman Novelist*. Oxford: Oxford University Press.

———. 1991. "In Body and Spirit: Representing Black Women Musicians." *Black Music Research Journal* 11, no. 2 (autumn): 177–92.

———. 1992. "Policing the Black Woman's Body in an Urban Context." *Critical Inquiry* 18, no. 4 (summer): 738–55.

———. 1994. " 'It Jus Be's Dat Way Sometime': The Sexual Politics of Women's Blues." In *Unequal Sisters: A Multicultural Reader in U.S. Women's History*, 2nd edition, ed. Vicki L. Ruiz and Ellen Carol DuBois, 330–41. New York: Routledge.

———. 1998. *Race Men*. Cambridge: Harvard University Press.

———. 1999. "The Sexual Politics of Women's Blues" and "Policing the Black Woman's Body in an Urban Context." In *Cultures in Babylon: Black Britain and African America*, 7–39. London: Verso.

Carson, Anne. 1998. "The Gender of Sound." In *Cassandra: Voices from the Inside*, ed. Freda Guttman, 62–81. Montreal: Orboro [orig. pub. in *Glass, Irony and God*. New York: New Directions, 1995].

Cavin, Susan. 1975. "Missing Women: On the Voodoo Trail to Jazz." *Journal of Jazz Studies* 3, no. 1 (fall): 4–27.

Chamberlain, Charles. 2001. "The Goodson Sisters: Women Pianists and the Function of Gender in the Jazz Age." *Jazz Archivist: A Newsletter of the William Ransom Hogan Jazz Archive* 15: 1–9.

Cheatham, Jeannie. 2006. *Meet Me with Your Black Drawers On: My Life in Music*. Austin: University of Texas Press.

Cixous, Hélène, and Catherine Clément. 1986. *The Newly Born Woman*, trans. Betsy Wing. Minneapolis: University of Minnesota Press.

Cleage, Pearl. 1993. *Deals with the Devil and Other Reasons to Riot*. New York: Ballantine.

Cohen, Cathy. 1999. *Boundaries of Blackness: AIDS and the Breakdown of Black Politics*. Chicago: University of Chicago Press.

Cook, Susan C. 1998. "Passionless Dancing and Passionate Reform: Respectability, Modernism, and the Social Dancing of Irene and Vernon Castle." In *The Passion of Music and Dance*, ed. William Washabaugh, 133–50. Oxford: Oxford University Press.

Cook, Susan C., and Judy Tsou. 1993. *Cecilia Reclaimed: Feminist Perspectives on Gender and Music*. Urbana: University of Illinois Press.

Cripps, Thomas. 1993. *Making Movies Black: The Hollywood Message Movie from World War II to the Civil Rights Era*. New York: Oxford University Press.

Currid, Brian. 2000. 'Ain't I People?': Voicing National Fantasy." In *Music and the Racial Imagination*, ed. Radano and Bohlman, 113–44.

Cusick, Suzanne G. 1994. "On a Lesbian Relationship with Music: A Serious Effort Not to Think Straight." In *Queering the Pitch: The New Gay and Lesbian Musicology*, ed. Phillip Brett, Elizabeth Wood, and Gary C. Thomas, 67–83. New York: Routledge.

———. 1999. "On Musical Performances of Gender and Sex." In *Audible Traces: Gender, Identity, and Music*, ed. Elaine Barkin and Lydia Hamessley, 5–48. Zurich: Carciofoli.

Dahl, Linda. 1984. *Stormy Weather: The Music and Lives of a Century of Jazzwomen*. New York: Limelight.

———. 1999. *Morning Glory: A Biography of Mary Lou Williams*. New York: Pantheon.

Davis, Angela Y. 1998. *Blues Legacies and Black Feminism: Gertrude "Ma" Rainey, Bessie Smith, and Billie Holiday*. New York: Pantheon.

DeVeaux, Scott. 1991. "Constructing the Jazz Tradition: Jazz Historiography." *Black American Literature Forum* 25: 526 [repr. in *The Jazz Cadence of American Culture*, ed. O'Meally, 483–512].

Dickerson, James L. 2002. *Just for a Thrill: Lil Hardin Armstrong, First Lady of Jazz*. New York: Cooper Square.

Dinerstein, Joel. 2003. *Swinging the Machine: Modernity, Technology, and African American Culture between the World Wars*. Amherst: University of Massachusetts Press.

DjeDje, Jacqueline Cogdell, and Eddie S. Meadows. 1998. *California Soul: Music of African Americans in the West*. Berkeley: University of California Press.

Driggs, Frank. 1977. *Women in Jazz: A Survey*. New York: Stash Records.

Early, Gerald. 1994. "Pulp and Circumstance: The Story of Jazz in High Places." In *The Culture of Bruising: Essays on Prizefighting, Literature, and Modern American Culture*, 163–206. Hopewell, N.J.: Ecco.

———, ed. 2001. *Miles Davis and American Culture*. St. Louis: Missouri Historical Society Press.

Ellison, Ralph. 1973. *Shadow and Act*. New York: Vintage.

Erenberg, Lewis. 1998. *Swingin' the Dream: Big Band Jazz and the Rebirth of American Culture*. Chicago: University of Chicago Press.

Fanon, Frantz. 1967. *Black Skins, White Masks*. New York: Grove.

Feather, Leonard. 1987. *The Jazz Years: Earwitness to an Era*. New York: Da Capo.

Fellezs, Kevin. 2004. "Between Rock and a Jazz Place: Intercultural Interchange in Fusion Musicking." Ph.D. diss., University of California, Santa Cruz.

Felski, Rita. 1995. *The Gender of Modernity*. Cambridge: Harvard University Press.

Findlay, Heather. 1994. "Queer Dora: Hysteria, Sexual Politics, and Lacan's 'Intervention on Transference.'" *GLQ: Journal of Lesbian and Gay Studies* 1, no. 3: 328.

Finkelstein, Sidney. 1948. *Jazz: A People's Music*. New York: Citadel.

Fischlin, Daniel, and Ajay Heble. 2004. *The Other Side of Nowhere: Jazz, Improvisation, and Communities in Dialogue*. Middletown: Wesleyan University Press.

Francis, Terri Simone. 2004. "Transatlantic Black Modernism, French Colonial Cinema and the Josephine Baker Museum." Ph.D. diss., University of Chicago.

Gabbard, Krin. 1995a. *Jazz among the Discourses*. Durham, N.C.: Duke University Press.

———. 1995b. *Representing Jazz*. Durham: Duke University Press.

———. 1996. *Jammin' at the Margins: Jazz and American Cinema*. Chicago: University of Chicago Press.

———. 2004. *Black Magic, White Hollywood, and African American Culture*. New Brunswick, N.J.: Rutgers University Press.

Gaunt, Kyra. 1997. "Translating Double-Dutch to Hip-hop: The Musical Vernacular of Black Girls' Play." In *Language, Rhythm, and Sound: Black Popular Cultures into the Twenty-first Century*, ed. Joseph K. Adjaye and Adrianne R. Andrews, 146–63. Pittsburgh: University of Pittsburgh Press.

———. 2006. *The Games Black Girls Play: Learning the Ropes from Double-Dutch to Hip-Hop*. New York: New York University Press.

Gehman, Mary, and Nancy Ries. 1988. *A History of Women and New Orleans*. New Orleans: Margaret Media.

Gendron, Bernard. 2002. *Between Montmartre and the Mudd Club: Popular Music and the Avant-garde*. Chicago: University of Chicago Press.

Gill, John. 1995. "Miles in the Sky." In *Queer Noises: Male and Female Homosexuality in 20th Century Music*, 58–67. London: Cassell.

Gilroy, Paul. 1993. *The Black Atlantic: Modernity and Double Consciousness*. Cambridge, Mass.: Harvard University Press.

Glenn, Susan A. 2000. *Female Spectacle: The Theatrical Roots of Modern Feminism*. Cambridge, Mass.: Harvard University Press.

gossett, hattie. 1984. "Swing thru the South: Journal of a Road Manager/Spring 1981." In *Speaking for Ourselves: Women of the South*, ed. Maxine Alexander. New York: Pantheon.

gossett, hattie, with carolyn johnson. 1979. "Jazzwomen." *Jazz Spotlite News*, August [repr. in *Rock She Wrote: Women Write about Rock, Pop, and Rap*, ed. McDonnell and Powers].

Gottschild, Brenda Dixon. 1996. *Digging the Africanist Presence in American Performance: Dance and Other Contexts*. Westport: Praeger.

———. 2000. *Waltzing in the Dark: African American Vaudeville and Race Politics in the Swing Era*. New York: St. Martin's.

———. 2003. *The Black Dancing Body: A Geography from Coon to Cool*. New York: Palgrave Macmillan.

Gourse, Leslie. 1995. *Madame Jazz: Contemporary Women Instrumentalists*. New York: Oxford University Press.

Gray, Herman S. 1995. "Black Masculinity and Visual Culture." *Callaloo* 18, no. 2: 401–5.

——. 2005. *Cultural Moves: African Americans and the Politics of Representation*. Berkeley: University of California Press.

Griffin, Farah Jasmine. 2001a. *If You Can't Be Free, Be a Mystery: In Search of Billie Holiday*. New York: Free Press.

——. 2001b. "Lady Sings Miles." In *Miles Davis and American Culture*, ed. Early, 180–87.

Guillory, Monique. 1998. "Black Bodies Swingin': Race, Gender, and Jazz." In *Soul: Black Power, Politics, and Pleasure*, ed. Monique Guillory and Richard C. Green, 191–215. New York: New York University Press.

Hajdu, David. 1996. *Lush Life: A Biography of Billy Strayhorn*. New York: Farrar, Straus, and Giroux.

Halberstam, Judith. 1998. *Female Masculinity*. Durham, N.C.: Duke University Press.

——. 2005. *In a Queer Time and Place: Transgender Bodies, Subcultural Lives*. New York: New York University Press.

Hammond, John, and Irving Townsend. 1977. *John Hammond on Record: An Autobiography*. New York: Ridge.

Handy, D. Antoinette. 1981. *Black Women in American Bands and Orchestras*, 2nd edn. Metuchen, N.J.: Scarecrow.

——. 1983. *The International Sweethearts of Rhythm*. Metuchen, N.J.: Scarecrow.

Haney, Lynn. 1981. *Naked at the Feast: The Biography of Josephine Baker*. New York: Dodd, Mead.

Harris, Hilary. 2000. "Failing 'White Woman': Interrogating the Performance of Respectability." *Theatre Journal* 52, no. 2: 183–209.

Harrison, Daphne Duvall. 1988. *Black Pearls: Blues Queens of the 1920s*. New Brunswick, N.J.: Rutgers University Press.

Hayes, Elaine M. 2004. "To Bebop or to Be Pop: Sarah Vaughan and the Politics of Cross-over." Ph.D. diss., University of Pennsylvania.

Hayes, Eileen M., and Linda F. Williams. 2007. *Black Women and Music: More Than the Blues*. Urbana: University of Illinois Press.

Hazzard-Gordon, Katrina. 1990. *Jookin': The Rise of Social Dance Formations in African American Culture*. Philadelphia: Temple University Press.

Heble, Ajay. 2000. *Landing on the Wrong Note: Jazz, Dissonance, and Critical Practices*. New York: Routledge.

Hentoff, Nat. [1961] 1975. *The Jazz Life*. New York: Da Capo.

——. 2001. "Testosterone Is Not an Instrument." *Jazz Times*, June, 166.

Higginbotham, Evelyn Brooks. 1992a. "African American Women's History and the Metalanguage of Race." *Signs* 17, no. 2: 251–74.

——. 1992b. "Rethinking Vernacular Culture: Black Religion and Race Records in the 1920s and 1930s." *The House That Race Built: Black Americans, U.S. Terrain*, ed. Wahneema Lubiano, 157–77. New York: Pantheon.

hooks, bell. 1981. *Ain't I a Woman*. Boston: South End.

——. 2004. *We Real Cool: Black Men and Masculinity*. London: Routledge.

Hunt, Danica Stein. 1994. "Women Who Play Jazz: A Study of the Experiences of Three Los Angeles Musicians." Ph.D. diss., University of California, Los Angeles.

Hunter, Tera. 1997. "Wholesome and Hurtful Amusements"; "Dancing and Carousing the Night Away." In *To Joy My Freedom: Southern Black Women's Lives and Labors after the Civil War*. Cambridge, Mass.: Harvard University Press.

———. 2000. "Sexual Pantomimes, the Blues Aesthetic, and Black Women in the New South." In *Music and the Racial Imagination*, ed. Radano and Bohlman, 145–66.

Hurston, Zora Neale. [1934] 1998. "Characteristics of Negro Expression." In *Jazz Cadence*, ed. Robert O'Meally, 298–310 [orig. pub. in Nancy Cunard, *Negro: An Anthology*. London: Wishart, 1934].

Jacques, Geoffrey, Sherrie Tucker, Scott DeVeaux, Krin Gabbard, and Bernard Gendron. 2001. "A Roundtable on Ken Burns's *Jazz*." *Journal of Popular Music Studies* 13, no. 2: 207–25.

Jones, LeRoi [Amiri Baraka]. 1963. *Blues People*. New York: William Morrow.

Julien, Kyle. 2000. "Sounding the City: Jazz, African American Nightlife, and the Articulation of Race in 1940s Los Angeles." Ph.D. diss., University of California, Irvine.

Kastinen, Arja. 2006. "Nica's Story: The Life and Legend of the Jazz Baroness." *Popular Music and Society* 29, no. 3 (July): 279–98.

Kelley, Robin D. G. 1993. " 'We Are Not What We Seem': Rethinking Black Working-Class Opposition in the Jim Crow South." *Journal of American History* 80, no. 1 (June): 75–112.

———. [1994] 1996. *Race Rebels: Culture, Politics, and the Black Working Class*. New York: Free Press.

———. 1999. "New Monastery: Monk and the Jazz Avant-Garde." *Black Music Research Journal* 19, no. 2 (fall): 135.

———. 2001. "Miles Davis: The Chameleon of Cool: A Jazz Genius in the Guise of a Hustler." *New York Times*, May 13.

———. 2002a. *Freedom Dreams: The Black Radical Imagination*. Boston: Beacon.

———. 2002b. "The Jazz Wife: Muse and Manager." *New York Times*, July 21, 24.

Kernodle, Tammy L. 2004. *Soul on Soul: The Life and Music of Mary Lou Williams*. Boston: Northeastern University Press.

Kibler, M. Alison. 1999. *Rank Ladies: Gender and Cultural Hierarchy in American Vaudeville*. Chapel Hill: University of North Carolina Press.

Koskoff, Ellen, ed. 1987. *Women and Music in Cross-cultural Perspective*. Westport: Greenwood.

Kristeva, Julia. 1981–82. "Women's Time." Trans. Alice Jardine and Harry Blake. *Signs* 7 (fall): 13–35.

Latham, Angela J. 2000. *Posing a Threat: Flappers, Chorus Girls, and Other Brazen Performers of the American 1920s*. Hanover, N.H.: University Press of New England.

Lavitt, Pamela Brown. 1999. " 'First of the Red Hot Mamas': Coon Shouting and the Jewish Ziegfeld Girl." *American Jewish History* 87, no. 4: 253–90.

Leonard, Neil. [1963] 1972. *Jazz and the White Americans*. Chicago: University of Chicago Press.

Leppert, Richard. 1993. *The Sight of Sound: Music, Representation and the History of the Body*. Berkeley: University of California Press.

Lewis, George. 1996. "Improvised Music after 1950: Afrological and Eurological Perspectives." *Black Music Research Journal* 16, no. 1 (spring): 91–122 [repr. in *The Other Side of Nowhere*, ed. Fischlin and Heble, 131–62].

Long, Alecia P. 2004. *The Great Southern Babylon*. Baton Rouge: Louisiana State University Press.

Lott, Eric. 1993. *Love and Theft: Blackface Minstrelsy and Working Class Culture*. New York: Oxford University Press.

Malone, Jacqui. 1996. *Steppin' on the Blues: The Visible Rhythms of African American Dance*. Urbana: University of Illinois Press.

McClary, Susan. 1991. *Feminine Endings: Music, Gender, and Sexuality*. Minneapolis: University of Minnesota Press.

McCracken, Allison. 1999. " 'God's Gift to Us Girls': Crooning, Gender, and the Recreation of American Popular Song, 1928–1933." *American Music* (winter): 364–95.

McDonnell, Evelyn, and Ann Powers. 1995. *Rock She Wrote: Women Write about Rock, Pop, and Rap*. New York: Delta.

McGee, Kristin Ann. 2003. "Some Liked It Hot: The Jazz Canon and the All-Girl Bands in Times of War and Peace, ca. 1928–1955." Ph.D. diss., University of Chicago.

McKeage, Kathleen M. 2003. "Gender and Participation in Undergraduate Jazz Ensembles: A National Survey." Ph.D. diss., University of Wyoming.

McPartland, Marion. 1987. *All in Good Time*. New York: Oxford University Press.

Meeker, David. 1977. *Jazz in the Movies: A Guide to Jazz Musicians, 1917–1977*. London: Talisman.

Mercer, Kobena. 1994. "Masculinity and the Sexual Politics of Race." In *Welcome to the Jungle*, 131–70. New York: Routledge.

Middlebrook, Diane Wood. 1998. *Suits Me: The Double Life of Billy Tipton*. Boston: Houghton Mifflin.

Miller, Norma, with Evette Jensen. 1996. *Swingin' at the Savoy: The Memoir of a Jazz Dancer*. Philadelphia: Temple University Press.

Mockus, Martha. 1999. "Lesbian Skin and Musical Fascination." In *Audible Traces*, ed. Barkin and Hamessley, 50–69.

Monson, Ingrid. 1995. "The Problem with White Hipness: Race, Gender, and Cultural Conceptions in Jazz Historical Discourse." *Journal of the American Musicological Society* 48, no. 3 (fall): 396–422.

———. 1996. *Saying Something: Jazz Improvisation and Interaction*. Chicago: University of Chicago Press.

———. 1997. "Music and the Anthropology of Gender and Cultural Identity." *Women and Music: A Journal of Gender and Culture* 1: 24–32.

Moraga, Cherríe, and Gloria Anzuldua, eds. 1981. *This Bridge Called My Back: Writings by Radical Women of Color*. Watertown, Mass.: Persephone.

Moten, Fred. 2003. *In the Break: The Aesthetics of the Black Radical Tradition*. Minneapolis: University of Minnesota Press.

Myers, Dana Reason. 2002. "The Myth of Absence: Representation, Reception, and the Music of Experimental Women Improvisers." Ph.D. diss., University of California, San Diego.

Ngo, Fiona Irene Brigstocke. 2003. "The Blue Set: Race, Gender, Sexuality, and Imperialism in Jazz Age New York." Ph.D. diss., University of California, Irvine.

Ogren, Kathy. 1989. *The Jazz Revolution: Twenties America and the Meaning of Jazz*. New York: Oxford University Press.

O'Meally, Robert. 1991. *Lady Day: The Many Faces of Billie Holiday*. New York: Arcade.

———, ed. 1998. *The Jazz Cadence of American Culture*. New York: Columbia University Press.

O'Meally, Robert G., Brent Hayes Edwards, and Farah Jasmine Griffin, eds. 2004. *Uptown Conversation: The New Jazz Studies*. New York: Columbia University Press.

Panish, John. 1997. *The Color of Jazz: Race and Representation in Postwar American Culture*. Jackson: University of Mississippi Press.

Pellegrinelli, Lara. 2000. "Dig Boy Dig: Jazz at Lincoln Center Breaks New Ground, but Where Are the Women?" *Village Voice*, November, 8–14.

———. 2005. "The Song Is *Who*? Locating Singers on the Jazz Scene." Ph.D. diss., Harvard University.

Placksin, Sally. 1982. *American Women in Jazz, 1900 to the Present: Their Words, Lives, and Music*. New York: Wideview [repr. as *Jazzwomen, 1900 to the Present: Their Words, Lives, and Music*. London: Pluto, 1985].

Poiger, Uta G. 2003. *Jazz, Rock, and Rebels: Cold War Politics and American Culture in a Divided Germany*. Berkeley: University of California Press.

Porter, Eric. 2002. *What Is This Thing Called Jazz? African American Musicians as Artists, Critics, and Activists*. Berkeley: University of California Press.

Radano, Ronald. 2000. "Hot Fantasies: American Modernism and the Idea of Black Rhythm." In *Music and the Racial Imagination*, ed. Radano and Bohlman, 459–82.

Radano, Ronald, and Philip V. Bohlman. 2000. *Music and the Racial Imagination*. Chicago: University of Chicago Press.

Ramsey, Guthrie P. 2003. *Race Music: Black Cultures from Bebop to Hip-Hop*. Berkeley: University of California Press.

Robinson, Jason. 2005. "Improvising California: Community and Creative Music in Los Angeles and San Francisco." Ph.D. diss., University of California, San Diego.

Rogin, Michael. 1996. *Blackface, White Noise: Jewish Immigrants in the Hollywood Melting Pot*. Berkeley: University of California Press.

Rustin, Nichole T. 1999. "Mingus Fingers: Charles Mingus, Black Masculinity, and Postwar Jazz Culture." Ph.D. diss., New York University.

———. 2005. "Mary Lou Williams Plays like a Man! Gender, Genius, and Difference in Black Music Discourse." *South Atlantic Quarterly* 104, no. 3 (summer): 445–62.

———. 2006. "*Cante Hondo*: Charles Mingus, Nat Hentoff, and Jazz Racism." *Critical Sociology* 32 (2–3): 309–31.

Rye, Howard. 1996–97. "What the Papers Said: The Harlem Play-Girls and Dixie Rhythm Girls (and Dixie Sweethearts)." In *Storyville*, ed. Laurie Wright. Chigwell, England.

Schlicht, Ursel. 2000. *It's Gotta Be Music First: Zur Bedeutung, Rezeption und Arbeitssituation von Jazzmusikerinnen*. Karben: Coda.

Scott, Joan Wallach. 1988. *Gender and the Politics of History*. New York: Columbia University Press.

———. 1991. "The Evidence of Experience." *Critical Inquiry* 17 (summer): 773–97.

Showalter, Elaine. 1985. *The Female Malady: Women, Madness, and English Culture, 1830–1980*. New York: Pantheon.

Sidran, Ben. [1971] 1983. *Black Talk*. New York: Da Capo.

Smith, Barbara, ed. 1983. *Home Girls: A Black Feminist Anthology*. New York: Kitchen Table, Women of Color Press.

Smith, Julie Dawn. 2001. "Diva-Dogs: Sounding Women Improvising." Ph.D. diss., University of British Columbia.

———. 2004. "Playing like a Girl: The Queer Laughter of the Feminist Improvising Group." In *The Other Side of Nowhere*, ed. Fischlin and Heble, 224–43.

Solie, Ruth. 1997. "Defining Feminism: Conundrums, Contexts, Communities." *Women and Music: A Journal of Gender and Culture* 1: 1–11.

Solis, Gabriel. 2001. "Monk's Music and the Making of a Legacy." Ph.D. diss., Washington University, St. Louis.

Spillers, Hortense. 1993. "Mama's Baby, Papa's Maybe: An American Grammar Book." *Diacritics* 17: 65–82.

Stanfield, Peter. 2005. *Body and Soul: Jazz and Blues in American Film, 1927–1963*. Urbana: University of Illinois Press.

Stearns, Marshall, and Jean Stearns. 1968. *Jazz Dance*. London: Macmillan.

Stewart, Jacqueline Najuma. 2005. *Migrating to the Movies: Cinema and Black Urban Modernity*. Berkeley: University of California Press.

Stowe, David. 1994. *Swing Changes: Big Band Jazz in New Deal America*. Cambridge, Mass.: Harvard University Press.

Stras, Laurie. 2007. "White Face, Black Voice: Race, Gender, and Region in the Music of the Boswell Sisters." *Journal of the Society for American Music* 1, no. 2: 207–55.

Summers, Martin. 2004. *Manliness and Its Discontents: The Black Middle Class and the Transformation of Masculinity, 1900–1930*. Chapel Hill: University of North Carolina Press.

Sunderland, Patricia. 1992. "Cultural Meanings and Identity: Women of the African American Art World of Jazz." Ph.D. diss., University of Vermont State Agricultural College.

Tickner, Lisa. 1987. *The Spectacle of Women: Imagery of the Suffrage Campaign, 1907–14*. London: Chatto and Windus.

Tucker, Sherrie. 1992. " 'Where the Blues and the Truth Lay Hiding': Rememory of Jazz in Black Women's Fiction." *Frontiers: A Journal of Women Studies* 13, no. 2: 26–44.

———. 1996–97. "West Coast Women: A Jazz Genealogy." *Pacific Review of Ethnomusicology* 8, no. 1 (winter): 5–22.

———. 2000. *Swing Shift: "All-Girl" Bands of the 1940s*. Durham, N.C.: Duke University Press.

———. 2001–2. "Big Ears: Listening for Gender in Jazz Studies." *Current Musicology*, nos. 71–73 (spring): 375–408.

———. 2002a. "When Subjects Don't Come Out." In *Queer Episodes in Music and Modern Identity*, ed. Sophie Fuller and Lloyd Whitesell, 293–310. Urbana: University of Illinois Press.

———. 2002b. "Historiography." In *The New Grove Dictionary of Jazz*, 2nd edition. New York: Grove Dictionaries.

———. 2002c. "Women." In *The New Grove Dictionary of Jazz*, 2nd edition. New York: Grove Dictionaries.

———. 2002d. "Uplift and Downbeats: What If Jazz History Included the Prairie View Co-eds?," *Journal of Texas Music History* 2, no. 2: 30–38.

———. 2004a. "Bordering on Community: Improvising Women Improvising Women-in-Jazz." In *The Other Side of Nowhere*, ed. Fischlin and Heble, 244–67.

———. 2004b. "A Feminist Perspective on New Orleans Jazz Women: A Research Study for the New Orleans Jazz National Historical Park."

———. 2006. "Women in Jazz." In *African American Music: A History*, ed. Mellonee V. Burnim and Portia K. Maultsby, 528–41. New York: Routledge.

Ulanov, Barry. 1952. *A History of Jazz in America*. New York: Viking.

Unterbrink, Mary. 1983. *Jazz Women at the Keyboard*. Jefferson, N.C.: McFarland.

Von Eschen, Penny M. 2004. *Satchmo Blows Up the World: Jazz Ambassadors Play the Cold War*. Cambridge, Mass.: Harvard University Press.

Wald, Gayle. 1997. "Mezz Mezzrow and the Voluntary Negro Blues." In *Race and the Subject of Masculinities*, ed. Harry Stecopoulous and Michael Uebel, 116–37. Durham, N.C.: Duke University Press.

———. 2003. "From Spirituals to Swing: Sister Rosetta Tharpe and Gospel Crossover." *American Quarterly* 55, no. 3: 387–416.

———. 2007. *Shout, Sister, Shout! The Untold Story of Rock-and-Roll Trailblazer Sister Rosetta Tharpe*. Boston: Beacon.

Wallace, Michele. 2000. "Uncle Tom's Cabin: Before and after the Jim Crow Era." *Drama Review* 44, no. 1 (spring), 137–56.

Whiteley, Sheila, ed. 1997. *Sexing the Groove: Popular Music and Gender*. London: Routledge.

Williams, Sherley Ann. 1972. *Give Birth to Brightness: A Thematic Study of Black Literature*. New York: Doubleday.

Wilmer, Valerie. 1977. *As Serious as Your Life: The Story of the New Jazz*. London: Quartet.

———. 1989. *Mama Said There'd Be Days Like This: My Life in the Jazz World*. London: Women's Press.

Wilson, Olly. 1999. "The Heterogeneous Sound Ideal in African-American Music." In

Signifyin(g), Sanctifyin', and Slam Dunking: A Reader in African American Expressive Culture, ed. Gena Dagel Caponi, 157–71. Amherst: University of Massachusetts Press.

Woll, Allen. 1989. *Black Musical Theatre from Coontown to Dreamgirls*. Baton Rouge: Louisiana State University Press.

X, Malcolm. [1964] 1973. *The Autobiography of Malcolm X*. New York: Ballantine.

Contributors

NICHOLE T. RUSTIN received her Ph.D. in American studies from New York University. Formerly an assistant professor at the University of Illinois, Urbana-Champaign, she is now an independent scholar completing a book entitled *Jazz Men: Race, Masculine Difference, and the Emotions in 1950s America*. She has published articles, reviews, and encyclopedia entries on jazz, gender, art, and race in the *South Atlantic Quarterly*, *Critical Sociology*, *Bill Traylor and William Edmondson and the Modernist Impulse*, *African American Lives*, *Radical History Review*, the *Journal of American History*, and *American Studies*.

SHERRIE TUCKER is an associate professor of American studies at the University of Kansas. In 2004–5 she was the Louis Armstrong Visiting Professor at the Center for Jazz Studies, Columbia University. She is the author of *Swing Shift: "All-Girl" Bands of the 1940s* (Duke University Press, 2000). Her articles on jazz and gender have appeared in numerous journals including *American Music*, *Black Music Research Journal*, *Current Musicology*, and *Women and Music: a Journal of Gender and Culture*, and edited volumes including Mellonee V. Burnim and Portia K. Maultsby (eds.), *African American Music: A History* (Routledge, 2006); Ajay Heble and Daniel Fischlin (eds.), *The Other Side of Nowhere: Jazz, Improvisation, and Communities in Dialogue* (Wesleyan, 2004); Sophie Fuller and Lloyd Whitesell (eds.), *Queer Episodes in Music and Modern Identity* (University of Illinois, 2002); and Vicki L. Ruiz and Ellen Carol DuBois (eds.), *Unequal Sisters: A Multicultural Reader in U.S. Women's History* (Routledge, 2000). She is currently serving as the team leader for the "Improvisation, Gender, and the Body" group for a Collaborative Research Initiative of the Social Sciences and Humanities Research Council of Canada: "Improvisation, Community, and Social Practice." She is currently completing a book entitled *Dance Floor Democracy: The Social Geography of Memory at the Hollywood Canteen*.

CHRISTINA BAADE is an assistant professor in Music and Communication Studies at McMaster University in Hamilton, Ontario. She has published work on American Klezmer and popular music broadcasting at the wartime BBC including a chapter in *Floodgates: Technologies, Cultural Ex/change and the Persistence of Place*, articles in *Popular Music, Atlantis: A Women's Studies Journal*, and *Feminist Media Studies*. This chapter relates to her current book project, *"Victory Through Harmony": The BBC, Performing Identity, and Popular Music in World War II*.

JAYNA BROWN is an assistant professor in the Media and Cultural Studies Department at the University of California, Riverside. Her book *Babylon Girls: Race, Performance, and the Modern Body* (Duke University Press, July 2008) examines the politics of transurban black expressivity, race, and the gendered body in the first half of the twentieth century. She has also published on early race film and the black filmmaker Oscar Micheaux.

FARAH JASMINE GRIFFIN is a professor in English and comparative literature at Columbia University. Griffin's major fields of interest are African American literature, music, history, and politics. She is the author of *If You Can't Be Free, Be a Mystery: In Search of Billie Holiday* (2001) and *Who Set You Flowin'?: The African American Migration Narrative* (1995); the editor of *Beloved Sisters and Loving Friends: Letters from Addie Brown and Rebecca Primus* (1999); and the coeditor of *Stranger in the Village: Two Centuries of African American Travel Writing* (1998). She is also the recipient of numerous honors and awards for her teaching and scholarship. In 2006–2007, Griffin was a fellow at the Cullman Center for Scholars and Writers at the New York Public Library. She received her Ph.D. from Yale University.

MONICA HAIRSTON received her M.M. in music literature from the University of Georgia and is currently a Ph.D. candidate in ethnomusicology at New York University. Her areas of interest include popular music and jazz in the United States (especially of the 1930s and 1940s) and theories and practices of gender, sexuality, race, class, and nation. Her dissertation focuses on Hazel Scott and the politics of gender at Café Society. She currently serves as interim executive director of the Center for Black Music Research at Columbia College, Chicago.

KRISTIN MCGEE is currently an assistant professor of popular music at the University of Groningen in the Netherlands. She received her

Ph.D. in ethnomusicology from the University of Chicago in 2003 and wrote her dissertation on the all-girl bands active during the 1930s and 1940s. She also played saxophone in many Chicago-area popular music bands.

TRACY MCMULLEN is a postdoctoral fellow at the University of Guelph as part of the "Improvisation, Community, and Social Practice" research initiative. She earned her Ph.D. in Critical Studies/Experimental Practices from the University of California, San Diego, in 2007 where she researched the connection between the staging of musical ensembles and the desire for a coherent identity. She is currently working on the idea of an "improvisative" as a countermodel to the performative. Her publications include articles in *Current Musicology* and the forthcoming *Encyclopedia of African American Music* (Greenwood Press, 2008). She is also a jazz saxophonist and has recorded with David Borgo, Anthony Davis, Mark Dresser, George Lewis, and others, and can be heard on the Cadence Jazz label.

INGRID MONSON is the Quincy Jones Professor of African American Music at Harvard University. She holds a joint appointment in the departments of music and African and African American studies. She is the author of *Freedom Sounds: Civil Rights Call Out to Jazz and Africa* (Oxford University Press, 2007) and *Saying Something: Jazz Improvisation and Interaction* (Chicago: University of Chicago Press, 1996). She edited a volume entitled *The African Diaspora: A Musical Perspective* (Garland Press, 2001). In the spring of 2005, she did fieldwork in southeastern Mali and is planning a book on the Senufo balafonist Neba Solo. Her articles have appeared in *Ethnomusicology, Critical Inquiry, Journal of the American Musicological Society, Black Music Research Journal, Women and Music*, and several edited volumes. She began her career as a trumpet player and has recently been studying contemporary Senufo balafon.

LARA PELLEGRINELLI received her Ph.D. in ethnomusicology from Harvard University in 2005, having completed a dissertation entitled "The Song is *Who?* Locating Singers on the Jazz Scene." She served as a visiting assistant professor at the University of Richmond from 2005 to 2007 and traveled the globe with Semester at Sea for the fall of 2007. Since 1998, she has combined her research on jazz vocals with popular writing for publications such as the *New York Times*, the *Village Voice*, and *Jazz Times*.

ERIC PORTER is an associate professor of American studies at the University of California, Santa Cruz. His research interests include black cultural and intellectual history, U.S. cultural history, critical race studies, and jazz studies. He is the author of *What Is This Thing Called Jazz? African American Musicians as Artists, Critics, and Activists* (University of California Press, 2002), which won the 2003 American Book Award.

URSEL SCHLICHT (Ph.D.) is an internationally active pianist, composer, improviser, scholar, and educator. She plays cutting-edge improvised music, jazz and intercultural styles, and new/experimental music. She is the author of *It's Gotta Be Music First. Zur Bedeutung, Rezeption und Arbeitssituation von Jazzmusikerinnen* (Coda 2000). She earned her doctorate degree from the University of Hamburg, Germany. She has taught courses on music and gender, improvisation, foundations/introduction to music, ear training, jazz piano/theory/history, currently at Ramapo College of New Jersey, also at Columbia University, Rutgers University, and the Universities of Kassel and Hamburg. Please visit www.ursel schlicht.com.

JULIE DAWN SMITH received her Ph.D. in interdisciplinary studies from the University of British Columbia in 2001. She is the executive director of Coastal Jazz and Blues Society and the Vancouver International Jazz Festival, and a Management Team Member/Outreach Coordinator of "Improvisation, Community, and Social Practice," a Social Sciences and Humanities Research Council of Canada Major Collaborative Research Initiative. She was the former executive director of the Jazz Institute of Chicago and coproduced the "Women of the New Jazz" festivals in Chicago during the 1990s.

JEFFREY TAYLOR (Ph.D., Michigan) is the director of Brooklyn College's Institute for Studies in American Music (ISAM) and teaches at the College's Conservatory of Music. He is also a faculty member of the CUNY Graduate Center, where he teaches doctoral seminars in jazz history and historiography. His articles have appeared in *Musical Quarterly, Black Music Research Journal, American Music,* the *ISAM Newsletter, The Oxford Companion to Jazz,* and other publications. He is currently working on the biography of jazz pianist Earl "Fatha" Hines, having published a critical edition of transcriptions of Hines's solos last year.

JOÃO H. COSTA VARGAS is an associate professor of the Department of Anthropology and Center for African and African American Studies,

University of Texas, Austin. He is the author of *Catching Hell in the City of Angels: Life and Meanings of Blackness in South Central Los Angeles* (University of Minnesota Press, 2006) and has a second book forthcoming entitled *Never Meant to Survive: Genocide and Utopia in Black Diaspora Communities* (Rowman & Littlefield).

Index

abjection, 185–86; of mother, 198

accompaniment, 21, 51

Ada Leonard and Her All-Girl Orchestra, 308, 400

Aebi, Irene, 7

Aerobleu, 143, 152 n. 40

aesthetics, 22, 325, 406; African 174; gendered, 27, 312

Africa, 217, 335–41, 356, aesthetic practices of, 174; in jazz origins narratives, 250, 257; South Africa, 188

African American dance, 23, 163–64. *See also* black dance

African American music: church, 51, 272; historiography of, 32, 34–35, 38, 44; identification by non–African Americans with, 283; vocal forms in, 32; vocal quartets in, 37. *See also* black music

African diaspora, 158, 175; music of, 280

African music, 280, 336

Afrocentricism, 340, 342

Afrofuturism, 219–23

age, 323, 333

agency, 78, 145, 342

Ahmed, Sarah, 259, 265 n. 62

Ake, David, 27

alcohol, alcoholism, 324, 365, 379, 385, 387

Alexander, William, 394, 396–97, 400–404, 406–8, 410, 413, 415

alienation, 163, 166, 219

Al-Islam, 320–21, 334–35, 339–42, 346–47 n. 13, 347 n. 14

Allen, Candace, 349

Allen, Geri, 13–14

All-Girl Jazz Bands, 397

all-woman bands, 27, 94, 307–8, 393, 397–99, 402–8; African American, 412, 414; gender segregation of dance bands and, 96–97; interracial, 394, 409, 415–16; marketing of, 104–5, 400; minstrelsy and, 410; repertoire of, 117–18; sidelining in films by, 409–14. *See also individual bands*

Alter, Louis, 252

America: Africanist presence in, 375; exceptionalism of, 139, 275, 378; jazz musicians as ambassadors of, 309; as nation, 117

American Federation of Musicians (AFM), 135, 367–68

American Labor Party, 67

Ammons, Albert, 73, 80, 256–57

Anderson, Marian, 69

Anderson, Tom, 36

Angelou, Maya, 268, 349, 351

Anglo-German Swing Club (AGSC), 296

antiracism, 256, 258–60, 286

anti-Semitism, 257, 340, 373

Appiah, Anthony, 286

appropriation, 16, 237, 240, 251, 258

Armstrong, Lillian Hardin, 21, 48–52, 54–56, 60, 143–44, 244–45, 255; Hines vs., 57–59

Armstrong, Louis, 34, 37, 57, 59, 142, 296, 394, 399, 416, 418 n. 6; Hot Five

Armstrong, Louis (*continued*)
  Sessions of, 48, 143, 301–2; in *New Orleans*, 235–36, 242, 246–47, 258; as standard for authentic jazz, 295, 302–3
Army Air Forces Technical Training Command (AAFTTC), 135
art/soul dichotomy, 219
Associated Negro Press, 401
Associated Producers of Negro Motion Pictures, 402–3
Association for the Advancement of Creative Musicians (AACM), 16, 28 n. 8
audiences, 324–25, 327, 329–30; American, in Germany, 294; German, 295–96; musicians' interaction with, 193, 322–23; perceptions of performers and, 276, 278–80; in segregated theaters, 165–66; of swing and dance music, 103; white, 395
Auer, Vera, 299, 313, 315
Austin, Lovie, 21, 48–60
authenticity, 22, 43, 93, 95, 137, 174, 363, 370–71; in British context, 94; at Café Society, 79–80; commercialism vs., 41–42, 132–33, 142–43; of discourse, 212; Hot Clubs and, 295, 301; inauthenticity vs., 267; in jazz, 41–42, 133; of jazz and female sexuality, 84; of jazz and race, 217–18
autobiography, 268. *See also* jazz autobiography

Baade, Christina, 22
Bacall, Lauren, 384–85
Baker, Dorothy, 26, 362–64, 368–69, 371, 374, 376, 379, 382, 384
Baker, Josephine, 394, 416
Baldwin, James, 356
Bambara, Toni Cade, 348–49, 351–52, 356–59
Baraka, Amiri (LeRoi Jones), 17–18
Barnett, Charlie, 134
Barrett, Sweet Emma, 245

Barrois, Briquette, 105
Bash, Carol, 8
Basie, Count, 13, 418 n. 6
Bass, Fontella, 351
BBC Radio, 22, 293; Benson and, 90–95, 104–14; *Radio Times*, 107
Beal, Charlie, 244
Beat Era, 218, 237
Beaver, Louise, 251
bebop: detractors of, 296, 382; modern black masculinity and, 245; as site of integration and democracy, 379–80. *See also* Jazz Wars
Bechet, Sidney, 36, 37, 42, 73
Beiderbecke, Bix, 362–63, 378, 388 n. 4
Benson, Ivy: BBC Radio and, 90–95, 104–14; in *The Dummy Talks*, 115; female exceptionalism and, 98–99; HMV recordings by, 112, 114–18; Ladies' Dance Orchestra of, 22, 90–118; "Stick of Licorice," 98
Berendt, Joachim Ernst, 32
Berliner, Paul, 1, 31
Berman, Marshall, 18
Biberman, Herbert, 254–55, 258
Bigard, Barney, 247
"Big Butter and Egg Man," 48
big ears, 1, 2, 6
Big Timers, The, 402, 410–13
Birch, Mae, 98
Black Arts Movement, 274, 338
black avant-garde, 220
Black Bottom, 168
black bourgeoisie, 82
Black Clubwomen's Movement, 15
black cultural politics, 24
black dance, 158–62, 164, 168–76; sexualization of, 414
black dancers, 164, 169–75; claiming bodies from labor, 168; as flaneurs, 23, 158–62, 165, 166, 176; "stealing," 159; as travelers, 158, 161–62
black female sexuality, 84

black feminism, 15, 26, 352, 359
black flanerie, 23, 158–62, 165, 166, 176
black freedom struggles, 26, 217, 269, 272–74, 352. *See also* Black Power Movement
black manhood, 167
black masculinity, 26, 355; authenticity of, 80, 133; heteronormativity and, 329–31, 343–44; hipness and, 17, 147; mystique of, 142–43; myths of, 24, 134; nonhegemonic, 331; "out-of-control" construction of, 134, 137; patriarchal, 329, 332, 339, 344; respectability and, 325–27, 332–33; white fantasies of, 16–17, 24, 41, 244
black men: criminalization of, 322, 332–33, 339, 341; emasculation by racism of, 382; as musicians, 217–18; objectification of, 371; representations of, 33–34; self-representations of, 17, 24
black middle class, 142
black music: as American music, 366; as art music, 217, 280; legitimacy of, 217–18; sexualization of, 383. *See also* African American music
black musicals, 415
Black Nationalism and the Revolution in Music, 346 n. 11, 355
blackness, 328, 338, 342; boundaries of, 321–22, 326, 330–34, 339–43; as emotional freedom, 368, 370–71, 377; heterosexuality and, 329; limitations of, 231; new technologies and, 220; white critics' romanticizing of, 350; white sexualization of, 373
Black Patti's Troubadours, 161
Black Power Movement, 12, 273–74, 334, 340, 351, 354
black press, 395
black radical traditions, 322, 334–35
black sound, 370, 374, 382–83
Black Woman: An Anthology, The, 352
black women: as blues musicians, 15,

356, 376; as dancers, 18, 406; feminism and, 15–16; as jazz musicians, 15, 325–31, 330, 334, 343–44, 408; representations as desexualized "Mammies" of, 406–7; representations as domestic workers of, 78, 82, 89 n. 54, 235–36, 241–43, 245–48, 251; representations as sexualized "Jezebels" of, 394; respectability of, 406; sexuality and, 329; as singers, 24; working, 160–61; white male gaze and, 407; as writers, 26, 348–50, 352–60
Blesh, Rudi, 32, 40, 43
blues, 21, 32, 40, 42–43, 73, 271, 280, 334, 346 n. 7, 356, 359, 396, 383, 404; body and sexuality linked to, 34; black masculinity and, 346 n. 7; classic, 33, 34; singers of, 34, 384, 394–95
body: anthropology of, 23–24; black, 24, 174; of black dancers, 168; black women's, 370, 407; embodiment, 23–25, 407; female, 187–89; instruments and, 188–90; of instrumentalists and instruments, 199, 203–4; music and, 24–26, 267, 273–76, 285–86; singing and, 33–34, 42–44; sonorous, 24, 199; white women's, 241, 248–49
Bogle, Donald, 236
Bohländer, Carlo, 294
Bolden, Buddy, 36, 39, 235, 362
boogie-woogie, 22, 74–81, 296
Boogie-Woogie Boys, 80
Bostic, Earl, 301–2
Boswell Sisters, 251
Bowman, Laura, 161–62
Boulez, Pierre, 224
Bourdieu, Pierre, 41
Bown, Patti, 133
Braddy, Pauline, 408
Bradley, Josephine, 101
Branch, Elizabeth, 130–31
Brandeis University, 210
Bressler, Judy, 278–79

bricolage, 224

British Broadcasting Company. *See* BBC Radio

Brooks, Gwendolyn, 352

Broonzy, Big Bill, 303

Brown, Elsa Barkley, 3, 19

Brown, Jayna, 18, 23, 234, 239, 246, 395

Brown, Oscar, Jr., 358, 360 n. 17

"Brown Baby," 358, 360 n. 17

Brown Sisters, 259–60

Brubeck, Dave, 301

Brun, Harry O., 39

burlesque, 36, 271, 412

Burns, Ken, 33, 41; Marsalis and, 141–42

Burnside, Vi, 404–5, 408

Butler, Judith, 19–20, 139, 145–46

Byron, Don, 278–79, 282, 284

Cabin in the Sky, 394

Café Society, 22, 71–82; authenticity and, 80; Holiday and, 247, 256; interracialism at, 72; Josephson and, 64

Cakewalk, 168

Calloway, Cab, 398, 416

Canaille (improvising collective), 184–85, 206–7 nn. 3–4

Cantor, Mark, 400, 402, 418 n. 5, 419 n. 14, 420 nn. 26–27

Carbone, Vince, 131

Carby, Hazel, 15, 17, 27, 407

Carey, Mutt, 236

Carmichael, Hoagy, 382

Carnegie Hall, 73, 214

Carole Adams and the Glamorettes, 410, 413

Carson, Anne, 180, 186, 204

Cartier, Xam, 349, 351

Cavin, Susan, 11, 13, 19, 21

Center for Jazz Studies, 5–7

Charcot, Jean Martin, 195–96

Charleston (dance), 172–75

Chase, James Hadley, 109

Chicago, 59–60; early jazz in, 52–53

chromaticism, 186

civil rights movement, 272–73, 335

Cixous, Hélène, 190, 197–98

class, 267, 283–84, 321–22, 325, 327, 331–34, 340, 342–43, 352, 373, 401, 406, 411; consciousness of, 185; privilege and, 93, 277; sexualization of class conflict, 71

classical music, 16, 18, 51–52, 210, 217, 270, 295; representations of, 242, 376, 386

Clément, Catherine, 197–98

Clinton, George, 221

Coalition Against Police Abuse, 322, 332

Cohen, Cathy, 342–43, 347

Cold War, 378, 382

Coleman, Ornette, 226, 228

Coleman, Steve, 220

Collette, Buddy, 367

Collier, James Lincoln, 34, 39, 41

colonial discourse, 165, 174, 176, 237, 250–52

color, colorism, 89 n. 54; African American all-woman bands and, 412, 414; chorus lines and, 395, 413; movie roles for African American women and, 78

Coltrane, Alice, 351

Coltrane, John, 17, 142, 273, 336, 346 n. 11, 348; black masculinity and, 327–28; discipline and, 337; emotion and, 328; nonblack men and, 327–28; spirituality and, 326–27, 337–38, 345 n. 5

Coltrane, Naima, 351

commerce, as inauthenticity, 370, 373–74, 377

Communist International Congress, 67

Communist Party, 67, 254

Communist Party of the United States of America (CPUSA), 68–70

Conant, Abbie, 146–47

Congo Square, 11

Congress of Industrial Organizations (CIO), 67

Connelly, Reg, 114
conservatories, 214, 275
Cook, Ann, 37
Cook, Susan, 23, 27
cool jazz, 16, 380
Cooper, Lindsay, 184
Corbett, John, 221–22
Cortez, Jayne, 349
Count Basie Orchestra, 13–14, 73, 403
Covent Garden Royal Opera House, 97
Cox, Ida, 397
Cripps, Thomas, 401
Crosby, Bing, 303
Crosby, Bob, 102
cross-dressing, 20, 130, 399; instruments and, 149 n. 4; "obedient transvestism," 139; sexual stereotypes and, 149 n. 4. *See also* "in-passing"
Crossfire, 257
Crouch, Stanley, 141
Cuba, 280
"Cubana Be, Cubana Bop," 214
cultural capital, 41, 42, 210
Curtiz, Michael, 26–27, 362–64, 379
Cusick, Suzanne, 190

Daaood, Kamau, 322, 338, 341, 346 n. 9
Dahl, Linda, 13, 15
Daily Worker, 73
Dameron, Tadd, 142
dance, 18, 23, 41, 394–96, 405, 412–13; debates over morality of, 296; Hot Club policies on, 296; interracial, 259–60; intraracial, 176; as modern art, 175; as phenomenological experience of modernity, 175. *See also individual dances*
Dance, Helen Oakley, 259
dance music, 90–96; disparagement of, 302; feminized, 303; as skilled masculine labor, 104; woman musicians and, 22, 97–98
dancers, 176, 394–96, 406–7, 413, 415
Darlings of Rhythm, 308

Daughters of the American Revolution, 81–82
Dave Schooler's 21 Swinghearts, 400, 417 n. 1, 419 n.13
Davis, Angela Y., 15, 18, 27, 240
Davis, Benjamin, 79, 84
Davis, F. James, 246
Davis, Miles, 17, 142, 273, 337
Davis, Richard, 273
Davis, Tiny, 404, 405
Day, Doris, 384, 385, 398
de Jong, Nanette, 16
Dee, Ruby, 406
Delaunay, Charles, 38, 43
democracy, 366, 368, 378, 399
Depression, 66, 164; emasculating effects of, 132
Desdoumes, Mamie, 37
Dessa Rose (S. A. Williams), 356
DeVeaux, Scott, 39, 40
Dial, Harry, 56, 62 n. 26
Dickerson, James L., 50
Diet Coke Women in Jazz Festival, 144–46
difference, 17, 21, 24, 187, 188; within difference, 78–79; gender and, 137; power, language, and, 198; race and, 137; subsuming of, 137, 139, 145; as women, 185
dissonance, 9, 267
"Diva Dog" paradigm (Julie Smith), 8
Dixieland, 366
D'Lange, Eddie, 252
domestic work, 162, 251
Donegan, Dorothy, 77–78
Dorsey, Tommy, 134, 303
Double Victory (Double V) Campaign, 81–82, 403, 409
Douglas, Kirk, 362, 384, 385
Douglass, Frederick, 244, 268
Down Beat, 229
"Do You Know What It Means to Miss New Orleans," 235, 238, 250, 252

drugs and alcohol, 248, 324, 333, 385–86

Du Bois, W. E. B., 33, 268

Duffy, Thomas, 129–40, 147–48

Early, Gerald, 17

East St. Louis massacre, 167

Ebony, 82–83, 243, 246

Edwards, Brent Hayes, 3

Ehrenberg, Lewis, 132–35

Electronic Sonata for Souls Loved by Nature (Russell), 214, 223

Ellington, Duke, 295–96, 394, 398, 403, 408

Ellison, Ralph, 19, 361, 368–69

embodiment, 23–25, 407

Emery, Lynne, 35

emotions, 23, 236, 325–26, 339, 366, 368, 370–72, 377–78; black masculinity and, 331; blues and, 33, 346 n. 7; playing without, 328–30, 363, 365

England, Sylvia, 98

Entertainments National Service Association (ENSA), 105

Epstein, Dena, 35

equal pay and equal access, 106

Ertegun, Nesuhi, 253

Eshun, Kodwo, 213; *More Brilliant than the Sun*, 222–23

ethnicity, 283, 286

ethnography, 26, 31, 268, 281–83, 321–22; insider/outsider, 325

European women, 185

European Women's Improvisng Group (EWIG), 184–85

Evans, Bill, 211

Everett, Anna, 246

Everett, Francine, 411, 414

exceptional woman, 22, 77, 88 n. 45, 306, 314–15; Benson as, 98, 99; Williams as, 78

exoticism, 303; of black women's bodies, 395, 407; of "ethnic" music cultures in soundies, 398–99

experience, 10, 24–25, 361–63, 377–79

"fallen woman" trope, 406. *See also* Jazz Whore

family and jazz musicians, 12, 13, 352; bands as families, 278, 384; family bands, 276; musical families, 96; representations of, 348, 351, 353–58, 366–67, 369, 372, 380–83

Fasteau, Kali Z., 8

Feather, Leonard, 236, 297

Federal Bureau of Investigation (FBI), 254

Federal Republic of Germany (FRG), 291

Feinstein, Sascha, 349

females, 92, 131, 186, 187

Feminine Endings, 16

femininity, 134, 192; American, 117; attractiveness and, 104; constructions of masculinity and, 377; danger and, 189; feminine competence as labor, 94, 103, 117–18; feminine sensibility, 193; as madness, 23, 187; maternal, 98; musical language and, 187; performances of, 118; sexuality and, 102, 113–14, 189–90; sonic excess and, 24, 186–87; spectacle and, 23, 182; wholesome, 111

feminism, 12, 202; black, 15, 26, 352, 359; cultural, 311–12; gender equality and, 277; hysteria linked with, 200–201

Feminist Improvising Group (FIG), 184–85, 206 n. 2

feminist musicology, 16

feminist theory and criticism, 23, 310; black, 15, 26, 352, 359; poststructuralist, 24–25, 145; psychoanalytic, 24, 145

Feminist Theory and Music Conferences, 16

femme bands, 103

Ferguson, Otis, 362–63, 378

Festersen, Else, 131

Fetchit, Stepin, 411

Fifth Street Dick's (Los Angeles), 336, 344 n. 1

film: black-cast musicals, 394, 402–4, 417; black filmmakers, 400–403; black independent sound film, 394, 401–2, 404, 410–11; Hollywood industry, 236, 254, 401–3, 407; race films, 401–4; sidelining by all-girl bands in, 409–14; "women's pictures," 117. See also jazz film

Finkelstein, Sidney, 17

First World War, 161–62, 365–66

flaneurs, 157; phraseology of the body, 158; black dancers as, 23, 158–62, 165, 166, 176; female, 160–61

Forsyne, Ida, 159–61

418th Army Air Forces Band, 134–35

Frankel, Elli, 313

Frankenberg, Ruth, 24, 240

Frankfurt, 294, 297

Frazier, George, 378

freedom, 215–16

free improvisation, 183–85, 198–99

free jazz, 189, 228, 348

Freud, Sigmund, 195–98, 390 n. 23

From Spirituals to Swing, 71, 73–75, 79

Fuelle, Ingigerd, 299, 304–7, 315

"Funky Blues," 271

Gabbard, Krin, 17, 27, 252, 382, 416; "Jazz Nerd" and, 238, 242

Gaines, Kevin, 27

Gates, Henry Louis, 145, 286, 346–47 n. 13

Gautier, Madeleine, 299, 313–14

gay and lesbian musicians, 55–56; 330; exclusions of, 344

Geller, Lorraine, 313

gender, 7, 66; aesthetics and, 27, 312; as analytic of power, 21; black masculinity and, 321, 325–26; class privilege and, 277; containment in jazz of, 15, 31, 76; difference and, 79, 92, 102, 112; essentialism and, 300–303, 307, 309–16; gender bias, 26; gender equality, 99; in Germany, 302, 305, 316; as improvisation, 19; mutability of, 9; nationality and, 118; norms and, 16, 132; as social category, 9; as performance, 19–20, 145–46; "playing cute," 328–31; polarized, 301–2; record collecting and, 301–2, 307; respectability and, 327, 329; sexuality and, 70; as social construction, 9, 304–6; socialization and, 273–5, 300–301, 304–6, 316; transgression, 277

gender and genre: bebop and modern black masculinity, 245; blues and black masculinity, 346 n. 7; blues as feminine, 33; classic blues as feminine, 42–43; cool jazz, 16; downhome blues as masculine, 42–43; gendered spheres of jazz, 15, 31, 76; popular jazz as feminized, 133; ragtime and gay men's masculinity, 55–56; ragtime as masculine, 33–34, 55

gender and instruments, 33–34, 42, 56, 78, 269, 277; bands as masculine, 131; drums, 291, 311–12; piano, 55, 83–84, 188–90; saxophone, 271; trumpets, 270, 273–76.

gender and listening, 303, 307–10, 315–16

gender studies, 60, 145

Gendron, Bernard, 3, 243–44

Gene Krupa (film), 386

Gennari, John, 27, 350

German Democratic Republic (GDR), 291, 294

German Jazz Federation, 297

Germany: dangers of listening to jazz in, 293, 296–97; Hot Clubs in, 294–97,

Germany (*continued*)
299–302; jazz and cultural definition
in, 296; jazz and racism in, 295; postwar jazz in, 24, 291–96, 305, 308, 316;
postwar reconstruction of, 291–92,
294, 305; Wehrmachtshelferinnen,
292; Wirtshaftswunder, 305
Gillespie, Dizzy, 81, 142, 214, 296–97
Giovanni, Nikki, 352
GI Shows, 294
Give Birth to Brightness, 353–54
glamour: at Café Society, 64; class and,
92; labor and, 110; mask of, 117; patri-
otic duty and, 92, 94, 97, 414
Gleason, Ralph J., 378–80, 389
Glenn Miller Orchestra, 22–23, 129–
30
Glenn Miller Story, 386
Gloria Gaye and Her Glamour Girl
Band, 96
Glucksman, Emmanuel, 401
Goffin, Robert, 37–38, 43, 60, 63
Golden Gate Quartet, 75, 256
Gonsoulin, Bertha, 244
Gonzales, Antonia, 37
Goodman, Benny, 133, 362, 403, 418
n. 6
Gordon, Dexter, 367
Gordon, Maxine, 8, 12, 13, 239
gossett, hattie, 11–12
Gottschild, Brenda Dixon, 23
Gramophone, 116–17
Gray, Herman, 17, 27, 142, 148; on
Afrofuturism, 220
Griffin, Farah Jasmine, 3, 7, 8, 26
Grosz, Elizabeth, 25
Gushee, Lawrence, 35, 38

hagiography, 361–63, 377–79. *See also*
jazz historiography
Hairston, Monica, 22
Halberstam, Judith, 131, 134
Hammersmith Palais, 101

Hammond, John, 17, 72–74
Hampton, Gladys, 12
Hampton, Lionel, 301
Handy, D. Antoinette, 13, 15
Handy, W. C., 38
Hans Koller Quartet, 297
hard bop, 188
hardship, 324–26, 332
Hare, Maude Cuney, 40
Harlem, 66, 164–66
Harlem Jam Session, 396
Harlem Renaissance, 40, 401, 407
Harrison, Daphne Duvall, 15
Harrison, Ruth, 98
Hartman, Johnny, 327
Hawkins, Coleman, 211–12, 215
Hayes, Eileen M., 15
Hayes, Roland, 40
Hazzard-Gordon, Katrina, 23
Heat's On, The, 64–66, 71, 82
Heble, Ajay, 9
Hentoff, Nat, 17
Herman, Woody, 251–52
Herskovitz, Melville, 39
heterosexuality: courtship and, 274, 374,
383–86, desire and, 131, as norm, 285;
performance of, 183, 276; romantic
love and, 194. *See also* sexuality
Higginbotham, Evelyn Brooks, 377
Higgins, Billy, 320–22, 337–38, 341, 344
n. 1
Hines, Earl, 58–59
hip hop, 334, 346 n. 9, 360 n. 18
hipness, 17; hipsters and, 238–39; unhip-
ness, 243, 267; white women and, 238,
253
Hipp, Jutta, 293–94, 297–99, 313–15
historiography, feminist, 10. *See also* jazz
historiography: women-and-jazz
Hitler, Adolf, 292–93
Hoeffler, Paul, 13, 14
Hoffman, Bernd, 295
Holiday, Billie, 4, 18, 76, 81, 297, 311,

397, 416; at Café Society, 247, at Carnegie Hall, 256, 258; Federal Reformatory for Women and, 258; at Metropolitan Opera House, 246, 251; in
New Orleans, 236, 242–43, 245–48,
256, 258; "Strange Fruit" and, 247,
252, 256; Town Hall, 247
Hollywood, 243, 257–58; film industry
in, 236, 254, 401–3, 407; music genre
films, 83, 403, 407
Holocaust, 292
home front, 91, 110, 134
homophobia, 269, 274, 281, 329, 343
homosexuality, 55–56, 62 n. 26. *See also*
gay and lesbian musicians; lesbians;
sexuality; sexual orientation
hooks, bell, 346 n. 7
Hope, Bertha, 8, 12
Horne, Lena, 76, 82, 358, 398, 418 n. 6
Hot Club Combo of Frankfurt, 294
Hot Club de France, 295
Hot Club Düsseldorf, 296
Hot Clubs, 308; activities in, 294–96,
299, 302, in France, 295; in Germany,
294–97, 299–302; women in, 295
hot jazz, 98, 303, 382, 408, 409, 414;
raced and gendered, 370, 374, 396,
412
House Un-American Activities Committee (HUAC), 243
"How 'bout That Jive?," 404
Hucko, Peanuts, 129
Hughes, Langston, 40
Hurston, Zora Neale, 353
Hutton, Marion, 134
Hylton, Jack, 107
hysteria: discursive history of, 191–93;
language and, 197; as medical discourse, 192–93, 200; performance and
performativity of, 24, 183, 193–95,
202–4; as protest, 197–98; psychoanalysis and, 195–98; subversive possibilities of, 197–98, 204–6

identity, 131, 137–38
"I Love You More Today Than Yesterday," 292, 297
Imitation of Life, 251
"Impressions," 320, 328
improvisation, 116, 130, 145–47, 198,
271, 320–29, 358; Afrological, 338;
bel canto eliminated from, 186; as category, 142; collective expression and,
324–25, 330–31; as dialogue with own
otherness, 200; in early jazz, 35; gender as, 24; as "inspired lunacy," 185;
beyond language, 193–95, 202, 204–5;
liberatory quality of, 322, 325, 331; as
process, 146; quotation in, 194; representations of, 189; as space of immediacy and displacement, 199; subjectivity and, 200, 205–6
improvising collectives, 16, 180;
women's, 183–85, 188. *See also individual collectives*
Ina Ray Hutton and Her Melodears,
397, 404, 409, 416
inauthenticity, 117
India, 217; music of, 280
individuality, 379–80, 382
"in-passing," 130–32, 137, 141, 146
Institute of Jazz Studies, 5
instruments: gender and, *see* gender and
instruments; genre and, 270–71, 273–
74; vocal effects of, 43–44
Intakt, 184
integration, 133, 364–65, 378–79
interiority, 159
internationalism, black, 335–38, 340–41,
409
International Sweethearts of Rhythm,
308, 393–97, 400–409, 413, 415–17
intersectional analysis, 7, 15, 19, 21, 24,
70; social categories and, 284–86; race
and class in, 185; sexualization of class
and, 71
interviews, 36, 282–83

Islam, 320–21, 334–35, 339–42, 346–47 n. 13, 347 n. 14
Ivy Benson and Her Ladies' Dance Orchestra, 22, 90–118

Jackson, George Pullen, 39
Jackson, Mahalia, 358, 360 n. 17
Jackson, Tony, 37
James, C. L. R., 172
James, Harry, 403
Jameson, Fredric, 138
jam sessions, 24, 320; black collective social life and, 324–25, 329–30, 344; exclusions from, 321–22, 325–26, 328–29, 344; gay musicians included in, 330; heterogeneity and, 330–32, 343; in Hot Clubs, 296; international nature of, 323; levels of expertise and, 322–25, 327–29, 344–45 n. 3; mythology of, 378; "playing cute" and, 328–31; representations of, 404; women included in, 297, 327–29, 330, 404. *See also* World Stage
jazz: as African American music, 280; as American music, 16–17, 366, 380; as art music, 39–42; authenticity of, 40–42, 84, 363; as black male space, 320–22, 325–34; as black music, 16–17; boogie-woogie, 79, 84; challenges to, 26, 147; as democracy, 4–5, 18, 19, 22, 141–42, 147, 364–66, 380; domestic partners of musicians, 12–13, 348–49, 351–59, 375–76, 380, 386–88; as emasculation, 296, 388; gender and, 218, 274–75, 291, 299, 310–13, 316, 382; German culture and, 293–97, 299–300, 312–15; identity formation and, 273, 275; improvisation and, 143; as industry, 217; as interracial fraternity, 5, 368–71, 374–75, 377–78, 380; jazz community, 6, 348–51, 356; as male domain, 5, 21, 26–27, 42, 273–75, 368; as modernist discourse, 18,

21; mythology of, 32, 38–39; as narrative, 32, 38–39; progressive movements symbolized by, 273–74, 315, 378–79; representations by black women writers of, 26, 348–50, 352–60; sexuality and, 24, 248–49, 296, 299, 372, 410; as site of racial transgression, 367–74, 376; sophistication of, 142, 296, 315; spirituality and, 42; youth culture and, 296
Jazz Age, 167–68, 364–65, 389 n. 13, 395, 397, 405, 407; "white primitives" and, 376–78
Jazz at Lincoln Center (JALC), 5, 130, 141–48
jazz autobiography, 13, 17, 36–37, 268, 387
jazz biography, 349, 377
jazz canon, 61 n. 4, 142, 148; race of, 388–89 n. 5
jazz clubs, 24, 357
jazz community, 22, 269, 273–76
jazz criticism, 2, 16–17, 22, 35, 43, 350–51, 366, 377, 378, 380
jazz culture, 286
jazz discourse: gendered, 6, 377–78; histories of injustice occluded from, 238; racialized, 377, 378
jazz drumming, 291, 311
jazz fans, 41, 293–95, 299, 312, 348–49, 357, 366; collectors vs., 309–10, 315; male, 300–301; in films, 240–52, 256; women, 8, 13, 24, 26, 237, 239, 252–60, 296, 302–9, 313–16
jazz fiction, 26, 348; race and gender represented in, 349–51, 362–77; virtuosic performance in, 356–58
jazz film, 24, 27, 362–63, 400–408; early sound, 397–98; Hollywood, 379–88; 414–15, 416–17; sidelining by all-woman bands and, 397, 399, 402, 409–14; soloists emphasized in, 412; women jazz musicians and, 393–417. *See also* film

jazz historiography, 19, 22–23, 27, 267, 364, 378; exceptional woman in, 76; gender analysis excluded from, 377; as "great man" history, 39, 151–52 n. 35; origins emphasized in, 11, 21, 32, 24, 28–29, 44; recordings emphasized in, 21, 38; singers vs. instrumentalists in, 15, 21, 31–35, 38, 41–44; soloists emphasized in, 21, 56; West Coast jazz in, 367–68; whites in, 366; women-and-jazz, 13, 15, 31; women erased from, 41, 42, 44, 143, 350–51, 377

Jazz Hot, 314

jazz knowledge, 253, 315–16

jazz magazines, 26, 291, 297, 299–301, 303–5, 309. *See also individual magazines*

jazz marketing, 142–43

jazzmen, 39, 212, 231, 383

jazz photography, 13, 142

Jazz Podium, 291, 297, 299–301, 308, 312–16

jazz poetry, 349

jazz polls, 297

jazz singing, 21, 31–44, 406

jazz studies, 1–3, 5–10, 28, 39–41, 44

jazz tradition narrative, 43–44, 142–43

"Jazz Virgin," 241

Jazz Wars, 243, 251, 253; bebop vs. cool, 380; bebop vs. swing, 311; gender and, 244–45; in Germany, 296, 303, 311; trad vs. swing, 41

"Jazz Whore," 241

Jerome, V. J., 240

Jet, 83

Jews: identity of, 149–50 n. 11, 283–85; as "coon-shouters," 239; music of, 278–79; as songwriters, 93

Jim Crow, 379, 409

Jitterbug, 100–101, 296

Jive, 101

Johnson, Bunk, 37, 244

johnson, carolyn, 11–12

Johnson, James Weldon, 164–66

Jones, Gayle, 349, 356

Jones, LeRoi (Amiri Baraka), 17–18

Josephson, Barney, 64, 83–84

Juilliard School, 81

Julian, Kyle, 17, 27

Jutta Hipp Combo, 297

Kelley, Robin D. G., 7, 12, 16–17, 27, 65, 68

Kernodle, Tammy, 8

Khalilullah, Rizza, 321

Kimball, Jeannette, 245

Kirby, John, 410, 420 n. 26

Klezmer, 68, 278–79

Klezmer Conservatory Band, 278

Knight, Doris, 111

Knueppel, Marianne, 299, 304, 306–15

Koller, Hans, 294, 297

Kondo, Dorinne, 146

Kristeva, Julia, 187, 206

Kulu Se Mama, 336, 346 n. 11

Kunst, Peter, 299–309, 312, 316

Kyser, Kay, 418 n. 6

Lady Sings the Blues, 4

Lala, Pete, 36

language: improvising beyond, 191, 193–95, 202, 204–5; linguistic excess, 185; music and, 187; power and, 198

Last of the Blonde Bombshells, The, 113–14

Latin music, 276–78

Lavitt, Pamela Brown, 239

Leadbelly, 303

Léandre, Jöelle, 180–85, 198–200, 202–4, 206

Lee, Peggy, 251

Lee, Spike, 281–82, 387–88

"Legend of Billy the Kid, The," 211

Leimert Park (Los Angeles), 320–21, 326, 332–44

Leonard, Neil, 17

Leppert, Richard, 188–89

lesbians, 186, 204, 274–75
Les Diaboliques, 180–85, 202–4, 206
Levin, Art, 253
Levin, Floyd, 253
Levine, Lawrence, 35
Lévi-Strauss, Claude, 224
Lewis, Edna, 20
Lewis, George, 7, 220, 338
Lewis, Juno Se Mama, 322, 335–39, 341, 344 n. 1, 346 n. 11
Lez Zeppelin, 146–47
Lincoln, Abbey, 352
Lincoln Motion Picture Company, 401–2
Lindy Hop, 168–72
Lippmann, Horst, 294, 297
listening, 181; challenges to notions of, 307; gendered, 309–10, 315–16
Little Harlem (Los Angeles), 259–60
Lock, Graham, 344
London, Frank, 276
Lorde, Audre, 352
Lorraine Page and Her Orchestra, 397
Los Angeles, 163, 380; Central Avenue, 367–68, 377; integration in, 259–60; Leimert Park, 320–21, 326, 332–44; segregation and racism in, 367–68; Watts, 163, 367. See also World Stage
Lott, Eric, 16, 238
Love Supreme, A, 327–28, 345 n. 5
Lowe, Lisa, 139
Lydian Chromatic Concept, 24, 211, 213–16, 214, 219, 224, 226–28
Lynch, Theodora, 251–52

Mackey, Nathaniel, 349
"Maiden Voyage," 358
Mairants, Ivor, 98
Malone, Jacqui, 23, 27, 174
marginalization: of improvised music, 185; (re)marginalization, 144; singing and, 31, 44; women and, 44, 185
Marijuana, 248

Marsalis, Wynton, 238; Burns and, 141–42; Jazz at Lincoln Center and, 5, 141–44, 146–48
Marshall, Paule, 356
masculinity, 95, 201, 361, 363–64, 368–72, 377–78, 382; authority and, 230; black, 133; British, 118–19 n. 5; competing versions of, 17, 387; genius as, 218; heterosexual desire and, 188; image of, 134
masculinity studies, 16–18; music and, 118 n. 5; normative, 133; sound and, 54–55; technology and, 54–55; women and, 201, 274
Maud Martha, 352
McClary, Susan, 16, 24, 118 n. 5, 180, 186
McClure, Kit, 8
McGee, Kristen, 27
McKinney, Nina Mae, 397, 420 n. 23
McMullen, Tracy, 7, 22–23
McRae, Carmen, 247
"Medley," 349, 356–59
Meeropol, Abel, 252
Meier, Rosmarie, 184
melodrama, 363, 379–80, 385–88, 391 n. 32
Melody Maker, 90, 93, 99–100, 104–5, 107
memory, 378–79; dance and, 168; national, 130, 137–38
meritocracy: as modernist ideal, 15, 280; women's bands excluded from, 104–5
Metropolitan Opera House, 251
Mezzrow, Mezz, 237, 283, 369–70
Micheaux, Oscar, 402
Miles, Lizzie, 245
military service: in Britain, 296; in United States, 134–35
Miller, Glenn, 22–23, 129, 132, 135–37, 140, 386, 403, 408; white masculinity and, 130, 133–34
Miller, Mark, 13–14

Miller, Norma, 176; Whitey's Lindy Hoppers and, 168–69

Mingus, Charles, 4, 219, 268, 357, 367, 387

minstrelsy, 16, 32–33, 36, 396, 399, 410; Topsy, 239; in *Uncle Tom's Cabin*, 239–40; white women and, 249

Minton's Playhouse, 75

miscegenation, 260, 407, 414

Mo' Better Blues, 387–88

modal jazz, 326

modern city, 158

modernism, 23, 28 n. 10; postwar, 18, 218

modernist ideals: of art, 18, 43; of meritocracy, 15, 280; of music, 18, 280

modernity, 364–65; abstract citizen of, 139; black, 18, 23; defined by black dancers, 158–59; feminist critiques of, 159–60; flaneurs and, 157; labor of black bodies crucial to, 172

modern subject, 18, 158–60

Moldy Figs, 41, 244. *See also* Jazz Wars

Monk, Nellie, 12

Monogram Theater (Chicago), 53, 61 n. 12

Monson, Ingrid, 1, 17, 23–26, 145, 238; on Russell, 216–17

Morden, Marili, 252–53, 257–60

Morel, Martine, 313–14

Morgenstern, Dan, 229

Morrison, Toni, 349, 352, 355–56, 374

Morton, Jelly Roll, 36–37, 53–56

mouvements brusques, 157, 163–64, 166

Muhammad, Don, 332

Mullen, Harryette, 349

Mumford, Brock, 36

Murphy, Rose, 78

Murray, Albert, 141

music: as cross-cultural experience, 277–78; healing and, 337; as masculine work, 109; mobility and, 355–56, 358

musical form, 218

music education, 269–71, 275, 300

musicians: health and, 320–21, 324, 387; nonsoloists, 51

Musicians' Union (MU), 99, 107

musicking, 66, 77, 80

Music Maids, 399

music notation, 54–55

musicology, 21

music theory, 215–16

music training, 269–71, 273–75

musique concrète, 224

Naison, Mark, 69–70, 73, 84–85 n 6, 85 n. 9

National Association for the Advancement of Colored People (NAACP), 246

national identity, 22, 137–38, 277, 292, 296; British, 90, 92, 94

nationalism and gender, 93, 118, 292

national memory, 130, 137–39

National Service (Britain), 99

Nazis, 172, 293, 296; mother cult images and, 292, 297

New Deal, 67–68

New England Conservatory of Music, 214, 275

New Grove Dictionary of Jazz, 34–35

New Orleans, 11, 21, 32–33, 36–38, 42–44, 251, 336, 338; fantasies of, 238, 245, 257, 386; style, 35, 41, 235–36, 240, 242–45, 248–53, 257–58, 366–68, 370–71, 380–81

New Orleans, 24, 235–37, 240–60

New York City, 158, 164–66

Nicols, Maggie, 180–85, 193–95, 202–6

"Night in Tunisia, A," 320

Nijinsky, Vaslav, 158

noise, 185–86

nostalgia, 23, 136, 147; performative, 130

Nurullah, Shanta, 8

O'Brien, Peter, 8

Office of War Information (OWI), 134, 400–401

Ogren, Kathy, 27, 365
Oja, Carol J., 18
Oliver, King, 244
O'Meally, Robert, 3, 6, 27, 247
openness, 335–39, 343–44
opera, 186
oral history, 8, 10, 13
Ory, Kid, 253, 257–58; in *New Orleans*, 235–36
Osborne, William, 146
Othering, 139

Pace, Robert, 210
palais de danse, 93, 95–101
Panassié, Hugues, 38–40, 43, 295, 314
Panish, Jon, 350–51
Paramount Records, 53
Parker, Charlie, 245, 271–73, 296, 345, 350
passing: gender, 20, 131; race, 131, 149 n. 5; sexuality, 285
pathways of identification, 238–39
Patrick, Dorothy, 235, 247
patriotism, 134, 136
Paul, Elliott, 255–56, 258
"paying dues," 323–26
pedagogy, 3, 7, 9, 210–13, 230–31, 268, 284–86
Pellegrinelli, Lara, 15, 21, 144
People's War, 90, 93–95
Perez, Manuel, 37
performance, 24–25, 163, 320–23, 326, 332, 357–58; gender as, 19–20, 145–46; of heterosexual femininity, 276; of hysteria, 195–96; 203–4; lesbian, 204; performance studies, 23; performative history, 141, 146; queer, 183, 204; of race, 396; of sexuality, 396
Perry, Lee, 221
Petry, Ann, 352, 356
Pettiford, Margie, 400
phallus, black, 133

Phil Spitalny and his Hour of Charm Orchestra, 114, 308, 400, 404, 417 n. 1, 420 n. 24
piano: accompanists on, 21, 55–57; as aesthetic feminized object, 188–89; child prodigies and, 95; economic and erotic economy of, 83–84, 188–89; European women and; 188–90; feminine sexuality and, 189; femininity and, 55, 83–84; uplift and, 83–84; women and, 21–22
Piazza, Countess Willie, 37
Pierce, Billie, 245
Placksin, Sally, 13, 15
"playing cute," 328–31
Poiger, Uta, 296
politics, 21–22, 147–48, 272–75, 286, 338, 341–42, 344; activism, 271–74; anti-imperialism, 68; antiracism, 68, 286; antiwar movements, 271–73
Pollard, Bud, 412–13
Pollard, Terry, 313
Popular Front, 22, 65–75, 79, 243
popularity, 36, 42, 133, 136, 372
Porter, Eric, 17, 24, 245
Porter, Lewis, 345 n. 5
postmodernism, 131, 138
postwar jazz, 222
Powell, Adam Clayton, Jr., 75
practice (discipline), 275
primitivism, 23, 41, 43, 174, 176, 231, 363, 370–71, 373, 376, 385–86, 407; assumptions about, 218, 222; in black entertainment, 395, 412–13, 416; writers and, 237
Progressive Party, 67
Prohibition, 365
public space, 163–66, 320–44
Purnell, Mattie, 170–71

queer activism, 205
queer performance, 183, 204
queer theory, 139, 205

Rabinowitz, Paula, 70, 78–79
race, 60; colorblindness and, 374, essentialism and, 339–41, 343–44; jazz historiography and, 39; manhood and, 370–72, 377; masculinity and, 16–17, 368, 371–72, 377; musical style and, 370, 373–74; as process, 369; reenactment and, 22–23; repertoire and, 328, 404; sound and, 295, 329, 373; racial traversing and, 130; transcendence of, 231
racism, 324–26, 373–74; African Americans and, 268–69, 279–80; life chances and, 280; racialized communities and, 330; scientific racialism and, 395; stereotypes and, 295, 398–99, 412–13, 417; in women's movement, 12
Radano, Ron, 17, 27
radio, 22, 293; BBC, 22, 90–95, 104–14; gender and, 102
Radio-Keith-Orpheum (RKO), 256
ragtime, 32, 44, 314, 396; masculinity of, 33–34, 55–56
Rainey, Gertrude "Ma," 18, 33, 38
Ramsey, Frederick, Jr., 33, 36, 39
Ramsey, Guthrie P., 18, 27
Rasula, Jed, 38
Ray, Carlene, 8
Ray, Kay D., 8
reading music, 277–79
Reagon, Bernice Johnson, 268, 272–73
Reason, Dana, 7
record collecting, 238, 295; jazz, 293–94, 301–2, 308–9, 315; as male activity, 301–2; women and, 305–6, 308, 315
records, 21; emphasis in jazz historiography on, 38; listening to, 316; popularity of blues women's, 38, 42; as source of knowledge, 315; race and, 395
Reefer Madness, 248
reflexive writing, 268–69

Regier, Muriel, 69
Reitz, Rosetta, 396–97
religion, 320–21, 334–35; Christianity, 342; Hinduism, 337; Islam, 320–21, 334–35, 339–42, 346–47 n. 13, 347 n. 14
repertoire, 327–28
repetition, 136, 146
"Replay," 137–40, 141, 143, 147–48
representations, 25, 185, 187; of ideal jazz man, 26–27, 368, 370–72; of jazz by black women writers, 26, 348–50, 352–60; of jazz musicians, 381; of nation, 138
respectability, 95, 322, 334, 342, 383; black masculinity and, 325–27, 332–33; black womanhood and, 406; feminine, 115; German women and, 296–97, 299; jazz and, 42; white womanhood and, 241
rhythm: masculine, 310–11; women's expertise on dance floor and, 313–15
rhythm and blues, 40
Rice, Johnny Mae, 404
Rita Rio and Her Mistresses of Rhythm, 308, 397, 400
Roberts, Matana, 7
Robeson, Paul, 40, 69
Robinson, Bill, 240
rock and roll, 273
Roelofs, Anne-Marie, 184
Rogers, Hattie, 37
Rogers, Sharon, 308
Rogin, Michael, 239
romantic artist, 219
Ross, Diana, 4
Royal Air Force (RAF), 91, 109
Ruben Guity y Su Orquesta, 276–78
Russell, George, 24, 213, 216–17, 219, 221–24, 226, 228–29, 231, 234 nn. 39–40; "The Future of Jazz" (television episode), 210–12, 214, 227, 230; tonal gravity, 211, 215

Russia, 159, 161–62
Russo-Japanese War, 161–62
Rustin, Nichole T., 4, 8, 17, 26

Said, Edward, 32, 39
Sanchez, Sonia, 349
San Francisco Museum of Modern Art,
    244
Sargeant, Winthrop, 39
Savage Mind, The (Lévi-Strauss), 224
Savoy Ballroom, 168–69, 170, 172
saxophone, 271
Scandinavian American, 267–68
Schiller, Greta, 396
Schlicht, Ursel, 25–26
school bands, 15, 269, 270, 271, 286
School of Jazz at Lenox, 210
Schuller, Gunther, 50
Schweizer, Irène, 180–85, 188–90, 202–
    4, 206
science: jazz as, 295; music as, 219; tech-
    nology and, 24, 220, 224
science fiction tropes, 221–22
scopophilic pleasure, 137
Scott, Hazel, 22, 74–79, 81, 85, 245, 255,
    418 n. 6; black audiences and, 84; Café
    Society and, 64–65; in The Heat's On,
    64–66, 71, 82; performances of black
    femininity by, 83–84; "swingin' the
    classics" and, 65
Scott, Joan, 7, 15, 24
Scottsboro Case, 67, 85 n.9
2nd Army Forces Training Command
    (AAFTC) Radio Union, 135
Second World War, 22–23, 129, 133,
    292–94, 296–97, 386, 399–403, 409–
    10, 413–14; commemorations of, 129,
    130, 138; Double Victory (Double V)
    campaign in, 81–82, 403, 409; Ger-
    man women in, 292–93, 296–97, 305;
    in Germany, 292–94, 296–97; Rosie
    the Riveter in, 307; Trummerfrauen
    in, 292, 298, 305; war effort, 92, 105

segregation, 163
Seldes, Gilbert, 210
sentimentality: Dorsey and, 303;
    effeminacy of, 94; excessive, 22, 111;
    female crooners and, 116; male
    crooners and, 93; Sinatra and, 303
Severinsen, Doc, 270
sexism: audiences and, 279; big bands
    and, 131, 275, 276; in jazz, 11, 12, 133,
    275, 321–22, 325, 406; music educa-
    tion and, 275, rehearsals and, 131, 275,
    276
sexuality: African Americans linked to,
    42; in early jazz, 36, 42; bodies, instru-
    ments, and, 190; blues and, 33, 271;
    difference and, 281–82, 330; hetero-
    normativity and, 329–31, 343–44;
    heterosexuality, 327, 329; homoerot-
    icism, 55–56, 190, 329–30, 371–72,
    382–83, 388; homophobia and, 281,
    343; ragtime pianists and, 55–56; rep-
    resentations of jazz musicians and,
    387; women in jazz spaces and, 270,
    334, 385. See also homophobia
sexualization: of black men, 371–72; of
    black music, 295, 373; of black
    women's bodies, 406–7; of class, 70–
    71; of jazz in marketing, 271
sexual orientation, 267–69, 275, 281–82,
    286; public disclosure of, 285; stereo-
    types and, 274, 285
sex workers, 36, 37, 43, 333
Shange, Ntozake, 349, 352, 359 n. 4
Shaw, Artie, 115–16, 134; "Begin the
    Beguine," 103
Shepp, Archie, 229
Showalter, Elaine, 196, 201, 202, 205
sidelining, 409–14
signifying practice, 131, 185
silence, breaking, 186
Simon, George T., 362
Simone, Nina, 358
Sinatra, Frank, 303

singing, 31; Armstrong and, 37; body linked to, 40–41, 43; crooning, 93, 116, 132; as feminine occupation, 92; jazz studies and, 43; instrumentalists' antipathy toward, 323; New Orleans and, 43–44; phrasing and timing in, 311; talking horns and, 43; women and, 358; "women's place" and, 276, as work, 92. *See also* women jazz singers

Singleton, Zutty, 175, 235

Smith, Anna Deveare, 146

Smith, Bessie, 18, 33, 38, 51, 73, 356, 420 n. 23

Smith, Charles Edward, 33, 36, 39

Smith, Julie Dawn, 7–8, 23–24

Snodgrass, Jeane, 276–77

Snow, Valaida, 349, 394, 395

Snowden, Shorty, 159, 170–71

social geography, 333, 334, 367, 368

socialization, 302, 304–6, 315

soul, 219, 228, 324

sound: competent femininity and, 114; excess, 180; feminized, 115, 132; heteromasculine, 274; madness and, 180; marginality and, 186, 204; pathology and, 183–85; racialized, 295, 373; social consciousness and, 273–74; women's, 185–87; women's reclaiming of, 187

soundies, 396–97, 408, 413–14, 417 n. 1, 418 n. 5, 419 n. 9, 420 n. 25; African American entertainers in, 400, 403; "ethnic" music cultures in, 398–99

Southern, Eileen, 34, 35, 41

Southern California Hot Jazz Society, 253

Spanish Civil War, 67, 255

spectacle, controlled, 189

Spillers, Hortense, 352

spirituals, 21, 32, 39, 40, 356

Stearns, Marshall, 32, 41, 293

Steck, Steven, 129

Stewart, Jacqueline Najuma, 401

Stork Club, 252

Storyville, 36, 37, 247

Stowe, David, 38, 73–74, 79

"Stratusphunk," 211

Strayhorn, Billy, 356

stride, 34

subject: black modern, 18, 23; normative model of, 160; subject formation, 18, 23–26, 395

"Subject Is Jazz, The," 210

subjectivity, 159–60; black female, 84; black modern, 18, 23; improvisation of, 145, 200, 205; white women's, 24, 246

Sun Ra, 221

sweet jazz, 116, 132, 133, 382. *See also* hot jazz

swing: bands, 131–33; classics and, 78, 81, 410, 420 n. 26; as dance music, 94; democratic nature of, 366; as genre, 41, 296, 366, 402, 403; in Germany, 296; masculinist language and, 71; patriotism and, 403; popularity of, 22, 101; as quality, 276, 329; revival of, 130; swing "era," 32

Symphony Hall, 251

Symphony in Black, 394

Syncopation, 256

Tabor, Charly, 294

Tall, Tan and Terrific, 402, 413–14

Tarzana, 412–13

Taylor, Jeffrey, 21

Taylor, Timothy, 224

Teachers College, 210

technique: lack of emotion and, 328–29; mastery of, 324–25; race and, 279; spirituality and, 337; women's, 406, 408

technology and modernity, 157–58

television: "The Future of Jazz" (episode), 210; "The Last of the Blond Bombshells," 113–14; Scott and, 77, 88 n. 50; "The Subject Is Jazz," 210

"Tell Martha Not to Moan," 349, 352–56

Temple, Shirley, 240
Texas Tommy (dance), 158
Tharpe, Sister Rosetta, 73–74, 397
That Man of Mine, 393–94, 396–408,
413, 415–17
Theater Owners' Booking Association
(TOBA), 42
theatrical shows, 394–96
Thelma White and Her All-Girl
Orchestra, 400
Third World Liberation, 217
Tickner, Lisa, 200–201
Tin Pan Alley, 42
Tirro, Frank, 32
Tracy, Sheila, 114
trad, 41, 244. *See also* Jazz Wars; New
Orleans: style
tribute bands, 22–23, 130, 137
Trummerfrauen, 292, 298, 305
trumpet: heteromasculinity linked to,
270, 273–76; Klezmer, 278–81; in
Latin music, 276–78; in western clas-
sical music, 270; women and, 24, 26,
83, 267, 269–70, 273–76, 279, 286
Tucker, Sherrie, 24, 38, 49, 349–51, 409
Tucker, Sophie, 162
Turkey Trot (dance), 158
Tyner, McCoy, 326, 328

utopia, 338, 341–44
Ulanov, Barry, 17, 39, 388 n. 5
Uncle Tom's Cabin (Stowe), 239
Underground Musicians Artists Associa-
tion (UGMA), 346 n. 9
United Service Organizations (USO), 308,
402, 410–13
universalism, 229–30
uplift, 83–84, 401–2, 405, 409, 415
Uptown Conversations, 3

Vargas, João H. Costa, 26
vaudeville, 33, 36, 42, 400, 413–14
venues and gender, 408

Vietnam War, 30, 140
virility, 93, 94, 132; British dance music
and, 22, 104, 108; Popular Front and, 71
virtuosity, 186, 271
Von Eschen, Penny, 27

Wald, Gayle, 356, 369–70
Walker, Alice, 352, 356
Walker, George, 161
Walker, T-Bone, 259–60
Wallace, Michele, 239
Washington, Salim, 238
Waterman, Ellen, 7
Waterman, Richard, 39
Waters, Ethel, 33, 48
Weiss, Andrea, 396
Welburn, Ron, 41
Welles, Orson, 244–45, 254–56
West, Cornel, 286
White, Hayden, 27
White, Lulu, 37
white dance orchestras, 370, 372–74,
377, 379, 383–84
white jazz musicians, 388–89 n. 5
white jazz scholars, 282–83, 286
Whiteman, Paul, 132–33, 362, 382,
388–89 n. 5, 410
white masculinity: black men's perceptions of, 328–29, 331; blackness and,
369–71; British, 23, 27, 93; controlled,
134, 137; constructions of, 361, 363; in
crisis, 377–79, 385; identity and, 361;
as nationalist archetype, 130, 145; normative, 136, 137; as patriarchy, 134
white men: black musicians and, 276;
blackness and, 133, 371–72, 379–81;
emasculation of, 328–29, 371; as emotionally lacking, 376–77; homosocial
interracial intimacy and, 372, 381; in
jazz, 368–71, 374, 377, 380–81;
racialized Other and, 369, 370, 372,
374; representations of, 24, 361–75,
378–88

whiteness: authenticity of black music "diluted" by, 73–74; black music and, 24–25, 268, 269, 274, 283, 284, 286; privilege and, 239, 284, 350; slumming and, 164, 235–36, 247–49, 376; whiteness studies, 17, 24; white supremacist ideology, 238

white people in jazz, 274, 283, 284, 286, 287

white womanhood, 24, 239–42, 258

white women, 236; as impediments to jazz subculture, 375–76, 383; "pure," 384; representations of, 235–37, 240–43

white women musicians, 275, 414

Whitey, George, 168, 172

Whitey's Lindy Hoppers, 168–69, 172–73

Wiebe, Rosemarie, 307–9, 315

Wiegman, Robyn, 369–70

Williams, Bert, 161

Williams, Clarence, 36–37

Williams, Edna, 404

Williams, Linda F., 15

Williams, Mary Lou, 8, 22, 51, 78, 308; black masculinity and, 80; boogie-woogie and, 74–77, 79–81; Father Peter O'Brien and, 8, 81; *Zodiac Suite*, 75

Williams, Rita, 116

Williams, Sherley Ann, 348–49, 352–54, 356, 359

Williams, Spencer, 37, 403

Wilmer, Val, 12, 348–49, 351–53

Wilson, Olly, 27

Winburn, Anna Mae, 404, 416

Windmöller, Eva, 299, 308–15

women-and-jazz history, 2, 10–11, 16; instrumentalists emphasized in, 13, 15, 31, 43; historians of, 13, 27, 237–38

womanhood: constructions of ideal, 292, 297, 299, 305; domesticity and, 292, 305; in Germany, 291–92, 296–97, 299, 305, 316

women jazz fans, 26, 252–60; independence of, 308, 315, 316; as partners and wives of male jazz fans, 303–6, 314; perceptions of, 303–4, 306; seriousness of, 308–10, 313, 315–16; strategies and tactics of, 315–16; women musicians and, 307–8, 313

women jazz instrumentalists, 15–16, 21–24, 26, 38, 130–31, 299, 307–8; 323, 328–30, 332, 334, 348–49; disrespect toward, 144–45, 269, 275–76; glamour and, 412–14, 416; horn players, 275, 279; perceptions of, 133, 270, 274; representations of, 143–45, 393–417; sexualized performance expectations and, 410, 413–14, 416–17; strategies and tactics of, 279–80, 416–17. *See also* "in-passing"

women jazz singers, 299, 346; diminutive titles of, 5, 32; representations of, 382–83, 411

Women's Army Corps (WAC), 413

women's history, 2, 10, 11, 13, 15, 31, 60

women's improvising collectives, 188

women's jazz festivals, 11, 13, 144–45, 153 n. 48

women's movement, 10, 13, 292, 305, 352, 396

"women's music," 11, 274

"women's place": in jazz, 144–45, 314–16; in the symbolic, 197

women's studies, 6, 7

women's suffrage, 200–201

Woode, Henri, 406

Woodman, Britt, 367

working women: black, 160–61; femininity and, 117; morality and, 105; female singers as, 92

World Stage (Los Angeles), 24, 322–27, 333, 335–37

X, Malcolm, 334, 351

Yale University Concert Band, 22–23, 129, 137–41

Yorston, Kay, 111, 113

"young man with a horn" trope, 26–27, 361

"Young Man with a Horn" (essay), 362–63, 378

Young Man with a Horn (film), 27, 362–63, 379–88

Young Man with a Horn (novel), 26, 361–77, 379, 382

young women, protection of, 300, 304, 316

Young, Lester, 211–12, 215

Z, Pamela, 220

Zodiac Suite, The, 75

Nichole T. Rustin received her Ph.D. in American studies from New York University. She is an independent scholar currently completing a book on race, masculinity, and jazz in the 1950s.

Sherrie Tucker is an associate professor of American studies at the University of Kansas. She is the author of *Swing Shift: "All Girl" Bands of the 1940s* (2000).

Library of Congress Cataloging-in-Publication Data

Big ears : listening for gender in jazz studies / edited by Nichole Rustin and Sherrie Tucker.   p. cm. — (Refiguring American music)
Includes bibliographical references and index.
ISBN 978-0-8223-4336-3 (cloth : alk. paper)
ISBN 978-0-8223-4320-2 (pbk. : alk. paper)
1. Jazz — History and criticism. 2. Jazz — Social aspects.
I. Rustin, Nichole T. II. Tucker, Sherrie, 1957–
ML3506.B53 2008   781.65082 — dc22
2008028462